Colonel H o w a r d's Regiment of Foot.		Dates of their present Commiſſions.	Dates of their firſt Commiſſions.
Colonel	Hon. Charles Howard	1 Nov. 1738.	10 Aug. 1715.
Lieutenant Colonel	Lord Sempill	11 June 1731.	July 1709.
Major	Richard Hawley	28 June 1710.	May 1692.
Captains	James Phillips	10 Jan. 1709.	Sept. 1702.
	Joſeph Stifted	11 Jan. 1714.	1 May 1709.
	Peter Franquefort	10 May 1732.	April 1694.
	William Petitot	26 Mar. 1737.	1721.
	Thomas Burton	1 Mar. 1737.	1724.
	William Mercer	31 Mar. 1737.	Jan. 1702.
Captain Lieutenant	Sir Warren Croſbie	Aug. 1707.	18 Oct. 1703.
Lieutenants	Michael Legge	23 Jan. 1711.	Oct. 1703.
	William Rousby	30 May 1720.	April 1715.
	Roger Crymble	11 July 1732.	Dec. 1717.
	James Grove	3 May 1728.	
	Matthew Bunbury	16 May 1733.	May 1720.
	Richard Hawley	18 Nov. 1736.	Sept. 1725.
	George Coote	31 May 1737.	Nov. 1729.
	Thomas Leake	1 Sept. 1725.	
	Nicholas Forde	7 Nov. 1739.	23 Dec. 1726.
	Henry Goddard	19 Jan. 1739.	1 Aug. 1728.
Enſigns	George Sempill	25 Sept. 1732.	
	Thomas Mainwaring	16 May 1733.	
	James Campbell	20 Nov. 1734.	
	Daniel Legrand	31 Mar. 1737.	
	Thomas Cuthbert	ditto.	
	Hugh Sempill		
	Patrick Cockran	19 Jan. 1739-40	
	Robert Douglaſs	7 Nov. 1739.	
	Charles Lumſden	4 Feb. 1739-40	

OFFICERS of The Green Howards,
FROM THE FIRST PRINTED ARMY LIST, 1740.

OFFICERS

OF

THE GREEN HOWARDS,

Alexandra, Princess of Wales's Own
(Yorkshire Regiment),

(Formerly the 19th Foot).

1688 to 1920.

BY

Major M. L. FERRAR.

(late 19th Foot).

LONDON, E.C.
EDEN FISHER & Co., Ltd.
1920.

PREFACE.

HAVING compiled several active service rolls for the Records of the Regiment as well as for *The Green Howards' Gazette*, I have been tempted to go a step further and make a complete roll of the Officers and their services from the raising of the Regiment in 1688 up to the present time.

In an Appendix I have added the names of the Officers of the Reserve and Territorial Battalions and those who had temporary commissions in the Regiment, who were all from time to time attached to the Regular Battalions during the Great War and who so well helped to maintain the honour and credit of THE GREEN HOWARDS on the various battle fronts.

In preparing the Roll I have made frequent use of **Mr.** Dalton's *Army Lists and Commissions Registers*, who before his death gave me full permission to do so, and I am also much indebted to Mr. W. R. Williams who is completing Mr. Dalton's work, for his valuable assistance and for the kindly interest he has taken in this Book. Mr. Percy Lewis, C.M.G., late Ceylon Civil Service has helped me greatly with the Ceylon period 1796—1820, and his work *The Tombstones and Monuments of Ceylon* contains a mass of information relative to the 19th Foot during the long time it was quartered in the Island. I have also to thank the Revd. H. B. Swanzy, Rector of Newry, Co. Down, for his unfailing help and for kindly placing at my disposal his valuable books, on several occasions. As regards the attached Officers, Captain Kenneth Hutchence late 6th Battalion has kept me posted with the services of all those who passed through the 3rd Reserve Battalion on their way to the front. Mr. Andrew Ross of Edinburgh and Major-General Granville Egerton, C.B., have sent me their notes on some of the Scotch names, and Mr. W. J. Somerville, late 19th Foot, an official of the British Museum, never could do enough for me in looking up any matter on which I required information. To these and all others who have assisted me I renew my grateful thanks.

M. L. FERRAR.

TORWOOD,
BELFAST.

July, 1920.

ROLL OF OFFICERS
1688-1920.

FRANCIS LUTTRELL

Baptized at Dunster, 16th June, 1659. Second son of Francis Luttrell of Dunster Castle, Somersetshire. Capt. and Col. 20th November, 1688. Was commissioned by the Prince of Orange to raise and equip a regiment of foot known in later years as the 19th Foot.

Represented Minehead as M.P. from 1679. In 1681 he was appointed by the Lord Lieut. of Somerset to be Col. of a regiment of foot in succession to Sir Halswell Tynte and was in command of the local forces when the Duke of Monmouth landed at Lynne in 1685. Was one of the first men of importance to join the standard of the Prince of Orange at Exeter in November, 1688.

Died on the 25th July, 1690, at Plymouth. Buried at Dunster.

Sir ROBERT PEYTON

Capt. 20th November, 1688.

Commanded one of the independent companies incorporated into Luttrell's in 1688.

EDMUND BOWYER

Son of Edmund Bowyer, of Beere, Co. Somerset. A connection by marriage of Col. Luttrell. Capt. 20th November, 1688; Major 28th February, 1694; left in 1694.

Commanded one of the independent companies incorporated into Luttrell's Regt. in 1688. In the list of Luttrell's 28th February, 1689, this officer's commission is marked " reinstated."

WILLIAM COWARD

Son of William Coward, M.P. for Wells. Capt., 20th November, 1688.

Commanded one of the independent companies incorporated into Luttrell's in 1688. In the list of Luttrell's 28th February, 1689, this officer's commission is marked " reinstated."

JOSEPH PRICMAN

Capt., 20th November, 1688.

Out of the regiment 1st March, 1690. In the list of officers of Luttrell's 28th February, 1689, his name is marked " reinstated." Commanded one of the independent companies incorporated into Luttrell's in November, 1688.

ROBERT CAREY

Capt., 20th November, 1688; Major, 14th May, 1695. Commission renewed in 1702.

In the list of Luttrell's Regt. 28th February, 1689, his commission is marked " reinstated." Commanded one of the independent companies incorporated into Luttrell's in 1688.

Served at Cadiz and in the West Indies, 1702-3.

Died on service at Guadeloupe in 1703.

WALTER VINCENT

Capt., 20th November, 1688.

Out of the Regt. 9th February, 1691. In the list of the regt. 28th February, 1689, his name is marked " reinstated." Commanded one of the independent companies incorporated into Luttrell's in 1688.

Petitioned the Treasury on behalf of himself and the officers of the regt. as to a debt due to the tradesmen who supplied the regt., dated 17th January, 1690. (Treasury papers.)

CHARLES BURRINGTON

Possibly son of Gilbert Burrington, of Newcombe, Co. Devon. Baptized at Crediton, 20th October, 1659. Capt., 20th November, 1688.

Commanded one of the independent companies incorporated into Luttrell's in 1688. Commission marked " reinstated " in the list of 28th February, 1689.

Bde.-Major in Holland 1st July, 1693; killed at the battle of Landen 19th July, 1693 (Rawdon papers).

JOHN SIMMONDS

Lieut., 20th November, 1688; Capt. Lieut., 28th February,. 1689; Capt., 29th December, 1692.

In the list of Luttrell's regt. of 28th February, 1689, his commission is marked " reinstated."

Probably the Capt. Jno *Symonds* who was placed on half-pay before 1700 but reappointed Capt. in Erle's Regt. 13th February, 1702. Major before 1703 (Dalton).

Served in the Cadiz Expedition of 1702 and at Guadeloupe in 1703.

WILLIAM NORCOTT

Capt. and Lieut.-Col. 1689; Col. of a regiment of foot, 16th February, 1694, which was disbanded in 1697.

Luttrell writing in his diary under date 17th Nov., 1688, says " several gentlemen of Devonshire we hear are gone to the Prince as Sir Fras. Drake, Sir Wm. Drake, Mr. William Cary, Major Norcott, Capt. Burrington, etc."

HENRY HAWLEY

Probably the Henry Hawley of St. James's, Westminster, who is mentioned in the marriage licence of Francis Lord Hawley, dated 3rd February, 1697. Half-brother to Gen. Thomas Erle, and brother to Col. Francis Hawley, of Princess Anne's Dragoons, who fell at Steenkirke (Dalton).

Lieut., Coldstream Guards 4th January, 1670; Duke of York's Marines 16th January, 1678; Major and Capt., Luttrell's Regt., 1689. Lieut.-Col. and Capt. 15th April, 1691. Commission renewed in 1702.

Left the regt. about 1708. Had the Queen's leave to be absent from the West Indian Expedition of 1702-3.

Died at Kinsale 17th July, 1724. There is a hatchment in St. Multose's Church, Kinsale, to his memory, " Vert, a saltier engrailed argent."

BALDWIN MALLETT

Born about 1650. Eldest son of Sir John Mallett, Kt. of Poyntington and St. Audries, Co. Cornwall.

Capt., 28th February, 1689. Out 9th February, 1691.

One of the first of the Somerset gentry to support William of Orange on his landing in England. Was Receiver-General for Somerset, 1702-3. Died in London in 1724.

ALEXANDER LUTTRELL

Baptized at Dunster 20th October, 1663. Third son of Francis Luttrell of Dunster Castle. Capt., 28th February, 1689; Lieut.-Col. of Col. Wm. Norcott's Regt. of Foot, 16th February, 1694; G. Villier's Regt. of Marines (31st Foot), 12th February, 1702; Col., 6th December, 1703.

" Expecting to succeed his brother in ye command of ye Regiment, which he justly might, his brother having raised it and laid out great sums of money thereon, but it being given to another, this Capt. Luttrell with several other officers of ye Regiment quitted ye same." (MS. at Dunster).

Served in all the wars in Flanders. Died 22nd September, 1711. Buried at Dunster.

THOMAS FINCH

Capt., 28th February, 1689. Out before 1694.

RICHARD WILLIAMS

Lieut., 28th February, 1689.

JOHN DODDINGTON

Lieut., 28th February, 1689; Adjt., 19th April, 1693. Out in 1694.

NICHOLAS SUMMERS or SIMMONS

Lieut., 28th February, 1689.

JOHN REDMORE

Lieut., 28th February, 1689; Capt., 1st January, 1694. Out of the Army before 1702.

WILLIAM WILLOUGHBY

Lieut., 28th February, 1689.

GEORGE PRATER

Lieut., 28th February, 1689 ; Capt., 1st March, 1690.

Served in Flanders, 1693-4.

" George Prater of Nunney, Somerset, Esqre., being forthwith going to my command in their Majesties' Army in Flanders against the French, in case I die unmarried without issue, etc." Will dated 12th April, 1694. Proved 15th June, 1699 by his brother, Richard Prater of Erle's Regt. (Brown's wills.)

R. WINDHAM

Lieut., 1689.

WILLIAM WEBB

Possibly son of John Webb, of Butleigh, Somerset, Esqre., whose will is dated 20th October, 1672. Lieut., 28th February, 1689.

JOHN CALMADY

Possibly fourth son of Francis Calmady, of Combeshead, in Stoke Climsland, Cornwall. Baptized, 20th July, 1674.
Lieut., 28th February, 1689 ; Capt., 9th February, 1691. Out before 1694.
Buried at Stoke Climsland, 24th October, 1726.

JOHN WEST

Son of Cromwell West, of Dromyvillan, Co. Down, and Monasterevan, Co. Kildare.

Succeeded Cromwell West between 10th July, 1680 and 20th March, 1685, as Lieut. in Sir Charles Vic's company in Sir Wm. King's Regt., but out of that Regt. on 1st March, 1686. Lieut. and Adjt. Luttrell's Regt. 28th February, 1689; Capt.-Lieut. 1st March, 1690; Capt., 1st February, 1691. Out of the Regt. before 1702.
Served in Flanders 1693-4.
Died October, 1701.
In his will dated 15th July, 1701, proved in Dublin 28th October, 1701, he mentions his friend Capt. Leonard Cradock, whom he appoints to collect the arrears due to him in Flanders and England.

HUGH MALLETT

Lieut., 1689.

WALTER SHEPCOT

Lieut., 28th February, 1689.

WILLIAM LEE

Lieut., 28th February, 1689.

JOSEPH LEWIS

Ensign, 28th February, 1689.

ABRAHAM HANCOCK

Ensign, 28th February, 1689; Lieut., 9th February, 1691. Left before 1st February, 1693.

CAPELL STOCKER

Fourth son of William Stocker, of Chilcompton, Co. Somerset. Ensign, 28th February, 1689; Lieut., 20th June, 1691.
Served in the Brest Expedition of 1694, and was killed at Camaret Bay. Widow granted a pension of £30.

THOMAS ADAMS

Ensign, 28th February, 1689.

JOHN SIDENHAM

Ensign, 28th February, 1689; Lieut., 20th June, 1691. Commission renewed in 1702. Out of the Regt. in 1705.

Probably the John Sydenham of Dulverton, Co. Somerset, whose will is dated 5th March, 1750, and proved 7th March, 1757. Executor, Penelope, his daughter. (Brown's wills.)

—— ENSATE

Ensign, 1689.

ROBERT NORCOTT

Ensign, February, 1689; Lieut. of Grenadiers, 1st April, 1690.

THOMAS ROBINSON

Ensign, 28th February, 1689; Lieut., 1st March, 1694. Serving as Lieut. in Ireland in 1706.

Took part in the Expedition to Cadiz and the West Indies, 1702-3.

THOMAS FREKE

Born 1665. Son of Robert Freke, of Upwey, Dorset. Ensign, 28th February, 1689.

Died in 1698.

THOMAS RISDON

Ensign, 28th February, 1689; Lieut., 9th February, 1691. Out of the Regt. in 1702.

Served in Flanders.

—— GREGOR

Ensign, 28th February, 1689.

LAWRENCE COWARD

Ensign, 28th February, 1689; Lieut., 1st April, 1690. Out of the Regt. before 1702.

Served in Flanders, 1694.

THEOPHILUS ALLEN

Chirugeon, 28th February, 1689. " Put out " of his Commission by Colonel Luttrell in 1690.

Presented a petition to Queen Mary for the restitution of money he had spent in medicines, etc. Petition shows that he had disbursed for medicaments for Col. Luttrell's and for Sir John Guise's Regts. 1or the use of the soldiers, £88 8s. He is a poor French Protestant who has been these 20 months soliciting the payment of the same and he prays for a speedy order to receive that debt (28th July, 1691.)

ARTHUR BALSON or BALSAM

Quarter-Master, 28th February, 1689.

HOPTON WYNDHAM

Third son of Thomas Wyndham, of Witham Friary, Somerset. Capt., 1st March, 1689. Out of the Regt. 1st March, 1690.

Died 13th February, 1697. Buried in Witham Friary churchyard where there is a memorial.

SANKEY GODFREY

Lieut., 28th March, 1689; Capt., 21st January, 1702.
Served in the Expedition to Cadiz, and the West Indies, 1702-3.
Died of wounds received in action at Guadeloupe in March, 1703.
Will proved in Dublin, 1703.

GEORGE NORMAN

Lieut. of Grenadiers, 28th March, 1689; Capt., 1st
September, 1694. Out before 1700.
Served in the Expedition to Cadiz, and the West Indies, 1702-3.

THOMAS BURRINGTON

Possibly son of Gilbert Burrington, of Newcombe, Devon.
Baptized at Crediton, 20th October, 1659. Capt., 28th March,
1689; Major and Capt., 20th November, 1696. Out of the Regt.
before 1702.

ZACHARY CLARKE

Ensign, 1st December, 1689; h.p. in 1697 in Col. Newton's
Regt. of Foot; Lieut. of a newly raised independent company
of foot formed of the invalid pensioners to keep guard at the
Tower of London under command of Capt. Robert D'Oyley,
8th March, 1711 (Dalton).

FRANCIS MAIDSTON

Capt., 1st March, 1690. Out of the Regt. in 1694.

SAMUEL SMITH

Quarter-Master, 1st March, 1690.

ARTHUR HORSEMAN

Ensign, 1st April, 1690; Lieut., 31st August, 1693; Capt.
Lieut., 20th November, 1696. Out of the Regt., 14th May, 1699.
Served in Flanders.

GEORGE SIDENHAM

Ensign, 1st April, 1690; Lieut. in 1702. Out before 1706.
Served in the Expedition to Cadiz, and the West Indies, 1702-3.
Probably brother of John Sydenham of Luttrell's. Mary Sandford,
of Minehead Flory, Somerset, in her will proved 2nd June, 1663,
mentions " my friend George Sydenham, of Combe, in the parish of
Dulverton."

THOMAS DENTON

Ensign, 1st April, 1690. Out before 1694.

PETER DIXON, Clk.

Chaplain, 31st May, 1690. Left the Regt., 1st June, 1693.

On the death of Col. Luttrell in July, 1690, the vacancy was not
filled till the 1st January, 1691, when Thomas Erle was appointed Col.
He retained command of his own battalion, formed in March, 1689, so
that till after the Peace of Ryswick in 1697, when it was disbanded, his
Regt. was composed of two battalions

The Right Hon. THOMAS ERLE, P.C.

Born in 1650. Second son of Thomas Erle, of Charborough, Dorset. Col. of a Regt. of Foot, 8th March, 1689; Br.-Gen., 22nd March, 1693; Major-Gen., 1st June, 1696; Lieut.-Gen., 11th February, 1703; Gen., 31st January, 1711.

Was M.P. for Wareham, 1678-9, 1680-5. Major in the Dorset Militia at the Revolution. One of the first officers to join the Prince of Orange. A Lord Justice for Ireland. Governor of Portsmouth, 1st July, 1694. Lieut.-Gen. of the Ordnance, 2nd May, 1705—21st June, 1712, and from 22nd September, 1714—19th March, 1717.

Took part in the Irish War in command of his battalion, and was present at the Boyne and first siege of Limerick. Distinguished himself at the battle of Aughrim where he was twice captured and twice rescued. Paid 14 days' pay (£16 16s. od.) on account of his wounds.

Present at Steenkirke and commanded a brigade at Landen (wounded). Commanded a division at the battle of Almanza, and, as Commander-in-Chief, an expedition against the coast of France in 1708.

Died at Charborough 23rd July, 1720.

ROBERT FREKE

Born at Upwey, Dorset, in 1655. Son of Robert Freke, of Upwey. Capt. and Lieut.-Col., 8th March, 1689; Bt.-Col., 16th February, 1694; Deputy Gov. of Plymouth in 1696.

Served in the Irish War and was wounded at Streamstown, Co. Westmeath, in December, 1690. Took part in the expedition to Cadiz and the West Indies 1702-3.

Died in 1709. Buried at Upwey.

FRANCIS DEVENISH

Possibly eldest son of Francis Devenish, who died 10th May, 1689, and to whom there is a tablet in Gillingham Church, Dorset (Hutchin's Dorset, Vol. iii., p. 64). Ensign in Capt. Robert St. Clair's Independent Co. at West Tilbury, 10th December, 1683; Lord Dartmouth's Regt. (7th Foot), 11th June, 1685; Major, T. Erle's Foot, 8th March, 1689.

Served in the Irish War. Had leave to go to England in 1690.

Killed at the battle of Aughrim, 1691.

THOMAS BULKELEY

Possibly the Capt. Thos. Bulkeley, of Dinas, Co. Carnarvon, who was third son of Viscount Bulkeley (Dalton). Capt., 8th March, 1689.

Not in any lists after October, 1689.

Served in the Irish War.

SAMUEL SOURTON

Capt., 8th March, 1689.

Served in the Irish War.

HENRY GOULD

Capt., 8th March, 1689.
Served in the Irish War.

ANDREW ABINGTON

Capt., 8th March, 1689; Col. T. Sanderson's Regt. of Marines (30th Foot), in 1702.

Served in the Irish War. The Very Revd. Rowland Davis, Dean of Cork, states in his diary that he met "Capt. Abbington of Earl's at Roscrea camp on 14th September, 1690, and talked to him on a matter of business."

VINCENT GOOKIN

Son of Vincent Gookin, Surveyor-General of Ireland. Capt., 8th March, 1689; Col. Richard Coote's Regt., 21st March, 1692.
Served in the Irish War.

———— WILLS

Capt., 8th March, 1689.
Served in the Irish War.

OXENBRIDGE HORWOOD

Ensign, Prince George of Denmark's Regt. of Marines (disbanded 28th February, 1689), from the ranks of the Royal Horse Guards, 24th May, 1687; Capt., T. Erle's Regt., 8th March, 1689.

Not in any list after 1689. Served in the ranks of the Royal Horse Guards at the battle of Sedgemoor. Received a bounty of £30 8s. 4d. for wounds. Took part in the Irish War. Was recommended by Col. Erle for a troop. in Col. Leigh's Dragoons, but another officer was appointed.

ROBERT LUCAS

Possibly son of Robert Lucas, of Chilton, Somerset.
Ensign, 8th March, 1689.

GEORGE CLARK

Ensign, 8th March, 1689.

EDWARD JONES

Ensign, 8th March, 1689. Capt.-Lieut., 2nd August, 1689; half-pay, 1689; Capt. before 1697.

JOHN ELLESDON

Capt., 8th March, 1689. Resigned, 2nd August, 1689.

HENRY HASTINGS

Lieut. and Adjt. Sir Bevill Skelton's Regt., 12th October, 1688; Lieut. and Adjt., T. Erle's Regt., 8th March, 1689; serving in 1695.

JOHN RAMSAY

Lieut., 8th March, 1689.

JOHN BOURNE

Ensign, 8th March, 1689.

CHARLES BINGHAM

Capt., Lord Roscommon's Regt. in 1689; transferred to T. Erle's Regt., when Roscommon's was broken, in 1690.

Served in the Irish War.

Killed at the battle of Aughrim, leaving a widow and three children in great distress. (Treasury papers.)

THOMAS PHILLIPS

Lieut., 28th June, 1689; Capt. before 1691; Gustavus Hamilton's Regt. (20th Foot), 31st January, 1692; Col. T. Farrington's Regt., 18th February, 1696; half-pay in 1698.

Served in the Irish War 1689-91. Story in his history states that Capt. Phillips of Erle's, in conjunction with Major Weldon of the Militia, killed thirteen rapparees near Mount Mellick on the 24th March, 1691.

A certain Edward Phillips, of Montacute, Somerset, who died 16th January, 1679, left his son Thomas £300 in his will (Brown's wills.)

GEORGE FREKE

Born 1670. Son of Robert Freke, of Upwey. Capt., 2nd August, 1689; Grenadier Company, 1st July, 1691; Major, 7th March, 1705; Lieut.-Col., 23rd March, 1709; Brig.-Gen., 12th February, 1710. Purchased the Colonelcy from General Erle, 22nd March, 1709, and sold the same to Brig.-Gen. R. Sutton, 3rd April, 1712.

Served in the Irish War, also in Flanders. Took part in the expedition to Cadiz and the West Indies in 1702-3.—Present at the battle of Malplaquet.

Died in 1730. Buried at Upwey. Will proved in Cork 1731.

CHARLES St LOO

Ensign, 2nd August, 1689.

There was a certain John Saint Loo, of Little Fontmell, Childe Okeford, Dorsetshire, who left his son Charles £400 in his will proved 18th November, 1668 (Brown's wills).

GEORGE WILLIAMS

Ensign, 2nd August, 1689; Lieut. in 1690; on leave in England in November, 1690.

Served in the Irish War.

―――― FITZHERBERT

Ensign, 2nd August, 1689.

JOSEPH DOLLING

Lieut. of Grenadiers, 1st November, 1689; Capt.-Lieut., 22nd April, 1695; half-pay in 1698; Earl of Huntingdon's Regt.

(33rd Foot), 10th March, 1703.

Paid 14 days' pay on account of wounds received at the battle of Aughrim (£3 5s. 4d)

WILLIAM LEIGH

Lieut., 1689; Capt., 1706; Capt. and Lieut.-Col., Coldstream Guards, 22nd July, 1715.

Present at the battle of Malplaquet.

Died 12th January, 1733.

—— DISCORISSIN

Lieut., 1690.

Served in the Irish War. Paid 14 days' pay (£3 5s. 4d.) on account of wounds received at the battle of Aughrim.

JOHN PEPPER

Third son of George Pepper, J.P. for Meath, 1662, of Ballygarth Castle, Co. Meath. Capt., Earl of Roscommon's Regt., 1689; T. Erle's Regt., 1690; Henry Cunningham's Dragoons, February, 1693: Major, 1st November, 1695; Lieut.-Col. before 1707; Col., 15th April, 1707; Brig.-Gen., 1707; Major-Gen., 1st January, 1710; Col., 8th Dragoons, by the fall of Gen. Robert Killegrew at the battle of Almanza, 15th April, 1707.

Served in the Irish War with T. Erle's Regt., being paid 14 days' pay (£7) on account of wounds received at the battle of Aughrim. Served in Spain and Portugal and commanded a cavalry brigade at the battle of Almanza where he distinguished himself, and gained additional fame at Saragossa. Taken prisoner at Brighuega in 1710. Was actively employed during the '15 in England. M.P. for Oban, 1715. Ranger of Epping Forest and Enfield Chase.

Died at Montpellier 22nd December, 1725. Will proved in Dublin, 1725.

JOHN PENNY

Ensign, 1690; Lieut., 1st January, 1694; 1st Lieut. Grenadier Co., 1702; out of the Regt. in 1706.

Served in the Irish War. Paid 14 days' pay (£2 11s. 4d.) on account of wounds received at the battle of Aughrim. Had the Queen's leave to be absent in England when the regt. went to the West Indies.

JOHN EVANS

Ensign, 1690; Lieut., 19th April, 1693.

Served in the Irish War.

NICHOLAS EVELEIGH

Lieut., 1st August, 1690; half-pay in 1697, when Erle's 2nd Battn. was disbanded.

The Dublin Record Office has a roll of Erle's officers wounded at the battle of Aughrim. Mr. Dalton's Commission Registers do not give it.

THOMAS COHAGAN

Capt., 1st August, 1690.

Served in the Irish War. Was paid 14 days' pay on account of wounds received at the battle of Aughrim (£3 5s. 4d.).

RICHARD HENNING

Born 1664. Fourth son of Robert Henning, of Hennings Crookson, Dorset. Ensign, 1689 ; Lieut., T. Erle's Regt., 26th December, 1690; Capt.-Lieut., 1st May, 1694; Capt., 22nd April, 1695; half-pay in 1698; Sir John Gibson's Regt. (28th Foot), 10th March, 1702.

A certain Ric. *Hemming* was appointed Capt. *en second* in Lord Mark Kerr's Regt. of Foot (29th Foot), and placed on half-pay in 1713 (Dalton.)

THOMAS WAGGET

Adjt., 26th December, 1690; Lieut., 1st August, 1691; Capt., 19th April, 1693; half-pay in 1698; Capt. of Grenadiers in Col. Thos. Brudenall's Regt. of Foot, 28th June, 1701.

Sir CHARLES WILLS, K.B.

Baptized at St. Gorran's, Cornwall, 23rd October, 1666. Son of Anthony Wills, of St. Gorran. Lieut., 1690; Capt., 1st July, 1691; Major, Col. T. Sanderson's Regt. (30th Foot), 6th November, 1694; Lieut.-Col., 1st May, 1697; half-pay 1697; Viscount Charlemont's Regt. (36th Foot), June, 1701; Col. of a regt. of Marines, 13th October, 1707; Brig.-Gen., 1st Jan., 1707; Major-Gen., 1st January, 1709; Col., 3rd Foot, 5th January, 1710; Lieut.-Gen., 21st June, 1727; Gen., 2nd July, 1730; Governor of Portsmouth, 1717; Lieut.-Gen. of the Ordnance, 22nd April, 1722; Knight of the Bath, 17th June, 1725; Col., 1st Foot Guards, 17th July, 1726. Commanding the Foot, 1739.

Served with Erle's at the battle of Steenkirke and as a Capt. was in the thick of the fight at Landen. Served with T. Sanderson's Regt. to the end of the war, including the seige and capture of Namur. Commanded Lord Charlemont's newly-raised regt. with great distinction at Cadiz in 1702 and at Guadeloupe the following year. Was Adjt.-Gen. of the expedition to Barcelona and at the capitulation of the town. Commanded two battalions of Marines in Catalonia at the victory of St. Estevan in January, 1706, where he assumed chief command on the fall of Major-Gen. Conyngham.

After the defeat of Almanza, Gen. Wills took part with his marines in the defence of Catalonia and commanded the British contingent at the desperate defence of Lerida.

In 1708, he commanded the troops in the capture of Cagliari and reduction of Sardinia. Was in command of the British infantry at the great victory of Saragossa and advance to Madrid. In the retreat, he specially distinguished himself at Brighuega, where the rear guard was overwhelmed. In 1715, he was in command at Chester and along the Welsh border, and when the Jacobites advanced he met them at Preston and captured some of their barricades, so effectually cowing their leaders that on the arrival of Gen. Carpenter next day with two regts. of dragoons, they surrendered without conditions.

Died in London 25th December, 1741.

Buried in Westminster Abbey. Memorial in the Guards' Chapel.

———— TREDENHAM
Ensign, 1691.

———— IZARD
Ensign, 1691.

CHARLES COOKIN
Ensign, 1691; half-pay in 1698; Lieut., 1st March, 1702; Qr.-Mr., 21st January, 1703; Capt. before 1706; appointed Deputy Governor of Pennsylvania in 1708.

Paid 14 days' pay (£3 5s. 4d.) on account of wounds received at the battle of Aughrim. Served in the expedition to Cadiz and the West Indies, 1702-3.

WILLIAM STRANGEWAYS
Capt., Grenadier Co., 1691.

Served in the Irish War and was killed at the seige of Athlone 30th June, 1691.

His brother-in-law, William Sympson, administrator of his estate, petitioned Government for the sum of £158 5s. 9d. due to him (State Papers.)

———— MONTGOMERY
Ensign, 1691.

———— HANSERD
Lieut., 1691.

ROBERT WINN
Ensign, 1691; Lieut., 1st March, 1694; half-pay in 1698.

———— ENGLIN
Ensign, 1691.

———— WARRING
Capt., 1691.

A certain Richard Warring was appointed Lieut. in the Grenadier Guards 28th February, 1694.

———— MERIMY
Lieut. of Grenadiers, 1691.

JAMES DELACOURT
Ensign, 1691; Capt., 1694.

———— St. MULLEN
Lieut., 1691.

———— TRIMLOE
Ensign, 1691.

——— DOBB

Lieut., 1691.

WILLIAM, 1st Earl CADOCAN, K.T., P.C.

Born at Liscartnan, 1672. Eldest son of Henry Cadogan, of Dublin, Counsellor at Law. Ensign, 1691; Capt., 4th March, 1694; Major, Inniskilling Dragoons, 1st August, 1698; Bt.-Col., 1st June, 1701; Qr.-Mr.-Gen., Flanders, 25th August, 1701; Col., 2nd Horse (5th Dragoon Guards), 2nd March, 1703; Brig.-Gen., 25th August, 1704; Major-Gen., 1st January, 1707; Lieut.-Gen., 1st January, 1709; Col., Coldstream Guards, 11th October, 1714; Gen., 12th July, 1717; 1st Foot Guards, 18th June, 1722.

Is supposed to have been at the Boyne. Served through all the wars in Flanders in the reigns of William III. and Queen Anne. Present at the battles of Schellenburg, Blenheim, Ramillies, and Malplaquet. Was wounded at the seige of Mons. Taken prisoner at the seige of Menin in 1706 but soon afterwards exchanged. Second in command to the Duke of York at close of the 1715 rebellion.

M.P. for Woodstock 1705-1716. Lieut. of the Tower 2nd January, 1707—11th January, 1712. Capt. and Governor of the Isle of Wight, 16th September, 1715. C.-in-C. Scotland, 25th February—12th May, 1716. K.T., 29th June, 1716, and advanced to an Earldom 8th May, 1718. Master-Gen. of the Ordnance, 10th June, 1722—3rd June, 1725.

"The one man whom Marlborough delighted to honour."

Died at his residence, Kensington Gravel Pits, on the 17th July, 1726. Buried in Westminster Abbey in King Henry VII.'s chapel. Memorial in the Guards' Chapel.

CHARLES DORRINGTON

Ensign, 9th February, 1691; Adjt., 19th April, 1693; Lieut., 8th July, 1693. Out of the Regiment in 1694.

JOHN WILLS

Ensign and Qr.-Master, 9th February, 1691; Lieut., 20th August, 1695. Commission renewed in 1702. Out before 1705

Served in the Irish War and was paid fourteen days' pay (£6 10s. 8d.) on account of wounds received at Aughrim. Present at the battle of Landen.

Died 12th August, 1728.

CHARLES WEEMYS

Lieut., 9th February, 1691.

AMBROSE EDGEWORTH

4th son of Sir John Edgeworth. Ensign, Lord Forbes' Regt. (18th Foot) 1686. Capt. Sir John Edgeworth's Regt., 1st March, 1689; T. Erle's Regt., 9th February, 1691; Major, Brig.-Gen. R. Gorges' Regt. (53th Foot) about 1704; Lieut.-Col., Thos. Allen's Regt., 19th August, 1707.

Several of the above names are taken from an undated MS. in the London Record Office. They are not mentioned in Mr. Dalton's lists.

Served in the expedition to Cadiz and the West Indies 1702-3. Served in Spain and was taken prisoner on his passage from Barcelona to England by a French cruiser, and carried to France. Died in 1710. Will proved in Dublin.

———— GRIMES

Ensign, 9th February, 1691.

JOHN PITT

Lieut. Lord Dartmouth's Regt. (7th Foot) 1685-1688 ; Capt., T. Erle's Regt., 9th February, 1691. Out before 1702.
Present at the battle of Landen.

JOHN TOOKE

Capt., 9th February, 1691 ; half-pay in 1697 ; Lord Mohun's Regt., 10th March, 1702.
One of this name was appointed Lieut. in the Earl of Oxford's Regt. of Horse Guards 31st December, 1688. (Dalton.)

RICHARD PRATER

Brother of George Prater, see ante. Ensign, 9th February, 1691 ; Lieut., 22nd May, 1694 ; Adjt., 22nd May, 1695. Half-pay in 1697. Capt., T. Erle's Regt., 1st March, 1702. Princess Anne of Denmark's Regt., 1st March, 1704. Bt.-Major, 1st January, 1707. Major, J. Churchill's Regt. (31st Foot) 25th April, 1708. Bt. Lieut.-Col., 1st January, 1712. Sir Harry Goring's reformed Regt. (31st Foot) 1st June, 1715.
Served in Flanders and in the Expedition to Cadiz and the West Indies 1702-3.

WILLIAM LANE

Lieut., 9th February, 1691. Out of the Regiment 20th June, 1692.

WILLIAM HICKMAN

Capt.-Lieut., 9th February, 1691. Out before 20th June, 1692.

THOMAS HAWKER

Ensign, 1st April, 1691.

SYLVANUS BRYAN

Ensign, 1st April, 1691-1694 ; 2nd-Lieut. to Capt. Courtenay's Grenadier Co., in Col. Wm. Norcott's Regt. of Foot, 26th February, 1697. Half-pay in 1698.

OSMOND BRYANSCOMBE or BRINSCOMB

Adjt., 1st April, 1691 ; Lieut., 1st February, 1693 ; Capt. before 1703. Capt. of Invalids at Chester, 13th May, 1697.
Served in the expedition to Cadiz and the West Indies 1702-3.

WILLIAM MORGAN

Ensign, Earl of Bath's Regt. (10th Foot) 1686 ; Lieut., 1687 ; T. Erle's Regt., 21st May, 1691 ; Adjt., 22nd May,

1694 ; Capt., 14th May, 1695 ; Major before 1702.

Served in the expedition to Cadiz and the West Indies. Wounded in action at Guadeloupe on the 12th March, 1703, and died on board the " Boyne " on the 27th.

THOMAS COWARD

Ensign, 20th June, 1691.   Half-pay, February, 1698.

CHRISTOPHER LEIGH

Capt.-Lieut., 20th June, 1691.   Out before 4th March, 1694.

JOHN FLOYER

Lieut., 1691.

RICHARD COHAGAN

Ensign, 1st August, 1691.

JOHN PERRY

Ensign, 1st August, 1691 ; Lieut., 22nd May, 1695.   Out in 1702.

Served in Flanders.

The Hon. ROBERT MACKAY

3rd son of John, 2nd Baron Reay. Lieut., Col. Mackay's Regt. of Foot, March, 1688 ; Capt., Grenadier Co., 1688 ; Major, 1688; T. Erle's Regt., 6th August, 1691 ; Lieut.-Col. in Army in 1694.   Colonel 21st Foot, 13th November, 1695.

Educated in Holland under the eye of his uncle, General Hugh Mackay of Scoury. At the revolution was appointed Captain of Grenadier Co. in his uncle's regiment. Took an active part in the battle of Killiecrankie, where he received eight broadsword wounds, and was left for dead on the field. Served in Ireland and in Flanders. (Dalton.)

Died at Tongue, Scotland, the family seat, in December, 1696.

CERVAIS LILLINCSTON

Capt., 31st January, 1692. Exchanged to Col. Luke Lillingston's (his brother) Regt. (6th Foot) 8th March, 1694 ; Major, 24th December, 1694.

Served in the West Indies, 1695.

RICHARD HAWLEY

Youngest son of Henry Hawley of Brentwood. Ensign, 7th March, 1692 ; Lieut., 13th August, 1695.   Capt., 21st January, 1703 ; Major, 11th June, 1710. Commission renewed, 20th June, 1727. Serving as Major in 1740, but not in any other list after that year.

Served in Flanders and in the expedition to Cadiz and the West Indies, 1702-3. Serving in Ireland in 1706. Present at the battle of Malplaquet.

RICHARD HILL

Ensign, Lord Lisburne's Regt., 1689 ; Capt., T. Erle's Regt., 21st March, 1692.

Served in Ireland and Flanders. This officer gained unenviable notoriety by his attempt in conjunction with Lord Mohun to carry off the celebrated actress, Anne Bracegirdle, on the 9th December, 1692, in Drury Lane. The actress was rescued, but two hours later Mohun and Hill waylaid Mountford, the famous actor, whom Hill looked upon as a rival, and in the quarrel which ensued between Mohun and the actor, Hill ran the latter through with his sword and killed him. The Grand Jury of Middlesex convicted Mohun and Hill of murder. The latter escaped and nothing more is recorded of him by the historian, but in the Record Office there is the following MS. petition to Queen Anne :—

"This humble petition of Captain Richard Hill showeth that your petitioner at the age of sixteen, after four years' service in Ireland and Flanders, under the command of Lieut.-Gen. Erle, was unhappily drawn into a quarrel with Mr. Mountford, wherein he had the misfortune to give him a mortal wound, for which inadvised act your petitioner has humbled himself before God these eleven years past, and since his misfortune went volunteer with Colonel Gibson to Newfoundland, who has given a character of your petitioner's behaviour there as Lieut.-General Erle has of his carriage and conduct in Ireland and Flanders, as appears by the certificates herewith annexed. May it therefore please your most Sacred Majestie, in consideration of your petitioner's past services, and in compassion to his youth, to extend your Royal mercy to your petitioner for a crime to which he was betrayed by his heat and folly of youth, that he may thereby be enabled to serve your Majestie and his country, as his earnest desire is to the last drop of his blood."

Lieut.-General Erle's certificate runs as follows :—

"Whereas Captain Richard Hill was under my command during the late Irish War and a volunteer with me in Flanders, I must needs give him this character, that he behaved himself on all occasions as a man of honour, and really with more courage and conduct than from one of his years could have been expected. For he was but twelve years old when he came into the army, and but sixteen when his misfortune hap'ned, which is eleven years since. Now the great concern for his misfortune and his earnest desire to serve Her Majesty again even in any post will, I hope, move her compassion and mercy in obtaining his freedom, which I am ready to certify to Her Majesty whenever 'tis thought convenient.

THO. ERLE."

There is reason to believe that Hill was pardoned, as in 1706 his name appears in a list of officers recommended by the Duke of Ormonde. (English Army Lists and Commission Register.)

JOHN PITT, Clk.

Chaplain, 22nd March, 1692. Serving in 1699.

JOHN ADAMS

Lieut. of Grenadiers, 22nd March, 1692, from half-pay in Lord Mark Kerr's Regt. of Foot. Capt., 26th December, 1726.

Reduced with his Company in 1729.

JOHN JACKSON

Ensign, 13th April, 1692 ; Lieut., Earl of Derby's (16th Foot) 1st March, 1696. Out of Regt., 1st May, 1709.

Wounded at Blenheim ; £28 bounty.

WILLIAM TULIP

Lieut., 20th June, 1692.   Out in 1702.

Served in Flanders.

SHELDON MARVIN

Ensign, 1st Febuary, 1693.   Out in 1702.

Served in Flanders in 1694.

JAMES GIBBONS

Lieut., 1st February, 1693 ; Capt., Col. Geo. McGill's Regt. before 1696 ; Geo. Hamilton's Regt., 1st June, 1696 ; T. Erle's Regt., 4th March, 1698.   Out in 1702.

HARRY FREKE

Born 1673.   Son of Robert Freke, of Upwey, Dorset. Ensign, 19th April, 1693; Capt.-Lieut., 6th December, 1706; Capt., 24th April, 1707.

Services untraced after 1709.   In Mr. Dalton's "Malplaquet Roll."

ANDREW ETTRICK

Ensign, 19th April, 1693; Lieut., 22nd April, 1695.   Out in 1698.

LEONARD CRADDOCK

Ensign, 25th August, 1693; Lieut., 15th April, 1696; Capt., 18th May, 1699; Bt.-Major, 7th March, 1706; Major, 23rd March, 1709.   Out of the Regt., 10th June, 1710.

Served in Flanders.   Had the Queen's leave to be absent when the Regiment went to the West Indies in 1702.   In the "Malplaquet Roll."

SAMUEL NORMAN

Ensign, 31st August, 1693; Half-pay in 1698; re-appointed Ensign in 1702; Lieut. before 1706; Capt.-Lieut., 1709.   Commission renewed, 11th January, 1715.   Out of the Regt., 2nd March, 1718.

Served in the expedition to Cadiz and the West Indies in 1702-3. His name is in the "Malplaquet Roll."

JOHN PRATT

Adjt., 31st August, 1693; Lieut., 1st July, 1694; Capt.-Lieut., 14th May, 1699 ; Capt., 2nd January, 1703.   Out in 1706.

Had the Queen's leave to be absent from the Regiment when it went to the West Indies in 1702.   Acted as agent for the Regiment during its absence abroad.

EDWARD EMMETT

Ensign, 30th November, 1693; Lieut., 1st March, 1696; Half-pay, 1698; Sir Richard Temple's Regt., 10th March, 1702; Capt of an Invalid Company, 19th March, 1711.

HENRY C. HAWLEY

Born 1679. Eldest son of Colonel Francis Hawley, killed at Steenkirke. Ensign, 10th January, 1694; Half-pay in 1698; Sir Ric. Temple's Regt. of Foot, 10th March, 1702 ; Cornet, Royal Horse Guards, 11th Sept., 1704; Capt., Princess Anne's Dragoons (4th Dragoons), 27th May, 1706; Major, 27th January, 1711; Lieut.-Col., 4th April, 1711; Bt.-Col., 16th October, 1712; Colonel G. Wade's Regt. (33rd Foot), 19th March, 1717; A.D.C. to the King, 25th June, 1727; Col., 13th Light Dragoons, 7th July, 1739, Royal Dragoons, 12th May, 1740 ; Lieut.-Gen., 26th March, 1743.

Probably present at the battle of Almanza, 1707. Wounded at the battle of Sherrifmuir. Took part in the expedition to Vigo, 1719. Present in the Flanders campaign, including the battles of Dettingen and Fontenoy, where he was second in command of the Horse. Was at the battle of Culloden. Defeated by the Jacobites at Falkirk, when he was in command. Governor of Portsmouth from 8th July, 1752, to his death. Nicknamed by the troops " The Hangman " on account of his severe methods of discipline. Died at Portsmouth in his house at West Green 23rd March, 1759.

THOMAS HOLLAND

Ensign, 1st March, 1694 ; Lieut., 21st January, 1703 ; Half-pay, 1713 ; Capt., T. Erle's, 6th December, 1716 ; Half-pay in 1718.

RICHARD WILLS

Probably a brother of Gen. Charles Wills (see ante). His father offered his services and those of his six sons to the Prince of Orange, who, it is said, gave them all commissions. (Dalton.) Lieut., 1st March, 1694 ; Capt.-Lieut., 21st January, 1703 ; Capt. of Grenadier Co., 1706.

Services untraced after 1709. Took part in the expedition to Cadiz and the West Indies in 1702-3. His name is in the " Malplaquet Roll."

HENRY HOLLAND

Ensign, 1st March, 1694; Qr.-Mr., same date; 2nd Lieut. of Grenadier Co., 20th November, 1696 ; 1st Lieut. of Grenadiers 18th May, 1699. Out of the Regt. in 1702.

WILLIAM WILKINSON

Capt.-Lieut., 1st March, 1694; Capt., 20th November, 1696. Meredyth's (37th Foot) in March, 1702.

ARTHUR O'NEAL

Ensign, 1st March, 1694. Out before 1702.

HENRY TRENCHARD

Baptized at Charminster, 3rd November, 1668. Son of George Trenchard, of Charminster, Dorset. Cousin to Gen. Thos. Erle.

Cornet, Marquis of Winchester's Horse, 1690 ; Lieut., T. Erle's Regiment, 1st March, 1694 ; half-pay in 1698 ; Lord Lucas's Regiment of Foot (34th Foot), 10th March, 1702.

Died 7th June, 1722.

STREAMER THOMAS

Ensign, 1st March, 1694 ; Lieut., 2nd May, 1696.

Luttrell, in his diary under date 11th May, 1699, says : " Captain Thomas of Col. Erle's Regt. was on Monday last in a duel in Hyde Park mortally wounded by another officer."

FARMER EDWARDS

Ensign, 1st May, 1694; Lieut., 1st March, 1702; Adjt. before 1705 ; Capt., 1st March, 1706. Out of the Regt., 24th April, 1707.

Served in Flanders and in the expedition to the West Indies, 1702-3.

WILLIAM WALD

Ensign, 1st May, 1694. Out before 1702.

EDWARD HOPKINS

Ensign, 22nd May, 1694 ; Lieut., 21st January, 1703. Out in 1706.

Served in Flanders and in the expedition to Cadiz and the West Indies, 1702-3.

———— SCARBOROW

Chaplain, 1st July, 1694.

WILLIAM ROLES

Ensign, 1st July, 1694; half-pay in 1698.

JOHN NIDLER

Chirugeon, 1st August, 1694.

JOHN STEELE

Ensign, 1st September, 1694. Commission renewed in 1702. Out in 1706.

Served in the expedition to Cadiz and the West Indies, 1702-3.

WILLIAM LEIGH

2nd Lieut., Grenadier Co., 1st September, 1694; commission renewed in 1702; Capt., before 1706; Bt.-Major, 10th April, 1707 ; Bt.-Lieut.-Col., 1st January, 1712 ; commission renewed, 11th January, 1715. Out of the Regt., 29th August, 1715.

Served in Flanders. Took part in the expedition to Cadiz and the West Indies in 1702-3.

IGNATIUS WHITE

Ensign, 8th Sept., 1694 ; Lord Mohun's Regt. of Foot, 10th March, 1702 ; Ensign of Chelsea Invalids, 9th June, 1711.

BENJAMIN MALFAQUERAT or MALSACUERAT

Chirugeon, 17th Sept., 1694. Out of the Regt. before 1702.

A French Huguenot naturalised 25th March, 1688.

ROBERT CLARK

Ensign, 27th November, 1694. Out before 1702.

PETER MINSHULL

Probably the Peter Minshull, Gentleman, of Redditch (or Reddish, near Stockport), administration of whose estate was granted at Chester, 1719. (Dalton.) Lieut., Viscount Castleton's Regt., 1st May, 1693; Capt., Col. Thos. Farrington's Regt. (29th Foot), 16th February, 1694; T. Erle's Regt., 18th February, 1695; half-pay in 1698; Capt., Grenadier Co. of Col. Thos. Stringer's Regt., 10th March, 1702; Major in John Livesay's Regt. (12th Foot), 10th October, 1702.

Served in Flanders and in the West Indies.

A certain Elizabeth, widow of Lieut.-Colonel Minshull petitioned the Lord High Treasurer. Her Majesty had granted her a pension of £50 a year in consideration of the loss of her husband, brother and son in Her Majesty's Service. Prays for payment. (Treasury Papers, 6th July, 1714.)

JOHN WILLIAMS

Ensign, 22nd April, 1695; half-pay, 1st May, 1698; reappointed Ensign in Erle's, 1702. Out of the Regt. in 1706.

Served in the West Indies, 1702-3.

GILBERT BURRINGTON

Ensign, 22nd April, 1695; half-pay in 1698; reappointed Ensign in Erle's, 1st March, 1702. Out in 1706.

Served in the West Indies, 1702-3.

JOHN TERTRE DECOPHAM

Born at Neuchatel, son of Ambroise du Tertre Deccpham. Capt., 14th May, 1695. Out before 1706.

Served in the Cadiz expedition in 1702.

A French Huguenot, naturalised 25th March, 1688.

FRANCIS FULFORD

Ensign, 22nd May, 1695. Out of the Regt. in 1702.

A certain Francis Fulford was Mayor of Exeter in 1690. (Domestic State Papers.)

LUCY or LOVEN CRAVEN

Eldest son of Loven Craven, of Philip Babington's Regt. (6th Foot), killed at Aughrim. Ensign, 23rd May, 1695; Lieut., 21st January, 1703.

Killed in action at Guadeloupe in 1703.

JOHN MADAN

Ensign, 13th August, 1695. Out of the Regt. in 1702.

Served in Flanders.

THOMAS NEW

Ensign, 20th August, 1695; Lieut. before 1706; Capt.-Lieut., 7th May, 1708 ; Capt., 23rd December. 1708. Untraced after 1709.

Served in Flanders and with the expedition to Cadiz and the West Indies.

In Mr. Dalton's "Malplaquet Roll."

EDWARD COX

Ensign, 1st March, 1696. Out of the Regt. in 1706.

Served in the expedition to Cadiz and the West Indies, 1702-3.

JOSEPH HENNING

Ensign, 1st March, 1696; half-pay in 1698.

WILLIAM STROUDE

Ensign, 1st March, 1696 ; Sir Ric. Tempie's Regt. of Foot, 10th March, 1702. Out in 1709.

JOHN MASSEY

Ensign, 15th April, 1696; commission renewed in 1702; 2nd Lieut., Grenadier Co. before 1706; commission renewed as Lieut., 11th January, 1715.

Served at Cadiz and with the expedition to the West Indies, 1702-3.

A certain John Massey was appointed Captain in Colonel Chas. Dubourgay's Regiment of Foot, 11th July, 1700, and another John Massey was placed on half-pay from Colonel James Leigh's Regiment of Foot in 1713. (Dalton.)

GEORGE TOULEY

Ensign, 2nd May, 1696. Out of the Regt. in 1702.

Probably the Lieutenant Touley who was killed in Jamaica when fighting a duel with Lieutenant John Oresby about 1703. (Dalton.)

WILLIAM NUTTALL

Qr.-Mr., 20th November, 1696; serving as such in 1702.

JOHN STRANGWICH

Lieut., 26th June, 1697 ; Sir Ric. Temple's Regt. of Foot, 10th March, 1702.

Probably meant for Robert Strangwich who was placed on half-pay as a Lieutenant when Erle's Irish battalion was disbanded in 1697. (Dalton). Served in Flanders.

ABRAHAM FOYE

Ensign, 26th June, 1697 ; half-pay in 1698.

Erle's Irish Battalion was disbanded after the Peace of Ryswick, signed in September, 1696, and many of the officers were placed on half-pay, whilst others were absorbed in his senior battalion.

PETER TOUSSIANT

Chirugeon, 18th May, 1699; commission renewed in 1702 and on 11th January, 1715.
Was with the West Indian expedition in 1702-3.

WILLIAM TAYLOR

Ensign, April, 1701; Capt. in Army, March, 1711; R. Sutton's Regt. (19th Foot), 2nd November, 1722; commission renewed, 20th June, 1727 ; serving in 1736 ; Independent Co. of Invalids at Jersey, 12th January, 1740; Co. of Invalids at Chester, 22nd August, 1744; succeeded, 16th June, 1759.
In the " Malplaquet Roll."

JOHN WHITEING

Ensign, 1702; Lieut., 7th May, 1708; commission renewed, 11th January, 1715; Capt.-Lieut., Hans Hamilton's Regt. (16th Foot) in 1715.
In the " Malplaquet Roll."

THOMAS PIERCY

Ensign, 1702; 2nd Lieut., Grenadier Co., 7th May, 1708; commission renewed as Lieut., 11th January, 1715. Out of the Regt. in 1727.
In the " Malplaquet Roll."

RICHARD GOODMAN

Ensign, 1702-6.
Died as Lieutenant in R. Sutton's Regiment in 1713.

THOMAS WOLF

Ensign, 1702.
Died as Lieutenant, 23rd July, 1713, when succeeded by Lieutenant R. Wenman.

ARTHUR GORE

Ensign, 1702-6.

THOMAS CLIFFE or CLIFT

Ensign, 1702-6 ; commission as Lieut. in Ric. Sutton's Regt. (19th Foot) ; renewed, 11th January, 1715.
Died 15th February, 1725. Will proved in Dublin same year.

ANDREW PLUNKETT

Chirugeon's Mate, 1702-6.
Died in 1736. Will proved in Dublin. Belonged to Athboy, Co. Meath.

———— SYNGE

Chaplain, March 1702. Was succeeded by Henry Cottingham same year.
Served in the West Indies.

HENRY COTTINGHAM, M.A.

Possibly son of the Very Revd. Henry Cottingham, Dean of Clonmacnoise and Archdeacon of Meath ; Chaplain, 1702. Out of the Regt. in 1708.

MAURICE WARREN

Lieut., 1702; 1st Lieut. in H. Mordaunt's New Marines, 10th March, 1702.

Served with the expedition to the West Indies, 1702-3.

WILLIAM MARTIN

Ensign, 1702; 2nd Lieut., Grenadier Co., 24th June, 1707; 1st Lieut., 1709. Untraced after 1709.

In the " Malplaquet Roll."

WILLIAM COURT

Ensign, 1702; Lieut., 5th April, 1708.

In the " Malplaquet Roll."

Tried by a General Court Martial held at Warde, Flanders, on 6th May, 1711. Charge : Making a complaint of a paper delivered to Colonel Freke, signed by several officers of the Regiment, reflecting on his honour and reputation. Captain James Phillips and several other officers gave evidence. Acquitted. The Court being unanimously of opinion that the accusation was grounded on errors.

RICHARD BENTLEY

Ensign, 21st January, 1703.

Served in the expedition to the West Indies, 1703.

WILLIAM MERCER

Ensign, 21st January, 1703; Lieut., 18th October, 1703; Capt., 31st March, 1727; commission renewed, 20th June, 1727; retired, 4th June, 1744.

In the " Malplaquet Roll."

ARTHUR HUBBARD

Ensign, 21st January, 1703. Out before 1706.

Served in the expedition to the West Indies, 1703.

WILLIAM CALVERT

Lieut., 21st January, 1703. Out before 1706.

Served in the expedition to the West Indies, 1703. Probably several of the officers who left before 1706 died in the West Indies.

WILLIAM NEW

Ensign, 21st January, 1703. Out before 1706.

Served in the expedition to the West Indies, 1703.

FRANCIS SAVAGE

Ensign, Sir Beville Granville's Regt. (10th Foot), 22nd March, 1694; Lieut., 2nd May, 1696; T. Erle's Regt. (19th Foot), 21st January, 1703-6.

JOHN MASSEY

Ensign, March, 1703; 2nd Lieut. of Grenadiers in 1706; commission renewed, 11th January, 1715.

Sir WARREN CROSBIE, Bart.

Elder son of Maurice Crosbie, of Crosbie Park, Wicklow. Ensign, 18th October, 1703; Lieut., 24th April, 1706; Grenadier Co. in 1723; Capt., 15th November, 1740. Retired, 17th June, 1746.

In the "Malplaquet Roll." According to the "Gentleman's Magazine," he served in all the great battles under the Duke of Marlborough. Died at Crosbie Park, 30th January, 1759. He had a pension of £200 a year in 1727.

MICHAEL LEGGE

Ensign, 18th October, 1703; Lieut., 23rd January, 1710; commission renewed, 11th January, 1715; Capt.-Lieut., 15th November, 1740; Capt., 27th January, 1741. Left the Service, 21st April, 1743.

In the "Malplaquet Roll."

THOMAS WOODHOUSE

Lieut., 21st September, 1705; Capt., 24th April, 1707; commission renewed, 11th January, 1715; half-pay, 23rd December, 1726.

In the "Malplaquet Roll."

THOMAS PRATT

Qr.-Mr., 21st September, 1705; Adjt., 6th December, 1706; Capt., Grenadier Co., January, 1715. Out of the Regt. 14th May, 1715.

In the "Malplaquet Roll."

RICHARD TOVEY

Lieut., 1706. Out of the Regt. in 1715.

In the "Malplaquet Roll."

MONIER SIMMONDS or SYMONDS

Lieut., 1706; Adjt. in 1713; commission renewed as Adjt., 11th January, 1715; Capt.-Lieut., 2nd March, 1718; Capt., 23rd December, 1726; commission renewed, 20th June, 1727. Out of the Regt. in 1733.

Served in the expedition to Cadiz and the West Indies in 1702-3. Died shortly before 24th December, 1732.

JAMES PHILLIPS

Ensign in Army, September, 1702; Lieut., T. Erle's Regt. in 1706; Capt. of Grenadier Co., 10th January, 1710; commission renewed, 11th January, 1715 and 20th June, 1727; Adjt., 18th November 1736—19th June, 1739 ; Major, 27th January, 1740 ; Lieut.-Col., 24th September, 1744. Out of the Regt., 6th February, 1746.

Served in Flanders. In the "Malplaquet Roll." Died 17th July, 1763.

RICHARD STONE

Capt., 7th March, 1706; commission renewed, 11th January, 1715.

In the "Malplaquet Roll." Died 6th December, 1716.

RICHARD EAGLESFIELD

Ensign, 25th November, 1706; T. Stanwix's Regt., 2nd August, 1707; Lieut., 1709; serving in T. Stanwix's newly-raised Regiment (12th Foot) in 1717. Lieut. of a Co. of Invalids at Carlisle, 3rd April, 1719.

In the "Malplaquet Roll." Died 21st May, 1743.

MATTHEW WALLER

Ensign, 24th April, 1707; commission renewed, 11th January, 1715. Out of the Regt., 25th February, 1718.

In the "Malplaquet Roll."

WILLIAM DAVENPORT

Ensign, 24th June, 1707. Services untraced after 1709.

In the "Malplaquet Roll."

THOMAS MALLET, Clk.

Chaplain, 1st August, 1707. Out of the Regt., 7th May, 1708.

Served in Flanders in 1694.

GABRIEL SIMONDS

Ensign, 1st August, 1707; Lieut., 16th November, 1713; half-pay in 1713.

CHARLES MAINWARING

Ensign, 24th March, 1708; Lieut., 24th June, 1710; commission renewed as 1st Lieut. in Grenadier Co., 11th January, 1715; Capt., 4th November, 1717; commission renewed, 20th June, 1727. Out of the Regt., 31st March, 1737.

Will proved in Dublin, 1737.

EDWARD RAWSON

Ensign, 5th April, 1708; commission renewed as Ensign, 11th January, 1715.

In the "Malplaquet Roll."

SAMUEL DUNSTER, Clk.

Chaplain, 1st Royal Regt. of Foot, 14th April, 1702, Erle's Regt., 7th May, 1708. Out of the Regt., 2nd November, 1713.

In the "Malplaquet Roll" Was Chaplain to the Duke of Marlborough for some years after 1713. Appointed Vicar of Rochdale in 1722 where he died in July, 1754.

"He was a dignified clergyman and a useful magistrate, though a poor and verbose preacher. He had high-church and non-juring leanings and was closely associated with the active Jacobite party at Manchester (D.N.B.).

WILLIAM BUTTS

Ensign, 7th May, 1708.
In the " Malplaquet Roll."

THOMAS INWOOD

Ensign, 7th May, 1708; Lieut. and Capt., 1st Foot Guards, 11th January, 1715; Capt. and Lieut.-Col., 18th July, 1718.

In the " Malplaquet Roll." Died 25th March, 1747, on the full pay list, whilst holding the appointment of Deputy Ranger of Enfield Chase. (Dalton.)

ERLE SIMMONDS

Qr.-Mr., 23rd March, 1709; half-pay in 1713.
In the " Malplaquet Roll."

GEORGE PAXTON

Capt., 23rd March, 1709. Untraced later.
In the " Malplaquet Roll."

JAMES HALES

Capt., 1711.
Succeeded by Captain A. Macdonell, 11th June, 1711.

ALEXANDER MACDONELL

Capt., 11th June, 1711.

Out of the Regiment before June, 1715. As Junior Captain, was in treaty with Br. R. Sutton for the Lieut.-Colonelcy of the Regiment, and had leave to go to Ireland to raise the money (£3,000), but could not do so, and it was bought by Major George Grove, of Br.-Genl. William Evans' Foot. Probably the same as Alex. McDonald, Lieut. of Lord Mark Kerr's newly raised Regiment of Foot, 1st January, 1706, so terribly cut up at Almanza.

RICHARD SUTTON

Born 1674; 2nd son of Robert Sutton, of Nottinghamshire, and nephew of the 1st Lord Lexington. Ensign, Viscount Castleton's Regt., 1st April, 1681; Capt., 1st June, 1693; Major, 1st August, 1697; Richmond Webb's Regt. (8th Foot), 14th April, 1701; Lieut.-Col., 10th September, 1702; Bt.-Col., 2nd August, 1704; Col. of Macartney's Regt., 23rd March, 1709; Br.-Gen., 1st January, 1710; Col. of Br.-Gen. Freke's Regt. (19th Foot), 3rd April, 1712-15; Col. of G. Grove's Regt. (19th Foot), reappointed, 24th October, 1729.

M.P. for Newark, 1710. Governor of Hull, 20th July, 1711. Commanding troops, Bruges, 3rd October, 1713. Governor of Guernsey, 1733. Lieutenant-General, 27th October, 1735. Took part in the seige of Namur, 1692-1695. Siege of Venloo and storming of Liege. Present at the battles of Schellenburg, Blenheim, Ramillies, and Oudenarde. Sieges of Menin and Aeth. Died in July, 1737.

A memoir of this distinguished officer appeared in The Green Howards' Gazette by Charles Dalton.

Note.—All the early Army Lists give the date of Br.-Genl. Freke's appointment as Colonel of the Regiment as 23rd March, 1709, but according to the Commission Registers it is stated that he bought the Colonelcy from General Erle on the 22nd January, 1712, and sold it to Br.-General Sutton on 3rd April following. I have, however, adhered to the Army List date. (M.L.F.)

RICHARD WENMAN

A Cadet of Viscount Wenman's family; Lieut., 23rd July, 1713, from half-pay. Again on half-pay in 1714. Cholmley's Regt. (16th Foot), 6th June, 1724 ; R. Regt. of Horse Guards, 9th September, 1726 ; Capt., 10th December, 1739.

Died shortly before 22nd March, 1744, when succeeded. A particular friend of Brigadier R. Sutton, brought into the Regiment by him over the heads of all the ensigns.

JOHN FURNESS

Capt. in 1713; commission renewed, 11th January, 1715. Out of the Regt., 4th November, 1717.

GEORGE GROVE

Ensign, Col. Ed. Fitzpatrick's Regt. (7th Foot), 21st May, 1692; 2nd Lieut. Grenadier Co., 25th August, 1693; Capt., Br.-Gen. Wm. Evans' Foot, 10th April, 1703 ; Lieut.-Col., Ric. Sutton's Regt., April, 1713; Col. of the Regt. (19th Foot), 5th August, 1715; commission renewed, 20th June, 1727.

Served with Fitzpatrick's Regiment in Flanders, 1693-97, and was taken prisoner at Steenkirke. Took part in the expedition to Cadiz and Vigo in 1702. At Malplaquet with Br.-Genl. Evans' Foot.

Governor of Dartmouth, 14th September, 1727.

Died 13th October, 1729, from the effects of a fall from his horse. Will proved in Dublin same year.

FRANCIS SYMONDS

Adjt., 24th June, 1713 " in room of Monier Symonds, who resigned to him."

BERNARD WILSON

Chaplain, 2nd November, 1713.

Probably succeeded by James Bramston, who was serving as Chaplain in 1721.

PHILIP CECIL

Ensign, 16th November, 1713; 2nd Lieut., C. Dubourgay's Regt. (32nd Foot), 10th June, 1725; commission renewed, 15th September, 1727. Out of the Regt., 17th July, 1734.

LEMYNG RICHARDSON

Born 1694; Ensign, 24th February, 1714; Lieut., 2nd March, 1719; Sir John Ligonier's Regt. of Horse (7th Dragoon Guards), 15th November, 1734; Capt.-Lieut., 19th September, 1743; Honywood's (11th Dragoons), 3rd May, 1748 ; Fort Major, Dungannon, 18th February, 1746. Out of the Army, 9th February, 1751.

A copy of his will dated 1752 is in the Record Office, Dublin.

THOMAS BROWN

Commission renewed as Ensign, 11th January, 1715. Out of the Regt., 11th December, 1717.

JOSEPH STYSTED

Lieut., Lord North and Grey's Regt. (10th Foot), 1st May, 1709; Capt., R. Sutton's Regt., 11th January, 1715; commission renewed as Captain in 1727. Out of the Regt., 1st April, 1744.

At the battle of Malplaquet with Lord North and Grey's (wounded).

ROBERT MOORE

Commission as Ensign renewed 11th January, 1715. Out of the Regt., 12th Dec., 1717.

JOSEPH FURNESS

Commission renewed as Ensign, 11th January, 1715; Lieut., 4th November, 1717. Out of the Regt., 14th June, 1731.

JOSHUA or JOSEPH GREEN

Commission renewed as Ensign, 11th January, 1715; Lieut., 25th February, 1719. Out of the Regt. in October, 1721.

WILLIAM BARTON

Commission renewed as Ensign, 11th January, 1715; serving in 1723. Out in 1727.

RANDOLPH BARON

Ensign, 24th March, 1715; Lieut., 1st July, 1719; Grenadier Co., September, 1723. Out of the Regt. before 1727.

WILLIAM ROUSBY

Ensign, 24th April, 1715; Lieut., 30th May, 1720; commission renewed, 20th June, 1727; Capt.-Lieut., 7th January, 1741. Left the Regt., 17th October, 1744.

Died at York, 6th April, 1761.

EDWARD BROWNE

Capt., 14th May, 1715. Out of the Regt., 22nd May, 1725.

THOMAS HANDASYDE

Son of Maj.-Gen. Thos. Handasyde (22nd Foot); Capt.-Lieut., Br.-Gen. T. Handasyde's Regt., 3rd April, 1712 ; Lieut., Col., Geo. Grove's Regt. (19th Foot), 5th August, 1715 ; commission renewed, 20th June, 1727.

Died 6th October, 1729.

ADAM WILLIAMSON

Probably son of Surgeon Adam Williamson, of Br. Meredyth's Regt. (37th Foot); Lieut. in Meredyth's Regt., 12th May, 1706; half-pay as Capt. in Br. Gen. Primrose's Regt. (24th Foot), 13th May, 1713; G. Grove's Regt., 29th August, 1715; 3rd Regt. of Guards, 6th November, 1717; Adjt.-Gen. to the Forces with rank of Colonel, 8th February, 1722; Br.-Gen., 2nd July, 1739; Major-Gen., 14th August, 1741; Lieut.-Gen., 3rd July, 1745.

Took part in the war of the Spanish Succession and was present at the battles of Ramillies, Oudenarde, and Malplaquet. Was A.D.C. to Lieut.-Gen. Meredyth and to Lord Cadogan.

The " London Gazette " under date 14th November, 1715, states : " On the 12th inst., in the evening, arrived Captain Williamson, Aid-de-Camp to Lieut.-Gen. Cadogan, with the treaty of the Barrier, signed at Antwerp on the 5th inst. O.S."

Deputy-Lieutenant of the Tower, 29th October, 1722, to 1747. Governor and Captain of Carisbrooke Castle, 1727. Governor of Gravesend and Tilbury, 1742. Held all three offices till his death. Author of " Military Maxims of Turenne," 1740. Died at Islington, of asthma, 9th November, 1747. Buried at Binfield, near Wokingham.

General Williamson's diary, 1722-1747, edited by John Charles Fox, F.R.H.S., has been published by the Camden Society.

NATHANIEL BLAND

Ensign, 4th November, 1717. Services untraced.

A certain Nathaniel Bland, LL.D., of Dublin, died in 1760. Will proved in Dublin.

PETER SMITH

Ensign, 4th November, 1717. Out of the Regt. before 1727.

Probably the Peter Smith, Cornet in J. Dormer's Regiment (14th Dragoons), 14th April, 1724 ; Lieut., 13th March, 1742 ; Capt.-Lieut., 3rd September, 1747. Out 2nd March, 1754.

ROGER CRYMBLE

Ensign, 12th December, 1717; Lieut., 11th July, 1722; commission renewed, 20th June, 1727. Left the Regt., 21st January, 1743.

The Hon. HENRY SOUTHWELL

Baptized 6th October, 1700 ; 2nd son of 1st Baron Southwell, M.P. for Limerick, 1729-1759; Ensign, 25th February, 1719; Lieut., 25th March, 1723; commission renewed 20th June, 1727; Grenadier Co. in 1731; Capt. in Jas. Dormer's Regt. (6th Foot), 28th January, 1736; T. Price's Regt. (14th Foot), 18th September, 1741 ; De Grangue's Dragoons (9th Dragoons), 17th March, 1743. Out of the Army, 4th March, 1745.

Deputy Governor of Limerick. Will proved in Dublin, 1765.

WILLIAM GARDINER

Ensign, 2nd March, 1719. Out of the Regt., 15th March, 1726.

BARTHOLEMEW STACKPOOLE

Ensign, 1st July, 1719. Out before 1727.

GEORGE SPEKE PETTY

2nd Lieut., Lord Tyrawly's Regt. (7th Foot), 12th May, 1715; Capt., Geo. Grove's Regt., 15th August, 1719.

Died in 1722. Will proved in Dublin.

MATTHEW BUNBURY

Ensign, 30th May, 1720; commission renewed 20th June, 1727; Lieut., 16th May, 1733; invalided as "incapable of serving," 22nd April, 1743.

A certain Matthew Bunbury died on the 11th August, 1786. His tomb is in Ballyoughtera Churchyard, Co. Cork.

JAMES BRAMSTON

Chaplain in 1721; 2nd Dragoon Guards, 21st June, 1721; resigned to the Rev. Thomas Vesey, 4th October, 1721.

THOMAS VESEY or VEZEY

Chaplain, Col. Peter Carle's Regt. of Foot; half-pay Col. Theodore Vezey's Regt. of Foot in 1714; Col. G. Grove's Regt., 4th October, 1721. Retired, 22nd March, 1726.

RICHARD DIXIE

Ensign, 10th October, 1721; commission as Ensign renewed, 20th June, 1727; serving in 1730.

Died, 25th December, 1732.

WILLIAM HOARE

Capt., Nicholas Sankey's Regt. (39th Foot), 3rd March, 1717; Geo. Grove's Regt. (19th Foot), 10th October, 1721; commission renewed, 20th June, 1727; Town Major of Dublin, 26th March, 1737. Succeeded, 22nd November, 1739.

JOHN FLETCHER

Lieut. in Lord Tunbridge's New Foot, 12th April, 1706; half-pay on disbandment in 1712; Geo. Grove's Regt. (19th Foot), 12th March, 1722, from half-pay in Br. Gen. Fras. Gore's Regt. Out of the Regt. in 1727.

NEWDICATE DALGARDNO

Ensign, 11th July, 1722; Adjt., 15th March, 1727; Lieut., 28th January, 1735. Succeeded 18th November, 1736.

Marked "dead" in a M.S. list of officers of 1736, in the Record Office, Dublin.

EDWARD LYSTER

Ensign, 22nd November, 1722; commission renewed, 20th June, 1727. Out of the Regt., 17th November, 1729.

THOMAS BURTON

Ensign, January, 1723; Lieut., 15th February, 1724; Capt.-Lieut., 23rd December, 1726; commission renewed, 20th June, 1727; Capt., 31st March, 1737; 2nd Regt. of Horse, Clement Neville's (5th Dragoon Guards), 10th May, 1740; Major, J. Mordaunt's Dragoons (12th Dragoons), 15th April, 1749. Out of the Army, 15th December, 1752.

JOHN CHACNEAU

Surgeon in 1723 in Ireland; commission renewed, 20th June, 1727. Out of the Regt., 31st October, 1728.

CHARLES COLLINS

Ensign, Br. Theodore Vesey's Regt., 16th February, 1716 (disbanded in June, 1717); Lieut., Lord Mark Kerr's Regt., 10th August, 1723 ; serving in Ric. Sutton's Regt. (19th Foot), in September, 1723 ; Adjt. to Lord Mark Kerr's Regt. (29th Foot), 22nd December, 1726 ; commission renewed in 1727 ; half-pay, Sir James Wood's Regt. (21st Foot), 14th June, 1734; Major, Lord Herbert's, 4th October, 1745 (disbanded, 23rd June, 1746). Major to Tower of London in 1761.

JOHN LYONS

Capt., 22nd April, 1724; commission renewed, 20th June, 1727. Out of the Regt., 3rd March, 1737.

THOMAS SOUTHWELL

Ensign, 15th February, 1725.
Removed, 22nd April, 1727. " Who is not big enough to be in the army."

NICHOLAS RYLAND

Fourth son of Charles Ryland, of Dungarvan, Co. Waterford. Ensign in Army, June, 1704; Lieut., 1st March, 1706; Adjt., Marquis de Montandre's Regt. of Foot, 1st June, 1710; Lieut., 16th February, 1716; half-pay on disbandment, 1717; Geo. Grove's Regt., 18th February, 1725; commission renewed, 20th June, 1727; Grenadier Co. in 1731; serving in 1737.
Died 7th November, 1739.

CEORGE DOBSON, Clk.

Chaplain, 22nd March, 1725; commission renewed, 20th June, 1727; serving in 1737.

DANIEL WEBB

Ensign, 1st Foot Guards, 20th March, 1721; Capt., 16th April, 1722; Geo. Grove's Regt., 22nd May, 1725; commission renewed, 20th June, 1727; 4th Horse (7th Dragoon Guards), 20th May, 1732; Major, 29th March, 1742; Lieut.-Col., 27th May, 1745; Colonel, 48th Foot, 11th November, 1755; Major-Gen., 23rd June, 1759; Gen., 1765; Col., 8th Foot, 18th December, 1766; 14th Dragoons, 22nd October, 1772.
Commanded a squadron at the Battle of Dettingen ; also the 7th Dragoon Guards at the battle of Fontenoy. Subsequently served in Germany under Prince Ferdinand of Brunswick, and commanded a brigade of Cavalry at the battle of Warburgh in 1760.
Died in Dublin, 11th November, 1773.

PHILIP SUCKLINC

Ensign, August, 1725.
Died, 1st September, 1725.

RICHARD HAWLEY

Son of Major Richard Hawley, of Erle's Regt.; Ensign, Ric. Sutton's Regt., 3rd September, 1710; half-pay in 1714; Geo. Grove's Regt. (19th Foot), 1st September, 1725; commission renewed, 20th June, 1727; Lieut., 18th November, 1736; half-pay, 18th February, 1749. Out of the Army List in 1752.

EDWARD GIBSON

Ensign, 1st September, 1725, but "vacated" the same day.

THOMAS LEAKE

Ensign in Army, September, 1710; Geo. Grove's Regt. (19th Foot), 1st September, 1725; commission renewed, 20th June, 1727; Lieut., 14th August, 1738; Adjt., 19th June, 1739; Capt., 31st January, 1743.

Taken prisoner at the battle of Roucoux, 1746.

Sir JOHN REDMOND FREKE, Bart.

Third and youngest son of Sir Ralph Freke, 1st Bart. of West Bilney, Norfolk. Ensign, 15th March, 1726; commission renewed, 20th June, 1727. Out of the Regt. in 1733.

Succeeded as 3rd Bart., 10th April, 1728.

Died, 13th April, 1764. (Title extinct.)

JAMES GROVE

Lieut., 9th June, 1726; half-pay on reduction in 1728; reappointed to Geo. Grove's Regt., 3rd May, 1728. Out of the Regt., 19th February, 1743.

RICHARD LOWNDES

Lieut., 3rd Sept., 1726; commission renewed, 20th June, 1727; serving in 1730. Out of the Regt., 16th May, 1733.

A certain Richard Lowndes was M.P. for Bucks in 1756. Eldest son of Robert Lowndes, Sheriff of Bucks, 1738. Died at Willesden, 6th November, 1775.

THOMAS WEBB

Born 1693; 3rd son of John Webb, of New Street, Wiltshire. 1st Lieut., Sir Charles Hotham's Regt. of Foot, 25th March, 1705; Capt., 10th March, 1708; half-pay on disbandment, Sept., 1713; Sir C. Hotham's new Corps, July, 1715; half-pay on disbandment in 1718; George Grove's Regt., 6th December, 1726; reduced with his company in 1728; half-pay in 1754.

Sir Charles Hotham's Regiment formed part of the garrison of Alicante, which stood a prolonged siege and was taken by the French in 1709. His new regiment marched to Scotland soon after Sherrifmuir and was quartered at Ayr and embarked for Ireland in 1717.

NICHOLAS FORDE

Born about 1705. 4th son of Matthew Forde, of Seaford, Co. Down, and Coolgrenny, Co. Wexford; brother of Francis Forde, Lord Clive's "right-hand man." Ensign, 24th December,

1726 ; Lieut., 7th November, 1739 ; Adjt., 21st January, 1743 ; Capt.-Lieut., 20th October, 1746; Capt., 2nd July, 1747.

Served in Flanders during the war of the Austrian Succession, and was present at the battles of Fontenoy, Roucoux, and Lauffeldt.

Lost at sea in the " Neptune " between Chester and Dublin about December, 1748. Administration of his estate granted January, 1749.

Petition by his widow, Mary Forde, to the Lord Lieutenant. (P.R.O., Dublin.)

The Humble Petition of Mary Forde, widow and Relict of Nicholas Forde, late Captain in the Regiment of the Right Honourable the Lord George Beauclerc.

Delivered to my Lord Lieutenant by Dean Delaney, 21st June, 1749.

" Most humble showeth that said Captain Nicholas Forde bought his first commission, was twenty-two years in the army, six of which he served in Flanders, and came to England with his Royal Highness, the Duke of Cumberland, at the time of the Rebellion in Scotland, but returned to Flanders immediately after the Rebellion was over, was ir every battle in Flanders except Dettingen—which the Regiment did not come up in time enough for. Bought the Adjutant's place which he sold to great loss upon being made Captain. In Germany he lost all his baggage, tents, bedding, horse and cloathes. When Ghent was taken, he lost his chest which he had there, and in it everything he had that was valuable. He was sent with a detachment to Bergen-op-Zoom and was within a quarter-of-a-mile of the town when it was taken ; there he lost his horse and furniture (which he valued at fifty pounds) by lending them to a wounded officer whom he met coming from the town, and afterwards they fell into the hands of the French. The truth of all these facts are well known to his (then) Colonel the Honourable Lieut.-General Charles Howard, to whom she also appeals for a more particular account of his faithful services. He was broke in Flanders, endured great hardships at sea between Flanders and England, and was lost between Chester and Dublin in the " Neptune." His money and bills (if he had any, as it is supposed he had) perished with him. Nothing belonging to him has been thrown up. His widdow and six children are helpless. His eldest son not quite ten years old ; and from these unhappy accidents, entirely unprovided for.

Most humbly hope, etc.,

(Sd.) MARY FORDE."

ELISHA GROVE

Qr.-Mr., 25th December, 1726 ; half-pay in 1728 ; omitted from half-pay list in 1745.

WILLIAM ARNAUD

Lieut., 26th December, 1726, from Cornet half-pay in Baron de Borle's Regt.; commission renewed, 20th June, 1727; reduced with Capt. Adams' Co. in 1729; from half-pay, Roger Handasyde's (16th Foot), to be Capt. of a new Co. of Invalids under Lieut.-Col. M. Crackerode (that sailed with Anson), 13th November, 1739.

JOHN LAMBERT

Ensign, 26th December, 1726; commission renewed, 20th June, 1727; reduced with his company in 1729.

JOHN ADAMS

Adjt., Lord Paston's Regt. of Foot, 25th March, 1705; Recruiting Service in England in 1709; Capt., Lord Mark Kerr's Foot, 27th April, 1710; disbanded on half-pay, 1712; Geo. Grove's (19th Foot), 26th December, 1726; reduced in 1729.

THOMAS MASTERS

Ensign, C. Wills' (3rd Foot), 13th September, 1717; Geo. Grove's Regt. (19th Foot), 26th December, 1726. Reduced with his Company in 1728.

EDWARD GIBBS

Ensign, 22nd April, 1727.
Died before August 1st, 1728.

HENRY GODDARD

Ensign, 1st August, 1728; Lieut., 19th January, 1740; Capt.-Lieut., 2nd July, 1747; 24th Foot, 29th April, 1754; succeeded, 11th January, 1764.

Wounded at the battle of Lauffeldt in 1747. The "Gentleman's Magazine" says he served in all the battles under the Duke of Cumberland. Died in October, 1770.

ALEXANDER MOORE

Surgeon, 31st October, 1728. Out in 1748.

FRANCIS FARQUHAR

Major, Sir James Wood's Regt. of Scotch Dutch, 6th December, 1709; Lieut.-Col., 20th December, 1715; half-pay on disbandment, 1716; Lieut.-Col. of Geo. Grove's (19th Foot), 18th October, 1729; Lord Mark Kerr's (13th Foot), 12th June, 1731.

He was examined for half-pay at Edinburgh, 15th July, 1726, his age then being 49, with 30 years' service. He had been on active service in Flanders.

Died shortly before 20th January, 1736.

He petitioned the House of Commons in 1721 in reference to arrears due to his and other Regiments, which had served on the Dutch establishment.

GEORGE COOTE

Born 1712. Second son of the Revd. Childey Coote, D.D. Ensign, 7th November, 1729; Lieut., 31st March, 1736; Capt.-Lieut., 23rd May, 1746; Capt., 20th October, 1746; H. Harrison's Regt. (15th Foot), 2nd February, 1747; Capt. of Invalids at Languard Fort, 8th November, 1756.

Wounded at the battle of Fontenoy. Died at Ipswich, 19th June, 1785.

BENEDICT BLAGDEN

Ensign, Royal Regt. of Ireland (18th Foot), 23rd March, 1711; Commission renewed in 1715; Lieut., 25th April, 1717;

Henry Grove's Regt. (10th Foot), 24th July, 1724 ; serving as Lieut. in R. Sutton's Regt. (19th Foot) in 1730 ; Independent Co. of Foot in Guernsey, 2nd November, 1733-1740 ; 74th Foot (disbanded 1768), 25th May, 1762.

Died, 3rd December, 1771.

JOHN MEAD

Ensign, 21st April, 1731.

Dead, 20th November, 1734.

HUGH, Lord SEMPILL

Fourth son of Francis Abercromby, afterwards Lord Glassford, and Anne, in her own right Baroness Sempill. Adjt., George Preston's Regt. (26th Foot), 1st December, 1708; Capt., 12th July, 1712; half-pay in 1713; Br.-Gen., Grant's Regt., 1715; Major, Br.-Gen. Preston's Regt. (26th Foot), 5th April, 1718; Lieut.-Col. Ric. Sutton's Regt., 12th June, 1731 ; Colonel of the Earl of Crauford's Regt. (42nd Foot), 14th January, 1741 ; Colonel of the Earl of Rothes' Regt. (25th Foot), 9th April, 1745; Br.-Gen., 9th June, 1745.

Served in Spain and Flanders under the Marquis of Ormonde and Marlborough. Was present at Malplaquet. Accompanied the 42nd Foot to Flanders in 1743. Distinguished himself in the defence of Aeth. Commanded the left wing of the Royal army at Culloden.

Died, 25th November, 1746, at Aberdeen whilst in command of the troops there.

WILLIAM RYAN

Ensign in the Army, August, 1710; Cornet, half-pay, of Sir Daniel Carroll's Regt. of Dragoons, reduced in 1711; Lieut. in R. Sutton's Regt. (19th Foot), 14th June, 1731; Capt. in Lowther's 3rd Marines, 29th November, 1739; Major in Wolfe's 1st Marines, 15th June, 1741 ; Lieut.-Col. of Pepperell's Foot, 1st September, 1745.

By affidavit dated Paris, 8-19 August, 1726, he was 33 years of age with 16 years' service, including Portugal.

Broke, 16th February, 1748.

PETER FRANKEFORTE

Lieut. in Army, 23rd April, 1694 ; half-pay, Col. Villiers' Regt. of Foot, 1701 ; Capt., 20th May, 1705 ; Col. Charles Churchill's Regt. of Marines, 23rd December, 1709; half-pay on reduction., 1713 ; Ric. Sutton's Regt., 21st May, 1732. Out of the Regt., 31st January, 1743.

Died 27th March, 1755. Buried at Portarlington. Will proved in Dublin, 1755.

GEORGE SEMPILL

Possibly second son of Hugh, Lord Sempill. Ensign, 25th December, 1732; Qr.-Mr., 25th June, 1739; Lieut., 15th November, 1740 ; Capt.-Lieut., 24th April, 1755 ; Capt. (53rd Foot), 19th October, 1755 ; Major, 31st January, 1766. Out of the Army, 20th August, 1768.

THOMAS MAINWARING

Possibly third son of Edward Mainwaring, of Whitmore, Co. Stafford. Ensign, 16th May, 1733; Lieut., 27th January, 1741 ; 2nd Lieut., Jeffrey's Regt. of Marines, 17th June, 1746. Out of the Army, 1752.

Died, 1776.

JAMES CAMPBELL

Ensign, 20th November, 1734; Lieut., 19th February, 1743. Killed at the battle of Roucoux, 1746.

WILLIAM PETITOT

Son of Jean Petitot, a celebrated miniature painter. First commission, 1721; renewed as Ensign in R. Murray's (37th Foot), 20th June, 1727; Lieut., 7th December, 1734; Town Major of Dublin, 11th May, 1735 ; Capt., Ric. Sutton's (19th Foot), 26th May, 1735; Major, 24th September, 1744; Lieut.-Col., 2nd July, 1747; Col., 71st Foot, 29th April, 1758; Major-Gen., 2nd March, 1761; half-pay in 1763.

Wounded at the battle of Fontenoy, 1745, and again at Lauffeldt, 1747.

Died at Northallerton, 26th July, 1764.

JOHN BRADSHAW

Chaplain, 10th April, 1736; resigned, 7th June, 1751.

JOHN McKENZIE

Ensign, 28th April, 1736; 1st Lieut., Wynward's 4th Marines, 2nd December, 1739; Capt., 15th April, 1741; half-pay on disbandment, 1748; Major of New Marines, 10th December, 1755.

DANIEL LEGRAND

Ensign, 31st March, 1737 ; Lieut., 21st January, 1743. Killed at the battle of Fontenoy, 1745.

THOMAS CUTHBERT

Born 1710. Ensign, 31st March, 1737; Lieut., 1st April, 1744; Capt.-Lieut., 3rd October, 1755; Capt., 28th August, 1756; retired, 19th July, 1770.

Wounded at the battle of Roucoux, 1746.

The Hon. HUGH SEMPILL

Third son of Hugh, Lord Sempill. Ensign, 14th August, 1738; Lieut., July, 1747; half-pay in 1748; reappointed to Lord G. Beauclerk's (19th Foot), 18th February, 1749; Capt.-Lieut., 25th August, 1756 ; Capt., Co. of Marines, 12th Nov., 1757.

Died at the Cape in January, 1764.

The Hon. Sir CHARLES HOWARD, K.B.

Second son of the third Earl of Carlisle. Ensign and Lieut., Coldstream Guards, 10th August, 1715 ; Capt., Ric. Viscount Irwin's Regt. (16th Foot), 21st April, 1717; Owen Wynne's (9th

Dragoons), 20th June, 1717; Capt. and Lieut.-Col., 2nd Foot Guards, 21st April, 1719; Col. and A.D.C. to the King, 23rd April, 1734 ; Col. of Ric. Sutton's Regt., 1st November, 1738 : Major-Gen., 4th July, 1743; Lieut.-Gen., 1747; Col., 3rd Dragoon Guards, 13th March, 1748; Gen., 22nd February, 1765.

Commanded a brigade at the battles of Dettingen and Fontenoy. At the latter was wounded in four places. Commanded the Infantry at the battles of Roucoux and Lauffeldt.

Was Deputy Governor of Carlisle, 24th March, 1725. Governor of Carlisle, 24th July, 1749. K.B., 2nd May, 1749. Governor of Fort George and Fort Augustus, 8th July, 1752.

Died at Bath, 25th August, 1765.

PATRICK COCKRANE

Ensign, 19th January, 1740; Lieut., 21st April, 1743; Capt., 1st April, 1744.

Wounded at the battle of Fontenoy, and died 23rd May, 1745.

CHARLES LUMSDEN

Born 1712. Ensign, 4th February, 1740; Lieut., 22nd April, 1743; Capt., 4th June, 1744; Major, 23rd April, 1758; succeeded, 24th November, 1761.

Served in Flanders. Wounded in the attack on Belle Isle, 7th April, 1761.

Lord GEORGE BENTINCK

Born December, 1715. Second son of Henry, first Duke of Portland. Ensign, 1st Foot Guards, 3rd November, 1735; Capt., Hon. Chas. Howard's Regt., 10th May, 1740; Capt. and Lieut.-Col., 1st Foot Guards, 27th May, 1745; A.D.C. to the King, 17th March, 1752; Col., 5th Foot, 20th August, 1754.

Present at the battle of Dettingen. M.P. for Droitwich, 1742-47 ; for Grampound, 1747-54 ; and for Hamesbury, 1754-57.

Died at Bath, 2nd March, 1759.

ROBERT DOUGLAS

Born 1716. Ensign, 7th November, 1740; Lieut., 21st January, 1743; Capt., 21st April, 1743; Major, 2nd July, 1747; Lieut.-Col., 10th April, 1758. Retired 17th June, 1767.

Wounded at the battle of Fontenoy. Commanded the Regiment at the first assault on Belle Isle, 1761. Appointed an acting Brigadier there 4th March, 1761.

Died at Strathendry, Scotland, 13th December, 1803.

ANTHONY ROTOLPH LADAVEZE

Born at The Hague, 1689. Second son of—De Ladaveze, Minister at The Hague. 2nd Lieut., Churchill's Regt. (31st Foot), 25th April, 1707; 1st Lieut., 6th May, 1710; Adjt., 5th February, 1712 ; Lieut. and Adjt., Sir H. Goring's reformed Regt. (31st Foot), 1st June, 1715; Capt.-Lieut., 15th May, 1716; Capt., 15th August, 1717; Major, 29th May, 1732; Lieut.-Col., Hon. C. Howard's Regt., 22nd January, 1741. Retired, 24th September, 1744.

Served in Flanders.

Died 25th November, 1771. Buried in the French Church of St. Patrick and St. Mary, Dublin.

CHARLES CRAVEN

Born, 24th October, 1718. Second son of Charles Craven and grandson of Loven Craven, of Erle's. Ensign, 26th January, 1741; Lieut., 4th June, 1744; Capt., 17th June, 1746; Major (new Corps), 51st Foot, 6th September, 1754; half-pay, 25th December, 1756. Omitted from the Army List, 15th March, 1786.

Served in Germany and in Scotland under the Duke of Cumberland. (Burke.)

ALEXANDER MURE

Son of James Mure, of Rhoddens, Co. Down. Ensign, 27th January, 1741; Capt.-Lieut., 17th October, 1744; Capt., 23rd May, 1746. Out of Regt., 1759.

Served in the Flanders campaign, 1744-47. Wounded at Fontenoy. (Burke.)

Died at Caldwell, near Glasgow, 3rd March, 1790.

ROBERT SKENE

Eldest son of David Skene, of Pitlour, Fifeshire. Ensign, 21st January, 1743; Lieut., 1st May, 1745; Adjt., 12th February, 1748; Capt., 59th Foot, 14th April, 1756; Bt.-Lieut.-Col., 14th October, 1758; Bt.-Col., 25th May, 1752; Col., 59th Foot, 25th May, 1772; Maj.-Gen., 29th August, 1772; Col., 99th Foot, 4th May, 1781; Lieut.-Gen., 10th November, 1782; Col., 48th Foot, 31st March, 1783.

Died at Manchester, 19th May, 1787, on his way to Scotland, where he was in command of the troops.

M.P. for Fifeshire, 1779, until unseated 1780, and again till his death.

ALEXANDER CHEAPE

Ensign, 21st January, 1743.

Wounded at the battle of Fontenoy, and is supposed to have died from his wounds 11th May, 1745.

FRANCIS WILLIAM SHEPPARD

Ensign, 19th February, 1743; Lieut., 23rd May, 1746; half-pay in 1749.

WILLIAM MARTIN

Ensign, 21st April, 1743; Lieut., 20th October, 1746; Capt., 51st Foot, 28th November, 1755.

Wounded at the battle of Fontenoy, 1745, and again at the battle of Roucoux, 1747. Out of the Army List of 1763.

ALEXANDER GIBSON

Ensign, 22nd April, 1743.

Killed at the battle of Fontenoy.

JAMES HALLIBURTON

Ensign, E. Fielding's Regt. (41st Foot), 20th June, 1735; Middleton's Regt. of Foot, 19th July, 1735; Capt., W. Graham's Regt. (43rd Foot), 27th January, 1741; Hon. C. Howard's Regt., 25th April, 1743; Bt.-Lieut.-Col., Army, 21st February, 1747; Capt. and Lieut.-Col., 3rd Foot Guards, 11th April, 1750. Retired, 6th June, 1753.

M.P. Orkney and Shetland 1747-1756.

GEORGE BROWN

Ensign, 1st April, 1744 ; Lieut., 17th June, 1746.

Served in Flanders.

Wounded at the battle of Lauffeldt, 1747. Superseded, 12th January, 1753.

BOYD PORTERFIELD

Son of Alexander Porterfield, of Duchal, Co. Renfrew. Ensign, 4th June, 1744; Lieut., 20th October, 1746 (latter commission cancelled owing to absence).

Wounded at the battle of Fontenoy. Died at Southsea, 4th May, 1794.

ROBERT FARMAR

Born 1718. Fifth son of Thomas Farmar, High Sheriff of Philadelphia and Mayor of Brunswick. Capt. in Col. Gooch's American Corps, 10th January, 1740 ; half-pay on reduction, 25th December, 1742 ; Hon. C. Howard's Regt., 25th June, 1744 ; Major, 34th Foot, 15th July, 1761. Sold out, 26th November, 1768.

Served in Flanders, and at the siege of Belle Isle with 19th Foot. Was Brigade Major in Scotland in 1761. Served in America with 34th Foot, and was Commandant, Fort Mobile, Florida, in 1764-5.

Died in 1776.

WILLIAM MURRAY

Born 1724. Ensign, Gooch's (American Regt.), 14th February, 1742; half-pay, 25th December, 1742; Hon. C. Howard's (19th Foot), 25th June, 1744; Lieut., 8th April, 1755; Qr.-Mr., 25th August, 1756; 66th Foot, April, 1758; Capt.-Lieut., 27th May, 1758; Capt., 86th Foot, 1st January, 1760; half-pay on reduction, 1763; Major, 42nd Foot, 7th September, 1771; Lieut.-Col., 27th Foot, 5th October, 1777.

Died, 3rd November, 1777.

LEWIS BROWN

Lieut., Gooch's (61st American Regt.), 9th June, 1740; half-pay on disbandment, 25th December, 1742; Hon. C. Howard's (19th Foot), 25th June, 1744. " Broke," 27th November, 1746.

WILLIAM OGILVIE

Born in New York. Ensign, Gooch's (61st American Regt.), 9th June, 1740; half-pay, 25th December, 1742; Hon. C.

Howard's Regt. (19th Foot), 25th June, 1744; Independent Co. at New York, 12th February, 1751. Was succeeded, 31st March, 1758.

"Lived in New York upon a small fortune and carryed arms six years in an Independent Co. there. He was appointed Ensign in Gooch's American Regiment, and went from that province upon the W. Indian Expedition, and was afterwards made a Lieutenant. Major-General Wentworth and Brig.-General Blakeney gave him a good character."— (Treasury Papers.)

GRIFFITH GRIFFITH

Ensign, 25th June, 1744. Half-pay, 1748 to 1755.

WILLIAM MASTERS

2nd Lieut., Wolfe's Marines, 13th August, 1740; 1st Lieut., 27th April, 1741 ; Capt. in Hon. C. Howard's (19th Foot), 25th June, 1744 ; 52nd (renumbered in 1756 the 51st Foot), 28th November, 1755 ; Major 36th Foot, 31st August, 1756 ; Lieut.-Col., 74th Foot, 25th April, 1758 ; Half-Pay on disbandment in 1763 ; 35th Foot, 22nd February, 1768 ; Sold out, 30th January, 1770.

Served in Flanders and was wounded at the battle of Lauffeldt, 1747.

WILLIAM CHOLMLEY

Ensign, William Handasyd's Regt. (31st Foot), 27th January, 1741 ; Lieut., 1st April, 1744 ; Capt., Hon. C. Howard's Regt., 24th September, 1744. Resigned, 24th April, 1755.

Served in Flanders.

WALTER (or WILLIAM) HAMILTON

Born 1723. Possibly son of Alexander Hamilton, of Greenge, Co. Ayr. Surgeon, 12th October, 1744 ; Commission renewed, 27th October, 1760.

Master Apothecary to the Belle Isle expedition, 20th July, 1761. Half-pay as Apothecary (Portugal).

Died, 10th September, 1793, on half-pay, as Apothecary to the Forces.

Shewn as WALTER in Army Lists, 1754-5, 1760-1 ; WILLIAM in Army Lists, 1756-59.

WILLIAM FARQUHAR

Ensign, 17th December, 1744 ; never a Lieut.; Capt., H. Harrison's Regt. (15th Foot), 30th April, 1746 ; Major, 12th March, 1754 ; Retired, 19th September, 1758.

Served in Flanders. Died, 9th July, 1767.

ANTHONY SHARPE

Born 1709. Ensign, 1st May, 1745 (from the ranks) ; Lieut., 27th November, 1746 ; Capt., 30th August, 1756 ; 66th Foot, April, 1758.

Served in Flanders. Died, 1759.

THOMAS PHILIPS

Ensign, 1st May, 1745 ; Lieut., 10th Mar., 1747 ; Half-Pay in 1748 ; Capt., 52nd Foot, 28th December, 1755 ; Retired, 3rd March, 1772.

Wounded at the battle Lauffeldt, 1747.

JAMES McFARLANE

Ensign, 1st May, 1745 ; Lieut., 22nd December, 1753 ; Capt., 55th Foot, 30th December, 1755 ; Major, 53rd Foot, 30th August, 1768 ; Sold out, 9th December, 1775.

Wounded at the battle of Roucoux, 1746.

JOHN BIRD

Born 1729. Son of Thomas Bird, of Devonshire. Ensign, 23rd May, 1746 ; Lieut., 24th April, 1755 ; Adjt., 14th April, 1756 ; Capt.-Lieut., 11th August, 1759 ; Capt., 15th July, 1761 ; Major, 26th May, 1769 ; Lieut.-Col., 15th Foot, 30th January, 1776.

Sent to discipline the Suffolk Militia in 1760. Brigade-Major of 1st Brigade at the Siege of Belle Isle, when Capt.-Lieut. Served in the American War, and was killed at Germantown, near Philadelphia, 4th October, 1777.

"Gen. W. Hoare spoke of his death as an event much to be lamented, he being an officer of experience and approved merit." (Hist. Record XVth Foot.)

FRANCIS HOUSTON

Ensign, 24th May, 1746 ; Half-Pay in 1748.

Omitted from the half-pay list 15th February, 1787.

NATHANIEL DOBSON

Ensign, 17th June, 1746 ; Lieut., 1st October, 1755 ; Adjt., 25th August, 1756.

Wounded at the battle of Lauffeldt, 1747.

Died, 5th June, 1758

JOHN JOHNSON

2nd Lieut., Jeffrey's Regt. of Marines, 13th Mar., 1744 ; Lieut., Hon. C. Howard's Regt., 17th June, 1746 ; Capt., 42nd Company of Marines, 11th March, 1755. Omitted from Marines List, 2nd August, 1762.

JOHN SCRYMSOUR

Born 1719. Ensign, 20th October, 1746 ; Lieut., 2nd October, 1755 ; Capt.-Lieut., 15th July, 1761 ; Capt., 17th December, 1761 ; Retired, 7th January, 1768.

Taken prisoner at the first attack on Belle Isle, 7th April, 1761.

WILLIAM GUN

Possibly 3rd son of William Gun, of Rattoo, Co. Kerry. Ensign, 20th October, 1746 ; Retired, 13th January, 1753.

Tried by court martial, 1st October, 1750, at Gibraltar, for beating men of the regiment. Found "guilty." Sentence "To be suspended for one calendar month from 29th September, 1750, and at the end thereof to make an acknowledgment before Lord George Beauclerk and the officers of the regiment." (Gibraltar Garrison Orders).

The Hon. GEORGE BYRON

Born, 22nd April, 1730. Fifth son of William, fourth Lord Byron. Ensign, 27th November, 1746 ; Cornet, the Duke of Cumberland's Dragoons, 27th September, 1747 ; Half-Pay on reduction, 1748 ; Lieut., W. Herbert's Regt. (14th Foot), 22nd May, 1749 ; Lieut. and Capt., 1st Foot Guards, 18th June, 1753 ; Capt, half-pay, 8th Marines, 30th December, 1755.

Died at Paddington, 6th May, 1789.

THOMAS CLARKE

Capt., Duke of Bedford's Foot (raised for the'45), 27th September, 1745 ; Half-Pay on disbandment, 1746, Hon. C. Howard's Regt. (19th Foot), 2nd February, 1747 ; Lieut. and Capt., Coldstream Gds., 15th May, 1749 ; Capt. and Lieut.-Col., 4th March, 1761 ; Bt.-Col., 11th June, 1773 ; 2nd Major, 8th September, 1775 ; Major-Gen., 29th August, 1777 ; Lieut.-Gen., 20th November, 1782 ; Gen., 3rd May, 1796 ; A.D.C. to the King, 27th July, 1773 ; Col., 31st Foot, 3rd May, 1780 ; 30th Foot, 8th February, 1792.

Took part in the expedition against Charlestown, South Carolina, under Sir Henry Clinton in 1779. Bailiff of Godmanchester, 1762, 1770, 1779, and 1797.

JAMES WILLIAMS

Born 1717. Third son of Sir John Williams, of Tendring Hall, Stoke Nayland, Lord Mayor of London. Ensign, W. Hargrave's Regt. (31st Foot), 20th January, 1735 ; Lieut., 1st Foot Gds., 1st July, 1739 ; Capt., J. Price's Regt. (46th Foot), 27th January, 1740 ; J. Cope's (7th Dragoons), 4th April, 1745 ; Lieut.-Col., Hon. C. Howard's Regt., 6th February, 1747.

Died of wounds received at the battle of Lauffeldt, 2nd July, 1747.

Francis Grose, the celebrated antiquarian, writing on the introduction of fifes to the Army, says :—

"The fife was not adopted in the marching regiments till the year 1747. The first regiment that had it was the 19th, then called the Green Howards, in which corps I had the honour to serve ; and I well remember a Hanoverian youth, an excellent fifer, being given by his Colonel to Lieut.-Col. Williams, then commanding that regt. at Bois-le-duc, in Dutch-Flanders."

THOMAS ALEXANDER FULLER

Ensign, 10th March, 1747 ; Lieut., 3rd October, 1755 ; 3rd Dragoons, 23rd March, 1756 ; Major, commanding German Volunteers, 6th July, 1762 ; Half-Pay when disbanded in 1763.

Wounded at the battle of Lauffeldt, 1747.

JAMES HEBDEN

Born 1729. Ensign, 2nd July, 1747, from a Volunteer ; Half-Pay in 1748 ; Re-appointed Ensign, 14th February, 1749 ; Lieut., 25th December, 1755 ; Adjt., 5th June, 1758 ; Qtr.-

Mstr., 22nd August, 1760 ; Capt.-Lieut., 17th December, 1761 ; Capt., 29th March, 1762 ; 94th Foot, 15th June, 1763 ; Half-Pay in 1763. Omitted from the half-pay list in 1787.

Wounded at the battle of Lauffeldt, when serving with the regiment as a volunteer.

MAGNUS VOLGER

Ensign, 21st September, 1747, from a Volunteer ; Half-Pay in 1748 ; Re-appointed Ensign, 9th February, 1749.

Died, 27th November, 1752.

JOHN MARRIOT

Born 1719. 2nd Lieut., Robinson's 2nd Marines, 20th November, 1739 ; Lieut., Cornwall's 7th Marines, 27th March, 1744 ; Capt., Hon. C. Howard's Regt., 2nd February, 1748 ; Half-Pay, 19th Foot, 15th October, 1754 ; 18th Dragoons, 11th March, 1760. Omitted from Army List, November, 1763.

Lord GEORGE BEAUCLERK

Born, 26th December, 1704. Sixth son of Charles, 1st Duke of St. Albans. Ensign, 1st Foot Gds., 29th July, 1723 ; Lieut., Philip Honywood's Dragoons (11th Hussars), 25th December, 1726 ; Capt., Royal Horse Gds., 1728 ; Capt. and Lieut.-Col., 1st Foot Gds., 13th August, 1736 ; Col. and A.D.C. to the King, 30th May, 1745 ; Col., 8th Marines, 1747 ; the Hon. C. Howard's Regt., 15th March, 1748 ; Maj.-Gen., March, 1755 Lieut.-Gen., 25th January, 1758.

M.P. for Windsor, 1741 to 1754 ; and in 1768. Governor of Landguard Fort, 25th December, 1753. Commander-in-Chief, Scotland. September, 1756.

Died, 11th May, 1768.

BENJAMIN RUDYARD

Great-great-grandson of Sir Benjamin Rudyard, 1572-1658. Ensign, Coldstream Gds., 5th July, 1737 ; Lieut., 13th February, 1741 ; Capt., Lord G. Beauclerk's Regt., 15th May, 1749 ; 47th Foot, 21st March, 1752.

Was, at the battles of Dettingen and Fontenoy with the Coldstream Guards.

Writing to the Hon. Mrs. Chaplin from a drumhead near Aeth, dated 13th May, 1745, Lieutenant Rudyard says :—

"I received many strokes from cannon and small shots which luckily only affected the arms which I carried, which were twice shattered, and one that grazed my neck without doing me any harm."

Received the public approbation of the Duke of Cumberland at the head of his regiment, the night after the battle of Fontenoy, for his conduct in the engagement. Several of his letters were published in 1841 by J. H. Manning, B.L.

WILLIAM CLEILAND

Ensign, R. Dalzell's Regt. (38th Foot), 16th February, 1740 ; Lieut., 28th September, 1743 ; J. Skelton's Regt. (32nd Foot), 25th June, 1744 ; Independent Co. at New York, 9th July, 1745 ; Half-Pay, 23rd June, 1746 ; Re-appointed, 25th

April, 1747 ; 19th Foot, 12th February, 1751 ; Superseded, 13th January, 1753 ; Appointed Lieut. of an Independent Co. of Invalids at Sheerness, 12th November, 1757, merged into the 82nd Invalids, 8th April, 1758 ; Appointed to Independent Co. at Sheerness in 1769.

Left or died between 1772 and 1779.

On the 1st July, 1751, all regiments were numbered, Lord George Beauclerk's becoming the 19th Foot in order of seniority.

GEORGE BURVILL

Born 1727. Son of Peter Burvill, of Boxley, Kent. Matriculated University College, Oxford, 12th March, 1743, aged 16 ; B.A., 12th March, 1747.

Chaplain, 7th June, 1751 ; Resigned, 8th September, 1759.

WILLIAM RICKSON

Born at Pembroke, 25th August, 1719. Only son of Joseph Rickson. Ensign, R. Onslow's Regt. (39th Foot), 4th February, 1739 ; Lieut., August, 1739 ; Capt., Peregrine Lascelles' Regt. (47th Foot), 23rd February, 1748 ; 19th Foot, 21st March, 1752 ; Bt.-Lieut.-Col., 13th January, 1760 ; Qtr.-Mstr.-Gen., North Britain, same date.

Present at the battles of Dettingen, Fontenoy, and Roucoux (severely wounded in the right arm).

Intimate friend of Major-General James Wolfe.

Died at Broughton, near Edinburgh, 19th July, 1770. Buried in Restalrig.

" He was an officer of much experience, excellent judgment and great bravery ; at the same time humane, agreeable, generous, friendly, affectionate." (Extract from notice on tombstone.)

HENRY MOORE

Ensign, 27th November, 1752 ; Cornet, 7th Dragoons, 10th February, 1753 ; Lieut., 2nd Dragoons, 25th December, 1755 ; Half-Pay on reduction of its Light troops, 1763 to 1772.

WILLIAM MORRIS

Ensign, J. Johnston's (33rd Foot), from Cadet, 1st May, 1745 ; Lieut., 11th October, 1748 ; Half-Pay, 1748 ; Lieut., 19th Foot, 12th January, 1753 ; Capt.-Lieut., 54th (renumbered in 1756 the 52nd Foot), 25th December, 1755 ; 72nd Foot, 28th August, 1756 ; Major, 12th October, 1762 ; Half-Pay on reduction in 1763 ; Bt.-Lieut.-Col., 25th May, 1772 ; Independent Co. of Invalids at Hull, 5th November, 1779 ; Co. of Invalids (41st Foot), 2nd February, 1784 ; Half-Pay on reduction, 25th December, 1787. Out of the Army List, 1st January, 1792.

WILLIAM PORTER

2nd Lieut. of an Independent Co. under Admiral Boscawen, 27th May, 1747 ; 1st Lieut., 4th August, 1749 ; Half-Pay on disbandment, 1750 ; Lieut., 19th Foot, 13th January, 1753 ; Succeeded, 22nd December, 1753.

JOHN BOWLING

Ensign, 13th January, 1753 ; Retired on half-pay of Churchill's 1st Marines, 29th May, 1754.

THOMAS CALCRAFT

Son of the Town Clerk of Grantham and brother of John Calcraft, M.P., the great Army agent. Ensign, 10th February, 1753 ; 2nd Foot Gds., 18th June, 1753 ; Capt., 7th Foot, 2nd October, 1755 ; 52nd Foot (renumbered in 1756 the 50th Foot), 8th November, 1755 ; Lieut.-Col., 91st Foot (new), 12th January, 1760 ; 50th Foot, 29th January, 1762 ; 36th Foot, 14th August, 1772 ; Bt.-Col., 25th May, 1772 ; Maj.-Gen., 29th August, 1777 ; Lieut.-Gen., 20th November, 1782 ; Col., 79th Foot, 16th December, 1777 ; 65th Foot, 6th January, 1779.

Was A.D.C. to Duke of Marlborough in the expedition to St. Maloes, May, 1758. A.D.C. to the Lord Lieutenant of Ireland, October, 1763 to 1765.

Died, 12th March, 1783.

JAMES LLOYD

Ensign, 2nd July, 1753 ; Lieut., 30th December, 1755 ; 1st Lieut., 85th Foot, 8th September, 1759. Out of the Army List, 1760.

CHRISTOPHER CHAMBRÉ

Ensign, 22nd December, 1753 ; Lieut., 53rd Foot, 4th January, 1756. Out of the Army List, 1767.

JOHN WOOD

2nd Lieut., 5th Marines, 5th February, 1740 ; 1st Lieut., 1st June, 1742 ; Capt.-Lieut., 30th July, 1745 ; Half-Pay on disbandment, 1748 ; 19th Foot, 29th April, 1754 ; Capt, 24th April, 1755 ; 116th Co. Marines, 19th March, 1757. Retired, 11th August, 1759.

ROBERT HARPUR

Born 1736. Ensign, 29th May, 1754 ; Lieut., 13th April, 1756 ; Adjt., 11th August, 1759, to 23rd September, 1761 ; Capt.-Lieut., 29th March, 1762 ; 100th Foot, 2nd April. 1762 ; 108th Foot, 22nd October, 1762 ; Half-Pay in 1764.

Served in the siege of Belle Isle as Adjutant to the Regiment.

Died, 20th July, 1777. Buried in Corrig Churchyard, Enniscorthy, Co. Wicklow.

WILLIAM BAINBRIDGE

Born 1737. Ensign, 8th April, 1755 ; Qtr.-Mstr., 20th December, 1755 ; Lieut., 14th April, 1756 ; Capt.-Lieut., 56th

Foot, 21st July, 1760 ; Capt., 24th October, 1760 ; Half-Pay, 110th Foot, 31st March, 1770. Out of the Army List, 20th January, 1832.

WILLIAM HATSELL

Born 1736. Ensign, 24th April, 1755 ; Lieut., 30th August, 1756 ; Capt., 2nd April, 1762 ; Major, 13th January, 1776 ; Retired, 17th November, 1780.

Took part in the siege of Belle Isle, 1761. Was Town Major of Gibraltar in 1769.

ROBERT SAVILLE

Born 1737. Ensign, 1st October, 1755 ; Lieut., 5th April, 1757 ; Capt.-Lieut., 15th June, 1763 ; Capt., 8th January, 1768. Out of the Army List, 20th July, 1781.

Was in Germany with drafts at the time of the attack on Belle Isle in 1761.

JAMES NUGENT

Born 1738. Ensign, 2nd October, 1755 ; Lieut., 25th September, 1757 ; Half-Pay 1763 ; Lieut., 70th Foot, 24th June, 1768 to 1769.

Taken prisoner in the first attack on Belle Isle, 7th April, 1761.

JOHN EVANS

Born 1733. Ensign, 3rd October, 1755 ; Lieut., 26th June, 1757 ; Capt.-Lieut., 8th January, 1768 ; Half-Pay, 106th Foot, 1st May, 1770. Out of the Army List, 14th February, 1806.

Recruiting in England during siege of Belle Isle.

JOHN LESLIE

Born 1740. Ensign, 4th October, 1755 ; Lieut., 27th September, 1757 ; Capt.-Lieut., 2nd March, 1770 ; Capt., 19th July, 1770 ; Resigned, 27th April, 1772.

Took part in the siege of Belle Isle.

JAMES HARGRAVE

Ensign, Stephen Cornwallis' Regt. (34th Foot), 2nd July, 1731 ; Lieut., 1st March, 1745 ; Capt.-Lieut., 28th March, 1751 ; Capt., 19th Foot, 5th October, 1755 ; 55th Foot, 13th November, 1755. Out of the Army List, November, 1763.

Sir WILLIAM GORDON, Bart.

Born 1736. Younger son of Sir John Gordon, 5th Bart. of Embo. Ensign, 30th October, 1755 ; Lieut., 28th September, 1757 ; Capt., 26th May, 1769. Out of the Regt., 12th November, 1778.

Adjutant and Paymaster to the West Norfolk Militia, 25th July, 1778 ; Lieutenant, 25th May, 1779 ; Captain-Lieutenant, 18th July, 1793 ; Captain, 27th February, 1798.

Took part with 19th Foot in the siege of Belle Isle.

Succeeded his brother, Sir James, of the Dutch Service, about 1786, as 7th Baronet.

Died at Colchester, 7th January, 1804.

"His funeral, which attracted many mourners, being extremely aweful—nothing could exceed the solemnity with which it was conducted." ("Gentleman's Magazine.")

JAMES COATES

Born 1738. Ensign, 25th December, 1755 ; Lieut., 29th September, 1757 ; 66th Foot, April, 1758 ; Capt.-Lieut., 24th August, 1761 ; Capt., 2nd April, 1762; Major, 3rd October, 1766 ; Bt.-Lieut.-Col., 11th September, 1765 ; Lieut.-Col., 19th Foot, 26th October, 1775 ; Bt.-Col., 16th May, 1781 ; Maj.-Gen., 28th April, 1790 ; Col., 2nd Foot, 20th December, 1794 ; Lieut.-Gen., 26th January, 1797 ; Gen., 29th April, 1802.

Took part in the American War in 1781, in command of the 19th Foot and was present at the fighting at Monk's Corner and the relief of Fort Ninety-Six. Served in the campaign in Holland, 1794-95 in command of a Brigade.

Died at Heslington, near York, 22nd July, 1822.

HENRY GODDARD

Born, 1739. Ensign, 4th May, 1756; Lieut., 30th September, 1757; 66th Foot, April, 1758; 108th Foot, 17th October, 1761 ; Capt., 17th May, 1762 ; out of the Army List, 1772.

RICHARD WIDMORE KNIGHT

Born, 1737. Ensign, 5th May, 1756 ; Lieut., 1st October, 1757 ; 66th Foot, April, 1758. Half-pay, 24th Foot, 1767 to 10th March, 1817.

JAMES PATERSON

Possibly son of Col. James Paterson of the Marines. Born, 1732. 2nd Lieut., Cornwallis' (7th Marines), 17th May, 1744 ; Lieut., 18th March, 1748 ; 31st Foot, 8th March, 1749 ; Capt., 18th Co. of Marines, 18th July, 1755 ; 19th Foot, 6th July, 1756 ; Major, 63rd Foot, 24th November, 1761 ; Lieut.-Col., 15th June, 1763 ; Bt.-Col., 29th August, 1777 ; Major-Gen., 20th November, 1782 ; Col., 28th Foot, 13th July, 1787.

Lost his arm in the second attack on Belle Isle in 1761. Served in the American war of Independence in command of 63rd Foot. Was Adjt.-Gen. to the Forces under Gen. Howe at Staten Island. Br.-Gen. in the expedition against Charlestown.

Died at Ballinarobe, Co. Mayo, in July, 1789, of apoplexy, in the act of mounting his horse to inspect the 8th Dragoons.

"His death is very much lamented by the gentlemen of the Army, by whom he was highly esteemed " (Walker's Hibernian Magazine).

JOHN PARR

Born, 1732. Ensign, 17th Foot, 20th August, 1751; Lieut., 19th Foot, 17th August, 1756 ; Capt., 21st February, 1760 ; Independent Co. at Senegal, 12th October, 1760. Half-pay, 97th Foot in 1773.

There was a John Parr, Major of the Tower of London in March, 1778—1784, and a certain John Parr died as Governor of Halifax, N.S., in 1791, aged 66.

A second Battalion was raised at Morpeth on the 25th August, 1756, and added to the regiment.

ROWLAND PHILLIPS

Eldest son of Rowland Phillips, Capt., 40th Foot. Born, 1717. Ensign, Ric. Phillips' (40th Foot), 13th October, 1732; Lieut., 19th January, 1741 ; Capt. in Gooch's Regt., 6th May, 1741; T. Wentworth's (24th Foot), 22nd September, 1742; Major, 19th Foot, 25th August, 1756 ; Lieut.-Col., 66th Foot, 23rd April, 1758 ; 9th Foot, 14th September, 1759. Retired, 1st July, 1763.

Served at the capture of Belle Isle in command of the 9th Foot. Also at the capture of Havannah in 1762.

Died in March, 1768.

DAVID HALDANE

Lieut. of Peperell's Foot (51st Foot), 31st September, 1754; 19th Foot, 25th August, 1756 ; Capt., 42nd Foot, 5th April, 1758. Out of the Army List of 1763.

ROBERT MANNING

Ensign, Shirley's Regt. (50th Foot), 1st September, 1745 ; Lieut., 19th March, 1746. Half-pay, Shirley's, 1748 ; 19th Foot, 25th August, 1756.

Died 10th February, 1758.

WILLIAM HARRISON

Ensign, 25th August, 1756 ; Lieut., 2nd October, 1757 ; 66th Foot, April, 1758.

A letter from Sergt. T. Crump, of Capt. Crosbie's Co. of Grenadiers, (66th Foot), dated Morocco, 1st January, 1759, narrates their being cast away on the 29th November last from the Somerset transport. Lieut. Wm. Harrison died 13th December. They were all made slaves. Ensign Bolton, of Lord Forbes' Regt., provided them with clothes (Universal Magazine).

ALGERNON WARREN

Born, 1731. Eldest son of Algernon Warren, Mayor of Kilkenny, 1736-37. Ensign, 17th Foot, 27th April, 1756 ; 19th Foot, 26th August, 1756 ; Lieut., 3rd October, 1757 ; 66th Foot, April, 1758 ; Capt., 26th August, 1764. Omitted from Army List of 1773.

Settled in Jamaica. Died in 1801.

THOMAS PEMBERTON

Born 1723. Ensign, J. Tyrrell's (17th Foot), 4th February, 1740 ; Lieut., 21st November, 1747 ; Capt.-Lieut., 30th March, 1754 ; Capt., 27th April, 1756 ; 19th Foot, 26th August, 1756 ; Retired, 2nd April, 1762.

Served at the siege of Belle Isle.

DUNCOMBE COLCHESTER

Born, 1729. Ensign, L. Dejean's (37th Foot), 20th August, 1752 ; Lieut., 59th Foot, 3rd January, 1756 ; 19th Foot, 26th August, 1756; Capt., 28th October, 1760; Independent Co. in North America, 12th January, 1761. Half-pay, 97th Foot in 1763. Omitted from the Half-pay List, 8th February, 1812.

RICHARD MERCER

Born, 1734. Ensign, P. Lascelles' (47th Foot), 8th June, 1749 ; Lieut., J. Mostyn's (7th Foot), 19th June, 1751 ; Capt., 19th Foot, 27th August, 1756 ; 66th Foot, 21st September, 1758. Out in 1760.

Was Town-Major of Dublin, 17th September, 1745.

JOHN PEARSON

Born, 1731. Ensign, 28th August, 1756 ; Lieut., 5th October, 1757 ; 66th Foot, April, 1758.

Died 23rd February, 1760.

ROBERT DREW

Born, 1723. Son of John Drew of Tercallen, Co. Wexford. Ensign, J. Wynward's Regt. (17th Foot), 30th October, 1745; Lieut., 60th Foot, 1st February, 1756 ; 19th Foot, 28th August, 1756 ; 66th Foot, April, 1758 ; Capt.-Lieut., 23rd February, 1760 ; Capt., 24th August, 1761.

Died, 2nd April, 1762.

ALEXANDER GORDON

Born, 1728. Son of Adam Gordon and grandson of Sir Adam Gordon of Dalpholly. Lieut., 29th August, 1756 from the Scotch-Dutch. Half-pay, 27th February, 1764.

Took part in the siege of Belle Isle. Died in November, 1781, leaving George, 4th Bart. of Invergordon, and Adam, 5th Bart.

ANDREW ROSS

Born, 1734. Ensign, 29th August, 1756 ; Lieut., 6th October, 1757 ; 66th Foot, April, 1758 ; 38th Foot, 18th March, 1760. Out of the Army List, November, 1761.

GEORGE DANSEY

Born, 1736. Ensign, 29th August, 1756 ; Lieut., 4th October, 1757; 66th Foot, April, 1758. Retired 20th January, 1764.

GEORGE DANIEL

Born, 1712. Lieut. in Gooch's (American Regt.), 29th July, 1742. Half-pay on reduction, 25th December, 1742 ; Independent Co. of Invalids in South Carolina, 25th December, 1744, disbanded about 1748 ; Capt.-Lieut. of Invalids at Newcastle, 13th October, 1755 ; Capt., 19th Foot, 29th August, 1756 ; 66th Foot, April, 1758. Half-pay, 88th Foot, 24th March, 1764. Out of the Army List, March, 1765.

WILLIAM COWLEY

Ensign, 30th August, 1756 ; Capt., 16th Foot, 27th August, 1757 (promoted from Ensign) ; 20th Foot, 28th February, 1759.

Killed at the battle of Minden, 1759.

ROBERT SINCLAIR

Born, 1712. Lieut., 31st August, 1756 from Sergeant, Coldstream Guards ; 66th Foot, April, 1758 ; 63rd Foot, 12th October, 1760. Half-pay, 83rd Foot, April, 1772 ; Capt., 73rd Foot, 27th September, 1778. Half-pay, 15th March, 1786. Omitted from Half-pay List, 10th August, 1799.

THOMAS RICHARD CROSBIE

Ensign, W. Graham's Regt. (43rd Foot), 27th March, 1745. Lieut., 19th March, 1750 ; Capt., 19th Foot, 31st August, 1756 ; 66th Foot, April, 1758 ; Capt. of a Company of Invalids at Tilbury Fort, 12th November, 1766. Succeeded, 9th May, 1768.

See William Harrison, ante.

JAMES NEWTON

Born, 1730. Ensign, H. Pulteney's Regt. (13th Foot), 12th January, 1747; Lieut., 20th May, 1752; Capt., 19th Foot, 1st September, 1756 ; 66th Foot, April, 1758.

Died, August, 1761.

GEORGE REYNOLDS

Born, 1734. Ensign, 1st September, 1756; Lieut., 7th October, 1757 ; 66th Foot, April, 1758 ; Capt., 106th Foot, 17th October, 1761; Half-pay on disbandment in 1763; 49th Foot, 15th August, 1775 ; Bt.-Major, 29th August, 1777 ; 96th Foot, 9th April, 1781. Retired, 25th April, 1781.

JOSEPH ACKMAN

Ensign, 2nd September, 1756. Left, 1757.

ANDREW AGNEW

Born, 1721. Lieut., 2nd September, 1756, from the ranks; 66th Foot, April, 1758; Half-pay in 1763. Out of the Army List, 10th January, 1803.

JOHN GILLAN

Born, 1708. 2nd Lieut., J. Campbell's Regt. (21st Foot), 10th March, 1746 ; Lieut., 8th August, 1755 ; Capt., 19th Foot, 2nd September, 1756 ; 66th Foot, April, 1758. Out of the Regt.. 4th March, 1767.

THOMAS WATSON

Born, 1722. Lieut., 3rd September, 1756, from the ranks; 66th Foot, April, 1758.

Died, 7th November, 1759.

ROBERT GREGORY

Born, 1739. Ensign, 3rd September, 1756 ; 66th Foot, 5th April, 1778 ; Lieut., 5th April, 1759. Retired, 6th October, 1762.

JAMES JOHNSTON

Born, 1727. 2nd Lieut., Alexander Majoribank's (Scotch-Dutch), 15th April, 1743 ; Lieut., 29th May, 1747 ; Capt., 19th Foot, 3rd September, 1756 ; 66th Foot, April, 1758 ; Major, 61st Foot, 1759; 112th Foot, 1st February, 1766; Half-pay in 1767. Out of the Half-pay List, 11th March, 1796.

JOHN HILL

Born, 1732. Lieut., 4th September, 1756, from Sergeant, 66th Foot, April, 1758.

Died, 22nd February, 1760.

JOHN MACHARG

Ensign, 8th December, 1756; Lieut., 8th October, 1757; 66th Foot, April, 1758 ; Capt., Independent Co., 20th October, 1760 ; Major, Colin Campbell's (100th Foot), 28th October, 1760.

Killed by Major Colin Campbell at Martinique in April, 1762. Major Campbell was tried by a Court Martial for murder, and sentenced to be cashiered, but owing to a flaw in the proceedings, the sentence was annulled, but Major Campbell was dismissed the Service (Gentleman's Magazine, May, 1764).

JOHN BARCAS

Born, 1735. Ensign, 5th April, 1757 ; Lieut., 10th February, 1758 ; Adjt., 66th Foot, 15th July, 1758 ; Capt.-Lieut., 23rd August, 1764.

Cashiered, 22nd February, 1768.

WILLIAM HEPBURN

Ensign, 29th April, 1757; 66th Foot, April, 1758; Lieut., 7th November, 1759. Superseded, 25th May, 1762.

Died, September, 1775.

WILLIAM GRIERSON

Born, 1727. Ensign, 19th Foot, 14th May, 1757 ; 66th Foot, April, 1758 ; Lieut., 5th June, 1758. Out of the Army List, 1769.

HENRY HUTCHINSON

Born, 1741. Ensign, 2nd September, 1757; Lieut., 5th April, 1759; Capt., 110th Foot, 19th October, 1761; Half-pay in 1763 ; out of the Army in 1769.

Took part in the siege of Belle Isle.

ANDREW FORBES

Born, 1725. Ensign in Army, 3rd June, 1745 ; Lieut., Dutch Service, 24th March, 1747 ; 19th Foot, 21st September, 1757; Half-pay, 27th December, 1764 to 1775.

Taken prisoner in the first attack on Belle Isle, 7th April, 1761.

JOHN MAJORIBANKS

Born, 1731. Ensign in Army, 24th May, 1749; Lieut., 21st October, 1749; 19th Foot, 22nd September, 1757, from the Dutch Service ; Adjt., 25th September, 1761 ; Capt.-Lieut., 108th Foot, 22nd October, 1761 ; 19th Foot, 2nd April, 1762 ; Capt., 15th June, 1763 ; Bt.-Major, 29th August, 1777 ; Major, 17th November, 1780.

Wounded during the siege of Belle Isle, 1761. Served in the American War, 1781, and was in command of the flank battalion at the battle of Eutaw Springs. Col. Stewart, writing to Gen. Cornwallis, says, " but to Major Majoribanks and the flank battalion under his command I think the honour of the day is greatly due." Died in South Carolina, 23rd October, 1781.

JAMES DOUGLAS

Surgeon, 24th September, 1757; 66th Foot, April, 1758.

ROBERT MENZIES

Born, 1740. Ensign, 26th September, 1757; Lieut., 8th September, 1759 ; Qr.-Mr., 2nd April, 1762 ; Capt.-Lieut., 10th July, 1769 ; Capt., 11th January, 1771 ; Major, 71st Foot (Frazer's Highlanders), 14th May, 1776.

Served with the 19th at the siege of Belle Isle.

" Shortly after his appointment to the 71st, the regiment was despatched to America, and on entering Boston harbour, which had been evacuated without their knowledge, the transport, with Major Menzies on board, was attacked by three privateers. These they beat off, but their ship, having been disabled, coming under the guns of a fort, where shot and shell were poured upon them, killing Major Menzies. His death was a great loss, as from his great military experience he was specially qualified to discipline the corps, which had not been drilled " (History of the Clan Menzies, 1884).

" An officer of great experience and approved talents " (Stewart's Highlanders). He was buried with the honours of war at Boston.

ARCHIBALD BOGLE

Ensign, 27th September, 1757; Lieut., 12th October, 1760; Half-pay in 1763. On recruiting service, 1762-3. Out of the Army, 1810.

Took part in the siege of Belle Isle. Died in 1820.

JOHN McGILL

Born, 1742. Ensign, 28th September, 1757; Lieut., 11th August, 1759; Adjt., 12th December, 1761; Capt., 19th July, 1769; Bt.-Major, 17th November, 1780; Major, 2nd June, 1790; Bt.-Lieut. Col., 18th November, 1790. Retired, 3rd June, 1794.

Was at the siege of Belle Isle. Served also in the American War in 1781, and in the campaign in Holland, 1793-94.

JOHN FORBES

Ensign, 30th September, 1757; 12th Foot, 4th October, 1757 ; Lieut., 25th August, 1759. Out of the Army in 1763.

Wounded at the battle of Minden.

THOMAS STUART

Ensign, 30th September, 1757 ; 56th Foot, 3rd October, 1757 ; Lieut., 24th October, 1760. Resigned, 3rd January, 1763.

ROBERT CARR
Ensign, 30th September, 1757. Left, 1758.

DOUGAL STUART
Born, 1743. Ensign, 1st October, 1757 ; Lieut., 12th January, 1761.
Killed at Port de Andro in the attack on Belle Isle, 7th April, 1761.

FRANCIS BINDON
Born, 1738. Ensign, 2nd October, 1757 ; 66th Foot, April, 1758 ; Lieut., 22nd March, 1762 ; Capt.-Lieut., 22nd February, 1768.
Died, 4th October, 1770.

THOMAS WILSON
Born, 1732. Ensign, 3rd October, 1757 ; Independent Co., 30th June, 1759 ; Lieut., 7th March, 1760 ; 59th Foot, 13th February, 1762 ; Capt., 26th December, 1778. Retired by sale, 9th November, 1793.

HUGH BELSHES
Ensign, 4th October, 1757. Left, 1758.

DAVID SCOTT
Born, 1740. Ensign, 4th Foot, 28th September, 1757 ; 19th Foot, 5th October, 1757 ; 66th Foot, April, 1758 ; Lieut., 24th November, 1759; 108th Foot, 19th October, 1761 ; Capt., 17th May, 1762. Out of the Army List, 20th March, 1779.

ISAAC SMITH
Born, 1733. Ensign, 6th October, 1757 ; 66th Foot, April, 1758 ; Lieut., 21st February, 1760. Out of the Army List, January, 1766.

GEORGE BORRADALE
Born, 1735. 2nd Lieut., 8th Foot, 12th March, 1755 ; Lieut., 31st August, 1756 ; Capt. in the Marines, March, 1757 ; Capt.-Lieut., 19th Foot, 16th November, 1757; Capt., 11th August, 1759. Resigned, 29th March, 1762.

HENRY WASTELL
Born, 16th March, 1738. 3rd son of the Revd. Henry Wastell, Rector of Simonburn, Co. Northumberland, of the Spital, Hexham. Ensign, 10th February, 1758 ; Independent Co., 12th June, 1759; Lieut., 95th Foot, 7th March, 1760; Half-pay on reduction in 1763. Out of the Army List, 12th February, 1813.

JOCELYN SHAWFORD
Born, 1732. Ensign, 7th March, 1758, from the ranks; 66th Foot, April 1758 ; Lieut., 22nd February, 1760. Out of the Army List, March, 1765.

RICHARD ELLIS

Born, 1740. 2nd son of Richard Ellis of Monaghan and Drumnalee, Co. Cavan. Ensign, 25th March, 1758 ; 66th Foot, April, 1758 ; Lieut., 23rd February, 1760 ; Capt.-Lieut., 4th October, 1770 ; Capt., 23rd December, 1771 ; Bt.-Major, 7th June, 1782. Sold out, 29th March, 1785.

Was admitted a freeman of Youghall, Co. Cork, 8th February, 1785.

Died in 1814.

Ancestor of the Ellis family of Abbey-feale, Co. Limerick.

In April, 1758, the 2nd Battalion was formed into the 66th Foot now 2nd Battn. of Princess Charlotte of Wales's (Royal Berkshire Regt.).

LEONARD CROSSLEY

Born, 1739. Ensign, 5th April, 1758 ; Lieut., Independent Co., 10th May, 1760. Not in any later Army List.

JOHN STUART

Born, 1740. Ensign, 5th June, 1758 ; Lieut., 9th April, 1761 ; Capt., 77th Foot, 16th July, 1762; Half-pay in 1763; 37th Foot, 25th December, 1770. Out of the Army in 1777.

Served at the siege of Belle Isle.

BACON WILLIAM WASTELL

Born 1st March, 1739. Third son of the Rev. Henry Wastell, Rector of Simonburn, Northumberland. Ensign, 11th August, 1759 ; Lieut., 15th July, 1761 ; retired, 1st October, 1761.

Served at the siege of Belle Isle. Died at Carlisle, 19th November, 1821.

WILLIAM MORETON

Ensign, 8th September, 1759 ; Lieut., 1st October, 1761 ; 108th Foot, 30th July, 1762 ; Half-pay on reduction, 1763. Omitted from the Army List, 1st January, 1812.

Was on recruiting service during the siege of Belle Isle.

EDWARD TAYLOR

Possibly son of Edward Taylor, of Kidderminster. Matriculated Christ Church, Oxford, 21st March, 1743, aged 16. Chaplain, 8th September, 1759 ; resigned, 10th June, 1764.

Took part in the siege of Belle Isle.

SAMUEL TOWNSEND

Third son of Samuel Townsend, of Castle Townsend, Co. Cork. Capt., 18th Light Dragoons, 8th December, 1759 ; Capt., 19th Foot, 11th March, 1760 ; Major, 15th June, 1763 ; Lieut.-Col., 34th Foot, 5th May, 1769 ; Half-pay, 20th May, 1776 ; Col. and A.D.C. to the King, 25th November, 1778 ; Major-Gen., 20th November, 1782 ; Lieut.-Gen., 12th October, 1793.

Took part in the siege of Belle Isle. A.D.C. to General Kingsley, 1761. Inspector-General of Recruiting, 1784-94.
Died in London, 17th May, 1794.
There is a portrait in the Convent, Gibraltar, in 19th uniform. Another in full dress at Whitehall House, Cape Clear.

WILLIAM WOOD

Ensign, 10th May, 1760 ; Lieut., 18th April, 1762 ; Half-pay in 1763 ; out of the Army in 1777.
Served at the siege of Belle Isle, 1761.

ROBERT HUTCHINSON

Ensign, 12th June, 1760 ; Lieut., 23rd July, 1762 ; Half-pay, 83rd Foot, 8th December, 1769 ; 71st Foot (Fraser's Highlanders), 24th November, 1775 ; Capt., 3rd August, 1778 ; retired, 13th January, 1784.
Took part in the siege of Belle Isle.

RICHARD FOLEY

Ensign, 12th June, 1760 ; Lieut., 19th February, 1762 ; Half-pay in 1763 ; 20th Foot, 25th December, 1770 ; out of the army, 2nd March, 1772.
Took part in the siege of Belle Isle. The "Gentleman's Magazine" for 1778 records the death of a certain Richard Foley at Newent, Gloucestershire.

GEORGE HENRIETTA KYFFIN

2nd Lieut., Royal Marines, 19th March, 1757 ; Lieut., 94th Foot, 3rd January, 1760 ; 19th Foot, 21st July, 1760 ; Half-pay in 1763 ; out of the army, January, 1797.
Was at the siege of Belle Isle, 1761.

ROBERT McGILL

Ensign, 12th October, 1760 ; Lieut., 15th June, 1763 ; Capt.-Lieut., 11th January, 1771 ; Capt., 25th May, 1772 ; out of the Regt., 20th Sept., 1773.
Present at the siege of Belle Isle.

NICHOLAS COLTHURST

Third son of James Coulthurst, of Dripsey Castle, Co. Cork. Ensign, 17th March, 1761 ; Lieut., same date ;. Capt.-Lieut., 106th Foot, 17th October, 1761 ; Half-pay in 1763 ; Capt., 68th Foot, 3rd February, 1773 ; out of the army, 30th June, 1780.
Served at the siege of Belle Isle. Was appointed Town Major of Cork in 1784, and admitted a freeman of the city 25th July, 1786.

WILLIAM GREEN

Ensign, 8th April, 1761 ; Lieut., 2nd April, 1762 ; Capt.-Lieut., 3rd September, 1773 ; retired, 28th August, 1775.

Sir WALTER FARQUHAR, Bart.

Born at Peterhead, October, 1738. Third son of Robert Farquhar, Minister of the Parish of Garioch and County of Aberdeen. Surg., 20th July, 1761 ; resigned, 9th August, 1769.

Took part in the siege of Belle Isle.
Died in London, 30th March, 1819.
Confidential advisor to Mr. Pitt and Lord Melville. One of the physicians to the Prince of Wales when Regent. F.R.C.P. Edinburgh. Matriculated at Glasgow University, 1760. Created a baronet 1st March, 1796. " He was considered a very able and successful physician, while his personal character won and secured for him many friends, but he is not known to have made any contribution to medical science or literature. His portrait by Raeburn was engraved by W. Sharp. His second son, Sir Robert Townsend Farquhar, Governor and Commander-in-Chief of Mauritius, was created a baronet in 1821." (Dict. N.B.)

RICHARD ARMSTRONG

Ensign, 19th August, 1761, from 97th Foot; retired, 30th May, 1766.

JOHN NICHOLAS SKERRETT

Ensign, 1st October, 1761 ; Lieut., 8th January, 1768 ; Capt.-Lieut., 27th May, 1775 ; Capt., 12th November, 1778 ; Bt.-Major, 18th November, 1790 ; Major 48th Foot, 7th December, 1791 ; Bt.-Lieut.-Col., 1st March, 1794 ; 8th West India Regt., 15th September, 1795 ; Col., Loyal Durham Fencibles, 1st January, 1798 ; Royal Newfoundland Fencibles, 9th July, 1803 ; Major-Gen., 1st January, 1805 ; Lieut.-Gen., 4th June, 1811.
Served in the American War, 1781, and in the Irish Rebellion, 1798. Died at Heavitree, near Exeter, in his 70th year, 18th August, 1813.

EVAN BAILLIE

Ensign, 4th Foot, 4th May, 1759. Lieut., 19th Foot, 27th January, 1762 ; Half-pay on reduction, 1763.
There was an Evan Baillie, M.P. for Bristol, 1802-1812. He was born in 1742, 3rd son of Hugh Baillie of Dochfour, Co. Inverness, and was a great West Indian-Bristol merchant. Several of the Dochfour men were in the Army. Possibly the M.P. was in the 19th.

The Hon. JOHN CHAPPLE NORTON

Born, 2nd April, 1746. Third son of the Rt. Hon. Sir Fletcher Norton, P.C., Speaker of the House of Commons, afterwards 1st Lord Grantley. Ensign, 2nd April, 1762 ; Lieut., 19th July, 1762 ; Capt., 94th Foot, 24th February, 1763 ; 19th Foot, 15th June, 1763 ; Major, 1st Foot, 14th July, 1769 ; Capt. and Lieut.-Col., 2nd Foot Gds., 1st June, 1774 ; Major, 1786 ; Major-Gen., 28th September, 1787 ; Col., 81st Foot, 25th March, 1795 ; 56th Foot, 24th January, 1797 ; Lieut.-Gen., 26th January, 1797 ; Gen., 29th April, 1802.
Served in the American War, 1776 to 1781, and was engaged in all the principal occurrences. Particularly distinguished himself in February, 1780, and was thanked in the following terms :—" His Excellency, Lieut.-Gen. Knyphausen, desires his thanks may be given in public orders to Lieut.-Col. Norton, of the Guards, for his good conduct and gallant behaviour in attacking and forcing a considerable body of rebels advantageously posted at Young's houses in the neighbourhood of White Plains."
Died at Wonersh, Surrey, on 19th March, 1818.

JOHN ASCOUGH

Ensign, 19th April, 1762 ; resigned, 20th June, 1766.

RALPH BALL

Ensign, 20th April, 1762 ; Lieut., 24th February, 1763 ; Half-pay, 4th April, 1763 ; out of the Army List, 8th February, 1812.

PHILIP CROSS

Ensign, 23rd June, 1762 ; Half-pay, 103rd Foot, 22nd July, 1763 ; omitted from the half-pay list, 20th July, 1781.

GEORGE ORMSBY

Ensign, 19th July, 1762 ; resigned, 14th March, 1766.

WILLIAM GILES

Ensign, 23rd July, 1762 ; Adjt., 2nd August, 1769 ; Capt.-Lieut., 12th November, 1778 ; Capt., 2nd June, 1790 ; retired, 20th March, 1793.

Served in the American War, 1781.

ROBERT MACLELLAN

Lieut., 108th Foot, 2nd November, 1761 ; 19th Foot, 30th July, 1762 ; Half-pay, 24th February, 1763 ; Lieut., 4th Foot, 28th October, 1763 ; omitted from the Army List, 28th April, 1783.

Was Major of Brigade, South Crabbe Island, West Indies, 1771 to 1782.

WILLIAM McCLINTOCK

Born at Dunmore. Second son of John McClintock, of Dunmore, Co. Donegal. Ensign, 103rd Foot, 4th September, 1761 ; 19th Foot, 22nd July, 1763 ; retired, 8th May, 1765.

GEORGE MACKENZIE

Born, 6th April, 1748. Fourth son of Sir Lewis Mackenzie, Bart., of Scotwell, Rosshire. Ensign, 23rd July, 1763 ; Lieut., 19th July, 1769 ; 78th Foot, 9th January, 1778 ; Major, 72nd Foot (renumbered), 13th September, 1780 ; Bt.-Lieut.-Col., 23rd November, 1790 ; sold out, 5th March, 1791.

Died at Ayr, 9th April, 1840.

DAVID JOHN BELL

Ensign, 24th July, 1763 ; Lieut., 27th March, 1770 ; Capt., 12th August, 1779 ; Bt.-Major, 1st March, 1794.

Took part in the American War, 1781. Served in the campaign in Holland, 1794-5.

Died, 11th May, 1795.

WILLIAM ADAIR

Son of William Robert Adair, of Ludlow, Salop. Matriculated at Worcester College, Oxford, 7th November, 1743, aged 19. Chaplain, 63rd Foot, 1st July, 1758 ; 31st Foot, 9th September, 1758 ; 19th Foot, 11th January, 1764 ; 3rd Dragoon Gds., 22nd July, 1767 ; retired, 3rd July, 1770.

JOHN SMITH

Ensign, 81st Foot, 22nd March, 1762 ; Lieut., 19th April, 1762 ; 19th Foot, 27th December, 1764 ; Capt., 28th August, 1775 ; Bt.-Major, 18th November, 1790 ; Bt.-Lieut.-Col., 1st March, 1794 ; retired, 28th March, 1795.

Took part in the American War, 1781, and in the campaign in Holland, 1794-5.

Died in St. James's Square, Edinburgh, 31st October, 1822.

JOHN MEADOWS

Ensign, 8th May, 1765 ; Lieut., 19th July, 1770 ; resigned, 15th April, 1774.

BRYDGES KEARNEY

Ensign, 14th March, 1766 ; Lieut., 25th December, 1770 ; resigned, 20th March, 1779.

THOMAS ASCOUGH

Ensign, 30th May, 1766 ; Lieut., 26th December, 1770 ; retired, 7th June, 1774.

ROBERT LONGFIELD

Ensign, 20th June, 1766 ; Lieut., 3rd September, 1773 ; 53rd Foot, 3rd February, 1776 ; retired, 19th April, 1779.

JOHN DENHOLME

Surgeon's Mate, 26th March, 1767 ; Surg., 2nd August, 1769 ; Staff-Surg. at Grenada, 28th March, 1787.

Died at Grenada about May, 1789. Served in the American War in 1781 with 19th Foot.

CHARLES MAWHOOD

Born 1729. Only son of Richard Mawhood, of Ardsley, Yorkshire. Cornet, 1st Royal Dragoons, 12th August, 1752 ; Lieut., 8th November, 1756 ; Capt.-Lieut., 15th Light Dragoons, 20th March, 1759 ; Capt., 6th December, 1759 ; Major, 3rd Foot, 17th May, 1763 ; Lieut.-Col., 19th Foot, 17th June, 1767 ; 17th Foot, 26th October, 1775 ; Col., 72nd Foot (Manchester Volunteers), 16th December, 1777.

Served in the American War of Independence in command of 17th Foot. " The bravery and abilities of Col. Mawhood deservedly gained him the highest applause at the fighting near Princetown, 4th January, 1777." (Beatson's Naval and Military Memoirs.)

Took part in the siege of Gibraltar with the 72nd Foot, and died there on the 29th August, 1780.

SAMUEL COOPER

Probably son of Thomas Cooper, of Post Comb, Oxford. Matriculated at Christ Church, Oxford, 30th May, 1754, aged 18. Chaplain, 14th August, 1767 ; 3rd Regt. of Dragoons (King's Own), 3rd July, 1770 ; replaced, 24th November, 1781.

JAMES ROBINSON

Son of Sir John Robinson, Bt., of Cranford, Northamptonshire. Ensign, 8th January, 1768 ; Lieut., 10th June, 1771.

Died in Kilkenny early in August, 1782.

He was a member of the Corps of Kilkenny Rangers. (Faulkner's Dublin Journal, 3rd-6th August, 1782.)

DAVID GRAEME

Eldest son of James Graeme, of Braco, Co. Perth. 1st Commission as Col., 105th Queen's Own Royal Regt. of Highlanders, 15th October, 1761 ; 49th Foot, 11th April, 1764 ; 19th Foot, 25th May, 1768 ; Major-Gen., 10th July, 1762 ; Lieut.-Gen., 25th May, 1772 ; Gen., 19th February, 1783.

Assisted to escort Princess Charlotte of Mecklinburg Strelitz to England for her wedding, and who, it is said, was responsible for the selection of that Princess as the Queen of George III. Was appointed Secretary to the Queen elect on the 5th September, 1761, and in the commission given him a month later to raise and command a regiment of two battalions under the title of The Queen's Own Royal Regiment of Highlanders may be seen a further mark of royal favour. (Military History of Perthshire.)

M.P. for Perthshire, 1764 to 1768, when he accepted the Chiltern Hundreds.

Died in George Street, Edinburgh, 24th January, 1797.

LEWIS NANNEY

Third son of John Nanney, of Maes-y-pandy, Merionethshire. Ensign, 26th May, 1769 ; Lieut., 15th April, 1774 ; sold out, 29th June, 1780.

JOHN BEST

Ensign, 19th July, 1769 ; retired, 16th April, 1771.

WILLIAM GREEN

1st Lieut., 85th Craufurd's Light Infantry Volunteers, 24th August, 1759; Lieut., 17th Light Dragoons, 5th November, 1759 ; 4th Dragoons, 22nd June, 1761 ; Half-pay in 1763 on reduction ; Lieut., 1st Dragoon Gds., 12th September, 1764 ; Half-pay, 83rd Foot, 27th December, 1765 ; Full-pay, 19th Foot, 8th December, 1769 ; retired, 27th March, 1770.

The Rt. Hon. Sir JAMES MURRAY-PULTENEY, Bt.

Eldest son of Sir Robert Murray, Bart., Receiver-General of Customs, Scotland. Lieut., 106th Foot, 25th December, 1762 ; Half-pay on reduction in 1763 ; 19th Foot, 2nd March, 1770 ; Capt., 57th Foot, 30th April, 1771 ; Major, 4th Foot, 31st January, 1778 ; Bt.-Lieut.-Col., 6th February, 1780 ; Lieut.-Col., 94th Foot, 2nd March, 1780 ; Half-pay on reduction, 1783 ; Col. and A.D.C. to the King, 21st November, 1789 ; Major-Gen., 1790 ; Col., 18th Foot, 26th February, 1794 ; Lieut.-Gen., 1799 ; Gen., 25th April, 1808.

Was at the capture of St. Lucia in 1778, with 4th Foot. Took part in the unsuccessful attempt on Charlestown, and was engaged in various minor operations in the vicinity of New York during the war of Independence. Wounded at the battle of Brandywine. Served in Flanders under the Duke of York in 1794 as Adjt.-Gen. He accompanied Sir R.

Abercromby to North Holland in 1799, and was shot in the right arm at the landing. Commanded an expedition against Ferrol, Spain, in 1800.

Privy Councillor and Secretary at War, 30th March, 1807-1809. M.P. for Weymouth, 1790 to 1811. Having married the Countess of Bath in 1794, he assumed the surname and arms of Pulteney.

Died at Beckenham, Norfolk, on 26th April, 1811, owing to an injury received from the explosion of a powder flask while out shooting.

JOHN TURNER

Ensign, 18th April, 1770; resigned, 16th April, 1771.

AENEAS McINTOSH

Ensign, 19th July, 1770; Lieut., 8th June, 1774; Half-pay, 10th July, 1776; Capt., 71st Foot, 3rd December, 1778; Half-pay on disbandment in 1783.

Died, 2nd June, 1792.

BACON BEDINGFIELD

Born, 16th May, 1746. Second son of Phillip Bedingfield, of Ditchingham, Norfolk. Chaplain, 4th October, 1770; out of the Army List, 1st January, 1798.

Died, 13th July, 1797.

WILLIAM MERCER

Born, 8th January, 1755. Third son of William Mercer, of Potterhill, Co. Perth. Ensign, 26th December, 1770; Cadet, Indian Army, 1781; Cornet, 1781; Lieut., 10th July, 1782; Capt., 5th Native Cavalry (Bengal), 29th May, 1800.

Joined the 19th Foot at Gibraltar in 1771, and sold out in Dublin.

Got a cadetship in the East India Co.'s Service. Sailed under a letter of exchequer on board the "Mount Stewart" in 1781. Captured on the voyage carried to Spain and exchanged. Started again and arrived in India after the convoy had been detained a year at Rio-de-Janiero. Major, commanding Warren Hastings' bodyguard from 1782 to 1801. Took part with the bodyguard in the 3rd Mysore War, 1790 to 1792.

Died at Ghazipore, 3rd August, 1801, the result of a duel.

JOHN BALNEAVES

Ensign, 18th February, 1771; Lieut., 27th May, 1776; Capt., 77th Foot (Athol Highlanders), 25th May, 1778; 74th Foot (Argyll Highlanders), 22nd January, 1783; half-pay in 1783.

Died, 24th June, 1785.

RICHARD GEM

Ensign, 16th April, 1771; Lieut., 10th July, 1776; Adjt., 12th April, 1782; Capt.-Lieut., 2nd June, 1790; Capt., 7th December, 1791; retired, 25th April, 1793.

Served in the American War, 1781.

Regimental Chaplains were abolished in the Army on the 23rd September, 1796.

HENRY BAYNTON

Cornet, Inniskilling Dragoons, 15th October, 1759; Lieut., 19th Foot, 28th June, 1771; resigned, 2nd October, 1771.

JAMES NESS

Ensign, 2nd July, 1771; resigned, 12th July, 1777.

THOMAS DAWSON

Lieut., 2nd October, 1771; half-pay, 104th Foot, 17th December, 1772. Omitted from the half-pay list, 1st January, 1802.

COLIN CAMPBELL

Eldest son of Sir James Campbell, Bart, of Aberuchill, Co. Perth. Ensign, 29th November, 1771; Lieut., 13th January, 1777; Capt., 30th June, 1780. Independent Co., 11th June, 1794; Bt.-Major, 29th November, 1794; Lieut.-Col., Perth Militia, 29th November, 1794.

Served in the American War and was taken prisoner in South Carolina, 24th December, 1781.

Died at Edinburgh, 3rd July, 1811. Buried at Restalrig Churchyard with military honours.

CHARLES CHURCHILL

Lieut., 7th Foot, 2nd November, 1760; Capt., 19th Foot, 27th April, 1772; retired, 7th August, 1779.

BENJAMIN TONG

Lieut., 104th Foot, 29th August, 1761; half-pay on reduction in 1763; Lieut., 19th Foot, 18th December, 1772; resigned, 15th December, 1777.

HENRY BROWN

Ensign, 15th April, 1774; Cornet, 18th Light Dragoons, 16th December, 1775; Lieut., 10th March, 1778. Out of the Army List, 30th June, 1780.

ALEXANDER GORDON

Son of Alexander Gordon of the Scotch-Dutch, 5th Laird of Carleton (Earlston family).

Ensign, 8th June, 1774.

Died at Waterford, 16th July, 1775.

WILLIAM SLEIGH

Born, 1758; son of Charles Bathurst Sleigh, of Arkendale, Co. York. Ensign, 28th August, 1775; Lieut., 15th December, 1777; Capt., 17th November, 1780; half-pay, 77th Foot, 20th July, 1785; 23rd Foot, 17th March, 1790; Major, 83rd Foot, 28th September, 1793; Lieut.-Col., 15th June, 1794.

Retired, 19th September, 1795. Served with the 19th in the American War and was present at the action of Eutaw Springs. J.P. for the North Riding and for Co. Durham. Was Colonel of Volunteers in the West Riding.

Died at Stockton-on-Tees, 13th February, 1825, aged 66.

HENRY WILLIAMSON

Ensign, 22nd September, 1775 ; 57th Foot, 26th November, 1775 ; superseded, 14th March, 1780.

ROBERT HICKMAN

Ensign, 21st December, 1775 ; Lieut., 25th May, 1778.

Served in the American War and was killed in action at the battle of Eutaw Springs, 8th September, 1781.

THOMAS MAWHOOD

Probably 2nd son of Richard Mawhood, Clerk of the Peace, Wakefield, Yorkshire.

Ensign, 24th December, 1775 ; Lieut., 1st July, 1778 ; Capt., 85th Foot (Westminster Volunteers), 4th September, 1779.

Died at Barbados, 24th September, 1780.

CHARLES MASTERSON

Ensign, 27th May, 1776 ; Lieut., 1st June, 1778 ; Capt. 30th Foot, 12th April, 1782 ; retired in 1789.

HENRY BOWYER

Born, 1743 ; 4th son of Sir William Bowyer, Bart., of Denham, Bucks ; Lieut., 68th Foot, 27th March, 1772 ; Capt., 19th Foot, 27th May, 1776 ; 66th Foot, 9th May, 1778 ; Bt.-Major, 10th January, 1781 ; Bt.-Lieut.-Col., 18th November, 1782 ; Major, 24th October, 1787 ; Lieut.-Col., 12th March, 1789 ; Major-Gen., 26th February, 1795 ; Col., 89th Foot, 2nd March, 1797 ; 16th Foot, 15th December, 1797 ; Lieut.-Gen., 8th May, 1798. D.A.A.G., Ireland, 30th September, 1776. Was Commander-in-Chief Windward and Leeward Islands.

Died in Ireland, 29th August, 1808.

WILLIAM M'LARIN

Direct Commission as Qr.-Mr., 10th July, 1776 ; retired, 2nd January, 1794.

Served in the American War, 1781.

GEORGE TAGGART

Ensign, 10th July, 1776 ; Lieut., 1st June, 1778 ; 29th Foot, 2nd March, 1791 ; Capt., half-pay, 1792 ; 55th Foot, 30th April, 1792.

Served in the American War, 1781.
Died, 27th January, 1795.

WILLIAM GORDON

Born, 1764 ; son of Sir William Gordon, 7th Bart. of Embo. Ensign, 5th October, 1776 ; Lieut., 72nd Foot, 4th January, 1778 ; Capt.-Lieut., 14th July, 1783 ; half-pay, 1784 ; 19th Foot, 25th September, 1787 ; Capt.-Lieut. and Adjt., 41st Foot, 25th December, 1787 ; Capt., 30th April, 1792 ; Bt.-Major, 9th September, 1794.

Served throughout the siege of Gibraltar, 1778-83. Took part in the Expedition against St. Domingo, with the 41st Foot.

Died at Port au Prince, St. Domingo, 30th June, 1794.

" Possessed of every virtue that can adorn human nature as a gentleman and a scholar, few could excel him in the knowledge of the world and polite literature. A severe loss to his country and particularly to the 41st Regiment in which his memory will ever be dear."— (Gentleman's Magazine.")

WILLIAM WRAY

Ensign, 13th January, 1777 ; Lieut., 1st June, 1778 ; retired, 11th February, 1789.

Served in the American War, 1781.

CHARLES PLEYDELL COLLEY

Ensign, 12th May, 1777 ; Lieut., 1st June, 1778. Omitted from the Army List, 30th April, 1782.

MATTHEW SCOTT

Son of Hibernicus Scott of Lisnalea or Flaxford, Co. Cork. Ensign, 12th July, 1777 ; Lieut., 1st June, 1778 ; Capt.-Lieut., 7th December, 1791 ; Capt., 30th May, 1794 ; Major, 4th November, 1795 ; Lieut.-Col., 28th Foot, 11th November, 1795.

Served in the American War, 1781, and in the Campaign in Holland, 1794-5.

Died in the West Indies, 12th July, 1796.

MARCUS LOWTHER CROFTON

Born, 13th June, 1757 ; 8th son of Sir Marcus Lowther Crofton, Bart., M.P. Ensign, 15th December, 1777 ; Lieut., 1st June, 1778. Half-pay, 27th January, 1786.

Served in the American War, 1781.

Died, 16th February, 1786.

CONWAY BLENNERHASSET

Ensign, 25th May, 1778 ; Lieut., 1st June, 1778.

Served in the American War, 1781.

Died, 17th July, 1786.

ARTHUR FLEMING

Ensign, 34th Foot, 3rd March, 1776 ; Lieut., 19th Foot, 1st June, 1778. Omitted from the Army List, 25th May, 1785.

EDWARD O'BRIEN

Ensign, 2nd June, 1778 ; 5th Foot, 19th March, 1781 ; retired, 30th December, 1783.

DAVID HAMILTON

Ensign, 3rd June, 1778 ; Lieut., 12th August, 1779 ; 66th Foot, 13th April, 1782 ; half-pay, 1784 ; 22nd Foot, 31st May, 1791.

Was at the taking of Port au Prince in 1794. A detachment of the 22nd formed part of the garrison of Fort Bizzotton, which was attacked by 2,000 of the enemy on the 5th December. The British defended their post with great gallantry and repulsed the assailants, and Lieut. Hamilton of the 22nd greatly distinguished himself (Records of the 22nd Foot).

Died at St. Domingo, 26th May, 1795.

STEPHEN BLOOMFIELD

Ensign, 4th June, 1778; Lieut., 8th March, 1780; 96th Foot, 20th September, 1780; half-pay on reduction, 1783. Omitted from half-pay list, 1st January, 1792.

ROBERT JOHNSTON

Ensign, 5th June, 1778; Lieut., 29th June, 1780. Out of the Army List, 30th April, 1782.

JAMES O'CONNOR

Ensign, 6th June, 1778; Lieut., 13th April, 1782; Independent Co., 3rd May, 1791. Half-pay on disbandment, December, 1791. Omitted from the half-pay list, 11th March, 1796.

PHILIP HOLMES

Ensign, 7th June, 1778; Lieut., 17th November, 1780; 5th Foot, 6th March, 1781; out of the Army List, 28th April, 1783.

WILLIAM PYNE

Ensign, 8th June, 1778; Lieut., 30th June, 1778; 103rd Foot, 3rd November, 1781; half-pay on reduction in 1784; 58th Foot, 25th June, 1789; Capt.-Lieut., 3rd July, 1794; Capt., 43rd Foot, 12th November, 1794.

Died, 21st April, 1798.

GEORGE BAILLIE

Lieut., 25th July, 1778; 5th Foot, 21st March, 1781; 68th Foot, 13th April, 1782; half-pay, 1783; 50th Foot, 4th January, 1786; half-pay, 100th Foot, 11th July, 1787.

Died near Carlow, 15th June, 1827.

RALPH HANSON

Lieut., 89th Foot (Highland Regt.), 21st October, 1759; 66th Foot, 27th May, 1771; Capt., 19th Foot, 9th November, 1778; retired, 12th April, 1782.

Served in the American War, 1781.

WILLIAM VINCENT

2nd son of John Vincent, of Limerick; Lieut., 12th November, 1778; Adjt., 23rd October, 1794; Capt., 2nd December, 1794; Major, 17th July, 1801; Lieut.-Col., 14th May, 1804; retired, 25th September, 1806.

Served in the American War, 1781. Also in the campaign in Germany, 1794-5. Commanded five companies of the 19th, destined for the siege of Seringapatam in 1799, where they arrived nine days after the fall of that fortress.

Died at Nice, 11th March, 1822.

WILLIAM BEAMISH

Born at Willsgrove, 13th May, 1760; 3rd son of Capt. William Beamish, R.N., of Willsgrove, Co. Cork. Entered Royal Navy. Afterwards Ensign, 19th Foot, 12th November, 1778; Lieut., 29th June, 1780; retired, 25th August, 1783.

Acted as Adjt. to 19th Foot during the War in America, 1781.
Died at Beaumont, Co. Cork, 17th April, 1828.
Founded a brewery in Cork, " Beamish and Crawford."

EDWARD BISHOP

Born, 1756; Surgeon's Mate, 1778; 35th Foot, 14th November, 1782; half-pay, 69th Foot, 23rd October, 1798 to 1805.

Served in the American War, 1781 with 19th Foot.
His name appears in list of superannuated Surgeons in 1818.
Died at Kinsale, 12th June, 1832.

JOHN CARDEN

Ensign, 60th Foot, 7th April, 1771; Lieut., 28th April, 1775; 19th Foot, 20th March, 1779; 5th Foot, 27th January, 1780; out of the Army List, 30th April, 1782.

JOHN BLOOMFIELD

Ensign, 20th March, 1779; Lieut., 9th September, 1781. Out of the Army List, 25th March, 1785.

Served in the American War, 1781.

CHARLES MACDONNELL

Born, 1761. Son of Charles James Macdonnell, of Kilkee, Co. Clare, Lieut.-Col. of the Clare Militia. Ensign, 8th March, 1780; Lieut., Irish Volunteers, 18th September, 1781; Capt., 105th Foot (Rawdon's), 21st March, 1782. Half-pay on reduction, 1783; 96th Foot (Murray's Regt.), 1st November, 1793; Major Macnamara's Foot (121st Foot), 10th June, 1794; Lieut.-Col., Earl of Belvidere's Regt., 27th November, 1794 (disbanded 1796); Col., 1st January, 1801.

Served in the American War, 1781. M.P. for Co. Clare and Yarmouth, Isle of Wight in 1803. Commissioner of accounts in 1802.
Died at Bath, 7th September, 1803.

WILLIAM CAULFIELD

Ensign, 29th June, 1780; Lieut., 12th April, 1782; retired, 30th June, 1790.

Served in the American War, 1781.

JOHN BARRINGTON PERRYN

Ensign, 29th June, 1780; Lieut., 12th April, 1782; retired, 9th June, 1786.

Served in the American War, 1781.

ROBERT BLOOMFIELD

Ensign, 30th June, 1780; Lieut., 25th August, 1783; retired, 23rd August, 1785.

Served in the American War, 1781.

Lord EDWARD FITZGERALD

Born at Whitehall, 15th October, 1763 ; 5th son of the 20th Earl of Kildare and 1st Duke of Leinster. Ensign, 96th Foot, 24th December, 1779 ; Lieut., 19th Foot, 20th September, 1780 ; Capt., 25th June, 1782 ; Major, 90th Foot, 12th February, 1783 ; half-pay, 31st March, 1784 ; 54th Foot, 23rd January, 1788.

Removed from the Army, 1st December, 1792 on political grounds. Served in the American War, 1781 as A.D.C. to Lord Rawdon. Present at the relief of Fort Ninety-Six, the engagement at Monk's Corner and battle of Eutaw Springs.

Whilst serving in Canada was inducted as a chief in the Great Bear tribe of Indians by David Palmer, the leader of the Six Nations. Sided with the Irish rebels in the rising of 1798. Apprehended in Dublin and after resistance severely wounded.

Died in prison in Dublin, 4th June 1798. Buried in St. Werburgh's Church, Dublin.

ARTHUR CAVENAGH

Ensign, 17th November, 1780 ; resigned, 4th October, 1786.

Took part in the American War, 1781.

WILLIAM GRANT

Ensign, 1781 ; Lieut., 14th December, 1785 ; Capt.-Lieut., 2nd May, 1795 ; Capt., 1st September, 1795 ; 88th Foot, 24th December, 1802. Half-pay, February, 1804 to 27th March, 1809.

Served in the American War in 1781, also in the campaign in Holland, 1794-5.

JOHN REYNOLDS

Ensign, 10th March, 1781. Half-pay, Waller's Corps, 26th January, 1785. Omitted from the half-pay list, 2nd January, 1797.

GEORGE FULLER

Ensign, 9th September, 1781 ; Lieut., 9th June, 1786 ; retired, 14th July, 1789.

JOHN LLOYD

Only son of John Lloyd, of Pound, Devon. Ensign, 64th Foot, 6th July, 1769 ; Lieut., 12th December, 1770 ; Capt., 23rd August, 1775 ; Major, 60th Foot, 22nd October, 1779 ; 19th Foot, 4th October, 1781 ; retired, 3rd May, 1782.

A.D.C. to General Clinton during the American War of Independence.

THOMAS LINDSAY

Ensign, 25th October, 1781. Out of the Army List, 15th March, 1786.

JOHN RAMSAY

Ensign, 12th April, 1782 ; 99th Foot, 1st November, 1782 ; Lieut., 101st Foot, 14th June, 1783. Omitted from the Army List, 15th March, 1786.

COLEBROOKE NESBITT

Natural son of Arnold Nesbitt, of Aldermanbury, M.P. for Crickdale and Winchelsea. Ensign, 32nd Foot, 7th June, 1773 ; Lieut., 25th October, 1775 ; Capt., 82nd Foot, 5th January, 1778 ; Major, 19th Foot, 3rd May, 1782 ; 52nd Foot, 9th May, 1789 ; Lieut.-Col., 21st June, 1789 ; Bt.-Col., 26th February, 1795 ; Local Maj.-Gen., 3rd May, 1796 ; A.D.C. to the King, 1797.

Took part in the assault on Fort Savendroog, Mysore, and the campaign of 1791. Was Inspector-Gen. of all the Foreign Corps in H.M's. Service.

Died in St. James' Place, London, 21st July, 1798.

JOHN SOUTHWELL BROWNE

Son of the Revd. John Browne, of Mount Browne, Co. Limerick. Ensign, 5th Foot, 14th September, 1782 ; 19th Foot, 25th December, 1782 ; Lieut., 21st September, 1787 ; Adjt., 28th December, 1791 ; Retired, 22nd October, 1793.

THOMAS LITTLETON

Ensign, 42nd Foot, 23rd November, 1772 ; Lieut., 7th December, 1775 ; 5th Foot, 7th October, 1777 ; Capt., 1st September, 1781 ; 19th Foot, 25th December, 1782 ; half-pay, 76th Foot, 26th April, 1786 ; omitted from the Half-pay List, 5th April, 1791.

JOHN LYNE

Son of the Revd. Phillip Lyne, D.C.L., of Treleven, Cornwall. Ensign, 12th January, 1783 ; Lieut., 25th February, 1788.

Died at Exeter, 19th March, 1793.

ALEXANDER GRAY

Ensign, 1st November, 1783 ; Retired, 17th October, 1786.

JOHN MAJORIBANKS

Ensign, Major H. Waller's Corps, 23rd October, 1782 ; Half-pay on disbandment, 1783 ; 19th Foot, 26th January, 1785; Lieut., 11th February, 1789 ; Capt., Independent Co., 3rd March, 1791 ; omitted from the Army List, 14th February, 1806.

WILLIAM HOWE HENNIS

Eldest son of Captain Peter Hennis, 59th Foot ; 2nd Lieut., 23rd Foot, 22nd November, 1777 ; 1st Lieut., 13th September, 1779 ; Capt., 19th Foot, 16th April, 1785 ; Half-pay, 15th March, 1786 ; 58th Foot, 28th February, 1787 ; Retired, 21st July, 1792. Was a Major in the South Cork Militia and Collector of Youghal after his father.

Died, 25th June, 1833, and was buried at Youghal, Co Cork.

THOMAS ELAND

Ensign, 11th May, 1785 ; Half-pay, 76th Foot, 17th March, 1787 ; omitted from the Half-pay List, 12th February, 1827, in consequence of no half-pay being issued to him for the last seven years.

Sir WILLIAM HOUSTON, Bart., G.C.B.

Born, 10th August, 1766. Only son of Andrew Houston, of Calderhaugh. Ensign, 31st Foot, 18th July, 1781 ; Lieut., Independent Co., 2nd April, 1782 ; 77th Foot, 1783 ; Capt., 13th March, 1783 ; half-pay, on disbandment for seventeen months ; 19th Foot, 20th July, 1785 ; Bt.-Major, 1st March, 1794 ; Major, 30th May, 1794 ; Lieut.-Col., 84th Foot, 21st March, 1795 ; 58th Foot, 11th June, 1795 ; Col., 29th April, 1802 ; Maj.-Gen., 25th October, 1809 ; Col., 4th Garrison Regt., 1st July, 1811 ; Lieut.-Gen., 4th June, 1814 ; Col., 20th Foot, 5th April, 1815 ; Gen., 10th January, 1837.

In command of 19th Foot during the campaign under the Duke of York in 1794. Present at the taking of Minorca in 1800 in command of 58th Foot. Was with the reserve in the landing in Egypt on 8th March, 1801. Commanded a brigade at the taking of Rosetta and at the surrender of Cairo and Alexandria (medal). Was in command of the reserve in the Walcheren Expedition when the enemy was defeated between Middleburg and Flushing, four guns being taken and the enemy driven into the latter town. Was in command of the 7th Division at the battle of Fuentes d' Onoro and at the 2nd siege of Badajos (mentioned in despatches, gold medal). K.C.B., 1815, G.C.B., 1830. Governor of Gibraltar 1831-35. Created a baronet, 19th July, 1836.

Died at Bromley, 8th April, 1842. Buried at Carshalton, Surrey.

THOMAS EDWARD HAY

Ensign, 14th December, 1785 ; Lieut., 25th June, 1790 ; 10th Foot, 11th May, 1791.

Died, 4th January, 1794.

JOHN GRANT

Ensign, 71st Foot, 8th December, 1775 ; Lieut., 14th October, 1778 ; Half-pay on disbandment, April, 1783 ; 19th Foot, 27th January, 1786 ; Capt., 55th Foot, 24th December, 1787 ; Retired, 25th December, 1787.

Died at Kincardine, 9th May, 1799.

SAMUEL GRAHAM

Born at Paisley, 20th May, 1756. Son of John Graham. Ensign, 31st Foot, 20th November, 1777 ; Lieut., 76th Foot, (Macdonald's Highlanders), 25th December, 1777 ; Capt.-Lieut., 9th April, 1779 ; Capt., 2nd February, 1784 ; half-pay, 2nd March, 1784 ; 19th Foot, 26th April, 1786 ; Bt.-Major, 1st March, 1794 ; Major, 13th May, 1795 ; Lieut.-Col., 2nd West India Regt., 20th May, 1795 ; 27th Foot, 18th January, 1797 ; Col., 29th April, 1802 ; Maj.-Gen., 25th October, 1809 ; Lieut.-Gen., 4th June, 1814.

Served with the 76th Foot in the War of Independence, and was taken prisoner with the Army under Lord Cornwallis at Yorktown.

Owing to the execution of Captain Joshua Huddy, an American officer, General Washington, demanded reparation, and Captain Graham was one of thirteen British officers who drew lots for his life.

"In one hat were the names of thirteen Captains, written on separate slips of paper, in the other were thirteen other slips upon one of which was marked "unfortunate." A drum boy drew a name while the other drew the slip, until the eleventh when the slip bearing the word came up after that of Captain Asgill."

Present with the 19th Foot in 1793 in the campaign in Holland and afterwards joined Sir Charles Grey who was besieged at Nieuport. Was A.D.C. to Gen. Crosbie in the 1794-5 campaign. Severely wounded in Jamaica when serving against the Charibs in 1795. Took part in the expedition to the Helder in 1799 and was wounded by a ball which deprived him of his right eye. Served in the expedition to Egypt under Sir Ralph Abercromby, and led the advance of one of the columns under Sir Eyre Coote. Deputy Governor of Stirling Castle, 4th April, 1800. Lieut.-Gov, 1802.

Died at Stirling, 25th January, 1831.

RICHARD PATERSON

Ensign, 19th July, 1786 ; Lieut., 14th July, 1789 ; 55th Foot, 27th October, 1790 ; Resigned, 28th June, 1791.

CHARLES DOLPHIN

Ensign, 4th October, 1786 ; Retired, 26th February, 1789.

GEORGE HENRY VANSITTART

Born, 16th July, 1768. Eldest son of George Vansittart, M.P. of Bisham Abbey, Berkshire. Ensign, 18th October, 1786; Lieut., 25th December, 1787 ; 38th Foot, 12th March, 1788 ; Capt., 18th Foot, 23rd June, 1790 ; Major, New South Wales Corps, 20th November, 1793 ; Lieut.-Col., 95th Foot, 21st February, 1794 ; Bt.-Col., 26th January, 1797 ; 68th Foot, 10th April, 1801 ; Col., 12th Reserve Batt., 9th July, 1803 ; Maj.-Gen., 25th September, 1803 ; Col., 1st Garrison Bn., 25th February, 1805 ; Lieut.-Gen., 25th July, 1810.

Took part in the defence of Toulon 1793, with the 18th Foot, and was the last man to leave. Accompanied the 95th Foot in the expedition under Sir Alured Clarke against the Cape of Good Hope in 1795. Was present at the capture of St. Lucia in June, 1803.

Died, 4th February, 1824.

CHARLES LIND

Surgeon, 28th March, 1787, from Hospital mate at Grenada; Surgeon to the Forces, 20th June, 1795 ; Apothecary, St. Domingo, 26th September, 1795 ; Surgeon, Jamaica, 23rd November, 1796 ; Assist.-Inspector of Hospitals, 14th May, 1802 ; Half-pay, 26th May, 1803 ; Retired, 25th June, 1805.

Died, 7th March, 1815.

JAMES MACDONALD

2nd son of Ranald Macdonald, of Clanranald. Ensign, 76th Foot (Macdonald's Highlanders), 2nd December, 1783 ; Half-pay, same year ; 19th Foot, 18th April, 1787 ; Lieut., 30th January, 1790 ; Capt., Independent Co., 26th February, 1791 ;

73rd Foot, 8th July, 1791 ; Bt.-Major, 1st January, 1798 ;
Major, 9th July, 1803 ; Lieut.-Col., 25th September, 1803.

Served in the East and West Indies (dangerously wounded). Dismissed the Service by sentence of a General Court Martial, 18th October, 1806.

Died in 1838.

PATRICK CHARLES O'CONNOR

Ensign, 24th September, 1787 ; Lieut., 2nd March, 1791 ;
Capt., Independent Co., 8th May, 1793 ; 60th Foot, 15th
October, 1794.

Died, 23rd January, 1796.

JOHN McGREGOR

Ensign, 25th September, 1787 ; Lieut., 5th March, 1793 ;
Resigned, 21st November, 1794.

KENNETH McKENZIE

Ensign, 83rd Foot, 13th June, 1781 ; Lieut., 18th December, 1782 ; Half-pay on reduction, June, 1783 ; 19th Foot, 6th
October, 1787. Out of the Army List in 1788.

JOHN CREIGHTON

Ensign, 2nd April, 1788 ; Lieut., 25th June, 1792 ; Capt.,
Hanger's Recruiting Corps, 26th April, 1798 ; Half-pay in 1799.

Served in the campaign in Germany, 1794-5.

Died, 7th April, 1853.

HENRY BENEDICT DOLPHIN, C.B.

2nd son of Redmond Dolphin, J.P., of Corr, Co. Galway.
Ensign, 27th February, 1789 ; Lieut., 14th March, 1793 ; Independent Co., 9th October, 1793 ; Capt., 4th West India Regt.,
1st July, 1795 ; Major, 1st July, 1804 ; Lieut.-Col., 6th West
India Regt., 12th April, 1807 ; Col., 4th June, 1814.

Served in the campaign in Holland, 1794-5 as A.D.C. to Major-Gen.
J. Coates (19th). Was at the capture of Guadeloupe in 1815 (Gold medal
and C.B.).

Died, 4th April, 1816.

JAMES DALRYMPLE

Ensign, 30th March, 1789 ; Lieut., 5th March, 1793 ;
Resigned, 13th June, 1795.

HENRY BARRY

Ensign, 52nd Foot, 10th March, 1768 ; Lieut., 23rd September, 1772 ; Capt., 4th January, 1777 ; Bt.-Major, 19th February,
1783 ; Major, 27th February, 1786 ; 19th Foot, 9th May, 1789 ;
Bt.-Lieut.-Col., 28th May, 1790 ; 71st Foot, 2nd June, 1790 ,
Lieut.-Col., 39th Foot, 8th December, 1790 ; Retired, 4th May,
1793.

WILLIAM WISHART

Ensign, 8th September, 1789 ; Lieut., 31st May, 1793 ;
Capt., 99th Foot, 13th February, 1794 ; 15th Foot, 1st Septem-

ber, 1799 ; Bt.-Major, 25th September, 1803.

Died, 10th December, 1805.

ALEXANDER NAPIER

Son of Alexander Napier, of Blackstone, Renfrew, Lieut. and Capt., Coldstream Gds., 1765. Ensign, 20th January, 1790 ; Lieut., 7th Foot, 11th May, 1791 ; Capt., 100th Foot, 12th February, 1794 ; Major, 92nd Foot, 12th March, 1796 ; Lieut.-Col., 5th April, 1801.

Served with the 92nd in the Irish Rebellion of 1798. Took part in the expedition to Holland in 1799, and was present at Egmont-op-zee. Served in the expedition to Denmark. Commanded the 92nd at the battle of Alexandria on the death of Col. Erskine, 13th March, 1801 (Gold medal for Egypt). Killed at the battle of Corunna, 16th January, 1809 (Gold medal).

" Whom every man in the 92nd adored and to whom he was more like an affectionate father than a commanding officer " (Diary of Sergt. Robertson, 92nd).

Sir JOHN WROTTESLEY, Bart., 1st Baron WROTTESLEY

Born at Wrottesley, Co. Stafford, 24th October, 1771. Son of Gen. Sir John Wrottesley, Bt. Col., 45th Foot. Ensign, 35th Foot, 24th September, 1787 ; Lieut., 19th Foot, 2nd June, 1790; 29th Foot, 25th June, 1790 ; Capt., 16th Light Dragoons, 26th February, 1793 ; Major, 32nd Foot, 28th April, 1794. Out of the Army List, 11th March, 1796 ; Lieut.-Col., West Staffordshire Militia, 1835 till death.

Present at the siege of Valenciennes, July, 1793 with 16th Light Dragoons. M.P. for Lichfield, 1796-1806, for Staffordshire, 1823-1832, and South Staffordshire, 1832-37. Created a Baron, 11th July, 1838.

Died at Wrottesley, 16th March, 1841.

ROBERT AENEAS STIRLING SHAW

Ensign, 25th June, 1790 ; Lieut., 6th June, 1793 ; Retired, 13th December, 1793.

Sir WILLIAM HUTCHINSON, K.C.H.

Ensign, 46th Foot, 1st June, 1780 ; Lieut., 20th January, 1783 ; 59th Foot, 6th September, 1786 ; 55th Foot, 3rd May, 1787 ; 19th Foot, 27th October, 1790 ; 13th Foot, 23rd November, 1791 ; Capt.-Lieut., 1st Foot, 7th November, 1792 ; Capt., 20th March, 1794 ; Major, West India Regt., 20th May, 1795 ; 49th Foot, 11th July, 1798 ; Bt.-Lieut.-Col., half-pay, 1st January, 1800 ; 83rd Foot, 9th June, 1803 ; Half-pay, 12th Garrison Btn., 6th May, 1805 ; Bt.-Col., 22nd July, 1810 ; Lieut.-Col., 48th Foot, 24th October, 1811 ; Major-Gen., 14th June, 1813 ; Lieut.-Gen., 27th May, 1825 ; Col., 75th Foot, 26th October, 1841 ; Gen., 23rd November, 1841.

Took part in the expedition against St. Domingo and was present at the taking of Jeremie and Cape St. Nicholas Mole in September, 1793 ; at the capture of Cape Tiberoun, 2nd February, 1794, and the storming of Fort L'Acul, 19th February, 1794. Served in the expedition to the Helder and was severely wounded at the battle of Egmont-op-zee. Accompanied the expedition to Copenhagen under Lord Nelson in 1801. Served for a short time on the staff in the Peninsula.

Died at Cheltenham, 27th August, 1845.

DAVID OSWALD

Son of George Oswald, of Scotstoun, Renfrew, and Auchencruive, Co. Ayr. Ensign, 20th Foot, 9th October, 1790 ; Lieut., 19th Foot, 24th January, 1791 ; Capt., 20th April, 1793 ; Major, 38th Foot, 2nd December, 1794.

Died in the West Indies, 9th December, 1797.

ALEXANDER HOUSTON

Eldest son of Colonel Andrew Houston, of Jordan Hill, Co. Renfrew. 2nd Lieut., 57th Foot, 20th March, 1788 ; Lieut., 2nd November, 1790 ; 19th Foot, 3rd March, 1791 ; Capt., 9th Foot, 5th March, 1793 ; Major, 88th Foot, 15th July, 1795 ; 57th Foot, 27th June, 1796 ; Lieut.-Col., 13th January, 1799 ; Rifle Brigade, 26th August, 1800.

Died at Gibraltar, 29th November, 1800.

JOHN LINDALL BORLAND

Ensign, 22nd Foot, 24th November, 1775 ; Lieut., 14th August, 1778 ; Half-pay, 71st Foot, 5th July, 1786 ; 10th Foot, 24th March, 1790 ; 19th Foot, 11th May, 1791 ; Capt., 38th Foot, 28th February, 1792 ; Major, 18th October, 1797 ; Bt.-Lieut.-Col., 29th April, 1802 ; Retired by sale, 11th April, 1807.

THOMAS ALEXANDER KENNEDY

Eldest son of Hugh Alexander Kennedy, M.D. Matriculated at Queen's College, Oxford, 27th May, 1787, aged 17. Ensign, 14th May, 1791 ; Lieut., 31st July, 1793 ; Capt.-Lieut., 1st September, 1795.

Served in the campaign in Germany, 1794-5. He commanded the detachment of the 19th consisting of the light company and four battalion companies, which formed part of the escort to General Macdowall's embassy to Kandy in March—May, 1800, and having been very ill from the day of its arrival (March 24th) at the King's Gardens which Captain Percival of the 19th, who was with the detachment, calls " Resue Ortie Palagomby Watty," situated on the bank of the Kelaniya River, within a mile of Rawanwella, was sent by water to Colombo where he died a fortnight later (15th April, 1800). Brother of Sir Robert Hugh Kennedy, K.C.H., Commissary to the Forces during the whole of the Peninsular War.

JOHN BRYNE SKERRETT

Son of Lieut.-Gen. John Nicholas Skerrett, (q.v.) ; Lieut., 79th Foot, 25th October, 1783 ; Half-pay, 1784 ; 19th Foot, 27th July, 1791 ; Capt., 103rd Foot, 27th August, 1794 ; 69th Foot, 23rd March, 1795 ; Major, 83rd Foot, 29th March, 1798 ; Bt.-Lieut.-Col., 23rd October, 1800 ; Lieut.-Col., 47th Foot, 16th January, 1804 ; Col., 25th July, 1810 ; Maj.-Gen., 4th June, 1813.

Served in the Peninsular War at Cadiz, and was in command of the troops at the siege of Tarifa and capture of Seville. Was also at the battle of Vittoria (gold medal), Present at Bergen-op-zoom, 8th March, 1814. Severely wounded and taken prisoner.

Died of his wounds, 12th March, 1814.

" This gallant and distinguished officer whose leg had been broken not many weeks before when proceeding to the siege of Williamstadt, was the first of his party who mounted the walls, when he was wounded in the hand, then in the thigh—still he went on—at last in the head, when, to use the hasty but expressive retort of an officer present, to the most afflicted of his survivors, 'Any other man would have been safe in his room, his leg retarded his progress' (Gentleman's Magazine).

JOHN NUGENT, C.B.

2nd son of James Nugent, of Clonlost, Co. Westmeath.

Ensign, 13th Foot, 3rd July, 1789; Lieut., 13th October, 1790; 19th Foot, 23rd November, 1791; Capt., 38th Foot, 30th July, 1793; Bt-Major, 29th April, 1802; Major, 1st August, 1803; Lieut.-Col., 8th February, 1807. Half-pay on reduction in 1804. Col., 4th June, 1814; Maj.-Gen., 19th July, 1821.

Was employed with the Army under the Duke of York in Flanders and was present at the actions on the 18th May and 13th June, 1794. Was at the capture of St. Lucia in 1796 and Trinidad in 1797. Present at the capture of the Cape of Good Hope in 1806. Took part in the actions of Maldonado and Montevideo in 1807. Was in command of the 38th at the capture of the Place de Toros at Buenos Ayres. Served in the Peninsular War, and was at the battles of Busaco, Fuentes d'Onoro, Badajos and Salamanca (gold medal and four clasps).

Died in Paris, 20th April, 1830.

HERBERT BEAVER

Born, 24th February, 1764. Son of the Revd. James Beaver, of Lewknor, Oxfordshire. Ensign, 48th Foot, 31st May, 1783; Lieut., 13th October, 1790; 19th Foot, 16th January, 1792; Capt., 2nd December, 1794; Major, 3rd September, 1803.

Served in the campaigns in Holland of 1793, 1794 and 1795 as A.D.C. to Br.-Gen. Coates and afterwards as Brigade-Major to Gen. Gordon. Took part in the Kandian campaign of 1803-4. For an account of his work see Cordiner, Vol. ii., p.p. 194-5. Highly recommended for his conduct, "London Gazette," 7th August, 1804. Took part in the Travancore War, 1809. Died at Colombo, 19th April, 1809. He received a public funeral A general order was issued by the Commander-in-Chief directing minute guns to be fired at the time of his funeral equal to the number of his years. "This last, though universal testimony to his merits," and his death was referred to "as severe a loss the society of this small settlement has perhaps ever sustained." There is a memorial tablet in Childry Church, Berkshire. When studying at Strasburg in 1784 he fought a duel with an arrogant French officer whom he succeeded in "pinning to the wall." Writing home from the Continent on the 9th January, 1795, he says: "Yesterday was one of the most trying days of either campaign; it was glorious for the troops, as they behaved like Britons. Still, it proved advantageous for the French. I have had some narrow escapes, yet am safe and sound. To give you an idea of what my health and constitution will bear, I have never laid down for an hour at a time for this last fortnight. I visited all the pickets of the brigade almost every hour of each night, and during the day was constantly riding about with orders. Not a boot off, not a change of linen. The cold is so intense that we crossed the Rhine yesterday with our cannon on the ice. Whenever we have marched it has been at night, and in the morning we have been obliged to fight. In short, this last business has been to the soldier equal in hardship to both campaigns put together. You will see in the account of yesterday that two Colonels of the 27th were wounded; the shot which struck the first passed me, and five minutes afterwards I was close to the second when his thigh was broken by a bullet."

ROBERT HONNER

Ensign, 25th January, 1792 ; Lieut., 16th September, 1793 ; Capt., 27th May, 1795 ; Major, 18th April, 1805.

Took part in the campaign in Germany, 1794-5. Served in the expedition against the king of Kandy in 1803 in command of the Grenadier Co., 19th Foot. Cashiered by sentence of a General Court Martial at Colombo, 13th January, 1806, for sending a message to the Captains of the 19th Regiment containing a misstatement derogatory to the character and subversive of the authority of the Commander of the Forces.

JOHN LEVESON-GOWER

Born, 25th June, 1774. Eldest son of Admiral the Hon. John Leveson-Gower. Ensign, 1st Foot, 6th February, 1791 ; Lieut., 19th Foot, 25th April, 1792 ; Capt., 9th Foot, 16th January, 1793 ; Major, New South Wales Corps, March, 1794 ; Lieut.-Col., 63rd Foot, 2nd July, 1794 ; Capt. and Lieut.-Col., Coldstream Gds., 17th June, 1799 ; 31st Foot, 17th October, 1799. Half-pay, 31st December, 1799 ; Bt.-Col., 1st January, 1800 ; A.D.C. to the King, 1st June, 1800 ; Col., 11th Garrison Btn., 1st June, 1803 ; Maj.-Gen., 30th October, 1805 ; Lieut.-Gen., 1st January, 1812.

Served in the West Indies at the sieges of Fort Bourbon, Martinique and capture of St. Lucia. Joined the 63rd in Holland and commanded it in the sortie from Nimeguen, also in front of Geldermalsen, and in the subsequent retreat of the army. Present at the relief of St. Vincent in 1796, and in the several attacks made by Sir Ralph Abercromby on the enemy's position at the Vigie and during the subsequent service in the Charib country. Was with the Coldstream Guards in the expedition to the Helder. On the staff of Lieut.-Gen. Whitelocke in South America. M.P. Truro 1796-1802.

Died at his seat in Berkshire, 14th September, 1816.

LEWIS MACDONELL

Possibly son of Duncan Macdonell, of Glengarry. Ensign, 31st January, 1793 ; Lieut., 14th December, 1793. Retired, 9th January, 1795.

ARCHIBALD CAMPBELL

Eldest son of Archibald Campbell, J.P., of Jura, Co. Argyll, Heritable Keeper of Craignish Castle. Ensign, 5th March, 1793 ; Lieut., 30th May, 1794 ; Capt., 84th Foot, 13th December, 1794 ; Bt.-Major, 1st January, 1805 ; Major, 19th December, 1807 ; Lieut.-Col., 31st March, 1810.

Died in India, 14th April, 1817.

JOHN WAUCHOPE

Eldest son of John Wauchope, of Edmonstone. Ensign, 63rd Foot, 3rd August, 1785 ; Lieut., 30th June, 1790 ; Capt., 19th Foot, 20th March, 1793 ; Major, 1st September, 1793 ; Bt.-Lieut.-Col., 1st January, 1801. Retired, 25th July, 1801.

Took part in the campaign in Germany, 1794-5. Lieut.-Col. Edinburgh Regt. of Militia, 13th October, 1802, to 13th November, 1809.

Died in June, 1837.

ALEXANDER BLACKWOOD VILANT

Ensign, 25th March, 1793 ; Lieut., 13th June, 1794 ; Capt., 28th March, 1799 ; Royal Staff Corps, 9th November, 1805 ; 50th Foot, 5th September, 1807. Retired by sale, 29th September, 1807.

Served in the campaign in Germany, 1794-5. Took part with escort in an embassy to the King of Kandy in March, 1800. Served in the Kandian campaign of 1803-4, including the advance on the capital. Acting Engineer at Kandy, 30th March, 1803.

JAMES McNAB

Ensign, 10th April, 1793 ; Lieut., 13th August, 1794 ; Capt., 25th June, 1803 ; Major, 26th November, 1809 ; Bt.-Lieut.-Col., 4th June, 1814.

Served in the campaign in Germany in 1794-5. Also in the war in Travancore in 1809.

Died at Trincomalee, 4th June, 1818.

JOHN HAMILTON, Earl of STAIR, K.T.

Born at Edinburgh, 15th June, 1771. Son of Sir John Dalrymple, Bart., of Cranstown. Ensign, 40th Foot, 28th February, 1790 ; Lieut., 30th April, 1792 ; Capt., 19th Foot, 26th April, 1793 ; 3rd Foot Gds., 28th May, 1793 ; Capt. and Lieut.-Col., 6th December, 1798 ; Col., 25th April, 1808 ; Maj.-Gen., 4th June, 1811 ; Lieut.-Gen., 19th July, 1821 ; Col., 92nd Foot, 20th July, 1831 ; Gen., 28th June, 1838 ; Col., 46th Foot, 31st May, 1843.

Took part in the Flanders campaign of 1794 and served on the Continent till the return of the army in 1795. In October, 1805, accompanied the expedition to Hanover. In July, 1807, went to Zealand and was present at the siege of Copenhagen. K.T., 1847. M.P. for Midlothian, 1832-34. Keeper of the Great Seal, 1840-1, 1846-52. Succeeded to the Earldom of Stair, 22nd March, 1840. Whilst a Captain in the Guards, he devoted considerable attention to the devising of means for providing a substitute for corporal punishment. (Dic. N.B.)

Died at Oxenfoord Castle, Edinburgh, 10th January, 1853.

HENRY MUSGRAVE LYDE

Ensign, 31st May, 1793 ; Lieut., 82nd Foot, 1st February, 1794 ; Capt., 30th January, 1795.

Died, 2nd December, 1796.

GEORGE ROBERT AINSLIE

Born 1774. Eldest son of Sir Philip Ainslie, of Pilton, Co. Edinburgh. Ensign, 14th June, 1793 ; Lieut., 85th Foot, 1793 ; Capt., 15th April, 1794 ; Major, 11th January, 1799 ; Lieut.-Col., Birmingham Fencible Infantry, 11th January, 1800. Half-pay in 1802. 5th Garrison Btn., 1807 ; 25th Foot, 21st May, 1807 ; Col., 25th July, 1810 ; Maj.-Gen., 4th June, 1813 ; Lieut.-Gen., 2nd May, 1825.

Served with the 19th Foot in Flanders in 1793. Also took part in the campaigns of 1794-5, including actions at St. André and Tuyl, and retreat from the Rhine. Served in the expedition to Holland in 1799. Was Governor of Eustatius, West Indies and Vice-Governor of Grenada, 1812.

Received a sword of honour value £200 for subduing the Maroons in Dominica, of which he was Governor in 1813. A celebrated numismatist. Author of " Anglo-French Coinage," 1830.

Died in Edinburgh, 16th April, 1839.

PERCY GROVES

Born in 1772. Ensign, 45th Foot, 8th August, 1792 ; Lieut., Independent Co., 10th April, 1793 ; 19th Foot, 28th August, 1793 ; Capt., 3rd Foot, 18th March, 1795 ; Major, 5th August, 1799. Retired by sale, 14th March, 1805.

Served with the 19th in the campaign in Germany, 1794-5.

Died at the Moat, Charing, Kent, 6th June, 1857.

JAMES LA HEY

Qtr.-Mstr., 2nd January, 1794.

Served in the campaign in Germany, 1794-5. Died at Trincomalee, 25th March, 1802, aged 37. Memorial at Fort Frederick, Trincomalee. He lived universally esteemed and died universally regretted by the Corps.

EDWARD HENRY MADGE

Ensign, 20th January, 1794 ; Lieut., 15th August, 1794 ; Capt., 28th January, 1802.

Took part in the campaign in Germany in 1794-5. Served in the war against the King of Kandy in 1803-4. General orders, Colombo, 13th July, 1803 : " Oppressed as the Governor is by grief and indignation at the atrocious act of perfidy and cruelty lately committed at Kandy, he has sincere satisfaction at noticing the spirited and successful conduct of the garrison of Fort Macdowall and Dambadinia. He requests Captain E. Madge, of H.M. 19th Regiment, to accept his thanks for his gallant defence of the former, and for the judicious manner in which he has brought off his garrison." A relative of Major Thomas Madge, H.E.I.C.S. Two of Captain Madge's sons are said to have given its name to Madge's Lane, Calcutta.

JOHN JEWELL

Ensign, 3rd April, 1794 ; Lieut., 3rd December, 1794 ; Capt., 3rd September, 1803. Retired by sale, 28th August, 1805.

Served in the campaign in Germany, 1794-5. Took part in the Kandian War of 1803-4, and marched into Kandy in 1803. Fort Adjt., Jaffna, 1797-9. Commandant, Jaffna, 1800. Commissioner of Revenue, Batticaloa, September-December, 1803.

JAMES HENRY KING

Son of Henry King, of Leicester. Ensign, 12th April, 1794 ; Lieut., 14th December, 1794.

Served in the war in Germany, 1794-5.

Died of a violent fever at Loningen, Munster, 26th March, 1795.

THOMAS WETHERILL OTTLEY

Fifth son of Thomas Ottley, sometime of St. Vincent and afterwards of Antigua. Ensign, May, 1794 ; Lieut., 24th August, 1794 ; Capt., 31st March, 1803 ; Major, 65th Foot, 2nd July, 1805.

Served in the campaign in Germany, 1794-5.

Died in India, 8th August, 1807.

JOHN FOLLIOTT POWELL

Born 1771. Third son of Richard Powell, of Stanage Park, Co. Radnor. Ensign, 30th May, 1794 (from volunteer) ; retired, 14th October, 1794.

Sometime of Sandy Brook, Co. Derby, and afterwards of Leamington. Died at Tempsford Hall, 9th November, 1839.

DENZIL ONSLOW

Eldest son of Middleton Onslow, M.P. for Rye, of Staughton House, Huntingdon. Ensign, 1st Foot Gds., 25th April, 1787 ; Lieut. and Capt., 25th April, 1793 ; Major, 19th Foot, 3rd June, 1794 ; 97th Foot, 6th June, 1794 ; Lieut.-Col., half-pay, 29th May, 1795 ; Col., 1st January, 1800 ; Maj.-Gen., 30th October, 1805 ; Lieut.-Gen., 1st January, 1812 ; Gen., 27th May, 1825.

Died at Great Staughton House, Huntingdon, 21st August, 1838.

DUNBAR JAMES HUNTER

Grandson of Robert Hunter, Professor of Greek, Edinburgh University. Ensign, 3rd Foot, 15th December, 1790 ; Lieut., Independent Co., 9th March, 1793 ; Capt., 31st October, 1793 ; 19th Foot, 11th June, 1794 ; Major, 4th November, 1795 ; Bt.-Lieut.-Col., 1st January, 1801 ; Commandant of Galle, 1798-1800 ; Commandant at Trincomalee in 1802.

Died at Trincomalee, 4th September, 1803. Buried in the Pettah Cemetery, Colombo. The following epitaph was written by Lieut. T. A. Anderson, 19th Foot :

Oh ye, who never left your native home!
Whose peaceful bosom never wish'd to roam,
Reflect awhile upon a soldier's doom,
And sigh one moment o'er his early tomb!
Severe his fate, on stranger shores to fall
In manhood's noon, beloved and mourned by all.

This epitaph was used 36 years later for the tombstone of a sergeant of the 18th Royal Irish, who was shot by a private.

JAMES CHRISTIE

2nd Lieut., 21st Foot, 9th April, 1794 ; Ensign, 19th Foot, 27th August, 1794. Resigned, 20th September, 1799.

Served in the campaign in Germany in 1794-5.

GEORGE HEWSON

Ensign, 8th October, 1794 ; Lieut., 44th Foot, 8th January, 1795 ; 17th Foot, 14th April, 1795. Superseded, 14th April, 1795.

Served in the campaign in Germany, 1794-5.

WILLIAM FENWICK HUTCHINSON

Ensign, 15th October, 1794 ; half-pay, 82nd Foot, 8th July, 1795 ; Lieut., 90th Foot, 18th September, 1804.

Served in the campaign in Germany, 1794-5.

Died, 26th April, 1808.

CHARLES ALBERT VIGOREUX, C.B.

Ensign, 3rd Foot, 18th December, 1793 ; Lieut., 19th Foot, 2nd December, 1794 ; Capt., Corsican Corps, 4th April, 1795 ; half-pay in 1798 ; 35th Foot, August, 1799 ; Lieut. and Capt., 1st Foot Gds., 20th December, 1799 ; Capt., 42nd Foot, 23rd November, 1804 ; 6th Foot, 16th May, 1805 ; 38th Foot, 2nd July, 1807 ; Bt.-Major, 25th April, 1808 ; Major, 30th Foot, 4th June, 1813 ; Bt.-Lieut.,Col., 21st June, 1813 ; Lieut.-Col., 7th September, 1820 ; 45th Foot, 20th December, 1826 ; Col., 22nd July, 1830 ; half-pay, 12th July, 1839 ; Maj.-Gen., 24th December, 1841, the day of his death.

Served in Holland in 1794-5, and was besieged in Nimeguen, 1794. Took part in the Peninsular War, and was at the battles of Fuentes d'Onoro, Salamanca and Vittoria (gold medal). Also served in the Netherlands, 1814-15, and was severely wounded at the battle of Waterloo (medal and C.B.). His decorations are in the 30th Mess.

Died at Cambridge Street, London, 24th December, 1841, aged 63.

GEORGE DALRYMPLE

Second son of Lieut.-Col. Campbell Dalrymple, 3rd Dragoon Gds., Governor of Guadeloupe. Ensign, 42nd Foot, 12th July, 1773 ; Lieut., 24th February, 1776 ; Capt., 25th August, 1778 ; Major, 16th March, 1791 ; Lieut.-Col., 19th Foot, 31st December, 1794 ; Col., 1st January, 1801. Retired, 20th December, 1803.

Served in the American War of Independence with 42nd Foot, and in the campaign in Germany, 1794-5, when he distinguished himself in the action at Geldermalsen.

Died at North Berwick, 19th January, 1804.

EDWARD DRUMMOND

Fifth son of the Hon. Robert Drummond, of Cadland, Hants, and Charing Cross. Ensign, 8th January, 1795 ; Lieut., 90th Foot, 4th February, 1795; 71st Foot, 25th February, 1795; Capt., 60th Foot, 8th November, 1798 ; Major, 11th June, 1801 ; Lieut.-Col., 29th December, 1804 ; 86th Foot, 2nd June, 1808 ; Col., 4th June, 1813. Retired by sale, 18th November, 1813.

Served at the taking of Bourbon, 1810, with the 86th Foot.

Died at Brighton, 4th May, 1859, in his 84th year.

JOHN NAIRN

Ensign, 8th January, 1795 ; Lieut., 3rd June, 1795.

Died, 8th August, 1799.

Sir WROTH PALMER ACLAND, K.C.B.

Born 1770. Third son of Arthur Acland, of Fairfield, Somerset. Ensign, 17th Foot, 25th April, 1787 ; Lieut., 17th June, 1790 ; Capt. Independent Co., 24th January, 1791 ; half-pay to December, 1791 ; 3rd Foot, 2nd March, 1793 ; Major, 19th Foot, 18th March, 1795 ; Lieut.-Col., 1st September, 1795 ; Coldstream Gds., 10th May, 1800 ; Col., 28th September, 1803 ; Major-Gen., 25th July, 1810 ; Lieut.-Gen., 4th June, 1814 ; Col.-

Commandant, 60th Foot, 9th August, 1815 ; K.C.B., 1815.

Served in Flanders with the Duke of York's army, 1794-5. Was with the expedition under Sir John Stuart in 1806 in Calabria, where he commanded a brigade at the battle of Maida (mentioned in despatches —gold medal). Was on the staff of Gen. Whitelock at Montevideo. Took part in the Peninsular War and commanded the 8th Brigade at Vimiera (mentioned in despatches—gold medal). Served in the Walcheren expedition of 1809, and was present at the siege of Flushing. Died at Bath, 8th March, 1816. Buried in Bath Abbey, where there is a memorial tablet.

ALEXANDER DALRYMPLE

Ensign, 21st April, 1795 ; Lieut., 1st September, 1795 ; half-pay, 46th Foot, December, 1804.

Died, 1st April, 1858.

GEORGE AUGUSTUS BYGRAVE

Ensign, 65th Foot, 26th December, 1778 ; Lieut., 5th April, 1780 ; 13th Foot, 16th October, 1792 ; Qtr.-Mstr., 14th December, 1792 ; Capt., 19th Foot, 20th May, 1795. Retired, 28th March, 1799.

CHARLES MORGAN CLAYFIELD

Son of Michael Clayfield, of Bristol. Matriculated at Oxford, 1st June, 1786, aged 15. Lieut., Independent Co., 19th May, 1794 ; 19th Foot, 21st May, 1795 ; Capt., 4th November, 1795 ; 85th Foot, 24th April, 1801. Sold out, 9th June, 1801.

Died at Downend, Gloucestershire, 20th September, 1828.

Sir JAMES COLQUHON, Bart.

Eldest son of Sir George Colquhon, Bart., of Tillyquhon. Ensign, 10th June, 1795 ; Lieut., 2nd September, 1795.

Served in the campaign in Holland, 1795. Died at Errood, 24th April, 1799, when on the march to Seringapatam.

ANDREW BOND

Surgeon, 16th June, 1795 ; to the Forces in the West Indies, 8th September, 1795 ; half-pay, 25th June, 1800 ; to the Forces, 25th July, 1803 ; half-pay, 25th September, 1803 ; full-pay, 20th February, 1809. Retired, half-pay, 25th May, 1810.

Died on half-pay at Tours, France, 1st June, 1827.

WILLIAM SHAW

Ensign, 43rd Foot, 9th November, 1779 ; Lieut., 82nd Foot, 5th May, 1782 ; half-pay, 1783 ; 19th Foot, 8th July, 1795. Retired, 2nd February, 1796.

JOHN DOHERTY

Fourth son of Richard Doherty, of Sairbank, and sometime of Kedragh, Co. Tipperary. Ensign, 102nd Foot, 15th May, 1784 ; 36th Foot, 12th June, 1785 ; Lieut., 75th Foot, 7th November, 1788 ; Capt., 29th Foot, 6th April, 1795 ; 19th Foot, 1st September, 1795.

Lost at sea, 18th April, 1798.

The Hon. FREDERICK FORBES

Born, 7th November, 1776. Third son of the 5th Earl of Granard. Served for a short time in the navy. Ensign, 14th Foot, 29th January, 1793 ; Lieut., 85th Foot, 1st March, 1794 ; Capt., 6th March, 1794 ; 19th Foot, 2nd September, 1795. Retired, 30th November, 1803.

Died at Sligo, 2nd February, 1817.

JOHN THOMAS EYRE

Second son of Walpole Eyre, of Burnham, Bucks. Ensign, 26th Foot, 5th June, 1789; Lieut., 19th March, 1793 ; Capt., 101st Foot, 11th March, 1794 ; 19th Foot, 3rd September, 1795 ; Bt.-Major, 25th September, 1802 ; Major, 24th Foot, 9th February, 1805 ; Staff Capt. for recruiting in the Isle of Wight in 1801. Sold out, 2nd November, 1805.

ARTHUR JOHNSTON

Born at Lifford, Co. Donegal, July, 1778. Eldest son of John Johnston, of Clare, Co. Tyrone. Lieut., 102nd Foot, 17th May, 1794 ; 19th Foot, 3rd September, 1795 ; Capt., 1st Celyon Regt., 17th August, 1804 ; Major, 3rd Ceylon, 30th November, 1811 ; half-pay, Royal Corsican Rangers, 25th July, 1816 ; Bt.-Lieut.-Col., 4th June, 1814.

Served in the Kandian War, 1803-4. His seizure of Kandy in 1804 was an achievement in oriental warfare not to be surpassed. With a detachment of 70 Europeans, chiefly 19th Foot, and 305 native troops, he penetrated 200 miles through a mountainous and most unhealthy part of the island and succeeded in gaining possession of the capital, notwithstanding the destructive modes of warfare practised by the natives. Not receiving any reinforcements, he was compelled to evacuate Kandy, and effected his retreat under extreme difficulties and sufferings, his ammunition spent, his men wasting under disease and harassed by day and night, he nevertheless reached Trincomalee with the loss of only eight Europeans and 48 natives. He published an account of the expedition.

Died at Shalden, Hants, 4th June, 1824.

" In the relations of private life the energy of his intellect, the moral dignity of his principles and the nobleness of his feelings, though acknowledged with esteem and respect by those who knew him, can only be appreciated by those only who had also earned his love. He lived in the exercise of many noble virtues, and died with a purity and fervour of Christian faith which, while it soothes the remembrance, cannot but influence the lives of those with whom he was connected." (Annual Biography and Obituary, 1826.)

" This excellent officer fell a sacrifice to his exertions in the service of his country, during his residence in Ceylon, the effects of which baffled every effort of human power to overcome." (" Gentleman's Magazine.")

ALEXANDER STEELE

Ensign, 69th Foot, 28th May, 1793 ; Lieut., Independent Co., 25th June, 1793 ; Capt., 101st Foot, 11th August, 1794 ; 19th Foot, 4th September, 1795 ; 52nd Foot, 31st August, 1798. Sold out, 13th October, 1801.

THOMAS COX

Lieut., 102nd Foot, 14th June, 1795 ; 19th Foot, 4th September, 1795. Resigned, 21st January, 1797.

JOHN CHARLES STRACIE

Cornet, 5th Dragoon Gds., 20th September, 1793 ; Lieut., 17th Light Dragoons, 22nd August, 1794 ; Capt., 107th Foot, 24th September, 1794 ; 102nd Foot, 30th May. 1795 ; 19th Foot, 5th September, 1795 ; half-pay, 91st Foot, 10th March, 1798. Out of the half-pay list, 10th August, 1799.

JOHN M. FITZCERALD

Ensign, Independent Co., 16th November, 1793 ; Lieut., 102nd Foot, 18th August, 1794 ; 19th Foot, 5th September, 1795 ; Capt., 10th Foot, 19th August, 1796 ; 71st Foot, 1st January, 1801. Retired by sale, 15th October, 1801.

JAMES THOMAS ROBERTSON

Son of Dr. William Robertson, Principal of the University of Edinburgh. Ensign, 2nd Btn. Scotch Brigade, 26th May, 1794 ; 102nd Foot, 17th December, 1794 ; Lieut., 19th Foot, 6th September, 1795 ; Capt., 3rd Ceylon Regt., 7th April, 1804 ; 6th Foot, 12th June, 1806 ; Major, 30th January, 1812 ; half-pay, 25th February, 1816 ; 82nd Foot, 26th November, 1818 ; Bt.-Lieut.-Col., 27th May, 1825 ; Lieut.-Col., half-pay unattached, 28th August, 1827. Resigned, December, 1827.

Took part in the advance to Kandy in 1803.

ROBERT PERCIVAL

Born 1765. Eldest son of Capt. William Percival. Ensign, 102nd Foot, 31st October, 1793 ; Lieut., 29th April, 1795 ; 19th Foot, 7th September, 1795 ; Capt., 18th Foot, 9th July, 1803 ; Bt.-Major, 4th June, 1814 ; Major, 4th September, 1823 ; retired by sale, 10th June, 1824.

Took part in the operations at the Cape with the 19th Foot in August, 1796. Accompanied the escort, 19th Foot, with the embassy to Kandy in 1800. Was with the original garrison of Curaçoa when in the 18th Foot. Killed by a fall from his horse in 1826. Author of "An Account of the Cape of Good Hope, containing an historical view of its original settlement " ; also " A History of Ceylon."

WILLIAM PORTER

Born, April, 1774, at Wearde, St. Stephen's, Cornwall. Son of Richard Porter, of Wearde. Ensign, 114th Foot, 28th October, 1794 ; Lieut., 19th Foot, 8th September, 1795 ; 76th Foot, 1st February, 1797 ; Capt. Reserve Btn., 9th July, 1803 ; 40th Foot, 3rd August, 1804. Retired, full-pay, Royal Veteran Btn., 23rd July, 1812, till disbanded, 1814 ; half-pay till death.

Present at the capture of Montevideo, and the attack on Buenos Ayres. Served in the Peninsular War, and was present at the battles of Roleia and Vimiera.

Died at St. Stephen's, near Saltash, Cornwall, 5th April, 1839.

DONOUGH O'BRIEN

Lieut., 102nd Foot, 20th December, 1794 ; 19th Foot, 9th September, 1795 ; 8th Foot, 28th October, 1795 ; Superseded, 12th April, 1796.

CHARLES STEWART

Ensign, 75th Foot, 6th November, 1788 ; Lieut., 16th January, 1793 ; half-pay, 63rd Foot, 8th August, 1793 ; Lord Conyngham's Regt., 30th October, 1794 ; 19th Foot, 11th September, 1795. Sold out, 16th February, 1797.

GEORGE GULLAND

Ensign, 26th Foot, 31st December, 1794 ; Lieut., 102nd Foot, 5th August, 1795 ; 19th Foot, 12th September, 1795. Retired, 16th December, 1795.

THOMAS CLARK, M.D.

Born, July, 1770. Surgeon's Mate, 65th Foot, 25th April, 1790 ; Surgeon, 113th Foot, 30th May, 1794 ; 19th Foot, 16th September, 1795 ; half-pay, 25th December, 1800.

Served in Ceylon with 19th Foot.
Died in London, 21st December, 1857.

DONALD MACDONALD

Born, 1778. Ensign, 12th October, 1795 ; Lieut, 12th April, 1796 ; Capt., 31st December, 1804 ; Major, 11th June, 1812 ; Bt.-Lieut.-Col., 29th October, 1818 ; half-pay, 25th April, 1826.

Served in Ceylon during the rebellions of 1815 and 1818. Fort Macdonald named after him. Died in Hans Place, Sloane Street, 22nd March, 1847. There is a memorial window in Preston Church, Brighton, put up by his son, Captain G. V. Macdonald, 19th Foot.

ALEXANDER MILLER

Ensign, 103rd Foot, 19th November, 1794 ; Lieut., 19th Foot, 21st October, 1795. Resigned, 1796.

JAMES DOWNING

Ensign, 103rd Foot, 22nd May, 1794 ; Lieut., 19th Foot, 21st October, 1795 ; half-pay in 1802 ; 57th Foot, 30th August, 1803 ; Capt., 61st Foot, 1st October, 1803 ; Major, 8th October, 1807.

Served in the Peninsular War from October, 1809, to July, 1812, with the 61st, and was at the battle of Busaco and siege of Salamanca.
Died of wounds received at Salamanca, 23rd July, 1812.

RANDOLPH McDONALD

Lieut., 4th Regt. of Fencible Infantry, 25th April, 1795 ; Ensign, 19th Foot, 24th October, 1795 ; Lieut., 14th April, 1796.

Died, 30th March, 1799.

WILLIAM EBHART

Son of Andreas Friedrich Ebhart, 1st Royal Regt. of Horse. Ensign, 24th October, 1795 ; Lieut., 9th December, 1795 ; 24th Light Dragoons, 12th April, 1796 ; 73rd Foot, 23rd May, 1799 ; 9th Light Dragoons, 28th July, 1803 ; Capt., 6th Dragoon Gds., 12th November, 1807 ; 72nd Foot, 10th May, 1810 ; Bt.-Major, 19th July, 1821 ; Major, unattached, 13th August, 1830 ; Staff Capt., York Hospital, Chelsea, 26th August, 1821. Retired, November, 1830.

Died, 31st January, 1833, in his 65th year.   Buried in Chelsea Hospital.

RICHARD YOUNG

Born, 10th August, 1778. Eldest son of Alexander Young, of Coolkeiragh, Co. Londonderry. Lieut., Lord Conyngham's Regt., 12th September, 1795 ; 19th Foot, 30th October, 1795 ; Capt., Ceylon Regt., 1st April, 1804 ; 39th Foot, 21st May, 1807 ; 3rd Garrison Btn., 4th February, 1811 ; Bt.-Major, 4th June, 1814 ; 40th Foot, 16th February, 1815. Retired by sale, 23rd February, 1815.

Died at Coolkeiragh, 4th December, 1858.

THOMAS BULLOCK

Ensign, 4th November, 1795.   Retired, 1st March, 1797.

GEORGE NIXON

Son of George Nixon, of Redmills, Co. Dublin. Lieut, 11th November, 1795 ; Capt., 3rd Ceylon Regt., 7th April, 1804 ; Major, 8th July, 1813. Retired, 12th September, 1816.

Served in the Kandyan campaign of 1803-4, and took part in the defence of Dambadenia.

Died at Southvale, Chapelizod, Co. Dublin, in May, 1839.

JOHN KER

Second son of Gilbert Ker, of Gateshaw, Co. Roxburgh. Ensign, 77th Foot, 9th February, 1792 ; Lieut., 19th Foot, 18th November, 1795 ; Adjt., 18th January, 1800.

Died at Colombo, 17th January, 1803.

BERKELEY VINCENT

Sixth son of John Vincent, of Limerick. Lieut., 16th December, 1795.

Killed in action near Lake Minnery, Ceylon, 14th October, 1804, when serving with Capt. A. Johnston's expedition.

" On the return march, about three days after leaving Kandy, somewhere in the jungle between Matale and Minnery, Lieut. Vincent, of the Grenadier Company, received a shot in the groin ; it had been rather spent. He marched on with the others until the blood was coming out over the top of his boot at the knee ; at length he became faint and was put in a doolie ; and also Ensign Smith, who was struck on the breast by a spent ball which knocked him down. They were sent off by a bye-road under the care of the guides with instructions to join again upon the route." (Howell's Life of Bombardier Alexander.) "The main body reached Minnery Lake on the 16th, to find Lieut. Virgo, Malay Regt., and the advanced guard, but without either Lieut. Vincent or Ensign

Smith and two wounded soldiers of the 19th, who had to be abandoned. The guard alleged that they had lost their way in the woods, and were nearly starved ; that the coolies had deserted them ; that they themselves were so exhausted as to be scarcely able to walk, and had no means of carrying the sick, whom they were under the necessity of abandoning ; that they were without guides, and found their way to the village where they were by mere chance." (Marshall's Conquest of Ceylon, p.p. 125-6.) There was considerable feeling on the part of the officers of the 19th, according to Dr. Marshall, against Lieut. Virgo, who was in command of the escort, on account of their abandonment, and he was tried by Court Martial and sentenced to go on half-pay and lose seniority for six months. Dr. Marshall is inclined to think that he could not help himself, and that he was badly treated, especially as he had lost an eye in the retreat.

Sir JAMES MACDONNELL, G.C.B., K.C.H.

Born at Glengarry, January, 1780, 3rd son of Duncan Macdonnell, of Glengarry, Inverness. Ensign, 25th January, 1796 ; Lieut., 2nd February, 1796 ; Capt., 85th Foot, 10th September, 1803 ; 5th Foot, 22nd October, 1803 ; Major, 78th Foot, 17th April, 1804 ; Bt.-Lieut.-Col., 7th September, 1809 ; 2nd Garrison Bn., 21st February, 1811 ; Capt. and Lieut.-Col., Coldstream Gds., 8th August, 1811 ; Bt.-Col., 12th August, 1819 ; Major, 25th July, 1821 ; Lieut.-Col. Commanding, 27th May, 1823; Col., 16th July, 1825; Major-Gen., 22nd July, 1830; Lieut.-Gen., 23rd November, 1841 ; Col., 79th Foot, 14th July, 1842 ; 71st Foot, 8th February, 1849 ; Gen., 20th June, 1854.

Served with the 2nd Bn. 78th in the expedition to Sicily and Calabria under Sir James Stuart in 1805-6, including the battle of Maida, the siege of Scylla, and capture of Cotroné (gold medal). Also served in the expedition to Egypt in 1807, including the capture of Rosetta, siege of Alexandria, and was in command of the party which destroyed the enemy's batteries in the Delta opposite Abumandur. Served in the Peninsular War, 1812-14, and was present at the battles of Salamanca, Burgos, Vittoria, Bidassoa, Nivelle and Nive (medal and four clasps). Served with the Coldstream Gds. in the campaign of 1815, and was in command of the regt. at Waterloo (medal). Was celebrated for having, with the assistance of Sergt. Graham of his regt., closed the gates of the Château of Hugomont on the advancing French. Was selected by the Duke of Wellington to receive a legacy of £500 left by the Revd. Mr. Norcross, of Framlingham, Suffolk, to the bravest man in the Army, which legacy was shared at his own request by Sergt. Graham. C.B. in 1815 ; K.C.B., 1838; G.C.B., 1855 ; K.C.H., 1837. Commanding Armagh District, 1831-8, Brigade of Gds. in Canada, 1838, and Troops in Canada till 1841. Knight of the Order of Maria Theresa, 4th Class Order of St. Vladmir.

Died at 15, Wilton Place, London, 15th May, 1857. Memorial in the Guards' Chapel.

WILLIAM TAYLOR

Ensign, 12th March, 1796 ; Lieut., 75th Foot, 11th May, 1798 ; Capt., 3rd March, 1809 ; sold out, 14th October, 1824.

ERASMUS PIERSON

Ensign, 12th April, 1796. Retired by sale, 6th April, 1797.

CHARLES HUME

Ensign, 26th August, 1796.

Died, 17th July, 1798.

The Hon. GEORGE TURNOUR

Born at Shillinglee Park, Sussex, 4th February, 1768. 3rd son of the 1st Earl of Winterton. Ensign, Bengal Native Infantry, 9th February, 1785 ; Lieut., 73rd Foot, 23rd February, 1789 ; 19th Foot, 29th August, 1796 ; Fort Adjt., Jaffna, Ceylon, in 1795 ; Commandant of Manaar, 1797-1800. Retired, 18th November, 1801.

Died at Jaffna, 19th April, 1813.

Appointed to the Ceylon Civil Service in 1807. Was at one time a tobacco merchant at Jaffna. Father of the Hon. George Turnour, Ceylon Civil Service, a celebrated oriental scholar. There is a tombstone to his memory on the floor of the Dutch Church, Jaffna, erected by his widow.

JASPER NIXON

Probably a son of George Nixon, of Redmills, Chapelizod, Co. Dublin and Queen's Co., merchant. Ensign, 17th November, 1796 ; Lieut., 28th March, 1799.

" Died at Colombo, in the Island of Ceylon, Lieut. G. Nixon, late of H.M's. 19th Regt. of Foot. This distinguished young officer was the eldest son of George Nixon, of Redmills, Co. Dublin. His death is a serious exaggeration of the grief of his parents by the recent loss of another promising youth, his brother, an officer in the same regt., on his return with a detachment from Seringapatam to join his regt." (Saunders' News Letter, 11th April, 1804).

There is some mistake here as Lieut. George Nixon, of the 19th, who joined in 1795, did not die till 1839. The writer may have mistaken him for Lieut. George Nixon of the 12th Foot, who died at Seringapatam in 1800 (M.L.F.).

WILLIAM S———— ANDREWS

Assist.-Surgeon, 25th December, 1796; Surgeon, 26th July, 1801 ; 67th Foot, 15th September, 1808 ; Superseded for absence, 24th December, 1808.

Served in the Kandyan campaign of 1803-4, including the advance to Kandy. Belonged to Richmond, Surrey.

DAVID BARCLAY

Ensign, 75th Foot, 7th January, 1797 ; Lieut., 19th Foot, 11th May, 1797. Retired, 14th April, 1799.

Sir SAMUEL HULSE, G.C.H.

Born, 1746. 2nd son of Sir Edward Hulse, Bt. Ensign, 1st Foot Guards, 17th December, 1761 ; Lieut. and Capt., 2nd August, 1769 ; Capt. and Lieut.-Col., 20th February, 1776 ; Col., 20th November, 1782 ; Maj.-Gen., 12th October, 1793 ; Lieut.-Gen., 1st January, 1798 ; Gen., 25th September, 1803 ; Field Marshal, 22nd July, 1830 ; Col., 56th Foot, 7th March, 1795 ; 19th Foot, 24th January, 1797 ; 62nd Foot, 25th June, 1810.

Served in Flanders in 1793, being present at the siege of Valenciennes and distinguished himself in the action of Lincelles on the 18th August, for which he was thanked in orders by the Duke of York. Was engaged in the operations before Dunkirk. Served in the 1794 campaign and was in command of a brigade before Tournay, and in the retreat to Holland. Under the Duke of York in 1799 was again in Holland, and was in several engagements from 19th September to 6th October. Served in London during the Gordon riots in 1780. Created a Privy Councillor, 5th January, 1787 ; Governor of Chelsea Hospital, 1807 to 19th February, 1820.

Died at Chelsea Hospital, 1st January, 1837.

" The loss of their venerable commander is unfeignedly regretted by the aged inmates of the Hospital, which he governed for so many years. Though his funeral was, by his own desire, conducted in a private manner, the corpse was dismissed from the Hospital with every mark of respect from its inhabitants. It was conveyed for internment to the family vault situated near Erith." (G.M.)

HUGH DALRYMPLE

Ensign, 76th Foot, 7th May, 1791 ; Lieut., 30th March, 1792 ; 19th Foot, 1st February, 1797 ; Capt., 1st Ceylon Regt., 1st November, 1802 ; Major, 12th June, 1805. Retired by sale, 8th August, 1807.

Served in the Mysore Campaign, 1791.

THOMAS DUNCAN

Born in Scotland, 11th June, 1771 ; Surgeon's mate, 78th Foot, 4th February, 1794 ; Assist.-Surgn., 19th Foot, 1st February, 1797 ; Surgeon, 15th Bn. Army Reserve, 9th July, 1803 ; 3rd Garrison Bn., 18th September, 1805 ; 99th Foot, 19th December, 1805 ; 71st Foot, 8th March, 1810 ; Staff-Surgeon, 8th August, 1811 ; Deputy Inspt.-Gen., 17th July, 1817 ; Half-pay, 25th September, 1825.

Died, 3rd November, 1848.
Saw a good deal of Service in the East Indies.

THOMAS JONES

Ensign, 57th Foot, 7th February, 1797 ; Lieut., 19th Foot, 16th February, 1797. Resigned, 16th January, 1800.

JAMES MOORE

Ensign, 17th February, 1797 ; Lieut., 73rd Foot, 23rd May, 1799 ; 51st Foot, 1st November, 1799.

Died at Colombo, 7th May, 1803.
Will proved in Dublin same year.

ISAAC GOUVERNEUR OGDEN

Born, 3rd October, 1783 in New York. Son of the Hon. Isaac Ogden, Judge of the Supreme Court, Montreal. Ensign, 72nd Foot, 3rd August, 1796 ; 19th Foot, 1st March, 1797 ; Lieut., 60th Foot, 11th January, 1800 ; 6th Foot, 14th March, 1801 ; 41st Foot, 15th October, 1803 ; 56th Foot, 13th September, 1810 ; Half-pay, 38th Foot, 16th July, 1825. Resigned, 1st February, 1830.

Died at Three Rivers, 19th January, 1868.

" He was a man of intelligence, mental equipment and executive ability, and one of the foremost men of his time, and for about 40 years Sheriff of the District of Three Rivers, Quebec Province (Family History).

Sir PATRICK ROSS, G.C.M.G., K.C.H.

Born, 26th January, 1778, eldest son of Patrick Ross, of Craigie and Inverethie, Co. Perth. Ensign, Independent Co., 12th May, 1794; Lieut., 100th Foot, 13th May, 1794; Capt., 101st Foot, 14th May, 1794; 91st Foot, 1st September, 1795; Half-pay on reduction in 1797; 19th Foot, 8th March, 1797; 22nd Light Dragoons, 15th March, 1798; Bt.-Major, 25th September, 1803; Major, 26th Foot, 12th December, 1805: 23rd Light Dragoons, 27th March, 1807; Lieut.-Col., 9th April, 1807; 10th Foot, 6th April, 1809; Half-pay, 8th Garrison Bn., 15th February, 1810; 48th Foot, 28th June, 1810; Half-pay, 8th Garrison Bn., 21st March, 1811; Col., 4th June, 1814; Lieut.-Col., 75th Foot, 12th October, 1815; Major-Gen., 19th July, 1821; K.C.M.G., 9th November, 1819; K.C.H., 1834; G.C.M.G., 17th May, 1837; Governor of Antigua, 18th February, 1826-1834; Governor of St. Helena, 27th June, 1846.

Served with the 25th (afterwards the 22nd) Light Dragoons in the Mysore campaign of 1799 under Lord Harris, including the battle of Mallavelly and siege of Seringapatam with the division under Sir A. Wellesley. Also in the campaign of 1801 against the Mahratta Chief, Doondiah Waugh. From February, 1802 to 1804, he served under Lt.-Gen. Stuart and Major-Gen. Campbell in the Mahratta country and at the reduction of the ceded provinces. Was in command of the 48th Foot (2nd Bn.) in the Peninsula in 1810 for one month when he had to return home on sick leave.

Died at St. Helena, 28th August, 1850.

RANDALL CHETHAM-STRODE

Born, 7th January, 1773. 3rd son of Thomas Chetham, of Mellor Hall, Co. Derby. Ensign, 6th April, 1797; Lieut., 19th April, 1799; Half-pay, 46th Foot, 17th February, 1803. Retired, April, 1827. Took the additional name of Strode in 1828.

Died in 1845.

JOHN CAMPBELL

Born, 31st May, 1766. Son of Sir James Campbell, Knt., of Inverneil, Argyllshire. Ensign, 82nd Foot, 16th March, 1797; Lieut., 19th Foot, 6th April, 1797; 21st Foot, 23rd August, 1804; Half-pay, 91st Foot, 12th June, 1806.

Death reported in the November, 1827, Army List.

WILLIAM MANSELL

Ensign, 22nd May, 1797; Lieut., 15th June, 1797. Resigned, 17th November, 1801.

HENRY SHADFORTH

Ensign, 23rd May, 1797; Lieut., 20th Foot, October, 1799; Capt., 57th Foot, 21st March, 1800; Major, 25th February, 1804; Half-pay, 1809; Bt.-Lieut.-Col., 4th June, 1811; 10th Foot; 22nd May, 1815; Half-pay, 25th February, 1816; Col., 27th May, 1825; Maj.-Gen., 10th January, 1837; Lieut.-Gen., 9th November, 1846; Gen., 20th June, 1854.

Served in Ceylon and on the Coromandel Coast, 1797-1801. Commanded in Brigade the Grenadier and Light Companies of the Regts. in Jersey, 1805. Probably brother to Tnomas Shadforth, Lieut.-Col. of the 57th Foot, 1830-31, whose son, Thomas, Lieut.-Col. of the 57th fell at the Redan in 1855.

Died at Newcastle-on-Tyne, 30th March, 1866, aged 88 years.

JOHN CARRINGTON-SMITH

Born, 8th May, 1766. Son of the Revd. John Smith, Rector of Ashwicken. Lieut., 25th Light Dragoons, 10th March, 1794; Capt.-Lieut., 25th March, 1795 ; Capt., 19th Foot, 20th March, 1798 ; Half-pay, April, 1799 ; Bt.-Major, 25th April, 1808 ; Bt.-Lieut.-Col., 4th June, 1814.

Died at St. Margaret's, Gloucestershire, 20th October, 1843.

RICHARD STARK

Ensign, 20th June, 1798. Resigned, 15th April, 1805.

JOHN GRAY

Ensign, 18th July, 1798 ; 33rd Foot, 12th September, 1798 ; Lieut., 74th Foot, 8th May, 1799 ; Capt., 8th W. India Regt., 4th April, 1808. Retired in 1813.

JOHN WILLIAM EVANS

Ensign, 52nd Foot, 16th June, 1780 ; Lieut., 27th June, 1781 ; Capt.-Lieut., 8th August, 1792 ; Capt., 4th July, 1793 ; 19th Foot, 31st August, 1798 ; Bt.-Major, 1st January, 1800 ; Commandant, Calpentyn, Ceylon, April, 1802-January, 1803 ; Commandant, Manaar, October, 1803.

Took part in the advance on Kandy in 1803, and was in command of the advance guard which entered the town.

Died at Jaffnapatam, 31st December, 1804.

SIMON PHILIP FRIEL

Ensign, 76th Foot, 18th February, 1798 ; 33rd Foot, 30th April, 1798 ; 19th Foot, 12th September, 1798. Resigned, 23rd July, 1799.

ALEXANDER ROBSON

Born, 1782. Ensign, 13th October, 1798 ; Lieut., 27th March, 1801 ; Capt., 31st December, 1804 ; Bt.-Major, 4th June, 1814 ; Half-pay, 25th October, 1821.

Took part in the advance to Kandy in 1803. Served in the Travancore War of 1809.

Died, 24th February, 1836.

CHARLES CUST

Ensign, 19th Foot, 6th December, 1798 ; resigned, 30th October, 1799.

EDWARD BARRY BEAUMAN

2nd son of John Beauman, of Co. Wexford. Ensign, 30th April, 1799. Resigned, 18th January 1800.

Died in India, 1800.

HECTOR McLAINE

Ensign, 23rd May, 1799 ; Lieut., 1st November, 1802.
Served in the Kandyan War, 1803. Killed at Watapulawa, near Kandy, 26th June, 1803.

THOMAS AJAX ANDERSON

Born, 1783. Ensign, 15th July, 1799 ; Lieut., 17th November, 1801 ; Capt., 4th October, 1809 ; Half-pay, 60th Foot, 8th April, 1819.

Accompanied Lieut.-Col. Barbut's force to Kandy in 1803. Left Kandy on the 20th March with twelve convalescent Europeans and an escort of 30 men of the Malay Regt., arriving at Trincomalee on the 28th thus escaping the debacle at Kandy. Commandant of Calpentyn, December, 1810, and of Batticaloa, 1815-6. Author of "The Wanderer in Ceylon" and other poems, written chiefly in India, the latter dedicated to Surgeon W. S. Andrews, 19th Foot.

Died, 8th January, 1824.

Awarded a temporary pension of £100 on 25th June, 1821, for injuries sustained in the performance of military duty in Kandy in 1815.

WILLIAM BLAKENEY

4th and youngest son of Charles Blakeney, of Feigh and Currenlarman, Co. Galway and Cloneera, Co. Roscommon. Ensign, 84th Foot, 9th July, 1795 ; Lieut., 19th Foot, 10th August, 1799.

Killed in action at Kandy, 24th June, 1803. The circumstances attending his death are thus described by Jan Egbertus Thoen, a Dutch Sergeant, belonging to the 5th Company of the 1st Bn. of the Bengal Artillery, who alone survived the massacre at the hospital on the 24th. He had heard the details from soldiers who came into the hospital after the fight. "There was a Malay chief called Sangalen in the King's Service, he was called a Captain ; this man advanced to a gun in the rear of the palace, this gun of ours had been playing grape on the road in the direction of the great tank. This Malay chief (who had a brother named Nouradeen in our service), attended by one armed follower, jumped upon this gun. Lieut. Blakeney advanced towards him, having his shirt and trousers on, with his sword in his hand. Sangalen jumped upon him and stabbed him with his creese, after which Lieut. Blakeney cut at him with his sword. They then grappled and fell together, and, as I understand, both died on the spot. Sangalen's follower was also killed by a shot, and the death of these two persons prevented any more from attempting to force their way into the palace by the rear." This narrative is appended to the "Wanderer in Ceylon," by T. A. Anderson, 19th Foot. (See also Cordiner, Vol. II., p., 208.) In Anderson's journal there is the following extract from a letter from Lieut. Blakeney to him dated Kandy, 14th June.

"I arrived here on the 4th after a very unpleasant march. It rained from the time I left Minery ; the roads were bad and the rivers deep and rapid. I need not attempt to picture to you the dreadful state of affairs here. Sickness and starvation, together with the treachery of the Adigars and the desertion of the Malays and Lascars. Combine these things with the General's sickness and departure and I fear not a man now will ever leave it. I will keep up my usual spirits and have plenty of employment. I hope, however, to see you again, if the Malays stand by us, and I believe the flank companies must be ordered up from Trincomalee to save our throats." (See also note under Qr.-Mr. John Brown).

PETER PLENDERLEATH

Possibly son of Patrick Plenderleath, born at Pittenweene,

Fifeshire, 20th March, 1778. Ensign, 20th September, 1799 ; Lieut., 18th November, 1801; "Adjt. and Qr.-Mr. to the detachment at Kandi," 31st March, 1803.

Mortally wounded at Kandy, 24th June, 1803.

On Lieut. Blakeney being stabbed by the Malay chief, "Lieut. Plenderleath and a private of the 19th ran two bayonets through the body of the Malay Captain. Captain Humphreys, of the Bengal Artillery, coming up loaded the field piece with grapeshot, which being fired, brought down 24 of the enemy. The Kandyan troops being intimidated by this loss withdrew to a greater distance and manned all the rising grounds from which they galled the garrison by the fire from their grass hopper guns. On this occasion, Lieut. Plenderleath was severely wounded and died of his wounds in Kandy," (Cordiner, Vol. 11, pp., 208-9, 216). Marshall in his "conquest of Ceylon," states he died the same day (See also note to Qr.-Mr. John Brown).

ROBERT BALL

Ensign, 1st West India Regt., 25th December, 1798 ; 19th Foot, 3rd October, 1799 ; Lieut., 9th June, 1803 ; Capt., 3rd Ceylon Regt., 7th April, 1804 ; 19th Foot, 25th October, 1809.

Died at Colombo, 17th June, 1811.

JAMES ALEXANDER MORLEY

Ensign, 21st March, 1800 ; Cornet, 8th Light Dragoons, 19th October, 1800 ; Lieut., 1st November, 1803 ; 75th Foot, 28th March, 1805. Sold out, 16th May, 1807.

ALEXANDER WILLIAM LAWRENCE

Born at Coleraine, 7th November, 1764, youngest son of William Lawrence, of Portrush, Co. Antrim. Ensign, 101st Foot, June, 1783, from Volunteer in the 36th Foot ; 52nd Foot, 23rd September, 1787 ; Lieut., 77th Foot, 20th November, 1788 ; Capt.-Lieut., 19th Foot, 17th April, 1800 ; Bt.-Major, 24th September, 1802 ; Capt., 7th June, 1803 ; Major, 21st September, 1809 ; Lieut.-Col., 4th Garrison Batt., 11th June, 1812.

Served in the long and arduous campaign under Colonel Fullerton in India. Took part in Lord Cornwallis' campaign against Tippoo Sahib, 1791-2, also in the siege and capture of Cochin under Colonel Petrie in 1795. Was with the expedition under Gen. Stewart against Colombo in 1796, and in the Cotiote country in 1797 under Colonels Dow and Dunlop (mentioned in despatches). Present in the action at Sedaseer, 6th March, 1799, and throughout the whole of the second siege of Seringapatam (severely wounded). He, on this occasion, commanded the Grenadier Co. of the 77th, and volunteered for the "forlorn hope" with three other subalterns. The latter were all killed and Lawrence was left for dead in the breach. Was with the 77th in the assault of the rockfortress of Jamalabad in South Canara, in August, 1799. Governor of Upnor Castle, 8th February, 1816.

Died at Clifton, Bristol, 7th May, 1835.

His five sons became, Colonel Alexander, Sir George, Sir Henry (Bart.), killed at Lucknow, John, 1st Lord Lawrence of the Punjab and Lieut.-Gen. Richard Lawrence, C.B.

EDWIN HEWGILL

Eldest son of the Revd. Henry Hewgill, Rector of Great Smeaton, Yorkshire. Ensign, Coldstream Gds., 19th March,

1782 ; Lieut., 13th January, 1790 ; Adjt., 5th September, 1787 —21st January, 1794 ; Capt. and Lieut.-Col., 22nd January, 1794 ; Bt.-Col., 26th January, 1797 ; Lieut.-Col., 19th Foot, 10th May, 1800 ; Major-Gen., 25th September, 1803 ; Colonel Yorkshire Light Infantry Volunteers, 29th August, 1808.

Served in the 1794-5 campaign in Flanders and Germany. Saved the Duke of York from being taken prisoner when pursued by some French dragoons by lending the Prince his horse. The bridle then used is in the Royal Arsenal, Woolwich. Private secretary to H.R.H. the Duke of York. Lieut.-Governor of Scilly, 11th July, 1804. Commanded the Garrison of Hull.

Died at Hull, 25th December, 1809, aged 40.

Published in 1792 a series of coloured prints of the Coldstream Gds. and other regts.

WILLIAM VAUGHAN

Ensign, 3rd September, 1800 ; Lieut., 28th January, 1802 ; resigned, 15th August, 1803.

GEORGE STEWART

Ensign, 16th September, 1800 ; Lieut., 25th June, 1803 ; Capt., 5th October, 1803 ; 3rd Ceylon Regt., 25th October, 1809 ; half-pay on reduction, 25th May, 1817 ; Capt., 2nd Ceylon, 5th January, 1818 ; half-pay on reduction, 25th August, 1822 ; Major, Ceylon Rifles, 16th August, 1831 ; retired by sale, 5th July, 1839.

For some years was Postmaster-General of Ceylon.

MARTIN HARLAND BYNE

Baptized at Alphington, 25th July, 1776, 6th son of Capt. Charles Byne, 3rd Dragoon Gds., of Alphington, Devon. Ensign, 76th Foot, 13th March, 1798 ; Lieut., 19th Foot, 1st November, 1800.

Served in the Kandyan War, 1803. Killed at Watapulawa, near Kandy, 26th June, 1803.

ROBERT SMITH

Ensign, 5th February, 1801.

Served in the Kandyan War, 1803, and was killed at Watapulawa, near Kandy, 26th June, 1803.

Extract from Asst-Surgeon Greeving's diary : " Two officers of the 19th Regt. sprang into the river and were drowned saying, ' We will not suffer ourselves to be killed by the hands of the Blacks.' " The M.S. of the diary is here annotated by another writer in red ink (a contemporary) as follows : " The two officers who plunged into the river are not known ; those of whom no account has been received are Lieuts. Byne and Maclaine, and Ensign Smith of the 19th, and Lieut. Mercer of the Malays. They are most probably all dead (See note under Qr.-Mr. John Brown).

THOMAS ALDERSEY JONES

Born at Maesmawr, 28th August, 1779, son of John Lloyd Jones, of Maesmawr Hall, Montgomeryshire. Ensign, 5th March, 1801 ; Lieut., 25th June, 1803 ; Capt., 28th August, 1805.

Served in the Travancore War, 1809 and in the Ceylon campaign of 1817-18.

Died at Batticaloa, 18th April, 1818. There are two memorials at Batticaloa and another at St. Peter's Church, Fort, Colombo.

"Captain Jones had always distinguished himself by the most scrupulous and honourable discharge of his military duties. The strictest attention to discipline was so tempered in him by a suavity of manners and soundness of judgment that he was regarded by his brother officers, without any invidious preference, as a pattern of military conduct and throughout his regt. he was universally respected and beloved " (Ceylon Gazette, 9th May, 1818).

GEORGE KEARNS

Ensign, 19th Foot ; resigned, 30th March, 1801.

Died at Trincomalee, 20th April, 1801.

Date of appointment not given in the London Gazette. Probably commissioned by the Governor of Ceylon.

THOMAS PEMBERTON

Ensign, 3rd April, 1801 ; retired, 20th October, 1801.

CHARLES PEARCE

Ensign, 35th Foot, 14th April, 1795 ; Lieut., 21st October, 1795 ; half-pay, 15th November, 1796 ; 13th Foot, 5th January, 1799 ; Capt., 85th Foot, 22nd May, 1800 ; 19th Foot, 24th April, 1801.

He was at Kandy with the 19th in the War of 1803, and left the town for Fort Macdowal, at Matale, on 15th April, with 55 rank and file of the 19th, under the command of Captain Madge, but returned to Kandy, as he was there on 31st May ill, and also on 10th June, still ill and " in great danger," but he recovered and returned to Fort Macdowal (see letters from Qr.-Mr. Brown and Lieut. Ormsby in Capt. Anderson's " poems written chiefly in India ").

Fort Macdowal had been in a state of siege from 25th to 27th June when Corpl. Barnsley arrived and made a formal deposition before the officers of the Garrison of the surrender of Kandy. Captain Pearce was in the retreat from Fort Macdowal to Trincomalee, which was begun on 27th June. Of the 35 men who garrisoned Fort Macdowall from Kandy, 19 were left behind sick and were massacred there, 13 reached Trincomalee on 3rd July, and the remainder must have died of disease (see Marshall, p.p. 104-6 also Capt. Johnston's narrative, p. 31).

Died at Colombo, 6th August, 1808.

RICHARD CHAMBERS

Ensign, 2nd October, 1801 ; sold out, 15th January, 1803.

JOHN BROWN

Qr.-Mr., 3rd April, 1802 (not from the ranks) ; appointed Paymaster to the Garrison at Kandy, 29th March, 1803.

Served in the Kandyan War, 1803, and was killed at Watapulawa, near Kandy, 24th June, 1803.

Three letters from Qr.-Mr. Brown written from Kandy in 1803 are appended to Lieut. Andersons's poems. Hitherto the principle authorities on the massacre at Kandy have been Dr. Marshall in his " History and Conquest of Ceylon," the Revd. J. Cordiner, and Capt. Robert Percival. Recently, however, a diary written at the time by Asst.-Surgeon Greeving has been discovered in the Colonial Office Records, by Miss V. M. Methley, F.R.S. He appears to have escaped from Kandy and his diary is annotated in red ink by some official in the Government Service. Obviously, as Miss Methley says, "his professional position would give him far better opportunities than native servants and private soldiers to watch the course of events, just as his education would qualify him the better to set them down." The following is an extract as to Qr.-Mr. Brown's death.

"Re 24th June : A moment before 5 o'clock in the morning when Mr. Brown intended to go out to shoot pigeons with a piece and the Fort Adjt. Barry (a civilian who entered into the Malay Regt.) was under the roof of the King's Dewal, a tall fat Malay Prince, commanding that nation as head, approached before the gate of the Battery and 15 or 16 paces behind the Prince, Kandians followed by thousands, also Malays, the most part of them deserters, and when Mr. Brown who was at a distance of 10 or 11 paces from that Prince, would shoot, that Prince with a swiftness pushed away the firelock and gave him a stab in the breast with a creese. Mr. Brown then fell down dead. Mr. Barry on perceiving this immediately ordered the alarm to be beaten, took a firelock in his hand, and gave a stab with its bayonet on the right side of the Malay Prince's head and when he became giddy and was falling down, Major Davie gave him a cut with his sword on the left side of his throat. The Prince, thereupon, fell down dead" (See also notes under Lieuts. Plenderleath and Blakeney.

WILLIAM HOPE

Asst. Surgeon, 12th June, 1802.

Served in the Kandyan War of 1803. Killed at Watapulawa, near Kandy, 26th June, 1803.

JOHN CROOKS

Adjt., 31st July, 1802 from Sergt.-Major ; Lieut., 27th June, 1803.

Served in the Kandyan War, 1803, and was in the advance to Kandy. Died, 28th January, 1804.

Sir FREDERICK HANKEY, G.C.M.G.

3rd son of John Hankey and grandson of Sir Thomas Hankey, Kt., Alderman of London. Ensign, 90th Foot, September, 1800 ; Lieut., 45th Foot, 2nd October, 1800 ; 51st Foot, 16th October, 1800 ; Capt., 88th Foot, 3rd December, 1802 ; 19th Foot, 24th December, 1802 ; Major, 50th Foot, 22nd September, 1808 ; 2nd Ceylon Regt., 13th July, 1809 ; Bt.-Lieut.-Col., 15th August, 1811 ; 15th Foot, 21st September, 1815 ; half-pay, 25th March, 1816 ; Col., 27th May, 1825 ; retired, August, 1826.

Served in the Kandyan War, 1803, and was severely wounded near Kandy in March, 1803, when acting as Brigade-Major to Col. Baillie. Took part in the Travancore War of 1809. Deputy Inspector Gen. of Colonial troops in Ceylon in 1811. Sent on a mission to Tunis in 1817. For many years Secretary to the Government of Malta. Private Secretary to Sir Thomas Maitland, Governor of Corfu. Secretary to the Order of St. Michael and St. George. G.C.M.G., 4th May, 1833. Companion of the Ionian order.

Died in Montagu Square, London, 13th March, 1855.

JOHN HAMES

Ensign, 15th January, 1803 ; sold out, 30th July, 1803.

HENRY LITTLETON SMITH

Born 1787, 3rd son of Ferdinando Smith, of Halesowen Grange, Co. Worcester, Col. of the Shropshire Militia. Ensign, 3rd February, 1803 ; Lieut., 15th August, 1803.

Killed in action at Lake Minnery, Ceylon, 14th October, 1804, when serving with Capt. Johnston's Expedition (See also note to Lieut. Berkeley Vincent).

JAMES PETER FITZGERALD

Born, 1786. Ensign, 46th Foot, 28th June, 1801 ; half-pay, 17th February, 1803 ; Lieut., 19th Foot, 17th February, 1803 : Capt., Grenadier Co., 24th March, 1807.

Served in the Tranvancore War, 1809.

Died at Trincomalee, 16th June, 1815.

There is a memorial in the cemetery, Trincomalee Esplanade.

RICHARD PARSONS

Born, 1778. Ensign, 14th April, 1803 ; Lieut., 1st December, 1804 ; Capt., 18th June, 1811.

Served in the Travancore War, 1809.

Died, 10th April, 1813.

THOMAS AUGUSTUS DOUCE

Born September, 1779, son of Thomas Augustus Douce, of Town Malling, Co. Kent. Ensign, 31st Foot, 1st August, 1798 ; Lieut., 4th Foot, 9th November, 1799 ; Capt., 15th January, 1801 ; half-pay in 1802 ; 19th Foot, 7th June, 1803 ; 60th Foot, 27th February, 1808 ; sold out, 22nd October, 1808.

EDMUND LOCKYER

Born at Plymouth, 21st January, 1784, 3rd son of Thomas Lockyer, of Wembury, near Plymouth. Ensign, 9th June, 1803 ; Lieut., 1st December, 1804 ; Capt., 29th August, 1805 ; Bt.-Major, 12th August, 1819 ; Major, 30th July, 1824 ; 57th Foot, 21st August, 1824 ; sold out, 8th November, 1827.

Served in the Ceylon War of 1815-16. In October, 1825, he was the first white man to explore the upper reaches of the Brisbane River under instructions of the Governor of New South Wales. In December, 1826, by direction of the British Government and under instructions of Sir Ralph Darling, Governor of N.S.W., was appointed commander of an expedition which included a detachment of the 39th Foot, to King George's Sound, W. Australia, for the purpose of hoisting the British flag. This action was taken on 27th December, 1826, in view of the fear that the French contemplated annexation. Prior to the above date only the eastern half of the Australian continent was claimed by the British crown, after it the whole continent became a British possession. Appointed Surveyor of roads and bridges, N.S.W., on 9th June, 1828. Serjeant at Arms, Legislative Council, N.S.W., 1st May, 1852. Usher of the Black Rod, 20th May, 1856.

Died at Lockyersleigh, Sydney, 10th June, 1860.

WILLIAM FLAMANT BLICK, M.D.

Asst.-Surgeon, July, 1803 ; 86th Foot, May, 1804 ; to the Forces, 1809 ; Surgeon, 10th Foot, 1812 ; to the Forces, 13th May, 1813 ; half-pay in 1814.

Wounded in Sicily. Served in the Peninsula with 10th Foot. Appointment to 19th not notified in " London Gazette." Probably a Ceylon Government appointment.

ARTHUR SAUNDERS

Ensign, 28th July, 1803 ; Lieut., 1st November, 1804.
Served in the Travancore War, 1809.
Died at Colombo, 17th January, 1810.

EDWARD SMITH

Ensign, 6th August, 1803 ; 1st Lieut., 1st Ceylon Regt., 1st June, 1805 ; Commandant at Chilon, 1817.
Died at Colombo, 15th November, 1818.

ROBERT NICHOLLS

Born, 1750 ; Paymaster, 14th August, 1803.
Died at Point de Galle, 28th August, 1819. Memorial in the Dutch cemetery, Galle.

" By amiable and affable virtues had endeared himself to the Colony at large, but only those who were intimately acquainted with him could know his worth (Ceylon Gazette, 4th September, 1819).

ALEXANDER ALEXANDER

2nd son of Archibald Alexander, of Boydstone and Black-shaw, Co. Ayr. Ensign, 75th Foot, 27th September, 1793 ; Lieut., 4th Foot, 1st June, 1796 ; Capt., 25th June, 1803 ; 19th Foot, 5th September, 1803 ; 3rd Ceylon Regt., 30th January, 1809 ; Bt.-Major, 4th June, 1814 ; half-pay, 4th Ceylon Regt., 22nd February, 1816 ; 5th Royal Veteran Bn., 24th February, 1820 ; retired, 6th September, 1822.

Was wounded in Holland in 1799. Served in the Travancore War of 1809.

Died, 21st October, 1843.

He is frequently mentioned in " Howell's life of Bombardier Alexander."

WILLIAM WILDEY

Born, 1785. Ensign, 24th December, 1803 ; Lieut., 2nd December, 1804 ; Capt., 29th September, 1808 ; retired, 27th April, 1815.

HUGH MORRIS JONES

Ensign, 16th January, 1804 ; resigned, 17th March, 1806.

THOMAS JAMES WEYMSS, C.B.

Born 1785, son of Col. James Weymss, Royal Marines of Southsea, Hants., D.L. for Carmarthen, who lost his arm at Trafalgar. Ensign, 65th Foot, 9th June, 1803 ; Lieut., 19th Foot, 1st March, 1804 ; Capt., 6th Garrison Bn., 30th November, 1806 ; 50th Foot, 12th November, 1807 ; Bt.-Major, 21st June, 1813 ; Bt.-Lieut.-Col., 21st January, 1819 ; Major 4th November, 1819 ; half-pay, 99th Foot, 10th February, 1820 ; Bt.-Col., 10th January, 1837 ; Major-Gen., 9th November, 1846; Col., 17th Foot, 31st May, 1854 ; Lieut.-Gen., 20th June, 1854 ; A.A.G., Northern District, 1833—1848.

Served in the Kandyan War of 1803-4 as A.D.C. to Major-Gen. D. D. Weymss. Took part in the Walcheren Expedition of 1809 and subsequently served in the Peninsula. Was Major of brigade to the 50th, 71st and 92nd Regts. from the formation of that brigade, under Lord Howard in 1810, to its final embarkation at Bordeaux in 1814. Was present in the different affairs during the retreat to the Lines near Lisbon, actions at Pombal, Redinha, Foz d'Aronce, battles of Fuentes d'Onoro, surprise of Gerrard at Arroyo dos Molinos, storm of Fort Napoleon and the bridge of Almarez, action of Alba de Tormes, defence of Bejar, battle of Vittoria (Bt. of Major) and the Pyrenees. Was at Maya, Lesacca, and Donna Maria (severely wounded) battles of the Nivelle, Cambo, Nive, St. Pierre (wounded), Hellette, Garris, St. Palais, Tarbes, Arriveriette, Orthes, Aire, and Toulouse, besides numerous minor affairs (medal and nine clasps). In receipt of a reward for distinguished service. Succeeded Sir Guy Campbell in command of the Athlone District.

Died at Green Park, Bath, 19th July, 1860.

CHARLES DOUGLAS

Ensign, 37th Foot, 9th March, 1803 ; Lieut., 19th Foot, 1st April, 1804.

The Army List of November, 1809, gives his death as having taken place recently.

THOMAS BLAKE

Born, 1775. Qr.-Mr. from Sergt.-Major, 12th April, 1804.

Served in the Travancore War, 1809.

Died at Colombo, 14th October, 1814.

GEORGE INGHAM

Born at Waterford, 4th June, 1787. Ensign, 22nd April, 1804 ; Lieut., 1st Ceylon Regt., 6th June, 1805 ; Capt., 4th Ceylon Regt., 19th March, 1812 ; half-pay, 25th June, 1817 ; Capt. and Bt.-Major, Ceylon Rifles, 22nd July, 1830 ; retired, 2nd August, 1839.

Served in the Travancore War of 1809 with the Ceylon Regt., and in the expedition to Kandy in 1815.

Died at Colombo, 25th December, 1843.

FRANCES FORESTER

Born, 19th August, 1774, 4th son of Lieut.-Col. Cecil Forester, M.P., of Rossall, near Shrewsbury, and brother of the 1st Lord Forester. Ensign, 47th Foot, 12th February, 1793 ; Lieut., Independent Co., 14th April, 1793 ; 95th Foot, 30th October, 1793 ; Capt., 11th June, 1794 ; 46th Foot, 4th May, 1798 ; 15th Light Dragoons, 23rd July, 1799 ; Bt.-Major, 25th September, 1803 ; Major, 19th Foot, 4th August, 1804 ; 15th Light Dragoons, 9th August, 1804 ; retired by sale, 31st August, 1809.

Served with the 15th Light Dragoons in the Peninsular campaign, including Sahagun, Benevente, etc., December, 1809, to January, 1810 (silver medal and clasp).

Died at 31, St. James' Place, London, 26th October, 1861.

WILLIAM AYLETT

Cornet, 15th Light Dragoons, 7th May, 1783 ; Lieut., 26th

October, 1787; Capt.-Lieut., 23rd January, 1793; Major, 1st March, 1794; Bt.-Lieut.-Col., 1st January, 1798; 19th Foot, 9th August, 1804; half-pay, 6th Garrison Bn., 18th March, 1805; Col., 25th April, 1808; Major-Gen., 4th June, 1811; Lieut.-Gen., 19th July, 1821.

Served in the campaign in Flanders and received the order of Maria Theresa for his share in the operations of his regt. for the relief of the Emperor of Austria. Bayoneted through the body in the charge at Villiers en Couché. He commanded the detachment of the 15th Light Dragoons on this occasion (gold medal). The following letter was addressed to Major Aylett in reference to this engagement.

Sir,

The Emperor remembers with satisfaction the distinguished proof of valour, that you, Sir, and the officers of the 15th Light Dragoons manifested on the 24th April, 1794, near Cambay.

His Majesty regrets that the statutes of the order of Maria Theresa confirmed by a constant custom, forbid the cross of this order, strictly national, being conferred on officers so worthy of being decorated with it.

But wishing to give you and also your honourable companions a public mark of his particular esteem, His Majesty has commanded a medal to be struck to perpetuate the remembrance of this brilliant action, and has ordered me to offer them, the only impressions which have been struck, except the one which is placed in the Imperial Cabinet at Vienna.

In fulfilling the intentions of His Imperial Majesty, I beg you, consequently, to receive for yourself, Sir, and distribute to the other officers, who on that memorable 24th of April, 1794, fought under your orders, the medals which I have delivered to Capt. Ryan.

I have the honour to join the assurance of the highest consideration, and have the honour to be, etc.

(Signed) Le BARON THUGNEY.

Vienna, March 5th, 1798.

To Lieut.-Col. Aylett.

Died in London, 7th July, 1834, aged 73.

BENJAMIN SMITH

Ensign, 69th Foot, 12th November, 1799; Lieut., 46th Foot, 14th June, 1800; half-pay in 1802; 19th Foot, 1st December, 1804; retired, 23rd June, 1808.

JAMES MEARES

Ensign, 1st December, 1804, from Trincomalee Pioneer Corps.

Died in Ceylon, 11th April, 1805.

This was probably a Ceylon appointment as there is no trace of it in the London Gazette.

JOHN LEATH, M.D.

Born in Norfolk in 1776; Hospital mate, 25th March, 1804; Asst.-Surgeon, 19th Foot, 1st January, 1805; Surgeon, 4th Ceylon Regt., 12th April, 1810; Staff, 4th April, 1813; half-pay, 25th May, 1817; full-pay, 13th December, 1826; retired on half-pay, 7th November, 1834.

Served in the Travancore War, 1809.

Died at 11, Notting hill Square, W., 21st October, 1859.

HENRY SAPTE

Born, 1773. Son of David Sapte, of London ; Lieut., 17th Foot, 25th July, 1797 ; Capt., 30th May, 1800 ; retired in 1802. Re-entered the Army as Ensign, 19th Foot, 5th January, 1805 ; Lieut., 1st October, 1805 ; Capt., 26th November, 1809; retired, 11th July, 1811.

Died in Rome, 20th October, 1816.

THOMAS DOBBIN

Born 1789. Ensign, 15th April, 1805 ; Lieut., 7th August, 1807 ; Capt., 10th April, 1813 ; Major, 3rd November, 1825 ; Lieut.-Col., unattached, 10th June, 1826 ; Col., 23rd November, 1841 ; Lieut.-Col., 3rd Dragoon Gds., 12th May, 1843 ; retired, 16th January, 1844.

Served in the Travancore War of 1809. Was at the capture of Kandy in 1815, and with the Grenadier Co. of the 19th throughout the Ceylon campaign of 1818, receiving the thanks of Sir Robert Brownrigg on three occasions in general orders for his services.

Died in Albany St., Regent's Park, 13th November, 1862.

HUGO WEMYSS

Born, 1788. 2nd Lieut., 1st Ceylon Regt., 3rd June, 1804; Lieut., 19th Foot, 2nd October, 1805 ; Capt., 11th June, 1812.

Served in the Travancore War, 1809.

Died on board the transport, "Arniston," on her way to the Cape, 29th April, 1815.

Sir JOHN BUCHAN, K.C.B.

Son of George Buchan of Kelloe, Co. Berwick. Ensign, Scots' Brigade, 1st August, 1795 ; Lieut., 21st October, 1795 ; Capt., 2nd Ceylon Regt., 15th March, 1802 ; Major, 30th June, 1804 ; Lieut.-Col., 4th West India Regt., 30th March, 1809 ; 7th Portuguese Infantry, 25th October, 1814 ; half-pay, 26th December, 1818 ; Bt.-Col., 12th August, 1819 ; Lieut.-Col., 29th Foot, 28th February, 1822 ; Major-Gen., 22nd July, 1830 ; Col., 95th Foot, 5th November, 1838 ; Lieut.-Gen., 23rd November, 1841 ; Col., 32nd Foot, 12th June, 1843 ; C.B.. 16th September, 1815 ; K.C.B., 13th September, 1831.

Served with the Scots' Brigade in the Mysore War against Tippoo Sahib and was present at the battle of Mallavallei and the assault upon Seringapatam in 1798 and 1799 (silver medal). Took part in the operations against the Southern Poligars in 1800 and 1801, on which occasion he resigned a staff appointment to join his regt. in the field. Subsequently held detached commands in Ceylon during the Kandyan War, 1803-4. Took part in the assault and capture of Guadeloupe in 1810. In 1811, served with Portuguese army as O/C. 4th Brigade and till 1814 was employed in Spain and Portugal, being present at the battles of Vittoria, Pyrenees, Nivelle, Nive, Orthes, and Toulouse (three times mentioned in despatches, gold cross and one clasp, silver medal and two clasps, and the order of the Tower and Sword of Portugal).

Towards the end of 1805 this officer was promoted by Lieut.-Gen. Maitland, Governor of Ceylon to a Lieut-Colonelcy in the 19th Foot and commanded the regt, till August, 1807, when His Majesty's disapproval of the appointment was received.

General orders Colombo, 22nd April, 1898, " Lieut.-Gen. Maitland entertains a full sense of the merit of Lieut-Col. Buchan's conduct during the period he commanded the 19th Regt. and shall feel it incumbent on him to state in due terms to H.R.H. the Commander-in-Chief for H.M's. information, his conviction of the benefit that corps has derived from the assiduity, zeal, and activity he has uniformly exhibited."

Died in Upper Harley St., London, 2nd June, 1850.

WILLIAM DUNBAR ROBERTSON

Born, 1787. Ensign, 10th April, 1806 ; Lieut., 9th August, 1807 ; Capt., 22nd February, 1816.

Served in the Travancore War, 1809, and in the campaign in Ceylon in 1815.

Died at Matura, Ceylon, 21st July, 1815.

WILLIAM COX

Born, 1783. Ensign, 1st May, 1806 ; Lieut., 8th August, 1807 ; Capt., 21st September, 1815 ; 54th Foot, 21st November, 1822 ; Bt.-Major, 10th January, 1837 ; retired, 6th December, 1844.

Served in the Travancore War, 1809, also in the Burmese War, 1825.

Died at Sidmouth, Devon, 27th July, 1859.

CHARLES DRIBURG

Born, 1788. Son of Friedrick Von Driburg, of Hanover. Ensign, 15th May, 1806 ; Lieut., 3rd July, 1808 ; Capt., 19th December, 1816 ; 1st Ceylon Regt., 19th March, 1818.

Served in the Travancore War of 1809, and in the Ceylon rebellion, 1817-18. Died of fever at Hambantotta, Ceylon, 8th October, 1826, where he was commandant from 1820 to 1826. His wife also died of fever the same day. " By the sudden removal of the heads of the family within four hours of each other, no less than seven children have been left totally unprovided for. To Captain Driburg's memory the Corps to which he belonged has borne honourable testimony, and the universally respected character of the parents has given rise to a great feeling of sympathy towards their offspring " (Ceylon Gazette, 4th November, 1826).

JOHN DORAN

Son of John Doran, of Wexford. Ensign, 29th May, 1806 ; 18th Foot, 16th September, 1806 ; Lieut., 5th December, 1806 ; Capt., 26th September, 1811 ; half-pay on reduction in 1814 ; 18th Foot, 25th May, 1815 ; Major, 14th January, 1826 ; retired by sale, 18th January, 1839.

Died at his residence, Ely House, Wexford, 30th October, 1866, aged 84 years.

JOHN McLEAN

Ensign, 7th August, 1806 ; retired, 10th October, 1809.

The Hon. Sir PATRICK STUART, G.C.M.G.

Born, 10th June, 1777, 2nd son of Alexander, 10th Lord Blantyre. Cornet, 2nd Life Gds., 26th September, 1793 ; Lieut. and Adjt., 6th June, 1794 ; Capt., 27th Light Dragoons, 12th April, 1796 ; Major, 95th Foot, 1st February, 1803 ; Lieut.-Col., 19th Foot, 25th September, 1806 ; Bt.-Col., 4th June,

1814 ; 15th Foot, 2nd November, 1815, to 24th March, 1816 ;
Maj.-Gen., 19th July, 1821 ; Lieut.-Gen., 10th January, 1837 ;
Col. Commandant, 60th Foot, 26th September, 1838 ; Col.,
44th Foot, 7th April. 1843 ; Gen., 11th November, 1851 ; In-
specting Field Officer of Militia in the Ionian Islands, 24th
March, 1816, to 19th July, 1821 ; Governor of Malta, 1843-1847;
G.C.M.G., 3rd July, 1843 ; Commanding the Forces in Scotland,
September, 1830 to 17th February, 1837.
Served in the Travancore War, 1809, in command of 19th Foot.
Died at Eagle's Carnie, Co. Haddington, 7th February, 1855.

JOHN GARDNER

Ensign, 2nd March, 1807 ; Lieut., 23rd June, 1808 ; sold
out, 18th March, 1809.

ROBERT WATTS

Born, 1785. Ensign, 59th Foot, 3rd September, 1803 ;
Lieut., 7th September, 1804 ; Capt., 19th Foot, 25th March,
1807 ; retired, 6th February, 1817.
Served in the Travancore War, 1809.

RICHARD PHEPOE NIXON

Born about 1770. Elder son of Adam Nixon, of Creeny,
Co. Cavan, late Ensign, 53rd Foot and Cornet, 13th Light
Dragoons ; 2nd Lieut., 2nd Ceylon Regt., 6th August, 1807 ;
Lieut., 19th Foot, 7th August, 1807 ; Adjt., 7th August, 1807.
Served in the Travancore War of 1809.
Died in Ceylon, 12th June, 1810.
Will dated, Point de Galle, 22nd May, 1810.

ROBERT BROWN DUKE

Born, 1787. 1st Lieut., 2nd Ceylon Regt., 20th November,
1805 ; Lieut., 19th Foot, 10th August, 1807 ; Adjt., 30th
March, 1810 ; Capt., 17th June, 1815.
Died, 5th December, 1816.

CHARLES HAY

2nd Lieut., 3rd Ceylon Regt., 25th March, 1806 ; Lieut.,
19th Foot, 11th August, 1807 ; 1st Lieut., 3rd Ceylon Regt.,
15th January, 1810 ; 2nd Ceylon, 25th April, 1815 ; 1st Ceylon,
25th April, 1817 ; Fort Adjt., Jaffna, 1st February, 1811 ;
Assist.-Deputy Commissary Gen., Jaffna, 1st January, 1814 ;
Magistrate and Asst. Customs Master, Calpentyn, 1st August,
1818.
Died at either Colombo or Calpentyn, 27th December, 1819.

JOHN BRADFORD

Ensign, 25th August, 1807 ; Lieut., 29th September, 1808 ;
retired, 19th December, 1811.

JAMES BAGNETT

Born 1783. Belonged to a Yorkshire family. Ensign, 26th

August, 1807 ; Lieut., 11th October, 1809 ; retired, half-pay, 4th Ceylon Regt., 16th May, 1816.

Died at Batticaloa, 26th September, 1821.

Was a Magistrate in Ceylon.

"Mr. Bagnett's mental powers arose far above mediocrity ; keen in his imagination and original in his wit which qualities were rendered more alluring by the unbounded generosity and fine sensibilites of a benevolent heart. His house has long been the asylum of the stranger and the afflicted His memory will be cherished with melancholy pleasure in the recollection of his friends who were best qualified to appreciate his numerous excellencies. Nor will the native population of this place suffer his integrity and kindness to be effaced from their memories, except oy the same stern foe which has numbered him among those who are alike insensible to pleasure or to pain " (Ceylon Government Gazette).

JOHN DUNCAN

Ensign, 27th August, 1807 ; Lieut., 12th October, 1809 ; 34th Foot, 17th March, 1814 ; cashiered in May, 1817.

——— BELL

Ensign, 1st October, 1807 ; resigned, 21st July, 1810.

ROGERSON MATHEWS

Ensign, Ceylon Regt., 8th June, 1793 ; 83rd Foot, 28th September, 1793 ; Lieut., Ceylon Regt., 20th July, 1794 ; 33rd Foot, 6th September, 1795 ; Capt., 1st Ceylon Regt., 29th April, 1803 ; Major, 19th Foot, 25th December, 1807 ; retired, 26th November, 1809.

Served in the Travancore War of 1809.

Died in Kilkenny, 1847.

VICTOR RAYMOND

Born, 1788. Ensign, 11th February, 1808 ; Lieut., 16th November, 1809 ; Capt., 7th April, 1825 ; half-pay, 40th Foot, 15th September, 1825 ; Paymaster, 27th Foot, 9th March, 1826; half-pay, 10th June, 1853.

Served in the Travancore War, 1809. Took part in the expedition to Kandy in 1815, and in the Ceylon rebellion of 1817-18.

Died at Kensington, 2nd September, 1859.

JOHN GORE LANGTON

Born 1791. 3rd son of William Gore Langton, of Newton Park, Somerset, Colonel of the Oxford Militia. Ensign, 26th May, 1808 ; Lieut., 15th January, 1810 ; Capt., 27th April, 1815.

Died at Katabowa, Ceylon, 6th May, 1818.

"In him the Service has lost an active and gallant officer, society an amiable and accomplished gentleman " (Ceylon Government Gazette).

SAMUEL DOWBIGGEN

Born 1784. Ensign, 24th Foot, 17th March, 1808 ; Lieut., 19th Foot, 17th March, 1808 ; Capt., 11th July, 1811 ; 38th Foot, 23rd December, 1813 ; half-pay, 3rd Garrison Btn., 14th

May, 1818. Omitted from the half-pay list, 15th January, 1836.

Served in the Travancore War of 1809.

Died at Porchester Terrace, London, 9th June, 1867.

CHARLES McANALLY

Born at Markethill, Co. Armagh, 1790, eldest son of Charles McAnally, Surgeon to the Armagh Militia. Ensign, 5th Garrison Bn., 26th November, 1806 ; Lieut., 31st December, 1807 ; 19th Foot, 9th April, 1808 ; 1st Garrison Bn., 16th June, 1808 ; 90th Foot, 10th October, 1809 ; retired, half-pay, 84th Foot, 5th October, 1820.

Died at Markethill, Co. Armagh, 2nd January, 1863.

HENRY O'SHEA

Ensign, 1st June, 1808 ; Lieut., 7th February, 1811 ; 13th Foot, 26th December, 1822.

Served in the Travancore War, 1809. Took part in the first Burmese War.

Killed in action at Rangoon, 1st December, 1824.

HENRY SAMUEL EYRE

Born 1770, eldest son of Walpole Eyre, of Burnham, Bucks. Ensign, 11th Foot, 23rd July, 1788 ; Lieut., 7th February, 1792 ; Capt., Independent Co., 24th July, 1793 ; 57th Foot, 25th October, 1793 ; half-pay, 28th October, 1795 ; 12th Reserve Bn., 9th July, 1803 ; Major, 3rd January, 1804 ; 82nd Foot, 1st August, 1804 ; Lieut.-Col., 19th Foot, 8th September, 1808 ; Capt. and Lieut.-Col., Grenadier Gds., 24th September, 1812. Retired, 1st July, 1813.

Served in the Peninsular War and was present at the battles of Roliea and Vimiera (gold medal).

Died at Bryanstone Square, London, 6th March, 1851.

WILLIAM WYBROW

Born, 27th March, 1773, son of William Wybrow ; Regtl. Mate, 1st Foot Gds., 8th July, 1795 ; Asst. Surgn, 25th December, 1796 ; Surgn., 3rd July, 1799 ; half-pay, 25th June, 1802 ; De Meuron's Regt., 9th February, 1804 ; 90th Foot, 22nd October, 1807 ; 19th Foot, 15th September, 1808 ; 17th Light Dragoons, 3rd August, 1815. Retired on half-pay, 11th September, 1828.

Served with the expedition to the Helder in 1799 with the Grenadier Guards.

Died in London, December, 1870. Buried in Kensal Green Cemetery.

RONALD McDONALD

Born 1784 ; 2nd Lieut., 2nd Ceylon Regt., 25th March, 1806 ; Lieut., 19th Foot, 1st December, 1808 ; Capt., 4th February, 1819. Sold out, 24th October, 1821.

Served in the Travancore War, 1809.

Died at Crieff, N.B., 31st October, 1822.

HENRY HARDY

Born 29th September, 1783, son of Thomas Hardy, of Hacketstown, Ireland, killed in June, 1798, fighting against the rebels. Ensign, 12th Foot, 7th March, 1800; Lieut., 17th September, 1802; Capt., 3rd Ceylon Regt., 16th August, 1804, 19th Foot, 30th January, 1809; Bt.-Major, 4th June, 1814; Bt.-Lieut.-Col., 3rd August, 1815; Major, 16th Foot, December 1821; half-pay, 17th January, 1822; 9th Foot, 8th June, 1826; Lieut.-Col., 19th Foot, 17th February, 1828.

Served in two campaigns in the South of India in the 12th Foot in 1804 under command of Major-Gen. Hay Macdowall, as Capt. in the 3rd Ceylon Regt., and in the year 1809 in the Travancore War. Took part in two campaigns in Ceylon under the comand of Lieut.-Gen. Sir R. Brownrigg, G.C.B., viz., in 1815 as A.D.C. and Military Secretary to the Lieut.-Gen., and in 1817-18 as D.A.Q.M.G. and acting D.A.G. to the Forces in the island Three times noted in General orders.

Died at Trinidad, 16th April, 1835.

Extract from a letter from the Governor of Trinidad to the officer commanding the troops: "His Majesty has lost in him one of his most loyal subjects, one of his most valuable military officers. The officers of the 19th Regt. have lost their friend, their adviser, their hospitable, cheerful companion, whose courteous manners and moral example secured the well-being and much contributed to establish the character of that corps for all that is correct and gentlemanlike.

The non-commissioned officers and privates of the 19th Regt. have lost in the lamented death of Lieut. Col. Hardy, a humane protector and charitable reliever of their wants and difficulties and a generous contributor to and superintendent of the education of their children.

Society at large has been deprived of a truly honest and honourable member, and I have to deplore the loss of a sincere friend."

"One of the best men that ever breathed—one of the most loyal subjects King ever possessed—one of the most chivalrous spirits that ever adorned the ranks even of the British Army."

From "Truths from the West Indies," by Captain Studholme Hodgson, 19th Foot.

THOMAS JAMES RODNEY

2nd son of Capt. the Hon. John Rodney, R.N., Chief Secretary to the Ceylon Government; 2nd Lieut., 2nd Ceylon Regt., 10th September, 1805; Lieut., 15th May, 1806.

Served in the operations in Travancore, 1809.

Died at Quilon, Travancore, 13th November, 1809, aged 19 years.

Memorial in St. Peter's, Fort Colombo.

His tombstone describes him as belonging to the 19th Regt., probably a local appointment as it was never notified in the London Gazette. His name also appears in a regimental return dated Quilon, 25th August, 1809 (M.L.F.).

The Hon. JOHN JAMES KNOX

Born 3rd April, 1790, 4th son of the 2nd Viscount Northland and 1st Earl of Ranfurly. Ensign, 52nd Foot, 17th August, 1808; Lieut., 19th Foot, 16th March, 1809; 52nd Foot, 11th May, 1809; Capt., 40th Foot, 8th October, 1812; 85th Foot, 25th June, 1813; Major, 22nd May, 1817; Bt.-Lieut.-Col., half-pay, 4th West India Regt., 24th June, 1819; Lieut.-Col., 65th Foot,

17th August, 1832 ; retired by sale, 24th August, 1832.

Served in the Peninsula, and was present at the battles of Vimiera, Vigo, Sabugal, Fuentes d'Onoro, storming of Ciudad Rodrigo, assault and capture of San Sebastian, battles of the Nivelle, Nive and Bayonne (medal and 6 clasps). Took part in the Walcheren expedition, 1809. Served in the American War and was wounded in the advance on New Orleans, 23rd December, 1814.

Died at Brighton, 9th July, 1856.

ROBERT CORMAC

Born, 1790. Ensign, 13th April, 1809 ; Lieut., 29th August, 1811 ; half-pay, 29th June, 1820.

Died at Thurso, N.B., 23rd March, 1822.

JAMES WILSON

Ensign, 52nd Foot, 18th June, 1805 ; Lieut., 18th December, 1806 ; 19th Foot, 11th May, 1809.

Died in France, 25th August, 1809.

PHILIP COSBY LANPHIER

Born at Waterford in 1789, 2nd son of Doctor Simon Lanphier ; 2nd Lieut., 3rd Ceylon Regt., 27th March, 1806 ; Lieut., 30th November, 1808 ; 19th Foot, 7th September, 1809 ; Capt., 19th April, 1818 ; retired, half-pay, 25th Foot, 6th October, 1825.

Died at Kinsale, 13th October, 1866.

JOHN BOWYER EDENSOR

Baptized at Newcastle-under-Lyme, 7th August, 1785, son of William Edensor, Alderman of Newcastle. Ensign, 11th October, 1809 ; Lieut., 20th July, 1812.

Died at Point de Galle, 31st October, 1814.

DONALD CAMPBELL

Born 1790, son of John Campbell. Ensign, 12th October, 1809 ; Lieut., 10th April, 1813.

Died at Jersey, C.I., 9th January, 1819.

DONALD McDONALD

Born, 1790. Ensign, 10th October, 1809 ; Lieut., 11th September, 1811 ; 34th Foot, 22nd April, 1814 ; retired on half-pay, 25th June, 1817. Omitted from the half-pay list, 12th February, 1827.

WILLIAM THOMÉ

Ensign, 84th Foot, 1st April, 1805 ; Lieut., 21st April, 1806 ; 19th Foot, 17th October, 1809 ; Capt., 1st Ceylon Regt., 30th August, 1810 ; 80th Foot, 30th June, 1812.

Died, 8th April, 1817.

EDMUND TUBBS

Born, 1776. Ensign, 56th Foot, 25th August, 1807 ; Lieut., 19th Foot, 18th October, 1809; 8th Royal Vet. Bn., 24th August,

1814 ; 7th Royal Vet. Bn., 1st November, 1818 ; retired, 25th April, 1821.

Died, 5th March, 1837.

GEORGE HALLILAY

Ensign, 7th Garrison Bn., 12th September, 1809 ; Lieut., 19th Foot, 19th October, 1809 ; half-pay, 4th Ceylon Regt., 25th December, 1815.

Took part in the expedition to Kandy in 1815.

Died at Point de Galle, 25th January, 1817.

HENRY WOODWARD

Ensign, 16th November, 1809 ; Cornet, 22nd Dragoons, 1st October, 1810.

Died in July, 1812.

LIONEL HOBART HUGHES

Born in Dublin, 17th January, 1791 ; 2nd Lieut., 3rd Ceylon Regt., 24th March, 1806 ; 1st Lieut., 1st July, 1808 ; Lieut., 19th Foot, 16th January, 1810 ; Capt., 8th April, 1825 ; Major, 17th April, 1836.

Taken prisoner in 1808 by the French frigate, "Piedmontese," and was recaptured by the "St. Fierenzo" frigate, 8th March, 1808. Served in the Travancore War of 1809. Took part in the Ceylon rebellion of 1817-18 under Lieut.-Gen. Sir Robert Brownrigg, G.C.B. Promoted over the three senior subalterns of the 19th by Lt.-Gen. Brownrigg in 1818 for meritorious conduct in the rebellion but the promotion was not confirmed by the Horse Guards.

Died at Buttevant, Co. Cork, 22nd January, 1837, "after a tedious illness brought on by long tropical service."

FRANCIS GOODALL

Born, 1792. Ensign, 3rd Ceylon Regt., 1st January, 1807 ; 2nd Lieut., 13th August, 1807 ; Lieut., 19th Foot, 18th January, 1810.

Drowned in the wreck of the "Arniston" on Lagullas reef off the Cape, 30th May, 1815, when out of a crew and passengers consisting of nearly 350, only six men reached the shore.

CHARLES HUNT LORIMER

Ensign, 91st Foot, 26th August, 1804 ; 8th West India Regt., 12th January, 1805 ; Lieut., 6th West India Regt., 28th April, 1806 ; 1st Foot, 27th December, 1807 ; 19th Foot, 29th March, 1810 ; 8th Veteran Bn., 9th November, 1815 ; retired, 25th June, 1816.

Served with the 3rd Bn. of the Royals with Sir David Baird's army in the north of Spain, and was severely wounded at the battle of Corunna. Served afterwards in the Walcheren expedition at the siege of Flushing and was wounded in both legs by the bursting of a shell (medal and clasp for Corunna).

Appointed a Military Knight of Windsor, 5th April, 1827.

Died at Windsor, 25th November, 1850.

"He carried to his death a bullet he received at Corunna and bore his protracted sufferings with infinite patience and was greatly respected at Windsor where he long resided" (G.M.)

HARRY BEAVER

Born in 1791. Ensign, Nova Scotia Fencibles, 14th July, 1806; Lieut., 27th Foot, 18th February, 1808; 19th Foot, 24th May, 1810.

Died at sea, 13th April, 1816, whilst on passage to the Isle of France and England for the recovery of his health.

ROBERT GARDINER

Ensign, 21st June, 1810; Lieut., 1st November, 1813.

Died at Trincomalee, 2nd June, 1815, aged 25 years.
Memorial in the Esplanade burial ground, Trincomalee.

Sir HEW WHITEFORD DALRYMPLE, Bart.

Born, 3rd December, 1750, only son of Capt. John Dalrymple, Enniskilling Dragoons. Ensign, 31st Foot, 3rd April, 1763; Lieut., 19th February, 1766; Capt., 1st Foot, 14th July, 1768; Major, 77th Foot, 1773; Lieut.-Col., 68th Foot, 21st September, 1781; Capt. and Lieut.-Col., 1st Foot Gds., 23rd May, 1783; Bt.-Col., 18th November, 1790; Major-Gen., 3rd October, 1794; Col., 37th Foot, 18th January, 1798; Lieut.-Gen., 10th November, 1799; Gen., 1st January, 1801; Col., 19th Foot, 25th June, 1810; 57th Foot, 27th April, 1811.

Served in the campaign of 1793 in the Grenadier Gds., and was present at the battle of Famars, the siege of Valenciennes and in the action before Dunkirk. Receiving orders to take over the command of the Army in Portugal in 1808 he arrived there in time to become responsible for the Convention of Cintra, by which treaty the French army evacuated the country.

Created a baronet, 6th May, 1815; Governor of Blackness Castle, 31st March, 1818.

Died in Upper Wimpole Street, London, 9th April, 1830.

WILLIAM McDONNELL, M.D.

Born in Inverness, 1790, 2nd son of Æneas McDonnell, 76th Foot (Macdonald's Regt.) of Scotus, Inverness; Hospital Mate, 20th May, 1809; Asst.-Surgeon, 19th Foot, 20th September, 1810.

Served in Portugal from June, 1809 until January, 1811.
Died on board the steam packet "St. George," off Bristol, 8th September, 1822.

RICHARD HOOPER

Born, 1781; Hospital mate for general service, 31st August, 1809; Asst.-Surg., 19th Foot, 20th September, 1810.
Died in Colombo, 14th May, 1818.

"Universally respected by his brother officers and the community in general, ever liberal and generous to all whom in his professional duties he assisted, his loss will be sincerely regretted" (Ceylon Government Gazette).

TIMOTHY RAPER

Born at Baldersby, Yorkshire, 21st December, 1790; son of George Raper. Ensign, 29th November, 1810; Lieut., 19th December, 1811; Capt., 6th February, 1817; half-pay, 19th

October, 1819; 19th Foot, February, 1822; Major, 10th June, 1826; Lieut.-Col., 17th April, 1835; retired by sale, 28th December, 1838.

Served in the campaigns of 1815 and 1817-18 under Sir Robert Brownrigg in Ceylon, the first occasion as Lieut. of the Light Co., the second as Capt. of that company. Employed in command of a flying camp, consisting of detachments of light troops from different corps. Noticed in gen. orders of Ceylon on different occasions for his conduct at Nalende and on the banks of the Mahavillaganga.

Died at his residence, Hoe Court, Herefordshire, 22nd July, 1862.

CHARLES MACDONALD

Ensign, 7th February, 1811; Lieut., 25th May, 1815; 47th Foot, 10th August, 1820; 86th Foot, 15th January, 1824; half-pay, 8th April, 1826; retired, October, 1830.

CROSBY MORGELL CHRISTIAN

Born, 1790; 2nd Lieut., 3rd Ceylon Regt., 2nd April, 1806; 1st Lieut., 1st June, 1809; Lieut., 19th Foot, 16th February, 1811; 34th Foot, 15th June, 1820; 87th Foot, 23rd September, 1824; 27th Foot, 8th April, 1825; Capt., half-pay, 27th April, 1827; retired, 31st January, 1829.

ROBERT LAYTON

Born, 1787. Ensign, 34th Foot, 12th March, 1809; 19th Foot, 7th March, 1811; Lieut., 26th June, 1815; 1st Lieut., 1st Ceylon Regt., 1st February, 1817.

Took part in the expedition to Kandy in 1815, and in the Ceylon rebellion of 1817-18.

Died at Hambantota Ceylon, 12th September, 1818.

Sir TOMPKINS HILGROVE TURNER, C.C.H., F.S.A., D.C.L.

Born at Uxbridge, 12th January, 1764; son of Richard Turner, M.D., of Uxbridge, a doctor in the Army. Ensign, 3rd Foot Gds., 20th February, 1782; Lieut. and Capt., 13th October, 1789; Capt. and Lieut.-Col., 12th November, 1794; Col., 1st January, 1801; Major-Gen., 25th April, 1808; Col., 19th Foot, 27th April, 1811; Lieut.-Gen., 4th June, 1813; Gen., 22nd July, 1830.

Served in Flanders in the campaign of 1793, including the battles of St. Amand and Famars, siege of Valenciennes and action of Lincelles. Was repeatedly engaged in 1794, commencing with the attack on Vaux, siege of Landrecies and battle of Cateaux. Present also at the battle of Tournay and actions at Roulaix, Monveaux and Templeuse. Served in the expedition to Egypt and was at the battles of the 8th, 13th and 21st March, 1801. Received a medal from the Grand Seigneur, and returned to England in charge of the Egyptian antiquities including the Rosetta Stone. Apptd. K.C.H. in 1820 and G.C.H. in 1827. Knight of the Crescent of Turkey, and of St. Anne of Russia. Lieut.-Governor of Jersey, 1814 to 1816, and Governor of Bermuda, 1825 to 1831.

Died at Gorey Lodge, Jersey, 7th May, 1843.

Author of "A short account of ancient chivalry, and a description of armour," London, 1799, "Thoughts and anecdotes, military and historical," London, 1811.

FORTESCUE WILLIAM HATHERLEY

Son of William Henry Hatherley, of Skibberton, Co. Devon.
Ensign, 8th May, 1811 ; Lieut., 24th August, 1815.

Took part in the Ceylon rebellion of 1817-18.

Died of fever at Katabowa, Ceylon, 20th July, 1818.

" This worthy young man endeared himself to his acquaintances
and friends by his many excellent and amiable qualities. The zeal and
correctness with which he performed his military duties gained him the
respect and esteem of his superiors, while his obliging disposition made
him universally beloved by his brother officers. He had been employed
in the Kandyan provinces from the commencement of the present
rebellion, during which time he, on many occasions, displayed an ardour
and ability in the execution of his duties that will ever reflect the
highest credit to his memory " (Ceylon Government Gazette).

JOHN RHODES

Born, September, 1789. Ensign, 9th May, 1811 ; Lieut.,
26th October, 1815 ; retired on half-pay, 25th December, 1818.

Died at Beaufoy Terrace, Maida Vale, London, 18th July, 1848.

THOMAS TAYLOE

Born, 25th December, 1790 ; son of William Tayloe, of
Chalford, Gloucestershire. Ensign, 29th August, 1811 ; Lieut.,
30th November, 1815.

Served in the Ceylon rebellion of 1817-18.

Died at Gravesend, 17th June, 1820.

His full dress uniform is to be seen in the museum of the Royal
United Service Institution, Whitehall, presented by his niece, Mrs.
Anderson.

HUGH MOORE

Born, 1788. Ensign, 56th Foot, 11th March, 1807 ; Lieut.,
16th July, 1808 ; 19th Foot, 17th September, 1811 ; 57th Foot,
19th October, 1815.

Died, 10th March, 1817.

DAVID BURNS

Born at Granard, 3rd August, 1793 ; son of David Burns,
of Granard, Co. Longford. Ensign, 17th October, 1811 ; Lieut.,
25th January, 1816 ; Capt., 20th July, 1830 ; Bt.-Major, 9th
November, 1846 ; retired, 12th October, 1849.

Actively employed in the Ceylon rebellion of 1818. Received the
approbation and thanks of Lieut.-Gen. Sir R. Brownrigg on three occasions, for a series of services against the insurgents and was mentioned
in despatches.

Died at Kingstown, Co. Dublin in 1850.

HENRY FREDERICK HAWKER

Born at St. Paul's, Covent Garden, 11th December, 1794.
Ensign, 24th October, 1811 ; Lieut., 22nd February, 1816 ;
Adjt., 22nd February, 1816—25th September, 1822 ; Capt.,
12th April, 1832 ; retired, half-pay, 12th Foot, 10th January,
1834 ; Adjt., Leicester Militia, 26th August, 1843 ; Staff Officer
of Pensioners, Leicester, 31st August, 1843 ; Bt.-Major, 9th

November, 1846 ; Bt.-Lieut.-Col., 20th June, 1854 ; Col., 1st May, 1856.

Died at Leicester, 20th October, 1856.

JOHN WILLIAM PRESTON

Ensign, 11th June, 1812 ; Lieut., 19th December, 1816 ; half-pay, 25th December, 1818 ; 76th Foot, 8th April, 1825 ; Qr.-Mr., 12th June, 1828 ; half-pay, 76th Foot, 9th February, 1849.

Died at Isleworth, London, 15th November, 1863.

GEORGE DENISON

Born, 1793. Ensign, 18th June, 1812 ; Lieut., 29th January, 1817 ; retired on half-pay, 20th July, 1820.

Served in the Ceylon rebellion of 1817-18.

Died about 1879.

WILLIAM HENRY RAINSFORD, C.B.

Born at St. Pancras, 2nd May, 1776 ; only son of General Charles Rainsford, 44th Foot, Governor of Chester. Ensign, 30th Foot, 15th March, 1793 ; 18th Foot, 22nd March, 1793 ; Grenadier Gds., 16th October, 1793 ; Lieut. and Capt., 10th September, 1795 ; Adjt., 23rd July, 1803—11th December, 1807 ; Capt. and Lieut.-Col., 10th September, 1807 ; Lieut.-Col., 19th Foot, 24th September, 1812 ; 89th Foot, 1st November, 1817 ; Bt.-Col., 4th June, 1814 ; Major-Gen., 19th July, 1821.

Served in Holland from September, 1794, till the evacuation of the country in 1795. Took part in the Walcheren expedition of 1809. C.B. in 1821.

Died at Malden, 20th May, 1823.

WILLIAM THORNTON

Born, 1796 ; son of Mrs. Thornton, of Haddington, near Edinburgh. Ensign, 21st January, 1813.

Died at Trincomalee, 6th September, 1816.

ADAM CALLANDER

Born, 1795. Possibly son of Adam Callander, of New Cavendish Street, London, of the Craigforth family. Ensign, 15th April, 1813.

Drowned in the wreck of the " Arniston," on Lagullas reef, off the Cape, 30th May, 1815.

FORBES ROBINSON

Ensign, 30th September, 1813 ; Lieut., 25th March, 1818 ; half-pay, 29th September, 1819 ; 20th Foot, 27th November, 1821.

Was in command of Chinna-Kandy post during the Ceylon rebellion of 1817-18.

Drowned on passage from Surat to Bengal, 7th February, 1824.

THOMAS HART DAVIS

Born, 1797. Ensign, 1st November, 1813 ; Lieut., 26th

March, 1818 ; half-pay, November, 1819 ; 30th Foot, 27th April, 1820 ; 35th Foot, 27th July, 1820 ; 94th Foot, 1st December, 1823 ; Capt., half-pay (unattached), 27th August, 1825 ; 8th Foot, 8th June, 1826 ; half-pay (unattached), 22nd February, 1833 ; 2nd Foot, 9th June, 1837 ; retired, 16th June, 1837.

WILLIAM NIHILL

Born, 1787. Ensign, 38th Foot, 1st August, 1804 ; Lieut., 7th May, 1805 ; Capt., 29th October, 1807 ; 19th Foot, 23rd December, 1813 ; sold out, 8th February, 1821.

GAVIN MILLER

Born, 1790. Probably son of Capt. G. Miller, Adjt. of the Derby Militia, 1798-1813 ; temporary Lieut., 25th December, 1813 from the Derby Militia ; half-pay, 26th September, 1814.

Died, 8th May, 1859, at Berkeley Place, North Road, London.

JAMES MARTIN SULLIVAN

Born, 1793. Ensign, 34th Foot, 18th May, 1809 ; Lieut., 20th June, 1811 ; 19th Foot, 17th March, 1814 ; retired on half-pay, 24th June, 1824.

Served in the Peninsula with the 34th and was present at the battle of Busaco and at Arroyo dos Molinos and Almaraz (medal and clasp). Took part in the expedition to Kandy in 1815.

Died, 26th November, 1856.

CHARLES STEWART

Ensign, 34th Foot, 25th July, 1809 ; Lieut., 17th October, 1811 ; 19th Foot, 22nd April, 1814 ; retired, half-pay, 4th Foot, 24th June, 1821.

Died, 14th January, 1854.

WILLIAM MORRIS

Born, 1784 ; Pte., 5th July, 1801 ; Corpl., 25th March, 1806 ; Sergt., 2nd September, 1807 ; Sergt.-Major, 17th July, 1808 ; Qr.-Mr., 15th October, 1814 ; retired on half-pay, 26th April, 1827.

Died at Cork, 22nd November, 1861.

CHARLES FORBES

Born, 1791. Ensign, Cape Regt., 16th July, 1806 ; 1st Lieut., 4th Ceylon Regt., 10th March, 1810 ; Lieut., 19th Foot, 24th June, 1815 ; Capt., half-pay, 24th October, 1821 ; 12th Foot, 14th March, 1822 ; Major (unattached), 15th August, 1826 ; 61st Foot, 4th July, 1834 ; Lieut.-Col., 28th June, 1838.

Was employed against the Kaffirs. Served as a volunteer with the 69th Foot at the capture of the Isle of France. Carried the regimental Colour at the storming of Fort Cornelis and was twice shot through the hand when planting it on the enemy's redoubt. Served in the Ceylon campaign of 1815 as D.A. Commissary General to one of the divisions operating in the Kandyan country.

Died at Aberdeen, 7th May, 1843.

WILLIAM JOHN BROWN PARKER

Born in Ireland, 1777 ; Hospital Asst, Army, 19th October, 1801 ; Asst.-Surgeon, 14th Foot, 8th November, 1804 ; Surgeon, 19th Foot, 3rd August, 1815 ; retired on half-pay, 26th October, 1826.

Was engaged with the French in the West Indies in 1803, and at the capture of Mauritius in 1810.

Died at St. Helier's, Jersey, 10th October, 1845.

HENRY WOOD RIDEOUT

Born at Woodmancote, Sussex, 9th December, 1797, son of the Revd. John Rideout, Rector of Woodmancote, Micheldever. Ensign, 21st September, 1815 ; Lieut., 19th April, 1818 ; retired on half-pay, 20th July, 1826.

Served in the Kandyan rebellion of 1818.

Died at Lansdown West, Bath, 19th March, 1876.

THOMAS TALBOT HAMILTON

Born at Norman's Cross, 1st December, 1799, son of Capt. John Hamilton, 5th Foot. Ensign, 57th Foot, 15th July, 1813 ; Lieut., 9th June, 1814 ; 19th Foot, 19th October, 1815 ; Capt., 8th November, 1825 ; Major, 23rd January, 1837 ; Lieut.-Col., 20th December, 1838 ; sold out, 30th August, 1842.

Died at Elgin Crescent, Notting Hill, London, 26th September, 1871.

ALEXANDER MILNE

Born, January, 1779, at Mill of Boyndie, Banff ; 3rd son of James Milne, of Boyndie. Ensign, 15th Foot, 13th September, 1798 ; Lieut., 26th November, 1799 ; Capt., 6th January, 1802 ; Major, 31st January, 1807 ; Bt.-Lieut.-Col., 4th June, 1813 ; Lieut.-Col., 19th Foot, 2nd November, 1815.

Died at Demarara, 5th November, 1827, when acting as Deputy Governor. The Colours of the 19th Foot were buried with him, his last dying request. There is a memorial tablet in the Cathedral Church, Demarara, erected by the officers of the regiment.

"No man had even been buried in the Colony so universally and sincerely regretted" (Extract from Captain Venable's account of the funeral).

GEORGE DURNFORD

Born, 1791. Ensign, Cape Regt., 27th June, 1806 ; 1st Lieut., 4th Ceylon Regt., 10th March, 1810 ; Lieut., 19th Foot, 25th December, 1815 ; Capt., half-pay (unattached), 25th April, 1826 ; commuted his half-pay, 13th February, 1827.

STEPHEN GRANBY BAGSHAW

Born at Trincomalee in 1800. Probably son of Granby C. Bagshaw, Master Attendant of Trincomalee, 1800-1803. Ensign, 25th January, 1816 ; Lieut., 6th July, 1820 ; 89th Foot, 25th January, 1821 ; retired, half-pay, 23rd Light Dragoons, 12th January, 1826.

Died, 17th November, 1843.

WILLIAM LEWIS

Born, 10th October, 1793; eldest son of Richard Hull Lewis, 68th Foot of Seaforth House, Co. Cork; 2nd Lieut., 4th Ceylon Regt., 12th March, 1810; Lieut., 10th May, 1814; 19th Foot, 22nd February, 1816; retired on half-pay, 20th July, 1820.

Served in the Ceylon rebellion of 1817-18.

Died at Cork, 17th October, 1883.

JOHN STIRLING

Born at Sandgate, Kent, 28th March, 1800; son of Major James Stirling, of Walworth, Co. Derry, late 63rd Foot. Ensign, 6th June, 1816; Lieut., 22nd July, 1824; Capt., 13th May, 1826.

Died at Malta, 25th January, 1841.

FRANCIS TYDD

Born in King's County, 29th October, 1787; 3rd son of Francis Tydd, of Dromoyle, King's County; Pte., 6th May, 1803; Corpl., 6th May, 1805; Sergt., 30th September, 1807; Sergt.-Major, 15th October, 1814; 2nd Lieut., 2nd Ceylon Regt., 12th July, 1816. Ensign, 19th Foot, 7th September, 1816; Adjt., 26th September, 1822; half-pay, 4th Ceylon Regt., 7th September, 1826; Paymaster, 19th Foot, 16th November, 1826.

Served with the 19th Foot in the Kandyan War of 1815, and in command of a detached post during the rebellion in Ceylon in 1817-18, for which he received a year's pay as Ensign.

Died at Trinidad, 11th February, 1835.

EDWARD CHARLES SODEN

Ensign, West India Rangers, 1st February, 1816; 19th Foot, 19th December, 1816; Lieut., 2nd West India Regt., 27th June, 1824; Capt., 10th November, 1834; Bt.-Major, 9th November, 1846; Major, 29th July, 1847.

Died in London, 30th June, 1851, of apoplexy, having just returned from Sierra Leone, aged 52 years.

JOHN MOFFATT

Ensign, 26th January, 1817; cashiered, 19th November, 1818, when attached to 4th Ceylon Regt.

EDWARD HUGHES

Ensign, 2nd West India Regt., 12th November, 1812; Lieut., 9th September, 1813; 1st Lieut., 1st Ceylon Regt., 17th March, 1814; Lieut., 19th Foot, 1st February, 1817; retired on half-pay, 25th December, 1818.

Died at Liverpool, 6th June, 1870.

JAMES EDWIN McCLASHAN, K.H.

Lieut., 2nd Light Battn. King's German Legion, 11th November, 1809; Capt., 22nd August, 1815; 1st Ceylon Regt., 25th December, 1815; 19th Foot, 25th May, 1817.

Served in the Peninsula and was present at the battles of Busaco and Albuera. Was A.D.C. to Major-Gen. Sir James Lyon, K.C.B., at Waterloo (medal and Knight of the Royal Hanoverian Guelphic order). Severely wounded at Morisco.

Died at Kandy, 2nd December, 1817, aged 26 years. Memorial at Kandy.

"Captain McGlashan had been only a short time in this island but his prepossessing appearance and polished manners had conciliated general regard. His last illness was soothed by the constant attention of his friend, Captain Kitson, who scarcely for a moment ever quitted his bedside. His Excellency the Governor and all the garrison of Kandy were present when the remains of this gallant soldier and accomplished gentleman were consigned with all military honours to the grave" (Ceylon Gazette, 29th November, 1817).

DONALD McBEAN

Ensign, Count Dillon's Regt., 1771 ; Lieut. and Adjt., Caledonian Volunteers, 1st May, 1778 ; Ensign, 71st Foot, 1st November, 1778 ; half-pay, 1783 ; 8th Foot, September, 1787 ; Lieut., 41st Foot, 25th December, 1787 ; Capt., June, 1794 ; Major, 89th Foot, 7th September, 1804 ; Bt.-Lieut.-Col., 25th July, 1810 ; Lieut.-Col., 28th November, 1810 ; 19th Foot, 1st November, 1817 ; Bt.-Col., 12th August, 1819.

As a Volunteer with the 71st, took part in the American War, and was taken prisoner in Boston Harbour in 1775. Rejoined in 1777. Retired from the Caledonian Volunteers to go with the expedition to Georgia with the 71st. Appointed a Cornet of Light Dragoons, 26th December, 1778. At the end of 1779 his troop was attached to Gen. Tarleton's famous British Legion till disbanded in 1783. Was at the capture of Savannah, Brian's Creek and at Charlestown. Present at the battle of Camden in 1778, and in the engagement at Guildford Court House. Taken prisoner at Yorktown. Took part in General Whitelock's expedition to Buenos Ayres. Several times wounded. Was in command of a Brigade sent from Ceylon to Madras in 1809 to quell the mutiny of the Madras army. Served in the Carnatic and Mysore in 1810. Inspecting Field officer during the American War of 1813.

Died at Point de Galle, Ceylon, 15th November, 1819.

Memorial at Galle in the Dutch cemetery.

MARK PRAEGER

Ensign, 2nd Foot, 30th July, 1803 ; 1st Lieut., 1st Ceylon Regt., 7th February, 1804 ; Capt., Nova Scotia Fencibles, 18th September, 1806 ; 1st Ceylon Regt., 13th November, 1806 ; 3rd Ceylon Regt., 20th March, 1809 ; half-pay, 25th May, 1817 ; 19th Foot, 3rd December, 1817 ; Bt.-Major, 12th August, 1819 ; 55th Foot, 8th November, 1821 ; Sub-inspector of Militia, Ionian Islands, 30th December, 1819 ; retired, 1st August, 1822.

LIONEL SMITH HOOK

Ensign and Lieut., 52nd Foot, 2nd January, 1796 ; Capt.-Lieut., 25th November, 1802 ; Capt., 2nd Ceylon Regt., 29th April, 1803 ; Bt.-Major, 4th June, 1813 ; Bt.-Lieut.-Col., 16th Foot, 3rd August, 1815 ; 19th Foot, 5th January, 1818 ; Major, 16th Foot, 8th March, 1821 ; Lieut-Col., Ceylon Rifles, 11th August, 1825 ; 16th Foot, 19th February, 1829.

Present at the capture of Kandy in 1815. Escorted the King as a prisoner to Colombo. Served also during the Ceylon rebellion of 1817-18. Died in camp at Secrole near Benares, 7th February, 1834.

ALEXANDER SCOTT

Born in Edinburgh, 20th September, 1796 ; 2nd Lieut., 3rd Ceylon Regt., 17th August, 1815 ; Ensign, 19th Foot, 2nd May, 1818 ; Lieut., 7th April, 1825 ; Adjt., 16th April, 1829—14th September, 1832 ; Capt., 23rd January, 1837 ; retired by sale, 20th May, 1842.

THOMAS BURT BAYLEY

Born, 8th October, 1801 ; son of Major Thomas Bayley, Ceylon Regt. 2nd Lieut., 3rd Ceylon Regt., 26th November, 1815 ; Ensign, 19th Foot, 3rd May, 1818; 20th Foot, 14th June, 1821 ; Lieut., 29th December, 1824 ; retired by sale, 20th August, 1829.

Died at the Cape.

JOHN WARDELL

2nd Lieut. 2nd Ceylon Regt., 6th February, 1812 ; Lieut., 19th Foot, 1st August, 1818 ; placed on half-pay, 20th July, 1820 ; omitted from the half-pay list in May, 1875.

ISAAC BRYNE ROBINSON

Born at Birmingham, 27th October, 1800. Ensign, 19th Foot, 17th December, 1818 ; Lieut., 3rd November, 1825 ; retired, half-pay, 92nd Foot, 8th February, 1834.

Died in Jersey, C.I., 30th May, 1881.
Memorial in St. Saviour's churchyard, St. Helier's, Jersey.

MONTGOMERY CAIRNES

Born, 1789 ; 3rd son of John Elliot Cairnes, of Savile Lodge and Kilnahussogue, Co. Tyrone. Ensign, 50th Foot, 17th April, 1806 ; Lieut., 56th Foot, 12th January, 1807 ; Capt., half-pay, 60th Foot, 7th September, 1815 ; 19th Foot, 8th April, 1819 ; 81st Foot, 17th January, 1821 ; sold out, 23rd March, 1825. Was A.D.C. to Sir Ronald Ferguson in Holland and to Sir George Don, Governor of Gibraltar.

Died at Spring Garden Parade, London, 12th March, 1877.

JOHN HENRY LEWIS

Born, 1794 ; son of Richard Hull Lewis, of Seaforth House, Co. Cork. Ensign, 86th Foot, 12th March, 1814, from Sergeant, 1st Foot Gds. ; Qr.-Mr., 33rd Foot, 19th October, 1815 ; 2nd Lieut., 1st Ceylon Regt., 4th December, 1818 ; Lieut., 19th Foot, 15th April, 1819; retired, half-pay, 83rd Foot, 24th June, 1824.

Died at Cork, 11th November, 1826.

EDWARD MATHIAS

Ensign, 22nd July, 1819 ; Lieut., 44th Foot, 20th November, 1822.

Died at Landour, Bengal, 13th August, 1839

HENRY HUBERT FARQUHARSON

Born in Bengal, 1st July, 1795. Ensign, 10th Foot, 20th May, 1813 ; Lieut., 5th June, 1815 ; Capt., 11th September, 1817 ; 19th Foot, 30th December, 1819 ; Major (unattached), 8th April, 1826 ; 1st Foot, 12th June, 1826 ; Lieut.-Col. (unattached), 10th March, 1837 ; retired in January, 1838.

Was at one time sub-inspector of Ionian Islands Militia. Barrack Master, 1846-53 at Hong Kong, Dublin, and Woolwich. Appointed Usher of the Black Rod to the Parliament of Victoria, N.S.W. when that office was created in November, 1856.

Died at his residence, Parliament House, Melbourne, 15th June, 1863.

Sympathetic reference was made to his death in the House of Parliament and the House adjourned at once as a mark of respect to so valuable an officer (Melbourne " Argus ").

WILLIAM WILDEY

Cornet, 25th Light Dragoons, 24th June, 1816 Lieut., half-pay, 13th Light Dragoons, 19th December, 1816 ; Paymaster, 19th Foot, 15th June, 1820 ; half-pay, 40th Foot, 6th March, 1823 ; 4th Queen's Own Light Dragoons, 12th March, 1824 ; half-pay, 24th January, 1828.

Died in January, 1837.

RICHARD CHAMBERS

Born at Newcastle-on-Tyne, 7th October, 1793. Ensign, 34th Foot, 13th May, 1813 ; Lieut., 5th July, 1819 ; 19th Foot, 15th June, 1820 ; Adjt., 7th September, 1826—15th April, 1829 ; Capt., 17th April, 1835 ; sold out, 29th March, 1838.

HUGH HENRY, Baron STRATHNAIRN of Strathnairn and Jhansi, G.C.B., G.C.S.I.

Born at Berlin, 6th April, 1801 ; son of the Right Hon. Sir George Henry Rose, G.C.B., Envoy Extraordinary and Minister Plenipotentiary at Berlin and Munich. Ensign, 93rd Foot, 8th June, 1820 ; 19th Foot, 6th July, 1820 ; Lieut., 24th October, 1821 ; Capt., 22nd July, 1824 ; Major (unattached), 30th December, 1826 ; 92nd Foot, 19th February, 1829 ; Lieut.-Col. (unattached), 17th September, 1839 ; Bt.-Col., 11th November, 1851 ; Major-Gen., 12th December, 1854 ; Col., 45th Foot, 20th July, 1858 ; Lieut.-Gen., 28th February, 1860 ; Col., 92nd Foot, 25th June, 1866 ; Gen., 4th February, 1867 ; Col., Royal Horse Gds., 3rd March, 1869 ; Field Marshal, 2nd June, 1877.

Served in Syria as Consul General, twice wounded at El Mejdol in 1841 (mentioned in despatches, naval medal and clasp, Turkish order of Nishan-i-Iftikhar in diamonds, gold medal and sword of honour from the Sultan, and order of St. John and Jerusalem from the King of Prussia for protecting the Christians). C.B., 23rd February, 1842. Queen's Commissioner in March, 1854 at Headquarters of French Army in the Crimea ; wounded before Sebastopol (medal with four clasps, 3rd Class of the Medjidieh, K.C.B., Legion of Honour and recommended for the Victoria Cross). Served in the Indian Mutiny in command of the force in Central India, including the relief of Saugor, capture of Raigur

Shahghur and Chundchree, siege and capture of Jhansi, Calpee and various other engagements, terminating in the storm and capture of Gwalior and the restoration of the Maharajah Scindia to his capital (medal and clasp, G.C.B.). Commander-in-Chief India, 1860-1865. K.C.S.I. in 1861 ; G.C.S.I. in 1866. Raised to the peerage as Baron Strathnairn of Strathnairn and Jhansi, 28th July, 1866. Commander-in-Chief, Ireland, 1865-1870.

Died in Paris, 16th October, 1885.

Buried at Christchurch Priory, Hants. Equestrian bronze statute at junction of Knightsbridge and Brompton Road.

" Rose was one of the bravest of men. He literally knew no fear. He was a fine soldier and among the many commanders brought to light by the Indian Mutiny, he was certainly the best " (D.N.B.).

CHARLES EDWARDS

Born, 1793. Ensign, 47th Foot, 27th September, 1813 ; Lieut., 24th December, 1818 ; 19th Foot, 10th October, 1820 ; retired, half-pay, 71st Foot, 3rd March, 1825.

Served in the Peninsula War with the 47th Foot from July, 1813 to the end of the war in 1814, including the second assault and capture of San Sebastian, the passage of the Bidassoa, Nivelle, Nive (9th to 13th December), and blockade of Bayonne (medal and three clasps). Served also in the campaigns of 1817 and 1818 in Malwa against the Mahrattas. Appointed Capt. of Invalids, 24th July, 1839.

Died at the Royal Hospital, Chelsea, 22nd August, 1866.

JOSEPH DOWLING

Born, 1794. Ensign, 66th Foot, 18th January, 1810 ; Lieut., 73rd Foot, 13th August, 1812 ; 87th Foot, 21st March, 1816 ; half-pay, 4th Foot, 4th March, 1818 ; 19th Foot, 21st January, 1821 ; half-pay, 20th December, 1821 ; 1st Royal Veteran Bn., 27th November, 1823 ; 96th Foot, 29th January, 1824 ; retired, half-pay (unattached), 26th July, 1827.

Served in the Peninsular War. Present at the battle cf Waterloo with 73rd Foot (medal).

Died in St. James' Park, London, 23rd August, 1845, when acting as Barrack Master at the Horse Guards.

LAMBERT COWELL

Born, 1800. Ensign, 73rd Foot, 24th August, 1815 ; Lieut., 22nd January, 1818 ; half-pay, 25th December, 1818 : 89th Foot, 7th December, 1820 ; 19th Foot, 25th January, 1821 ; half-pay, 25th October, 1821 ; 99th Foot, 4th January, 1833 ; Capt., half-pay (unattached), 16th January, 1846 ; 15th Foot, 3rd October, 1848 ; retired by sale, 3rd October, 1848.

Served in the Kandyan rebellion, 1817-18. Appointed a Military Knight of Windsor in June, 1867.

Died at Windsor, 24th August, 1867.

Sir EDWARD McARTHUR, K.C.B.

Born at Bath, 1787 ; eldest son of John McArthur, of Camden Park, N.S. Wales, late Capt., 102nd Foot, the "Father" of N.S. Wales. Ensign, 60th Foot, 27th October, 1808 ; Lieut., 39th Foot, 6th July, 1809 ; Capt., 19th Foot, 8th February, 1821 ; Major, half-pay (unattached), 10th June, 1826 ; Lieut-

Col., 23rd November, 1841 ; Col., 20th June, 1854 ; Major-Gen., 26th October, 1858 ; Col., 100th Foot, 28th September, 1862 ; Lieut.-Gen., 14th June, 1866.

Present with the 60th at the battle of Corunna. Afterwards served with the 39th in Sicily and again in Spain, when he was engaged at Vittoria, the Pyrenees, Nivelle, Nive, Bayonne, Orthes and Toulouse, where he served on the staff of Sir Robert O'Callaghan. Accompanied his regt. from Bordeaux to Canada and afterwards served with it in the army of occupation in France (medal and seven clasps). Lieut.-Governor of New South Wales, 1856. C.B., 17th July, 1857. K.C.B., 23rd July, 1862.

Died in London, 4th January, 1872.

WILLIAM BROOMFIELD

Ensign, 15th Foot, 28th November, 1800 ; 16th Foot, 19th July, 1802 ; Lieut., 25th March, 1804 ; Capt., 8th October, 1807 ; Major, 19th Foot, 8th March, 1821 ; retired, 22nd July, 1824.

Died at Boulogne in February, 1825.

EDWARD CHENEY

Born, 1803 ; 2nd son of Lieut.-Gen. Robert Cheney, Grenadier Gds., of Badger Hall, Shropshire. Ensign, 20th Foot, 28th December, 1820 ; 19th Foot, 14th June, 1821 ; half-pay, 25th October, 1821 ; 97th Foot, 25th October, 1824 ; Lieut., 19th January, 1826 ; Capt., half-pay, 20th March, 1827 ; omitted from the half-pay list, 20th January, 1843.

Died at Badger Hall, Shifnal, Shropshire, 16th April, 1884.

ROBERT WATSON GORDON

Born, 1786. Ensign, 8th Foot, 31st December, 1803 ; Lieut., 6th Foot, 16th March, 1805 ; Capt., 16th September, 1813 ; half-pay, 31st December, 1816 ; 81st Foot, 21st December, 1820 ; 19th Foot, 17th June, 1821 ; Major, half-pay (unattached), 19th September, 1826 ; 93rd Foot, 23rd December, 1836 ; retired by sale, 30th December, 1836.

Will proved in Dublin in 1848.

JOHN DOUGLAS COGAN

Ensign, 24th October, 1821 ; 68th Foot, 24th May, 1823.

Killed by lightning at Quebec, 9th June, 1824.

WILLIAM JAMES SHIELL, M.D., F.R.C.S.I.

Born, 1794 ; Hospital Asst. Medical Dept., Ireland, 25th June, 1819 ; Asst-Surgeon, 19th Foot, 26th September, 1822 ; half-pay, 25th April, 1825 ; 9th Light Dragoons, 15th June, 1826 ; half-pay, 25th April, 1828 ; commuted his half-pay, 6th September, 1831.

Served in St. Helena in 1816.

Died at Bagwell Street, Clonmell, 3rd March, 1870.

ALEXANDER GORDON MOORHEAD

Born, 1798. Ensign, 44th Foot, 26th May, 1822 ; 19th Foot, 20th November, 1822 ; Lieut., 3rd December, 1825 ; half-pay (unattached), 10th August, 1826; 26th Foot, 15th February, 1839; Capt. (unattached), 3rd March, 1848; retired by sale, 16th June, 1853.

Sir EDMUND CONVILLE BROMHEAD, Bart.

Born, 22nd January, 1791; 2nd son of Lieut.-Gen. Sir Gonville Bromhead, Bart. Ensign, 8th Foot, 18th January, 1808; Lieut., 54th Foot, 23rd March, 1809; Capt., 27th June, 1822; 19th Foot, 21st November, 1822; Major, half-pay (unattached), 13th May, 1826; retired, 24th January, 1831.

Lost an eye in Jamaica when on active service. Present at the battle of Waterloo with 54th Foot. Succeeded his brother as 3rd baronet, 14th March, 1855.

Died at Thurlby Hall, Lincolnshire, 25th October, 1870.

GEORGE BOOTH

Ensign, 87th Foot, 8th September, 1815; half-pay, 25th March, 1817; 87th Foot, 29th May, 1817; Lieut., 11th December, 1821; 19th Foot, 25th December, 1822; 88th Foot, 27th October, 1825; half-pay, 26th March, 1828; omitted from the Army list, 15th June, 1836.

NATHANIEL FAREWELL

Son of the Revd. Samuel Farewell, of Wincanton, Somerset. Ensign, 36th Foot, 17th September, 1803; Lieut., 22nd December, 1804; Capt., 23rd February, 1809; Capt., 40th Foot, 25th December, 1813; half-pay in 1814; Paymaster, 19th Foot, 6th March, 1823; 29th Foot, 25th May, 1826.

Served with the 36th Foot in the Walcheren expedition, 1809.

Died at Plymouth, 16th November, 1838.

CHARLES CRAUFORD HAY

Born in Kent, 17th February, 1807; 4th son of General Sir James Hay, K.C.H., for many years Governor of Edinburgh Castle. Ensign, 24th June, 1824; Lieut., 24th December, 1825; Capt., 26th September, 1826; Major, 16th June, 1837; Lieut.-Col., 30th August, 1842; half-pay (unattached), 7th April, 1854; Major-Gen., 26th October, 1858; Col., 58th Foot, 25th November, 1864; Lieut.-Gen., 20th January, 1867; Col., 93rd Foot, 29th August, 1868; 1st Commandant of the School of Musketry, Hythe, in 1854 to 1867; Commanding troops in Cape Colony, 1868-1873.

Died at Freshwater, Isle of Wight, 27th September, 1873.

SAMUEL VIGNOLES

Born at Portarlington, 23rd April, 1796; 4th son of the Revd. Jean Vignoles, formerly a Major, 39th Foot, of Cornahair, Westmeath, for 24 years Minister of the French church at Portarlington. Ensign, 41st Foot, 1811; resigned and entered R.M.A., Woolwich, 13th November, 1811; 2nd Lieut., Royal Artillery, 11th December, 1815; 1st Lieut., half-pay, 24th December, 1821; Lieut., 19th Foot, 24th June, 1824;

Capt., 8th April, 1826 ; retired, 4th September, 1834.

Was chief magistrate of police at Ennis, Co. Clare for some years. Kane's list of the Royal Artillery says that he became a celebrated engineer, famous for building bridges, but this is evidently a mistake (M.L.F.).

RICHARD FRANCIS GIBSON POORE

Born, 1804 ; 2nd son of Edward Poore, B.L. and half-brother of Sir Edward Poore, Bart. Ensign, 22nd July, 1824 ; Lieut. (unattached), 3rd December, 1825 ; half-pay, 28th February, 1828 ; 4th Foot, 11th June, 1830 ; Capt., 15th Light Dragoons, 7th July, 1843.

Died at Clevedon, Somerset, 4th September, 1852.

EDWARD LENN

Son of Mrs. Lenn, of Watford, Hertford. Ensign, 17th Foot, 10th August, 1799 ; Lieut., 23rd March, 1800 ; 80th Foot, 16th June, 1803 ; Capt., 3rd Ceylon Regt., 7th April, 1804 ; Bt.-Major, 4th June, 1814 ; Major, 8th February, 1816 ; 57th Foot, 2nd May, 1822 ; 19th Foot, 21st October, 1824.

Died at the barracks, Cork, 24th October, 1825. Buried in St. Finn Barr's Cemetery.

CHARLES BERKELEY BERKELEY

Ensign, 68th Foot, 19th August, 1813 ; Lieut., 14th April, 1814 ; half-pay, 92nd Foot, 17th April, 1817 ; 91st Foot, 22nd July, 1819 ; 71st Foot, 20th May, 1824 ; 19th Foot, 3rd March, 1825 ; Capt., half-pay (unattached), 21st November, 1828 ; retired by sale, 1st February, 1830.

PHILIP HENRY MICHELL

Born, 1802. Ensign, 63rd Foot, 24th October, 1821 ; half-pay in 1823 ; 19th Foot, 7th April, 1825 ; Lieut., 8th April, 1826 ; 76th Foot, 24th August, 1826 ; Capt., 22nd October, 1829 ; 47th Foot, 1st May, 1835 ; Sub-inspector of Ionian Islands Militia, 27th April, 1832 ; retired by sale, 19th October, 1838.

JOHN PERRY ELLIOTT

Ensign, 72nd Foot, 28th December, 1814 ; half-pay, 1816 ; 19th Foot, 7th April, 1825 ; Lieut., 40th Foot, 26th June, 1827 ; Capt., half-pay (unattached), 8th April, 1842.

Died, 23rd January, 1843.

THOMAS ATKINS

Born, 22nd April, 1808 ; son of Robert Atkins, of Mallow, Co. Cork. Ensign, 8th April, 1825 ; Lieut., 19th September, 1826.

Died in Demerara, 24th June, 1828.

HENRY HARDING

Born at Mount Mellick, 24th November, 1796. Ensign, 18th Foot, 24th June, 1812 ; Lieut., 16th September, 1813 ;

half-pay, 24th June, 1817 ; 89th Foot, 26th March, 1824 ; 31st Foot, 25th January, 1825 ; 19th Foot, 8th April, 1825.

Died at Trinidad, 5th August, 1833.

CORBETT COTTON

Born, 10th August, 1808 ; youngest son of General Sir Willoughby Cotton, G.C.B., K.C.H., of Cadogan Place. Ensign, 9th April, 1825 ; Cornet, 16th Light Dragoons, 29th June, 1826 ; Lieut., 29th March, 1827 ; Capt., 2nd West India Regt., 4th May, 1834 ; 94th Foot, 9th August, 1835 ; Major, 5th June, 1844 ; 49th Foot, 6th December, 1844 ; Lieut.-Col. (unattached), 20th April, 1849 ; Bt.-Col., 28th November, 1854; Major-Gen., 6th July, 1863 ; Lieut.-General., 5th January, 1872 ; Col., 101st Foot, 29th December, 1873 ; Gen., 1st October, 1877. A.D.C. to G.O.C.,Tasmania, 31st March, 1831 —3rd April, 1833. A.D.C. to G.O.C., Northern Division, 1st October, 1834—30th September, 1836. Brig.-Major to Inspector Gen. of Cavalry, 8th March, 1852—21st August, 1854. A.A.G., Cavalry, 21st August, 1854—4th October, 1859 ; retired, 10th August, 1878.

Died at 65, Warwick Square, Belgravia, 30th April, 1885.

DAVID WILLIAM ARCHIBALD DOUGLAS

Born, 13th September, 1798 ; eldest son of Col. William Douglas ; 2nd Lieut., 21st Foot, 29th June, 1815 ; half-pay on reduction, 24th March, 1816 ; 20th Foot, 2nd March, 1818 ; Lieut., 21st November, 1821 ; 19th Foot, 21st July, 1825 ; half-pay, 55th Foot, 10th November, 1825 ; Lieut., 38th Foot, 20th September, 1839. Unable to join the 19th Foot in consequence of hemiplegia by which he was attacked near Bangalore in July, 1824 ; sold out, 31st September, 1839.

Died in 1841.

ARCHIBALD TAYLOR

Ensign, Royal Staff Corps, 23rd November, 1804 ; Lieut., 28th May, 1809 ; Capt., 60th Foot, 20th September, 1810 ; 37th Foot, 14th February, 1811 ; half-pay, 40th Foot, 3rd May, 1821 ; 19th Foot, 15th September, 1825 ; Major, half-pay (unattached), 13th May, 1826.

Died in Dublin, 29th March, 1828.

JAMES PRICE HELY, K.H

2nd son of Br.-Gen. Patrick Hely, 11th Foot, killed at Ostend, 1798. Ensign, 69th Foot, 4th April, 1795 ; Lieut., 9th July, 1803 ; half-pay, 25th Foot, 18th July, 1822 ; Capt., 57th Foot, 15th February, 1810 ; 19th Foot, 6th October, 1825; Major, half-pay, 41st Foot, 1st August, 1826 ; Lieut.-Col., 23rd November, 1841 ; Col., 20th June, 1854 ; Major-Gen., 26th October, 1858.

Served with Lord Hill's division in the Peninsula in 1800, and was present at the battle of Busaco, in the actions of Pombal and Redinha, the first siege of Badajos, battle of Albuera (twice wounded), the

Pyrenees, Nivelle, Nive, Bayonne (13th December, 1813), and Orthes ; affairs of Perache, Aire and Tarbes, and battle of Toulouse. Sailed for Canada at the end of the war ; returned after the peace with America. landing at Ostend. Marched to Paris and served with the army of occupation until it broke up (medal and 6 clasps and Knight of the Hanoverian order).

Died at Norfolk Crescent, Bath, 17th October, 1861, aged 76.

ROBERT THOMAS FLETCHER

Ensign, 88th Foot, 28th November, 1822 ; Lieut., 21st July, 1825 ; 19th Foot, 27th October, 1825 ; half-pay (unattached), 9th April, 1826 ; 58th Foot, 18th January, 1827 ; half-pay, 6th West India Regt., 21st November, 1828 ; retired in May, 1829.

JOHN BAKER GRAVES

Son of the Revd. John Graves, Rector of Ballingarry, Co. Limerick. Ensign, 18th Foot, 4th March, 1812 ; Lieut., 13th May, 1813 ; 55th Foot, 5th May, 1815 ; half-pay, 55th Foot, 25th March, 1817 ; 19th Foot, 10th November, 1825 ; Capt., half-pay, 24th December, 1825 ; 87th Foot, 15th February, 1833.

Died at Kandy, 14th July, 1865, aged 66.

"After leaving the Army, Capt. Graves was a stipendiary magistrate in Ireland. Subsequently on May 7th, 1851, he was appointed Police Magistrate of Kandy and became District Judge of Kurunegala on 1st March, 1861. He was generally known as "Paddy Graves," and his character was in accordance with his nickname. The stories about him and his friend, Denis Purcell, also of the Ceylon Civil Service, would have suited the pages of Charles Lever" (From Tombstones and Monuments in Ceylon, by J. Penry Lewis, C.M.G.).

WILLIAM BERNARD

Born, 14th March, 1808. Ensign, 17th November, 1825 ; Lieut., 25th January, 1828 ; Capt., 26th January, 1841 ; half-pay (unattached), 4th February, 1845.

Died at Berwick House, Walthamstow, 7th January, 1881.

JAMES MILLS

Born, 1802. Ensign, 3rd December, 1825 ; Lieut., 12th December, 1826 ; 79th Foot, 26th February, 1829 ; half-pay, 30th Foot, 3rd September, 1829.

Died, 4th June, 1852.

GEORGE WILLIAMSON

Born in London, 25th February, 1805. Ensign, 3rd December, 1825 ; Lieut., 28th September, 1826 ; Capt. (unattached), 1st November, 1832.

Died in Maddox Street, London, 20th June, 1835.

CHARLES WILLIAM CLARKE

Born, January, 1806 ; 5th son of Major-Gen. Sir William Clarke, Bart., of Rossmore, Cork, Governor of Seringapatam. Ensign, 24th December, 1825 ; Lieut., 31st October, 1826 ; half-pay, Glengarry Fencibles, 19th December, 1827.

Died in July, 1830.

SEYMOUR ROBERT DELME'

5th son of John Delmé, of Cams House, Fareham, Hants. Ensign, 8th April, 1826 ; 53rd Foot, 6th July, 1826 ; Lieut., 15th September, 1829 ; retired by sale, 29th December, 1835.

Died, 12th March, 1894, aged 86.

Memorial on west wall of St. Peter's Church, Tichfield, erected by the Vicar and Church Wardens.

FRANCIS PRICE

Born at Bath, 11th March, 1804 ; 3rd son of Sir Rose Price, Bart. Ensign, 95th Foot, 12th May, 1825 ; 78th Foot, 16th June, 1825 ; half-pay (unattached), 18th February, 1826 ; 19th Foot, 9th April, 1826 ; Capt., 7th February, 1834 ; retired, 11th September, 1840.

Died at Charlton Kings, Cheltenham, 14th September, 1863.

JOHN JAMES SARGENT

Ensign, 60th Foot, 26th October, 1809 ; Lieut., 13th October, 1810 ; 41st Foot, 16th January, 1823 ; 69th Foot, 13th September, 1823 ; Capt., 19th Foot, 13th May, 1826 ; 58th Foot, 8th June, 1826 ; 18th Foot, 14th December, 1838 ; Bt.-Major, 16th May, 1841 ; retired, 26th January, 1844.

Took part in the China War and was severely wounded in the attack on Canton in May, 1841.

Died at Point de Galle, Ceylon, 19th August, 1844, in his 54th year, from the effects of a fever contracted whilst serving in China. Memorial at Galle, erected by his children.

WELBORE ELLIS SWENY

Born in Ireland, April, 1796. Ensign, 34th Foot, 1st February, 1813 ; Lieut., 1st February, 1817 ; half-pay, 1823-25 ; Capt. (unattached), 19th November, 1825 ; 19th Foot, 8th June, 1826 ; half-pay, 9th Foot, 21st September, 1830 ; Bt.-Major and Bt.-Lieut-Col., 64th Foot, 8th February, 1856 ; retired on commutation in March, 1856.

Died at 6, Burlington Road, Dublin, about 1860.

NEVILLE CUSTANCE

Born, 2nd July, 1790 ; 5th son of John Custance, of Weston House, Norfolk ; 2nd Lieut., 23rd Foot, 2nd July, 1812; 1st Lieut., 9th September, 1813 ; half-pay, 25th March, 1814 ; 7th Light Dragoons, 19th April, 1815 ; 25th Light Dragoons, 16th July, 1818 ; half-pay, 25th December, 1818 ; 37th Foot, 8th April, 1826 ; Capt., 19th Foot, 15th June, 1826 ; Bt.-Major, half-pay, 1st Royal Vet. Bn., 12th October, 1826.

Granted a pension of £100 for wound at Bayonne, 1814.

Died at 34, Tregunter Road, Kensington, 11th September, 1880.

GEORGE JAMES HYDE

Born at St. James', London, 12th May, 1801 ; Hospital Asst. Staff, October, 1825 ; Asst.-Surgeon, 19th Foot, 15th June, 1826.

Died at Southampton, 11th June, 1825, when on leave of absence.

GEORGE PIPON, K.H.

Son of Thomas Pipon, of La Moye, Jersey, Col., 5th South West Regt. of Jersey Militia. Ensign, 26th Foot, 17th April, 1806 ; Lieut., 4th February, 1808 ; Capt., 28th July, 1814 ; Major, half-pay (unattached), 10th September, 1825 ; 19th Foot, 19th June, 1826 ; 26th Foot, 29th August, 1826 ; half-pay (unattached), 25th December, 1828 ; Bt.-Lieut.-Col., 28th June, 1838 ; retired, 17th December, 1841.

Served in the Peninsula and was present at the battle of Corunna. Took part in the Walcheren expedition and was at the siege of Flushing in 1809. Served again in the Peninsular war in the campaigns of 1811 and 1812, and in April, 1813 was at the battle of Castalla (medal and clasps). K.H. in 1836.

Died in Jermyn Street, London, 12th July, 1852, aged 60.

ROBERT GRANT

Ensign, 29th June, 1826 ; unattached, 18th July, 1826 ; Lieut., 67th Foot, 17th May, 1827 ; Capt., 11th December, 1828 ; half-pay (unattached), 11th June, 1830.

Died, 28th July, 1849.

ROBERT LOVELACE

Born at Quidenham Hall. Attleborough, Norfolk, 17th October, 1806 ; son of Lieut.-Col. Robert Lovelace, Coldstream Gds. Ensign, 53rd Foot, 9th April. 1825 ; 19th Foot, 6th July, 1826 ; Lieut., 12th April, 1832 ; Capt., 16th June, 1837 ; retired, 4th September, 1840.

Served with the Osmanli Irregular Cavalry in the Crimea. Was Commandant at Varna. Local rank of Major and Lieut.-Col. Settled in Canada after his retirement.

Died at Montreal, 18th May, 1888.

JOHN SEMPLE

Born at Liverpool, 6th March, 1807 ; son of John Semple. Ensign, 20th July, 1826 ; Lieut., 28th September, 1830 ; Capt., 5th September, 1834 ; Major, 30th August, 1842 ; retired by sale, 7th August, 1846.

Died at Moorside House, Neston, Cheshire, 21st April, 1891.

JAMES FRERE MAY

Ensign, 52nd Foot, 28th April, 1814 ; Lieut., 29th January, 1818 ; half-pay on reduction, 25th December, 1818 ; Capt., 19th Foot, 1st August, 1826 ; 41st Foot, 10th August, 1826.

Present at the battle of Waterloo with the 52nd Foot (medal).

Died at sea on board the " Orontes " near the Cape, on passage home from Madras, 2nd June, 1837.

Major May's youngest daughter, Catherine Anne, married, 19th June, 1858, Lord Nigel Kennedy, 8th son of 13th Earl of Cassilis.

CONSTANTINE YEOMAN

Born at Woodlands, 1789 ; 3rd son of Lieut.-Col. Henry Walker Yeoman, Whitby Volunteers, of Woodlands, Whitby ; Cadet, R.M.A., Woolwich, 19th November, 1806 ; 2nd Lieut.,

Royal Artillery, 5th March, 1810; 1st Lieut., 21st October, 1813; half-pay, R.A., 8th April, 1822; Capt., 19th Foot, 10th August, 1826; half-pay, Royal Staff Corps, 13th December, 1832.

Died at Whitby, 27th July, 1852.

JOHN HENRY SLADE

Born, 8th July, 1796; eldest son of Gen. Sir John Slade, Bart., G.C.H., of Maunsell Grange, Co. Somerset; Lieut., 12th Light Dragoons, 6th April. 1815; Capt., half-pay, 2nd Ceylon Regt., 24th October, 1821; 19th Foot, 10th August, 1826; Major (unattached), 5th June, 1827; 1st Dragoon Gds., 7th December, 1838; half-pay (unattached), 11th June, 1841; Lieut.-Col., 23rd November, 1841.

Served in the Peninsular War, May, 1813, to April, 1814, and was present at the battle of Toulouse. Was at the battle of Waterloo with the 12th Light Dragoons (medal).

Died at Barnes, 30th October, 1843.

JOHN EDWARD EDWARDS

Born at Milton House, Long Parish, Hants, 14th April, 1792. Cornet, 20th Dragoons, 20th February, 1812; Lieut., 30th December, 1813; 76th Foot, 8th April, 1825; 19th Foot, 24th August, 1826; half-pay (unattached), 7th March, 1839; Royal Canadian Regt., 16th July, 1841; retired by sale, 31st May, 1844.

Served in Spain, 1812-1814 under Sir H. Clinton, and was at the siege of Tarragona under Gen. Lord W. Bentinck.

Died at Brighton, 5th May, 1850.

DONALD CAMPBELL

Born in Argyllshire in May, 1784; son of Alexander Campbell, of Raschoillie. Ensign, 60th Foot, 3rd August, 1800; Lieut., 36th Foot, 15th August, 1801; half-pay, 25th August, 1802; 92nd Foot, 9th July, 1803; 17th Foot, 27th June, 1804; Capt., 1st August, 1811; Major, 19th Foot, 29th August, 1826; retired, 16th June, 1837.

Present at the siege of Fort Comona, E.I., in November, 1807, and Fort Chanowrie in December, 1807, under Major-Gen. Dickens. Took part in the campaigns on the Nepaul frontier in 1814-15 under Major-Gen. J. S. Wood, and in January, 1815, in the action at Geetghur. Served in the campaign in the Mahratta country in 1817-18, including the action at Jubbulpore in December, 1817, under Brig.-Gen. Hardyman. Twice wounded at the storming of Fort Comona. Received £191 12s 6d. batta money.

Died at Newtown, Inverary, 28th November, 1865. Buried in Kilmalen Churchyard, Inverary.

JOSEPH FRAZER WILSON

Born, 1788. Ensign, 63rd Foot, 5th April, 1810; Lieut., 77th Foot, 10th June, 1810; 4th Ceylon Regt., 28th February, 1812; half-pay on reduction, 17th September, 1816; 19th Foot, 7th September, 1826; Capt., half-pay (unattached), 13th February, 1827; omitted from the Army List, 1st April, 1862.

ROBERT STANSFELD

Born at Sowerby, Yorks, 5th December, 1805 ; 2nd son of Robert Stansfeld, of Field House, Halifax. Ensign, 19th September, 1826 ; Lieut., 2nd November, 1832 ; retired, half-pay, 20th Foot, 3rd August, 1837 ; Capt., 2nd West Yorkshire Militia, 1852 ; Major, 6th West Yorkshire Militia, 25th April, 1854 ; Lieut.-Col., 26th March, 1872 ; Hon. Col., 16th May, 1874.

Died at Field House, Halifax, 19th October, 1885.

THOMAS WILLIAMS, M.D.

Born at Cork, 2nd December, 1802 ; Hospital Asst. Staff, 3rd November, 1825 ; Asst.-Surgeon, 19th Foot, 28th September, 1826 ; Surgeon, 57th Foot, 26th January, 1841 ; Staff Surgeon, 1st Class, 15th June, 1849 ; half-pay, 5th November, 1852.

Died at Ebury Place, Pimlico, 12th October, 1869.

JOHN SPRING HAMILTON

Born at Dingle, Ireland, 5th June, 1784 ; son of Capt. John Hamilton, 5th Foot. Ensign, 5th Foot, 30th October, 1799 ; Lieut., 12th November, 1800 ; half-pay, 5th Foot, June, 1803 ; Capt., 25th February, 1808 ; 99th Foot, 25th December, 1818 ; half-pay, 1st Royal Vet. Bn., 13th January, 1824 ; Bt.-Major, 27th May, 1825 ; 19th Foot, 12th October, 1826 ; Major (unattached), 12th October, 1830 ; retired, 20th January, 1832.

Was present at the storming of Buenos Ayres, 5th July, 1807, under Gen Whitelocke. Served in the Peninsula and was at the battles of Salamanca (22nd July, 1812), Vittoria and Nivelle.

WILLIAM FINNIE

Born, 1793 ; Hospital Asst. Army, 25th June, 1812 ; Asst.-Surgeon, 1st Foot, 12th November, 1812 ; Surgeon, 19th Foot, 26th October, 1826 ; 8th Foot, 13th August, 1829 ; 1st Class Surgeon, Royal Hibernian School, 25th March, 1836 ; half-pay, 5th March, 1841.

Served in the Waterloo campaign with the 1st Royals (medal).
Died at Glasgow, 7th January, 1863, at his brother-in-law's house, 19, Kew Terrace.

LEWIS WYNNE

Born in August, 1808. Ensign, 2nd November, 1826 ; Lieut., 7th February, 1834 ; retired on half-pay, 26th December, 1837.

CHRISTOPHER SANDERS

Born at Weymouth, 12th July, 1808 ; son of William Sanders, of Deer Park, Charleville. Co. Cork. Ensign, 30th November, 1826 ; Lieut., 31st May, 1833 ; half-pay, 38th Foot, 24th February, 1837 ; 88th Foot, 2nd November, 1838 ; sold out, 1st March, 1839.

Died, 22nd November, 1839.

GODFREY BALDWIN

Born in Co. Cork, 15th July, 1806 ; 5th son of William Baldwin, of Green House, Kinsale. Ensign, 12th December, 1826 ; 8th Foot, 2nd November, 1830 ; half-pay, 1st June, 1832 ; 84th Foot, 11th October, 1833 ; retired, 13th December, 1833.

Died at Brookfield House, Bandon, 22nd May, 1877.

JOHN GURWOOD, C.B.

Born at Hoddesdon, Co. Herts, 7th April, 1788; 2nd son of one Gurwood, whose widow married H. Okey. Ensign, 52nd Foot, 30th March, 1808 ; Lieut., 3rd August, 1809 ; Capt., Royal African Corps, 6th February, 1812 ; 9th Light Dragoons, 30th July, 1812 ; 10th Hussars, 12th November, 1814 ; Bt.-Major, 6th March, 1817 ; half-pay, 1st West India Regt., 16th May, 1822 ; 19th Foot, 30th December, 1826 ; Bt.-Lieut.-Col., 15th March, 1827 ; Major, half-pay (unattached), 20th July, 1830 ; Col., 23rd November, 1841.

Served in the Peninsula with the 52nd Foot from August, 1808, to June, 1812, and was present at Vimiera, Vigo, Coa, Busaco, Pombal, the Redinha, Casa Nova, Foz d' Aronce, Sabugal (slightly wounded), Cuidad Rodrigo, Vittoria, Nivelle, Nive, Orthes and Toulouse. As a subaltern commanded the forlorn hope at the lesser breach in the assault on Cuidad Rodrigo and received a severe wound in the head. On this occasion he took the Governor, General Barrié, prisoner, whose sword was presented to Gurwood by Wellington. Was Brigade-Major to General Lambert's brigade at the Nivelle, Nive, Orthes and Toulouse. Served with the 10th Hussars at Waterloo (medal and C.B.). Was private secretary to the Duke of Wellington. Deputy Lieut. of the Tower, 22nd November, 1839. Editor of the "Wellington Despatches," and was awarded a Civil pension of £200 a year for his literary services.

Died at Brunswick Square, Brighton, 25th December, 1843. Buried in the Tower Chapel where there is a memorial.

JAMES JACKSON

Ensign, 94th Foot, 12th May, 1812, from Sergt.-Major ; Lieut., 30th March, 1815 ; half-pay, 25th December, 1818 ; 19th Foot, 13th February, 1827 ; half-pay, 8th Foot, 6th March, 1828 ; retired in May, 1832.

Severely wounded at the battle of Vittoria. Was also present at the Nivelle, Nive, Orthes, Vic Bigorre and Toulouse.

Died at St. Mary's Jamaica, in 1835.

GEORGE TOLSON

Born at Darlington, 9th February, 1793 ; Corpl., 4th May, 1811 ; Sergt., 24th June, 1813 ; Sergt.-Major, 2nd March, 1816 ; Qr.-Master, 26th April, 1827 ; retired, 27th February, 1835.

JAMES RALPH

Ensign, 59th Foot, 17th June, 1813 ; Lieut., 26th May, 1814 ; half-pay in 1816 ; 30th Foot, 18th December, 1819 ; Capt., 19th Foot, 5th June, 1827 ; half-pay (unattached), 5th February, 1829 ; 22nd Foot, 9th July, 1829 ; sold out, 16th July, 1829.

FREDERICK DEACON

Born at Portsmouth, 26th May, 1807. Ensign, half-pay (unattached), 8th October, 1825 ; 19th Foot, 26th June, 1827 ; Lieut., 49th Foot, 27th January, 1832 ; 19th Foot, 8th February, 1834 ; Adjt., 27th September, 1842 ; Capt., 7th March, 1845 (unattached list).

Died at Lordswood, near Southampton, the residence of his brother, 10th August, 1864.

JOSEPH THOMAS

Born at Lymington, 23rd June, 1803 ; son of Lieut.-Col. John Thomas, 28th Foot, of Lymington. Ensign, 101st Foot, 15th February, 1816 ; half-pay, 24th July, 1816, on disbandment ; 87th Foot, 7th November, 1822 ; Lieut., 23rd August, 1825 ; half-pay, 24th August, 1827 ; 19th Foot, 1st November, 1827 ; retired, 31st May, 1833.

Served in the Burmese campaign, 1825-6, as Lieut. in 87th Foot, under Major-Gen. Archibald Campbell.

JAMES STEWART

Born at Glenavy, Co. Antrim, in 1792 ; possibly son of William Stewart, Surgeon to H.M. Forces in Upper and Lower Canada, and grandson of John Stewart, of Glenavy. Ensign, 100th Foot, August, 1806; Lieut., Glengarry Regt., 6th February, 1812 ; half-pay in 1817 by reduction of the Corps ; 19th Foot, 20th December, 1827 ; retired by sale, 21st February, 1836.

Commanded a company on board the gunboats for three months on the River St. Lawrence in 1812 ; employed in cutting off the supplies of the enemy. Commanded a company in action of Fort George 27th May, 1813, also at the action of Stoney Creek, at 40 Hill Creek, and at the siege of Fort George. Was at the battles of Lundy's Lane, Cook's Mills, Chippawa Black Creek, and during the whole of the siege of Fort Erie in 1814. Distinguished himself in cutting off a picquet of the enemy under the guns of Fort Erie in 1814. The troops under his command for this service consisted of a company of the Glengarry Regt. and a company of the 6th Foot (wounded in the left thigh on the Niagara Frontier in 1813, and again at Crooks Mills).

Died before 1846.

GEORGE ISAAC WILLIAM LANDMANN

Born at Gosport, 24th January, 1805 ; son of Lieut.-Col. George Thomas Landmann, Royal Engineers. Ensign, 3rd April, 1828.

Died at Burnley, 2nd March, 1832.

THOMAS ROBERT TRAVERS

Born at Cork, 21st October, 1808. Ensign, 97th Foot, 7th April, 1825 ; Lieut., 10th June, 1826 ; 19th Foot, 5th June, 1828 ; Paymaster, 23rd November, 1838.

Died at Montreal of cholera, 23rd August, 1849. There was a memorial in the Cathedral erected by his brother officers of the 19th. The Cathedral was destroyed by fire in 1856, and the memorial is not in the new building.

CHARLES HIGHMORE POTTS

Born at Carlisle, 18th May, 1794. Ensign, York Rangers, 8th February, 1816; Lieut., 18th November, 1817; 54th Foot, 24th May, 1818; Capt. (unattached), 31st December, 1825; 19th Foot, 5th February, 1829; Bt.-Major, 28th June, 1838; Bt.-Lieut.-Col., 11th November, 1851; Bt.-Col., 28th November, 1854, on retirement.

Died at Worthing, 12th February, 1883.

JOHN BENJAMIN WATERSON

Born at Emyvale, Co. Monaghan in 1791; Hospital Mate Staff, 5th June, 1809; Asst.-Surgeon, 3rd West India Regt., 22nd March, 1810; 15th Foot, 28th January, 1813; half-pay, 5th Royal Vet. Bn., 27th June, 1816; Asst. Staff Surgeon, 25th March, 1825; Surgeon, Staff, 31st January, 1828; 19th Foot, 13th August, 1829; retired, 25th February, 1835.

STUDHOLME JOHN HODGSON

Born near Ipswich in December, 1804; son of General John Hodgson, Col., 4th Foot, and grandson of Field Marshal Studholme J. Hodgson, Col., 4th Foot. Ensign, 50th Foot, 30th December, 1819; 45th Foot, 12th August, 1820; Lieut., 83rd, Foot, 2nd February, 1825; Capt., half-pay (unattached), 30th December, 1826; 39th Foot, 12th November, 1827; 19th Foot, 21st September, 1830; Major, 28th December, 1838; Lieut.-Col. (unattached), 8th August, 1845; Bt.-Col., 20th June, 1854; Major-Gen., 11th April, 1860; Lieut.-Gen., 29th August, 1868; Col., 54th Foot, 13th March, 1868; Gen., 2nd February, 1876; Col., 4th Foot, 21st November, 1876.

Served in the Burmese War with the 45th Foot, under Major-Gen. Sir H. Campbell, G.C.B. (medal and clasp). Commanded troops in Ceylon, 1865-1869. Author of " Truths from the West Indies," London, 1838. Three generations of his family Colonels of the 4th Foot.

Died at Argyll Hall, Torquay, 31st August, 1890.

RICHARD AUGUSTUS MEIR FRANKLIN

Born, 18th October, 1811. Ensign, 28th September, 1830: Lieut., 17th April, 1835; Adjt., 29th July, 1836—2nd August, 1839; half-pay, 55th Foot, 25th October, 1844; Staff Officer of Pensioners, December, 1844; retired, August, 1850.

Died in New Zealand.

Sir MARK ANTHONY HENRY TUITE, Bart.

Born in Dublin, 24th March, 1810; eldest son of Sir George Tuite, Bart., 19th Light Dragoons. Ensign, 3rd November, 1830; Lieut., 21st February, 1834; Capt., 20th May, 1842; retired by sale, 14th August, 1848.

Succeeded to the Baronetcy in 1841; was M.P. for Co. Westmeath.

Died at Kilruane, Nenagh, Co. Tipperary. 10th March, 1898.

For forty years past he had applied himself assiduously to the perfecting of experiments for the production of flying machine mechanism and also was engaged in other inventions.

THOMAS BECKHAM

Born at Yarmouth, 29th January, 1795. Ensign, 43rd Foot, 7th May, 1811 ; Lieut., 23rd May, 1813 ; half-pay, 24th October, 1819, by reduction ; 39th Foot, 13th August, 1820 ; 79th Foot, 15th February, 1821 ; 31st Foot, 25th March, 1824 ; 61st Foot, July, 1825 ; 66th Foot, 18th November, 1828 ; Capt., 1st West India Regt., 8th June, 1830 ; 19th Foot, 3rd December, 1830 ; half-pay (unattached), 8th March, 1845 ; Major, 9th November, 1846 ; Lieut.-Col., 20th June, 1854 ; Capt., St. Helena Regt., 24th October, 1856 ; retired, 1st April, 1857.

Served in the Peninsular War, 1812-14, and in France, 1815-18. Adjt., East Norfolk Yeomanry Cavalry, 25th March, 1825. Staff Officer of Pensioners, Preston. Omitted from the Army List, 1st April, 1866.

CHARLES JOSEPH FREEMAN

Born in Worcestershire, 7th May, 1813 ; son of the Revd. Keelings Freeman, of Pedmore Hall, Worcestershire. Ensign, 3rd February, 1832 ; Lieut., 3rd September, 1834 ; sold out, 26th May, 1837.

Died at Trim, Co Meath, 15th October, 1853.

THOMAS HILTON

Born at Selling, Kent., 12th December, 1813 ; son of Henry Hilton, of Sale Street House, Kent. Ensign, 3rd March, 1832 ; Lieut., 29th July, 1836 ; Capt., 30th March, 1838 ; retired, 4th April, 1845.

JOHN FORMAN

Born in Edinburgh, 2nd February, 1796 ; Pte., 71st Foot, 19th February, 1811 ; Corp., 19th Foot, 19th February, 1821 ; Sergt., 19th July, 1821; Cr.-Sergt., 25th January, 1822; Sergt.-Major, 25th July, 1827. Ensign, 12th April, 1832 ; Adjt., 14th September, 1832.

Was present at the action of the Pyrenees, crossing of the Nive, battles of Bayonne, Orthes, Aire, Toulouse, and Waterloo (medal). Granted the regimental medal for exemplary conduct, 14th October, 1816. Dismissed the Service by sentence of a General Court Martial held at Barbados in January, 1836.

ANTHONY WALSHE

Born at Belfast, 27th December, 1815 ; eldest son of Lieut.-Col. Blaney Townley Walshe, Royal Artillery, of St. Catherine's, Carrickfergus. Ensign, 2nd November, 1832; Lieut., 23rd January, 1837 ; Paymaster, 2nd Foot, 10th September, 1841 : half-pay in 1845 ; 59th Foot, 20th June, 1845 ; half-pay (unattached), March, 1849 ; 1st Lieut., 89th Foot, 3rd April, 1849; retired by sale, 16th July, 1852.

JOHN DUKE SIMPSON

Born at Armagh, 20th October, 1812 ; son of Thomas Simpson, of Armagh. Ensign, 31st May, 1833 ; Lieut., 26th

May, 1837 ; Capt., 28th December, 1838 ; Major, 8th August, 1845 ; retired by sale, 6th August, 1847.

Died at Southampton.

SAMUEL GEORGE BEAMISH

Born at Kinsale, 22nd June, 1810 ; eldest son of William Beamish, of Mount Prospect, Co. Cork. Ensign, 5th Foot, 19th April, 1831 ; 19th Foot, 22nd November, 1833 ; retired, 2nd May, 1834.

Died in London, 23rd April, 1889.

CHARLES KENNEY

Ensign, 52nd Foot, 17th August, 1809 ; Lieut., September, 1810 ; half-pay, 12th Foot, 4th September, 1823 ; Capt., 52nd Foot, 9th September, 1819 ; 1st West India Regt., 19th December, 1822 ; 19th Foot, 10th January, 1834 ; sold out, 7th February, 1834.

Served in the Peninsula with 52nd Foot. Present at Pombal, Redinha, Casa Nova, Foz d' Aronce, Sabugal, Fuentes d' Onoro, Cuidad Rodrigo, Vittoria, Pyrenees, Vera, Bidassoa, Orthes, Tarbes (wounded) and Toulouse. Slightly wounded in the attack of La Petite La Rhune, 10th November, 1813 (medal and 7 clasps). Present at Waterloo (medal).

JAMES HANNOVER GEORGE TUITE

Born in Dublin, 29th March, 1813 ; son of Sir George Tuite, Bart. Ensign, 7th February, 1834 ; Lieut., 1st West India Regt., 31st May, 1839 ; 19th Foot, 7th June, 1839 ; Capt. (unattached), 12th January, 1849.

Died at Calais, 1st September, 1853.

THOMAS BUTLER STONEY

Born at Portland, Roscrea, Tipperary, 22nd March, 1813 ; eldest son of Richard Falkiner Stoney, of Portland. Ensign, 21st February, 1834 ; retired by sale, 5th May, 1837.

Died, 10th March, 1893.

The Right Hon. Sir FRANCIS SEYMOUR, Bart., G.C.B., P.C.

Born in Belfast, 2nd August, 1813 ; eldest son of Henry Augustus Seymour, M.A., of Pembroke College, Cambridge. Ensign, 2nd May, 1834 ; Lieut., 16th June, 1837 ; Capt., 4th September, 1840 ; Scots Fusilier Gds., 21st January, 1842 ; Capt. and Lieut.-Col., 28th June, 1850 ; Major, 14th June, 1858 ; Bt.-Col., 28th November, 1854 ; Major-Gen., 10th September, 1864 ; Lieut.-Gen., 14th April, 1873 ; Colonel, 11th Foot, 7th February, 1874 ; Gen. 1st October, 1877.

Embarked for the East with the Scots Fusilier Gds., on 28th February, 1854, in which he served without intermission throughout the Crimean Campaign to the fall of Sebastopol, 8th September, 1855, when he returned to England in consequence of a severe wound in the head which he received in the trenches before Sebastopol while Field officer commanding the right attack, on the 24th August, 1855. He was present at the battle of the Alma where he was highly commended for his gallant conduct, battle of Balaclava, the repulse of a sortie the day after, and the battle of Inkerman, where he received a gunshot wound in the hand, and succeeded to the command of the battalion at an early part of the day. Was recommended for the Victoria Cross for gallant conduct when Field officer in the trenches on 24th August, 1855, as well as for his conduct at the battle of the Alma (medal with 4 clasps, C.B., officer of the Legion of Honour, 2nd Class of the Medjidie and Turkish medal).

Equerry to the Prince Consort. Approved by King Leopold I. to accompany his nephew, the Prince Consort, in his travels. He joined H.R.H. at Florence in January, 1839, and went with him in his journey to Italy and Switzerland. Groom-in-waiting to Queen Victoria. Comander of the order of Leopold of Austria. Knight Grand Cross of the Saxe-Ernestine order. Was in command of the troops in Malta, 1872-74.

Died at Kensington Palace, 10th July, 1890.

JAMES TEMPLE BOWDOIN

Born at Rome, 17th March, 1815 ; only son of James Temple Bowdoin and grandson of Sir John Temple, Bart. Ensign, 12th September, 1834; Lieut., 30th March, 1838; Capt., 11th September, 1840 ; 4th Dragoon Gds., 16th February, 1844 ; sold out, 29th January, 1847.

EDWARD BRICE

Born at Carlingford, 12th August, 1782 ; Pte., 46th Foot, 1798 ; Sergt., 1798 ; Sergt.-Major, Qr.-Mr. General's Dept. 1808 ; Qr.-Mr., 3rd West India Regt., 16th December, 1810 ; half-pay, 23rd June, 1825 ; 19th Foot, 6th March, 1835.

Died at Trinidad, 29th October, 1835.

JOHN WYER

Born at Wyloft, Lincolnshire, 17th February, 1791 ; Hospital Mate Staff, 5th February, 1811 ; Asst-Surgeon, 88th Foot, 9th September, 1813 ; half-pay, 25th May, 1816 ; Staff, 25th Jun, 1823 ; Surgeon, 74th Foot, 13th April, 1832 ; 19th Foot, 13th March, 1835 ; retired on half-pay, 18th October, 1839.

Present before Ciudad Rodrigo, January, 1812 ; Badajos, 6th April, 1812, and Salamanca as Hospital Asst. Was at the Nivelle, Orthes, and Toulouse as Asst.-Surgeon, 88th Foot (medal and 5 clasps).

Died at Whitchurch, Dorset, 23rd February, 1883.

JAMES COCHRANE

Born in Bombay, 25th June, 1818. Ensign, 5th June, 1835 ; Lieut., 28th December, 1838 ; Capt. (unattached), 5th October, 1849 ; retired, 18th June, 1852.

ALEXANDER CAMPBELL

Born at Little Dunkeld in 1807 ; Hospital Asst. Staff, 27th February, 1827 ; Asst. Surgeon, 29th July, 1830 ; 19th Foot, 12th June, 1835 ; Staff, 22nd November, 1836 ; 22nd Foot, 15th December, 1840 ; Surgeon, 30th September, 1842 ; 55th Foot, 17th September, 1847 ; half-pay, 5th April, 1850 ; Staff, 12th December, 1851 ; 59th Foot, 3rd December, 1852.

Served with the 22nd Foot in the campaign of Scinde under Sir Charles Napier, and was present at the destruction of the fort of

Imaumghur and at the battle of Meanee (medal). He served also in the campaign of 1844 in the Southern Mahratta country, and was present at the investment and storming of Panulla and Pownghur.

Died at Hong Kong, 18th June, 1853.

RICHARD BARRETT

Born at Cork, 25th December, 1794 ; Pte., 8th April, 1813; Corpl., 25th October, 1818 ; Sergt., 31st July, 1820 ; Sergt.-Major, 12th April, 1832 ; Qr.-Mr., 30th October, 1835. Ensign and Adjt., 13th June, 1845 ; Lieut., 14th August, 1848 ; Capt., 6th June, 1854 ; unattached, 2nd October, 1855 ; Hon. Major., 28th August, 1857 on retirement.

Served with 19th Foot in command of a detached post in Ceylon during the insurrection of 1817-18.

Died at 140, Pembroke Road, Dublin, 24th March, 1882.

PATRICK FLEMING

Born at Strabane, 17th July, 1788 ; Asst.-Surgeon, Clare Militia, September, 1811 ; half-pay on reduction, November, 1814 ; Clare Militia, July, 1815—April, 1816 ; Staff-Surgeon, October, 1822 ; half-pay, 24th June, 1829 ; Paymaster, 56th Foot, 9th August, 1833 ; 19th Foot, 27th May, 1836.

Died in Dublin, 6th September, 1838.

HENRY CALLEY

Born, 22nd May, 1818 ; 2nd son of John James Calley, late 12th Lancers, of Blunsden, St. Andrew, Wiltshire. Ensign, 29th July, 1836 ; Lieut., 2nd February, 1839 ; Adjt., 2nd August, 1839—13th June, 1845 ; Capt., 30th August, 1842 ; Major, 7th August, 1846 ; retired by sale, 15th February, 1853.

Died, 3rd May, 1881.

EDWARD JOHN ELLERMAN

Born at Antwerp, 15th December, 1818. Ensign, 17th Foot, 10th February, 1837 ; 19th Foot, 11th February, 1837 ; Lieut., 4th September, 1840 ; Capt., 9th July, 1850 ; 98th Foot, 61th June, 1851 ; Bt.-Major, 14th February, 1860 ; Major, 10th May, 1864 ; retired with rank of Lieut.-Col., 6th March, 1867.

Served with the Peshawar Expeditionary Force on the Euzofzie frontier under Sir Sidney Cotton, in April and May, 1858, and at the affair with the Hindostan fanatics on the heights of Sittana on the 4th May (medal and clasp).

Died in 1891.

ROBERT HENRY BUNBURY

Born at Tullow, 29th September, 1799. Ensign, 88th Foot, 31st August, 1815 ; 2nd Royal Vet. Bn., 24th March, 1823 ; 95th Foot, 23rd December, 1823 ; Lieut., 7th April, 1825 ; half-pay, 24th September, 1825 ; 66th Foot, 24th March, 1827 ; 94th Foot, 24th October, 1828 ; half-pay, 25th May, 1832 ; 96th Foot, 17th August, 1832 ; half-pay, 22nd July, 1836 ; 19th Foot, 23rd February, 1837 ; retired on half-pay, 38th Foot, 2nd November, 1838.

Died, 30th May, 1839.

HENRY BUTLER STONEY

Born at Portland, Tipperary, 28th September, 1816 ; 3rd son of Richard Falkiner Stoney, of Portland. Ensign, 5th May, 1837 ; Lieut., 11th September, 1840 ; Capt. (unattached), 28th May, 1852 ; Paymaster, 99th Foot, 12th October, 1852 ; 40th Foot, 19th August, 1856 ; Hon. Major, 12th October, 1862 ; half-pay (unattached), 4th December, 1863 ; sold out, 5th August, 1864.

ROBERT SANDERS, C.B.

Born at Charleville, 25th December, 1814 ; 3rd son of William Sanders, of Deer Park, Charleville, Co. Cork. Ensign, 26th May, 1837 ; Lieut., 26th January, 1841 ; Capt., 3rd February, 1843 ; Major, 6th August, 1847 ; Lieut.-Col., 14th April, 1854 ; Col., 28th November, 1854 ; half-pay, 10th November, 1856 ; Depot Batt., 23rd October, 1857 ; sold out, 25th September, 1860.

Served in the Crimea. Severely wounded and horse killed at the Alma. (C.B., mentioned in despatches, medal and clasp and Turkish medal.)

Died at Salthill, Monkstown, Co. Dublin, 1st November, 1860.

FREDERICK AUGUSTUS JEFFREYS

Born in London, 28th August, 1820 ; 3rd son of Henry Jeffreys. Ensign, 10th June, 1837 ; retired by sale, 4th September, 1840.

Died at Kyneton, Port Phillip, 24th March, 1853.

GEORGE RICHARD LANGLEY

Born at Sporle, Norfolk, 6th October, 1796 ; son of Collin Langley. Cornet, Royal Waggon Train, 24th November, 1812 ; Lieut., 7th January, 1814 ; half-pay, 25th June, 1814 ; Royal Waggon Train, 25th May, 1815 ; half-pay, 25th October, 1816, on reduction ; Royal West India Rangers, 2nd January, 1817 ; half-pay, 4th October, 1819, on reduction ; 20th Foot, 24th August, 1832 ; half-pay, 14th July, 1837 ; 19th Foot, 4th August, 1837 ; Capt. (unattached), 26th April, 1844.

Took part in the campaign in Holland under Sir Thomas Graham in 1813, and in Spain and Belgium under the Duke of Wellington.

Died at Stockwell, 7th April, 1882

GEORGE ADAMSON STANLEY

Born in Dublin, 17th November, 1796. Ensign, Royal African Corps, 17th February, 1814 ; Lieut., 25th May, 1815 ; half-pay, 15th Foot, 30th May, 1816 ; Royal Newfoundland Volunteer Corps, 25th July, 1824 ; 40th Foot, 30th January, 1828 ; 19th Foot, 26th December, 1837 ; Capt., half-pay (unattached), 10th September, 1841 ; sold out, 31st July, 1846.

Died in Bloomfield Avenue, Dublin, 11th November, 1872.

JAMES KER

Born at Edinburgh, 2nd June, 1819 ; eldest son of James Ker, of Blackshields, Co. Haddington. Ensign, 30th March,

1838 ; Lieut., 12th October, 1841 ; Capt., 7th August, 1846.

Took part in the battle of the Alma, and was mortally wounded at Inkerman, dying on 7th November, 1854.

THOMAS BYRNE

Born in Dublin, 23rd July, 1803. Ensign, 38th Foot, 15th March, 1821 ; half-pay, 12th February, 1826 ; Lieut., 18th September, 1828 ; 19th Foot, 20th November, 1838 ; 32nd Foot, 30th August, 1839; half-pay (unattached), 13th May, 1842.

Died 27th March, 1844.

ROBERT JOHN SOUTHCOTE MANSERGH

Born at Fermoy, 8th April, 1818 ; youngest son of John Southcote Mansergh, of Greenane, Co. Tipperary. Ensign, 2nd West India Regt., 14th September, 1838 ; 19th Foot, 28th December, 1838 ; Lieut., 16th November, 1841 ; retired by sale, 6th August, 1847.

Died 31st May, 1871.

ROBERT CROSBY

Ensign, 3rd West India Regt., 26th August, 1814 ; Lieut., 11th April, 1816 ; half-pay, 15th October, 1819 ; 19th Foot, 1st February, 1839 ; retired by sale, 1st February, 1839.

JOHN PHILLIPS

Born at Hereford, 18th October, 1820. Ensign, 2nd February, 1839 ; Lieut., 20th May, 1842 ; retired, half-pay, 57th Foot, 21st March, 1851.

JAMES YOUNG, M.D.

Born, 21st April, 1800 ; Hospital Assist., 18th May, 1824 ; Assist.-Surgeon Staff, 14th August, 1824 ; 50th Foot, 4th May, 1826 ; 78th Foot, 12th April, 1827 ; Surgeon, 19th Foot, 18th May, 1839 ; 13th Light Dragoons, 30th May, 1843 ; 48th Foot, 16th August, 1850 ; half-pay, 18th February, 1853.

Served in Africa from 1824-1827 inclusive, and was present at the battle of Doodwa against the Ashantees, 7th August, 1826 (mentioned in despatches).

Died at Ayr, N.B., 27th October, 1866.

HUGH JOHN MONTGOMERY CAMPBELL

Born at the Hollies, near Enville, Staffordshire, 18th August, 1822 ; eldest son of Hugo Montgomery Campbell. Ensign, 31st May, 1839 ; Lieut., 30th August, 1842 ; Capt., 4th April, 1845 ; retired by sale, 21st November, 1851.

Died at 29, Cambridge Terrace, London, 16th February, 1852.

WILLIAM DILLON

Born at Clifton, 12th July, 1817 ; son of Sir Charles Drake Dillon, Bart., of Lismullen, Co. Meath. Ensign, 32nd Foot, 18th February, 1835 ; Lieut., 15th February, 1839 ; 19th Foot,

30th August, 1839 ; retired, 9th June, 1843.

Died at Monkstown, Co. Dublin, 18th July, 1843.

ARTHUR PELHAM ATHERLEY

Born at Exeter, 19th July, 1822 ; eldest son of the Revd. Arthur Atherley, Vicar of Heavitree, Exeter. Ensign, 30th Foot, 14th February, 1840 ; 19th Foot, 14th February, 1840 ; 92nd Foot, 24th June, 1842 ; retired by sale, 30th June, 1843.

Died at Bath in August, 1847.

HENRY EDWARD McGEE

Born at Port of Spain, Trinidad, 29th March, 1820 ; son of James French McGee, of Trinidad. Ensign, 4th September, 1840 ; Lieut., 3rd February, 1843 ; Capt., 8th August, 1845 ; Major, 14th April, 1854 ; Bt.-Lieut.-Col., 12th December, 1854 ; Lieut.-Col., half-pay, 31st August, 1855 ; 3rd West India Regt., 25th March, 1859 ; Col., 19th June, 1860 ; half-pay, 28th August, 1863 ; 9th Foot, 3rd June, 1864 ; retired by sale, 3rd June, 1864.

Served in the Crimean War. Slightly wounded at the Alma. Present at Inkerman, and before Sebastopol. (Medal and 3 clasps, Knight of the Legion of Honour, 5th Class of the Medjidieh, Bt. of Lieut.-Col. and Turkish medal).

Died at Hauteville, St. Peter's Port, Guernsey, 28th April, 1866.

WILLIAM TEMPLE PARRATT

Born in London, 25th February, 1821 ; youngest son of Lieut.-Col. Hildebrand Meredith Parratt, R.A., of Effingham House, Surrey. Ensign, 5th September, 1840 ; Lieut., 9th June, 1843 ; Capt., 58th Foot, 24th October, 1845 ; Bt.-Major, 15th January, 1858 ; 14th Foot, 28th January, 1859 ; half-pay (unattached), 4th September, 1860 ; 1st Foot, 11th February, 1862 ; 58th Foot, 23rd September, 1862 ; retired by sale, 12th June, 1863.

Died at Snodland, Kent, 27th November, 1877.

JOHN LEWIS RICHARD ROOKE, C.B.

Born at Taunton, 23rd July, 1822 ; son of Lieut. Lewis Rooke, Royal Marines who fought at Trafalgar. Ensign, 11th September, 1840 ; Lieut., 20th August, 1844 ; Capt., 2nd April, 1847 ; Major, 12th December, 1854 ; Lieut.-Col., 15th September, 1855.

In general orders received the thanks of Gen. Berkeley, when in command of a detachment in Tobago in 1847, on the occasion of a hurricane.

Served in the Crimea. Present at the battles of the Alma and Inkerman, siege of Sebastopol (October, 1854, to 9th July, 1855). Commanded the reserve of the Light Division in the attack on the Great Redan, 18th June, 1855 (medal and 3 clasps, Knight of the Legion of Honour, C.B., and Turkish medal).

Died at Fort William, Calcutta, of cholera, 27th November, 1857.

A brother officer wrote as follows:—

"I need not tell you how sincerely he is regretted by the Regiment. Besides, he was so good an officer and there was so much confidence in him that all were delighted at the prospect of going on service with him. There were few more promising officers in the Service, and his untimely end is not only a misfortune to the Regiment, but a loss to the Army in general."

THOMAS JOHN COGHLAN, M.D.

Born at Colombo, in June, 1816, probably son of Surgeon John Coghlan, 86th Foot ; Asst.-Surgeon, Staff, 29th March, 1839 ; 19th Foot, 11th September, 1840.

Died in London, 20th January, 1843.

ROBERT SMITH

Born at Cromarty, N.B., 15th August, 1807 ; Asst.-Surgeon, Staff, 26th September, 1834 ; 21st Foot, 21st November, 1834 ; 19th Foot, 26th January, 1841 ; 2nd Class Staff-Surgeon, 8th December, 1845 ; 23rd Foot, 7th August, 1846 ; Surgeon-Major, 28th March, 1854 ; retired as Hon. Deputy Inspector-Gen., 21st September, 1860.

Died at Stuttgart, 29th September, 1880.

WILLIAM MACDONALD MACDONALD

Born at Belfast Bks., 26th May, 1822 ; only son of Major-Gen. James Alexander Farquharson, of Oakley, Co. Fife, Governor of the Windward Islands. Ensign, 19th February, 1841 ; retired, 30th April, 1841.

J.P. and D.L. Cos. Forfar and Perthshire. Commanded 13th Perthshire Rifle Volunteers. Succeeded his cousin, William Macdonald, of Ranaltan and St. Martin's, in 1841, and took the name and arms of Macdonald.

Died in 1895.

WILLIAM LEWIS PENNEFATHER

Born near Cawnpore, 21st July, 1822. Ensign, 30th April, 1841 ; Lieut., 6th Foot, 31st July, 1846 ; resigned, 11th May, 1849.

ROBERT WARDEN, C.B.

Born at Stirling, 8th November, 1822 ; only son of Robert Warden, of Park Hill, Co. Stirling. Ensign, 12th October, 1841; Lieut., 4th April, 1845 ; Capt., 6th August, 1847 ; Bt.-Major, 12th December, 1854 ; Major, 31st August, 1855 ; Bt.-Lieut.-Col., 2nd November, 1855 ; Lieut.-Col., 26th September, 1856 : Col., 15th August, 1862 ; Hon. Major-Gen., 28th June, 1868 ; Hon. Lieut.-Gen., 7th June, 1880 ; Hon. Gen., 1st July, 1881.

Served in the Crimea. Severely wounded at the Alma. Present at Inkerman and before Sebastopol, including the final assault on the Redan (mentioned in despatches, brevets of Major and Lieut.-Col., C.B., Knight of the Legion of Honour, medal with 3 clasps, 5th Class of the Medjidieh and Turkish medal). Afterwards awarded a distinguished service pension.

Died in Edinburgh, 15th June, 1890. Was first commanding officer of the 2nd Btn. 19th Foot, when it was raised in 1858.

" A Scot, honourable and true as steel, handsome, tall and spare—reserved and silent for the most part—one who by the mesmeric influence of his nature drew men to him as are steel filings to a magnet."—Extract from a letter from a brother officer.

CLELAND CUMBERLEGE

Eldest son of Joseph Cumberlege, Notary at Bombay. Cornet, 4th Light Dragoons, 31st December, 1825 ; Lieut., 25th August, 1829 ; 5th Foot, 11th June, 1830 ; half-pay, 1st Foot, 28th September, 1830 ; 19th Foot, 12th October, 1841 ; retired, 12th October, 1841.

Served in Spain with the Legion under Gen. de Lacy Evans. For some years was consul at Tampico, Mexico.

Died in 1861 on board the " Seine," off the island of St. Thomas, West Indies, where he was buried.

JAMES McCLINTOCK

Born, 1793 ; 5th son of John McClintock of Hempstead Hall, Co. Londonderry. Ensign, 88th Foot, 12th May, 1812 ; Lieut., 23rd November, 1815 ; half-pay, 25th February, 1816 ; 19th Foot, 10th November, 1841 ; sold out, 29th January, 1842. For many years Adjt. of the Londonderry Militia.

Died at the Strand, Derry, 15th April, 1850.

GEORGE ANSON, Baron BYRON

Born at Cheltenham, 30th June, 1818 ; eldest son of George Anson, 7th Baron Byron. Ensign and Lieut., Scots Fusilier Gds., 8th July, 1836 ; Lieut. and Capt., 18th May, 1841; Capt., 19th Foot, 21st January, 1842 ; retired by sale, 3rd February, 1843.

Succeeded his father as 8th Baron, 1st March, 1868.

Died at Rochdale, Co. Lancashire, 28th November, 1870, after a lingering illness.

HENRY MACDONALD BURNS

Born at Longford, 28th July, 1825 ; son of Major David Burns, 19th Foot. Ensign, 20th May, 1842 ; lieut., 24th Foot, 23rd June, 1848 ; Capt., 20th July, 1856.

Died at Aldershot, 15th April, 1864.

JOHN MARGITSON

Born at Ditchingham, Norfolk, 20th August, 1821 ; only son of James Taylor Margitson, of Ditchingham House. Ensign, 24th June, 1842 ; Lieut., 18th August, 1845 ; Capt., 15th August, 1848 ; 48th Foot, 8th August, 1851 ; retired by sale, 2nd April, 1852. Was a Capt. in the Suffolk Volunteers.

Died at Thun, Switzerland, in July, 1878.

CHARLES KYD SKEETE

Born at Barbados, 17th January, 1824 ; youngest son of the Hon. Braithwaite Skeete, President of Barbados, 1820-1833. Ensign, 30th August, 1842 ; Lieut., 24th October, 1845 ; Capt., 12th October, 1849 ; retired by sale, 23rd January, 1852 ; Capt., Royal Wiltshire Militia, 1854-64.

Died at Wanstead, Essex, 28th February, 1898.

JOHN HAY MOORE

Born at Ickford. Bucks, 11th February, 1823. Ensign, 3rd February, 1843 ; Lieut., 7th August, 1846 ; Capt., 21st November, 1851 ; retired by sale, 23rd December, 1853

Sir WARREN MARMADUKE PEACOCKE, K.C.H.

Eldest son of Marmaduke Peacocke of London. Ensign 85th Foot, December, 1780 ; Lieut., May, 1782 ; Capt.-Lieut., half-pay, 88th Foot, 14th May, 1783 ; 2nd Foot Gds., 6th November, 1793 ; Bt.-Major, March, 1794 ; Capt. and Lieut.-Col., 9th May, 1800 ; Bt.-Col., 25th April, 1808 ; Major-Gen., 4th June, 1811 ; Lieut.-Gen., 1821 ; Gen., 28th June, 1838 ; Col., 19th Foot, 31st May, 1843 to 22nd August, 1849.

Took part in the suppression of the Irish Rebellion of 1798, and was present at Antrim and Ballynahinch. Was with the expedition to Egypt in 1801, being present at all the actions the Guards were engaged in (medal). Took part in the attack on Copenhagen in 1807. In command of a brigade in the Peninsula, and was at the passage of the Douro. Governor of Lisbon 1809-1814. Knighted by the Prince Regent in 1832. Knight of the Tower and Sword of Portugal and Knight of the Crescent.

Died at Coulson's Hotel, Brook Street, London, 22nd August, 1849, aged 83.

Sir ROBERT ONESIPHORUS BRIGHT, G.C.B.

Born at Abbotsleigh, 7th July, 1823 ; 2nd son of Robert Bright, of Abbotsleigh, Bristol, High Sheriff of Bristol. Ensign, 9th June, 1843 ; Lieut., 2nd April, 1847 ; Capt., 23rd June, 1852 ; Major, 15th September, 1855 ; Bt.-Lieut.-Col., 26th December, 1856 ; Lieut.-Col., 28th November, 1857 ; Col., 24th May, 1862 ; Major-Gen., 6th March, 1868 ; Lieut.-Gen., 13th April, 1880 ; Col., 19th Foot, 27th October, 1886 ; Gen., 1st April, 1887 ; placed on retired list, 30th April, 1887.

Served in the Crimea. Present at the Alma, Inkerman and the whole siege of Sebastopol from October, 1854, to 9th September, 1855, including the attacks on the Redan, 18th June, and final assault, 8th September, 1855 (mentioned in despatches, Bt. of Lieut.-Col., medal and 3 clasps, Knight of the Legion of Honour, 5th Class of the Medjidieh and Turkish medal). Served in India during the Mutiny. Commanded as Brigadier the 1st Brigade Hazara Field Force of 1868 including the expedition against the tribes on the Black Mountain (mentioned in despatches, thanked by the Government of India, medal and clasp, C.B.). Served in the Afghan war of 1879-80 in command of the Khyber Line Field Force including the operations in the Hissarik Valley, and the expedition against the Wazeeree Khugianis (mentioned in despatches, received the thanks of both Houses of Parliament, medal and K.C.B.). Was created G.C.B. on Queen Victoria's birthday, 1894. Was in possession of a meritorious service reward.

Died at his residence, Normandy Park, Guildford, 15th November, 1896.

"In his prime, one of the smartest officers in Her Majesty's service, and in every respect the beau-ideal of a Commanding Officer. No one who ever came under his command was unjustly treated, and he was absolutely worshipped by both officers and men." (Extract from G.H.G.)

"No one ever took greater interest in the welfare of the 19th Regiment, and his death will be deeply felt, not only by those who had the honour to serve under his command but also by all ranks of the regiment which he at one time so ably commanded and for which he did so much."—(Extract from 1st Bn. Orders.)

WILLIAM O'DELL, M.D.

Born in Dublin, 17th March, 1807 ; son of Col. William O'Dell, The Grove, Limerick, M.P. Hospital Asst. Staff, 14th February, 1828; half-pay, 15th September, 1829; Asst-Surgeon, 7th November, 1830 ; 60th Rifles, 12th July, 1833 ; half-pay, 30th October, 1835 ; Staff, 28th October, 1836 ; Surgeon, 19th Foot, 9th June, 1843 ; Staff, 3rd March, 1853 ; 1st Class Surgeon, half-pay, 3rd March, 1854 ; Hon. Deputy Inspector-Gen., 15th May, 1862.

Served at Gibraltar during the greater part of the cholera epidemic with the 60th Foot. Served with 19th Foot during the cholera epidemic of 1849.

Died at Carrigafoyle, Co. Kerry, 3rd June, 1865.

MILDMAY CLERK

Born at Southampton, 10th September, 1810 ; son of John Clerk of Worthy, Hants. Cornet, 17th Lancers, 4th May, 1832 ; Lieut., 7th March, 1834 ; 4th Dragoon Gds., 27th May, 1836 ; Capt., 10th March, 1843 ; 19th Foot, 16th February, 1844 ; 12th Light Dragoons, 19th January, 1845 ; sold out, 26th November, 1847.

Died at Spratton, Northamptonshire, in September, 1877.

JOHN FOWKE

Ensign, 68th Foot, 20th February, 1812 ; Lieut., 19th August, 1813 ; half-pay, 25th August, 1818 ; Lieut., 19th Foot, 19th August, 1844 ; retired by sale, 19th August, 1844.

WILLIAM HENRY LEE WARNER

Born at Tyberton Court, Hereford, 16th April, 1825 ; 8th son of the Revd. Daniel Henry Lee Warner of Walsingham Abbey, Norfolk. Ensign, 20th August, 1844 ; Lieut., 6th August, 1847 ; retired by sale, 18th September, 1849.

Died, 20th July, 1896.

JOHN MAGUIRE

Ensign, 55th Foot, 7th February, 1840 ; Lieut., 4th July, 1843 ; 19th Foot, 25th October, 1844 ; 60th Rifles, 27th June, 1845 ; Adjt., 1st Bn., 2nd June, 1849 ; Capt., 20th June, 1854 ; Bt.-Major, 20th June, 1858 ; Bt.-Lieut.-Col., 5th August, 1864 ; half-pay, 1st April, 1866 ; retired, 4th February, 1871.

Served with the 55th Regiment in China and was present at the attack and capture of Amoy, second capture of Chusan, attack and capture of Chinhae and operations up the Yangtsekiang (medal). Served with the 60th Rifles throughout the Punjab campaign of 1848-9, including the siege and storm of the town and capture of the citadel of Mooltan, battle of Goojerat, pursuit of the Sikh army until its final surrender at Rawal Pindi, occupation of Attock and Peshawar and expulsion of the Afghan force beyond the Khyber Pass (medal and 2 clasps). Served throughout the campaign of Rohilcund in 1858, including the actions of Bugawalla and Nugena, relief of Moradabad, action of the Dojura, assault and capture of Bareilly, attack and bombardment of Shahjehanpore, defeat of the rebels and relief of the garrison ; capture of the fort of Bunnai, pursuit of the enemy to the left bank of the Goomtee, and destruction of the fort of Mahomdee ; commanded a wing of the 1st Btn. 60th at the attack and destruction of Shahabad (Brevet of Major) ; commanded the battalion in the action of Bunkagong (medal, three times mentioned in despatches, and recommended for an unattached majority by Lord Clyde for service in the field, in lieu of which he subsequently received the brevet of Lieut.-Col.).

Installed a Military Knight of Windsor, 26th June, 1895.

Died at Windsor, 11th January, 1904.

The Hon. CHARLES ROBERT WELD FORESTER

Born, 28th December, 1811 ; 3rd son of Cecil Weld, 1st Lord Forester. Cornet, 12th Lancers, 18th December, 1827 ; Lieut., 3rd August, 1830 ; Capt., 20th August, 1833 ; 19th Foot, 17th January, 1845 ; half-pay, unattached, 4th April, 1845 ; Major, 9th November, 1846.

Died in Cavendish Square, London, 16th September, 1852.

GEORGE BINGHAM JENNINGS

Born at Mount Jennings, Hollymount, Co. Mayo, 8th May, 1821. Son of Benjamin Jennings, of Mount Jennings.

Ensign, 9th Foot, 21st July, 1843 ; 2nd Lieut., 60th Rifles, 13th October, 1843 ; 1st Lieut., 4th April, 1845 ; Lieut., 19th Foot, 27th June, 1845 ; Capt., 1st July, 1853 ; Major, 30th September, 1856 ; Lieut.-Col., 18th April, 1868.

Served in the Crimea, including the siege of Sebastopol, from 7th October, 1854, to 29th December, 1854, under Lord Raglan. Present also before Sebastopol from 17th October, 1855, to end of the war (medal with clasp and Turkish medal). Commanded the district of Dacca during the Indian Mutiny in 1858, and received the approbation of the Government. Also commanded part of the force in the Sikkim campaign of 1861.

Died of cholera at Fort William, Calcutta, 6th March, 1870.

JOHN HODGSON FEARON

Born, 28th June, 1801. Ensign, Royal African Corps, 10th October, 1827 ; Lieut., 4th February, 1832 ; 63rd Foot, 18th September, 1833 ; Capt., 3rd November, 1837 ; half-pay, 14th January, 1842 ; 19th Foot, 4th April, 1845 ; retired by sale, 2nd April, 1847.

Acted as Brigade Major and Ordnance Storekeeper under Lieut.-Col. Kingston against the King of Bana. Also in command of a gunboat from the French brig of war " La Birdelaise " (Captain Couvelle). Received the thanks of H.M. Government in a letter from the Rt.-Hon. John Vincent Goderich dated 29th January, 1831, for a mission he was sent on to the King of Salun in the interior of Africa.

HENRY BRADDELL

Born at Mallow, Cork, 23rd November, 1827 ; only surviving son of Henry Braddell, J.P., of Modeligo, near Fermoy.

Ensign, 18th April, 1845; Lieut., 6th August, 1847; retired, 21st December, 1849.

Died at Modeligo, 9th March, 1913.

WILLIAM HARRIS

Born at Cardiff, 28th December, 1825. Ensign, 8th August, 1845; Lieut., 15th August, 1848; 32nd Foot, 2nd November, 1849; retired by sale, 31st December, 1852.

ALEXANDER HENDRY

Born at Killenmair, Scotland 6th February, 1797; Pte., 79th Foot, 6th February, 1813; 19th Foot, 20th February, 1822; Corpl., 10th June, 1822; Sergt., 29th August, 1822; Qr.-Mr.-Sergt., 9th September, 1836; Qr.-Mr., 2nd September, 1845; Depôt Bn. at Winchester, 7th April, 1854; retired, half-pay with hon. rank of Capt., 8th August, 1862.

Served with the 79th in the campaign of 1815, and was present at the battles of Quatre Bras, Waterloo, and capture of Paris (medal).

Created a Military Knight of Windsor in December, 1862.

Died at Great Malvern, 16th February, 1865.

GODFREY WILLIAM HUGH MASSY

Born in Tipperary in October, 1825; 4th son of the Revd. William Massy, Rector of Clonbeg, Tipperary, and Prebendary of Dysart. Ensign, 24th October, 1845; Lieut., 2nd February, 1849; Capt., 21st May, 1852; Major (unattached), 20th June, 1856.

Served in the Crimean War. Present at the battles of the Alma and Inkerman, and during the siege of Sebastopol till 22nd June, 1855, when he was invalided home (medal and 3 clasps, Knight of the Legion of Honour and Turkish medal).

Died in Albermarle Street, London, 4th June, 1862.

THOMAS WALLER BARROW, M.R.C.S., L.S.A.

Born in London, 24th May, 1817; son of Doctor John Barrow, Berkeley Square, London. Asst.-Surgeon, 2nd Foot, 8th June, 1841; 19th Foot, 23rd March, 1846; to the Forces, 9th September, 1851; Surgeon, 26th December, 1851; Surgeon-Major, 8th June, 1861; Deputy Inspector-Gen., 9th May, 1865; Hon. Inspector-Gen., 20th June, 1868, on retirement.

Served with the Queen's in the campaign of 1844 in the southern Mahratta country, including the storming of the fortress of Pancella and that in the Concan in 1845. Also during the Kaffir War in 1852-3 (medal). Promoted Deputy-Inspector-Gen. for highly meritorious services during the epidemic of yellow fever in Bermuda. Served in the Crimea

Died at Nightingale Place, Woolwich, 1st July, 1900.

JOHN GRATTAN ANDERSON

Ensign, 31st July, 1846; 37th Foot, 13th November, 1846; Lieut., 1st March, 1850; retired, 25th August, 1854.

Killed by the mutineers at Cawnpore in June, 1857.—(Smith's obituary.)

HENRY WELLINGTON PALMER, C.B.

Born at Tallaght House, Co. Dublin, 18th June, 1831 ; only son of Major James Palmer, 14th Foot. Ensign, 7th August, 1846 ; 74th Foot, 29th December, 1846 ; Lieut., 10th November, 1848 ; Capt., 17th August, 1852 ; Bt.-Major, 8th August, 1864 ; Major, 90th Foot, 9th September, 1864 ; Lieut.-Col., 1st April, 1873 ; Col., 1st April, 1878 ; retired with rank of Major.-Gen., 13th November, 1878.

Served with the 74th throughout the Kaffir War of 1851-3 (medal). Also in the Kaffir War of 1878, in command of the 90th L.I., and was three times thanked in general orders for his conduct in command of the operations in Fort Beaufort district (clasp and C.B.).

Died in Dublin, 14th January, 1891.

GEORGE VARNHAM MACDONALD

Born in Wilton Place, London, 2nd March, 1828 ; only son of Lieut.-Col. Donald Macdonald, 19th Foot. Ensign, 13th November, 1846 ; Lieut., 18th September, 1849 ; retired by sale, 3rd February, 1854 ; Exon Yeoman of the Guard, 6th February, 1855.

Died at Laureston Castle, Montrose, N.B., 22nd September, 1881. Memorial in Preston Churchyard, Brighton. erected by his brother officers.

JAMES COLE TAYLOR

Born in Dublin, 7th April, 1825. Ensign, 74th Foot, 31st July, 1846 ; 19th Foot, 29th December, 1846 ; retired, 18th February, 1848.

FREDERIC CHARLES ASHWORTH

Born in London, 25th December, 1829 ; son of Sir Charles Ashworth, K.C.B. Ensign, 2nd April, 1847 ; Lieut., 12th October, 1849 ; Capt., 15th February, 1853 ; retired by sale, 4th November, 1853.

Died at Chester Terrace, London, 15th December, 1889.

HENRY HILL DAWSON

Born at Lambeth, 2nd September, 1827 ; son of Frederick Dawson, B.L., of the Middle Temple. Ensign, 6th August, 1847 ; Lieut., 21st December, 1849 ; retired, 6th December, 1850.

Died at Hove, Brighton, 21st June, 1911.

HUGH FRANCIS MASSY

Born in Tipperary, 12th August, 1828 ; son of the Revd. William Massy, Rector of Clonbeg, Tipperary, and Prebendary of Dysart. Ensign, 7th August, 1847 ; Lieut., 9th July, 1850 ; Capt., 3rd February, 1854 ; retired on half-pay, 2nd June, 1865.

Served in the Crimea, including the capture of Egerton's rifle pits, 19th April, 1855 ; attack on the Quarries, 7th June, 1855 ; and on the Redan, 18th June, 1855, (medal and clasp, and Turkish medal).

Died at New Court, Bray, 3rd February, 1900.

RICHARD DENNY

Born at Doncaster, 18th December, 1815, second son of the Rev. Barry Denny, of Churchill, near Tralee, Co. Kerry.

Ensign, 58th Foot, 13th May, 1836 ; Lieut., 12th October, 1838 ; Capt., 30th December, 1842 ; Bt.-Major, 7th July, 1846 ; 19th Foot, 28th January, 1848.

Commanded the Light Co. of the 58th at the destruction of Pomares pah on the 30th April, 1845. At Mawie, 8th May. Present at the attack and destruction of the Winkadi pah, 16th May, at the storming of Kawitis pah at Ohiawai on the 1st July, and destruction of the same on 10th July. Again at the destruction of Arratna's pah on the 16th July. At the storming of Kawitis pah on 11th January, 1848.

Died at Quebec, 4th June, 1850.

Memorial in Quebec erected by his brother officers and the n.c.o.'s. and men of his company.

GEORGE LIDWILL

Born at Dromard, 3rd June, 1828, only son of Frederick Lidwill, of Dromard, Co. Tipperary.

Ensign, 18th February, 1848 ; Lieut., 6th December, 1850 ; Capt., 6th November, 1854 ; retired by sale, 24th July, 1857.

Served in the Crimea. Took part in the battles of the Alma and Inkerman. Was on picquet duty on the occasion of the sortie of 26th October, 1854. Before Sebastopol to 30th May, 1855 (medal and 3 clasps, Turkish medal). For 22 years was Adjt. of the 19th West Surrey Volunteers from which he retired 1st April, 1883, with honorary rank of Major (Volunteer Decoration).

Died at Dromard, 14th October, 1908.

OSWALD JAMES AUGUSTUS GRIMSTON

Born, 27th August, 1831, eldest son of Oswald Grimston, of Mersham House, Hants.

Ensign, 23rd June, 1848 ; Lieut., 21st November, 1851 ; Capt., 14th April, 1854. Retired, 26th October, 1855. Major, 1st Warwick Militia, 15th November, 1860 ; Lieut.-Col. Commanding, 15th April, 1874 ; retired with rank of Col., 18th December, 1888.

Served in the Crimea from 5th January, 1855, to 21st July, 1855, when he was invalided (medal with clasp and Turkish medal).

Died at the Lodge, Itchen, 13th October, 1916.

" A prominent figure in public and well-known in yachting circles in the South of England. Among the yachts he owned was the schooner " Chonita " and the cutter " Pauline," and for several years he was the Rear-Commodore of the Royal Yacht Club, and long associated with the sailing committee. In conjunction with Colonel Bucknill and others he set on foot the Solent Classes Racing Association of which he was Vice-President for several years, and succeeded the Earl of Dunraven when the latter retired from the Presidency, holding the position until a year or so before the great war broke out " (Extract from the " Field ").

THOMAS GOODRICKE PEACOCKE

Born in Dublin, 25th August, 1829 ; son of the Revd. George Peacocke, of Holy Cross, Tipperary.

Ensign, 15th August, 1848 ; 84th Foot, 6th July, 1849 ; Lieut., 9th January, 1855 ; 30th Foot, 1st May, 1855 ; Capt.,

24th Foot, 17th April, 1858 ; 94th Foot, 5th August, 1859 ; retired by sale, 19th December, 1862.

Served in the Crimea with the 30th Foot.

LEONARD DOUGLAS HAY CURRIE

Born in London, 6th March, 1832, son of Leonard Currie, of Bromley, Bow, Middlesex, and Manor House, Tunbridge Wells.

Ensign, 2nd February, 1849 ; Lieut., 23rd January, 1852 ; Capt., 29th December, 1854 ; sold out, 15th October, 1861.

Served in the Crimea. Severely wounded at the Alma (medal with clasp and Turkish medal). Served in the American Civil War as A.A.G. to a division of the Army of the Potomac. Present at the seven days' fighting before Richmond (horse killed). In command of the 133rd New York Regt. of Infantry. Severely wounded in the assault on Fort Hudson. Present at New Orleans, Batôn Rouge, and in Sheridan's operations in the Shendoah Valley.

Died at 31, Colville Square, Bayswater, 3rd January, 1907.

EDMUND KER VAUGHAN-ARBUCKLE

Born at Woolwich, 3rd April, 1829, son of Gen. Benjamin Hutcheson Vaughan-Arbuckle, R.A., J.P. for Kent.

Ensign, 84th Foot, 10th December, 1847 ; 19th Foot, 6th July, 1849 ; Lieut., 21st May, 1852 ; 3rd Foot, 12th October, 1852 ; Capt., 29th June, 1855 ; retired by sale, 16th May, 1868.

Served throughout the campaign of 1860 in China (medal with clasp for the Taku Forts). Living in Hastings in October, 1919.

Sir GEORGE CLAY, Bart.

Born in London, 14th August, 1831 ; son of Sir William Clay, Bt., M.P. for Tower Hamlets.

Ensign, 18th September, 1849 ; Lieut., 31st December, 1852 ; Capt., 29th December, 1854 ; Major, half-pay, 1st May, 1866 ; Lieut.-Col., 2nd August, 1875.

Served in the Crimea at the battles of the Alma and Inkerman, and from the commencement of the siege of Sebastopol to February, 1855 (medal and 3 clasps, 5th Class of the Medjidieh and Turkish medal). A.D.C. to the Governor of Ceylon, 1874-5. Succeeded his brother as 3rd Bart., 14th October, 1876.

Died at 17, Cavendish Square, London, 30th June, 1878. Buried at All Saints', Bradfield, Co. Devon.

GEORGE RIDGE BEADON

Born at Brampton, Kent, 26th December, 1829 ; only son of Major Valentine Beadon, Royal Marines.

Ensign, 19th October, 1849 ; Lieut., 15th February, 1853 ; retired by sale, 19th February, 1854.

Died, 8th February, 1859.

EDWARD CHIPPINDALL, C.B.

Born at Cheetham Hill, Manchester, 4th October, 1827 ; 3rd son of John Chippindall, J.P., D.L.

Ensign, 32nd Foot, 10th December, 1847 ; Lieut., 30th October, 1848 ; 19th Foot, 2nd November, 1849 ;

Capt., 23rd December, 1853 ; Bt.-Major, 2nd March, 1855 ; Major, 28th November, 1857 ; Bt.-Lieut.-Col., 9th March, 1865 ; Lieut.-Col., 7th March, 1870 ; Col., 14th August, 1870 ; half-pay, 23rd January, 1878 ; Commanding Brigade Depot, 3rd April, 1878 : half-pay, 18th May, 1881 : Major-Gen., 13th February, 1883 ; Col., 19th Foot, 16th November, 1886 ; Hon. Lieut.-Gen., 22nd December, 1886 on retirement.

Present during the latter part of the siege operations before Mooltan 5th to 21st January, 1849, and the surrender of the fort and garrison on the 22nd January. Was at the surrender of the fort and garrison of Cheniote on the 9th and the battle of Gujerat, 21st February, 1849, under Gen. Lord Gough (medal with 2 clasps). Took part in the battles of the Alma and Inkerman, the whole of the siege operations before Sebastopol, including the attacks on the Redan, 18th June and 8th September (slightly wounded). Brigade-Major to the Light Division, 24th October, 1855, to 10th June, 1856 (Brevet of Major, mentioned in despatches, medal with 3 clasps, Knight of the Legion of Honour, 5th Class of the Medjidieh, Turkish medal, and C.B.). Served in India during the Mutiny. Commanded the 19th Foot during the Hazara campaign of 1868, including the expedition against the hill tribes on the Black Mountain. Mentioned in Major-Gen. Wilde's despatch (25th October, 1868), as " being a most distinguished officer and commanded his regt. admirably." Also in Brig.-Gen. R. O. Bright's despatch " for untiring energy and zeal " (medal and clasp). A.D.C. to Queen Victoria, 13th August, 1872—12th February, 1883.

Died at Quendon Court, Newport, Essex (the residence of Major R. Biscoe, late 19th Foot), on the 12th September, 1902.

CECIL RIVERS

Born at Winchester, 30th December, 1823 ; 3rd son of the Revd. Sir Henry Rivers, Bart., of Chafford, Kent. and Martyr Worthy, Hants.

Ensign. 1st Foot, 20th May, 1842 ; Lieut., 36th Foot, 29th December, 1846 ; 19th Foot, 23rd November, 1849 ; retired by sale, 31st December, 1852

Drowned in the Thames near Kingston, 3rd February, 1862.

HENRY TURNER UNIACKE

Born at Larne, Wales, 31st October, 1830 ; son of John Uniacke, of Kerminchan and Broughton Hall, Cheshire.

Ensign, 21st December, 1849 ; Lieut., 1st July, 1853 ; Capt., 31st August, 1855 ; retired, 2nd March, 1860.

Served in the Crimea and was present at the Alma and before Sebastopol, including both attacks on the Redan (medal with 2 clasps, 5th Class of the Medjidieh and Turkish medal). Served in India during the Mutiny. Adjt., 3rd Staffordshire Militia, 1st September, 1863 to 1st October, 1869.

Died at Sheringham, Norfolk, 19th August, 1907.

ANDREW CLENDINNING

3rd son of George Clendinning of Westport, High Sheriff, Co. Mayo.

Ensign, 45th Foot, 25th April, 1827; Lieut., 9th April, 1829 ; Paymaster, 19th Foot, 25th January, 1850 ; Provisional Bn., 7th December, 1855 ; retired on half-pay, 25th January, 1858.

Served in the Crimea from 24th September, 1854, to 8th March, 1855 (medal with clasp and Turkish medal).

Died in Paris, 8th March, 1858.

RAMSAY WARDLAW

Born in Midlothian, 29th May, 1831 ; youngest son of Lieut.-Gen. John Wardlaw, Col., 55th Foot, of Pennington House, Lymington.

Ensign, 16th August, 1850 ; Lieut., 4th November, 1853.

Mortally wounded at the battle of the Alma. Died on board the s.s. "Andes" after amputation of his leg, 27th September, 1854.

EDWARD WENTWORTH BENNETT

Born at Cadbury, Somerset, 18th June, 1831 ; son of James Bennett, J.P., of Cadbury.

Ensign, 13th December, 1850 ; retired by sale, 16th September, 1851.

MAURICE LYNCH BLAKE

Born at Ballinafad, Co. Mayo, 15th October, 1821 ; 2nd son of Maurice Blake of Ballinafad House.

Cornet, 4th Hussars, 11th March, 1842 ; Lieut., 15th Hussars, 5th September, 1843 ; 57th Foot, 5th November, 1846 ; 19th Foot, 21st March, 1851 ; Capt., 29th December, 1854 ; retired by sale, 14th September, 1855.

Died in Dublin, 30th March, 1870.

LAWRENCE SHADWELL, C.B.

Born at Old Windsor, Berkshire, 6th July, 1823 ; son of the Rt. Hon. Sir Lancelot Shadwell of Barn Elms, Surrey.

Ensign, 98th Foot, 16th April, 1841 ; Lieut., 17th March, 1843 ; Capt., 7th February, 1851 ; 19th Foot, 6th June, 1851 ; Bt.-Major, 12th December, 1854 ; Bt.-Lieut.-Col. (unattached), 31st August, 1855 ; Lieut.-Col., 2nd November, 1855 ; Col., 4th September, 1861 ; Major-Gen., 6th March, 1868 ; Lieut-Gen., 27th April, 1879 ; Hon. Gen., 1st July, 1881 ; retired, 25th June, 1881.

Served with the 98th Foot in China and was present at the capture of Chinkiang Foo, and at the investment of Nankin (medal). Was extra A.D.C. to Sir Colin Campbell at the battles of Chillianwallah and Goojerat (medal with 2 clasps). As A.D.C. to Sir Colin Campbell, and subsequently as Asst.-Q.M.-Gen., was present at the battles of the Alma, Balaclava, and Inkerman and before Sebastopol (medal with 4 clasps, Brevets of Major and Lieut.-Col., Knight of the Legion of Honour, Sardinian and Turkish medals, and 5th Class of the Medjidieh). Awarded the C.B., 27th April, 1869. In receipt of a distinguished service reward, 1874.

Died at Reading, 16th August, 1887. Memorial in the Garrison Chapel, Portsmouth, erected by his widow, relatives and friends.

Author of "A Life of Lord Clyde."

SAMUEL JOHN MACLURCAN

Born at Belfast, 4th March, 1826 ; only son of Dr. Thomas Maclurcan, M.D., of Belfast.

Ensign, 48th Foot, 28th August, 1846 ; Lieut., 13th October, 1848 ; Capt., 7th March, 1851 ; 19th Foot, 8th August, 1851 ; retired by sale, 21st May, 1852 ; Major, 1st Devon Militia, 25th May, 1855.

Died at 17, Henrietta Street, Bath, 2nd March, 1868.

PETER GODFREY

Born at East Bergholt, Suffolk, 15th October, 1834 ; only son of Edward Godfrey of Old Hall, Suffolk.

Ensign, 16th September, 1851 ; Lieut., 23rd December, 1853 ; Capt., 31st August, 1855.

Served in the Crimea and was at the battles of the Alma and Inkerman. Mortally wounded at the final assault on the Redan, 8th September, 1855, and died on the 13th September.

HENRY LADBROKE WELLER CLARKE

Born at Aneton, Isle of Wight, 31st May, 1833, eldest son of Henry Danvers Clarke of Swakeleys, near Uxbridge.

Ensign, 21st November, 1851 ; Lieut., 3rd February, 1854 ; resigned, 10th November, 1854.

Served in Bulgaria, 11th May, 1854, to July, 1854.

EDWARD ROBERT WARD BAYLEY

Born in London, 7th December, 1833 ; son of John W. Bayley, F.R.S., 4 Suffolk Square, Cheltenham.

Ensign, 13th February, 1852 ; Lieut., 17th February, 1854 ; Capt., 14th February, 1855 ; sold out, 1st March, 1864.

Served in the Crimea. Present at the Alma and before Sebastopol, including the attacks on the Redan, 18th June, 1855, and 8th September, 1855. Slightly wounded in the trenches in June, and again in September (medal with two clasps, 5th Class of the Medjidieh, Sardinian and Turkish medals). Appointed a Military Knight of Windsor, 27th February, 1902.

Died at the International Hospital, Naples, and was buried, 8th May, 1912.

RICHARD DOYLE BARRETT

Born at Youghal, Cork, 18th February, 1830 ; son of Major Richard Barrett, late 19th Foot.

Ensign, 1st West India Regt., 14th April, 1846 ; Lieut., 9th April, 1848 ; 19th Foot, 28th May, 1852 ; Capt., 29th December, 1854 ; Bt.-Major, 14th May, 1866 ; Major, 28th September, 1866 ; Bt.-Lieut.-Col., 27th February, 1876 ; Lieut.-Col., 23rd January, 1878 ; 100th Foot, 29th September, 1880 ; half-pay, 29th September, 1882 ; Commanding 19th Regtl. District, 23rd February, 1883 ; retired with hon. rank of Major-Gen., 31st December, 1887.

Served in the Crimea. Present at the battles of the Alma and Inkerman. Siege of Sebastopol from its commencement to February, 1855. Slightly wounded by a shell, 31st October, 1854 (medal with 3 clasps, 5th Class of the Medjidieh and Turkish medal). Granted a meritorious service reward. Inventor of a new equipment for soldiers and a new signalling whistle.

Died at Blackheath, 21st April, 1905.

EDWARD LEVETT

Born at Hollybank, Staffordshire, 18th December, 1832 ; 3rd son of John Levett, of Wychnor Park, Staffordshire.

Ensign, 17th August, 1852 ; Lieut., 6th June, 1854 ; 10th Light Dragoons, 7th September, 1855 ; Capt., 24th November, 1857 ; Major, 16th October, 1860 ; retired by sale, 16th January, 1863.

Served in the Crimea with 19th Foot to 13th July, 1855. Present at Inkerman and siege of Sebastopol, including the assault on the Redan, 8th September, 1855 (medal and 2 clasps and Turkish medal).

Adjutant, Derbyshire Rifle Volunteers (Bakewell), 20th May, 1867 —6th April, 1881.

Died at 2, Place Duplaa, Pau, France, 28th December, 1899.

RICHARD FIELDING MORRISON

Born in Dublin, 20th June, 1829 ; only son of Richard H. Morrison of Coolegegan King's Co.

Ensign, 3rd Foot, 12th January, 1849 ; Lieut., 16th July, 1852 ; 19th Foot, 12th October, 1852 ; Capt., 29th December, 1854 ; 51st Foot, 17th August, 1855 ; retired, 17th November, 1857. Rejoined Army as Cornet, 16th Lancers, 30th March, 1858 ; Lieut., 24th December, 1858 ; Capt., 10th July, 1863 ; 7th Foot, 9th October, 1863 ; 5th Dragoon Gds., 29th March, 1864 ; half-pay, 8th August, 1868 ; 5th Lancers, 5th June, 1875 ; Bt.-Major, 1st October, 1877 ; retired as hon. Lieut.-Col., 1st July, 1881.

Served in the Crimea with 19th Foot. Present at the Alma and before Sebastopol (medal and 2 clasps and Turkish medal).

Died at Larkfield, Ballybrack, Co. Dublin, 19th July, 1902.

THOMAS WOORE SCOTT

Born in Londonderry, 15th February, 1831 ; son of the Revd. Henry Scott, Rector of Inch, Co. Derry.

Ensign, 18th February, 1853 ; Lieut., 6th June, 1854.

Died at Foyle Hill, Derry, 9th July, 1855.

AMES GOREN

Born in London, 26th September, 1832.

Ensign, 11th March, 1853 ; Lieut., 6th November, 1854 ; Capt., 28th November, 1857 ; retired by sale, 22nd January, 1869.

Served in the Crimea and was at the battle of Inkerman and before Sebastopol, including the attacks on the Redan, 18th June, and 8th September, 1855. Slightly wounded in the trenches, 28th July, 1855, and dangerously in the attack on the 8th September (medal and 2 clasps, 5th Class of the Medjidieh and Turkish medal). Served in India during the Mutiny.

Died at Brighton, 30th November, 1910.

AMBROSE MARSHALL CARDEW

Born at Dum Dum, India, 17th April, 1836 ; son of Ambrose Cardew, Bengal Horse Artillery.

Ensign, 1st July, 1853 ; Lieut., 23rd September, 1854 ; Adjt., 17th March, 1854—21st September, 1855 ; Capt., 27th June, 1856 ; half-pay, 10th November, 1856 ; 9th Foot, 23rd October, 1857 ; Adjt., Depôt Bn., 28th October, 1868 ; half-pay, 16th June, 1870 ; Staff Officer of Pensioners, Omagh, 1st October, 1870 ; Bt.-Major, 5th July, 1872 : Bt.-Lieut.-Col., 31st December, 1878 ; Col., 31st December, 1883 ; retired, 17th April, 1893.

Served in the Crimea. Severely wounded at the Alma and horse shot (medal with clasp and Turkish medal). Was the last Staff Officer of Pensioners.

Died at 9, Cambridge Place, Falmouth, 4th March, 1895. Memorial brass in Truro Cathedral.

WILLIAM FREDERICK HOTHERSALL PHIPPS

Born at Westbury, Wilts, 16th April, 1835 ; 2nd son of T. H. Hele Phipps of Leighton House, Wiltshire.

Ensign, 4th November, 1853.

Served in the Crimea and carried the Queen's Colour at the Alma. Died of cholera, 25th September, 1854.

HENRY MITFORD

Born in London, 16th July, 1833 ; 2nd son of Henry Revely Mitford, J.P., D.L., of Exbury, Southampton ; twin brother of Percy Mitford, 43rd Foot and Scots Fusilier Gds.

Ensign, 23rd December, 1853 ; Lieut., 23rd September, 1854 ; Capt., 8th August, 1856 ; 98th Foot, 26th September, 1856 ; 27th Foot, 13th March, 1857 ; retired by sale, 12th June, 1863.

Served in the Crimea. Present at the Alma and Inkerman and before Sebastopol to 28th December, 1854 (medal and 3 clasps and Turkish medal).

Died at Godesberg on the Rhine, 17th February, 1910.

GEORGE DICKSON THOMAS STOCKWELL

Son of Lieut.-Col. Thomas Stockwell, H.E.I.C.S.

Ensign, 46th Foot, 16th December, 1853 ; 19th Foot, 3rd February, 1854.

Killed at the battle of the Alma whilst carrying the Regimental Colour, aged 19.

The Colour belt with a suitable inscription is in the officers' mess, 1st Bn. The following letter was received by Mrs. Stockwell :—

Scutari, September 23rd.

" My dear Madam,—You will, before you receive this, be aware that my regiment has been in action in the Crimea on the 20th of this month. With the deepest regret, I have to inform you of the loss of your son, who fell in that action. He was carrying the Colours, and immediately before the charge, I ordered him to wave them which he did gallantly, but he was immediately shot down, the ball passing through his head. He was buried on the field where he fell. He was highly esteemed by us all and we sincerely feel his loss, and, indeed, he will be a great loss to the regiment. I especially recommended him for promotion to Lord Raglan, and he would have been promoted but for his early death. Having been shot through the leg myself and confined to bed, you will excuse my writing at greater length and sincerely sympathizing with you in the sad loss you have just received, believe me,

Yours sincerely,

ROBERT SANDERS,

Lieut-Col., 19th Regt.

Mrs. Stockwell.

JOHN HENRY KIRKE

Born at Retford, Notts, 16th December, 1833 ; son of William Kirke, B.L., J.P., of Mirfield Hall, Notts.

Ensign, 17th February, 1854 ; Lieut., 10th November, 1854 ; Capt., 30th April, 1858 ; Bt.-Major, 5th July, 1872 ; half-pay, 14th April, 1875 ; Bt.-Lieut.-Col., 25th March, 1880 ; retired, 1st July, 1881.

Served in the Crimea before Sebastopol from 28th December, 1854, to 26th July, 1855, including the attack on the Redan, 18th June, 1855 (medal with clasp and Turkish medal). Served in India during the Mutiny.

Died at Kempston Manor, Bedford, 24th February, 1892.

JOHN PEILE

Born at Kilcullen, Co. Kildare, 10th January, 1826.

Asst.-Surgeon, 1st Dragoon Gds., 8th January, 1847 ; 19th Foot, 24th March, 1854 ; resigned, 16th June, 1854.

WILLIAM MARSHALL WEBB, L.R.C.S.I.

Born at Tenby, Pembrokeshire, 6th July, 1833 ; 3rd son of Capt. John Wynne Webb, 79th Foot.

Asst.-Surgeon, 28th March, 1854 ; Staff, 15th November, 1859 ; Surgeon, 15th January, 1864 ; Surgeon-Major, 1st March, 1873 ; Brig.-Surgeon, 27th November, 1879 ; Deputy-Surgeon-Gen., 31st December, 1887 ; retired on half-pay, 6th July, 1893.

Served in the Crimea. Present at the Alma, Inkerman, and siege of Sebastopol (medal with 3 clasps and Turkish medal). Served in India during the Mutiny.

Died at Cairo, 18th March, 1899.

WILLIAM RICHARD GRYLLS, M.D.

Born in Cornwall, 3rd June, 1825 ; son of Canon John Couch Grylls.

Asst.-Surgeon, 7th April, 1854 ; 19th Foot, 28th April, 1854 ; 6th Inniskilling Dragoons, 1st May, 1855 ; resigned, 17th October, 1856.

Present at the battles of the Alma, Inkerman and siege of Sebastopol up to May, 1855 (medal with 3 clasps and Turkish medal).

Died at Coconada, Madras, 1st July, 1871.

ALEXANDER FRASER UNETT

Born at Beverley, 23rd December, 1831 ; son of Lieut.-Col., Thomas Unett, C.B., 19th Foot.

Ensign, 14th April, 1854 ; Lieut., 8th December, 1854 ; retired by sale, 19th September, 1856.

Served in the Crimea to December, 1854, when he was invalided (medal with clasp and Turkish medal).

Died in March, 1884.

THOMAS PALMER

Born at Great Gunnerby, 12th May, 1815.

Pte., 28th October, 1831 ; Corpl., 1st October, 1833 ; Sergt., 9th September, 1836 ; Col.-Sergt., 29th November, 1836 ; Qr.-Mr.-Sergt., 2nd September, 1845 ; Qr.-Mr., 21st April, 1854 ; Paymaster, 7th December, 1855 ; Hon. Capt., 7th December, 1860.

Served in the Crimea. Present at the battles of the Alma and Inkerman and before Sebastopol (medal and 3 clasps and Turkish medal). In possession of the medal for long service and good conduct.

Died at Nowshera, India, of apoplexy, 29th June, 1867.

GODFREY BALDWIN

Born in London, 17th April, 1836 ; 3rd son of Edward Calcott Baldwin.

Ensign, 6th June, 1854 ; Lieut., 8th December, 1854 ; Capt., 25th August, 1862 ; Bt.-Major, 8th October, 1876 ; Bt.-Lieut.-Col., 24th November, 1877 ; retired, 1st October, 1878.

Served in the Hazara campaign of 1868, including the expedition against the hill tribes of the Black Mountain (medal and clasp).

Died at Limpsfield, Surrey, 3rd February, 1880.

EDWARD WILLIAM EVANS

Born at Cloughjordan, Tipperary, 28th May, 1836 ; youngest son of Capt. Evans, 38th, 45th and 78th Foot, of South Park, Ballingarry, Tipperary.

Ensign, 7th June, 1854 ; Lieut., 8th December, 1854 ; Adjt., 19th March, 1860, to 15th July, 1862 ; Capt., 5th February, 1866 ; Bt.-Major, 4th November, 1868 ; Major, 15th March, 1879 ; Adjt., North York Rifles, 26th November, 1874 —27th April, 1879 ; retired, 7th June, 1879, with hon. rank of Lieut.-Col.

Served in the Crimea during the siege of Sebastopol, including the attack on the Quarries, 7th June, 1855, severely wounded (medal with clasp and Turkish medal). Served in India during the Mutiny. Took part in the Hazara campaign of 1868, including the expedition against the tribes on the Black Mountains, as Brigade-Major to Brig.-Gen. R. O. Bright, C B. (mentioned in despatches, medal and clasp).

Died at 12, Mowbray Road, Upper Norwood, London, 16th January, 1910.

Sir WILLIAM ROWAN, G.C.B.

Born in the Isle of Man, 18th June, 1789 ; 8th son of Robert Rowan, of Mullans, Co. Antrim.

Ensign, 52nd Foot, 4th November, 1803 ; Lieut., 15th June, 1804 ; Capt., 19th October, 1808 ; Major, 3rd March, 1814 ; Lieut.-Col., 21st January, 1819 ; Col., 10th January,

1837 ; Major-Gen., 9th November, 1846 ; Lieut.-Gen., 20th June, 1854 ; Gen., 30th August, 1862 ; Field Marshal, 2nd June, 1877 ; Col., 19th Foot, 15th June, 1854 ; 52nd Foot, 10th March, 1861.

Served with the 52nd in Sicily in 1806-7. In the expedition to Sweden in 1808. In the Peninsula under Sir John Moore, 1808-9. At Walcheren in 1809, including the bombardment and surrender of Flushing. In Portugal from 26th January, to 1st June, 1811, including the action of Sabugal. Subsequently in the Peninsula and South of France, 10th January, 1813 to end of war in 1814. Present at Vigo, Vittoria, Pyrenees, Vera, passage of the Bidassoa, Nivelle, Nive, Orthes, VicBigorre, Tarbes, and Toulouse, together with intermediate affairs. Served also in the campaign of 1815, and was present at Waterloo. Brevet-Major for Orthes and Bt.-Lieut-Col. for former services in the field (war medal with 6 clasps and medal for Waterloo). Commanding troops in Canada, 1849-1855. K.C.B., 5th February, 1856 ; G.C.B., 28th March, 1865.

Died at Bath, 25th September, 1879
Memorial in Landsdown cemetery, Bath

During the latter part of his life he resided at Bath at No. 9, Gay Street, in front of which there is still the raised stone on the kerb for the Field Marshal to mount his horse.

He was by nature reserved and reticent on the subject of his own services, marking the personal exploits dispersed throughout the memoranda which he left for publication about his campaigns "strictly private." Still, in his old age, he was fond of referring to the singular coincidence that on three of his birthdays he was in a stand-up fight, adding "never a scratch either, despite all the scrimmages big and little, I've taken part in, and save those of my country, I can safely say I never had an enemy."

EXHAM LONG HIFFERNAN

Born at Aglish Glebe, Co. Cork in September, 1830 ; son of the Revd. Thomas Exham Hiffernan, Curate of Aglish.

Asst.-Surgeon, 16th June, 1854 ; Staff, 18th March, 1862 ; 5th Foot, 1865 ; Surgeon, 19th Foot, 10th July, 1866 ; Surgeon-Major A.M.D., 1st March, 1873 : Brig.-Surgeon, 27th November, 1879.

Served in the Crimea with 19th Foot. Present at the Alma and Inkerman and during the siege of Sebastopol to 3rd July, 1855 (medal with 3 clasps and Turkish medal). Served in India during the Mutiny.
Died at Netley Hospital, 24th April, 1881.

ERNEST CHRISTIAN WILFORD

Born at Chapel Izzod, Dublin, 20th May, 1798.

Ensign, 35th Foot, 2nd December, 1814 ; Royal Staff Corps, 26th January, 1815 ; Lieut., 14th March, 1828 ; Capt., half-pay, 19th April, 1831 ; Bt.-Major, 9th November, 1846 ; Bt.-Lieut.-Col., 20th June, 1854 ; 19th Foot, 7th July, 1854 ; School of Musketry, Hythe, 27th June, 1856 ; Bt.-Col., 25th April, 1858 ; Lieut.-Col., 11th May, 1860 ; retired by sale, 10th June, 1862.

Chief Instructor, Hythe, 27th June, 1856. Author of " A Class book for the School of Musketry," 1861.
Died in 1880.

THOMAS THOMPSON

Born at St. Helier's, Jersey in December, 1818 ; son of Sergeant Thompson, 19th Foot.

Boy, 5th January, 1833 ; Pte., 5th December, 1833 ; Corpl., 26th June, 1839 ; Sergt., 14th February, 1844 ; Co.-Sergt., 1st January, 1849 ; Qr.-Mr.-Sergt., 29th July, 1854 ; Ensign, 11th August, 1854 ; Lieut., 12th January, 1855 ; Adjt., 21st September, 1855.

Served in the Crimea. Present at the Alma and Inkerman and before Sebastopol to 14th February, 1855 (medal with 3 clasps, Sardinian and Turkish medals). Served in India during the Mutiny.

Died at Capetown whilst on passage to England, 18th March, 1860.

Memorial in Forton Churchyard, near Gosport, erected by his brother officers. " The Commanding Officer cannot help bearing testimony to the exemplary manner in which he performed the duties of the responsible position which he held in the regiment, as also to the sterling worth of his character, which made him beloved and respected by all who knew him " (Extract from 1st Bn. orders).

GEORGE ALEXANDER WARBURTON

Born at Sible Hedingham, Essex, 5th January, 1829 ; son of the Revd. H. Warburton, Rector of Sible Hedingham and Rural Dean.

Ensign, 96th Foot, 15th March, 1850 ; Lieut., 9th July, 1852 ; 19th Foot, 15th August, 1854 ; Capt., 15th September, 1855 ; retired by sale, 23rd December, 1858.

Served in the Crimea. Present during the siege of Sebastopol from 22nd January, 1855, to 29th March, 1856. Acted as Adjt. at the assault on the Redan, 8th September, 1855 (medal with clasp, Sardinian and Turkish medals). Served in India during the Mutiny. Capt., the King's Own L.I. (Militia), 11th February, 1859.

Died at Folkestone, 19th May, 1891.

WILLIAM GODFREY DUNHAM MASSY, C.B.

Born in Dublin, 24th May, 1838, eldest son of Major H. W. Massy of Granstown, Tipperary.

Ensign, 27th October, 1854 ; Lieut., 9th February, 1855 ; Capt., Military Train, 20th February, 1857 ; 5th Light Dragoons, 26th February, 1858 ; Major, 23rd January, 1863 ; Lieut.-Col., 31st October, 1871 ; Bt.-Col., 31st October, 1876 ; half-pay, 15th March, 1879 ; Major-Gen., 28th August, 1886 ; Lieut.-Gen., 21st January, 1893 ; Col., 4th Dragoon Gds., 11th December, 1894 ; 5th Lancers, 4th October, 1896 ; C.B., 21st June, 1887 ; A.A.G., Bengal, 1st November, 1867—31st January, 1872 ; Brig.-Gen., Bengal, 10th April, 1879—9th April, 1884 ; Commanding Troops, Ceylon, 1st April, 1888, to 31st March, 1893 ; retired, 1st April, 1898.

Served in the Crimea. Took part in the battle of the Tchernaya and in the final assault on the Redan, 8th September, 1855, when he was dangerously wounded (mentioned in despatches, promoted Capt., Knight of the Legion of Honour, medal with clasp and Turkish medal). Presented with a sword of Honour by the students of Trinity College, Dublin, on his return from the Crimea. Served in the Afghan War, 1879-80. Commanded the Cavalry Brigade at the battle of Charasiah, 6th

October, 1879, and subsequent operations up to the fall of Kabul. Was at the capture of Sherpur, action in the Shardel Valley, sortie from Sherpur, and final pursuit of the enemy. Captured by a surprise attack, 80 guns, without the loss of a single man. Two of the field pieces, mounted on their original carriages, were presented to him by the Government and have since adorned the turrets of Granstown Hall (twice mentioned in despatches, medal with 2 clasps). Granted a reward for meritorious service.

Died at Granstown, Tipperary, 20th September, 1906. A memorial archway has been erected to his memory at Rawal Pindi, at the entrance to the Bazaar, as well as a spacious market, built by Sirdar Surjan Singh at a cost of £20,000.

ARTHUR WELLESLEY KIRBY

Ensign, 5th November, 1854 ; Lieut., 14th February, 1855.

Served in the Crimea and was present at the battle of the Alma and during the siege of Sebastopol. Was specially promoted from the ranks for service in the field.

Cashiered, 30th August, 1855.

THOMAS BEWLEY MONSELL

Born at Londonderry, 5th November, 1836 ; eldest son of the Revd. John Samuel Bewley Monsell, Rector of St. Nicholas, Guildford, Surrey, and hon. Chaplain-in-ordinary to Queen Victoria.

Ensign, 10th November, 1854 ; Lieut., 9th February, 1855.

Died on board the s.s. " Crœsus," on passage to Malta, 16th February, 1855.

HERBERT BLAKE

Born in Galway, 4th May, 1828 ; 7th son of Henry Blake of Renvyle, Co. Galway.

Ensign, 15th November, 1854.

Accidentally killed at Walmer Barracks owing to the discharge of his pistol when cleaning it, 20th April, 1855. Tombstone in the old Cemetery at Walmer, next the Marine Barracks.

FREDERICK ARTHUR

Ensign, 15th November, 1854, from Sergt., 19th Foot.

Served in the Crimea and was wounded at the Alma. Cashiered, 30th August, 1855.

HENRY JOHN BROWNE

Born in London, 14th February, 1832 ; 3rd son of Lieut.-Col. John Browne of Breaghwy, Co. Mayo.

Ensign, 22nd November, 1854 ; Lieut., 17th February, 1855 ; retired by sale, 25th August, 1861.

Served in the Crimea, including siege of Sebastopol, 2nd August to 9th September, 1855, and was present at the attack on the Redan (medal with clasp and Turkish medal). Served in India during the Mutiny.

Died in Queensland, 10th March, 1878.

RICHARD MOLESWORTH

Born in Dublin, 3rd May, 1836 ; eldest son of the Hon. Anthony Oliver Molesworth, Royal Artillery.

Ensign, 23rd November, 1854 ; Lieut., 9th March, 1855 ; Capt., 4th June, 1861 ; 1st Royal Dragoons, 16th July, 1861 ; retired by sale, 29th March, 1864.

Served in the Crimea from 1st June to 9th September, 1855. Severely wounded at the attack on the Redan (medal and clasp and Turkish medal). Served in India during the Mutiny.

Adjt. to 6th Royal Lancashire Militia, 5th January, 1865, to 31st December, 1873, retiring with the rank of Major. Appointed a Military Knight of Windsor in June, 1896.

Died at Salisbury Tower, Windsor Castle, 2nd April, 1900.

JAMES ROBERT DALTON

Born in London, 30th June, 1838 ; only son of Major-Gen. Charles Dalton, Royal Artillery.

Ensign, 24th November, 1854 ; Lieut., 9th March, 1855 ; Capt., 15th October, 1861.

Served in the Crimea from 9th March, 1856, to end of war. Served in India during the Mutiny.

Died at Battramsley House, Lymington, Hants, 4th February, 1866.

EDWARD St. JOHN GRIFFITHS

Born at Luz, France, 23rd June, 1835 ; 3rd son of John Rogers Griffiths, J.P., of Pilton, Co. Devon.

Ensign, 58th Foot, 27th October, 1854 ; 19th Foot, 15th December, 1854 ; Lieut., 9th March, 1855 ; Capt., 24th July, 1857 ; Major, 18th April, 1868 ; half-pay, 22nd March, 1876 ; Lieut.-Col., 31st March, 1877 ; retired with hon. rank of Col., 1st July, 1881.

Served in the Crimea from 3rd October, 1855, to end of war. Served in India during the Mutiny. Took part in the Hazara Campaign of 1868, including the expedition against the hill tribes on the Black Mountain (medal and clasp).

EDWARD NASSAU MOLESWORTH KINDERSLEY

Born in Madras, 28th August, 1836 ; eldest son of Nathaniel W. Kindersley, Madras Civil Service.

Ensign, 15th December, 1854 ; Lieut., 9th March, 1855 ; Capt., 7th August, 1857 ; retired by sale, 6th March, 1870.

Served in the Crimea from 6th November, 1855, to end of the war. Served in India during the Mutiny.

Died at Sherborne, Dorset, 11th November, 1907.

GEORGE STEWART NUTTING

Born at Kamptee, Madras, 28th August, 1833 ; son of Major Nutting, Grosvenor, Bath.

Ensign, 48th Foot, 13th December, 1853 ; Lieut., 19th Foot, 29th December, 1854 ; retired by sale, 18th December, 1856.

Served in the Crimea ; siege of Sebastopol, 10th August to 9th September, 1855 (medal with clasp and Turkish medal).

Died in Canada.

FRANCIS DAVIS

Born at Dromoyle, King's Co., in June, 1836 ; son of John Davis of Dromoyle.

Ensign, 5th January, 1855 ; Lieut., 11th May, 1855 ; Capt., 24th December, 1858.

Served in the Crimea before Sebastopol, 2nd to 9th September, 1855, and to end of the war (medal with clasp and Turkish medal).

Died at Parsonstown, Tipperary, of cholera, 20th October, 1866.

GEORGE FORBES

Born at Ferrintosh, Invernesshire, 1st March, 1837 ; eldest son of John Forbes of Haddo, Co. Banff.

Ensign, 12th January, 1855 ; Lieut., 10th July, 1855 ; Capt., 24th May, 1857 ; 78th Foot, 15th January, 1861 ; Bt.-Major, 5th July, 1872 ; Major, 11th July, 1877 ; Bt.-Lieut.-Col., 8th November, 1880 ; Lieut.-Col., 1st July, 1881 ; Col., 8th November, 1884.

Served in the Crimea from 1st August, 1855, to end of the war, including the final assault on the Redan (medal with clasp and Turkish medal). Served in India during the Mutiny.

Died at Victoria Hospital, Netley, 26th December, 1884.

"He was an excellent officer and was much beloved by his brother officers, and by all who knew him—in particular by the men of his regiment, in whose welfare and comfort he took the deepest interest. When he left Lucknow, as it turned out for the last time, the General of the district and his staff and all his brother officers attended at the station to bid him good-bye. He was the life and soul of any company in which he was, and his kindly, genial Scot's humour and fund of anecdotes was irresistible. He was an enthusiast in bagpipe playing, and was one of the best amateur players in Scotland. He was generally judge of pipe music at the Highland meeting at Inverness."—(Extract from the " Edinburgh Courant.")

ROBERT CONOLLY MARTIN

Born at Glanmire, Cork, 26th January, 1837 ; only son of Robert Martin, of Castle Jane Villa, Glanmire, Co. Cork.

Ensign, 26th January, 1855 ; Lieut., 31st August, 1855 ; Capt., 31st May, 1859 ; half-pay, 22nd April, 1862 ; Bt.-Major, 5th July, 1872 ; Bt.-Lieut.-Col., 13th November, 1880 ; Staff Officer of Pensioners ; retired as hon. Col., 24th August, 1881.

Served in the Crimea from 31st August, 1855, including the final assault on the Redan, where he was severely wounded in the neck (medal with clasp and Turkish medal). Served in India during the Mutiny.

Died at Cloone Grange, Mohill, Co. Leitrim, 13th December, 1903.

ROBERT JACKSON

Ensign, 22nd Foot, 12th December, 1851 (from Sergeant) ; Lieut., 19th Foot, 2nd February, 1855.

Died at Chatham, 13th February, 1855.

SACKVILLE HAMILTON MOLESWORTH EATON

Born at Castle Comer, Kilkenny, 4th May, 1828 ; son of Sackville Hamilton Eaton, 62nd Foot.

Ensign, 2nd West India Regt., 19th February, 1847;
Lieut., 14th August, 1849; 26th Foot, 31st October, 1851;
10th Foot, 13th February, 1852; 19th Foot, 9th February,
1855; retired by sale, 12th December, 1856.

CHARLES VINCENT HIFFERNAN

Born at Aglish Glebe, Co. Cork, 19th January, 1839; son
of the Revd. Thomas Exham Hiffernan, Rector of Aglish.

Ensign, 13th February, 1855; Lieut., 15th September,
1855; Capt., 28th September, 1866; 108th Foot, 13th November, 1872; retired by sale, 29th December, 1876.

Served in India during the Mutiny.

WALTER WILLIAM YOUNG

Born in Dublin, 26th July, 1838; second son of Andrew
Knight Young, M.D., of Monaghan.

Ensign, 20th February, 1855; Lieut., 14th September,
1855; 78th Foot, 10th March, 1857; retired, 16th September,
1859.

Served in the Crimea. Severely wounded at the final assault on
the Redan, 8th September, 1855 (medal with clasp and Turkish medal).
Presented with a sword of honour by the Corporation of Belfast. Also
with a massive silver salver by the County of Monaghan in appreciation
of his heroic conduct at the assault on the Redan.

Died at the Alexandra Redoubt, Auckland, N.Z., 21st August, 1865,
of rapid consumption. He was a Lieut. in the 2nd Waikato Regiment
at the time of his death.

WILLIAM HENRY MOFFATT

Born in Athlone, 7th September, 1834; son of the Revd.
James Robert Moffatt, Rector of Athlone.

Ensign, 16th March, 1855; Lieut., 12th December, 1856;
Capt., 4th February, 1862; Bt.-Major, 28th April, 1875; retired
as hon. Lieut.-Col., 13th March, 1878.

Served in the Crimea, including the fall of Sebastopol to the end
of the war (medal with clasp and Turkish medal). Served in India
during the Mutiny, and towards the close of 1860 was twice in command
of patrols engaged against the hill tribes of Sikkim. Took part in the
Hazara Campaign of 1868, including the expedition against the tribes
on the Black Mountain (medal and clasp). Appointed a Military Knight
of Windsor in March, 1904.

Died at Windsor, 20th June, 1915.

DIGBY COTES PEDDER

Born at Clevedon, 8th February, 1837; younger son of the
Revd. William Newland Pedder, Vicar of Clevedon, 1830-1871.

Ensign, 29th March, 1855; retired, 5th March, 1857;
rejoined the Service as Ensign, Indian Army, 12th March, 1860;
Lieut., 16th March, 1862; Capt., 12th January, 1872; Major,
12th March, 1880; retired as hon. Lieut.-Col., 2nd December,
1882.

Served in the Crimea from 7th September, 1855. In the trenches
during the attack on the Redan (medal with clasp and Turkish medal).
Died at Ogbourne St. George, Wiltshire, 8th September, 1918.

EDWARD HALES

Born at Enniskillen, 20th April, 1836 ; youngest son of the Revd. Edward Hales, Rector of Rossinver, Co. Leitrim.

Ensign, 30th March, 1855 ; Lieut., 24th July, 1857.

Served in the Crimea from 28th December, 1855, to end of the war. Served in India during the Mutiny.

Died at sea on passage to England in s.s. " Indus," 3rd November, 1858.

JOHN HEDLEY

Ensign, 32nd Foot, 25th February, 1848 ; Lieut., 4th April, 1851 ; 50th Foot, 24th August, 1852.

Dismissed the Service by sentence of a General Court Martial, 24th June, 1853, for ragging a brother officer.

Reinstated in his former rank and appointed to a Lieutenantcy in the 19th Foot, 30th March, 1855; 60th Foot, 11th May, 1855 ; retired by sale, 19th September, 1856.

Sir ALEXANDER BROOKE MORGAN, K.C.B., p.s.c.

Born at Secunderabad, 23rd October, 1837 ; son of Surgeon Alexander Braithwaite Morgan, 55th and 57th Foot.

Ensign, 6th April, 1855 ; Lieut., 28th November, 1857 ; Capt., 9th January, 1863 ; Bt.-Major, 15th April, 1877 ; Major, 11th May, 1878 ; 9th Foot, 7th August, 1878 ; Lieut.-Col., 21st July, 1882 ; Col., 1st April, 1889 ; retired, 11th January, 1893.

His first experience of fighting was at the Cape during the Kaffir War of 1851, while still a boy. Served in the Crimea from 28th December, 1855, to end of the war. Took part in the Indian Mutiny. Served in the Hazara Campaign of 1868, including the expedition against the tribes on the Black Mountain (medal with clasp). Served in the Afghan War, 1879-80, during the operations round Jugdullack, relief of Sherpur, and affair at Saidabad (medal and clasp). Was A.A.G. to the Indian contingent in the expedition to Egypt in 1882 (mentioned in despatches, C.B., medal with clasp, 3rd class of the Medjidieh and Khedive's star). Served in the Burmese Expedition, 1887-89 (mentioned in despatches, clasp). Also in the Chin-Lushai Expedition (mentioned in despatches, clasp). In possession of a Staff College certificate and a reward for distinguished service. K.C.B. on King's birthday, 1907.

Died at Ilkley, Yorkshire, 13th August, 1911.

The Hon. HENRY SUTTON FANE

Born, 14th January, 1804 ; 2nd son of the 10th Earl of Westmoreland.

Ensign, 63rd Foot, 18th July, 1822 ; half-pay, 29th August, 1822 ; 93rd Foot, 20th November, 1823 ; Lieut., 27th November, 1823 ; Capt. (unattached), 22nd October, 1825 ; 34th Foot, 24th October, 1825 ; Major, 18th December, 1828 ; Lieut.-Col., 9th May, 1834 ; half-pay (unattached), 9th February, 1838 ; Col., 9th November, 1846 ; Lieut.-Col., 19th Foot, 7th April, 1855 ; retired, 14th April, 1855.

M.P. for Lyme Regis, 1826-1830.

Died at Upper Brook Street, London, the residence of his sister, Lady Georgiana Fane, 7th May, 1857.

SAMUEL JOSEPH BAYFIELD

Born in London, 9th February, 1831 ; son of Samuel J. Bayfield, Surgeon, St. Thomas' Street, London.

Asst.-Surgeon, Staff, 5th May, 1854 ; 19th Foot, 1st May, 1855. To the Forces, 1st August, 1856 ; Staff-Surgeon, 25th July, 1865.

Served in the Crimea, 1st May, 1855, to 23rd July, 1856, with 19th Foot (medal and clasp and Turkish medal).

Died at sea on board the s.s. "Mooltan" on passage to Madras, 22nd October, 1865.

WALTER LACY ROGERS

Born in London, 26th January, 1831 ; 3rd son of Francis James Newman Rogers, Q.C., Recorder of Exeter.

Ensign, 4th May, 1855 ; resigned, 12th September, 1856.

Served in the Crimea from 28th December, 1855. to 27th June, 1856. M.A. of Baliol College, Oxford, 1864. B.L. Author of "Men at the Bar" and "Eton School List."

Died at Rainscombe, Marlborough, Wiltshire, 18th April, 1885.

HENRY THOMPSON

Born at Quebec, 6th December, 1836.

Ensign, 11th May, 1855 ; Lieut., 26th March, 1858 ; Indian Army, 23rd March, 1863 ; Capt., 11th May, 1867 ; Bt.-Major, 11th September, 1872 ; Major, 11th May, 1875 ; Lieut.-Col., 11th May, 1881 ; retired as hon. Col., 13th March, 1885.

Served in the Crimea from 9th March, 1856, to end of the war. Served in India during the Mutiny. Was Adjt. to the Bijnour Rajput levy during the operations in Bundlecund under Br.-Gen. Wheeler in 1859. Took part in the Looshai Expedition, 1871-2 (mentioned in despatches, Bt. of Major, medal and clasp). Served in the Afghan War of 1880 (medal).

JAMES KNOX

Born at Arcot, India, 16th July, 1837 ; son of Superintending Surgeon George Knox, Madras Army.

Ensign, 73rd Foot, 30th April, 1855 ; 19th Foot, 15th May, 1855 ; Lieut., 26th March, 1858 ; Adjt., 16th July, 1862, to 20th October, 1866; Capt., 21st October, 1866 ; half-pay, 15th April, 1871 ; 33rd Foot, 13th November, 1875 ; half-pay, 1st April, 1876; retired by sale, 16th March, 1880.

Served in the Crimea from 28th December, 1855, to end of the war, and in India during the Mutiny. Governor of Kingswood Reformatory, 1870-72 ; Governor of Gloucester Prison, 1874-1894 ; Governor of Leeds Prison, 1894-1896 ; Governor of Wandsworth Prison, 1896-1907.

Died at Melfort Road, Norbury, London, 17th December, 1912.

FRANCIS EDWARD BIDDULPH

Born at Portarlington, 2nd June, 1834 ; eldest son of Nicholas Biddulph of Congor, Borrisokane, Tipperary.

Ensign, 15th May, 1855 ; Lieut., 26th March, 1858 ; Capt., 17th July, 1863 ; 9th Foot, 5th November, 1870 ; Bt.-Major, 1st October, 1877 ; retired as hon. Lieut.-Col., 16th February, 1878.

Served in India during the Mutiny, 17th November, 1857, to 7th September, 1858.

Died at 21, Brading Avenue, Southsea, the residence of his daughter, Mrs. Fitzgerald, 16th May, 1919. Full military honours were rendered by the 3rd Bn. Leinster Regt. at Southsea, where he was buried.

CONYNGHAM JONES BACKAS

Born at Butlerstown Castle, Waterford, 24th February, 1835.

Ensign, 3rd August, 1855 ; Lieut., 26th March, 1858.

Served in India during the Mutiny.

Died at Meerut of cholera, 17th August, 1861.

GEORGE DOUGLAS HARRIS

Born in London, 10th January, 1834. Brother of the Revd. A. E. O. Harris, Vicar of Stoke, Kent.

Ensign, 17th August, 1855 ; Lieut., 15th June, 1858 ; Capt., 1st March, 1864 ; retired by sale, 20th September, 1864.

Served in the Crimea from 31st March, 1856, to 27th June, 1856. Served in India during the Mutiny.

Died at Villa d'Este, Ryde, 14th June, 1878. Memorial in Ryde Cemetery.

Took his degree as Bachelor of Laws. According to the author of " A Mingled Yarn," he served in the China War, attached to a native regiment, and was at the sacking of the Summer Palace, where he obtained much loot.

WILLIAM LEMPRIERE FREDERICK SHEAFFE

Born at Newport, Isle of Wight, 25th November, 1827 ; son of Capt. William Sheaffe, 58th Foot.

Ensign, 57th Foot, 5th December, 1844 ; 51st Foot, 31st December, 1844 ; Lieut., 6th August, 1847 ; Capt., 2nd April, 1855 ; 19th Foot, 17th August, 1855 ; retired by sale, 24th May, 1859.

Served in Burmah from June, 1852, to the end of the war, and was present in action with the enemy on the heights opposite Prome, on 12th November, 1852, and at the repulse of the night attack on Br.-Gen. Sir John Cheape's division at Prome, 8th December, 1852 (medal and clasp for Pegu). Served in the Crimea from 27th October, 1855, to August, 1856. Served in India during the Mutiny.

Died at Port Bowen, Queensland in 1863, where he was Commissioner of town lands.

GEORGE FREDERICK WEBSTER

Born at Montrose, Forfarshire, 9th May, 1831.

Ensign, 2nd West India Regt., 17th June, 1851 ; 98th Foot, 31st October, 1851 ; Lieut., 19th Foot, 31st August, 1855 ; retired by sale, 7th December, 1858.

CRANMER KENRICK

Born at Melksham, Wilts, 14th January, 1837; son of Surgeon George Cranmer Kenrick.

Ensign, 31st August, 1855; resigned, 22nd August, 1856.

FREDERICK THOMAS ONGLEY HOPSON

Born at Rochester, Kent., 6th May, 1828. Cornet, 3rd Light Dragoons, 15th August, 1848; Lieut., 15th March, 1853; half-pay, 22nd July, 1853; 10th Hussars, 4th November, 1853; 19th Foot, 7th September, 1855; Paymaster, 3rd Light Dragoons, 15th February, 1856; Hon. Capt., 15th February, 1861; 15th Foot, 20th February, 1863; Hon. Major, 15th February, 1866; retired on half-pay, 3rd April, 1878.

Served in the Crimea from 17th April to 15th July, 1855 (medal with clasp and Turkish medal). Out of the Army List, 17th January, 1881.

CHARLES HENRY LAMBERT

Born at Stoke Edith Park, Hereford, 4th March, 1830; 3rd son of Sir Henry John Lambert, Bt.

Ensign, 52nd Foot, 13th October, 1848; 36th Foot, 16th August, 1850; Lieut., 28th January, 1853; Capt., 19th Foot, 14th September, 1855; retired by sale, 4th June, 1861.

Served in India during the Mutiny.

Died in Queensland, 4th July, 1872.

HENRY AUGUSTUS JACKSON

Ensign, 80th Foot, 27th August, 1815; Lieut., 8th April, 1825; Capt., 18th December, 1835; half-pay (unattached), 19th August, 1836; Paymaster, 5th Dragoon Gds., 15th December, 1837; Bt.-Major, 9th November, 1846; half-pay (unattached), 30th June, 1848; Bt.-Lieut.-Col., 20th June, 1854; Capt. and Bt.-Lieut.-Col., 19th Foot, 2nd October, 1855; sold out, 9th October, 1855.

Died at 24, Upper Berkeley Street, Portman Square, 2nd January, 1856, aged 58 years.

WALTER MONTEFORD WESTROPP-DAWSON

Born at Malton House, Palace Kennery, Co. Limerick, 26th September, 1827; 4th son of Monteford Westropp, of Mellon, Co. Limerick.

Ensign, 76th Foot, 4th June, 1847; Lieut., 2nd January, 1854; Capt., 19th Foot, 9th October, 1855; retired by sale, 7th August, 1857.

Served in the Crimea from 25th March, 1856, to 27th June, 1856. Assumed the name of Dawson in 1859 on inheriting Charlesfort, Co. Limerick, from his uncle, Walter Dawson.

Died at The Lodge, Marston, Oxford, 17th April, 1896. Buried in Headington Cemetery, Oxford.

THOMAS DENNIS REW

Born at Westfield, Hertford, 26th March, 1828 ; son of George Rew.

Ensign, 26th October, 1855 ; Lieut., 15th June, 1858 ; Capt., 20th January, 1868 ; retired as hon. Major, 10th November, 1877. Granted the hon. rank of Lieut.-Col., 1st July, 1881.

Served in India during the Mutiny.

Died at Manor Cottage, Hertingfordbury, Herts, 3rd October, 1913.

DONALD MACLEOD FARRINGTON

Born at Cawnpore, 5th July, 1829.

Ensign, 94th Foot, 17th December, 1847 ; 98th Foot, 7th January, 1848 ; Lieut., 28th August, 1849 ; Capt., 19th Foot, 26th October, 1855 ; half-pay, 10th November, 1856 ; 4th Foot, 23rd October, 1857.

Died at Sallara, India, 15th January, 1866.

WILLIAM ROBERT ILES

Born at Laleham, Staines, 8th February, 1836 ; son of the Revd. Thomas Hodgens Iles, of Osmanthorpe, Surrey.

Ensign, 16th November, 1855 ; Lieut., 15th June, 1858 ; Capt., 2nd April, 1869 ; retired as Major, half-pay, 12th July, 1878.

Served in India during the Mutiny.

Died, 30th December, 1880.

WILLIAM RAWDING

Born at Besthorpe, Notts, 1st September, 1823 ; Pte., 60th Foot, 28th December, 1843 ; Corpl., 19th Foot, 24th February, 1846 ; Sergt., 28th February, 1848 ; Col.-Sergt., 12th April, 1854 ; Qr.-Mr., 7th March, 1856.

Served in the Crimea. Present at the Alma, severely wounded, fracture of the leg by shell and rifle fire (medal and clasp and Turkish medal). Served in India during the Mutiny.

Died at Barrackpore of fever, 5th June, 1858. Tombstone erected there by the officers of the regiment.

ROBERT HENRY HACKETT

Born at Parsonstown, King's Co., 26th August, 1339 ; 3rd son of Thomas Hackett, of Moore Park, King's Co.

Ensign, 4th April, 1856 ; Lieut., 15th June, 1858 ; Capt., 20th September, 1864 ; 90th Foot, 20th February, 1865 ; Bt.-Major, 1st October, 1877 ; Bt.-Lieut.-Col., 29th November, 1879 ; retired on pension, 15th June, 1880.

Served in India during the Mutiny. Took part in the Kaffir War of 1878, including actions of Waterkloof, Tchelen Kloof, Intaluk Udodo and Perie Bush. In the Zulu War till March, 1879. Present at the engagement at Zunguin Nek. Dangerously wounded at the battle of Kambula, whilst leading two companies, losing the sight of both eyes permanently (mentioned in despatches, Bt. of Lieut.-Col., medal and clasp).

Died at Riverstown, Parsonstown, 30th December, 1893. Buried at Lockeen Churchyard.

" A man of long service, old enough to be the father of the junior Captains, he has, I believe, been for many years the bedrock of the 90th Light Infantry. An excellent regimental officer, ever ready to counsel or aid those of his brothers whose follies or scanty purses brought them into trouble."—(Extract from a letter to the Military Secretary from Colonel Evelyn Wood.) See also Sir E. Wood's reminiscences.

RICHARD YOUNG

Son of Capt. Richard Sparkman Young, Royal Engineers.

Ensign, 98th Foot, 22nd July, 1842 ; Lieut., 28th July, 1844 ; Capt., 15th March, 1853 ; 19th Foot, 26th September, 1856 ; Adjt., Depôt Bn., Perth, 31st October, 1856 ; Capt., 15th Foot, 9th March, 1858 ; Adjt., 19th Depôt Bn., 30th April, 1858 ; Major, 3rd February, 1860 ; Lieut.-Col., half-pay, 4th September, 1865 ; retired by sale, 1st February, 1873. Local Lieut.-Col. when employed as Asst.-Inspector of Volunteers, 11th February, 1862—October, 1865.

Served with the 98th Foot in the Punjab Campaign of 1848-49 (medal).

ARTHUR WESTBROOKE BURTON

Born in Daventry, Northampton, 24th May, 1839 ; son of Edmund Singer Burton of Churchill House, Co. Northampton.

Ensign, 2nd December, 1856 ; Lieut., 16th July, 1858 ; sold out, 22nd September, 1865.

Served in India during the Mutiny.

Died on board the s.s. " Behar " off Ceylon, 29th December, 1865. Memorial in All Saints' Cemetery, Galle.

FREDERICK GEORGE FRITH

Born in Dublin, 30th May, 1839 ; eldest son of Henry Frith, Ordnance Office, Dublin Castle.

Ensign, 3rd March, 1857 ; Lieut., 4th November, 1858 ; Capt., 17th April, 1866 ; 74th Foot, 29th May, 1866 ; 65th Foot, 2nd October, 1866 ; retired, 20th July, 1867.

Served in India during the Mutiny.

Died at Barton Tower, Canterbury, 30th October, 1905.

For several years was Governor of H.M.'s Prisons at Gloucester and Canterbury.

JAMES CASTOR SMITH

Born in Co. Mayo, 1st September, 1832.

Asst.-Surgeon, Staff, 1st September, 1854 ; 21st Foot, 3rd August, 1855 ; to the Forces, 1st August, 1856 ; 19th Foot, 14th July, 1857.

Served in the Crimea with the 21st Foot. Siege of Sebastopol and expedition to Kinburn (medal with clasp and Turkish medal). Served in India during the Mutiny.

Died at Ferozepore, Punjab, 13th February, 1864, of hepatitis.

GEORGE VALENTINE MUNDY, C.B.

Born at Brighton, 14th February, 1819 ; 4th son of Gen. Godfrey Basil Mundy of Bramcote, Notts.

Ensign and Lieut., Coldstream Gds., 27th February, 1835 ; Lieut. and Capt., 1st May, 1840 ; 33rd Foot, 10th September, 1841 ; Bt.-Major, 11th September, 1851 ; Bt.-Lieut.-Col., 12th December, 1854 ; Major, 20th December, 1854 ; Lieut.-Col., 19th Foot, 17th July, 1857 ; Col., 24th April, 1860.

Served with the Coldstream Gds. during the Canadian Rebellion of 1838-39. Took part in the Crimean War—battles of the Alma (horse shot), Inkerman and siege of Sebastopol (twice mentioned in despatches, twice slightly wounded and once severely, medal and 3 clasps, Knight of the Legion of Honour, 5th class of the Medjidieh, Sardinian and Turkish medals). Served in India during the Mutiny.

Died at 42, Bryanstone Street, Portman Square, London, 14th May, 1863.

He was a page of honour to Queen Victoria. "Brimful of wit and humour, an excellent billiard player (the amateur championship rested between him and the late Lord Eglinton), and the most fertile raconteur in the British Army" ("A Mingled Yarn," by E. Spencer Mott, 19th Foot).

WALLER LANGFORD SAINSBURY

Born, 18th May, 1838 ; son of the Revd. Sainsbury Langford Sainsbury, Beckington, Frome, Somerset.

Ensign, 25th August, 1857 ; 60th Foot, 18th September, 1857 ; Lieut., 16th December, 1859 ; sold out, 11th September, 1860.

A second battalion was formed at Exeter in March, 1858, and added to the regiment.

PHILIP DOYNE VIGORS, p.s.c.

Born at Burgage, Co., Carlow, 23rd December, 1825 ; 7th son of the Revd. Thomas Mercer Vigors of Burgage.

Ensign, 11th Foot, 9th October, 1846 ; Lieut., 19th July, 1850 ; Adjt., 27th May, 1856 ; Capt., 19th Foot, 9th March, 1858 ; Major, 7th March, 1870 ; Bt.-Lieut.-Col., 1st October, 1877 ; Lieut.-Col., 15th March, 1879 ; retired, 12th January, 1881.

Died at Holloden, Bagnalstown, Co. Carlow, 30th December, 1903. There is a carved oak episcopal throne in Leighlin Cathedral to his memory.

High Sheriff, Co. Carlow, 1894. F.R.S.A. Ireland. Founder of the association for the preservation of the memorials of the dead in Ireland. "Whatever his hand found to do, he did it with all his might. He was a cultured, scholarly man, who in every relationship of life strove faithfully to do his duty." (Extract from the journal of the above association.)

JAMES DAY COCHRANE

Born at Devonport in 1823 ; 2nd son of Col. James Johnston Cochrane, Scots Fusilier Gds.

Ensign, 91st Foot, 31st December, 1841 ; Lieut., 13th October, 1843 ; Capt., 4th May, 1849 ; half-pay (unattached), 7th September, 1855 ; 19th Foot, 9th March, 1858 ; retired in June, 1858.

Served with the 91st in the operations against the Kaffirs and was severely wounded (shot through the body and left hand) on the 18th April, 1846, when covering the rear of Col. Somerset's division, during the retreat from the Amatola mountains to Block Drift. Served with the regiment in Greece in 1855.

Died at 46a, Pall Mall, S.W., 3rd March, 1867.

WILLIAM SERJEANT ARNOLD

3rd son of Thomas Arnold of Hopperford Hall, Warwickshire.

Ensign, 67th Foot, 13th August, 1847 ; Lieut., 31st January, 1857 ; Capt., 19th Foot, 9th March, 1858 ; 67th Foot, 13th April, 1858.

Died at Barrackpore, 10th August, 1859.

JOHN ANDERSON

Born in Dublin, 5th May, 1828 ; son of John Anderson, County Inspector, Royal Irish Constabulary, Summerhill, Nenagh.

Ensign, 51st Foot, 25th June, 1847 ; Lieut., 18th April, 1851 ; Capt., 19th Foot, 9th March, 1858 ; Major, 11th May, 1878 ; Bt.-Lieut.-Col., 11th May, 1878 on retirement.

Served with the 51st throughout the Burmese War of 1852-3. Was on board the East India Co.'s steam frigate " Sesostris " during the naval action and destruction of the enemy's stockade on the Rangoon river, and served during the succeeding three days' operations in the vicinity and at the storm and capture of Rangoon, and assault and capture of Bassein, 19th May, 1852 (medal with clasp).

Died at the Lawn, Staplegrove, Taunton, 20th June, 1899.

EDWIN FLETCHER FOSTER

Born in Ceylon, 18th June, 1828 ; son of Lieut-Col. Isaac Foster, Ceylon Rifles and 3rd West India Regt.

Ensign, 70th Foot, 23rd April, 1847 ; 84th Foot, 30th April, 1847 ; 50th Foot, 6th July, 1849 ; Lieut., 80th Foot, 7th January, 1853 ; 81st Foot, 27th May, 1853 ; Capt., 19th Foot, 9th March, 1858 ; retired by sale, 27th February, 1865.

His father, when in the Ceylon Rifles, was taken prisoner by the Kandians in 1818, and was rescued when the rebels were in the act of suspending him from a tree (Smith's Obituary).

GEORGE LEWIS DIVE AMIEL

Ensign, 64th Foot, 20th December, 1839 ; Lieut., 55th Foot, 1st July, 1842 ; 89th Foot, 30th August, 1844 ; 10th Foot, 2nd May, 1845 ; Capt. (unattached), 9th March, 1855 ; 48th Foot, 10th March, 1855 ; half-pay, 7th Foot, 2nd May, 1856 ; 19th Foot, 9th March, 1858 ; retired by sale, 30th April, 1858.

Served with the 10th Foot in the Sutlej Campaign of 1845-48, including the battle of Sobraon (medal). Also in the early part of the siege operations against Mooltan in 1848, and in the action of Soorjkoond (medal). Appointed a Military Knight of Windsor, 16th June, 1883.

Died at Windsor, 22nd June, 1890.

JOHN RICHARDSON STUART

Son of Col. William Keir Stuart, C.B., 86th Foot.

Ensign, 86th Foot, 23rd March, 1844 ; Lieut., 13th December, 1847 ; Capt., 19th Foot, 9th March, 1858 ; retired by sale, 30th December, 1859.

Served in India during the Mutiny.

Died at Victoria, 15th May, 1872.

CHARLES HEREFORD

Born at Tenby, South Wales, 12th October, 1835 ; 3rd son of Richard Hereford, of Sufton Court, Hereford.

Ensign, 39th Foot, 17th August, 1855 ; Lieut., 17th July, 1857 ; 19th Foot, 23rd March. 1858 ; Capt., 30th December, 1859 ; Bt.-Major, 5th July, 1872 ; Major, 29th November, 1876 ; Lieut.-Col., 12th January, 1881 ; half-pay, 4th March, 1885 ; retired as Hon. Major-Gen., 8th July, 1885.

Died at Twickenham, 14th July, 1891.

JOHN RINNIE MACKENZIE

Born in Lancashire, 25th June, 1833.

Ensign, 30th Foot, 17th August, 1855 ; Lieut., 4th December, 1857 ; 19th Foot, 23rd March, 1858 ; Capt., 2nd March, 1860 ; 1st Foot, 23rd June, 1863 ; retired by sale, 21st August, 1866.

FRANK WILLIAM DUNDEE

Born, 21st May, 1828.

Paymaster, 3rd Middlesex Militia, 14th April, 1855 ; 19th Foot, 23rd March, 1858 ; 3rd Foot, 4th August, 1863 ; Hon. Major, 23rd March, 1873 ; Staff Paymaster, 1st April, 1878 ; retired as hon. Lieut.-Col., 16th July, 1887.

Died at Worthing, 27th March, 1898.

Sir LUMLEY GRAHAM, Bart.

Born in London, 28th February, 1828 ; 2nd son of Sir Sandford Graham, Bart., of Kirkstall, York.

Ensign, 43rd Foot, 13th August, 1847 ; Lieut., 28th February, 1851 ; Capt., 41st Foot, 7th July, 1854 ; Bt.-Major, 12th December, 1854 ; Major, 9th March, 1856 ; Bt.-Lieut.-Col., 6th June, 1856 ; 19th Foot, 25th March, 1858 ; Bt.-Col., 4th December, 1864 ; 18th Foot, 29th September, 1865 ; retired on half-pay, 25th September, 1869.

Served in the Kaffir War, 1851-53 (medal). In the Crimean War, being present at the Alma, Inkerman, and siege of Sebastopol, severely wounded, right arm amputated (medal with 3 clasps, Knight of the Legion of Honour, 5th class of the Medjidieh, Turkish medal, Brevets of Major and Lieut.-Col.).

Died at Arlington Manor near Wantage, 25th October, 1890, the result of a carriage accident.

Succeeded to the baronetcy, 2nd May, 1875. Author of " Remarks on Infantry Tactics," Sandgate, 1866 ; " A New System of Infantry Tactics " ; " The best mode of providing recruits and forming reserves for the British Army," London, 1874.

WILLIAM BENNETT, D.S.O.

Born at Athlone, 15th November, 1835; son of Captain Thomas Bennett, 14th Hussars.

Ensign, 26th March, 1858; Lieut., 30th December, 1859; Capt., 25th August, 1871; Major, 12th January, 1881; Lieut.-Col., 4th March, 1885; Bt.-Col., 4th March, 1889; half-pay, 17th July, 1889; Capt.-Instructor, Hythe, 31st July, 1877—28th February, 1878; D.A.A.G. Musketry, Aldershot, 1st March, 1878—28th February, 1881; retired, 15th November, 1890.

Served in the Hazara campaign of 1868, and in the expedition against the tribes of the Black Mountain (medal with clasp). Took part in the Nile expedition, 1884-5, on the Staff (medal with clasp and Khedive's star). Commanded 1st Bn. 19th Foot in the Soudan expedition of 1885-6, including the action of Ginnis (Distinguished Service Order).

Died at Whitby, Yorkshire, 2nd August, 1912.

A musketry expert and in his day one of the best shots in the Army.

JOHN CAMPBELL TAYLOR HUMFREY

Born at Niagara, 31st August, 1840; son of Dr. William Charles Humfrey, M.D., C.B., Inspector General of Hospitals.

Ensign, 27th March, 1855; Lieut., 19th March, 1860; Adjt., 8th November, 1870; Capt., 16th August, 1873; 9th Foot, 10th February, 1877; Paymaster, 8th August, 1880; Hon. Major, 8th August, 1885; Staff-Paymaster, 16th August, 1892; Lieut.-Col., 16th August, 1897; retired, 20th January, 1902.

Served in the Hazara expedition of 1868, including the expedition against the tribes on the Black Mountain (medal with clasp). Served in the Jowaki campaign of 1877-8 (clasp). Also in the Afghan War of 1878-80 in charge of field treasure chest, and as Provost-Marshal on the Staff of Sir R. O. Bright, K.C.B. (medal and clasp for Ali Musjid).

Died at Blackheath, 28th January, 1905.

JOHN JAMES MACDONALD

Qr.-Mr., 30th March, 1858, from the 2nd Jagers British-German Legion; 71st Foot, 29th July, 1862; retired on half-pay, 16th November, 1866.

Died at Maidstone, 14th July, 1867.

FREDERICK MONTAGUE ALISON

Born at Possil House, near Glasgow, 11th May, 1835; 2nd son of Sir Archibald Alison, Bt., the Historian.

Ensign, 72nd Foot, 17th October, 1851; Lieut., 1st September, 1854; Capt., 19th Foot, 13th April, 1858; Bt.-Major, 26th April, 1859; unattached, 28th January, 1862; Major, 4th February, 1862; Lieut.-Col., 4th June, 1870.

Served in the Crimea, 13th June, 1855, to May, 1856, including the expedition to Kertch as A.D.C. to Sir Colin Campbell, and attack on the Redan on 18th June (medal with clasp and Turkish medal), was A.D.C. to Lord Clyde in India from August, 1857 to July, 1860. Present at the relief of Lucknow (wounded), battle of Cawnpore, 6th December, 1857, action of Kala Nuddee, siege and fall of Lucknow. Took part in the Rohilcund campaign, including the actions and occupation of Shahjehanpore and Bareilly, also in Biswarra and Transgogra campaigns, and actions of Dondiakara, Musjidia, Burgidia, and final action on the Raptee (Brevet of Major, medal and 2 clasps).

Died at Innes House, Elgin, 1st February, 1872.

WILLIAM BRETTON KITTSON

Ensign, 13th April, 1858 ; resigned, 22nd November, 1858.

HENRY SOLLERS GUNNING SPARKS KNIGHT

Born at Grahamstown, Cape Colony, 12th September, 1828 ; son of Thomas Sollers Knight, Cape Mounted Rifles.

Ensign, 21st Foot, 2nd September, 1845 ; Lieut., 3rd June, 1847 ; 67th Foot, 22nd December, 1848 ; Capt., 30th October 1857 ; 19th Foot, 13th April, 1858 ; Bt.-Major, 5th July, 1872 ; Major, 29th November, 1876 ; retired as hon. Lieut.-Col., 29th November, 1876.

Died at the Observatory, Littleton, Winchester, 13th October, 1904.

GEORGE FRANCIS VESEY

Born at Long Ditton, West Surrey, 2nd May, 1839 ; 3rd son of Captain George Vesey, 9th Lancers.

Midshipman R.N., 1854. Ensign, 19th Foot, 14th April, 1858 ; Lieut., 24th December, 1858 ; Capt., 8th May, 1866 ; 43rd Foot, 14th September, 1866 ; Bt.-Major, 31st December, 1878 ; Major, 1st July, 1881 ; Lieut.-Col., 8th July, 1885 ; Col., 8th July, 1889 ; retired, 1st July, 1891.

Served as a midshipman in the Baltic fleet, 1854 (medal). Served in India during the Mutiny. With a detachment of the 43rd, attacked and destroyed a party of Mopla fanatics at Colotore, Malabar, on the 8th September, 1873, when he was thanked by the Madras Government.

Died at the Vicarage, Whitchurch, Hants, 26th July, 1899.

THOMAS HARTWELL KIRBY

Born at Limerick, 23rd March, 1838 ; son of P. M. Kirby, Controller in H.M's. Customs.

Ensign, 15th April, 1858 ; Lieut., 11th February, 1859 ; Capt., 7th August, 1863 ; 22nd Foot, 22nd June, 1870 ; Major. 1st July, 1881 ; retired as hon. Lieut.-Col., 23rd March, 1888.

Served with the 22nd in the Burmese campaign of 1887-89 (medal with clasp).

Died in Dublin, 11th April, 1904. Buried in Southsea.

HENRY WALTER HOPE

Born, 17th August, 1839, at Ditton Park, Slough, 2nd and eldest surviving son of George William Hope, D.L., M.P., of Luffness, Co. Haddington.

Ensign, 23rd April, 1858 ; Ensign and Lieut., Grenadier Gds., 7th December, 1858 ; Lieut. and Capt., 3rd October, 1862 ; retired, 8th August, 1865.

After his retirement he joined the Berwickshire Yeomanry and left with the rank of Major after twelve years' service. Provincial Grand

Master of the East Lothian Freemasons. From 1869-1871, Master of the East Lothian Hunt. In 1875 bought large properties in Algeria, and was one of the Commissioners appointed by the Governor General, Gen. Chauzy, to arrange and direct the railway development of Algeria. Pioneer of golf in East Lothian and laid out the first 18-hole course between Edinburgh and London.

Died at Luffness, 25th October, 1913.

HORACE ARTHUR WELLS

Born in the Isle of Thanet, 5th July, 1840.

Ensign, 24th April, 1858 ; Lieut., 2nd December, 1859.

Died at Nowshera, 28th June, 1867.

MARCUS WILLIAM O'RORKE

Son of the Revd. John O'Rorke, of Moylough House, Galway, and Rector of Foxford, Co. Mayo.

Ensign, 25th April, 1858 ; 60th Foot, 28th May, 1858 ; Lieut., 16th April, 1861 ; Capt., 24th April, 1869.

Died at Beckenham, Kent, 19th April, 1871.

PHILIP DOWNES WILLIAMS

Born, 4th June, 1841 ; son of Penry Williams, J.P., D.L., of Penpont, near Brecon.

Ensign, 26th April, 1858 ; Lieut., 2nd December, 1859 ; Capt., 18th April, 1868.

Died at Penpont, 1st March, 1869.

BRUMHEAD ROGERS

Ensign, 30th April, 1858 ; Lieut., 2nd March, 1860 ; sold out, 18th July, 1862.

Died at Tooting, Surrey, 10th November, 1908, aged 68.

WILLIAM READ

Sergt.-Major, Royal Engineers, 1st April, 1853 ; Ensign and Adjt., 19th Foot, 7th May, 1858 ; Lieut., 4th June, 1861 ; half-pay, 29th December, 1865 ; retired with rank of Capt., 1st July, 1881.

DONALD MACPHERSON

Born in London, 6th October, 1833.

Asst.-Surgeon, Staff, 10th March, 1858 ; 19th Foot, 7th May, 1858 ; Surgeon, Army Med. Dept., 1st March, 1873 ; Surgeon-Major, 1st April, 1873.

Died at Fort Grange, Gosport, 12th May, 1873, from blood poisoning. Buried at Haslar Hospital.

DUNCAN CAMPBELL AFFLECK

Probably son of Surgeon Duncan Affleck, 95th and 74th, Foot, who was married at St. Mary's Newry, 29th September, 1838, to Margaret Anne, daughter of Lt.-Col. Campbell, K.H., 95th Foot.

Ensign, 14th May, 1858 ; 42nd Foot, 5th November, 1861 ; retired, 21st December, 1862.

WILLIAM JOHN FOSTER

Born at Southsea, 27th January, 1835 ; son of the Revd. W. Foster.

Ensign, 46th Foot, 21st February, 1855 ; Lieut., 2nd October, 1855 ; 19th Foot, May, 1858 ; Capt., 8th July, 1859 ; half-pay, 5th July, 1872 ; retired in July, 1875, with rank of Major.

Served in the Crimea from 18th August, 1855, with the 46th Foot (medal with clasp and Turkish Medal).

Died at Hillsborough, Bath, 18th November, 1910.

EDGAR ANGELO DICKENSON

Born in Dublin, 12th September, 1838.

Ensign, 28th May, 1858 ; Lieut., 18th August, 1861 ; retired by sale, 3rd March, 1868.

GEORGE ROGERS

Ensign, 49th Foot, 15th January, 1856 ; Lieut., 19th Foot, 15th June, 1858 ; retired by sale, 19th August, 1862.

Capt., West Yorkshire Militia, 26th April, 1873.

Died at 19, Gloucester Terrace, Hyde Park, on the 27th June, 1917, in his 80th year.

JOHN T—— U—— COXEN

Ensign, 25th June, 1858 ; 60th Foot, 2nd July, 1858 ; superseded for absence without leave, 8th April, 1859.

WILLIAM FREDERICK THOMAS MARSHALL

Born at Mauritius, 21st October, 1829 ; son of Colonel George Marshall, Royal Marines.

Ensign, 65th Foot, 13th March, 1840 ; Lieut., 7th February, 1851 ; 70th Foot, 18th October, 1851 ; Capt., 19th Foot, 2nd July, 1858 ; Major, 1st April, 1870 ; half-pay, 1st April, 1870 ; retired by sale, 17th July, 1872.

Served in the Indian Mutiny, 1857-8 as Station Staff-Officer at Murree, Punjab, when attacked by a large force of hill men on the night of 1st September, 1857, and during the following three days. Joined the army at Delhi, 24th September, 1857 (medal). Served in the Hazara campaign of 1868, including the expedition against the tribes on the Black Mountain (medal and clasp).

Died at Teignbridge House, near Newton Abbot, Devon, 29th September, 1872.

GEORGE EDWARD CHARTRES BISSETT   •

Born at Swanage, 21st August, 1831.

Ensign, 56th Foot, 20th October, 1848 ; Lieut., 8th November, 1850 ; 55th Foot, 4th April, 1851 ; Capt., 21st September, 1854; half-pay, 17th April, 1857 ; 19th Foot, 2nd July, 1858 ; retired by sale, 31st May, 1859.

Served in the Crimea, including the battle of the Alma (severely wounded), and siege of Sebastopol, 6th September, to fall. (Medal with 2 clasps and Turkish medal).

Died at Dinan, France, of acute bronchitis, 26th March, 1865.

THOMAS MADDEN

Qr.-Mr., 24th Foot, 12th October, 1849 ; Ensign and Adjt., 12th December, 1851 ; Lieut., 11th October, 1854 ; Capt., 19th Foot, 2nd July, 1858 ; sold out, 8th July, 1859.

Served with the 24th in the Punjab campaign of 1848-9, including the passage of the Chenah, and battles of Sadoola, Chillianwallah, and Goojerat (medal and clasps).

AUGUSTUS MOURANT HANDLEY

Born at Dorchester, 28th November, 1838 ; son of the Revd. Augustus Bernard Handley, Rector of West Fordington, Dorchester.

Ensign, 2nd July, 1858 ; Lieut., 15th October, 1861 ; Capt., 23rd January, 1869 ; Major, 7th June, 1879 ; Lieut.-Col., 29th September, 1882 ; Col., 29th September, 1886 ; retired, 29th September, 1888.

Served in the Hazara campaign of 1868, including the expedition against the tribes on the Black Mountain (medal and clasp).

Died at Clifton, Bristol, 27th February, 1906.

Extract from a letter from the Secretary of the National Association for the employment of Reserve Soldiers : " To place on record in the minutes their great appreciation of the late Colonel Handley's services, extending over so long a period in connection with this Society, and to say how deeply they feel the loss of one who so unsparingly and zealously devoted himself to the interests of the Association and the welfare of ex-soliders."

RALPH FITZGIBBON LEWIS

Ensign, 86th Foot, 27th October, 1846 ; Lieut., 30th July, 1849 ; Capt., 19th Foot, 2nd July, 1858 ; 86th Foot, 8th July, 1858 ; Bt.-Major, 23rd March, 1860 ; sold out, 31st January, 1868.

Served with the Central India Field Force in 1858, and commanded three companies 86th Foot during the siege of Chandaree, and was slightly wounded at the storming of the fort ; present at the battle of Betwa and siege and capture of the town and fortress of Jhansi (twice wounded, once dangerously, mentioned in despatches, brevet of Major, medal and clasp).

" Severely wounded at Jhansi by a sword cut which extended from the right shoulder to the left hip and presented a frightful spectacle. To the astonishment of all he recovered " (Historical Record Royal Irish Rifles).

JAMES FRANCIS FRASER

Born at Frankfort, 5th February, 1840 ; elder son of Col. A. Fraser of Rugby.

Ensign, 3rd July, 1858 ; Lieut., 18th July, 1862 ; Capt., 26th November, 1874 ; retired with hon. rank of Major, 27th April, 1881.

Served in the Hazara campaign of 1868, including the expedition against the tribes on the Black Mountain (medal and clasp).
Died at Culduthel, Richmond, Yorkshire, 27th April, 1910.

FRANCIS HERBERT EVANS

Born at St. Helier's, Jersey, 5th December, 1839 ; son of George Edward Evans.
Ensign, 4th July, 1858 ; retired, 14th September, 1861.

THOMAS CONWAY LLOYD

Born at Brecon, 23rd July, 1828 ; eldest son of John Lloyd, of Dinas House, Co. Brecon.
Ensign, St. Helena Regt., 18th April, 1851 ; Adjt., 26th November, 1852 ; Lieut., 4th Foot, 24th April, 1855 ; Capt., 19th Foot, 13th July, 1858 ; 84th Foot, 4th May, 1860 ; retired by sale, 18th April, 1865.
Served in the Crimea, 27th February to 21st July, 1856. Colonel Commandant 1st Breconshire Volunteers (South Wales Borderers). J.P. and D.L. for Brecon. In possession of the Volunteer decoration.
Died at Dinas House, 29th October, 1893.

BEAUCHAMP COLCLOUGH

Born in Dublin, 16th August, 1828 ; son of Beauchamp Urquhart Colclough, of Elm Grove, Carlow.
Ensign, 62nd Foot, 4th July, 1855 ; Lieut., 19th Foot, 13th July, 1858 ; Adjt., 21st September, 1864—7th March, 1870 ; Capt., 7th March, 1870 ; retired, 28th October, 1873.
Died at 25, Victoria Grove, Southsea, 30th March, 1900.

CHARLES JAMES FORBES-SMITH

Son of the Revd. James Smith, Rector of Vere, Jamaica.
Ensign, 32nd Foot, 27th July, 1855 ; Lieut., 19th Foot, 13th July, 1858 ; retired by sale, 17th April, 1860.

ROBERT CAYER TRAILL

Born at Ballylough, Co. Antrim, 21st November, 1839 ; 2nd son of William Traill of Ballylough.
Ensign, 14th July, 1858 ; Lieut., 5th November, 1861 ; Capt., 3rd March, 1870 ; retired, 20th March, 1880.
Served in the Hazara campaign of 1868, including the expedition against the tribes on the Black Mountain (medal and clasp). Called to the Irish Bar, 1895. For over ten years was a resident magistrate in Ireland, 1880-1893.
Died at Belfast, 5th March, 1908.

HENRY EDWARD JEROME, V.C.

Born at Antigua, 26th February, 1830 ; son of Captain Joseph Jerome, 86th Foot.
Ensign, 86th Foot, 21st January, 1848 ; Lieut., 30th April, 1852 ; Capt., 19th Foot, 23rd July, 1858 ; Bt.-Major, 1st July, 1859 ; Bt.-Lieut.-Col., 15th September, 1870 ; Major, 62nd Foot, 23rd May, 1873 ; half-pay, 15th July, 1876 ; Col., 31st July, 1879 ; retired on hon. Major-Gen., 9th September, 1885.

Served in the Indian Mutiny, 1857-59, including the storming and capture of Chundaree, operations against the rebel tribes of Goojerat, siege and capture of Jhansi (mentioned in despatches). Action of Koonch, and various engagements before Calpee (severely wounded mentioned in despatches). Distinguished himself at the siege of Thausi, when under a murderous fire he assisted in rescuing Ensign Sewell who was severely wounded. He was conspicuous for gallantry against a superior force of the enemy at Calpee, and was also mentioned in despatches for leading a storming party at the capture of Chundaree (Victoria Cross, Bt. of Major, medal and clasp). Served in the Hazara campaign of 1868, including the expedition against the tribes on the Black Mountain (medal and clasp). In receipt of a reward for meritorious and distinguished service. Was recommended for the Victoria Cross on three separate occasions, viz., 17th March, 3rd April, and 28th May, 1858.

Died at Bath, 25th February, 1901. There is a memorial to him at Lansdown, Bath.

" In stature and appearance, he much resembled Napoleon, being short, and towards the last years of his life inclined to stoutness. Pallid, with a face slightly acquiline, destitute of beard, the hair scanty above a high forehead, deeply scored where the Imperial lock was set, by a rebel shot at Calpee. Nor did the similarity end here for Jerome—part French in blood—was, like the great Emperor by dispostion, reserved, brooding, silent, and of that mystic turn of mind prone to the study of metaphysical science and abstruse doctrines " (Extract from letter to G.H.G.).

CORTLANDT SKINNER

Born at Dacca, India, 3rd September, 1839; 3rd son of Russell Morland Skinner, of Shirley Park, Surrey.

Ensign, 7th August, 1858 ; Lieut., 25th February, 1862 ; Capt., 29 October, 1873 ; sold out, 24th February, 1877.

ROBERT BATES

Ensign, 45th Foot, 6th June, 1834 ; Lieut., 25th December, 1838 ; Capt., 15th October, 1845 ; Bt.-Major, 6th June, 1856 ; Major, 9th March, 1858 ; 19th Foot, September, 1858 ; 83rd Foot, 1st July, 1863 ; retired with rank of Lieut.-Col., 2nd May, 1865.

Served with the 45th in the Kaffir campaign of 1846-7 (medal).
Died at Folkestone, 12th July, 1894, aged 77 years.

CHARLES USHERWOOD

Born at Worsboro' Dale, Yorkshire, 7th July, 1831.

Private, 6th January, 1852 ; Corpl., 25th February, 1854 ; Sergt., 10th May, 1854 ; Col.-Sergt., 23rd September, 1857 ; Qr.-Mr.-Sergt., 2nd July, 1858 ; Qr.-Mr., 7th September, 1858 ; 8th Foot, 25th February, 1862 ; half-pay, 20th May, 1864.

Served in the Crimea. Present at the Alma, Inkerman, and during the siege of Sebastopol up to the evacuation of the Crimea (medal with 3 clasps and Turkish medal). Served in India during the Mutiny.
Died at Usk, South Wales, 22nd December, 1880.

GEORGE HEWETSON REYNOLDS

Born at The Mullens, Ballyshannon, Co. Donegal, 21st January, 1837 ; eldest son of Robert Reynolds of The Mullens.

Ensign, 15th October, 1858 ; Lieut., 19th August, 1863 ;

Capt., 24th June, 1876 ; Major, 1st July, 1881 ; retired, 18th November, 1882.

Died at The Mullens, 18th May, 1895.

"Few men at one time were better known in the Service than " Joe " Reynolds. He was an authority on horse-flesh, full of high spirits and an inveterate practical joker. A thoroughly capable officer, devoted to his regiment and beloved by his comrades of all ranks. There are few Green Howards who will hear unmoved that he has passed suddenly away " (G.H.G.).

CONSTANTINE CHARLES BARROW TRIBE

Born at Chatham, 11th November, 1839.

Ensign, 19th November, 1858 ; Lieut., 25th August, 1862 ; Capt., 94th Foot, 27th September, 1876 ; Army Pay Dept., 16th May, 1879.

Served in the Hazara campaign of 1868, including the expedition against the tribes on the Black Mountain (medal and clasp). King's Scholar, Rochester, 1854.

Died at the camp, Aldershot, 12th May, 1879, when attached as Paymaster to 41st Foot.

MARTIN TUCKER

Ensign, 24th December, 1858 ; Lieut., 9th January, 1863 ; sold out, 6th March, 1867.

WILLIAM KELMAN CHALMERS, M.D.

Born at Fraserburgh, Aberdeenshire, 31st July, 1825.

Asst.-Surgeon, 18th Foot, 13th November, 1846 ; Surgeon, 12th January, 1855 ; 34th Foot, 5th June, 1857 ; 19th Foot, 31st December, 1858 ; half-pay, 2nd September, 1862 ; Staff, 9th October, 1863.

Served with the 18th Foot in the Burmese War of 1852-53 (medal) ; also in the trenches at the siege and fall of Sebastopol (medal with clasp and Turkish medal).

Died at Capetown, 2nd March, 1864.

HENRY FOWLE SMITH, M.D.

Born at Weyhill, Andover, 13th December, 1824.

Asst.-Surgeon, 16th Foot, 23rd March, 1847 ; Staff, 16th March, 1854 ; Surgeon, 12th January, 1855 ; 19th Foot, 31st December, 1858 ; Staff, 16th August, 1859 ; Surgeon-Major, 23rd March, 1867 ; retired on half-pay as Deputy Surgeon-Gen., 24th April, 1875.

Served in the Crimea, 1854-55. Was attached to Head Quarters, and was not absent a single day from duty. Had medical charge of the staff belonging to the Adjutant and Quarter-Master General's Departments, and subsequently on the personal staff of Sir James Simpson and Sir William Codrington. Present at the Bulganac, Alma, Balaclava, Inkerman, siege and fall of Sebastopol (medal with 4 clasps, 5th Class of the Medjidieh and Turkish medal).

Died at Gretna, 5th August, 1906.

THOMAS HEWLETT

Born at Abingdon, 29th June, 1835 ; son of —— Hewlett, Headmaster of Abingdon Grammar School, 1829-1849.

Assist.-Surgeon, 1st February, 1859; resigned, 13th November, 1861.

Died at 102, Nicholson Street, Fitzroy, Victoria, 28th September 1904. For 42 years in active practice in Fitzroy.

ALEXANDER BREDIN

Born at Prospect Forgney, 10th October, 1837; son of Thomas Bredin, of Prospect Forgney, Ireland.

Ensign, 11th March, 1859; Lieut., 5th February, 1866; Indian Army, 23rd February, 1869; Capt., 23rd February, 1873; Major, 11th March, 1879; Lieut.-Col., 11th March, 1885; Col., 11th March, 1889; placed on the unemployed supernumerary list, 10th October, 1894.

WILLIAM JOSEPH LYNCH

Born in Galway, 1835; youngest son of Patrick Marcus Lynch, of Duras and Renmore, Co. Galway.

Ensign, 18th March, 1859; Lieut., 17th July, 1863; half-pay, April, 1871.

Died at St. Leonard's-on-Sea, 14th December, 1874.

HENRY STOKES

Born in London, 19th January, 1842.

Ensign, 31st May, 1859; Lieut., 1st March, 1864; retired, 2nd December, 1868; Captain, Middlesex Militia, 11th May, 1872, and retired from it in 1883.

Died at Millhill House, Crowmarsh, Preston, Oxford, in June, 1906.

GEORGE ARCHIBALD WARDEN

Eldest son of George Warden, of Liverpool.

Ensign, 3rd June, 1859; Lieut., 19th September, 1864; 66th Foot, 10th November, 1865; sold out, 1st August, 1868; Captain, Carlow Militia, 4th March, 1869.

DANIEL JAMES MANSERGH

Born, 3rd November, 1836; eldest son of the Revd. James Wentworth Mansergh, Rector of Kilmore, Diocese of Cashel.

Ensign, 14th June, 1859; Lieut., 14th August, 1859; sold out, October, 1863.

Capt., Tipperary Militia, 14th April, 1864; Major, 5th Bde., South Irish Dn. Royal Artillery Militia, 23rd November, 1881; Hon. Lieut.-Col., 6th June, 1885; Hon. Col., 5th August, 1885.

Died at Grallagh Castle, Tipperary, 27th April, 1907.

ALEXANDER DUNLOP ANDERSON

Born, 3rd February, 1841; son of Alexander Dunlop Anderson, M.D., of Glasgow.

Ensign, 10th Foot, 4th September, 1858; 19th Foot, 15th July, 1859; Lieut., Indian Army, 1862; Capt., 4th September, 1870; Major, 4th September, 1878.

Took part in the Abyssinian War, 1868, being present at the action of Arogee, 10th April, and at the storming and capture of Magdala, 13th April (mentioned in despatches, medal). Served in the Afghan War of 1878 with the 23rd Punjab Pioneers.

Killed in the attack on the Peiwar Kotal, 2nd December, 1878.

HENRY BOLTON HASSARD, C.B.

Born at Cava House, Fermanagh, 28th November, 1829; son of Capt. Jason Hassard, 74th Highlanders, of Rockingham, Co. Waterford.

Asst.-Surgeon, Cape Mounted Rifles, 14th March, 1851 ; Surgeon, Staff, 28th January, 1858 ; 19th Foot, 16th August, 1859; Surgeon-Major, 14th March, 1871; 56th Brigade Depôt, 29th October, 1873 ; Deputy Surgeon-Gen., 13th February, 1879; Surgeon-Gen., 20th November, 1884 . retired, 29th November, 1888.

C.B., 22nd February, 1881. P.M.O., Ireland, 1884-88. In receipt of a reward for distinguished and meritorious service, 1888.

Took part in the Kaffir War, 1851-53 (medal). Served in the Hazara campaign of 1868, including the expedition against the tribes on the Black Mountain (medal with clasp). Took part in the Afghan War, 1878-79, with General Bright's column (medal).

Died at Portsmouth, 2nd July, 1892.

CHARLES EDWARD WIKELEY, M.R.C.S., L.S.A.

Born at Leeds, 26th April, 1833 ; son of Thomas Wikeley, of Leeds.

Asst.-Surgeon, Staff, 12th January, 1859 ; 19th Foot, 15th November, 1859 ; Staff, 25th December, 1867 ; Surgeon, 1st March, 1873 ; Surgeon-Major, 1st April, 1874 ; retired as hon. Brigade Surgeon, 2nd February, 1884.

WILLIAM IRVINE

Born at Hull, 6th August, 1842 ; eldest son of Lieut.-Col. Charles Irvine, of Cookstown, Co. Tyrone.

Ensign, 9th March, 1860.

Died at Kurachee, 31st March, 1864.

JAMES GORDON MOIR

Born at Fateghur, India, 16th March, 1842 ; only son of George Gordon Moir.

Ensign, 10th March, 1860 ; Lieut., 16th May, 1865 ; Adjt., 10th June, 1867—22nd February, 1870 ; Capt., 7th September, 1871 ; retired, 28th October, 1871.

Served in the Hazara campaign of 1868, including the expedition against the tribes on the Black Mountain (medal and clasp).

Died at 87, Elgin Crescent, London, W., 11th July, 1903. Buried in Kensal Green.

MONTGOMERY WILLIAMS

Born at Walcot, Bath, 22nd August, 1837 ; son of Capt. Lawrence Blount Williams, R.N.

Ensign, 67th Foot, 22nd July, 1856 ; 84th Foot, 14th

August, 1857; Lieut., 29th November, 1857; Capt., 21st February, 1860 ; 19th Foot, 4th May, 1860 ; Bt.-Major, 5th July, 1872 ; Major, 23rd January, 1878 ; 100th Foot, 13th March, 1878; Lieut.-Col., 1st July, 1881; Col., 1st July, 1885 ; half-pay, 29th September, 1886 ; Commanding 100th Regtl. District, 25th November, 1886 ; half-pay, 25th November, 1891 ; retired, 22nd August, 1894.

Served in the Indian Mutiny in the Shuhabad district until its suppression there, 6th March, 1858 to 2nd September, 1859 (medal). Took part in the Hazara campaign of 1868, including the expedition against the tribes on the Black Mountain (medal and clasp).

EDWARD TURNER

Ensign, 15th June, 1860 ; sold out, 15th October, 1861.

CHARLES GILBERT FRYER

Born in 1845 ; son of the Revd. Henry Edmund Fryer, M.A., of Burley Wood, Hants.

Ensign, 14th August, 1860 ; 60th Foot, 4th September, 1860 ; Lieut., 6th October, 1864 ; Capt., 2nd January, 1873 ; half-pay, 28th April, 1875 ; retired by sale in January, 1877.

Died at Winchester, 23rd September, 1919.

FREDERICK KNOWLES

Born at Meerut, 1st October, 1835 ; son of Captain Frederick Knowles, 3rd King's Own Light Dragoons.

Ensign, Indian Army, 13th August, 1857 ; 19th Foot, 22nd September, 1860 ; Indian Army, 4th September, 1863 ; Capt., 4th September, 1872 ; Major, 13th August, 1877 ; Bt. Lieut.-Col., 18th November, 1882 ; Lieut.-Col., 13th August, 1883 ; Col., 18th November, 1886 ; retired, 13th August, 1889.

Served as assist. field engineer at the siege and capture of Delhi. Was at the siege and capture of Lucknow and relief of Azinghur (wounded, medal and clasps and one year's service). Served with the 2nd Bengal Cavalry in the Egyptian War of 1882, and was present at the action of Kassasin (9th September), and at the battle of Tel-el-Kebir and capture of Cairo (mentioned in despatches, Bt. of Lieut.-Col., medal with clasp, 3rd Class of the Medjidieh and Khedive's Star). Received his first commission for service in the field.

Died at 29, Tisbury Road, Brighton, 1st April, 1900.

WILLIAM ROBERT THORNHILL

Born at Skerries, Co. Dublin, 10th February, 1840 ; son of William Thornhill, M.D., of Dublin.

Ensign, 25th September, 1860 ; Lieut., 22nd September, 1865 ; Capt., 29th November, 1876 ; Army Pay Dept., 1st April, 1878 ; Hon. Major, 1st April, 1883 ; Staff Paymaster, 16th January, 1884 Hon. Lieut.-Col., 16th January, 1891.

Served in the Egyptian War of 1882 with the 42nd Foot (medal and Khedive's Star), and in the Nile expedition of 1884-85 (clasp).

Died at St. Thomas' House, London, 27th September, 1894.

WILLIAM McGREGOR ARCHER

Born in Edinburgh, 6th September, 1825.

Ensign, 10th Foot, 1st April, 1842; 78th Foot, 8th April, 1842 ; Lieut., 28th October, 1844 ; Capt., 13th December, 1856; 19th Foot, 15th January, 1861.

Served in the Persian War at the bombardment of Mohumrah under Sir J. Outram (medal with clasp). Served in India at Bithoor under General Havelock, at Bunterah under General Grant, relief of Lucknow under Sir John Campbell, defence of the position of the Alumbagh under Sir J. Outram, siege and capture of Lucknow, campaign in Rohilcund, capture of Bareilly under Sir Colin Campbell (medal and 2 clasps).

Died at Clifton, 1st April, 1861.

GEORGE ALBERT MACDONNELL

Ensign, 8th February, 1861 ; 18th Foot, 18th February, 1862 ; Lieut., 18th December, 1867.

Died at Naples, 29th July, 1872.

Sir ABRAHAM JOSIAS CLOETÉ, K.H., K.C.B.

Born in 1794 ; 2nd son of the Hon. Peter Lawrence Cloeté, of the Elms, Southampton, Member of Council, Cape of Good Hope.

Cornet, 15th Hussars, 29th June, 1809 ; Lieut., 17th May, 1810 ; Capt., 5th November, 1812 ; Bt.-Major, 21st November, 1822 ; Bt. Lieut.-Col., 10th January, 1837 ; Major, 12th September, 1848 ; Col., 11th November, 1851 ; Major-Gen., 31st August, 1855 ; Col., 19th Foot, 10th March, 1861 ; Lieut.-Gen., 21st December, 1862 ; Gen., 25th October, 1871.

Served as A.D.C. to Lord Charles Somerset at the Cape from 1814-17 from where he was sent in command of a detachment to take military possession of the island of Tristan d' Acunha. Served with a squadron of his regiment detached as a field force during the Pindaree and Mahratta war from 1817-19. In 1842, commanded the successful expedition sent to Natal to relieve a detachment besieged by insurgent Boers. Served as Deputy Qr.-Mr. General in the Kaffir campaign of 1846 (C.B.). During the Kaffir war of 1851-53 served as chief of the Staff to the Army in the field, including the operations in the Basuto country and the battle of Bereia, where he commanded a division (medal). In acknowledgement of his services received the honour of knighthood and was subsequently nominated K.C.B. In possession of a reward for distinguished service, 30th August, 1853. In command of the Windward and Leeward Islands, 1855-1861.

Died in London, 26th October, 1886.

Sir GEORGE DIGBY BARKER, G.C.B., p.s.c.

Born at Clare Priory, Suffolk, 9th October, 1833, son of John Barker, of Clare Priory.

Ensign, 78th Foot, 21st January, 1853 ; Lieut., 16th March, 1855 ; Adjt., 5th November, 1858, to 1st April, 1861 ; Capt., 19th Foot, 2nd April, 1861 ; Bt.-Major, 17th September, 1861 ; 64th Foot, 26th November, 1861 ; Major, 94th Foot, 21st January, 1874 ; Bt.-Lieut.-Col., 23rd April, 1872 ; Col., 1st October, 1877 ; Major-Gen., 14th May, 1887 ; Lieut.-Gen., 1st January, 1895 ; Gen., 6th April, 1900 ; Col., North Staffordshire Regt., 7th February, 1905 ; Seaforth Highlanders, 20th August, 1911 ; placed on retired list, 30th January, 1902.

Served in the Persian War of 1857, under Sir J. Outram. Present at the battles of Khosab, bombardment of Mohumrah and expedition to Ahwaz (medal and clasp). Served in Bengal with Havelock's column from its first taking the field in 1857, including the actions at Futtehpore, Aoung, Pandoo Nuddee, Cawnpore, Onoa, Busseratgunge (first and second), Boorhea-ke-chowkee, and the several actions leading to and ending in the relief of the Lucknow Residency, and subsequent defence, including several sorties (wounded). Was with Outram's force at Alumbagh and in the operations ending in the final capture of Lucknow, where he officiated as D.A.A.Q.M.G., 1st Division (mentioned in despatches). Served in the Rohihcund campaign of 1858, and capture of Bareilly (mentioned in despatches, Bt. of Major, medal and two clasps, and a year's service for Lucknow). C.B. in 1889, K.C.B. in 1900, and G.C.B. in 1912. Granted a distinguished service reward in May, 1893. Commanded the troops in China and Hong Kong, 1890-1895, and was Governor of the Bermudas 1896-1902.

Died at Clare Priory, Suffolk, 15th April, 1914.

His letters home from Persia and India, 1857-1859, were published in 1915.

GEORGE OAKES

Born at Bury St. Edmund's, 23rd January, 1843, 4th son of the Revd. Hervey Aston Adamson Oakes, Rector of Nowton, Suffolk.

Ensign, 11th June, 1861 ; Lieut., 29th December, 1865 : Capt., 16th June, 1877 ; Major, 1st July, 1881 ; Lieut.-Col., 28th July, 1886 ; Bt.-Col., 28th July, 1890 ; half-pay, 28th July, 1892 ; retired, 10th May, 1893.

Proceeded to the Cape with drafts during the Zulu War, 1879, and served with the Field Force during the latter phase of the war.

Died at " The Branthams," near Ipswich, 26th November, 1896. Buried at Stowmarket.

WALTER BALFE

Born, 16th July, 1835, son of Christopher Walter Balfe, of Heathfield, Co. Roscommon.

Cornet, 1st Dragoons, 27th January, 1857 ; Lieut., 19th February, 1858 ; Capt., 16th October, 1860 ; 19th Foot, 16th July, 1861 ; 17th Lancers, 2nd December, 1862 ; half-pay, 12th July, 1865 ; 13th Hussars, 29th June, 1866 ; Bt.-Major, 29th August, 1873 ; Major, 3rd April, 1878 ; Lieut.-Col., 18th May, 1881 ; Col., 18th May, 1885 ; half-pay, 18th May, 1886 ; retired, 16th July, 1890.

Died in Dublin, 4th May, 1899.

ARTHUR EDWARD TROTTER TROTTER

Born at Wimbledon, 1st February, 1843, son of William Trotter Brown, of Horton Manor, Surrey.

Ensign, 23rd August, 1861 ; Lieut., 17th April, 1866 ; Capt., 28th October, 1871 ; retired, 7th August, 1880.

Assumed the name of Trotter, 3rd December, 1868.

Died at Folkestone, 3rd June, 1887.

GEORGE FEARON THORP

Eldest son of George Thorp, of Upper Gloucester Street, Dublin.

Ensign, 15th October, 1861 ; Lieut., 28th September, 1866 ; Indian Army, 1st March, 1871.

Died at Poungday, 9th March, 1873, when acting as Assist. Commissioner of Burmah.

SAMUEL GORDON M'DAKIN

Only son of Captain M'Dakin, of Boultham, Lincoln.

Ensign, 42nd Foot, 23rd October, 1855 ; Lieut., 24th May, 1861 ; 19th Foot, 5th November, 1861 ; half-pay, 22nd December, 1863 ; retired, 6th July, 1869.

Served with the 42nd Highlanders in the campaign of 1857-58 against the mutineers of India, including the actions at Cawnpore (6th December, 1857), Seriaghat, Khoda-gunzi, and Shumsabad, siege and fall of Lucknow, and assault of Martinière and Bank's bungalow, attack and capture of Bareilly, attack on the fort of Rooyah, and action of Allygunge (medal and clasp).

GODFREY LYON KNIGHT

Born at Boulogne, 3rd November, 1827, only son of Col. Edward Knight, late 15th Hussars and Portuguese Service.

Ensign, 63rd Foot, 28th February, 1845 ; Lieut., Ceylon Rifles, 17th March, 1848 ; 64th Foot, 9th January, 1849 ; Capt., 29th November, 1857 ; 19th Foot, 26th November, 1861.

Served in the Persian campaign of 1857, including bombardment of Mohumrah (medal and clasp). Took part in the Indian Mutiny, 1857-58, including operations around Cawnpore under Major-Gen. Windham, defence of Cawnpore, defeat of the Gwalior mutineers and action of Kallee Nuddee (medal).

Died on passage to India, 24th August, 1862.

THEODORE BOSVILLE EMERSON

Born at Bath, 12th July, 1843, son of the Revd. Alexander Lyon Emerson, B.A., of West Buckland, Somerset.

Ensign, 13th December, 1861 ; Lieut., 8th May, 1866 ; Capt., 10th November, 1877 ; Major, 1st July, 1881 ; retired, 17th December, 1881 ; Lieut.-Instr., School of Musketry, Hythe, 1st October, 1874—8th June, 1877.

Died at Abbey View Villa, Bath, 15th November, 1883.

AGATHUS HENRY ELSTER

Born in London, 8th August, 1843.

Ensign, 20th Foot, 8th February, 1861 ; 19th Foot, 28th January, 1862 ; retired, 18th July, 1862.

EDWARD SPENCER MOTT

Born at Wall Grange, Lichfield, 7th April, 1844, 2nd son of William Mott, J.P., D.L.

Ensign, 18th February, 1862 ; Lieut., 5th June, 1866 ; retired by sale, 30th October, 1869.

Known as "Nathaniel Gubbins," a constant contributor to the "Pink 'un." Author of "A Mingled Yarn," in which he tells of his life in the Green Howards. "Cakes and Ale," "Clear the Course,"' "Wanted a Wife," "The Flowing Bowl," "My Hostess," etc., etc. Died at Gresham College, Ewell, Epsom, 5th January, 1910.

JOHN WYNN GRIFFITH

Born at Llanfair, 23rd September, 1843.

Ensign, 25th February, 1862 ; 86th Foot, 5th May, 1863 ; sold out, 11th October, 1864.

JOHN KEATINGE

Born in Dublin, 13th August, 1828.

Pte. 8th Foot, 9th April, 1846 ; Corpl., 13th June, 1849 ; Sergt., 1st January, 1852 ; Qr.-Mr.-Sergt., 19th November, 1858 ; Qr.-Mr., 23rd September, 1859 ; 19th Foot, 25th February, 1862 ; 63rd Foot, 19th September, 1871.

Served in the Indian Mutiny, siege and capture of Delhi, actions of Bolundshur Allyguch and battle of Agra (10th October, 1857). Relief of Lucknow, under Sir Colin Campbell, defeat of the rebels at Cawnpore, action of Kallee Nuddee (medal and 2 clasps). Recommended for the Victoria Cross for saving the life of an officer. Served in the Hazara campaign of 1868, including the expedition against the tribes on the Black Mountain (medal and clasp). Died at Hazareebaugh, India, 21st March, 1872.

RICHARD THOMAS SWEENEY

Ensign, 83rd Foot, 1st December, 1848 ; Lieut., 3rd June, 1851 ; Capt., 2nd September, 1858 ; half-pay, Royal Waggon Train, 6th June, 1860 ; 19th Foot, 22nd April, 1862 ; retired by sale, 8th May, 1863.

Died at his brother's residence, Alma Road, Monkstown, Co. Dublin, 30th January, 1865.

THOMAS PERCIVAL PALMER

Born, 2nd November, 1839, eldest son of Thomas Palmer, J.P., of Summerhill, Co. Mayo.

Ensign, 20th Foot, 16th May, 1862 ; 19th Foot, 18th July, 1862 ; sold out, 10th November, 1865.

JOHN JAMESON

Born at Glasgow, 26th September, 1843, son of John Jameson, Solicitor, Penrith, Cornwall.

Ensign, 18th July, 1862 ; Lieut., 7th August, 1866 ; Capt., 24th November, 1877 ; Major, 1st July, 1881 ; retired as hon. Lieut.-Col., 19th July, 1882.

Served in the Hazara campaign of 1868, including the expedition against the tribes on the Black Mountain (medal and clasp). Died at Ardunan, Strathblane, Stirling, 4th January, 1899.

FRANCIS PATRICK STAPLES, M.R.C.P.I., M.R.C.S.

Born at Creg House, Mayglass, Wexford, 14th December, 1838, son of James Staples, of Creg.

Assist.-Surgeon, Staff, 1st April, 1861 ; half-pay, 16th

September, 1861 ; Staff, 22nd April, 1862 ; 19th Foot, 29th July, 1862 ; Staff, 18th August, 1869 ; Surgeon-Major, 1st April, 1876 ; Bgde.-Surgeon Lieut.-Col., 20th September, 1887 ; retired, 1st February, 1888.

Served in the Hazara campaign of 1868, including the expedition against the tribes on the Black Mountain (medal and clasp).

JAMES TWIGG

Qr.-Mr., 71st Foot, 20th September, 1860, from half-pay, British Swiss Legion ; 19th Foot, 29th July, 1862 ; retired, 2nd December, 1862.

ABNEY HASTINGS CAMERON

Born at Frankfort, 16th April, 1842, son of Lieut.-Gen. Cameron, late 95th Foot.

Ensign, 19th August, 1862 ; Lieut., 21st October, 1866.

Served in the Ashantee expedition of 1873, under Captain Glover, R.N., as Assist. Commissioner. Was placed in charge of Addah Fo and the Volta, where he was employed in disciplining the new levies of Houssas and Yourabas. Crossed the Volta with a large force as 2nd in command on 23rd December, and was in action the next day. Passed through Coomassie with the rear guard in February, 1874 (medal and clasp).

Died at Parkhurst Barracks, 6th October, 1877.

WILLIAM TYDD HARDING, L.R.C.S.I.

Born at St. Vincent, 4th January, 1832, son of Captain Henry Harding, 18th Foot.

Assist.-Surgeon, 12th Depôt Bn., 13th May, 1853 ; 25th Foot, 25th September, 1860 ; Surgeon, Staff, 28th January, 1862 ; 19th Foot, 2nd September, 1862 ; Staff, 14th September, 1866 ; 56th Foot, 1st February, 1867 ; Staff, 4th August, 1870 ; Surgeon-Major, 1st March, 1873 ; half-pay, 27th May, 1879, when he retired as Hon. Deputy Surgeon-Gen.

Died at Rathmines, Dublin, 30th November, 1892.

WILLIAM CALDERHEAD

Qr.-Mr., 2nd December, 1862, from Sergt.-Major.

Served in the Crimea before Sebastopol (medal and clasp and Turkish medal).

Died at Thayetmyo, Burmah, 20th June, 1864, aged 46 years.

JOHN GIBSONE

Born in Edinburgh, 4th May, 1838, eldest son of General John Charles Hope Gibsone, J.P., D.L., late 7th Dragoon Gds., of Pentland, Co. Edinburgh.

Cornet, 17th Lancers, 8th December, 1854 ; Lieut., 26th February, 1856 ; Capt., 27th May, 1859 ; 19th Foot, 2nd December, 1862 ; retired by sale, 17th July, 1863 ; Adjt., Leicester Yeomanry Cavalry, 18th September, 1863--1st January, 1885 ; Hon. Major, 12th February, 1885.

Served with the 17th Lancers in the Crimea, including the battle of the Tchernaya and siege and fall of Sebastopol (medal with clasp and Turkish medal). Took part in the Indian Mutiny campaign under Sir John Michel, action of Baroda and minor affairs, 1858-59 (medal).

Died at Redcross Lodge, Leamington, 12th May, 1913.

HERBERT LEIGH GIPPS

Born in London, 6th April, 1845.

Ensign, 9th January, 1863 ; Lieut., 3rd April, 1867 ; Capt., 24th November, 1877 ; Adjt., North York Rifles, 28th April, 1879—27th April, 1884 ; retired as hon. Lieut.-Col., 6th August, 1884.

Died at Llandrindod Wells, 19th June, 1905. Buried in Hambledon Churchyard, Canterbury.

REGINALD CHALMER, C.B.

Born at Lambert House, near Falkirk, 12th July, 1844, 2nd son of Major Francis Day Chalmer, 7th Dragoon Gds., of Larbert, Stirlingshire.

Ensign, 17th March, 1863 ; Cornet, 1st Dragoon Gds., 23rd June, 1863 ; Lieut., 21st February, 1865 ; 60th Foot, 14th September, 1866 ; Adjt., 10th November, 1869—5th November, 1873 ; Capt., 2nd April, 1874 ; Bt.-Major, 2nd March, 1881 ; Major, 1st July, 1881 ; Lieut.-Col., 15th October, 1890 ; Bt.-Col., 15th October, 1894 ; retired, 15th October, 1894.

Served with the 60th Rifles in the Afghan War from February, 1879, to November, 1880, during the occupation of Candahar and as Bde.-Major to Br.-Gen. Barter's brigade, and was present in the engagement at Ahmed Kheyl and Urzoo, near Ghuznee (mentioned in despatches), and in the subsequent operations in the Logan Valley ; accompanied Sir F. Roberts in the march to Candahar as Bde.-Major to Br.-Gen. Macgregor's brigade, and was present at the battle of Candahar (mentioned in despatches, medal and 2 clasps and bronze star). Also served as Bde.-Major to Br.-Gen. Macgregor in the Marri expedition (mentioned in despatches). Served in the Boer War of 1881 with the 60th Rifles in the Natal Field Force. Took part in the Manipur expedition in 1891, in command of 4th Bn. 60th (mentioned despatches, medal with clasp and C.B.). D.A.A. and Q.M.G., Aldershot, 1882-1887.

Died in London, 28th December, 1911.

GEORGE ONSLOW

Born, 30th April, 1839, 4th son of Richard Foley Onslow, of Stardene, Gloucestershire.

Ensign, 58th Foot, 26th February, 1858 ; Lieut., 20th July, 1859 ; Capt., 27th May, 1862 ; 1st Foot, 23rd September, 1862 ; 19th Foot, 24th March, 1863 ; retired by sale, 7th August, 1866.

Died, 6th March, 1880.

FREDERICK SALE SOWLEY BRIND

Born at Dum Dum, Bengal, 29th March, 1839, son of Col. Frederick Brind, C.B., Bengal Horse Artillery.

Ensign, 44th Native Infantry, 4th March, 1857 ; Lieut., 30th April, 1858 19th Foot, 24th March, 1863 ; Capt., half-pay, 1st April, 1870 ; 17th Foot, 24th September, 1870 ; Bt.-Major,

22nd November, 1879 ; Major, 1st July, 1881 ; retired as hon. Lieut.-Col., 27th September, 1882.

Served in the Indian Mutiny, 1857-60, with the 66th Ghoorka N.I., at the actions of Huldwharree and Charpoorah, in the second Oude campaign, and with Ross' Camel Corps in Central India as Adjt. and Qr.-Mr., and commanded detachments engaged in clearing the Marawara district of rebels (medal). Served in the Hazara campaign of 1868, including the expedition against the tribes on the Black Mountain, as orderly officer to Br.-Gen. R. O. Bright (mentioned in despatches, medal and clasp). Took part in the Afghan War, 1878-79, with the Peshawar Valley Field Force, and was present at the action of Futtehabad (mentioned in despatches, Bt. of Major, medal).

Died at Bournemouth, 18th January, 1912.

For many years in charge of the Liverpool and Manchester Division of the Corps of Commissionaires, from which he retired in 1898.

HERBERT BOULCOTT

Born at Clapham, Surrey, 6th February, 1842, 2nd son of John Almond Boulcott of Ryde, I. of W.

Ensign, 86th Foot, 14th February, 1860 ; 19th Foot, 5th May, 1863 ; Lieut., 20th April, 1867 ; retired by sale, 10th May, 1870.

Served in the Hazara campaign of 1868 (medal and clasp).

Died at Upcross, Westend, Hants, 18th February, 1909.

WALTER St. JAMES YOUNG

Ensign, 23rd June, 1863 ; 38th Foot, 28th August, 1863 : Lieut., 2nd October, 1866 ; Capt., 29th July, 1874 ; retired by sale, 24th March, 1875.

HENRY DE RENZY PIGOTT

Born at Eagle Hill, Loughrea, Galway, 18th May, 1825, youngest son of Captain Henry Pigott, 82nd Foot, J.P., Co. Galway.

Ensign, 83rd Foot, 22nd July, 1845 ; Lieut., 19th September, 1848 ; Capt., 7th May, 1854 ; Major, 19th December, 1862 ; 19th Foot, 30th June, 1863 ; Lieut.-Col., 25th August, 1871 ; 70th Foot, 14th August, 1872 ; Col., 25th August, 1876 ; Commanding, 40th Regt. District, 1st April, 1881 ; retired as hon. Major-Gen., 8th February, 1882.

Served in the Indian Mutiny, including the reduction of the fort of Arrah, January, 1858, siege of Kotah and its capture by assault, 23rd March, 1858 ; action of Sangeneer, 8th August, defeat of the Gwalior rebels in Bumar's River, 14th August, 1858 (medal and clasp). Asst. Executive Engineer, Sinde, March, 1856, to August, 1857. Deputy Judge Advocate, Central India Field Force, Musserabad, 9th February to July, 1859. Served in the Afghan War of 1878 with the Chotiah Field Force (medal).

Died at Elkhorn, Manitoba, 14th November, 1889.

"He was a commanding officer of the old school, an accomplished soldier, and a fine horseman ; his stern system of discipline kept his regiment in a high state of efficiency and made a permanent impression on the character of those who served under him" (Records of the East Surrey Regt.).

ALFRED JAMES PATERSON, p.s.c.

Born in Edinburgh, 15th February, 1846, son of Dr. James Paterson, M.D., 42nd Foot.

Ensign, 17th July, 1863 ; Lieut., 29th June, 1867 ; Adjt., 22nd February, 1870—19th February, 1878 ; Capt., 1st January, 1878 ; Major, 1st July, 1881 ; Lieut.-Col., 29th September, 1886 ; Col., 29th September, 1890.

Bde.-Major, Aldershot, 4th February, 1882 to 18th September, 1886 ; Asst.-Inspector of Musketry, 14th Depôt Bn., 9th November, 1866—16th November, 1868 ; retired, 29th March, 1893.

Died at the Red House, Fleet, Hants, 23rd December, 1914.

" He was a keen and energetic officer, alert and very capable ; with a marvellous memory and knowledge of every detail of drill and office work ; impatient it may be with those less active than himself in mind and body, but always genial and kindly. There are few who cannot recall acts of personal kindness received from him. He will be remembered best as an exceptionally good Adjutant at a time when the chief burden of the work of the battalion centralized in that office " (G.H.G.).

JAMES WRAY

Paymaster, 1st Light Infantry British-Swiss Legion, 9th July, 1855, from the Victoria Rifles ; 5th Foot, 7th November, 1857 ; Hon. Capt., 7th November, 1862 ; 19th Foot, 11th August, 1863 ; 3rd Foot, 30th October, 1866 ; Hon. Major, 14th April, 1871 ; Staff-Paymaster, 1st April, 1878 ; Hon. Lieut.-Col., half-pay, 21st June, 1884 ; omitted from the half-pay list, 31st March, 1895.

HENRY WALKER

Born at King's Lynn, Norfolk, 29th August, 1830.

Asst-Surgeon, Staff, 12th January, 1859 ; half-pay, 21st July, 1860 ; 19th Foot, 27th August, 1863 ; Staff, 30th October, 1869 ; 3rd Foot, 3rd July, 1872 ; Surgeon, Army Medical Staff, 1st March, 1873 ; Surgeon-Major, 1st April, 1874.

Died in Cape Colony, 25th June, 1879.

LORNE ROBERT HENRY DICK CAMPBELL, C.B.

Born in India, 11th February, 1846, eldest son of Major-Gen. Archibald Lorne Campbell, Bengal Cavalry.

Ensign, 28th August, 1863 ; Lieut., 20th January, 1868 ; Indian Army, 28th July, 1869 ; Capt., 28th August, 1875 ; Major, 28th August, 1883 ; Lieut.-Col., 28th August, 1889 ; Bt.-Col., 15th January, 1895 ; Col., 3rd November, 1899 ; hon. Major-Gen., unemployed supernumerary list, 14th February, 1903 ; Col., 38th Dogras, 13th May, 1904 ; retired, 1st January, 1904.

Served in the Hazara campaign of 1868 as orderly officer to Br.-Gen. Wilde, C.B., C.S.I. (medal and clasp). Took part in the Dour Valley expedition, 1872, and the Afghan War, 1878-9, including action in the Kundil Pass and Baghao, and affair at Synd Boot (mentioned in despatches, medal). Served in the Mahsood Wazeeree expedition in 1881, attached to the signalling department (mentioned in despatches). Also in the China expedition of 1900 in command of the lines of communications (mentioned in despatches, C.B., medal and clasp).

Died at Cheltenham, 27th May, 1913.

CROSBIE BARTON

Born in Dublin, 29th June, 1845, 3rd son of Samuel William Barton, of Rochestown, Co. Tipperary.

Ensign, 29th August, 1863; Lieut., 4th March, 1868; Capt., 23rd January, 1878; Major, 17th December, 1881; retired as hon. Lieut.-Col., 13th October, 1886.

Served in the Boer War with 18th Imperial Yeomanry (mentioned in despatches, medal and clasps, promoted Lieut.-Col., Reserve of Officers).

Died at the Lodge, Frampton-on-Severn, Gloucestershire, September, 1902.

ANDREW STEWART

Ensign, 98th Foot, 26th February, 1856; Lieut., 7th May, 1858; 84th Foot, 17th January, 1859; half-pay, 19th December, 1862; 19th Foot, 22nd December, 1863; 64th Foot, 22nd December, 1863; resigned his commission, 9th September, 1864.

Served with the 98th Foot in the Peshawar Expeditionary Force on the Euzofzie Frontier, under Sir Sydney Cotton in April and May, 1858, and at the affair with the Hindostanee fanatics on the heights of Sittana, 4th May (medal and clasp).

JOHN FRANCIS JAMES MILLER

Born at Bombay, 22nd October, 1846, son of J. B. Miller, of Inneyshields, Renfrewshire.

Ensign, 1st March, 1864; Lieut., 8th September, 1868; Indian Army, 15th April, 1869; Capt., 1st March, 1876; Major, 1st March, 1884; Lieut.-Col., 1st March, 1890; retired, 6th March, 1899.

Served in the Hazara campaign of 1868, including the expedition against the tribes on the Black Mountain (medal and clasp). Served in the Afghan War, 1879-80 with 23rd Pioneers, and as field engineer, Kurram Valley Field Force (medal).

Died at Pershore, Worcestershire, 7th January, 1917.

CHARLES JAMES MAYNARD HALLEWELL

Born, 16th November, 1833, youngest son of Edmund Gilling Hallewell, of Stratford Park, Stroud.

Ensign, Cape Mounted Rifles, 13th February, 1858; Lieut., 19th Foot, 22nd March, 1864; retired by sale, 5th June, 1866.

Died at Deepdene, Bathampton, Bath, 20th October, 1919.

D'URBAN WILLIAM FARRER BLYTH

Ensign, 43rd Foot, 7th March, 1856; Lieut., 24th May, 1858; Capt., 19th Foot, 2nd May, 1864.

Served with the 43rd in the Indian Mutiny from December, 1857, to January, 1860, including actions at Sahao Dooleypore, and Parraha.

Commanded a detachment of the 43rd at Putowrie. Thanked by the Governor-General (medal). Also served in the New Zealand War, 1864-65, including expeditions in province of Taranaki, destroying many pahs and fortified villages.

Died at Rangoon, 19th January, 1868.

WILLIAM MALONEY

Pte. 80th Foot, 13th October, 1839 ; Corpl., 2nd March, 1842 ; Sergt., 6th May, 1843 ; Col.-Sergt., 27th November, 1845 ; Qr.-Mr.-Sergt., 13th April, 1852 ; Qr.-Mr., 23rd October, 1855 ; 6th Foot, 10th March, 1860 ; Depôt Bn., 17th November, 1863 ; 19th Foot, 20th June, 1864 ; 74th Foot, 16th May, 1865 ; 5th Depôt Bn., 23rd October, 1867 ; Hon. Capt., half-pay, 20th June 1869 ; retired, 1st July, 1881.

It is on record that he was shipwrecked on the voyage from New South Wales to India on 12th November, 1844. It appears that he and others were on voyage to India in the transport "Briton," which was wrecked on one of the lesser Andaman Islands which was uninhabited. They suffered terrible privations for 51 days. Ultimately they constructed a boat in which a party embarked, and after being 21 days at sea reached the Burmah coast, when relief was despatched.

Served with the 80th Foot in the Sutlej campaign of 1845-46, including the battles of Moodkee, Ferozeshah and Sobraon (medal and two clasps). Also served in the Burmese War of 1852-3, including the capture of Martaban, operations before Rangoon, and capture of Prome (medal with clasp for Pegu). Served in the Indian campaign of 1858-59, including the affairs of Hurra, Simree, Bera, Dhoondeakeira and Busingpore (medal).

Appointed a military Knight of Windsor in March, 1875, and Governor, 24th April, 1896.

Died at Windsor, 17th August, 1905.

HENRY BADELEY

Born at Chelmsford, 27th May, 1842, son of John Carr Badeley, F.R.C.P., Guy Harlings, Chelmsford.

Ensign, 28th June, 1864 ; Lieut., 2nd December, 1868 ; 98th Foot, 17th April, 1869 ; retired, 22nd July, 1871.

Died, 17th November, 1880.

ALFRED WESTERN HATCHELL HORNSBY-DRAKE

Born at St. Helena, 30th November, 1845, son of Major Romaine Hornsby, Royal Artillery.

Ensign, 100th Foot, 26th July, 1864 ; 19th Foot, 20th September, 1864 ; Lieut., 23rd February, 1869 ; Indian Army, 21st September, 1869 ; Capt., 26th July, 1876 ; Major, 26th July, 1884 ; retired as hon. Lieut.-Col., 29th September, 1887.

Served in the Afghan War (medal). Also in the Burmese expedition, 1886-87, as D.A.A. and Q.M.G. (mentioned in despatches, medal and clasp). Appointed a Gentleman-at-Arms, 20th April, 1895. Assumed the additional name of Drake.

ALBERT SEAGRIM

Born at Winchester, 3rd April, 1834, son of Charles Seagrim, Barrister-at-Law.

Ensign, 36th Foot, 12th March, 1852 ; Lieut., 1st Foot,

12th January, 1855 ; Capt., 90th Foot, 11th February, 1862 ; 19th Foot, 20th February, 1865 ; Indian Army 8th March, 1866 ; Bt.-Major, 17th September, 1871 ; Major, 12th March, 1872 ; Bt.-Lieut.-Col., 1st October, 1877 ; Bt.-Col., 12th March, 1878 ; retired, 24th June, 1881.

Served in the Crimea with 1st Foot, including siege and fall of Sebastopol from 20th August, 1855 (medal with clasp and Turkish medal). Served with the 42nd Foot in the campaign of 1857-58 against the Mutineers in India, including the actions of Cawnpore (6th December, 1857), Seringhat, Khoodajung, and Shumsabad, siege and fall of Lucknow and assault of the Martinière, and Bank's bungalow, attack on the fort of Roozah, action of Allygunge, attack and capture of Bareilly (medal and clasp).

Died at a nursing home in Kensington, 21st April, 1919.

ALEXANDER ROCHE

Born in London, 25th June, 1844.

Ensign, 16th May, 1865 ; Lieut., 18th April, 1868.

Died at Alcester, 10th June, 1877.

CHARLES M'LAGAN

Born at Alyth, Perthshire.

Pte. 74th Foot, 11th October, 1849 ; Corpl., 14th January, 1852 ; Sergt., 13th September, 1853 ; Sergt.-Major, 12th November, 1858 ; Qr.-Mr., 22nd October, 1861 ; 19th Foot, 16th May, 1865 ; 7th Foot, 31st October, 1871.

Served with the 74th Highlanders in the Kaffir War of 1851-53 (medal), also in the Indian Mutiny campaign in 1858, and was present at the storm and capture of Shorapore (medal).

Died at Portsmouth, 11th September, 1872.

STEPHEN WESTON BENT

Born at Wexham Lodge, Bucks, 25th April, 1835, 5th son of Major John Bent, J.P., D.L., 5th Foot, of Wexham Lodge, Slough.

Ensign, 66th Foot, 19th January, 1855 ; Lieut., 4th Foot, 8th August, 1858 ; Capt., 29th March, 1864 ; 5th West India Regt., 22nd November, 1864 ; 19th Foot, 2nd June, 1865 ; retired by sale, 9th September, 1871.

Served in India during the Mutiny.

Died at the Cape in 1880 in the neighbourhood of Maticla, Cape Colony, at the time of the rising of the Basutos who attacked his house.

WILLIAM GRAHAM WAUGH McCLINTOCK

Born at sea, 24th October, 1846, son of George Frederick McClintock, Indian Civil Service.

Ensign, 4th August, 1865 ; Lieut., 23rd January, 1869 ; Capt. 13th March, 1878 ; Major, 4th February, 1882 ; Lieut.-Col., 28th July, 1892 ; Bt.-Col., 28th July, 1896 ; half-pay, 28th July, 1896 ; retired, 23rd December, 1896.

Served in the Hazara campaign of 1868, including the expedition against the tribes on the Black Mountain (medal and clasp). Served in the Nile expedition of 1885, and with the Soudan Field Force, 1885-86, including the action at Ginnis (medal and Khedive's Star).

WILLIAM GEORGE CURRIE JOHNSTONE

Born, 24th May, 1844.

Ensign, 8th August, 1865 ; Lieut., Indian Army, 18th May, 1869 ; Capt., 8th August, 1877 ; Major, 8th August, 1885 ; Lieut.-Col., 8th August, 1891 ; placed on the unemployed supernumerary list, 24th May, 1897.

Served with the Burmese expedition in 1887-88 (medal and clasp).

FREDERICK AUGUSTUS REMMINGTON

Born, 26th May, 1846.

Ensign, 22nd September, 1865 ; 88th Foot, 10th November, 1865 ; Lieut., Indian Army, 18th September, 1869 ; Capt., 22nd September, 1877 ; retired, 22nd August, 1884.

Served in the Afghan War, 1878-79 (medal).

BONAR MILLET DEANE

Born at Bighton Rectory, near Alresford, Hants, 30th September, 1834, son of the Revd. George Deane.

Ensign, 22nd Foot, 12th March, 1853 ; Lieut., 2nd November, 1855 ; Adjt., 6th June, 1856 ; Capt., 25th September, 1857 ; Major, 24th November, 1863 ; 18th Foot, 19th April, 1864 ; 19th Foot, 29th September, 1865 ; Bt.-Lieut.-Col., 29th December, 1873 ; Lieut.-Col., 14th April, 1875 ; Col., 29th December, 1878 ; half-pay, 14th January, 1879.

Served in the Boer War of 1881. Killed at the battle of Laing's Nek, 28th January, 1881, whilst in command of the Natal Field Force, at the head of a storming party, ten yards in front of the foremost man.

Memorial in St. George's Churchyard, Aldershot, and at Mount Prospect, Natal.

" I have specially to deplore the death of Colonel Deane, commanding Natal Field Force, in whom this force has suffered an irreparable loss. His experience and knowledge of all staff and regimental work, and his unremitting attention to every detail, having for its object the comfort, the efficiency, and the security of the men under his command, coupled with his charm of manner, had made him alike beloved and looked up to by all serving with him ; and his death was in keeping with his character as a chivalrous gentleman and officer " (Extract from report of Major-Gen. G. Pomeroy Colley).

GEORGE DALTON MICHELL

Born in Dublin, 12th October, 1835, 2nd son of George M. Berkeley Michell.

Ensign, 66th Foot, 11th March, 1859 ; Lieut., 18th May, 1865 ; 19th Foot, 10th November, 1865 ; Capt., 27th February, 1877 ; retired with a gratuity, 24th November, 1877.

Died at Milford, Surrey, 17th March, 1908.

GEORGE EDWARD LANGFORD

Born in the Punjab, 29th October, 1845, son of John Langford, H.E.I.C.S.

Ensign, 10th November, 1865 ; Lieut., 2nd March, 1869 ; Capt., 23rd July 1878 ; Army Pay Department, 4th October,

1878 ; hon. Major, 4th October, 1883 ; hon. Lieut.-Col., 6th December, 1892 ; retired, 25th June, 1898.

Served in the Hazara campaign of 1868, including the expedition against the tribes on the Black Mountain (medal and clasp).

Re-employed during the South African War (hon. rank of Colonel, 18th October, 1902).

Died at Lagos, Bournemouth, 1st February, 1915.

"One of the most talented and most genial officers that ever wore the uniform of the Green Howards. He was an excellent company officer ; a thorough all-round sportsman, and keen shot—the numerous trophies now at the Depôt, bear witness to his skill. He had a strong artistic and literary vein and was devoted to music—indeed, the Band owed much to his knowledge and keen interest in their work " (G.H.G.).

WILLIAM ALEXANDER CURTIS

Born at Nagpur, 9th September, 1845, 3rd son of Augustus John Curtis, Madras Cavalry.

Ensign, 21st November, 1865 ; Lieut., 23rd March, 1869 ; retired, 8th June, 1872.

Served in the Hazara campaign of 1868, including the expedition against the tribes on the Black Mountain (medal and clasp).

CHARLES GARLING DRURY

Born, 31st December, 1845, son of Lieut.-Col. Charles Harrison Drury, Madras Staff Corps.

Ensign, 29th December, 1865 ; Indian Army, 19th December, 1868

Died on board H.M.S. Crocodile, 19th March, 1874.

WILLIAM WOOKEY

Lieut., Turkish Contingent, 8th February, 1856 ; half-pay, 11th August, 1856 ; 19th Foot, 29th December, 1865 ; retired, 29th December, 1865.

JAMES BUTLER

Born, 14th March, 1846, son of Colonel John Butler, H.E.I.C.S., of Empshott, near Petersfield.

Ensign, 20th February, 1866 ; Lieut., 9th July, 1868 ; Indian Army, 17th September, 1868 ; Capt., 20th February, 1878 ; Major, 20th February, 1886 ; Lieut.-Col., 20th February, 1892 ; retired on unemployed supernumerary list, 14th March, 1901.

THOMAS MORRIS JENKINS

Born, 6th September, 1846, son of Major Thomas Askwith Jenkins, Madras Army.

Ensign, 99th Foot, 2nd March, 1866 ; 19th Foot, 17th April 1866 ; Lieut., Indian Army, 19th June, 1869 ; Capt., 2nd March, 1878 ; Major, 2nd March, 1886 ; Lieut.-Col., 2nd March, 1892 ; retired in March, 1899.

Employed on civil duties in the Burmese expedition, 1885-87 (medal and clasp).

Died at Southampton, 10th February, 1904.

HENRI CAMPBELL

Born at Dieppe, 6th November, 1830, son of Captain Archibald Montgomery Campbell, late Royal Horse Artillery.

Ensign, 63rd Native Infantry, 11th December, 1849; Lieut., 12th February, 1854; Capt., 16th December, 1863; 19th Foot, 8th May, 1866; retired by sale, 20th April, 1867.

Served in the Southal campaign, 1855-56, under Br.-Gen. Bird. Noticed with approbation for his energy and ingenuity by H.E. the Commander-in-Chief, 1857.

Died in Bayswater, London, 15th July, 1874.

JOHN HENRY BARNARD, C.B., C.M.G., A.D.C.

Born at Hastings, Sussex, 26th October, 1846, eldest son of John Wyatt Barnard, M.D.

Ensign, 8th May, 1866; Lieut., 28th July, 1869; Capt., 101st Foot, 7th March, 1877; Bt.-Major, 2nd March, 1881; Major, 1st July, 1881; Lieut.-Col., 20th May, 1889 Col., 23rd April, 1890; Commanding 101st Regtl. District, 28th October, 1894 to 29th July, 1896; Commanding Mandalay District, 18th August, 1896.

Served with 19th Foot in the Hazara campaign of 1868, including the expedition against the tribes on the Black Mountain (medal and clasp). Served as a volunteer under Capt. Glover, R.N., in the Ashanti War of 1873-4. Led the advanced guard at the capture of Abogoo. Commanded for five days a detached force of 650 men which captured Jaashi and Adomassie. With a detachment of 150 men drove the enemy out of their camps on the north bank of the Anoon. Present at the capture of Comassie (mentioned in despatches for "great discretion and judgment," and on two occasions for "gallant conduct" (C.M.G., medal and clasp, and promoted Captain). Served in the Afghan War in 1879-80 as A.D.C. to Lieut.-Gen R. O. Bright, first with the Peshawar Valley Field Force and afterwards with the Khyber Line Force, including the expedition to Hisarak (mentioned in despatches, Bt. of Major, medal). Served in the Soudan expedition of 1885 under Sir Gerald Graham, as D.A.A.G. (medal with clasp and Khedive's Star).

A.D.C. to Govr. of Newfoundland, 27th April, 1877, to 20th September, 1877. A.D.C. to Major-Gen., Bengal, 22nd October, 1878—5th November, 1883. A.D.C. to Queen Victoria, 23rd April, 1890.

Died at 36, Gloucester Gardens, London, 11th May, 1901. Buried in Paddington Cemetery.

WILLIAM SHAPTER HUNT

Born at Exeter, 25th March, 1834, son of Lieut.-Col. Robert Hunt, 57th and 49th Regiments.

Ensign, 74th Foot, 6th July, 1852; Lieut., 30th June, 1854; Capt., 17th November, 1863; 19th Foot, 29th May, 1866; Indian Army, 30th November, 1870; Bt.-Major, 6th July, 1872; Major, 30th November, 1876; Bt.-Lieut.-Col., 6th July, 1878; Lieut.-Col., 7th March, 1880; Bt.-Col., 6th July, 1882; Col., 8th June, 1890; placed on unemployed supernumerary list, 25th March, 1889.

Died at 11, Wilson Grove, Southsea, 24th April, 1913.

WILLIAM AUGUSTUS BURNETT

Born at Sialkot, 8th February, 1848, 3rd son of Major-Gen. Francis Claude Burnett, Bengal Artillery, of Gadgirth, Tarbotton, Ayrshire.

Ensign, 5th June, 1866 ; Lieut., 21st September, 1869 ; Capt., 24th July, 1878 ; 103rd Foot, 12th April, 1879 ; Paymaster, 11th April, 1882 ; hon. Major, 11th April, 1892.

Served in the Hazara campaign of 1868, including the expedition against the tribes on the Black Mountain (medal and clasp). Served in the Nile expedition, 1884-85 (medal with clasp and Khedive's Star).

Died at Springfield, Mannamead, Plymouth, 29th December, 1897.

THOMAS RICHARD MARTYR

Born at Tavoy, Burmah, 3rd May, 1847, eldest son of Major-Gen. James Smyth Martyr, Indian Army.

Ensign, 7th August, 1866.

Drowned at Barracow, on the Murree Road, 20th August, 1867. Tomb in Rawal Pindi Cemetery.

STUART ERSKINE ROLLAND

Born at Bundah, Madras, 7th November, 1846, son of Captain C. W. Rolland, Madras Artillery.

Ensign, 9th November, 1866 ; Lieut., Indian Army, 9th December, 1868 ; Capt., 9th November, 1878 ; Major, 9th November, 1886 ; Bt.-Lieut.-Col., 1st July, 1887 ; Lieut.-Col., 9th November, 1892 ; Col., 29th August, 1893 ; Br.-Gen., India, 31st December, 1896—18th January, 1900. Placed on Unemployed Supernumerary List, 7th November, 1903. Granted rank of Br.-Gen., 24th August, 1912 ; Col., 86th Carnatic Infantry, 15th August, 1913.

Served in the Burmese expedition, 1886-89, in command of Eastern frontier, and afterwards of Mappah and movable column (severely wounded), including the engagement at Segu (mentioned in despatches, medal with two clasps and Bt. of Lieut.-Col). Received the thanks of the Bombay Government for services rendered during the plague (14th February, 1900).

JOHN JOSEPH WESTENRA SMITH

Born in Dublin, 20th January, 1823, son of Robert Smith, of Mountjoy Square, Dublin.

Paymaster, 27th November, 1866 ; half-pay, 17th Lancers, 27th November, 1871 ; retired as hon. Capt., 8th April, 1874.

Died in Dublin, 10th October, 1878.

HENRY FAWCETT

Born at New Cross, Middlesex, 31st January, 1848.

Ensign, 6th March, 1867 ; Lieut., 8th December, 1869 ; retired by sale, 7th July, 1875.

Died at Carlsbad, Bohemia, 9th June, 1877.

CECIL LUMSDEN HORNBY

Born at Blackburn, 25th July, 1843, 5th son of William Henry Hornby, J.P., D.L., M.P., of Blackburn.

Ensign, 3rd April, 1867 ; Lieut., 58th Foot, 4th January, 1871 ; Capt., 9th September, 1879 ; retired with a gratuity, 26th June, 1883.

Served in the Zulu War, 1879. Took part with the 58th in the advance of General Newdigate's column on Ulundi. Remained on detachment at Fort Evelyn from the date of its construction till the conclusion of the war. Served in the Boer war and was present at the battle of Laing's Nek and at the passage of the Ingogo. Taken prisoner at Majuba Hill.

Died at Leamington, 27th February, 1896.

GEORGE BARRINGTON BEHAN

Born at Assyghur, Bombay, 15th November, 1847.

Ensign, 20th April, 1867 ; Lieut., 7th March, 1870 ; retired by sale, 24th September, 1873.

Became a schoolmaster in Canada.

Died about 1894.

CHARLES ARCHIBALD MERCER

Born at Jullundur, Bengal, 7th July, 1847, 2nd son of General Thomas Warren Mercer, Indian Army.

Ensign, 34th Foot, 8th June, 1867 ; 19th Foot, 8th June, 1867 ; Lieut., Indian Army, 18th January, 1870 ; Capt., 8th June, 1879 ; Major, 8th June, 1887 ; Lieut.-Col., 8th June, 1893 ; Bt.-Col., 8th June, 1897 ; Col., 29th August, 1901 ; placed on the unemployed supernumerary list, 1st July, 1904.

Served in the Hazara campaign of 1868, including the expedition against the tribes on the Black Mountain (medal and clasp). Served in the Chin Lushai expedition, 1871-2 (clasp). Took part in the Afghan War, 1878-80, and was at the capture of Ali Musjid, the operations at and around Kabul in December, 1879, operations in Maidan, Wardak, and Kohistan, affair at Saidabad, march from Kabul to the relief of Kandahar and battle of 1st September. Also served in the Mari expedition. (Medal with three clasps, mentioned in despatches and bronze decoration). Served in the Waziristan expedition, 1894-95 (clasp).

FRANCIS OPENSHAW SARGEANT-OPENSHAW

Born at Coventry, 12th September, 1836, son of Francis Sargeant.

Ensign, 37th Foot, 28th May, 1858 ; Lieut., 21st October, 1862 ; Paymaster, 59th Foot, 20th July, 1866 ; 19th Foot, 30th October, 1867 ; hon. Major, 20th July, 1876 ; Staff Paymaster, 1st November, 1879 ; Chief Paymaster and hon. Lieut.-Col., 1st November, 1887 ; retired, 12th September, 1896.

Served in the Hazara campaign of 1868, including the expedition against the tribes on the Black Mountain (medal and clasp).

Died at Fairlawn, Winchester, 5th February, 1917.

ALFRED CHARLES LE QUESNE

Born at St. Helier's, Jersey, 16th July, 1848, son of William V. Le Quesne, of St. Helier's.

Ensign, 83rd Foot, 6th November, 1867 ; 19th Foot, 6th November, 1867 ; Lieut., Indian Army, 18th November, 1869 : Capt., 6th November, 1879.

Served in the Afghan and Waziristan campaigns (medal).
Died of cholera at Jhelum, Punjab, 20th September, 1881. Memorial tablet in the parish church of St. Helier's.

GEORGE ATKINSON, M.B.

Born at Firhill, Tipperary, 15th October, 1840, son of George Guy Atkinson, J.P., of Ashleigh Park, Nenagh.

Asst.-Surgeon, Staff, 31st March, 1864 ; 19th Foot, 24th December, 1867 ; Surgeon, 28th April, 1876.

Served in the Bhootan expedition of 1865, and in the Hazara campaign of 1868 (medal and clasp). Took part in the Afghan war and was present at the battle of Ahmed Khel (medal).

Died at Hafaizai, near Ghuznee, of pneumonia, 25th April, 1880. There is a memorial tablet in Nenagh Church.

GRANVILLE SHARPE

Born at Reasby, Lincoln, 6th August, 1847.

Ensign, 4th March, 1868 ; Lieut., 18th May, 1870 ; Capt., 18th October, 1878 ; retired by sale, 11th October, 1879.

GEORGE BURRIDGE ROGERS

Born, 9th September, 1848. Ensign, 1st April, 1868 ; 48th Foot, 13th June, 1868 ; Lieut., 28th October, 1871 ; Capt., 1st May, 1881 ; retired with a gratuity, 20th June, 1883.

HARRY JULIAN CHARRINGTON

Born at Chigwell, Essex, 20th February, 1849, son of Edward Charrington, D.L., of Mile End, Middlesex and Bury's Court, Reigate.

Ensign, 18th April, 1868 ; Lieut., 4th March, 1870 ; Capt., 21st August, 1878 ; retired, 25th September, 1883.

HENRY WARREN WALKER

Born at Quebec, 27th December, 1846.

Ensign, 83rd Foot, 22nd January, 1867 ; 19th Foot, 13th June, 1868 ; retired by sale, 10th May, 1871.

WILLIAM FRANCIS HUNGERFORD GREY

Born at Calcutta, 18th February, 1849, son of Sir William Grey, K.C.S.I., Indian Civil Service.

Ensign, 29th Foot, 3rd June, 1868 ; 19th Foot, 20th June, 1868 ; Lieut., 28th October, 1871 ; Indian Army, 27th May, 1872 ; Capt., 3rd June, 1880 ; Major, 3rd June, 1888 ; Lieut.-Col., 3rd June, 1894 ; retired, 24th March, 1901.

WILLIAM GILLON

Born, 21st December, 1849, son of Andrew Gillon, of Wall House, Linlithgow, J.P., D.L.

Ensign, 2nd December, 1868, 71st Foot, 28th December, 1868 ; Lieut., 28th October, 1871 ; Capt., 6th November, 1878 ; retired with a gratuity, 31st January, 1888.

JOHN CORSE-SCOTT

Born at Nusseerabad, 6th January, 1846, eldest son of Edward William Corse-Scott, H.E.I.C.S.

Ensign, 56th Foot, 16th May, 1865 ; 4th Foot, 2nd June, 1865 ; 19th Foot, 12th December, 1868 ; Indian Army, 13th May, 1869 ; Capt., 16th May, 1877.

Served in the Abyssinian campaign as Sub.-Assist. Commissary General (medal).

Died in August, 1888, at Dharmsala when 2nd in command of 2nd Bn. 1st Ghoorkhas.

EDWARDS WERGE

Born, 12th February, 1850, son of the Revd. John Werge, Rector of Somersal, Derbyshire.

Ensign, 23rd December, 1368 ; 2nd Foot, 3rd February, 1869 ; Indian Army, 22nd March, 1871 ; Capt., 23rd December, 1880.

Died at Satara, E.I., 13th June, 1886.

EDWARD ARCHIBALD BRUCE

Born at Secunderabad, 1st September, 1849, son of Br.-Gen. Edward Brice, C.B., R.A., Indian Army, Inspector of Artillery, Madras.

Ensign, 23rd January, 1869 ; Lieut., 28th October, 1871 ; Adjt., 8th December, 1873—14th September, 1878 ; Capt., 1st March, 1879 ; Major, 29th September, 1882 ; Lieut.-Col., 29th March, 1893 ; Col., 29th March, 1897 ; half-pay, 25th March, 1905 ; retired, 5th September, 1905.

Changed his name to Bruce, 17th June, 1875. Adjt., Scarborough Volunteers, 1st August, 1884—14th December, 1888. In command of 19th Regtl. District, 25th March, 1900, to 25th March, 1905.

Died at The Hove, Brighton, 13th November, 1918.

" To few has it been given to wear the uniform of the old Nineteenth for over 36 years ; and fewer still have enjoyed the popularity, esteem, and affection that Colonel Bruce held. He was an excellent Adjutant, a keen company officer, a commanding officer under whom it was a real pleasure to serve. It was never his good luck to see active service, but he was a born leader of men, and lacked only the opportunity of proving his ability in the Field. Dauntless and straight himself, he abhorred crooked ways, and feared neither man nor devil when upholding what he knew to be right ; at all manly sports he was hard to beat in his day " (G.H.G.).

GEORGE HENRY ASHINGTON CHRISTOPHER

Born at Rhotas, India, 6th December, 1850, 2nd son of Maj-Gen. Leonard Raisbeck Christopher, of the Warren, Ealing.

Ensign, 3rd February, 1869.

Died at Rawal Pindi of ague and continuous fever, 20th June, 1869. Memorial in Rawal Pindi cemetery.

WILLIAM WILKINSON SCOTT

Born at Benares, 11th July, 1850, son of Capt. A. W. Scott.

Ensign, 7th March, 1869 ; Lieut., 27th Foot, 9th September, 1871 ; retired by sale, 24th June, 1873.

GEORGE HAWKINS ·

Born, 5th May, 1851, son of Clement James Hawkins, Surgeon, 24, Cambray Place, Cheltenham.

Ensign, 24th March, 1869 ; Lieut., 86th Foot, 1st November, 1871 ; resigned, 27th March, 1872.

Died in December, 1908.

HENRY JOHN GOODWIN ROBINSON

Born at Goodwin Paddock, Lydd, Kent, 21st September, 1843, son of John Robinson, J.P., of Goodwin Paddock.

Ensign, 98th Foot, 2nd September, 1862 ; Lieut., 10th November, 1865 ; 19th Foot, 16th April, 1869 ; half-pay, 24th February, 1871 ; retired, 13th November, 1872.

For some time resident in Queensland and at Maryland, N.S. Wales. For many years employed with Hart's Army List.

Died at a nursing home in London, 22nd May, 1916.

HARRY MICHAEL STAPLETON

Born in Dublin, 13th April, 1847, probably son of Michael Stapleton, M.D., of Dublin.

Ensign, 99th Foot, 22nd February, 1868 ; 19th Foot, 5th May, 1869 ; retired, 14th March, 1873.

Died at Waverley, N S. Wales, 1st October, 1900.

ROBERT ALFRED PLASSEY HALLIFAX

Born at Plassey, 4th September, 1849, son of Br.-Gen. Robert Dampier Hallifax, 75th Foot.

Ensign, 7th July, 1869 ; Lieut., 28th October, 1871 ; Capt., 7th June, 1879 ; half-pay, 11th March, 1881 ; retired by sale, 20th May, 1882.

Died at Bedford, 1st February, 1905.

GEORGE RYAN

Born in Dublin, 16th May, 1845, son of Patrick Ryan, J.P., of Balyard, Co. Kerry.

Asst.-Surgeon, Staff, 31st March, 1868 ; 19th Foot, 18th August, 1869 ; Surgeon, 1st March, 1873 ; Surgeon-Major, 1st January, 1881 ; half-pay, 24th July, 1878—24th April, 1879 ; Surgeon-Lieut.-Col., 1st January, 1889 ; retired, 16th January, 1889.

Served in the Zulu war of 1879 (medal and clasp).

Died at Ryde, 7th October, 1904.

GEORGE ALEXANDER KENNEDY SKIPTON

Born in Londonderry, 16th August, 1849, eldest son of Henry Stacy Skipton, M.D., of Beechill, Co. Derry.

Ensign, 22nd Foot, 18th November, 1868 ; 19th Foot, 9th October, 1869 ; Lieut., 28th October, 1871 ; retired by sale, 10th March, 1875.

Died in London, 15th January, 1906.

NOEL NORCOTT WINTER

Born, 24th December, 1851, son of Captain Winter, of Canterbury.

Ensign, 30th October, 1869 ; 13th Foot, 10th November, 1869 ; Lieut., 28th October, 1871 ; 96th Foot, 27th June, 1874; Capt., 6th December, 1879 ; half-pay, 22nd December, 1880 ; retired by sale, 22nd December, 1890 ; Capt., 4th Bn. South Staffordshire Regt., 16th February, 1881 ; hon. Major, 8th May, 1886 ; Major, 7th December, 1889 ; hon. Lieut.-Col., 1st January, 1890 ; retired from Militia, 11th April, 1891.

JOHN LEADER

Born at Duhalow, Dromhariffe, Co. Cork, 26th June, 1843, 2nd son of John Leader, M.D., J.P., of Keale, Millstreet, Co. Cork.

Asst.-Surgeon, Staff, 31st March, 1868 ; 19th Foot, 30th October, 1869 ; Staff, 13th February, 1871 ; Surgeon, 1st May, 1873 ; Surgeon-Major, 31st March, 1880 ; half-pay, 27th February, 1889.

Died at Cahir, 12th September, 1892.

THOMAS OTHO FITZGERALD

Born at Glin Castle, Co. Limerick, 23rd February, 1849, 5th son of John Fraunceis Eyre Fitzgerald, Knight of Glin.

Ensign, 10th November, 1869 ; Lieut., 28th October, 1871; Indian Army, 12th June, 1875.

Killed in action at Ali Musjid, 21st November, 1878, when acting as Adjt. to the 27th Native Infantry. Buried at Peshawar.

WILLOUGHBY PITCAIRN KENNEDY, C.S.I.

Born, 10th December, 1850, son of General Sir Michael Cavenagh Kennedy, R.E., K.C.S.I.

Ensign, 8th February, 1870 ; 44th Foot, 7th October, 1871; Lieut., 28th October, 1871 ; Indian Army, 9th January, 1874 ; Capt., 8th February, 1882 ; Major, 8th February, 1890 ; Lieut., Col., 8th February, 1896 ; Col., 15th December, 1899 ; retired, 31st March, 1906.

Served in the Afghan War, 1880, as Assistant to the Agent to the Governor-General in Baluchistan (medal). Special political agent, Cambay. Administrator, Jamnagar State, Kathiawar, 1895-1901. Political agent and agent to the Gurcar Kathiawar, 1901-1905. C.S.I. in 1906.

GEORGE HAWKES

Born in Darjeeling, 10th October, 1851, son of Colonel Robert Hawkes, 80th Foot.

Ensign, 19th February, 1870 ; Lieut., 28th October, 1871 ; Indian Army, 12th February, 1874 ; Capt., 19th February, 1882 ; Major, 19th February, 1890 ; Lieut.-Col., 19th February, 1896 ; Col., 19th February, 1900 ; placed on unemployed supernumerary list, 10th October, 1908.

Served in the Rumpa Rebellion, 1880, also in the Hazara campaign of 1888 (medal and clasp). Hazara, 1891 (clasp). Isazai expedition, 1892.

LIONEL HENRY MOCATTA LEVIN

Born at Wellington, N.Z., 10th December, 1849, son of N. W. Levin.

Ensign, 20th February, 1870 ; Lieut., 28th October, 1871 ; Capt., 28th July, 1879 ; Major, 1st August, 1884.

Died in London, 31st March, 1886.

JOHN FRANCIS SIMONET

Born at Radier, Jersey, 6th April, 1852, son of Francis John Simonet, of Jersey.

Ensign, 21st February, 1870 ; Lieut., 28th October, 1871 ; Capt., 11th October, 1879 Paymaster, 16th May, 1884 ; hon. Major, 16th May, 1894 ; Staff-Paymaster, 12th October, 1898 ; Lieut.-Col., 12th October, 1903 ; retired, 27th April, 1909.

Died at Ivanhoe, Charlton Road, Weymouth, 19th December, 1911.

MORTON FREDERICK THRUPP

Born, 18th July, 1840, son of the Revd. Edward Thrupp, Vicar of Feltham, Hounslow.

Ensign, 4th Foot, 5th July, 1860 ; Lieut., 9th October, 1863 sold out, 1st February, 1868 ; re-entered the Army as Ensign, Royal Canadian Rifle Regt., 14th October, 1868 ; Cape Mounted Rifles, 1st April, 1869 ; 19th Foot, 31st March, 1870 ; Lieut., 45th Foot, 27th August, 1870 ; Capt., 29th June, 1878 ; Major, half-pay, 18th July, 1882 ; Lieut.-Col., 18th July, 1887 ; retired, 9th January, 1889.

Inspector of Army Signalling, Aldershot, 1880-1889.

Died at Tadworth, Surrey, 12th February, 1917.

LAWRENCE RICHARD DOWDALL

Born at New Ground, Guernsey, 11th February, 1843, younger son of Major Aylmer Dowdall, 54th and 89th Foot.

Ensign, Royal Canadian Rifles, 21st November, 1865 ; 19th Foot, 31st March, 1870 ; Lieut., 18th Foot, 20th September, 1871 ; 102nd Foot, 25th June, 1873 ; Capt., 1st September, 1877 ; Army Pay Dept., 1st October, 1879 ; hon. Major, 1st October, 1884 ; hon. Lieut.-Col., 2nd April, 1895 ; hon. Col., 16th February, 1899 ; retired, 30th May, 1905.

Served in Canada during the Fenian raids of 1866 and 1870 (medal and two clasps).

Died at 158, Cromwell Road, S. Kensington, 5th November, 1908.

GEORGE EDWIN BORRADAILE

Born, 3rd September, 1835, 2nd son of George Borradaile, of Cheltenham.

Ensign, Indian Army, 10th June, 1854 ; Lieut., 1st June, 1857 ; Capt., 10th June, 1866 ; 19th Foot, 29th November, 1870 ; half-pay, 22nd July, 1871 ; 63rd Foot, 9th June, 1877 ; Bt.-Major, 15th March, 1879 ; retired as hon. Lieut.-Col., 26th May, 1880.

Justice of the Peace for Straits Settlements, 1859, and for the

Madras Presidency, 1862. Police Magistrate and Commissioner of Court of requests, Strait Settlements, 1859-60. Cantonment Magistrate, Madras Presidency, 1862. Magistrate of Police, Madras town, 1867-8. An advocate for the High Court of Judicature, Madras, 20th October, 1868. Called to the Bar, 26th February, 1867.

Died at Tunbridge Wells, 24th December, 1899.

HENRY ERNEST HALDANE

Born at Devonport, 18th January, 1850.

Ensign, 4th January, 1871 ; 49th Foot, 2nd August, 1871 ; Lieut., 28th October, 1871 ; Capt., 64th Foot, 29th September, 1880 ; retired with a gratuity, 4th January, 1884.

Served in the Zulu War, 1879 (medal and clasp).

Selected in 1886 by the British Govt. to proceed to Australia and there to organise and instruct the newly-formed Defence Force for which he received the thanks of the Minister of Defence.

Died at 60, Park Street, Durban, 26th December, 1915, from injuries received in a motor car accident ten months previously.

E. E. de PENTHENY de PENTHENY-O'KELLY

Born, 25th December, 1831, 3rd son of Edmund de Pentheny O'Kelly.

Paymaster, British-German Legion, 23rd August, 1855 ; 17th Lancers, 28th December, 1860 ; hon. Capt., 28th December, 1865 ; 19th Foot, 2nd May, 1871 ; hon. Major, 4th July, 1874 ; 24th Foot, 28th April, 1875 ; 32nd Foot, 1st February, 1878 ; Staff-Paymaster, 1st April, 1879, with rank of Lieut.-Col. ; retired, 25th December, 1890.

Died at Bournemouth, 11th November, 1913.

JOHN PYNE

Born, 27th July, 1838. Ensign, 16th Foot, 5th July, 1855 ; Lieut., 1st October, 1858 ; Adjt., 16th November, 1866 ; Capt., 1st April, 1870 ; half-pay, 8th April, 1870 ; 19th Foot, 10th May, 1871 ; Army Pay Dept., 1st April, 1878 ; Staff-Paymaster and hon. Lieut.-Col., 23rd August, 1882 ; retired, 23rd August, 1889.

Served in the Egyptian war of 1882 (medal and Khedive's Star).

Died at Croydon, 8th January, 1897.

WINDLE HILL St. HILL

Born at St. Omer, France, 11th July, 1837, youngest son of Henry Charles St. Hill, Colonial Secretary of Trinidad.

Ensign, 65th Foot, 12th February, 1858 ; Lieut., 28th January, 1862 ; Capt., half-pay, 8th June, 1867 ; Bt.-Major, 8th June, 1867 ; 19th Foot, 22nd July, 1871 ; Bt.-Lieut.-Col., 24th June, 1876 ; retired, 25th August, 1881.

Served in the New Zealand war, 1860-65. Attack and capture of Kohea pah (March 17th-18th, 1860). Expedition to Warea, attack and capture of pah's, action at Kaherera (17th July, 1863). Storming and capture of rifle pits and pah at Rangiriri (20th-21st November, 1863). Attack and capture of Rangrarhia and Kazaria (horse shot). Attack and capture of pah at Pake, action at Nukumaru and skirmish at Kakaramea

(mentioned in despatches four times, Bt. of Major for " distinguished conduct in the field," and medal).
  A.D.C. to Governor of New Zealand, Sir Duncan Cameron, 1863-65. A.D.C. to G.O.C., Shorncliffe, 1866-1867, and to Commander-in-Chief, Madras, 1867-1875.

JAMES LINFORD

Born at Phillipstown, King's Co., 4th November, 1823. Pte. 63rd Foot, 29th January, 1839; Corpl., 19th April, 1843; Sergt., 1st March, 1844 ; Col.-Sergt., 16th August, 1844 ; Qr.-Mr.-Sergt., 17th July, 1852 ; Qr.-Mr., 28th December, 1855 ; 19th Foot, 19th September, 1871 ; 108th Foot, 12th November, 1872 ; retired as hon. Major, 6th September, 1881.

Served in the Crimea. Present at the battles of the Alma, Inkerman, and Balaclava. Expedition to Kertch, bombardment and capture of Kinburn (medal and four clasps, medal for distinguished conduct in the field, annuity of £20, and Turkish medal).

GEORGE WINGATE, C.I.E.

Born, 21st November, 1852. Ensign, 23rd September, 1871 ; Lieut., 28th October, 1871 ; Indian Army, 7th September, 1875 ; Capt., 23rd September, 1883 ; Major, 23rd September, 1891 ; Lieut.-Col., 23rd September, 1897 ; Col., 23rd September, 1901 ; placed on unemployed supernumerary list, 21st November, 1909.

Served in the Naga Hills expedition, 1879-80 (mentioned in despatches, medal and clasp). Took part in the operations in Chitral, 1895, with the relief force (medal and clasp), operations on the N.W.F. of India, 1897-98, and served as chief commissariat officer with the Tochi Valley Force (mentioned in despatches, clasp). C.I.E. in 1901.

THOMAS MURPHY

Qr.-Mr., 7th Foot, from Sergt., 4th April, 1856 ; 19th Foot, 31st October, 1871 ; half-pay, 9th August, 1873, with hon. rank of Capt. Commuted his half-pay in January, 1874.

Served with the 7th Fusiliers in the Crimea, 1854-56, as Hospital Sergeant (medal and clasps and Turkish medal). Took part in the Indian frontier war of 1863, with the Eusofzie field force. Present in the defence of the sangars at the Umballa Pass and at the attack and storming of the conical hill and destruction of Lalloo on the 15th December. Also in the action at Umbeyla and destruction of the bridge at the foot of the Bonair Pass on the 16th December, which ended in the complete rout of the enemy and submission of the hill tribes on the 17th December (medal and clasp).

On Christmas Day, 1856, he was presented with a silver breakfast service by his brother officers as a token of esteem and appreciation of his services in the Crimea.

JOHN HENRY EDEN

Born at Etherby, Durham, 10th May, 1851, eldest son of Canon John Patrick Eden, Rector of Sedgefield, Co. Durham. Lieut., 3rd July, 1872 ; Capt., 11th February, 1880 ;

By Royal Warrant of the 30th October, 1871, the ranks of Cornet and Ensign were abolished, and officers were gazetted as Sub-Lieutenants, altered a few years later to 2nd Lieutenants.

Major, 4th March, 1885 ; Lieut.-Col., half-pay, 4th March, 1892 ; retired, 16th March, 1892.

Served in the Nile expedition, 1885, and with the Soudan frontier field force, 1885-86, and was present at the action of Ginnis (medal and Khedive's Star).

Chief Constable, Durham, 1892-1902. H.M.s Inspector of Constabulary for England and Wales, 1902—May, 1916.

Awarded the King's Coronation Medal, 1911.

WILLIAM SPENCER COOPER

Born at Greenock, 22nd May, 1827, son of Lieut. John Cooper, 78th Foot.

Ensign, 3rd West India Regt., 5th June, 1843 ; Lieut., 31st October, 1845 ; 70th Foot, 26th May, 1848 ; Capt., 26th January, 1855 ; Major, 16th May, 1865 ; Lieut.-Col., 17th May, 1867 ; Bt.-Col., 17th April, 1872 ; 19th Foot, 14th August, 1872, to 10th March, 1875 ; Major-Gen., 1st October, 1882 ; retired, 11th July, 1888 ; Col., 19th Foot, 14th September, 1902.

Served with the 18th Foot as interpreter throughout the Burmese campaign of 1852-53, including the capture of Rangoon, Prome and other minor affairs (medal and clasp). Served in the Indian Mutiny, 1857-58 (medal). Was A.Q.M.G. to the expeditionary force on the Eusofzai frontier, under Sir S. Cotton in 1858, and in the same capacity with the expeditionary force in the Wazeeree country under Br.-Gen. Chamberlain in December, 1859 (clasp).

Died at Grosvenor Place, London, 1st October, 1906. Buried in Brompton Cemetery.

MONTGOMERIE CROFTON CAULFEILD

Born at Quebec, 24th August, 1851, eldest son of Lieut.-Col. William Montgomerie Stewart Caulfeild.

Sub-Lieut., 31st August, 1872 ; Lieut., 31st August, 1872 ; superseded for absence, 5th January, 1876.

CHARLES SHEA HUNT

Born at Plymouth, 3rd May, 1836, son of Warwick A. Hunt of Burleigh, near Plymouth.

Ensign, Indian Army, 4th July, 1855 ; Lieut., 108th Foot, 23rd November, 1856 ; Capt., 15th January, 1866 ; 19th Foot, 13th November, 1872 ; Major, 16th September, 1878 ; retired as hon. Lieut.-Col., 11th February, 1880.

Served in the Indian Mutiny, 1858-59, with the Saugor field division as baggage master in actions of Kerivee, Punwarree and on the banks of the Jumna (mentioned in despatches, medal and clasp).

Died at Cosham Park House, Hants, 20th February, 1898. Buried in Wymering cemetery.

JAMES HEDINGHAM

Born in Suffolk, 12th January, 1837.

Pte., 21st February 1854 ; Corpl., 1st July, 1856 ; Sergt., 24th September, 1858 ; Col.-Sergt., 12th March, 1861 ; Sergt.-Major, 1st April, 1868 ; Qr.-Mr., 13th November, 1872, to 31st January, 1882 ; 4th Bn., 19th April, 1882.

Served in the Crimea and was present at siege of Sebastopol (medal and clasp and Turkish medal). Also in the Hazara campaign of 1868, including the expedition against the tribes on the Black Mountain (medal and clasp). Awarded the medal for long service and good conduct.

Died at Southsea, 22nd December, 1883.

GEORGE WARBURTON MARSH

Born, 16th November, 1850, son of the Revd. Peter Marsh, of Ballinaminton, Birr, King's Co. and Rector of O'Meath, Co. Louth.

Sub-Lieut., 23rd November, 1872 ; resigned, 23rd October, 1875.

WILLIAM HUNT

Born. 20th February, 1839. In ranks, 14 years 120 days ; Sub-Lieut., 26th March, 1873 ; Qr.-Mr., 9th August, 1873 ; 77th Foot, 25th August, 1880 ; retired as hon. Major, 21st December, 1887.

Died, 19th July, 1902.

RICHARD PHAYRE, O.B.E.

Born, 31st October, 1853, 2nd son of General Sir Robert Phayre, G.C.B.

Lieut., 9th August, 1873 ; Adjt., 19th February, 1878—20th March, 1880 ; Capt., 20th March, 1880 ; Major, 1st April, 1885 ; Lieut.-Col., half-pay, 1st April, 1892 ; retired, 6th April, 1892.

Served in the Afghan War, 1880, as A.D.C. to the G.O.C. Southern Afghanistan Reserve division and lines of communications between Kandahar and Sabi, including the march from Quetta to the relief of Kandahar (mentioned in despatches, medal). Awarded the order of officer of the British Empire for services as chief organiser of Beachcroft Auxiliary Hospital, Woking, during the Great War.

REGINALD MOLESWORTH SIMPSON

Born at Bath, 8th April, 1853, son of William Henry Simpson, C.B., Royal Artillery.

Lieut., 12th November, 1873 ; resigned, 5th May, 1877.

HUGH CECIL CHOLMONDELY, C.B., C.B.E.

Born, 1st December, 1853, at Sledmere, York, eldest son of the Hon. Thomas Grenville Cholmondely, of Abbot's Moss, Northwich, Cheshire.

Lieut., 12th November, 1873 ; Rifle Brigade, 24th December, 1873 ; Adjt., 1st May, 1878—11th January, 1881 ; Capt., 12th January, 1881 ; retired on a gratuity, 23rd September, 1887.

Regimental Surgeons and Assistant Surgeons were abolished by Royal Warrant dated 1st March, 1873, which established an Army Medical Department.

Served in the Afghan War, 1878-79, with the Peshawar Valley field force, including capture of Ali Musjid and the expedition to the Bazar and Lughman Valleys (medal and clasp). Commanded as Lieut.-Col. the City Imperial Volunteer Mounted Infantry in the South African War (twice mentioned in despatches, medal and 6 clasps, C.B.). Hon. Br.-General, 1917. Vice-Chairman of the Shropshire Territorial Force Association. Mentioned in home despatches, August, 1918, for services rendered during the Great War. C.B.E., 3rd June, 1919.

JAMES HARRY SCHWABE

Born at Liverpool, 9th March, 1855.

Sub-Lieut., 12th November, 1873 ; resigned, 23rd January, 1875.

RICHARD FOORD

Born at Foxholes, 21st September, 1852, eldest son of the Revd. Richard Henry Foord, Rector of Foxholes, Ganton, Yorkshire.

Lieut., 28th February, 1874 ; resigned, 26th February, 1876.

Died at Galway, 2nd July, 1892.

FREDERICK BARFF BRIGGS

Born, 25th February, 1855 ; son of Rawdon Briggs, of Birstwith Hall, Yorkshire.

Sub-Lieut., 13th June, 1874 ; Adjt., 15th September, 1878—28th September, 1880 ; Capt., 29th September, 1880 ; Bt.-Major, 15th June, 1885.

Served with the Mounted Infantry, 19th Foot, at Suakin in 1885 (medal and clasp and Khedive's Star).

Died at Cairo, 15th September, 1885.

Sir WILLIAM EDMUND FRANKLYN, K.C.B., p.s.c.

Born at Ventnor, Isle of Wight, 14th May, 1856, eldest son of the Revd. Thomas Edmund Franklyn, of Barton Grange, Cheshunt.

Sub-Lieut., 13th June, 1874 ; Lieut., 13th June, 1874 ; Capt., 30th March, 1881 ; Major, 20th April, 1886 ; Lieut.-Col., 28th July, 1896 ; Bt.-Col., 20th May, 1898 ; Col., 29th September, 1898 ; Major-Gen., 1st April, 1904 ; Lieut.-Gen., 31st August, 1910 ; Col., 19th Foot, 2nd October, 1906.

Served in the Tirah Expedition of 1897-98, under Sir William Lockhart in command of 2nd Bn. 19th Foot, and was present at the capture of the Sampagha and Arhanga Passes, the reconnaissance of the Saran Sar, operations at and around Dwatoi, operations against the Khani-Khel Chamkanis, operations in the Bazar Valley (Bt. of Colonel mentioned in despatches, medal and two clasps).

D.A.A.G., Aldershot, 4th May, 1888—3rd May, 1893 ; A.A.G., Scotland, 29th September, 1898—8th October, 1899 ; Asst. Military Secretary, War Office, 9th October, 1899—14th October, 1902. Director of Personal Services, 28th March, 1904—31st May, 1906. Military Secretary to the Secretary of State for War and Secretary of the Selection Board, 6th October, 1911. C.B., August, 1902 ; K.C.B., King's birth-day, 1912. In October, 1914, he was sent on an important and delicate commission to the Front.

Died at Luton Hoo, Hertford, 27th October, 1914, when in command of the 3rd Army, Central Force.

The King and Queen sent the following message of sympathy to Lady Franklyn :—" The King and Queen have learnt with much regret of the grievous loss which you have sustained, and I am desired to express their Majesties' sympathy with you in your sorrow. The King had met Sir William Franklyn quite recently when inspecting a portion of his command."

" Stamfordham."

From Queen Alexandra :—" I offer you my most sincere and heart-felt sympathy in the terrible sorrow which has befallen you in the death of your distinguished husband, Sir William Franklyn. His loss will be most deeply felt, not only by his regiment of which I am Colonel-in-Chief, but by the whole Army."

FRANK MILES BARCLAY

Born at Quilon, India, in 1855, 6th son of Surgeon-Gen. Charles Barclay, Madras Army.

Sub-Lieut., 11th February, 1875 ; 44th Foot, 11th February, 1875 ; Indian Army, 11th February, 1875.

Severely wounded near Maidenak in the Shinwari country, 17th March, 1879, when with a surveying party under Lieut. E. P. Leach, R.E.

Died of his wounds at Landi Kotal in the Khyber Pass, 31st March, 1879.

JAMES HENRY ERSKINE READ

Born, 20th April, 1856. Sub-Lieut, unattached, 11th February, 1875 ; 19th Foot, 11th February, 1875 ; Lieut., 11th February, 1875 ; 25th Foot, 29th January, 1876 ; Capt., 21st June, 1885 ; Major, 10th September, 1894 ; Lieut.-Col., half-pay, 12th June, 1901 ; Col., 1st July, 1904 ; retired on half-pay, 1st July, 1906.

Served throughout the Afghan War of 1878-80, first in Northern Afghanistan with the 25th Foot, under Sir Frederick Maude, including the Bazar Valley Expedition, afterwards in Southern Afghanistan with the 3rd Bombay Light Cavalry, including the mutiny and subsequent pursuit of the Wali of Kandahar's troops at Girishk ; the battle of Maiwand in command of a squadron (wounded), and the defence of Kandahar (mentioned in despatches, medal).

O'DONNELL COLLEY GRATTAN, D.S.O.

Born, 13th June, 1855, son of Henry Colley Grattan.

Sub-Lieut., unattached, 10th March, 1875 ; 19th Foot, 10th March, 1875 ; 8th Foot, 29th January, 1876 ; Lieut., 10th March, 1877 ; Capt., 20th September, 1882 ; Major, 26th October, 1892 ; Lieut.-Col., 17th February, 1900 ; Col., 10th February, 1904 ; retired, 11th October, 1905.

Served in the Afghan War of 1878-80, including action of 28th November, 1878, in Kurram Valley and battle and capture of the Peiwar

Kotal, also in the affair of Ali Khel (medal and clasp). Served in the Boer War, 1899-1900, with 8th Foot, and took part in the operations in Natal in 1899, including the actions at Reitfontein and Lombard's Kop, and in the defence of Ladysmith (mentioned in despatches, medal and clasp and D.S.O.). Served in the Great War in command of an Infantry Brigade at home and as Commandant, Prisoners of War Camp. Granted hon. rank of Br.-General, 9th October, 1919.

GILBERT HAMILTON FEARON MATHISON

Born at Nuremburg, 30th November, 1856, son of Captain C. M. Mathison, R.N.

Sub-Lieut., unattached, 10th March, 1875 ; 19th Foot, 10th March, 1875 ; Lieut., 10th March, 1877 ; Capt., 14th November, 1883 ; Major, 1st April, 1892 ; retired, 18th November, 1896.

Served in the Nile Expedition, 1885, and with the Soudan Field Force, 1885-6, including the engagement at Ginnis (medal and Khedive's Star). Served with a field column in Burmah in February and March, 1893, in operations in the Katchin Hills (medal and clasp).

WILLIAM ALBERT STRATTON, m.c.c.

Born at Brighton, 7th April, 1825, 2nd son of Robert Stratton, of Dibden Lodge, Hants.

Ensign, 6th Foot, 27th May, 1842 ; Lieut., 19th November, 1844 ; Capt., 30th March, 1849 ; Major, 15th April, 1856 ; Lieut.-Col., 6th May, 1858 ; half-pay, 24th May, 1862 ; Bt.-Col., 30th June, 1863 ; Lieut.-Col., 19th Foot, 10th March, 1875 ; half-pay, 13th April, 1875 ; Major-Gen., 2nd June, 1877 ; retired with hon. rank of Lieut.-Gen., 14th April, 1883.

Served in the Indian Mutiny, 1858-59, in command of 6th Foot and a body of drafts, in the operations at Perai and in the jungle (mentioned in despatches, medal).

Died at Hove, Brighton, 27th November, 1893.

ANDREW MUNRO

Born at Tongue, Sutherland, 8th September, 1830, son of Neill Munro, of Tongue.

Pte., 7th Foot, 18th October, 1850 ; Corpl., 14th January, 1852 ; Sergt., 1st March, 1854 ; Qr.-Mr.-Sergt., Land Transport Corps, 1st October, 1855. Ensign, 29th January, 1856 ; half-pay, 1st April, 1857 ; Military Train, 30th July, 1858 ; Lieut., 31st January, 1860 ; Capt., half-pay, 1st April, 1870 ; 19th Foot, 28th April, 1875 retired as hon. Lieut.-Col., 1st July, 1881.

Served in the Crimea and was present at the Alma, Inkerman, affairs of the Bulganac and McKenzie's farm, capture of Balaclava, and sortie of the 26th October. Siege of Sebastopol (medal and 3 clasps, Turkish medal).

Died at Westminster, 16th June, 1899. Buried at Nunhead Cemetery.

ALEXANDER SYDNEY GODOLPHIN JAUNCEY

Born, 20th November, 1827. Captain, Renfrew Militia, 5th January, 1855 ; Paymaster, 24th Foot, 1st February, 1868 ; hon. Capt., 1st February, 1873 ; 19th Foot, 28th April, 1875 ; 67th Foot, 19th July, 1876 ; 12th Lancers, 30th June, 1877 ; hon. Major, Army Pay Dept., 1st February, 1883 ; retired, 11th March, 1886.

Died at Brighton, 1st August, 1904.

CHARLES JOHN SPOTTISWOODE

Born at Bath, 16th December, 1856, son of Major-General Molyneux Capel Spottiswoode, Indian Army.

Sub-Lieut., unattached, 5th June, 1875 ; 19th Foot, 5th June, 1875 ; Lieut., 5th June, 1876 ; Capt., 29th September, 1882 ; Major, 11th May, 1890 ; Lieut.-Col., 29th September, 1898 ; Col., 29th September, 1902 ; half-pay, 30th September, 1902 ; retired, 20th April, 1904.

Served on the Nile during the expedition of 1885.

Died at Courtmacsherry, Co. Cork, 8th September, 1919.

In " Spot " as he was affectionately called, we have lost an old comrade and very dear friend, whose death will be widely mourned. No keener sportsman ever lived, and what he did not know about fishing and shooting was not worth knowing. It will be remembered that when the 1st Battalion was at Halifax, N.S., he spent all his long leave—six months at a time—in the woods, and wherever quartered, he seldom failed to find occasion to gratify his passion for sport. Since his retirement, he had resided at Southsea, with which he had long been connected, and he was an old and most popular member of the Royal Albert Yacht Club " (G.H.G.).

JAMES HENRY SCOTT-DOUGLAS

Born at Edinburgh, 27th May, 1853, eldest son of Sir George Henry Scott-Douglas, Bart., M.P., late 34th Foot, of Springwood Park, Kelso.

Lieut., 20th November, 1875 ; 21st Foot, 5th January, 1876.

Served in the Zulu War as chief of the signalling staff of the 2nd Division. Was surprised in company with Corporal Cotter, 17th Lancers, at Kwanagwasa by the enemy on 3rd July, 1879. Lieut. Scott-Douglas was able to discharge five chambers of his revolver and then fell pierced to the heart by an assegai. His body was found on 11th July, lying near that of Corporal Cotter, who had also stood his ground most gallantly. The two were buried with military honours, side-by-side, in graves marked with crosses and sheltered by a luxuriant growth of wild cactus.

" Of the soldierlike, manly bearing and social virtues of Lieut. Scott-Douglas," wrote Colonel Collingwood, 21st Fusiliers, " I his commanding officer cannot speak too highly. He was the ideal type of an officer and a gentleman in the highest sense in which that term can be applied."

GERARD GORDON ELRINGTON

Born at Cairo, 15th March, 1855, eldest son of Richard J. Crook Elrington.

Lieut., 29th January, 1876 ; 54th Foot, 15th September, 1877 ; Capt., 27th July, 1885 ; retired, 14th December, 1892.

JOHN WILLIAM ROBINSON PARKER, C.B., F.S.A.

Born at Browsholme, 6th October, 1857, son of Colonel Thomas Goulborne Parker, of Browsholme, Yorkshire.

Sub-Lieut., unattached, 12th February, 1876 ; 19th Foot, 12th February, 1876 ; Lieut., 12th February, 1876 ; Capt., 18th June, 1881 ; Major, 2nd May, 1890 retired, 27th May, 1896. Lieut.-Col., 3rd Bn. East Lancashire Regt., 26th March, 1902 ; retired from Militia, 13th Ocober, 1911.

Served with the Soudan Field Force in 1886. Served in the Boer War, 1900-01, with the 3rd Bn. East Lancashire Regt. in command most of the time. Commandant at Vet River and Smalldeel (mentioned in despatches, Queen's medal and 2 clasps, King's medal and 2 clasps).

In charge of Territorial Force Records, 28th April, 1915, to 18th January, 1918, (mentioned in home despatches).

Best shot in the Army, 1883. Best shot amongst officers of the Militia, 1903. C.B. (Civil) King's birthday, 1910. King's coronation medal, 1911.

Has calendared and edited two volumes of early Lancashire Assize Rolls. Editor, " The Green Howards' Gazette," April, 1893,—March, 1896, November, 1914,—September, 1919.

HENRY PONTING NORTHCOTT, p.s.c.

Born, 16th October, 1856, 2nd son of Dr. W. Northcott, of Staines.

Sub-Lieut., unattached, 12th February, 1876 ; 19th Foot, 12th February, 1876 ; Lieut., 12th February, 1877 ; 2nd West India Regt., 30th November, 1878 ; Capt., 12th February, 1886 ; Leinster Regt., 8th September, 1886 ; Major, 17th October, 1894.

Served in the expedition to Sherbro, West Africa in 1883 (mentioned in despatches). Took part in the operations in Zululand in 1888 as D.A.A.G. Served with the expedition to Ashanti under Sir Francis Scott in 1895 (star). Served in the Boer War, 1899, on the staff of Lord Methuen.

Killed at the battle of Modder River, 28th November, 1899.

Lieut.-Gen. Lord Methuen in his despatches, 1st December, 1899, wrote, " The Army has lost one of the ablest officers in the Service and I cannot express the grief his death has caused me."

CHARLES STANIFORTH GREENWOOD

Born, 1st May, 1857, 2nd son of John Greenwood, of Swarcliffe Hall, Leeds.

Sub-Lieut., unattached, 12th February, 1876 ; 19th Foot, 12th February, 1876 ; 10th Hussars, 17th January, 1877 ; Lieut., 12th February, 1877 ; Capt., 27th August, 1884 ; retired on a gratuity, 16th March, 1889. Lieut.-Col., 2nd West Yorkshire Yeomanry Cavalry, 7th November, 1891, to 1894.

Served with the 10th Hussars in the Afghan War of 1878-79, with the Khyber Line Force, and was present at the capture of Ali Musjid and in the second expedition into the Bazar Valley, including the affairs at Deb Sarak and Futtehabad (medal and clasp). Also served in the Soudan Expedition in 1884, and was present at the engagements at El Teb and Tamai (medal and clasp and Khedive's Star).

JOHN ROSE VINCENT

Born at Kurrachee, 5th May, 1855 ; Lieut., 1st Dragoon Gds., 20th November, 1875 ; 19th Foot, 26th February, 1876 ; resigned, 20th June, 1879.

HENRY BOWLES, C.B.

Born at Milton Hill, Berkshire, 25th June, 1854, son of John Samuel Bowles, J.P., D.L., of Milton Hill, Steventon.

Sub-Lieut., unattached, 26th February, 1876 ; 19th Foot, 26th February, 1876 ; Lieut., 28th February, 1877 ; Capt., 26th September, 1883 ; Bt.-Major, 15th June, 1885 ; Major, 4th March, 1892 ; Bt.-Lieut.-Col., 20th March, 1898 ; Lieut.-Col., 29th March, 1899 ; Col., 1st June, 1903 ; half-pay, 29th March, 1903 ; Director of Army Schools, 1st June, 1903, to 31st May, 1907 ; half-pay, 1st June, 1907 ; retired, 7th June, 1909.

Served in the Nile Expedition, 1884-85, as Staff Officer, Assouan, (mentioned in despatches Bt. of Major). Took part in the operations on the N.W. Frontier of India, 1897-98, with the Tirah Expeditionary Force, under Sir Wm. Lockhart, and was present at the capture of the Sampagha and Arhanga Passes, the capture of Bagh, the Dwatoi reconnaissance, the crossing of the Kahu Darra, the reconnaissance of the Saran Sar and engagements of 11th November, and the operations against the Khani Khel Chamkanis (mentioned in despatches, Bt. of Lieut.-Col., medal and 2 clasps). Served in the Boer War in command of 1st Bn., and was present in the operations round Colesberg in January, 1900, (mentioned in despatches). In the march along the Modder River, including the Relief of Kimberley, the engagement at Paardeberg (severely wounded), the advance on Dewetsdorp, including the engagement at Leuukop, the march from Bloemfontein to Pretoria, the engagements at Brandfort, Kroonstadt, and Johannesburg, and the advance to the Eastern Transvaal, including the battles of Diamond Hill and Belfast (mentioned in despatches, C.B., Queen's medal with 5 clasps, and King's medal with 2 clasps).

Commanded a Brigade at home, 1915-16, (mentioned). Granted hon. rank of Br.-General, 7th May, 1919.

EDWARD WHYTE

Born at Loughbrickland House, 17th September, 1837, 3rd son of Captain Nicholas Charles Whyte, R.N., J.P., D.L., of Loughbrickland, Co. Down.

Ensign, Royal Canadian Rifle Regt., 30th March, 1858 ; Lieut., 8th April, 1859 ; Capt., 12th May, 1863 ; Major, 13th June, 1868 ; half-pay, 10th October, 1870 ; 19th Foot, April, 1876 ; retired, 24th June, 1876.

Died at Monkstown, Co. Dublin, in August, 1905.

GEORGE FRENCH STEHELIN

Born at Mullingar, 14th July, 1834.

Ensign, 60th Rifles, 7th April, 1855 ; Lieut., 26th October, 1855 ; Capt., 22nd May, 1863 ; 83rd Foot, 17th October, 1863 ; half-pay, 31st August, 1869 ; 19th Foot, 24th June, 1876 ; 4th Foot, 17th January, 1877 ; Bt. Major, 1st October, 1877; Major,

1st July, 1881 ; retired as hon. Lieut.-Col., 9th August, 1882. Was for some time Secretary for the employment of discharged soldiers. Died in London, 26th August, 1890.

WILLIAM HUGHES

Born at Aghanloo, Co. Derry, 5th September, 1838, youngest son of the Revd. William Hughes, Rector of Killymard and Prebendary of Raphoe, Co. Donegal.

Ensign, 24th Foot, 22nd March, 1864, from ranks of 12th Foot ; Paymaster, 85th Foot, 20th November, 1867 ; hon. Capt., 20th November, 1872 ; 19th Foot, September, 1876 ; Army Pay Dept., April, 1878 ; Major, 22nd March, 1879 ; Staff Paymaster, 14th March, 1881 ; Chief Paymaster and Lieut.-Col., 24th December, 1884 ; Col., 1st November, 1887 ; retired, 5th September, 1898. Died at Stockbridge, Chichester, 19th September, 1908.

ARTHUR HENRY THISTLEWAYTE

Born, 25th March, 1857, 2nd son of Thomas Thistlewayte, of Southwick Park, Hants.

Sub-Lieut., 11th October, 1876 ; Lieut., Grenadier Gds., 10th November, 1877 ; Capt., 23rd April, 1887 ; retired with a gratuity, 22nd January, 1892.

REGINALD HOPE PARKINSON

Born, 31st July, 1856, son of C. E. Parkinson of Harrogate.

Lieut., 19th Foot, 29th November, 1876 ; 33rd Foot, 29th September, 1877 ; 80th Foot, 30th March, 1881; retired with a gratuity, 24th February, 1889 ; Capt. and hon. Major, 4th Bn. Highland L.I., 4th May, 1889. Died at Morningside, Edinburgh, 23rd April, 1915.

GEORGE WILLIAM HUGHES

Born at Edinburgh, 13th May, 1841, son of George Hughes, Writer to the Signet, 10, Rutland Square, Edinburgh.

Ensign, 4th Foot, 28th May, 1858 ; Lieut., 18th June, 1861 ; Capt., 30th March, 1870 ; 19th Foot, 17th January, 1877 ; 41st Foot, 17th May, 1879 ; retired as hon. Major., 19th May, 1880. Granted hon. rank of Lieut.-Col., 1st July, 1881.

Served in the Abyssinia Expedition of 1868, with the 4th King's Own, and was present at the action of Arogee and capture of Magdala (medal). Died at Southsea, 15th September, 1895.

REGINALD EDWARD HUXHAM

Born, 10th July, 1834. Ensign, 31st Foot, 27th February, 1856 ; Lieut., 22nd April, 1862 ; Capt., 9th Foot, 1st April, 1870 ; half-pay, 1st June, 1870 ; 19th Foot, 9th February, 1877; retired as hon. Major, 25th September, 1878. Granted hon. rank of Lieut.-Col., 25th June, 1881.

Served with the 31st Foot throughout the campaign of 1860 in China, including the action of Sinho and storming of Tangka (medal and clasp for Taku forts). Served against the Taeping rebels in the vicinity of Shanghai, 1862.

EDWARD JOHN BENTLEY BUCKLE

Born at Bedale, 11th May, 1857, son of Major John Edward Buckle, North Yorkshire Militia, of Scruton, Bedale, Yorkshire.

Second Lieut., 8th December, 1877 ; Lieut., 8th December, 1877 ; Capt., 1st August, 1884 ; Major, 28th July, 1892 ; retired, 12th January, 1898 ; Major, 6th Bn. P.W.O. West Yorkshire Regt., 18th March, 1915 ; Temporary Lieut.-Col., 5th November, 1915.

Served in the Nile Expedition, 1885, and with the Soudan Frontier Force, 1885-86 (medal and Khedive's Star). Employed on recruiting duty during War of 1914-18 (mentioned). Granted hon. rank of Colonel, 1st January, 1919.

THOMAS DAVID KIRKPATRICK

Born at Larne, Co. Antrim, 25th December, 1857, son of Thomas Kirkpatrick, of Larne.

Second Lieut., 8th December, 1877 ; Lieut., 1st January, 1878 ; Capt., 16th August, 1884 ; Major, 28th March, 1894 ; retired, 25th December, 1905.

Served in the Boer War, 1899-1900, and took part in the operations round Colesberg in January, 1900, and in the march along the Modder River, including the Relief of Kimberley and the battle of Paardeberg (dangerously wounded. Queens' medal and 2 clasps). Served in India with the 6th Bn. Devonshire Regt. during the Great War, from 12th December, 1914, to 23rd November, 1917, succeeding to the command on 1st July, 1916.

JOHN COLIN WARDLAW

Born at Edinburgh, 19th July, 1856, son of Major James Wardlaw, J.P., D.L., of Mimlochy, Rosshire.

Second Lieut., 8th December, 1877 ; 34th Foot, 23rd January, 1878 ; Lieut., 16th August, 1880 ; Adjt., 19th September, 1880—19th January, 1886 ; Capt., 20th January, 1886 ; Major, 16th June, 1896 ; retired, 26th August, 1896.

Died at Largs, Twynholm, Kircudbrightshire, 9th November, 1905.

EDWARD ROGER JACSON

Born, 10th October, 1857, 3rd son of the Revd. Edward Jacson, Rector of Thruxton, Hereford.

Second Lieut., 19th December, 1877 ; superseded for absence, 12th November, 1878.

Sir JAMES HAMLYN WILLIAMS WILLIAMS-DRUMMOND, Bart., C.B.

Born at Clovelly Court, Devon, 13th January, 1857, eldest son of Sir James Walker Williams-Drummond, Bart., of Hawthornden, Midlothian.

Regimental Paymasters were abolished by Royal Warrant, dated 22nd October, 1877, when the Army Pay Department was established.

Second Lieut., 29th December, 1877 ; Grenadier Gds., 13th March, 1878 ; Lieut., 1st July, 1881 ; resigned, 13th April, 1883. Major and hon. Lieut.-Col., Carmarthen Artillery Militia, 6th May, 1893 ; Lieut.-Col., 20th December, 1902.

Lord Lieut., Co. Carmarthen, 1898 ; C.B., 1909.

Died at Edwinsford, Llandilo, S. Wales, 15th June, 1913.

JAMES AHMUTY FEARON

Born in London, 27th October, 1856, son of Captain P. S. Fearon, H.E.I.C.S.

Second Lieut., 23rd January, 1878 ; Lieut., 28th January, 1878 ; Adjt., 20th March, 1880—19th March, 1887 ; Capt., 16th August, 1884 ; Major, 29th March, 1893 ; Bt. Lieut.-Col., 29th November, 1900 ; Lieut-Col., 29th September, 1902 ; Bt. Col., 29th October, 1904 ; retired, 29th September, 1906.

Served in the Nile Expedition, 1885. Took part in the campaign on the N.W. Frontier of India under Sir Wm. Lockhart with the Tirah Expeditionary Force, and was present at the taking of the Sampagha and Arhanga Passes, the capture of Bagh, the Dwatoi reconnaissance, the crossing of the Kahu Darra, the reconnaissance of the Saran Sar, and engagement of 11th November, 1897, and the operations against the Khami Khel Chamkanis (medal and two clasps).

Served in the Boer War, 1899-1902, and took part in the operations round Colesberg in January, 1900, the march along the Modder River, including the Relief of Kimberley, the battle of Paardeberg, 18th February, 1900, and commanded 1st Bn. in the subsequent actions at Kitchener's Kop, Poplar Grove, and Driefontein. Also took part in the advance on Dewetsdorp and action at Leuukop, the march from Bloemfontein to Pretoria, including the actions at the Vet and Zand Rivers, and engagements at Brandfort and Kroonstadt, and occupation of Johnannesburg and Pretoria. Was with the advance to the Eastern Transvaal and actions at Diamond Hill and Belfast (mentioned in despatches, Bt. of Lieut.-Col., Queen's medal and 6 clasps, King's medal and two clasps). In possession of the Delhi Coronation medal. In the Great War served as A.A.G. to a Division at home from 4th August, 1914, to January, 1916.

REGINALD HAYES-SADLER

Born in London, 5th September, 1856, 2nd son of Colonel Sir James Hayes-Sadler, K.C.M.G.

Second Lieut., 30th January, 1878 ; Lieut., 13th March, 1878 ; resigned his commission, 13th January, 1885 ; Major, 3rd Bn. King's Own Yorkshire L.I., 19th May, 1894 ; resigned, 1904.

Served in the Egyptian campaign of 1882, on the lines of communications, and was present at Kafrdwar and subsequently attached to the 38th Foot (medal and Khedive's Star). Served in the operations in Matabeleland in 1893 as special correspondent to the Army and Navy Gazette (medal). Served as a special service officer to the 7th Hussars during the operations in Mashonaland in 1897 (clasp). Took part in the Boer War on the Staff as Commandant, Rest Camp, Pretoria, afterwards as Asst. Provost Marshal, Standerton district (Queen's medal and 3 clasp, King's medal and 2 clasps). Served on special service in the Natal rebellion as Commandant, Tongaat district, 1906 (medal). Employed on the Staff in East Africa during the War of 1914-1918 (Bronze Star).

EDWARD WILLIAM MILLS

Born at Mian Mir, Punjab, 29th May, 1857, son of Lieut.-Col. Charles Edward Mills, Indian Army.

Second Lieut., 30th January, 1878 ; Lieut., 13th July, 1878 ; Capt., 1st April, 1885 ; D.A.C.G., Commissariat and Transport Staff, 8th February, 1885, to 10th December, 1888 ; retired, 18th November, 1896.

WILLIAM JAMES LASCELLES

Born at Goldsborough Hall, 22nd August, 1858, eldest son of the Revd. the Hon. James Walter Lascelles, Rector of Goldsborough, Knaresborough.

Second Lieut., 30th January, 1878 ; Rifle Brigade, 25th May, 1878 ; Lieut., 7th August, 1880 ; resigned, 26th November, 1884.

CHARLES STUART MOLONY

Born in Dublin, 21st October, 1856, only son of Colonel Charles Preston Molony, Indian Army.

Second Lieut., 16th February, 1878 ; Lieut., 24th July, 1878 ; Capt., 18th April, 1885 ; retired, 1st February, 1888 ; Capt., 6th Bn. Rifle Brigade, 1888-1902.

Served with the Militia in the Boer War (medal and clasps).

Was champion quarter mile runner in the Army.

JOHN DAVIES

Born, 23rd January, 1857, son of Captain John Davies, Adjt. and Qr.-Master, R.M.C., Sandhurst.

Second Lieut., 16th February, 1878 ; Lieut., 21st August, 1878 ; Indian Army, 26th April, 1882 ; Capt., 16th February, 1889 ; Major, 16th February, 1898 ; Lieut.-Col., 16th February, 1904 ; retired, 9th November, 1911.

CHARLES TULIN HENNAH

Born at East Cowes, 31st October, 1856, son of the Revd. William Veale Hennah, R.N., Vicar of East Cowes.

Second Lieut., 2nd March, 1878 ; Lieut., 25th September, 1878 ; Adjt., 22nd January, 1881—22nd December, 1886 ; Capt., 18th April, 1885 ; Adjt., 4th Bn. Yorkshire Regt., 1st May, 1889—1st May, 1894 ; retired, 17th October, 1894; Capt., 1st North Riding Volunteer Royal Garrison Artillery, 6th March, 1895 ; Major, 11th June, 1904 ; hon. Lieut.-Col., 12th July, 1905.

During the Boer War was Adjutant of the 19th Depôt, from 1st March, 1900,—13th July, 1901 ; and during the Great War from 21st August, 1914,—17th March, 1918 (mentioned in home despatch, 24th February, 1917). Comptroller and Private Secretary to the Marquess of Zetland since 1894.

HENRY EDWARD DAVIDSON

Born at Quebec, 16th August, 1838, son of Henry Edward Davidson, B.L., of Quebec.

Ensign, 100th Foot, 29th June, 1858 ; Lieut., 3rd July, 1860 ; Capt., 7th April, 1863 ; Major, 29th September, 1877 ; 19th Foot, 13th March, 1878 ; Lieut.-Col., 1st July, 1881 ; Bt. Col., 1st July, 1885 ; half-pay, 29th September, 1886 ; Commanding, 19th Regtl. District, 5th January, 1888, to 5th January, 1893 ; retired, 16th August, 1895.

Died at Woodchester, Stroud, 4th November, 1915.

"Under his command the 2nd Bn. earned very high praise for smartness and discipline. He was strict no doubt, very punctilious as to dress, severe on those who did anything to bring disgrace on the regiment. But he ruled by kindness and tact and a personal charm peculiarly his own. An excellent horseman ; there was little about horseflesh with which he was not acquainted, and he keenly encouraged those of his officers who had similar tastes. It was never his good fortune to see active service, but he was a good soldier and his regiment would have followed him anywhere " (G.H.G.).

GERALD CARLILE STRATFORD HANDCOCK

Born at Dunmore, 16th February, 1858, eldest son of John Stratford Handcock, of Carantrila Park, Co. Galway.

Second Lieut., 10th April, 1878 ; Lieut., 1st March 1879 ; Capt., 24th May, 1885 ; Major, 27th May, 1896 ; retired, 16th February, 1906.

Served in the Nile Expedition, 1885, and with the Soudan Frontier Field Force, 1885-86 (medal and Khedive's Star).

Served with the 4th Bn. Mounted Infantry in the Boer War, 1899-1902, and was present at the operations round Colesberg in January, 1900, the march along the Modder River, including the Relief of Kimberley, the battle of Paardeberg, the advance on Bloemfontein, and engagement at Poplar Grove. Took part in the march to Pretoria, the engagements at Brandfort, Kroonstadt and Johannesburg, and actions at the Vet and Zand Rivers, the occupation of Pretoria, and the march Eastwards, including the battles at Diamond Hill and Belfast (Queen's medal and 6 clasps, King's medal and 2 clasps).

Was employed on recruiting duties during war of 1914-18.

ALEXANDER HUGH DOBBS

Born in Dublin, 9th September, 1859, son of Arthur Macauley Dobbs, of Dublin.

Second Lieut., 1st May, 1878 ; 43rd Foot, 5th September, 1878 ; Indian Army, 20th May, 1880 ; Capt., 1st May, 1889 ; Major, 1st May, 1898 ; Lieut.-Col., 1st May, 1904 ; retired, 1st May, 1910.

Served in the Burmese Expedition, 1888-89 (medal and clasp).

WILLIAM HARRIS-BURLAND

Born, 1st August, 1835, son of John Harris-Burland, J P., of Bradby House, Wooton-under-Edge, Gloucestershire.

Ensign, 9th Foot, 25th August, 1854 ; Lieut., 7th March, 1855 ; Capt., 25th September, 1860 ; Bt. Major, 1st June, 1873 ; Major, 21st July, 1877 ; 19th Foot, 6th August, 1878 ; Lieut.-Col., 1st July, 1881 ; half-pay, 13th September, 1881 ; 19th Foot, 7th January, 1882 ; Col., 24th October, 1885 ; half-pay, 28th July, 1886 ; retired as hon. Major-Gen., 27th April, 1887.

Served in the Crimea from 16th June, 1855, including the assault on the Cemetery, 18th June, and the fall of Sebastopol (medal with clasp and Turkish medal). Served in the Nile Expedition, 1885, and with the Soudan Field Force, 1886.

Died at Sydenham, 28th July, 1890. Buried in Elmer's End Cemetery.

MATTHEW VILLIERS ELRINGTON SANKEY

Born, 1st April, 1856, only son of Captain Jacob Hiram Sankey, R.N., J.P., of Coolmore, Fethard, Tipperary.

Second Lieut., 25th September, 1878 ; Lieut., 7th June, 1879 ; 5th Dragoon Gds., 12th December, 1883 ; resigned, 22nd July, 1884.

Died at Blackheath, 26th October, 1907.

WILLIAM AUSCHAR CHAUNCY

Born at Leamington, 5th August, 1858, eldest son of Henry Carter Chauncy.

Second Lieut., 30th October, 1878 ; Lieut., 21st June, 1879 ; Capt., 27th July, 1885 ; Major, 28th July, 1896 ; retired, 16th November, 1896.

Served in the Nile Expedition, 1885, and with the Soudan Frontier Field Force, 1885-86, including the engagement at Ginnis (medal and Khedive's Star). During the Great War was employed as Chief Recruiting Officer, 35th Regtl. District, from 29th September, 1914, to 15th October, 1917, and afterwards under the Ministry of National Service till April, 1918 (mentioned in home despatch).

EDWIN LOUD HERAPATH

Born in London, 24th April, 1854, son of Edwin John Herapath, Barrister, Middle Temple, of Kidbrooke Park, Blackheath.

Sub Lieut., 1st West India Regt., 13th November, 1875 ; Lieut., 13th November, 1876 ; 19th Foot, 30th November, 1878 ; Capt., 24th May, 1885 ; Army Pay Dept., 22nd January, 1890 ; hon. Major, 24th May, 1894 ; Major, February, 1899 ; retired, 17th September, 1902.

GEORGE O'NEILL SEGRAVE

Born in London, 22nd July, 1858, son of Stephen Segrave.

Second Lieut., 108th Foot, 13th November, 1878 ; 19th Foot, 4th December, 1878 ; Lieut., 28th July, 1879 ; Capt., 9th September, 1885 ; retired, 16th March, 1889 ; Capt., 3rd Militia Bn., Bedfordshire Regt., 16th March, 1889 ; hon. Major, 8th May, 1889 ; Major, 17th March, 1894 ; hon. Lieut.-Col., 13th January, 1897 ; retired, 4th November, 1899.

ARTHUR de SALIS HADOW

Born in London, 12th July, 1858, son of Patrick Douglas Hadow, B.L., of Sudbury Priory, Middlesex.

Second Lieut., 4th December, 1878 ; Lieut., 11th October, 1879 ; Capt., 8th November, 1885 ; Major, 4th December, 1896 ; Lieut.-Col., 29th September, 1906 ; Bt. Col., 29th

September, 1909 ; retired, 29th September, 1910.

Served in the Nile Expedition, 1885, and with the Soudan Frontier Force in charge of regimental Camel Corps, 1885-6. Appointed to the command of the 10th Service Battalion, 21st September, 1914. Killed in action at Hill 70, Loos, 26th September, 1915.

" The period of his command was one to which the 2nd Battalion can look back with pride. No one more strongly fostered that esprit-de-corps which has ever been characteristic of the Green Howards, and no one more thoroughly carried out the precepts which he enjoined " (G.H.G.).

ALFRED GRAHAM CARTWRIGHT

Born in London, 29th July, 1858, youngest son of Samuel Cartwright, F.R.C.S., of Old Burlington Street, London.

Second Lieut., 1st January, 1879 ; Lieut., 11th February, 1880 ; Capt., 1st September, 1886 ; Major, 16th December, 1896 ; retired, 29th July, 1906.

Served in the Nile Expedition, 1885, and with the Soudan Frontier Field Force, including the engagement at Ginnis (medal and Khedive's Star). Served in the campaign on the N.W. Frontier of India, under Sir William Lockhart in 1897-8, with the Tirah Expeditionary Force, and was present at the capture of the Sampagha and Arhanga Passes, the capture of Bagh, the Dwatoi reconnaissance, the crossing of the Kahu Darra, the reconnaissance of the Saran Sar and engagement of 11th November, and the operations against the Khani Khel Chamkanis. Also in the Bazar Valley (medal and two clasps).

Served in France from July, 1915, to November, 1915, at Voormelles, and Hooge, with 7th Service Battalion (Bronze Star). In command of a training Reserve Battalion at home from April, 1916 (twice mentioned in despatches).

Died at Benton, near Newcastle-on-Tyne, 5th August, 1917.

" In the mud, discomfort and fighting of Flanders, his unvarying cheerfulness and dis-regard of danger won the admiration of the whole Division. Several times he was offered the command of other units, but he always refused to accept promotion outside the regiment. Gifted with a keen sense of humour and of a tolerant and kindly disposition, Colonel Cartwright was not only punctilious in the performance of his own duties, but an excellent disciplinarian, as those who served under him will remember. Yet no one was a keener champion of the unfortunate, if a wrong were to be righted, an injustice remedied, or more ready to help a subordinate in trouble. His subalterns, in particular, knew that they would never be forgotten if a chance occurred to do them a good turn ; and, though he never mentioned his kindly acts, it is certain that nobody ever appealed to him in vain " (G.H.G.).

COLQUHON GRANT MORRISON, C.M.G., p.s.c.

Born in Dublin, 28th January, 1860, son of Lieut.-Col. Richard Fielding Morrison, late 19th Foot and 5th Lancers.

Second Lieut., 22nd January, 1879 ; Rifle Brigade, 23rd July, 1879 ; Lieut., 18th June, 1881 ; Capt., 18th Hussars, 27th May, 1889 ; Major, 1st Royal Dragoons, 15th September, 1897 ; Lieut.-Col., half-pay, 28th January, 1908 ; Col., 4th October, 1911.

Served in the Boer War, 1899-1902, as Station Commandant, Middleburg, and as administrator No. 16 area (Queen's medal and 3 clasps). Served in France as President of Claims' Commission as temporary Br.-General (mentioned in despatches, C.M.G.).

Died at Amiens, 23rd May, 1916, from the result of a motor car accident.

Author of "Notes on Military Law, Organization, etc," 1896; "Tactics of the Drill Books, 1899.

JAMES TREVELYAN COTESWORTH

Born at Walthamstow, 21st January, 1858, son of William Cotesworth, J.P., of Cowdenknowes, Earlston, Co. Berwick. Second Lieut., 22nd January, 1879 ; Lieut., 20th March, 1880 ; Capt., 11th January, 1888 ; Adjt., 20th March, 1887—15th January, 1889 ; Major, 12th January, 1898 ; retired, 21st January, 1906.

Served with the Soudan Expedition in 1885 with the Mounted Infantry and was present at the engagements of Hasheen, Tamai and Takdul (medal with clasp and Khedive's Star). Also with the Frontier Force on the Nile in 1886. Served with the Tirah Expeditionary Force under Sir William Lockhart in 1897-98, and was present at the capture of the Sampagha and Arhanga Passes, the capture of Bagh, the Dwatoi reconnaissance, the crossing of the Kahu Darra, the reconnaissance of the Saran Sar and engagement of the 11th November. In the operations against the Khani Khel Chamkanis, and in the Bazar Valley (medal and two clasps). Served in the Boer War, 1900-02, and took part in the advance to the Eastern Transvaal, including the battle at Belfast (Queen's medal and 3 clasps, King's medal and 2 clasps).

During the War of 1914-18, served as 2nd in command of the 7th Service Battalion the Buffs, till appointed Deputy Assistant Censor of Cables, 31st July, 1915, to 21st March, 1916. Editor "The Green Howards' Gazette, November, 1899—June, 1900.

ALEXANDER DINGWALL FORDYCE

Born at Blackheath, 21st March, 1860, 5th son of Lieut.-Gen. Sir John Fordyce, K.C.B., Royal (Bengal) Artillery. Second Lieut., 22nd January, 1879 ; 16th Foot, 15th March, 1879 ; Lieut., 2nd July, 1879 ; Indian Army, 16th August, 1880; Capt., 22nd January, 1890 ; Major, 22nd January, 1899 ; retired, 11th February, 1899.

Served in the Burmese Expedition of 1886-7 (medal and clasp).

HENRY FREDERICK TUCKER MACARTNEY

Born, 11th June, 1856, 3rd son of William Merton Macartney, B.L., of Muckamore, Co. Antrim. Second Lieut., 22nd January, 1879 ; Lieut., 29th September, 1880 ; Indian Army, 2nd October, 1880 ; Capt., 22nd January, 1890 ; Major, 22nd January, 1899 ; Lieut.-Col., 22nd January, 1907 ; retired, 19th March, 1907.

Served in the Hazara Expedition, 1891 (medal and clasp). Served in the China Expedition of 1900 (medal). Employed on recruiting duties during the War of 1914-18.

GEORGE LAWRENCE MELLISS

Born, 25th September, 1860. Second Lieut., 22nd January, 1879 ; 66th Foot, 27th September, 1879 ; Lieut., 28th July, 1880 ; Indian Army, 9th April, 1881.

Served in the Afghan War, 1879-80, and was present at the action of Ghirisk, defence of Kandahar, battle of Maiwand, sortie from Kandahar of 16th August, and battle of 1st September (medal and clasp). Died at Bombay, 5th February, 1889.

LEONARD WILKINSON CLEVELAND KERRICH

Born, 25th August, 1850, son of General Walter D'Oyley Kerrich, Col. Commandant, Royal (Madras) Artillery.

Second Lieut., 22nd January, 1879 ; 13th Foot, 8th March, 1879 ; Lieut., Indian Army, 1st September, 1880 ; Capt., 22nd January, 1890 ; Major, 22nd January, 1899 ; Lieut.-Col., 22nd January, 1905 ; Col., 2nd June, 1907 ; retired, 22nd January, 1911.

Served in the Boer War, 1900-02, as transport officer, including the Relief of Kimberley, operations in the Orange Free State, February to May, 1900, and the operations at Paardeberg, 17th to 26th February, actions at Poplar Grove, Driefontein, Karee Siding, Vet River (5th and 6th May), and Zand River. In the operations in the Transvaal in May and June, 1900, including actions near Johannesburg, Pretoria and Diamond Hill (11th and 12th June), and East of Pretoria, July to 29th November, 1900, including actions at Reitvlei and Belfast, 26th and 27th August (Queen's medal and 6 clasps ; King's medal and 2 clasps).

LIONEL HOOK

Son of Colonel Lionel Smith Hook, 19th and 16th Foot.

Ensign, 16th Foot, 5th September, 1834 ; Lieut., 9th Foot, 4th December, 1838 ; Adjt., 13th December, 1844 ; Capt., 27th April, 1849 ; Ceylon Rifles, 21st May, 1852 ; Bt. Major, 18th January, 1861 ; Major, 13th March, 1861 ; Lieut.-Col., half-pay, 3rd February, 1872 ; 19th Foot, 12th February, 1879; retired as hon. Col., 15th March, 1879.

Served with the 9th Foot throughout the campaign of 1842 in Afghanistan (medal) under Sir George Pollock, and was present at the forcing of the Khyber Pass, storming of Mamookail, and the heights of Jugdulluck, affair in Tezeen Valley and Huft Kotal mountain, occupation of Kabul, expedition to Kohistan, storm, capture and destruction of Istaliff. Served as Adjt. to the 9th Foot in the Sutlej campaign of 1845-46, and was present at the battles of Moodkee, Ferozeshah (horse shot) and Sobraon (medal and two clasps). Awarded a meritorious pension in 1873.

Died at 79, Abingdon Road, Kensington, 8th October, 1904, aged 89 years.

HENRY HENZEL FRASER PIDCOCK-HENZEL

Born at Bareilly, 1st February, 1849, eldest son of Henry Pidcock, B.C.S., J.P., D.L., of Oakfield Manor Worcestershire.

Ensign, 63rd Foot, 24th March, 1869; Lieut., 28th March, 1870 ; 103rd Foot, 22nd March, 1871 ; Capt., 1st October, 1878 ; 19th Foot, 12th April, 1879 ; retired, 10th June, 1881 ; Major, Middlesex Militia, 1886-89.

JOHN OLAUS CHAMPION MÖLLER

Born at Chatham, 13th September, 1847, son of Major John Olaus Möller, 50th Foot, killed before Sebastopol, 1854.

Ensign, 41st Foot, 27th November, 1866 ; Lieut., 1st

December, 1869; Capt., 13th November, 1878; 19th Foot, 17th May, 1879; Major, 2nd May, 1883; Lieut.-Col., half-pay, 2nd May, 1890; retired, 7th May, 1890.

Served in the Nile Expedition of 1885, and with the Soudan Frontier Field Force, including the engagement at Ginnis (medal and Khedive's Star).

ARTHUR BAYARD ELTON

Born, 6th November, 1857, 4th son of Frederick Bayard Elton, H.E.I.C.S.

Second Lieut., 13th August, 1879; Lieut., 2nd October, 1880; Capt., 4th May, 1888; Major, 14th December, 1898; half-pay, 21st January, 1902; retired, 2nd August, 1902.

Served with the Tirah Expedition, 1897-98, under Sir William Lockhart, including the expedition to the Bazar Valley (medal and two clasps).

Died at Brighton, 11th January, 1916.

EDWARD KNATCHBULL-HUGESSEN, 2nd Baron BRABOURNE

Born at Malvern, 5th April, 1857, eldest son of 1st Baron Brabourne.

Second Lieut., 13th August, 1879; Coldstream Guards, 13th August, 1879; retired, 23rd March, 1881.

M.P. for Rochester, 1886-1892. Succeeded his father as 2nd Baron, 6th February, 1893.

Died in London, 29th December, 1909.

Sir EDWARD CHARLES WILLIAM MACKENZIE-KENNEDY, C.B., K.B.E.

Born, 6th July, 1860, 3rd son of the Revd. Chessborough de la Poer Mackenzie-Kennedy.

Second Lieut., 13th August, 1879; Lieut., 30th March, 1881; Indian Army, 3rd May, 1882; Capt., 13th August, 1892; Major, 13th August, 1899; Bt. Lieut.-Col., 29th November, 1900; Lieut.-Col., 1st June, 1904; Bt. Col., 10th February, 1904; Major-Gen., 9th June, 1908; Col., 61st (King George's Own) Pioneers, 23rd April, 1912.

Served in the Burmese Expedition, 1885-87, advance and occupation of Mandalay (medal and clasp). Hazara Expedition of 1891 (clasp), and in the China Expedition of 1900, including the relief of Pekin (mentioned in despatches, Bt. of Lieut.-Colonel, medal and clasp). C.B., King's birthday, 1910. Appointed to command 26th (New Army) Division on its formation, 18th September, 1914. Served with it in France and the Balkans till 22nd March, 1917 (mentioned in despatches, Bronze Star and Knight of the British Empire).

CHARLES HENRY ROBERT M'NAIR

Born, 16th March, 1860, son of Captain M'Nair.

Second Lieut., 13th August, 1879; 65th Foot, 27th September, 1879; Lieut., 1st July, 1881; Indian Army, 30th August, 1883.

Died at Midnapore, Bengal, 26th January, 1885.

CLEMENT HENRY BILLINGS

Born at Meerut, 11th August, 1858.

Second Lieut., 13th August, 1879 ; 30th Foot, 7th January, 1880 ; Lieut., 1st July, 1881 ; Indian Army, 6th March, 1882 ; Capt., 13th August, 1890 ; half-pay, 12th November, 1895 ; retired, 24th December, 1898.

Died at St. Leonard's, 31st March, 1899.

ALFRED ERNEST STUART SEARLE

Born at Bangalore, 16th March, 1860, son of Major-Gen. George Archimedes Searle, Madras Army.

Second Lieut., 13th August, 1879 ; Lieut., 8th June, 1881 ; Indian Army, 5th April, 1882 ; Capt., 13th August, 1890 ; Major, 13th August, 1899 ; Lieut.-Col., 17th September, 1904 ; Col., 7th March, 1908; retired, 13th August, 1911.

Served with Burmese Expedition, 1885-6 (medal and clasp). Served in East Africa, 1902-4, during the operations in Somaliland (medal and clasp). Served in the War of 1914-18, as a draft conducting officer and also in command of a labour battalion.

MICHAEL HARRISON ORR, D.S.O.

Born at Ballymena, 23rd December, 1859, son of William Orr, of Hugomont, Ballymena, Co. Antrim.

Second Lieut., 14th January, 1880 ; Lieut., 1st July, 1881 ; Capt., 29th September, 1888 ; Major, 21st January, 1902 ; retired, 23rd December, 1907.

Served in the Nile Expedition, 1885, and with the Soudan Field Force, 1885-6 (medal and Khedive's Star). Served in the Boer War, 1899-1902, and took part in the operations near Colesberg in January, 1900 (wounded, mentioned in despatches). In the march from Bloemfontein to Pretoria, including the engagements at the Vet and Zand Rivers, Brandfort, Kroonstadt, Johannesburg and occupation of Pretoria. In the advance eastwards, including actions at Diamond Hill and Belfast (mentioned in despatches, D.S.O., Queen's medal and 5 clasps, King's medal and 2 clasps).

FRANK WILLIAM McTIER BUNNY

Born in London, 16th June, 1860, 3rd son of Major-Gen. Arthur Bunny, C.B., Royal Artillery.

Second Lieut., 14th January, 1880 ; 66th Foot, 25th February, 1880 ; Lieut., 29th September, 1880 ; Capt., 16th November, 1886 ; Ordnance Dept., 11th August, 1887 ; Major, 1st May, 1899 ; Lieut.-Col., 1st February, 1904 ; Col., 2nd August, 1909 ; retired, 22nd July, 1915.

Served in the Afghan War in Southern Afghanistan, 1880 (medal).

DONALD GRANT

Born, 11th July, 1856, eldest son of Major John Hayes Grant, Bengal Artillery.

Second Lieut., 14th January, 1880 ; Lieut., 1st July, 1881 ; Capt., 28th August, 1889 ; retired, 17th February, 1892.

Promoted Major, Reserve of Officers, 18th October, 1902, for service at home with the Army Service Corps during the Boer War. Appointed a temporary Lieut.-Col., Army Service Corps, 21st April, 1916 (mentioned for home service, 24th February, 1917).

HUGH WOOLCOMBE WOOLCOMBE-BOYCE

Born at the Priory, Cheltenham, 20th March, 1861, 3rd son of the Revd. William Woolcombe-Boyce, M.A., Rector of Elkston, Gloucestershire.

Second Lieut., 14th January, 1880 ; Lieut., 1st July, 1881 ; 19th Hussars, 11th March, 1884 ; Capt., 5th Lancers, 22nd November, 1888 ; 6th Dragoon Gds., 6th February, 1889.

Served in the Nile Expedition, 1884-5, with the 19th Hussars, and was present at the battle of Kirbekan (medal with 2 clasps and Khedive's Star).

Died in London, 1st March, 1890, the result of a fall from his horse at Sandown Park the same day, when riding in the Hunter's Steeplechase.

" The sad death of Captain Boyce came as a shock to a large circle of friends, both in the Army and in what for lack of a better term we may call sporting circles. He was a good cross-country rider and an excellent shot, but, like other good men in the Army, he did not allow his amusements to interfere with his duties, which from the day he entered the Army he discharged with zeal and enthusiasm."

An officer of his late regiment, the Carabineers, writes : " He was an excellent officer and most zealous in the performance of all his duties and very popular with all ranks, and his loss is much regretted by the regiment." An officer of the 19th Hussars also writes : " He was a great favourite in the regiment and a hard-working soldier. He served in the Egyptian campaign with us where he did very good work " (Broad Arrow).

HARRY OTHO DEVEREUX HICKMAN, C.B., p.s.c.

Born at Kinver, Worcestershire, 13th November, 1860, 2nd son of H. T. Hickman of Chorton House, Leamington, Warwickshire.

Second Lieut., 14th January, 1880 ; Lieut., 1st July, 1881 ; Capt., 28th August, 1899 ; Royal Inniskilling Fusiliers, 8th January, 1890 ; Major, 25th February, 1900 ; Lieut.-Col., 27th January, 1908 ; Col., 4th October, 1911 ; retired, 2nd July, 1913.

Served in the Nile Expedition, 1884-85, with the Egyptian Army (medal and clasp and Khedive's Star). In the Soudan Expediton, 1889, including the action at Gamaizeh (clasp, 4th Class of the Osmanieh). In the South African War, and took part in the operations in Natal, March to June, 1900, and in the Transvaal, East of Pretoria, July to November, 1900 inclusive ; actions at Belfast and Lydenberg (medal and 4 clasps). Commanded the 66th Infantry Brigade in France and Macedonia from July, 1915, to December, 1916 (mentioned in despatches, Bronze Star). Commanded the 19th Training Reserve Brigade from March, 1917, to 9th February, 1918 (mentioned in home despatches, C.B.). Hon. rank of Br.-General, 9th February, 1918.

Asst. Military Secretary and A.D.C. to Governor of Bermuda, 24th June, 1896, to 24th February, 1900 ; D.A.A.G., Western District, 1st August, 1901, to 31st October, 1904 ; 2nd in command, R.M.C., Sandhurst, 19th February, 1910, to 3rd May, 1912 ; Asst. Director Territorial Force, 9th April, 1912, to July, 1913 ; G.S.O., 1st Grade, War Office, 10th August, 1914, to 5th July, 1915.

MICHAEL LLOYD FERRAR

Born in Belfast, 8th January, 1861, 2nd son of Augustus Minchin Ferrar, D.L., of Belfast.

Second Lieut., 14th January, 1880 ; Lieut., 1st July, 1881 ; Capt., 2nd May, 1890 ; Bt. Major, 29th November, 1900 ; Major, 29th September, 1902 ; retired, 18th February, 1905.

Served in the Nile Expedition, 1885, and with the Soudan Frontier Field Force, 1885-6, as Acting District Officer, Royal Engineers, Korosko, and took part in the engagement at Ginnis (medal and Khedive's Star).

Served in the Boer War, 1899-1902, and was present during the operations round Colesberg in January, 1900, in the march along the Modder River, including the Relief of Kimberley, the actions at Paardeberg, Kitchener's Kop, Poplar Grove, and Driefontein, and occupation of Bloemfontein (mentioned in despatches). In the advance on Dewetsdorp and action at Leeukop. In the march from Bloemfontein to Pretoria, including the engagements at Brandfort, Kroonstadt, the Vet and Zand Rivers, and occupation of Johannesburg and Pretoria. Also in the advance eastwards, including the actions at Diamond Hill and Belfast. Was Commandant, Springs, Transvaal, from October, 1901, to end of war (mentioned in despatches, Bt. of Major, Queen's medal and 6 clasps, King's medal and 2 clasps).

In the Great War was D.A.A. and Q.M.G., 19th Division, from October, 1914, to October, 1915, including the operations near Festubert in September, 1915 (Bronze Star). Employed with 83rd Depôt, October, 1915, to August, 1918.

Author of "With the Green Howards in South Africa," 1904. "Historical Record of the Green Howards," 1911. Editor of "The Green Howards' Gazette," April, 1896—November, 1899, November, 1902—November, 1914, October, 1919, to date.

EDWARD EDWIN BULLEN OLDFIELD

Born at Mauritius, 30th October, 1860, son of Major Edwin John Oldfield, 5th Fusiliers.

Second Lieut., 17th April, 1880 ; 5th Foot, 12th March, 1881 ; Lieut., 1st July, 1881 ; Capt., 7th February, 1890 ; retired on half-pay, 4th March, 1892.

Died at Southsea, 20th March, 1893.

ARTHUR JAMES CRAIG WARD

Born, 20th August, 1860, son of Lieut.-Col. James Ward, C.B., V.D., London Irish Rifles, of Lisburn, Co. Antrim.

Second Lieut., 17th April, 1880.

Died at Halifax, Nova Scotia, 12th December, 1880, of typhoid fever.

GEORGE PEARSON

Born in London, 29th September, 1856.

Second Lieut., 12th Lancers, 30th October, 1878 ; 19th Foot, 23rd June, 1880 ; Lieut., 1st July, 1881 ; Capt., 11th May, 1890 ; retired, 29th September, 1901.

Served in the Nile Expedition, 1884-5, with the Egyptian Army (medal and clasp, Khedive's Star). Served in the Boer War, 1899-1900, including the operations round Colesberg in January, 1900. In the march along the Modder River, the Relief of Kimberley, battle of Paardeberg, and attack on Kitchener's Kopje (severely wounded, medal and two clasps). Was employed on recruiting duties during war of 1914-18. Captain of Invalids, Chelsea Hospital, since 26th June, 1902.

GEORGE HOPE

Born, 30th September, 1834, son of George Hope, 77th Foot, Qr.-Master, 4th South Middlesex Militia, 1854-1878.

In the ranks 13 years 300 days. Qr.-Master, 77th Foot, 27th July, 1866 ; 19th Foot, 25th August, 1880 ; hon. Capt., 1st July, 1881 ; retired as hon. Major, 29th November, 1881.

Served throughout the Eastern campaign of 1854-55, including the battles of the Alma and Inkerman, siege and fall of Sebastopol, assaults on the Redan, 18th June, and 8th September (medal with 3 clasps and Turkish medal).

Died at Southsea, 18th December, 1889.

ARTHUR WHICHCOTE TURNER

Born, 10th October, 1847, 3rd son of the Revd. Canon Turner, Rector of Aldford, Chester.

Ensign, 99th Foot, 27th February, 1867 ; Lieut., 28th October, 1871 ; Capt., 19th Foot, 4th September, 1880 ; retired, 11th March, 1881.

Served with the 99th Foot in the Zulu War, being present at the engagements of Inyezani and Ginghilovo, when he acted as Adjt. to the companies under Lieut.-Col. Walker in the latter action (medal and clasp).

Accidentally drowned at Menindie, New South Wales, 2nd March, 1888.

HENRY COOK, C.B.

Born, 21st October, 1837. Ensign, 32nd Foot, 15th June, 1855 ; Lieut., 31st August, 1855 Capt., 100th Foot, 1st June, 1858 ; Major, 7th April, 1863 ; Bt. Lieut.-Col., 23rd May, 1873 ; Lieut.-Col., 29th September, 1877 ; 19th Foot, 28th October, 1880 ; Col., 23rd May, 1878. In command of 30th Regtl. District, 1883-88. Major-Gen., 5th August, 1888 ; retired, 5th August, 1893 ; Colonel, Dorsetshire Regt., 17th June, 1910.

Present with the 32nd Foot in the action of Chenut, 30th June, 1857, and throughout the defence of the Lucknow Residency. Commanded the troops at Innes' House during the first part of the siege and at Sago's House during the latter part. Commanded two sorties, in one of which he took a gun in battery at the head of twenty men, for which he was mentioned in General Inglis' despatch as "having highly distinguished himself" (medal and clasp and a year's service). Awarded the C.B., King's birthday, 1907.

WILLIAM LINDSAY MERCER

Born at Edinburgh, 23rd April, 1858, eldest son of Major William Drummond Mercer, J.P., of Huntingtower, Co. Perth, late 16th Lancers, and grandson of William Mercer, 19th Foot and H.E.I.C.S.

Second Lieut., 22nd January, 1881 ; Lieut., 1st July, 1881 ; Capt., 9th April, 1891 ; retired, 27th April, 1898.

Served in the Nile Expedition, 1885, and with the Soudan Frontier Field Force, 1885-86, and was present at the action of Ginnis (medal and Khedive's Star).

Promoted Major, Reserve of Officers, 18th October, 1902, for services at home during the Boer War.

Editor, The Green Howards' Gazette, July, 1900, to October, 1902.

ARTHUR TRISTRAM HERBERT NEWNHAM

Born at Clifton, 17th January, 1861, son of William Heurtley Newnham, Bombay Civil Service.

Second Lieut., 22nd January, 1881 ; Lieut., 1st July, 1881 ; Indian Army, 11th April, 1883 ; Capt., 22nd January, 1892 ; Major, 22nd January, 1901 ; Lieut.-Col., 22nd January, 1907 ; retired, 22nd January, 1913.

WILLIAM JOSEPH TODD

Born at Dover, 28th September, 1858, son of Joseph Todd.

Second Lieut., 1st Foot, 23rd October, 1880 ; 19th Foot, 23rd March, 1881 ; Lieut., 1st July, 1881 ; Capt., 27th June, 1891 ; retired, 29th December, 1900.

Served in the Tirah Campaign, 1897-98. Present at the capture of the Sampagha and Arhanga Passes ; the reconnaissance of the Saran Sar and action of 9th November ; operations at and around Dwatoi, and action of 24th November ; operations against the Khani Khel Chamkanis and in the Bazar Valley, 25th to 30th December, 1897 ; affair at Shinkamar, 29th January, 1898 (medal and two clasps). During the war, 1914-15, was employed as temporary Major, 6th Bn. Shropshire L.I.

Died at 20, Jermyn Street, London, 17th March, 1917.

See "The Green Howards' Gazette," vol. xxiv, pp. 153-4, for an obituary notice.

ALFRED CHARLES FRYER

Born at Hagley, Worcestershire, 19th July, 1846, son of F. W. Fryer of Hawford, Bournemouth, and Westmoor, Dorset.

Ensign, 61st Foot, 16th March, 1867 ; Lieut., 7th May, 1870 ; 106th Foot, 12th March, 1881 ; Capt., 19th Foot, 30th March, 1881 ; Major, 1st April, 1886 ; Adjt., 1st Vol. Bn., 20th April, 1886—20th April, 1891 ; Lieut.-Col., half-pay, 28th March, 1894 ; retired, 3rd October, 1894.

For many years Secretary to the Royal Cambridge Asylum for soldiers' widows.

PERCY LEES

Born at Middleton, Lancashire, 4th February, 1860, 5th son of James Lees, of Alkrington Hall, D.L., J.P., Lancashire.

Second Lieut., 23rd April, 1881 ; Lieut., 1st July, 1881 ; Adjt., 22nd December, 1886—7th November, 1888 ; Capt., 4th March, 1892 ; half-pay, 30th January, 1894 ; retired, 8th May, 1895.

Died at Colorado Springs, U.S.A., 20th August, 1903.

AUBREY WALTER WASHBOURNE MONEY-KYRLE

Born at Homme House, Co. Hereford, 12th September,
1846, 2nd son of Lieut.-Col. John E. Money-Kyrle, 32nd Foot.
Ensign, 55th Foot, 27th July, 1866 ; Lieut., 28th October,
1871 ; Capt., 19th Foot, 8th June, 1881 ; Major, 28th July,
1886 ; retired, 28th August, 1889.
Died at Much Marche, near Ledbury, 28th October, 1908.

FRANCIS PETTITT

Born, 3rd October, 1847. In ranks of 19th Foot 13 years
75 days. Hon. Lieut. and Qr.-Master, 17th December, 1881 ;
hon. Capt., 17th December, 1891.
Died at Wellington, Madras, 7th April, 1894.

GEORGE HEDINGHAM

Born, 24th March, 1847. Pte., 22nd March, 1862 ; Corpl.,
2nd January, 1866 ; Sergt., 22nd June, 1868 ; Sergt.-Major,
5th April, 1875 ; Qr.-Master, 19th April, 1882 ; 3rd (Militia)
Bn., 8th May, 1883 ; 107th Foot, 4th October, 1884 ; 15th
Foot, 9th November, 1892 ; hon. Capt., 19th April, 1892 ; retired, 7th April, 1897.
Served in the Hazara Expedition of 1888 (medal and clasp).
Died at Angell Road, Brixton, 21st December, 1912.
"Captain Hedingham was a splendid type of soldier, of fine
presence, a commanding manner and a strict disciplinarian. His fearless, straightforward character left one in no doubt as to his ideals in
the fulfilment of a duty, and the splendid example he set to all, won
for him the universal regard and esteem of officers and men alike"
(Regtl. Journal of the 15th Foot).

ARTHUR GEORGE BOILEAU LANG

Born, 14th July, 1861, eldest son of Colonel Arthur Moffatt
Lang, Royal Engineers.
Lieut., 10th May, 1882 ; 22nd Foot, 9th August, 1882 ;
Indian Army, 16th February, 1884 ; Capt., 10th May, 1893 ;
Major, 10th July, 1901 ; Lieut.-Col., 30th September, 1907 ;
retired, 20th May, 1914.
Served in the Waziristan Expedition, 1894 (severely wounded, medal
and clasp). Served in the war of 1914-18 in command of the 8th Service
Bn., South Lancashire Regt., 18th September, 1914-16. Afterwards in
command of the 12th Reserve Bn., King's Own Royal Lancaster Regt.,
and 76th Bn. Training Reserve.

EDWARD MALCOLM ESSON

Born in Edinburgh, 6th December, 1862, son of George
Auldjo Esson, of Edinburgh.
Lieut., 10th May, 1882 ; Capt., 1st April, 1892 ; Major,
6th September, 1903 ; Lieut.-Col., 5th April, 1907 ; retired,
28th March, 1911.

On the 1st July, 1881, all 2nd Lieutenants were ordered to be styled
Lieutenants in conformity with the provisions of the Royal Warrant of
25th June, 1881, by which the rank of 2nd Lieutenant was abolished.
The establishment of Lieut.-Colonels in all battalions was increased from
one to two and the Majors from two to four.

Served in the Nile Expedition, 1885. Served in the Boer War, 1899-1902, and was present at the operations round Colesberg in January, 1900, in the march along the Modder River, including the Relief of Kimberley, the actions at Paardeberg, Kitchener's Kopje, Poplar Grove and Driefontein and capture of Bloemfontein. Was with the advance on Dewetsdorp and the engagement at Leuukop. Also with the advance on Pretoria, including the engagements at Brandfort, Kroonstadt, the Vet and Zand rivers, and occupation of Johannesburg and Pretoria. Took part in the advance eastwards, and was at the actions of Diamond Hill and Belfast (mentioned in despatches, Queen's medal and 6 clasps, King's medal and 2 clasps). During the war of 1914-18 commanded the 19th Regtl. Depôt from 5th August, 1914, to 16th August, 1917.

GERALD NEILL PRENDERGAST

Born, 7th May, 1861, eldest son of Colonel Lenox Prendergast, Royal Scots Greys.

Lieut., Leinster Regt., 10th May, 1882 ; 19th Foot, 10th June, 1882 ; 60th Foot, 4th April, 1883 ; Capt., 16th July, 1890 ; Major, 29th December, 1898 ; retired, 9th August, 1905.

Served in the Soudan Expedition, 1884, and was present at the battle of Tamai (medal and clasp and Khedive's Star). Served in the Boer War, 1899-1902, and was at the operations in Natal in 1899, and on the march to June, 1900. Took part in the operations in Cape Colony, March to 31st May, 1902 (Queen's medal and two clasps, King's medal and two clasps). Was wrecked off Reunion with four companies 1st Bn. 60th Rifles, in the " Warren Hastings," 14th January, 1897, " when Captain Prendergast's knowledge of French was of the greatest service." In the war of 1914-18, was posted to the 13th Service Bn., 60th Rifles, 7th November, 1914, to the 14th Reserve Bn., 60th, 17th August, 1915, and to the 17th Bn. Training Reserve, 1st September, 1916.

WALTER JOHN BOYES

Born at Graham's Town, C.C., 18th January, 1841, son of Captain Robert Nairne Boyes, 85th and 55th Regiments, Military Knight of Windsor.

Ensign, 12th Foot, 21st March, 1858 ; Lieut., 6th July, 1864 ; Adjt., 9th June, 1866, to 12th November, 1872 ; Capt., 13th November, 1872 ; Bt. Major, 2nd March, 1881 ; half-pay, April, 1881 ; Major, 1st July, 1881 ; 19th Foot, 23rd August, 1882 ; retired as hon. Lieut.-Col., 2nd May, 1883.

Served in the Duffla Expedition, 1874-5. Also in the Jowaki Expedition, 1877-78, as D.A.A.G., under Br.-General Campbell Ross, C.B. (medal and clasp). Took part in the Afghan War, 1879-80, as Asst. Adjt.-Gen. on the Staff of Lieut.-General R. O. Bright and Major-Gen. C. Ross, including action at Saidabad (mentioned in despatches, Bt. of Major, medal).

Died at Haslemere, 12th May, 1918.

For many years Secretary to the Soldiers' and Sailors' Employment Society, and Secretary to Cooper's Hill, Indian College of Engineering from 1902 till it was abolished.

CLARENCE DALRYMPLE BRUCE, C.B.E.

Born at North Berwick, 8th July, 1862, son of Major Edward Jackson Bruce, R.A.

Lieut., 9th September, 1882 ; West Riding Regt., 25th October, 1882 ; Capt., 30th November, 1888 ; Major, 21st

February, 1902 ; retired, 17th November, 1906. Hon. Lieut.-Col., Essex Yeomanry, 25th March, 1907.

Served with the China Expeditionary Force in 1900, including the relief of Tientsin and Pekin (severely wounded, medal and clasp). A.D.C. to Major-Gen., Bengal, 15th February, 1886—31st March, 1889. Superintendent, Shanghai Municipal Police, 8th August, 1907. Police advisor to the Chinese Govt., 1913. Appointed a Tempy. Br.-Gen., 7th January, 1915, and was awarded the C.B.E. for services rendered during the war, 1914-1918. Granted hon. rank of Br.-Gen., 14th June, 1919.

Author of "In the footsteps of Marco Polo," "Overland from Simla to Pekin." Went on a mission to Belgium and France in 1919, in connexion with missing British soldiers.

ARTHUR LENOX NAPIER, O.B.E.

Born at Cheltenham, 8th December, 1863, 4th son of the Revd. John Warren Napier-Clavering, Axwell Park, Co. Durham.

Lieut., 9th September, 1882 ; Capt., 28th July, 1892 ; Adjt., 4th Bn. (Militia), 1st May, 1894—30th April, 1899 ; retired, 2nd March, 1904.

Served in the Boer War, 1902 (medal and two clasps).

Secretary to the Northumberland Territorial Force Association, and was awarded the order of O.B.E. for services in connection with the war, 1914-1918 (mentioned in home despatch).

CHARLES ARTHUR CECIL KING

Born at Capetown, 6th February, 1863, son of James King, of Belsize Park Gardens, London.

Lieut., 9th September, 1882 ; Capt., 15th February, 1893 ; Adjt., 3rd Bn. (Militia), 20th November, 1896—19th May, 1902 ; Bt. Major, 22nd August, 1902 ; Major, 18th February, 1905 ; Lieut.-Col., 29th September, 1910 ; Col., 16th December, 1913.

Served in the Nile Expedition, 1885, and with the Soudan Frontier Field Force, 1885-6, including the action at Ginnis (medal and Khedive's Star). Served with a column in Burmah in 1892 (medal and clasp for Katchin Hills). Took part in the Boer War, 1900-02, as Adjt., 3rd Bn. (Queen's medal and two clasps, King's medal and two clasps, twice mentioned in despatches, and Bt. of Major). Awarded the King's Coronation medal, 1911. Commanded the 2nd Bn. in the Expeditionary Force in Belgium and France (twice mentioned in despatches).

Killed at Ypres, 25th October, 1914. Memorial tablet in Richmond Parish Church, Yorkshire.

"This bold statement of his distinguished services would show that in him the Army has lost a valuable and experienced soldier, but it in no way conveys the sense of a personal bereavement which is felt by those of all ranks who had the privilege of serving with him. The cheeriest, kindliest and most generous of friends, he was beloved both by his brother officers and by the men who served under him, taking a keen interest in all sports, he encouraged and shared in all their amusements. How many a dull hour did he brighten for his comrades, how many a dreary station became the happier and livelier for his presence! No kinder or more genial host could be found ; his hospitality was proverbial, and he was never happier than when entertaining his friends.

Of the thrilling story of those last few eventful days before his death, we at present know but little, but we do know that it is a story of brave deeds and cheerful devotion to duty, a story that will live long in the annals of our Army, telling of a heroic struggle against well-nigh overwhelming odds. In this struggle he played a splendid part" (G.H.G.).

THOMAS ADAM FISCHER

Born, 20th May, 1863, 3rd son of Thomas Halhed Fischer, Q.C., of Walton Oaks, Epsom.

Lieut., 10th March, 1883 ; Indian Army, 19th November, 1884 ; Capt., 10th March, 1894.

Served in the Burmese Expedition, 1885-89 (medal and 2 clasps).

Died at Wardha, Central Provinces, India, 9th May, 1900, while engaged in famine relief work.

GEORGE LYCETT ENGLEDUE MAY

Born at Warminster, Wiltshire, 16th January, 1850, son of George May, of Croydon.

Ensign, 84th Foot, 13th June, 1868 ; 76th Foot, 27th June, 1868 ; Lieut., 9th August, 1871 ; Adjt., 16th February, 1878, to 21st November, 1878 ; Capt., 22nd November, 1878 ; Major, 19th Foot, 4th April, 1883 ; 20th Foot, 28th November, 1883 ; Lieut.-Col., 25th September, 1897 ; half-pay with rank of Col., 25th September, 1901 ; retired, 9th April, 1902.

CHARLES ORGAN, M.V.O.

Born at Woolwich, 13th October, 1853, son of Charles Organ.

Pte., 13th January, 1873 ; Corpl., 11th October, 1873 ; Sergt., 15th August, 1874 ; Cr.-Sergt., 27th August, 1875 ; Sergt.-Major, 20th April, 1882 ; Qr.-Master, 8th August, 1883 ; hon. Capt., 8th August, 1893 ; hon. Major, 29th November, 1900 ; retired, 13th October, 1908.

Served in the Nile Expedition, 1885, and with the Soudan Frontier Force, 1885-6, including the engagement at Ginnis (medal and Khedive's Star). Served in the Boer War, 1899-1902, and took part in the operations round Colesberg in January, 1900, and in the march along the Modder River, including the Relief of Kimberley, the actions at Paardeberg, Kitchener's Kopje, Poplar Grove and Driefontein, and the occupation of Bloemfontein ; was with the advance on Dewetsdorp, and action at Leuukop ; in the march to Pretoria, actions at Brandfort, Kroonstadt, Vet and Zand rivers, and Johannesburg ; took part in the advance Eastwards, including the battles of Diamond Hill and Belfast (mentioned in despatches, hon. rank of Major, Queen's medal with 6 clasps, King's medal and 2 clasps). Qr.-Master, Chelsea Hospital, 1st October, 1903—1st September, 1912. Was employed at 19th Regtl. Depôt, and on recruiting duties during the war of 1914-18.

BASIL WILLETT CHARLES HOOD

Born at Croydon Lodge, Surrey, 5th April, 1864, youngest son of Sir Charles Hood, of Croydon Lodge.

Lieut., 25th August, 1883 ; Capt., 31st December, 1893 ; retired, 30th January, 1895 ; Captain, 3rd Bn., 30th January, 1895, to 22nd June, 1898.

Private Secretary to Director-General of the Territorial Force, 1914-1917.

Died at 88, St. James's Street, 6th August, 1917.
Dramatic author. Author of "Gentleman Joe," "The French Maid," "Dandy Dan," "The Rose of Persia," "The Emerald Isle," "Merrie England," "Sweet and Twenty," "Her Royal Highness," etc., etc.

Lieut.-Gen. Sir E. C. Bethune, K.C.B., Director-General of the Territorial Force wrote as follows :—

"Captain Hood acted as my private Secretary in the War Office from the first day of the war until August, 1916, when his health gave way and he had to take a rest. During these two years he worked incessantly and brilliantly in the Territorial Directorate, of which I was the head, and he rendered splendid service for the country and for the Territorial Force in particular. In my opinion his breakdown and death were entirely attributable to his hard work at the war office, and to no other cause, and he gave his life for the country as surely as if he had fallen in the trenches."

HORACE ROBERT FRANCIS ANDERSON

Born at Kurrachee, 14th August, 1863, son of Major-Gen. Horace Searle Anderson, C.B., Indian Army.

Lieut., 25th August, 1883 ; 20th Foot, 10th October, 1883 ; Indian Army, 22nd January, 1885 ; Capt., 25th August, 1894 ; Major, 25th August, 1901.

Died on board the s.s. "Oriental" on passage to Aden, 20th August, 1903.

EDWARD STANLEY NEWTON-DICKENSON

Born in Guernsey, 26th September, 1847, eldest son of the Revd. E. Newton-Dickenson.

Cornet, 5th Lancers, 8th May, 1867. Ensign, 20th Foot, 6th July, 1867 ; Lieut., 13th June, 1870 ; Adjt., 20th August, 1872—23rd August, 1873 ; Capt., 20th April, 1878 ; Major, 11th May, 1883 ; 19th Foot, 28th November, 1883 ; Adjt., 4th Bn. (Militia), 28th April, 1884—30th April, 1889 ; retired, 21st May, 1890.

In 1865 he was injured in the Staplehurst railway accident ; all the other passengers in his carriage were killed. He was rescued from the debris by Charles Dickens. Served in Ireland during the Fenian disturbances. Appointed High Seneschal of Canterbury Cathedral in 1895.

Died at "The Precincts," Canterbury, 20th May, 1910. There is a memorial tablet in Canterbury Cathedral erected by the Dean and Chapter "in gratitude for the devoted and able service in the Cathedral."

WILLIAM RICHARD NORTON ANNESLEY, D.S.O.

Born at Colchester, 12th June, 1863, eldest son of Major-Gen. William Richard Annesley, Bay's Hill Terrace, Cheltenham, late 97th Foot.

Lieut., 6th February, 1884 ; Royal West Kent Regt., 27th February, 1884 ; Capt., 15th July, 1891 ; Major, 16th July, 1902 ; retired, 13th December, 1905.

Served in the Nile Expedition, 1884-85 (medal with clasp and Khedive's Star). Also with the Soudan Frontier Field Force in 1885-86, and was present at the engagement at Ginnis and the attack on Ambigol

Wells (Distinguished Service Order). Served with the Egyptian Army, 1888-90.

Lecturer on Military subjects at St. Andrew's University, N.B., 1905
Died in London, 29th November, 1914.

FRANCIS CONNOP

Born at Crediton, 22nd May, 1864, son of Newell Connop, of King's Lympton Park, Chumleigh, North Devon.

Lieut., 6th February, 1884 ; Adjt., 16th January, 1889, to 15th January, 1893 ; Capt., 28th March, 1894.

Served in the Nile Expedition, 1885, and with the Soudan Frontier Force, 1886.

Died at Fifehead Neville, Dorset, 5th May, 1896, owing to a fall from his horse. Buried at Bradfield Churchyard, Berkshire.

Master of the Regimental Harriers in Cyprus, 1888-89 Master of the Jersey Draghounds, 1892-93.

" A smart and active officer, a straight and daring rider with an excellent seat ; his bright and sunny nature—happy himself and making others happy—his singularly attractive appearance and warm generous heart, all combined to make him a great favourite with his brother officers and the men of his regiment, and, indeed, with all with whom he came in contact " (Local paper).

" Captain Connop was an accomplished horseman and a bold rider to hounds, and a better sportsman never wore the uniform of the old 19th " (The Field).

HENRY HONNER

Born in Dublin, 6th May, 1847.

In ranks of 19th Foot 19 years 145 days ; Sergt-Major 2 years 289 days ; Qr.-Master, 16th April, 1884 ; 11th Foot, 5th June, 1889 ; hon. Capt., 16th April, 1894 ; retired with hon. rank of Major, 1st January, 1903.

COLLIN CAMPBELL BOILEAU

Born, 25th May, 1863, 4th son of Lieut.-Col. George Wilson Boileau, Indian Army.

Lieut., 14th May, 1884 ; 9th Foot, 11th June, 1884 ; Indian Army, 2nd April, 1886 ; Capt., 14th May, 1895 ; Major, 14th May, 1902 ; resigned, 1st April, 1903.

Served in the Burmese Expedition in 1886 (medal and clasp).

ARCHIBALD COLIN BALDWIN

Born, 18th April, 1862, eldest son of Colonel Archibald Thomas Baldwin, Indian Army.

Lieut., 14th May, 1884 ; 1st Foot, 4th June, 1884 ; Indian Army, 14th May, 1887 ; Capt., 14th May, 1895 ; Major, 14th May, 1902.

Served with the Bechuanaland Expedition of 1884-5 Served in the Burmese Expedition, 1887 (medal and clasp), also in Burmah, 1892-94 (clasp for Chin-hills, 1892-3).

Died at Rangoon, 29th January, 1908.

DESMOND LAMBERT HARTLEY

Born, Beechpart, Clonsilla, 29th March, 1862, 2nd son of Colonel Richard Wilson Hartley, of Clonsilla, Co. Dublin, late 8th King's Regt.

Lieut., 14th May, 1884 ; Capt., 17th October, 1894 ; Adjt., 1st Vol. Bn., 1st July, 1896—15th March, 1901 ; retired, 6th July, 1904 ; Major and Lieut.-Col., 5th Bn. Royal Dublin Fusiliers, 6th July, 1904—6th July, 1910.

Served in the Boer War with 4th Bn. Mounted Infantry, and on special service, including operations in the Transvaal, March, 1901, to 31st May, 1902 (Queen's medal and 5 clasps). During the war of 1914-18 was in command of the 7th Bn. Royal Irish Rifles from 17th October, 1914, to 10th February, 1916, and served with it in France (Bronze Star). Was Section Commandant on No. 2 and No. 4 Lines of Communication from March, 1916, until protection was withdrawn from the railways. Also served in command of the 10th Bn. Royal Defence Corps from 10th October, 1917, until disbandment of the coast battalions in June, 1918.

BOLTON JAMES ALFRED MONSELL

Born at Coleraine, 27th December, 1840, eldest son of the Revd. John Samuel Bewley Monsell, LL.D., Rector of St. Nicholas, Guildford, Surrey, and hon. Chaplain in Ordinary to Queen Victoria.

Ensign, 73rd Foot, 7th September, 1858 ; Lieut., 29th October, 1861 ; Capt., 20th April, 1866 ; Major, 31st December, 1878 ; 19th Foot, 3rd September, 1884 ; retired as hon. Lieut.-Col., 25th September, 1886.

A.D.C. to Sir Richard Airey, G.C.B., Governor of Gibraltar, 1865-1870 ; Adjt., Tower Hamlets Volunteers, 1871-1873 ; Adjt, Royal Victoria Hospital, Netley, 1874-1882 ; Commandant, Discharge Depôt, Fort Brockhurst, 1882-84 ; Headquarters Recruiting Staff, 1885-86 ; Chief Constable, Metropolitan Police, London, 1886-1910.

Died at 1, Tedworth Square, London, 2nd February, 1919.

GEORGE CROFT

Born, 25th September, 1846. In ranks 17 years 271 days ; Qr.-Master, Royal Sussex Regt., 23rd August, 1882 ; 19th Foot, 4th October, 1884 ; hon. Capt., 23rd August, 1892 ; hon. Major, 1st January, 1903 ; retired, 25th September, 1901.

Served in the Boer War with 3rd Bn. Yorkshire Regt. (medal and two clasps).

Sir EDWARD STANISLAUS BULFIN, K.C.B., C.V.O.

Born, 6th November, 1862, son of Patrick Bulfin, J.P., of Woodtown Park, Rathfarnham, Co. Dublin.

Lieut., 12th November, 1884 ; Capt., 30th January, 1895 ; Bt. Major, 29th November, 1900 ; Bt. Lieut.-Col., 26th June, 1902 ; Major, Manchester Regt., 28th November, 1903 ; 23rd Foot, 15th October, 1904 ; Bt. Col., 17th November, 1906 ; Col., 4th July, 1908 ; Major-Gen., 26th October, 1914 ; Colonel, 19th Foot, 28th October, 1914 ; Lieut.-Gen., 1st January, 1919.

Served in Burmah in 1893 in command of a column during the operations in the Katchin Hills (medal and clasp). Served in the Boer

War, 1899-1902, on the Staff. Took part in the advance on Kimberley, including the actions at Belmont, Enslin, Modder River and Majesfontein (three times mentioned in despatches) ; the operations in the Transvaal, west of Pretoria, July to November, 1900, including the action at Venterskroom ; operations in the Orange River Colony, May to November, 1900, including actions at Lindley and Rhenoster River ; operations in the Transvaal, 30th November, 1900, to 31st May, 1902, and on the Zululand frontier of Natal in September and October, 1901 ; commanded a mobile column from 12th December, 1901 (mentioned in despatches, brevets of Major and Lieut.-Col., Queen's medal and 4 clasps, King's medal and 2 clasps).

Landed in France, 13th August, 1914, in command of 2nd Infantry Bde., 1st Div., 1st Army Corps. Took part in the advance and retreat to Mons, the Marne and Aisne. Held line in Chemin des Dames till replaced by French troops. Commanded two brigades at battle of Pilken, capturing German trenches and 600 prisoners with machine guns (promoted Major-Gen. for distinguished service in the field). Present at 1st battle of Ypres (severely wounded, 1st November). Again landed in France with 28th Division, 15th February, 1915. Held left of line at 2nd battle of Ypres. Remained in Ypres salient until 15th September, when he proceeded to Loos and took part in the operations there. On appointment to the command of the 60th London Division in December, 1915, took over the Vimy Ridge, N. of Arras in June, 1916, and remained there till September, when the division moved to the Somme. Sailed with the 60th to Salonika in December, 1916, and remained on the Doiran front till May, 1917. Landed in Egypt in June, 1917, and was appointed to command of 21st Army Corps, 3rd August, 1917. Present at the 3rd battle of Gaza, Junction Station, Askelon, Kuryet-el-Enab and Nebi Samwell, four miles from Jerusalem. Handed over Jerusalem line to 20th Corps in November, 1917, and proceeded to Jaffa and Aujah line. Commanded 120,000 men in operations commencing 19th September, 1918, at battle of Sharon, capturing Kilkilieh, Jibjilieh, Tul Keram, Messudieh and Nablus. Occupied Haifa, Tyre, Sidon, Beirut and Tripoli, and later Ladikiya, Alexandretta, Antioch, Adana, Mersina, and the Taurus tunnel. In these operations captured 253 field guns, several hundred machine guns, and 12,875 prisoners (promoted Lieut.-Gen. for distinguished service in the field). Acted as C. in C. for General Sir Edmund Allenby in March, 1919, when disturbances broke out in Egypt, and later was appointed G.O.C., Egypt, Assouan to Alexandria (frequently mentioned in despatches, K.C.B. for capture of Jerusalem, Commander of the Order of Savoy, 2nd Class Order of the Nile, Officer of the Legion of Honour). Awarded C.V.O., 7th November, 1910 ; C.B., King's birthday, 1913. LL.D. (honoris causa) Dublin University.

ALBERT ALEXANDER McCALL

Born at Glasgow, 12th May, 1863, son of Thomas McCall, of Glasgow.

Lieut., 12th November, 1884 ; Highland L.I., 14th January, 1885 ; resigned, 14th August, 1888.

The Hon. ANDREW DAVID MURRAY

Born at Scone Palace, Perthshire, 28th September, 1863, 2nd son of Viscount Stormount.

Lieut., 12th November, 1884 ; 79th Foot, 24th December, 1884 ; Capt., 11th March, 1893.

Served in the Nile Expedition 1884-85 (medal with clasp and Khedive's Star), and with the Soudan Frontier Field Force 1885-86, including the actions at Kosheh and Ginnis. Served also in the Soudan campaign of 1898 and was present at the actions of the Atbara and

Omdurman (twice mentioned in despatches, Bt. of Major, medal and Khedive's medal with 2 clasps). Served in the Boer War in command of Lovatt's Scouts, including actions at Johannesburg, Pretoria, Diamond Hill and Wittebergen (Bt. of Lieut.-Col., three times mentioned in despatches).

Killed in action at Quaggafontein, Orange River Colony, 20th September, 1901.

FREDERICK WILLIAM TEMPLETOWN ROBINSON, D.S.O.

Born at Montserrat, W.I., 21st April, 1863, son of Sir William Cleave Francis Robinson, G.C.M.G.

Lieut., 12th November, 1884 ; Capt., Royal Sussex Regt., 8th April, 1896 ; Major, Royal Garrison Regt., 17th December, 1902 ; half-pay, 7th December, 1905 ; retired, 21st July, 1906.

Commandant Freemantle Rifle Volunteers Corps 1894 (thanked by the Australian Govt.).

Served in the Boer War 1900-02 as Commandant Bethulie and Hoopstad. Took part in the operations in the Free State Feb. to May, 1900, including the action at the Zand River, operations in the Orange River Colony 30th November, 1900, to February, 1901, and in Cape Colony March, 1902, to end of war (mentioned in despatches, Queen's medal and 3 clasps, King's medal and 2 clasps, D.S.O.). Served in the war of 1914-18 in the 16th Bn. County of London Regt.

ADAM BRACK-BOYD WILSON

Born, 12th May, 1863, eldest son of William B. Boyd, of Ormiston, Kelso, N.B.

Lieut., 12th November, 1884 ; 6th Dragoons, 7th April, 1886 ; Capt., 8th June, 1891 ; 19th Hussars, 15th August, 1894; retired, 26th May, 1897 ; Major, Reserve of Officers, 18th October, 1902.

Served with the Soudan Frontier Field Force 1885-86, and was present at the action of Ginnis (medal and Khedive's Star). Served in the Boer War 1899-01 with Thorneycroft's Mounted Infantry, and took part in the battles of Colenso, Spion Kop, Vaal Kranz, Pieter's Hill, Alleman's Nek and relief of Ladysmith. Was attached to the South African Constabulary 1901, and to Remount Depôt 1901 to end of war (Queen's medal and 3 clasps, King's medal and 2 clasps). Was second in command of the Natal Rangers in 1906, which he assisted to raise and equip, and with them served through the Zulu rebellion of 1906, being present at the engagement of Mome Gorge (medal and clasp).

Died at Cambridge, New Zealand, 14th November, 1911.

ARCHIBALD FRANCIS PINKNEY PAXTON

Born in Madras, 6th December, 1862, son of Major-Gen. George Paxton, Indian Army.

Lieut., 28th February, 1885 ; Indian Army, 14th June, 1887 ; Capt., 28th February, 1896 ; Major, 28th February, 1903 ; Retired, 23rd March, 1909.

Served with the Soudan Frontier Field Force 1885-86, including the action at Ginnis (medal and Khedive's Star). Took part in the Burmah Expedition 1887-9 (medal and 2 clasps).

Died at Brookfield, Emsworth, Hants, 19th December, 1915.

ERNEST SOMERVELL

Born at Hendon, 9th November, 1863, son of William Somervell, of Hendon.

Lieut., 28th February, 1885 ; Capt., 28th July, 1896 ; retired, 19th May, 1905 ; Capt. and hon. Major, 4th Bn., 20th May, 1905.

Served with the Soudan Frontier Field Force 1885-6, and was present at the action at Ginnis (medal and Khedive's Star). Served in the Boer War 1899-02, Asst.-Railway Transport officer to 6th July, 1900. Operations in the Transvaal, 30th November, 1900, to 31st May, 1902 (Queen's medal with 3 clasps, King's medal and 2 clasps).

HARDRESS GILBERT HOLMES, C.M.G., C.B.E.

Born at Nenagh, Co. Tipperary, 7th July, 1862, son of William Bassett Holmes, of St. David's, Nenagh.

Lieut., 9th May, 1885 ; Capt., 18th November, 1896 ; Bt. Major, 26th June, 1902 ; Adjt., 3rd (Militia) Bn., 8th September, 1902—7th September, 1905 ; Major, 25th December, 1905 ; retired, 4th February, 1908.

Served in the campaign on the N.W. Frontier of India, 1897-98, under Sir William Lockhart, and was present at the capture of the Sampagha and Arhanga Passes, the capture of Bagh, the Dwatoi reconnaissance, crossing of the Kahu Darra, reconnaissance of the Saran Sar and engagement of 11th November, the operations against the Khani Khel Chamkanis and in the Bazar Valley (medal and 2 clasps).

Served in the Boer War 1900-02, and took part in the advance on Dewetsdorp and action of Leuukop. Was with the advance from Bloemfontein to Pretoria, including the engagements at Brandfort, Kroonstadt, Vet and Zand Rivers and Johannesburg. Also in the action at Diamond Hill. Served with the 4th Bn. Mounted Infantry during the Eastern advance and in the action at Belfast (mentioned in despatches). Commanded the 15th M.I. during the operations in the Free State 1901, and a mobile column from September, 1901, till the end of the war (mentioned in despatches, Bt. of Major, Queen's medal and 5 clasps, King's medal and 2 clasps).

Served in the war of 1914-18 as Lieut.-Col. Commanding 9th Service Bn. till promoted Br.-Gen., 11th December, 1916. Took part in the operations on the Somme, 1916, including the capture of Contalmaison. Present at the fighting before Arras in 1917 (wounded), and in front of Ypres in September, 1917 (four times mentioned in despatches, Bt. of Lieut.-Col., bronze star and C.M.G.). Awarded the C.B.E. for services at home as Br.-Gen. in command of Newcastle-on-Tyne defences.

WILLIAM STAFFORD BROOKSBANK

Born, 22nd April, 1864, 4th son of Edward Brooksbank, of Healaugh Old Hall, Tadcaster.

Lieut., 23rd May, 1885 ; Adjt., 7th April, 1891.

Died at Bangalore of smallpox, 18th June, 1891.

"A good comrade, a zealous soldier and an ornament to his profession " (G.H.G.).

Sir CECIL LOTHIAN NICHOLSON, K.C.B., C.M.G., p.s.c.

Born in London, 1st November, 1865, son of General Sir Lothian Nicholson, K.C.B., Governor of Gibraltar.

Lieut., 29th August, 1885 ; Adjt., 7th November, 1888— 7th April, 1891 ; Capt., 4th December, 1896 ; Major, Worcester-

shire Regt., 8th March, 1905 ; Lieut.-Col., East Lancashire
Regt., 17th February, 1912 ; Bt.-Col., 17th February, 1915 ;
Major-Gen., 3rd June, 1918.

Served in the Tirah Campaign 1897-98, and was present at the
capture of Bagh, the Dwatoi reconnaissance and the crossing of the
Kahu Darra (medal and 2 clasps). Served in the war of 1914-18 in
command of the 2nd Bn. East Lancashire Regt., and was wounded at
Neuve Chapelle in March, 1915. Was promoted to the command of a
brigade 16th June, 1915, and as Major-Gen. commanded the 34th Division
in the fighting on the Western front in 1918 (seven times mentioned in
despatches, Bt. of Colonel, promoted Major-Gen., K.C.B., C.M.G.,
bronze star, Commander of the Legion of Honour, and French Croix
de Guerre, Commander of the Order of Leopold and Croix de Guerre).

WILLIAM MELVILLE DOUGLAS

Born at Saugor, India, 27th January, 1864, son of Claud
Barwell Douglas.

Lieut., 25th November, 1885.

Died at Korosko, Nile, 13th April, 1886.

HUGH EDWARD WALKER

Born, 22nd August, 1865, only son of Frederick J. Walker,
M.V.O., of 24, Lennox Gardens, London and Mezzo Monte,
Cannes.

Lieut., 25th November, 1885 ; 23rd Foot, 6th January,
1886 ; Capt., 1st July, 1895 ; half-pay, 28th March, 1896 ;
omitted from the half-pay list May, 1901.

Served in the Burmese Expedition 1886-87 (medal and clasp).

EDWARD SNELL WALLIS

Born, 7th June, 1864, son of Surgeon-Major William Beale
Wallis.

Lieut., 25th November, 1885.

Served on the Soudan Frontier, 1886.

Died at Portsmouth, 25th March, 1890.

SHELLEY ALEXANDER SEALE

Born, 14th September, 1859 ; Lieut., 28th November, 1885,
from the ranks of the Worcestershire Regt. ; half-pay, 16th
March, 1889 ; retired, 16th March, 1894.

Served on the Soudan Frontier in 1886.

HENRY ROTHES STEWART MAITLAND

Born, 26th April, 1865, 6th son of Lieut.-General John
Maitland, R.A., of Balgreggan House, Sandhead, Wigtown-
shire.

Lieut., 30th January, 1886 ; half-pay, 26th July, 1894 ;
19th Foot, 30th January, 1895 ; Capt., 9th March, 1897 ; retired, 11th January, 1899.

Served in the Tirah Expedition, 1897-98, under Sir William Lock-
hart, including the operations in the Bazar Valley (medal and 2 clasps).
Served in the Boer War, 1900-02, and took part in the operations in the
Transvaal, May and June, 1900, including the actions at Johannesburg,

Pretoria and Diamond Hill, and in the advance eastwards, including the action at Belfast (Queen's medal and 3 clasps, King's medal and 2 clasps, and promoted Major, Reserve of Officers, 18th October, 1902).
Died at Perrymead House, Bath, 16th May, 1911.

CHARLES WILLIAM GALE

Born at Chepstow, Co. Monmouth, 12th August, 1866, son of Charles William Gale, of St. Arvan's, Co. Monmouth.

Lieut., 30th January, 1886 ; Adjt., 16th January, 1893— 16th January, 1897 ; Capt., 4th December, 1896 ; half-pay, 1st May, 1899 ; retired, 4th November, 1899.

Served on the Soudan Frontier in 1886.

BERKELEY COLE WILMOT WILLIAMS

Born at Herringston, 4th May, 1865, eldest son of Captain Edward Wilmot Williams, H.E.I.C.S., of Herringston, Dorset.

Lieut., 30th January, 1886 ; Capt., 27th April, 1898 ; retired, 22nd November, 1902.

Served on the Soudan Frontier in 1886. Served in Burmah in 1893 with a column operating against the Katchins (medal and clasp). Served in the Tirah Expedition of 1897-8, and was attached to the 18th Foot in the operations on the Samana range. Was with the 19th Foot at the capture of the Sampagha and Arhanga Passes, the capture of Bagh, the Dwatoi reconnaissance and the crossing of the Kahu Darra (severely wounded, medal and 3 clasps).

Served in the Boer War, 1899-02, and took part in the operations near Colesberg in January, 1900, in the march along the Modder River, including the relief of Kimberley, actions at Paardeberg, Kitchener's Kop, Poplar Grove, Driefontein, and occupation of Bloemfontein. Was with the advance on Dewetsdorp and in the action of Leuukop. Also in the march to Pretoria, including actions at Brandfort, Kroonstadt, Vet and Zand rivers, Johannesburg, and occupation of Pretoria. In the advance eastwards, including actions at Diamond Hill and Belfast (Queen's medal and 6 clasps, King's medal and 2 clasps). In the war of 1914-18, was employed at the 19th Regtl. Depôt, and was Adjt. from 19th March, 1918 (mentioned in home despatch).

LESLIE MICHAEL FARRELL

Born at Paris, 14th February, 1864, son of Michael Farrell, of Ellenfield, Drumcondra, Co. Dublin.

Lieut., 18th Hussars, 12th May, 1886 ; 19th Foot, 11th August, 1886 ; retired, 17th August, 1898.

MORTON HENRY EDEN

Born at Sheerness, 24th October, 1865, eldest son of Lieut.-Col. Morton Parker Eden, R.A.

Lieut., 1st September, 1886.

Died in London, 5th November, 1889.

METCALFE STUDHOLME BROWNRIGG

Born at Government House, Montreal, 5th July, 1845, 3rd son of General John Studholme Brownrigg, Colonel, 95th Foot.

Ensign, 83rd Foot, 1st December, 1863 ; 52nd Foot, 29th March, 1864 ; Lieut., 3rd April, 1867 ; Capt., 10th November, 1869 ; Major, 11th March, 1882 ; 19th Foot, 6th November,

1886 ; half-pay, 11th January, 1888 ; Lieut.-Col., 31st July, 1892 ; Col., 25th November, 1896 ; retired, 5th July, 1902.

Adjt. 3rd Cambridge Rifle Vols., 15th October, 1877, to 3rd April, 1882. On Recruiting Staff, 30th December, 1891, to 29th November, 1896. Commanded 30th Regtl. District, 30th November, 1896, to 17th December, 1901. Commanded Wilts. and Dorset Volunteer Infantry Brigade, 1902-09.

GERARD CHRISTIAN, C.B., C.I.E., D.S.O.

Born at Valetta, 2nd June, 1867, son of Alfred Christian, C.M.G., of Valetta.

Second Lieut., 5th February, 1887 ; Lieut., 2nd May, 1890 ; Adjt., 16th January, 1897—15th January, 1901 ; Capt., 17th August, 1898 ; Major, 21st January, 1906 ; Lieut.-Col., 28th March, 1911 ; Col., 15th June, 1914 ; retired with hon. rank of Br.-General. 1st January, 1920.

Served in the Boer War, 1899-1902, and was present at the operations round Colesberg in January, 1900. Took part in the march along the Modder River, including the relief of Kimberley, the engagements at Paardeberg, Kitchener's Kop, Poplar Grove and Driefontein. Was with the advance on Dewetsdorp and action at Leuukop, and towards the Eastern Transvaal, including the action at Belfast (mentioned in despatches, D.S.O., Queen's medal and 4 clasps, King's medal and 2 clasps).

In the war of 1914-18 commanded the Rawal Pindi Bde. and the 4th Inftry. Bde. on the N.W. Frontier in 1915, and the 36th Bde. in Mesopotamia with the Indian Expeditionary Force. Was later appointed an inspector of Infantry in India. Commanded the 6th Brigade in the operations against the Afghans in 1919 (several times mentioned in despatches, C.B., C.I.E., 3rd Class order of the White Eagle with Swords (Serbia), and bronze star).

JOHN JOCELYN DOYNE SILLERY

Born at Hobart Town, 5th November, 1866, son of Major-Gen. Charles Jocelyn Cecil Sillery, formerly 12th Foot.

Second Lieut., 5th February, 1887 ; Lieut., Indian Army, 27th February, 1888 ; Capt., 5th February, 1898 ; Major, 5th February, 1905 ; retired, 5th February, 1912.

Killed in action at Gallipoli, 7th August, 1915, when serving with the 11th Bn. Manchester Regt.

EDWARD FRANCIS TWIGG

Born, 21st February, 1868, 6th and youngest son of the Revd. Thomas Twigg, Canon of Swords and St. Patrick's Cathedral, Dublin.

Second Lieut., 5th February, 1887 ; Lieut., Indian Army, 27th February, 1888 ; Capt., 5th February, 1898 ; Major, 5th February, 1905 ; Lieut.-Col., 5th February, 1913.

Served in East Africa, 1895-96, in the operations against the Mazru rebels (medal).

In 1887 the rank of Second Lieutenant was re-established and the second Lieut.-Colonel abolished in all regiments.

RONALD D'ARCY FIFE, C.M.G., D.S.O.

Born at Scarborough, 19th March, 1868, 2nd son of William Henry Fife, of Lee Hall, Northumberland.

Second Lieut., 14th September, 1887 ; Lieut., 10th September, 1890 ; Adjt., 12th October, 1896—15th December, 1900 ; Capt., 17th August, 1898 ; Major, 16th February, 1906 ; retired, 3rd December, 1913.

Served in the Tirah Expedition, 1897-98, and was present at the capture of the Sampagha and Arhanga Passes, the capture of Bagh, the Dwatoi reconnaissance, the crossing of the Kahu Darra, the reconnaissance of the Saran Sar, and engagement of 11th November. In the operations against the Khani Khel Chamkanis and in the Bazar Valley and affair at Shinkamar, 29th January, 1898 (medal and 2 clasps). King's Coronation medal, 1911. In the war of 1914-18, went to France in July, 1915, in command of the 7th Service Bn., and took part in the fighting at Voormezeele and Hooge, etc. Wounded at Sailly-Saillisel on 14th February, 1917 (four times mentioned in despatches, C.M.G., D.S.O., and bronze star, and retained rank of Lieut.-Col.).

EDWARD LOVELACE VANS-AGNEW

Born at Horsham, 26th November, 1867, 5th son of John Vans-Agnew, Ladbroke Grove, Bayswater.

Second Lieut., 14th September, 1887 ; Lieut., 9th April, 1891 ; Capt., 12th November, 1898 ; Major, 29th July, 1906 ; retired, 4th March, 1908.

Served in the war of 1914-18 as press censor, and embarkation officer at Folkestone and Liverpool (mentioned in home despatch).

HAROLD FUTVOYE LEA, C.M.G., D.S.O.

Born in London, 19th September, 1867, son of His Honour Judge George Harris Lea, of Broadlands, Hereford.

Second Lieut., 14th September, 1887 ; Lieut., 8th May, 1891 ; Adjt., 19th June, 1891—4th February, 1895 ; Capt., 11th January, 1899 ; Major, 29th September, 1906 ; retired, 28th October, 1908.

Served in the Boer War, 1901-2 as Station Staff Officer, 30th October to 4th December, 1901, afterwards on Staff as Asst. Provost Marshal. Operations in the Transvaal and Orange River Colony to end of war. Placed on the list of officers considered qualified for Staff employment in consequence of service on the Staff in the field (Queen's medal and 5 clasps).

Went to France in January, 1917 as D.A.A.G. to the 62nd Division, having previously served as Brigade-Major to the 76th Brigade at home. Was appointed A.A. and Q.M.G. to the Division on the 29th December, 1917, and served with it in that capacity till the end of the war with the temporary rank of Lieut.-Col. Was present at the battles of the Ancre, Bullecourt and Cambrai in 1917 ; Bucquoy, the Marne, Ardre Valley, Mory and Vaux, Havrincourt, Marcoing and Flesquières, Soulesmes, La Selle and Mauberge in 1918 (four times mentioned in despatches ; C.M.G., D.S.O., Legion of Honour (Croix de Chevalier) and Belgian Croix de Guèrre).

MAURICE HILLIARD TOMLIN

Born in London, 28th June, 1868, 3rd son of J. L. Tomlin of Thiernswood, Richmond, Yorkshire.

Second Lieut., 29th February, 1888 ; Lieut., 19th June,

1891 ; Capt., 1st April, 1900 ; Bt. Major, 26th June, 1902 ; Major, 5th April, 1907 ; retired, 3rd July, 1907.

Served with the West African Frontier Field Force, 13th November, 1897, to 15th December, 1898, in the operations on the Niger, including the expedition to Lapaie and Argeyah (mentioned in despatches, medal and 2 clasps). Served in the Boer War, 1899-00, with the 2nd Bn. Mounted Infantry and as Staff-Lieut., Headquarters, in the general advance from Modder River. Served also in 1901 in command of the Northern Company 2nd M.I., and in 1902 in command of the 9th Battn. M.I., and also of a mobile column in the Orange River Colony (twice mentioned in despatches, Bt. of Major, Queen's medal and 3 clasps, King's medal and 2 clasps). Chief Constable, London Metropolitan Police, 5th December, 1912.

FERDINAND HARPER HODGE

Born at Aldershot, 5th June, 1867, son of General Sir Edward Cooper Hodge, G.C.B.

Second Lieut., 10th October, 1888 ; Lieut., 13th January, 1892 ; resigned, 19th June, 1895 ; Captain, 3rd Bn., 27th July, 1897.

WILFRID HARRY DENT

Born at Hunsingore, 5th June, 1867, son of the Revd. Canon Joseph Jonathan Dent, M.A., Vicar of Hunsingore, Witherby, Yorkshire.

Second Lieut., 10th November, 1888 ; Lieut., 4th March, 1892 ; Adjt., 5th February, 1895, to 6th June, 1896 ; Capt., Durham L.I., 11th November, 1899 ; retired, 8th June, 1907.

Served in Burmah, 1892-93, with the Intelligence Department in the Katchin Hills (dangerously wounded, received the thanks of the Government of India, medal and clasp). Was attached to the Chinese Regiment, 15th December, 1898, to January, 1907, and served with the China Expeditionary Force in 1900, including the relief of Tientsin and Pekin, actions of Pietsang and Yangtsun (mentioned in despatches, medal and clasp). Appointed temporary Major in the 10th Service Battn., 20th November, 1914, and went with it to France.

Killed in action at Hill 60, Loos, 25th September, 1915.

EDWARD HUGH BROOME RAYMOND, D.S.O.

Born, 6th September, 1868, 3rd son of the Revd. Slade Baker-Stallard-Penoyre, of Sandbourne, Bowdley, Co. Worcestershire. Changed his name to Raymond in 1898.

Second Lieut., 23rd March, 1889 ; 1st Foot, 17th April, 1889 ; Lieut., 15th November, 1891 ; Capt., 12th August, 1896; retired, 9th September, 1908.

Served in the Boer War, 1899-02, and took part in the operations in Cape Colony, 1899-00, including actions at Loperberg, Bird's River, Penhoek and Labus-Chagnes Nek. Also in the Orange River Colony with the 3rd Division during the relief of Wepener, before Dewetsdorp, 20th-25th April, 1900, and about Middleburg, including affair at Paardeplatz, January, 1902, with Colonel Urmston's column (Queen's medal with 3 clasps, King's medal and 2 clasps). In the war of 1914-18, served as second in command of the 13th Service Bn., Royal Scots (mentioned in despatches, D.S.O.).

HARRY ELLIOTT RAYMOND

Born at Birr, 28th March, 1868, son of Lieut.-Col. Elliott Arthur Raymond, late 44th Foot.

Second Lieut., 24th April, 1889 ; Lieut., 1st April, 1892 ; Capt., 28th December, 1900 ; half-pay, 19th May, 1904 ; 19th Foot, 20th September, 1904 ; Major, 3rd July, 1907 ; half-pay, 11th February, 1911 ; 19th Foot, 1st September, 1914 ; Bt. Lieut.-Col., 3rd June, 1919 ; retired, 2nd March, 1920.

Served in the Tirah Expedition as Provost Marshal, 2nd Brigade, and was present at the capture of the Sampagha and Arhanga Passes, the crossing of the Kahu Darra, the reconnaissance of the Saran Sar, and engagements of the 11th November, and at Shinkamar, 29th January, 1898, and in the operations against the Khani Khel Chamkanis, also in the Bazar Valley (medal and 2 clasps). Served in the Boer War, 1900-01, as Asst. Provost Marshal, 9th Division in the Free State and Transvaal (Queen's medal and 3 clasps). In the war of 1914-18, served at home on the Staff (twice mentioned in home despatches).

JOSEPH GEALE DOWNES

Born, 9th December, 1844. In ranks 22 years and 71 days. Lieut. and Qr.-Master, 11th Foot, 18th February, 1885 ; 19th Foot, 5th June, 1889 ; hon. Capt., 18th February, 1895 ; retired, 9th December, 1899.

ARTHUR FRANCIS OWEN-LEWIS, D.S.O., O.B.E.

Born at Booterstown, Co. Dublin, 6th August, 1868, only surviving son of Henry Owen-Lewis, of Inniskeen, Co. Monaghan, J.P., D.L., sometime M.P. for Carlow.

Second Lieut., 8th June, 1889 ; Lieut., 28th July, 1892 ; Capt., 29th December, 1900 ; retired, 25th June, 1904 ; Capt., 6th Bn. Lancashire Fusiliers, 26th June, 1904 ; Major, 21st March, 1909.

Served as Adjt., 6th Bn. Lancashire Fusiliers, during the Boer War (mentioned in despatches, D.S.O., Queen's medal and 3 clasps, King's medal and 2 clasps). Commandant, Carnarvon, Cape Colony, for eight months. Presented with an address and a piece of plate by the residents there in recognition of the services he rendered.

During the Great War, served on the Staff in Ireland as G.S.O., and afterwards in France, December, 1916, to March, 1918, as A.Q.M.G. (twice mentioned in despatches, O.B.E.) Has been Governor of Dundalk and Mountjoy Prisons, and Inspector of Prisons in Ireland.

HUBERT ARTHUR STANSFELD

Born at Weetwood Grove, Leeds, 29th February, 1868, son of Thomas Wolryche Stansfeld, of Weetwood Grove.

Second Lieut., 21st December, 1889 ; Lieut., 26th July, 1893 ; Capt., 29th December, 1900 ; Adjt., 2nd Vol. Bn., 15th December, 1898—1st February, 1904 ; retired, 9th May, 1906 ; Capt., 3rd Bn., 9th May, 1906 ; hon. Major, September, 1907 ; resigned, 15th March, 1913. Appointed D.A.A. and Q.M.G. to the 21st Division, 19th September, 1914.

Died suddenly at Bournemouth, 8th December, 1914.

"Excelling in all active sports, he captained the Army Rugby Team in 1891, was useful both with bat and ball, and was well-known in the hunting field. The sadness of his end will be lost to sight in the remembrance of Jock Stansfeld as we knew him best—full of fun and brightness, an all-round sportsman and a good soldier " (G.H.G.).

JAMES WILLIAM BRADFORD SILVERTHORNE, O.B.E.

Born at West Hoathly, Sussex, 9th April, 1859, son of Colonel J. W. Silverthorne, J.P., D.L., Royal Sussex Artillery Militia.

Second Lieut., 108th Foot, 19th February, 1881 ; Lieut., 1st July, 1881 ; Capt., 31st October, 1888 ; 19th Foot, 8th January, 1890 ; retired, 3rd May, 1899.

Served with the Tirah Expeditionary Force, 1897-98 (medal and 2 clasps). Promoted Major, Reserve of Officers, 18th October, 1902, for services at home during the Boer War. Served in France during the war of 1914-18, on the Staff as Asst. Military Landing Officer, Marseilles (three times mentioned in despatches, O.B.E.).

SPENCER CLAY

Born, 14th September, 1869, 3rd son of Major-General Charles Henry Clay, Bengal Staff Corps.

Second Lieut., 3rd May, 1890 ; Indian Army, 26th September, 1891.

Died at Kherwarra Rajputnana, 3rd September, 1897.

CHARLES MORRIS KEMBLE

Born at East Harptree, Bristol, 5th June, 1870, son of Charles Adams Kemble, M.A., J.P., of Hallatrow, Bristol.

Second Lieut., 28th June, 1890 ; Lieut., 31st December, 1893 ; Army Service Corps, 1st April, 1894 ; Capt., 7th September, 1898.

Served with the Soudan Expedition of 1898, and was present at the battle of Omdurman (medal and Khedive's medal and clasp). Served in the Boer War in the advance along the Modder River.

Died at Bloemfontein of enteric fever, 29th March, 1900.

ALFRED FOTHERGILL ROBINSON

Born in Liverpool, 22nd May, 1868, son of H. Robinson of Chislehurst, Sefton Park, Liverpool.

Second Lieut., 28th June, 1890.

Died at Brighton, 4th September, 1893.

" His death at the early age of 25 will be much felt by all ranks of his comrades, to whom he had endeared himself by his genial and kindly disposition."

WILLIAM ALEXANDER FINISTON WILLIAMSON

Born in Derry, 15th May, 1867, 3rd son of Edward Augustus Williamson, Paymaster R N., of Culmore, Co. Derry.

Second Lieut., 28th June, 1890 ; Lieut., Army Service Corps, 15th September, 1891 ; Capt., 4th July, 1895 ; Major, 16th June, 1902.

Died at Hendon, London, N.W., on 8th June, 1911. Memorial in St. George's Garrison Church, Aldershot.

DAVID EDWARD OSBORNE JONES

Born at Llandovery, S. Wales, 8th June, 1870, son of E. Jones, of Velindre, Llandovery.

Second Lieut., 17th June, 1891 ; Lieut., 28th March, 1894.

Served in the Tirah campaign, and was killed during the advance on Dwatoi, 22nd November, 1897, whilst attempting with three men to dislodge a party of the enemy concealed amongst woods and trees.

" A most promising officer, a capital rider, polo player, and sportsman all round ; popular with his comrades, he was one of those whom the Army can ill afford to lose " (G.H.G.).

ERNEST HENRY LEE-WARNER

Born in Dublin, 10th May, 1869, son of Biddulph Lee Warner, 21st Foot and Army Service Corps.

Second Lieut., 10th October, 1891 ; Lieut., 26th July, 1894 ; Capt., 29th December, 1900 retired, 10th October, 1908.

Served in the Boer War, 1900-02, with the Railway Pioneer Regt. and 3rd Bn., also with 1st Bn. towards close of the war (Queen's medal and 3 clasps, King's medal and 2 clasps). During the war of 1914-18, was employed in the Record Offices at Cork, Hounslow and York (twice mentioned in home despatches).

ERNEST GREGORIE CAFFIN

Born at Durham, 8th November, 1869, son of the Revd. Benjamin Charles Caffin, Vicar of Northallerton.

Second Lieut., 10th October, 1891 ; Lieut., 17th October, 1894 ; Capt., 5th Foot, 9th May, 1900 ; Major, 19th Foot, 23rd December, 1907 ; retired on account of ill-health caused by wounds with hon. rank of Lieut.-Col., 7th June, 1919.

Served in the campaign on the N.W. Frontier of India in 1897-98, with the Tirah Expeditionary Force, and was present at the capture of the Sampagha and Arhanga Passes, and in the operations in the Maidan (severely wounded). Took part in the reconnaissance of the Saran Sar and engagement of 11th November, and against the Khani Khel Chamkanis (medal and 2 clasps).

Served in the Boer War, 1899-00, and took part in the operations in Natal in 1899, including the actions at Elandslaagte, Reitfontein, and Lombard's Kop, defence of Ladysmith, and sortie of the 7th December, 1899 (severely wounded, medal and 2 clasps). In the war of 1914-18, served with the 9th Service Bn., and as temporary Lieut.-Col., 11th Service Bn., 5th Fusiliers, and took part in the fighting at Armentières, Calonne, Souchez, and Ploegsteert, and also on the Somme (mentioned in despatches). Commanded the 19th Regtl. Depôt from 16th August, 1917, to June, 1919. Secretary to the North Riding Territorial Association, 1919.

REGINALD EDWIN BOND

Born at Meerut, 28th October, 1870, son of Lieut.-Col. Charles Frederick Bond, 105th Madras Light Infantry.

Second Lieut., 9th January, 1892 ; Lieut., 19th June, 1895; Indian Army, 14th July, 1896 ; Capt., 10th July, 1901 ; Major, 9th January, 1910.

Killed in action at Ahwaz, Persia, 3rd March, 1915.

ALEXANDER BREDIN

Born near Trimulgherry, E.I., 22nd February, 1871, son of Colonel Alexander Bredin, Indian Army, formerly 19th Foot.

Second Lieut., 9th January, 1892 Lieut., 8th April, 1896 ; Indian Army, 9th July, 1896 ; Capt., 10th July, 1901 ; Major, 9th January, 1910 ; Lieut.-Col., 28th August, 1917.

HERBERT ALBRECHT FULTON, D.S.O.

Born at Bangalore, 3rd October, 1872, son of Major-General Graeme Auchmuty Fulton, Indian Army.

Second Lieut., 27th January, 1892 ; Lieut., 14th July, 1896 ; Capt., Worcestershire Regt., 20th June, 1900 ; Adjt., 5th October, 1900—4th October, 1904 ; Major, 2nd March, 1911.

Served in the Tirah Expedition, 1897-98, and was present at the capture of Bagh, the Dwatoi reconnaissance and reconnaissance of the Saran Sar and engagement of the 11th November. Operations against the Khani Khel Chamkanis. Also in the Bazar Valley (medal and 2 clasps). In the war of 1914-18, served on the Staff and in command of the 9th Bn. Scottish Rifles (wounded, twice mentioned in despatches and D.S.O.).

HENRY GEORGE LYON CORBETT

Born at Dartmouth, 9th June, 1870, son of Admiral Sir John Corbett, K.C.B.

Second Lieut., 9th April, 1892 ; Lieut., Indian Army, 23rd September, 1894 ; Capt., 10th July, 1901 ; Major, 9th April, 1910 ; retired, 9th April, 1915.

WALTER LORENZO ALEXANDER

Born at Rathmindon, Co. Carlow, 8th September, 1872, youngest son of George Alexander, of Erindale, Co. Carlow.

Second Lieut., 18th May, 1892 ; Lieut., 28th July, 1896 ; Capt., 29th December, 1900 ; Major, 4th February, 1908 ; Lieut.-Col., 29th September, 1914.

Served in the Tirah Expedition of 1897-98, and was present at the capture of the Sampagha and Arhanga Passes, the capture of Bagh, the Dwatoi reconnaissance, the reconnaissance of the Saran Sar and engagements of 11th November, and at Shinkamar on 29th January, 1898. Also in the operations against the Khani Khel Chamkanis and in the Bazar Valley (medal and 2 clasps). Awarded King Edward's Delhi Coronation medal, 1903. Proceeded to Zeebrugge in October, 1914, with 2nd Bn. and took part in the fighting at Ypres (wounded at Gheluvelt). Returned to the front in December and commanded the battalion at the battle of Neuve Chapelle, 12th March, 1915.

Killed by a shell at Festubert, 14th May, 1915. Buried at Le Touret.

" The battalion has suffered an irreparable loss in the death of Lieut.-Col. W. L. Alexander, who was killed instantaneously by a shell while inspecting the trenches held by part of the battalion. It seems but yesterday that we were congratulating him and ourselves on his appointment to the command. No one could have wished to serve under a better commanding officer, whose first thought was for the Regiment and his last for himself. All ranks loved, respected and honoured him."
—G. H. G.

EARLS AINSLIE HOSFORD

Born at Lea, Kent, 27th July, 1872, son of Thomas Stroud Hosford, M.D., of Tulse Hill, London.

Second Lieut., 19th November, 1892 ; Lieut., 12th October, 1896 ; Adjt., 16th December, 1900—1st October, 1903 ; Capt., 29th December, 1900 ; Adjt., 2nd Vol. Bn., 1st February, 1904—3rd March, 1908 ; Major, 4th March, 1908.

Served in the Tirah Expedition of 1897-98, and was present at the capture of the Sampagha and Arhanga Passes, the reconnaissance of the Saran Sar, and engagement of 11th November. Also in the expedition to the Bazar Valley and in the affair at Shinkamar, 29th January, 1898 (medal and 2 clasps).

Died at Leeds, 11th February, 1914. Buried at Richmond, Yorks.

" Nature had gifted him with unusual abilities, and the best qualifications for a leader, but, by the irony of fate, health, that greatest of all boons, was denied to him, and having once broken never could be regained. Quiet and unassuming though he was, it was impossible to be in his society without becoming aware of the sterling qualities and great abilities which he possessed. Given the opportunity, it is quite certain that he would have made his mark, and that he would have taken a high place in his profession. But since it is certain that no life of great example is ever lived in vain, we who knew him shall always value the lesson of these last years of his life ; the lesson that no accumulation of misfortune, no continued run of bad luck, need ever diminish the spirit of a brave man and a good soldier."—G. H. G.

FRANCIS STIRLING DE MONTALT MAUDE

Born at Emsworth, 25th April, 1867, only son of Colonel Francis Cornwallis Maude, V.C., C.B., Royal Artillery.

Second Lieut., 17th May, 1893, from ranks of the North Staffordshire Regt. ; resigned, 27th February, 1895 ; Capt., Royal Northern Reserve Regt., 26th May, 1900 ; Adjt., 2nd June, 1900 ; Capt., Royal Garrison Regt., 9th August, 1902 ; Major, 25th February, 1903 ; half-pay, 26th January, 1906 ; Provisional Bn., 12th September, 1906 ; half-pay, 4th April, 1909 ; West African Regt., 8th December, 1909 ; retired, 21st June, 1917.

EDWARD BOUVERIE PUSEY

Born at St. Leonard's, 19th March, 1873, eldest son of Captain Edward Bouverie Pusey, R.N.

Second Lieut., 9th September, 1893 Lieut., 18th November, 1896 ; resigned, 17th November, 1901.

Served in the Tirah Expedition of 1897-98 (medal and 2 clasps).

RALPH ELLIOT NOYES

Born at Milford Haven, 23rd November, 1873, son of Col. George Augustus Noyes, Royal Artillery.

Second Lieut., 21st October, 1893 ; Lieut., 4th December, 1896 ; Capt., 12th March, 1901 ; Major, 29th September, 1910 ; retired, 4th November, 1911.

Served in the Tirah Expedition of 1897-98, and was present at the capture of Bagh, the Dwatoi reconnaissance, the crossing of the Kahu

Darra, the reconnaissance of the Saran Sar, and engagement of 11th November, the operations against the Khani Khel Chamkanis and in the Bazar Valley (medal and 2 clasps). Was posted to the 10th Service Bn., 4th October, 1914, and proceeded with it to France.

Killed at Hill 60, near Loos, 26th September, 1915.

JAMES GREER

Born at Sandgate, Kent, 17th November, 1859.

Boy service one year and 273 days. In ranks 18 years 236 days. Hon. Lieut. and Qr.-Master, 11th July, 1894 ; hon. Capt., 11th July, 1904 ; retired as hon. Major, 11th July, 1909.

Served in the Tirah Expeditionary Force, 1897-98, and was present at the capture of the Sampagha and Arhanga Passes, the capture of Bagh, the crossing of the Kahu Darra, the reconnaissance of the Saran Sar and engagement of 11th November, operations at and around Dwatoi. In the operations against the Khani Khel Chamkanis, and in the Bazar Valley and affair at Shinkamar, 29th January, 1898 (medal and 2 clasps).

Appointed Qr.-Mr. to the 4th Bn. Royal West Surrey Regt., 16th December, 1911, and was promoted Lieut.-Col., 3rd June, 1918, for services connected with the Great War. In possession of the medal for long service and good conduct.

CHARLES JOHN HERBERT HAY NOBLE

Born, 27th June, 1870, son of Colonel C. S. Noble, of Innerwick, Murrayfield, Edinburgh.

Second Lieut., 12th September, 1894, from ranks of 16th Foot ; Lieut., 16th January, 1897 ; Capt., Manchester Regt., 9th June, 1900.

Served in the Isazai Expedition, 1892 (mentioned in despatches). Took part in the Tirah Expedition of 1897-98 as regimental transport officer, and was present at the capture of the Sampagha and Arhanga Passes, the capture of Bagh, the Dwatoi reconnaissance, and engagement of November 11th. Also in the operations in the Bazar Valley (mentioned in despatches, medal and two clasps). Served in the Boer War, 1899-01, as transport officer during the siege of Ladysmith (mentioned in despatches, 7th May, 1901).

Killed in action at Ochapie near Bethlehem, Orange River Colony, 12th November, 1901.

General Sir Leslie Rundle on hearing of his death wired to sympathise with the Manchester Regt. saying, " He was an example of bravery to all of us."

WILLIAM HORSBROUGH LANE

Born at Amraoti, Behar, India, 2nd August, 1874, son of Colonel Clayton Turner Lane, C.I.E., Bengal Staff Corps, of Downfold, Guildford, Surrey.

Second Lieut., 10th October, 1894 ; Lieut., 9th March, 1897 ; Indian Army, 10th August, 1897 ; Capt., 10th October, 1903 ; Major, 10th October, 1912.

Served in the arms traffic operations in the Persian Gulf from January, 1913, to August, 1914. In the war of 1914-18, served in the Persian Gulf operations from August, 1914, to January, 1916. In the operations against the Mohmands and Wahsuds between October, 1916, and June, 1917. During the remainder of the war served with the Mesopotamian Field Force (mentioned by the C.-in-C., India, in his despatch of 9th June, 1916).

GEORGE CUTHBERT DILLON MASTERSON

Born, 17th July, 1872. Second Lieut., 12th December, 1894 ; Army Service Corps, 1st October, 1896 ; Lieut., 1st October, 1897 ; Capt., 1st January, 1901 ; resigned, 12th May, 1906.

Served in the operations in Sierra Leone in 1898-99 with the Protectorate Expedition (medal and clasp). Served in the Boer War, 1899-02, as supply officer to a division, including the advance on Kimberley, actions of Belmont, Enslin, Modder River and Majesfontein. Operations in the Orange River Colony, May to 29th November, 1900, including actions at Biddulphsberg, Wittebergen, 1st to 29th July, and Caledon River. Operations in O.R.C., 30th November, to 31st May, 1902 (Queen's medal with 4 clasps, King's medal and 2 clasps). Appointed Capt, 10th Reserve Bn., Royal Lancaster Regt., 16th February, 1915.

EDWARD HENRY CHAPMAN

Born at Budleigh, Salterton, 25th April, 1875, eldest son of Edward Henry Chapman, of Carr Hall, Whitby.

Second Lieut., 20th February, 1895 ; Lieut., 18th August, 1897 ; Capt., 29th September, 1901 ; Major, 11th February, 1911.

Served in the Tirah Expedition of 1897-8, and was present at the capture of Bagh, the Dwatoi reconnaissance, the crossing of the Kahu Darra, the reconnaissance of the Saran Sar and engagement of 11th November, and in the operations against the Khani Khel Chamkanis. Also in the Bazar Valley (medal and 2 clasps). On the outbreak of the war in 1914, was appointed to the command of the 6th Service Battn., and accompanied it to Gallipoli.

Killed in action at the taking of Lali Baba, 7th August, 1915.

"The raising of the 6th Battalion was a task for which he was eminently suited. A thorough and conscientious soldier, his chief aim was the welfare and correct training of his men: He was a keen all-round sportsman, a plucky horseman, a very fair shot and good cricketer ; at lawn tennis and hockey, far above the average" (G.H.G.).

MATTHEW ROBERT LIDDON

Born at Preston, 7th June, 1873, son of Captain Matthew Liddon, 8th Foot.

Second Lieut., 29th May, 1895 ; Lieut., 13th November, 1897 ; Capt., 21st January, 1902 ; half-pay, 28th November, 1903 ; Staff Officer, Recruiting, London, 28th August, 1905 ; half-pay, 28th August, 1909 ; 19th Foot, 5th August, 1914 ; Bt. Major, 1st January, 1917 ; half-pay, 31st October, 1919.

Served in the Boer War, 1900-1902. Took part in the march to Pretoria, including engagements at Brandfort Kroonstadt, Vet and Zand Rivers, and Johannesburg. In the advance eastwards and actions at Diamond Hill and Belfast. Was severely wounded in the Origstadt Valley when serving with the 4th Bn. Mounted Infantry (Queen's medal and 5 clasps, King's medal and 2 clasps).

In the war of 1914-18, served on the Staff at Southampton (mentioned in home despatch, Bt. of Major).

CHRISTOPHER VAUGHAN EDWARDS, C.M.G., D.S.O.

Born at Llanfair, Anglesey, 13th January, 1875, son of the Revd. W. J. Edwards, The Rectory, Llanfair.

Second Lieut., 28th September, 1895 ; Lieut., 23rd Novem-

246

ber, 1897 ; Capt., 19th May, 1904 ; Major, 28th March, 1911 ; Bt. Lieut.-Col., 3rd June, 1918 ; Lieut.-Col., 1st January, 1919.

Served in the Tirah Expedition, 1897-98, and was at the capture of the Sampagha and Arhanga Passes, the capture of Bagh, the crossing of the Kahu Darra, the Dwatoi reconnaissance, the reconnaissance of the Saran Sar and engagement of 11th November. Also in the operations against the Khani Khel Chamkanis (medal and 2 clasps). Served in the Boer War, 1900, and took part in the operations around Colesberg in January, the march along the Modder River, including the Relief of Kimberley and action at Paardeberg (severely wounded, mentioned in despatches, medal and 2 clasps). Served in the Somaliland Expedition of 1904, with the mounted infantry, including the action at Jidballi (medal and 2 clasps).

In the war of 1914-18, served with the 1st Bn. in India and with 2nd Bn. from October, 1916, and was present in the fighting at Arras in April, 1917. In the German advance in March, 1918, was wounded when in command of 2nd Bn. After recovery was appointed to the command of the 64th Brigade in June, and took part in all the fighting on the Western front till the end of the war (four times mentioned in despatches, C.M.G., D.S.O., Belgium Order de la Couronne of Leopold and Croix de Guerre). Was awarded the Distinguished Service Order for conspicuous gallantry and devotion to duty in going forward under shell and rifle fire and making a daring personal reconnaissance in order to clear up an obscure situation. By his action he not only managed to ascertain the actual situation and to take the necessary measures, but also set a fine example of coolness and greatly encouraged both officers and men. He had previously displayed great judgment and gallantry under fire.

CHARLES FRANCIS CRACROFT JARVIS, O.B.E.

Born at Kettlethorpe Hall, 3rd May, 1875, only son of the Revd. Francis Amcotts Jarvis, Vicar of Burton-on-Stather, Doncaster.

Second Lieut., 6th June, 1896 ; Lieut., 27th April, 1898 ; Capt., 25th June, 1904 ; retired, 12th May, 1909 ; Capt., 3rd Bn. Lincolnshire Regt., 12th May, 1909 ; Bt. Major, 1st January, 1918 ; Major, 4th April, 1918.

Served in the Boer War, 1899-1901, and was present during the operations round Colesberg in January, 1900. Took part in the march along the Modder River, the Relief of Kimberley, and the actions at Paardeberg and Kitchener's Kop. Was in the advance on Dewetsdorp and action at Leuukop. In the march from Bloemfontein to Pretoria, including engagements at Brandfort, Kroonstadt, the Vet and Zand Rivers and occupation of Johannesburg and Pretoria. Also in the advance eastwards and actions at Diamond Hill and Belfast (mentioned in despatches, Queen's medal and 7 clasps). In the war of 1914-18, served on the Staff as Asst. Military Landing Officer, Staff Captain and D.A.Q.M.G. in France (five times mentioned in despatches, bronze star Bt. of Major and O.B.E.).

MAUNTON EDWARD THOMAS GUNTHORPE

Born at Akola, E.I., 19th February, 1876, only son of Colonel Edward James Gunthorpe, Indian Army.

Second Lieut., 9th December, 1896 ; Lieut., 1st July, 1898 : Adjt., 16th January, 1901—16th January, 1905 ; Capt., 25th June, 1904 ; seconded Egyptian Army, 5th April, 1906.

Served in the Boer War, 1899-1902, and was attached to the Royal Irish Rifles during the operations round Stormberg. Took part in the operations round Colesberg in January, 1900, and in the march along the Modder River, the Relief of Kimberley and actions at Paardeberg and Kitchener's Kop (wounded). In the advance on Dewetsdorp and action at Leuukop. In the march from Bloemfontein to Pretoria, including the engagements at Brandfort, Kroonstadt, Vet and Zand Rivers, Johannesburg and occupation of Pretoria. Also in the advance eastwards and actions at Diamond Hill and Belfast (mentioned in despatches, Queen's medal and 5 clasps, King's medal and 2 clasps).

Died at Roseires, Soudan, of blackwater fever, 7th September, 1907, when serving with the Egyptian Army. Memorial window in St. George's Garrison Church, Aldershot. Monument at Roseires erected by his brother officers.

The Sirdar sent the following telegram to Colonel Gunthorpe :

" Accept heartfelt sympathy in loss of your gallant son. Egyptian Army has been deprived of excellent and capable officer, and we all deplore death of a good comrade and friend."

OLIVER CYRIL SPENCER WATSON, V.C., D.S.O.

Born in London, 7th September, 1876, son of W. Spencer Watson, F.R.C.S., Henrietta Street, London.

Second Lieut., 20th February, 1897 ; Lieut., 17th August, 1898 ; retired, 16th January, 1904.

Served in the Tirah Expedition, 1897-98, and was present at the capture of the Sampagha and Arhanga Passes, the Dwatoi reconnaissance (severely wounded), the reconnaissance of the Saran Sar and engagement of 11th November ; in the operations against the Khani Khel Chamkanis (medal with two clasps). Served in the China Expedition of 1900 (medal and clasp). In the war of 1914-18, as a captain in the London Yeomanry ; took part in the expedition to Gallipoli (bronze star). As Major in the 5th Bn. King's Own Yorkshire L.I., served in France, and was wounded at Bullecourt (mentioned in despatches and D.S.O.). The " London Gazette" detailing the award of the Distinguished Service Order states :

On the 3rd May, 1917, during the attack near Bullecourt, Lieut.-Col. W. Watson, commanding the battalion, was killed. Major O. C. S. Watson was sent up to take his place. On arriving at the railway cutting, he found men of all units of the brigade who had returned there after the first unsuccessful attack. Displaying the highest soldierly qualities, he organised these men, inspired them with his own coolness and confidence and personally led them forward to a second attack. This attack was eventually brought to nothing by machine gun fire, but Major Watson continued to advance alone in an endeavour to reach the men still holding on in front until he was badly wounded. All units of the brigade were talking about his great gallantry and fine leadership.

Killed at Rossignol Wood, Bucquoy-Hebuterne, France, 28th March, 1918.

On 8th May, 1918, the Victoria Cross was awarded " For most conspicuous bravery, self-sacrificing devotion to duty, and exceptionally gallant leading during a critical period of operations. His command was at a point where continual attacks were made by the enemy, in order to pierce the line, and an intricate system of old trenches in front, coupled with the fact that his position was under constant rifle and machine gun fire, rendered the situation still more dangerous. A counter attack had been made against the enemy position, which at first achieved its object, but as they were holding out in two improvised strong points, Lieut.-Col. Watson saw that immediate action was necessary, and led his remaining small reserve to the attack, organizing bombing parties and leading attacks under intense rifle and machine gun fire. Out-numbered, he finally ordered his men to retire, remaining himself in a communication trench to cover the retirement, though he faced almost certain death by so doing.

The assault he led was at a critical moment and without doubt saved the line. Both in the assault and in covering his mens' retirement he held his life as nothing, and his splendid bravery inspired all troops in the vicinity to rise to the occasion and save a breach being made in a hardly tried and attenuated line. Lieut.-Col. Watson was killed while covering the withdrawal."

WILFRID BECKETT WALKER

Born at Scarborough, 5th August, 1876, 2nd son of Captain Edwyn Walker, 15th Hussars.

Second Lieut., 20th February, 1897 ; Lieut., 15th October, 1898 ; Capt., 25th June, 1904 ; Major, 3rd December, 1913.

Served in the Boer War, 1900-02. Operations in the Orange River Colony, including actions at the Vet and Zand Rivers. In the advance eastwards, actions at Diamond Hill and Belfast. With the 2nd Bn. Mounted Infantry in operations in the Transvaal, 30th November, 1900, to end of the war (mentioned in despatches, Queen's medal and 4 clasps, King's medal and 2 clasps).

Proceeded to Zeebrugge with 2nd Bn. in October, 1914, and was killed at Ypres, 29th October, 1914.

"He was a most capable and reliable officer, whose loss will be deeply felt in the regiment. Under a quiet and somewhat cynical exterior, there was a true and brave heart. No one did kinder things than he, and certainly no one took more pains to conceal the fact that he had done them. He always had a way out of a difficulty and worked for the good of the regiment " (G.H.G.).

MERVYN DOBREÉ CAREY

Born in Guernsey, 8th January, 1877, son of Julius Carey, Receiver General of Guernsey.

Second Lieut., 20th February, 1897 ; Lieut., 12th November, 1898 ; Capt., 1st October, 1904 ; Major, 12th February, 1914 ; Bt. Lieut.-Col., 3rd June, 1919.

During the war of 1914-18, served in India, most of the time in command of the 1st Bn. on the North West Frontier and in the operations in Afghanistan, 1919 (Brevet of Lieut.-Colonel).

THOMAS WOLRYCHE STANSFELD, C.M.G., D.S.O.

Born at Leeds, 30th June, 1877, son of Thomas Wolryche Stansfeld, J.P., of Weetwood Grove, Leeds.

Second Lieut., 24th March, 1897 ; Lieut., 15th December, 1898 ; Capt., 6th Foot, 19th February, 1902 ; re-appointed to 19th Foot, 8th January, 1908 ; Major, 29th September, 1914 ; Bt. Lieut.-Col., 3rd June, 1916 ; Bt. Col., 3rd June, 1919. (Adjt., M.I., South Africa, 22nd June, 1906—21st June, 1909 ; Adjt., 3rd Reserve Battn., 9th October, 1910—9th October, 1913).

Served in the Boer War, 1899-1902, and took part in the operations near Colesberg in January, 1900. In the march along the Modder River, including the Relief of Kimberley and actions at Paardeberg, Kitchener's Kop, Poplar Grove and Driefontein. Occupation of Bloemfontein. Was with the advance on Dewetsdorp, and action at Leuukop. In the advance to Pretoria and engagements at Brandfort, Kroonstadt, Vet and Zand Rivers. With the 4th M.I. in the fighting at Johannesburg and occupation of Pretoria, also in the advance to Komati Poort, including actions at Diamond Hill and Belfast (mentioned in despatches, D.S.O., promoted Captain, Queen's medal and 6 clasps, King's medal and 2 clasps).

Landed with the 2nd Bn. at Zeebrugge in the war of 1914-18, and took part in the battle of Ypres, October, 1914 (wounded, bronze star and clasp). Present at the battles of Festubert, 16th May, 1915 ; Givenchy, 15th June, 1915, and Hulloch, September—October, 1915 (mentioned in despatches, Bt. of Lieut.-Col.). Appointed to command a brigade, 6th April, 1917, and was present at the fighting at Hargicourt Quarries, April, 1917, the third battle of Ypres, 26th September, 1917, Cambrai, November to December, 1917 (twice mentioned in despatches and Legion of Honour, Croix d' Officier). Was engaged at Bullecourt, 21st—24th March, 1918 ; Mount Kemmell, 12th—19th April ; Mercatel, 23rd August, and advance from Lestrem to Tournai and Lille, September and October, 1918 (mentioned in despatches, C.M.G., Bt. of Colonel and Croix de Guerre).

CHARLES TEMPLE MORRIS

Born at Lucknow, 9th January, 1876, son of A. T. Morris.

Second Lieut., 15th May, 1897 ; Lieut., 11th January, 1899 ; Indian Army, 12th April, 1900 ; Capt., 15th May, 1906 ; Major, 15th May, 1915.

Served in the Tirah Expedition of 1897-98, on the N.W. Frontier of India, including affair at Shinkamar, 29th January, 1898 (medal and 2 clasps). Took part in the North West Frontier campaign of 1908, operations against the Mohmands, including engagement at Kargha (medal and clasp).

ROBERT HENRY DARWIN

Born at Arthington, Yorkshire, son of Francis Darwin, J.P., of Creskeld Hall, near Leeds, D.L. for West Riding.

Second Lieut., 15th May, 1897 ; Lieut., 22nd October, 1899 ; Capt., 1st November, 1904 ; retired, 15th May, 1912.

Served in the Boer War, 1899-02, and took part in the operations, near Colesberg in January, 1900, and in the March along the Modder River, including the Relief of Kimberley and actions at Paardeberg, Kitchener's Kop, Poplar Grove, Driefontein and occupation of Bloemfontein. Was with the advance on Dewetsdorp and action at Leuukop. In the advance on Pretoria and engagements at Brandfort, Kroonstadt, Vet and Zand Rivers and occupation of Johannesburg and Pretoria. Also with the advance eastward, including actions at Diamond Hill and Belfast (Queen's medal and 6 clasps, King's medal and 2 clasps).

WILLIAM JOSEPH ROSKELL

Born at St. Edmonsbury, Lucan, Co. Dublin, 29th August, 1875, son of Nicholas Robert Roskell, of Warwick Gardens, Kensington.

Second Lieut., 15th May, 1897 ; Lieut., 24th March, 1900 ; Capt., 18th February, 1905 ; retired, 21st December, 1912 ; Capt., 4th Bn. North Staffordshire Regt., 21st December, 1912 ; Major, 1st March, 1913.

Served in the Tirah Expedition of 1897-98, on the N.W. Frontier of India (medal and 2 clasps). In the Great War was temporary Lieut.-Col. in command of 4th Bn. North Staffordshire Regt. on home service from 10th August, 1915, to 8th December, 1916 (mentioned in home despatch and granted honorary rank of Lieut.-Colonel).

NORMAN EDWARD SWAN, p.s.c.

Born at Middlesbcrough, 27th September, 1876, son of Norman Arthur Swan, of Middlesborough.

Second Lieut., 1st December, 1897 ; Lieut., 12th April, 1900 ; Capt., 18th February, 1905 ; Adjt., 1st October, 1903— 1st December, 1906 ; Major, 30th October, 1914 ; Bt. Lieut.-Col., 1st January, 1919.

Served in the Tirah Expedition of 1897-8 on the North West Frontier of India (medal and clasp). As Brigade Major to the 163rd Brigade took part in the landing at Suvla Bay and was present at the attack and capture of Anafarta. Was severely wounded whilst making a reconnaissance with a view to advancing the line (bronze star). Organised and commanded No. 8 Officers' Cadet Battalion. Served in Egypt on the Staff and also as G.S.O.2 to the 21st Corps in Palestine. Appointed to the Staff of the British Military Mission, Portugal, October 1918, to May, 1919, latterly acting as military attaché (Bt. of Lieut.-Col., Chevalier of the Legion of Honour, Commander of the Order of Avis and Commander Ordeur do Cristo of Portugal).

ERNEST VIVIAN LIVESEY WARDLE, D.S.O.

Born at Boroughbridge, Yorkshire, 28th June, 1878, son of Captain T. Livesey Wardle, of Birchington, Kent.

Second Lieut., 22nd December, 1897 ; Lieut., 9th May, 1900 ; Capt., 14th February, 1908 resigned, 25th August, 1909.

Served in the Boer War, 1899-1902, and took part in the operations near Colesberg in January, 1900. Was with the advance along the Modder River, including the Relief of Kimberley, the actions at Paardeberg and Kitchener's Kop (wounded). In the march on Dewetsdorp and action at Leuukop. Also in the march to Pretoria and engagements at Brandfort, Kroonstadt, Vet and Zand Rivers, and Johannesburg. With the advance eastwards and actions at Diamond Hill and Belfast (mentioned in despatches, D.S.O., Queen's medal and 5 clasps, King's medal and 2 clasps). During the War of 1914-18 was employed on recruiting duties.

PATRICK HOUSTON KEEN

Born, 19th September, 1877, son of Sir Frederick Keen, G.C.B., of Kingswood, Woking.

Second Lieut., 16th February, 1898 ; Lieut., 9th June, 1900 ; Indian Army, 16th August, 1900 ; Capt., 16th February, 1907 ; Major, 1st September, 1915 ; Bt. Lieut.-Col., 1st January, 1919.

Served with the Egyptian Expeditionary Force in the Great War (mentioned in despatches).

WILLIAM GODFREY TARBET, D.S.O.

Born at Liverpool, 18th January, 1878, son of E. G. Tarbet, of Liverpool.

Second Lieut., 16th February, 1898 ; Lieut., 20th June, 1900 ; Capt., Worcestershire Regt., 13th Apil, 1904 ; Adjt., 6th September, 1906—5th September, 1909.

Served in the Boer War, 1899-1902, with the 4th Bn. Mounted Infantry. Took part in the march along the Modder River, including the Relief of Kimberley, the actions at Paardeberg (slightly wounded), and Poplar Grove, and occupation of Bloemfontein. With the advance on Pretoria and engagements at Brandfort, Kroonstadt, Vet and Zand Rivers and Johannesburg. In the advance to Komati Poort and engagement at Belfast (slightly wounded, twice mentioned in despatches, D.S.O., Queen's medal and 4 clasps, King's medal and 2 clasps).

Died at Jhansi, India, 20th April, 1911, the result of a fall from his horse whilst pigsticking Tombstone at Jhansi Cemetery, erected by the officers, N.C.O's. and men of the 2nd Bn. Worcestershire Regt.

" The universal opinion of him was that he was an excellent soldier, a brave man, and a very good friend " (G.H.G.).

CHARLES HAMILTON de St. PIERRE BUNBURY

Born in Dublin, 23rd September, 1877, eldest son of Colonel Charles Thomas Bunbury, Rifle Brigade.

Second Lieut., 16th February, 1898 ; Lieut., 1st August, 1900 ; Capt., 25th January, 1905 ; Major, 28th March, 1915.

Served in the Boer War, 1899-1902, and was present at the operations near Colesberg in January, 1900. Took part in the march along the Modder River, including the Relief of Kimberey, the actions at Paardeberg, Kitchener's Kop, Poplar Grove, Driefontein, and occupation of Bloemfontein. Was with the advance on Dewetsdorp and action at Leuukop. In the march to Pretoria, including engagements at Brandfort, Vet and Zand Rivers, Kroonstadt and Johannesburg. Also in the advance eastwards and actions at Diamond Hill and Belfast (Queen's medal and 6 clasps, King's medal and 2 clasps). During the war of 1914-18, served on the Staff in India. Joined 2nd Bn. in France in May, 1917, and with it till appointed to command 2nd Bedfordshire Regt. Took part in the 3rd battle of Ypres. From December, 1917, to February, 1918, was in command of a Service Bn. of the Lancashire Fusiliers.

ARTHUR LOWTHIAN GODMAN, C.M.G., D.S.O.

Born at Smeaton, Yorkshire, 20th September, 1877, son of Colonel Arthur Fitzpatrick Godman, C.B., V.D., D.L., late 6th Carabineers.

Second Lieut., 4th May, 1898 ; Lieut., 17th November, 1900 ; Capt., 16th January, 1906 ; Major, 8th August, 1915 ; Wing Commander, Royal Air Force, 1st August, 1919.

Served with the Mounted Infantry in the Somaliland Expedition, 1904 (medal and clasp). Went to Belgium in October, 1914, as Staff Captain to 21st Brigade of the 7th Division, and was severely wounded in the fighting at Ypres, 30th October, 1914. Served in France from August, 1915, to July, 1917, on the staff of the Royal Flying Corps, and afterwards under the Air Ministry (bronze star and clasp, three times mentioned in despatches, C.M.G. and D.S.O.).

MALHERT MARTIN HUYSHE NEVILE

Born at Doncaster, 14th May, 1877, 3rd son of Percy Sandford Nevile, late 22nd Foot.

Second Lieut., 4th May, 1898 ; Lieut., 16th December, 1900 ; Capt., 5th Foot, 19th April, 1902 ; 7th Foot, 20th May, 1908 ; retired, 29th January, 1910 ; Captain, 3rd (Reserve) Battn., 29th January, 1910 ; Major, 24th August, 1917 ; resigned, 30th March, 1920.

Served in the Boer War, 1899-1902, with 4th Bn. Mounted Infantry, and took part in the march along the Modder River, the Relief of Kimberley, the actions at Paardeberg, Poplar Grove, and occupation of Bloemfontein. In the march to Pretoria, including actions at Brandfort, Vet and Zand Rivers, Kroonstadt and Johannesburg. Also in the advance to Komati Poort and actions of Diamond Hill and Belfast (twice mentioned in despatches, specially promoted Captain, Queen's medal and 6 clasps, King's medal and 2 clasps). In the Great War served in France as A.D.C. to General Maxse, Commanding 18th Division, from

April, 1915, to January, 1917, and afterwards to February, 1919, as Camp Commandant. Present at the fighting on the Somme, 1916, and later at Armentières, also at Paschendaele, St. Quentin, and in the retreat of the 5th Army in March, 1918 (three times mentioned in despatches, bronze star and Belgium Croix de Guerre).

WILLIAM SHAFTO CRASTER

Born, 11th April, 1873, 2nd son of Lieut.-Col. William Robert Craster, late R.A., of Otterington House, Northallerton.

Second Lieut., 18th May, 1898, from ranks of 20th Hussars ; Lieut., Indian Army, 28th December, 1900 ; Capt., 26th July, 1907 ; Major, 18th May, 1916.

ERNEST SCOTT BROUN

Born at Orchard Carluke, N.B., 7th December, 1879, son of James Broun, of Orchard Carluke.

Second Lieut., 4th February, 1899 ; Lieut., 29th December, 1900 ; Capt., 6th April, 1906 ; A.D.C. to Sir L. Probyn, K.C.M.G., Governor of Barbados, 19th July, 1911.

Served in the Boer War, 1899-1902, and was present at the operations near Colesberg in January, 1900, and in the march along the Modder River, including the Relief of Kimberley, actions at Paardeberg, Kitchener's Kop, Poplar Grove, Driefontein, and occupation of Bloemfontein. Was with the advance on Dewetsdorp and action at Leuukop. In the march to Pretoria and actions at Brandfort, Vet and Zand Rivers, Kroonstadt and Johannesburg. In the advance eastwards, in actions at Diamond Hill and Belfast (Queen's medal and 6 clasps, King's medal and 2 clasps). Proceeded to France with 2nd Bn., and was killed near Ypres on the 30th October, 1914 (mentioned in despatches).

" He was a very popular member of society in Barbados, possessing an exceedingly genial disposition and urbanity of manner. His early death is greatly to be deplored, but consolation is to be taken from the fact that he died at the post of honour where a good soldier loves to die " (Bridgetown Paper).

EUSTACE CLEMENTI-SMITH

Born at Singapore, 8th November, 1879, 3rd son of Sir Cecil Clementi-Smith, P.C., G.C.M.G., Governor of the Straits Settlements.

Second Lieut., 11th February, 1899, Indian Army, 29th September, 1900 ; Lieut., 11th May, 1901 ; Capt., 25th January, 1908 ; Major, 1st September, 1915.

Served on the North West Frontier, 1902, in the operations against the Darwesh Khel Waziris. In the war of 1914-18, served on the North West Frontier, and took part in the actions of Spina Khaisora, 7th January, 1915, and Miranshaw, 26th March, 1915. Was also engaged in the Mohmand Blockade (twice mentioned in despatches). Employed with the North Waziristan Militia, September, 1913—April, 1917. Raised the Mohmand Militia in January, 1918, and afterwards the 2/28th Punjabis, which he commanded.

JAMES ALEXANDER SKENE THOMSON

Born in London, 6th September, 1855, son of J. Thomson of Dunstable House, Richmond, Surrey.

Lieut., 100th Foot, 24th March, 1877 ; Capt., 24th January,

1883 ; West Riding Regt., 5th March, 1884 ; Major, 15th March, 1894 ; 19th Foot, 29th March, 1899 ; retired, 6th September, 1903.

Served with the 3rd Ghoorkas in the Afghan War in 1880, and was present in the engagement at Ahmed Kheyl and Urzoo, near Ghuznee, and in the subsequent operations in the Logar Valley (medal and clasp). Served in the Bechuanaland Expedition in 1884-85 with the Corps of Guides, under Sir Charles Warren.

ARTHUR CORMAC NEAVE

Born, 4th June, 1877, son of Francis Digby Spencer Neave, of Okeover, Upper Riccarton, Christchurch, New Zealand.

Second Lieut., 22nd November, 1899.

Served in the Boer War, 1899-1900, with the New Zealand Mounted Rifles and 1st Bn. (mentioned in despatches).

Killed in action at Paardeberg, 18th February, 1900. Memorial Cross at Paardeberg, erected by officers and men of the regiment.

JOHN SHERIDAN

Born at Doncaster, 30th June, 1861, son of Jonas Sheridan. Pte., 31st July, 1879 ; Sergt., 1st January, 1882 ; Cr.-Sergt., 4th June, 1883 ; Qr.-Mr.-Sergt., 9th June, 1888 ; Sergt.-Major, 13th October, 1897 ; hon. Lieut. and Qr.-Mr., 13th December, 1899 ; hon. Capt., 13th December, 1909.

Served in the Tirah Expedition, 1897-98, as acting Sergt.-Major 2nd Bn. (medal and 2 clasps). Served in the Boer War with 4th Bn.. Operations in Cape Colony, April to 31st May, 1902 (Queen's medal and 2 clasps). In possession of the medal for long service and good conduct.

Died at Richmond, Yorkshire, 5th March, 1913.

" The respect in which the late Captain Sheridan was held, not only by the military, but by the civil population of Richmond, was signified by the enormous crowds that lined the route from the Parish Church to the Cemetery on the day of the funeral " (G.H.G.).

ATWELL CHARLES DENNET PEARSON

Born in the Punjab, 5th May, 1878, son of Colonel Pearson.

Second Lieut., 20th December, 1899 ; half-pay, 27th July, 1901 ; 19th Foot, February, 1902 ; resigned, 27th April, 1904.

Served in the Boer War, 1901-2 (medal and 2 clasps).

Died at Bromley, Kent, 9th December, 1914.

HAROLD VERMUDEN BASTOW, D.S.O.

Born at Eastnor, Herefordshire, 2nd July, 1878, son of the Revd. Thomas Claude Vermuden Bastow, Rector of Peatling Parva, Leicestershire.

Second Lieut., 20th December, 1899 ; Lieut., 16th January, 1901 ; Capt., 4th March, 1908 ; Major, 29th December, 1915.

Served in the Boer War, 1900-02, and took part in the march from Bloemfontein to Pretoria, including actions at Brandfort, Vet and Zand Rivers, Kroonstadt and Johannesburg. Also in the advance eastwards and actions at Diamond Hill and Belfast. Served with the Mounted Infantry in the Transvaal, 30th November, 1900, to end of the war (Queen's medal and 5 clasps, King's medal and 2 clasps). Was employed with the Northern Nigerian Police from September, 1903, to January, 1905.

In the Great War, served from April, 1915, to March, 1916 in Mesopotamia as A.D.C. to Major-Gen. Sir Charles Townshend, K.C.B., and took part in the actions at Amara, Kut-el-Amara, and Ctesiphon (mentioned in despatches). Was afterwards 2nd in command of 5th Bn. Somersetshire L.I. In 1917, was Camp Commandant to the Sir Mark Sykes-Picot Mission to Palestine and Hedjaz, including second action at Gaza. In 1918 (January to April) commanded the 5th Bn. Royal Scots Fusiliers in Palestine till appointed to the command of the 1/5th Bn. Devonshire Regt., and was present at the actions on the Nablus Road. Took this battalion to France in May and was at the battle of Rheims, July, 1918 (wounded) ; Bapaume, 23rd August ; crossing of the Selle River, Havrincourt, September ; Solesmes, and the capture of Mauberge, 9th November, 1918 (three times mentioned in despatches, bronze star, Croix de Guerre, D.S.O.). Was awarded the D.S.O. under the following circumstances.

"For conspicuous gallantry and devotion to duty. He commanded his battalion, which was new to the particular conditions of warfare they encountered, in a successful attack, which was brilliantly carried through to the objective under heavy machine gun fire, in spite of the flank being entirely exposed. The spirit and fighting quality shown by all ranks of the battalion was largely due to the fine example he has always shown of personal courage and able leadership."

JOHN CECIL MORGAN

Born in London, 24th October, 1875, son of John Hammond Morgan, C.V.O., F.R.C.S.

Second Lieut., 20th December, 1899 ; Lieut., 12th March, 1901 ; Capt., 9th May, 1906 ; resigned, 8th September, 1909.

Served in the Boer War, 1900-02 and took part in the march from Bloemfontein to Pretoria, incuding the actions at Brandfort, the Vet and Zand Rivers, Kroonstadt and Johannesburg. Also in the advance eastwards and actions at Diamond Hill and Belfast (Queen's medal and 5 clasps, King's medal and 2 clasps). Was appointed to the 6th Service Bn. on 4th October, 1914, and proceeded with it to Gallipoli.

Killed in action at the taking of Lali Baba, 7th August, 1915.

FRANCIS GREY OKE SANDERSON

Born, 26th September, 1879, son of the Revd. Lancelot Sanderson, of Elstree, Yorkshire.

Second Lieut., 18th April, 1900 ; Lieut., 29th September, 1901 ; Indian Army, 10th October, 1903 ; Capt., 18th April, 1909 ; Major, 1st September, 1915.

Served in the Boer War, 1900, and took part in the advance from Pretoria to the eastern Transvaal, and actions at Diamond Hill and Belfast (Queen's medal and 5 clasps).

CHARLES HOWARD MARSDEN, O.B.E.

Born at Manchester, 1st March, 1876, eldest son of the Revd. Maurice Howard Marsden, M.A., Moreton Rectory, Dorset.

Second Lieut., 23rd May, 1900 ; Lieut., 19th February, 1902 ; Capt., 10th October, 1908 ; Major, 29th December, 1915 ; retired, 25th January, 1920.

Served in the Boer War, 1900-02. Operations in the Transvaal, 30th November, 1900, to end of war (Queen's medal and 5 clasps). During war of 1914-18, served at home as a Musketry Staff Officer (twice mentioned, O.B.E.).

HUGH WILLIAM McCALL, C.M.G., D.S.O.

Born in London, 28th September, 1878, son of Robert Alfred McCall, K.C., LL.D., Attorney General for the Duchy of Lancaster.

Second Lieut., 23rd May, 1900 ; Lieut., 11th April, 1902 ; Capt., 29th June, 1906 ; Adjt., 2nd Vol. Bn., 27th July, 1910—27th October, 1913 ; Major, 1st September, 1915 ; Bt. Lieut.-Col., 1st January, 1918.

Served in the Boer War, 1900-02. Operations in the Transvaal 30th November, 1900, to end of the war (Queen's medal and 5 clasps). In the war of 1914-18, proceeded with the 2nd Bn. to Belgium, and was present in the fighting at Ypres (wounded, bronze star and clasp). Served in France on the Staff of the 60th Division as D.A.A., and later as A.A. and Q.M.G., and was present at the operations at Vimy Ridge, June to October, 1916. With the 60th served on the Macedonian front, and took part in the operations at Lake Doiran in April, 1917. Also served with the 60th Division in Egypt and in the Palestine campaign, and was at the capture of Beersheba, the battle of Sheria, the capture of Jerusalem and Jericho, as well as in the operations east of the Jordan, between March and May, 1918. Was also present at the operations in Palestine and Syria in October, 1918 (twice mentioned in despatches, C.M.G. D.S.O., Bt. of Lieut.-Col., 4th Class Order of the Nile, Chevalier of the Legion of Honour).

EDWARD GEORGE CLARKSON BAGSHAWE

Born at Hampstead, 17th September, 1879, youngest son of His Honour, Judge William Henry Gunning Bagshawe.

Second Lieut., 4th August, 1900 ; Lieut., 19th August, 1902 ; half-pay, 17th October, 1905 ; 19th Foot, 16th March, 1906 ; resigned, 6th March, 1907.

Served in the Boer War, 1900-02, with the 3rd Bn., and on the staff as transport officer, and was present at the engagement at Reitvlei. With the 1st Bn. was in the action at Belfast (Queen's medal and 3 clasps). He was gazetted a Captain in the 5th Bn. on 29th August, 1914, and eight months after left with it for France, but was shortly afterwards invalided home. He went out again and was attached to the 9th Bn.

Killed in action in France, 20th July, 1916.

In the " Saturday Review," of 29th July, 1916, there is a fitting tribute to his memory. See also The Green Howards' Gazette, Vol. XXIV, page 75.

CHARLES LIONEL DAVID HERBERT WHITAKER

Born at York, 10th March, 1881, son of Colonel Charles Hildyard Thornton Whitaker, M.V.O., late King's Own Yorkshire L.I. of Runagry, Ballina, Co. Mayo.

Second Lieut., 11th August, 1900 ; Lieut., 1st May, 1902 ; Indian Army, 29th May, 1903 ; Capt., 11th August, 1909 ; Major, 1st September, 1915.

Served with the Bushire Field Force in 1919 (mentioned in despatches).

WILLOUGHBY LUGARD HOGG

Born, 29th December, 1881. Second Lieut., 11th August, 1900 ; Lieut., Indian Army, 13th August, 1903 ; Capt., 30th October, 1909 ; Major, 30th October, 1915.

BERTRAM HENRY LEATHAM, D.S.O.

Born at Heath, near Wakefield, Yorkshire, 2nd March, 1881, son of Samuel Gurney Leatham, J.P., of Hemsworth Hall, Wakefield.

Second Lieut., 11th August, 1900 ; Lieut., 26th April, 1902 ; Capt., 21st July, 1906 Adjt., 16th January, 1908—16th January, 1911 ; Bt. Major, 6th September, 1915.

Served in the Boer War, 1901-2, with 1st Bn. and 4th Bn. Mounted Infantry (Queen's medal and 5 clasps). Joined the 2nd Bn. in France on 5th December, 1914, and remained with it till July, 1915, when he was specially selected to take command of the 2nd Bn. Wiltshire Regt. (mentioned in despatches, Bt. of Major, D.S.O. and bronze star).

Killed in action at Hulloch, 26th September, 1915.

The following letter was received by Mrs. Leatham from General H. P. Gough, Commanding the IVth Corps :—

" I want to send you one line of the very deepest sympathy in the great loss of your gallant husband. I had the very greatest respect and admiration for him as an officer, showing the highest ideals of honour, a most resolute unflinching courage, and great energy. His loss is immense to the army and our cause. If he had been spared, I hoped to see him a general in a few months. His loss to you, I know must be terrible, but let us share it a little with you, as we who knew him out here really do. In reforming and leading the Wiltshire Regiment I asked him to undertake a very hard task. . . . What he did in so short a time for that regiment was just grand, and the proof of his success and his great influence was shown in the unflinching gallantry displayed by that battalion who never wavered. We can ill afford to lose these great souls ; but yet they have not died in vain if they lived long enough to set us their great example as your husband did."

Memorial in Richmond Parish Church.

HERBERT JAMES KIRKPATRICK

Born, 24th June, 1878. Second Lieut., 3rd October, 1900.

Died at Benares, 16th April, 1902.

BRYAN SEYMOUR MOSS-BLUNDELL, D.S.O., O.B.E.

Born at Hessle, Hull, 14th February, 1878, son of John Seymour Moss-Blundell, J.P., of Tranby Rise, Hessle.

Second Lieut., 29th December, 1900 ; Lieut., 29th May, 1903 ; Capt., 29th July, 1906 ; Major, 29th December, 1915.

Proceeded to Belgium and was engaged in the fighting near Ypres, October and November, 1914 (wounded, mentioned in despatches, bronze star and clasp and D.S.O.). Employed on the staff in France as Bde. Major and D.A.A. and Q.M.G. for the remainder of the war (twice mentioned in despatches and O.B.E.).

KENNETH WILLIAM LEE SIMONET

Born in Jersey, 14th March, 1881, son of William Simonet, of Radiez, Jersey.

Second Lieut., 5th January, 1901 ; Lieut., 16th January, 1904 ; Capt., 1st April, 1909.

Killed in action in Mesopotamia, 21st January, 1916, when attached to the Black Watch.

" In him the Regiment has lost not only an excellent officer, but one of the most sympathetic of men, and he will be deeply mourned by his comrades. He was a nephew of the late Lieut.-Colonel J. F. Simonet, who served for 14 years in the 19th " (G.H.G.).

BRERTON CHARLES DALTON NASH-WORTHAM, M.C.

Born at Royston, 1st July, 1879, son of H. D. Nash-Wortham, of Deepdene, Haslemere.

Second Lieut., 5th January, 1901 ; Lieut., 19th September, 1903 ; Adjt., 16th January, 1905—16th January, 1908 ; Capt., 20th March, 1909 ; 9th Lancers, 23rd April, 1913.

Served in the Boer War 1900-02, with 3rd and 1st Battalions (Queen's Medal and 3 clasps, King's Medal and 2 clasps).

Served in France with Expeditionary Force (wounded, bronze star). Afterwards served with Imperial Yeomanry and on the staff in Palestine (mentioned in despatches, M.C.).

BURTON HOWARD HALL

Born, 10th January, 1882, younger son of the Revd. Samuel Howard Hall, Rector of Sproatley, Yorkshire.

Second Lieut., unattached, 8th January, 1901 ; 19th Foot, 9th March, 1901 ; Lieut., Indian Army, 3rd February, 1904 ; Capt., 8th January, 1910.

Killed in action with the Germans at Tanga, East Africa, 4th November, 1914

FRANCIS CLAUDE SHELMERDINE, O.B.E.

Born at Churchill, Chipping Norton, 25th October, 1881, younger son of the Revd. Nathaniel Shelmerdine, Great Comberton Rectory, Pershore.

Second Lieut., unattached, 2nd January, 1901 ; 19th Foot, 9th March, 1901 ; half-pay, 12th January, 1904 ; 19th Foot, 12th April, 1904 ; Lieut., 25th June, 1904 ; resigned, 27th August, 1904 ; 6th Service Bn., 24th August, 1914 ; temp. Capt., 29th October, 1914 ; Adjt., 23rd October, 1914 ; 11th Service Bn., 25th May, 1915 ; Wing Adjt., Royal Flying Corps, 1st November, 1915 ; Capt., Reserve of Officers, 19th Foot, 1st January, 1917 ; Bt. Major, 1st January, 1918 ; Lieut.-Col., Royal Air Force, 1st April, 1918; unemployed list, 9th July, 1919.

During the Great War, served at home with the 6th and 11th Service battalions. Appointed S.O.2 in the Royal Flying Corps, 28th December, 1916, and S.O.1 on 22nd June, 1917. Served with the Royal Flying Corps in Egypt, 1915-16. Has lately been employed under the Controller-General of Civil Aviation at the Air Ministry. Awarded the Order of the British Empire, 1st January, 1919.

SEATON DUNHAM MASSY, D.S.O.

Born, 25th April, 1882, eldest son of Lieut.-Col. Charles Francis Massy, Indian Army.

Second Lieut. (unattached), 8th January, 1901 ; 19th Foot, 9th March, 1901 ; Lieut., Indian Army, 5th September, 1903 ; Capt., 8th January, 1910 ; Bt.-Major, 3rd June, 1915 ; Major, 8th January, 1916.

Served in the Boer War, 1901 (Queen's medal and 5 clasps). In the war of 1914-18, served with the Royal Flying Corps in Egypt and India, including the campaign against the Mahsuds, March to August, 1917 (four times mentioned in despatches, Bt. of Major, Distinguished Service Order and 4th Class Order of the Nile).

RICHARD FITZROY HOWARD

Born, 14th April, 1879, son of Lieut.-Col. Frederick Compton Howard, late Rifle Brigade.

Second Lieut., 4th May, 1901 ; resigned, 21st November, 1903.

Served in the Boer War, 1902 (Queen's medal and 4 clasps). Appointed Lieut., 7th Service Bn., 22nd September, 1914. Relinquished his commission, 24th December 1915.

CHARLES JAMES HOOKHAM GARDNER, C.B.E.

Born at Plaistow, London, 18th July, 1875, son of Capt. Gardner, R.N.

Second Lieut., 27th July, 1901, from ranks of the Royal Dragoons ; Lieut., 27th April, 1904 ; Capt., 22nd July, 1909 ; retired, 23rd August, 1913.

Served in the Boer War, 1899-1901, and was present at the Relief of Ladysmith, including the operations on the Tugela Heights, 14th to 27th February, 1900. Operations in Natal, including action at Laing's Nek, operations in the Transvaal, 30th November, 1900, to June, 1901, and operations in Orange River Colony, June to December, 1901 (Queen's medal and 6 clasps, King's medal and 2 clasps). In the war of 1914-18, served with the 21st Bn. Northumberland Fusiliers and on the Staff (three times mentioned in despatches, promoted Major in the Reserve of Officers and Commander of the British Empire).

CLAUD GIFFORD JEFFERY

Born at Manningham, Bradford, 13th April, 1880, son of Herbert J. Jeffery, of Bradford.

Second Lieut., 14th September, 1901 ; Lieut., 12th May, 1904 ; Capt., 25th August, 1909 ; Adjt., 1st March, 1910—12th April, 1912 ; Egyptian Army, 12th April, 1912—12th April, 1914. ...

Served with the Volunteer Company in the Boer War, 1900-02, and took part in the march from Bloemfontein to Pretoria, including the actions at Brandfort, Vet and Zand Rivers, Kroonstadt and Johannesburg. Also in the advance eastwards and actions at Diamond Hill and Belfast (Queen's medal and 5 clasps, King's medal and 2 clasps). Proceeded to Belgium with 2nd Bn. in October, 1914. Whilst leading a party of volunteers to repel an attack by a large force of the enemy near Becelaire, he was wounded in the groin, on the 22nd October (mentioned in despatches).

Died in hospital, near Ypres, 24th October, 1914.

An officer who was with him in hospital said that Captain Jeffery was one of the most gallant men he ever met, popular with all officers and beloved by his men. When men from the regiment were brought in wounded to the hospital their first question was "How is Captain Jeffery?"

ARTHUR JOHN HUGHES

Born, 18th February, 1865 ; Pte., Coldstream Gds., 14th February, 1884 ; Sergt.-Major, 1st Bn. 19th Foot, 8th September, 1897 ; hon. Lieut. and Qr.-Mstr., 5th October, 1901 ; retired on half-pay, 14th October, 1908.

Served with the Coldstream Guards in the Suakin Expedition of 1885 (medal and clasp and Khedive's Star). Served in the Boer War, 1899-02, and took part in the operations near Colesberg in January, 1900, and in the march along the Modder River, including the Relief of

Kimberley, the actions at Paardeberg, Kitchener's Kop, Poplar Grove, and Driefontein. In the march on Dewetsdorp, and action of Leuukop. In the advance eastwards from Pretoria and actions at Diamond Hill and Belfast (mentioned in despatches, promoted Qr.-Master, 3rd Bn., Queen's medal and 5 clasps, King's medal and 2 clasps).

Died at Marrow in Lincoln, 9th February, 1909.

GEORGE CLARKE DENTON

Born at St. Vincent, W.I., 22nd April, 1881, only son of Sir George Chardin Denton, K.C.M.G., Governor of the Gambia, 1901-1911.

Second Lieut., 19th October, 1901 ; Lieut., 25th June, 1904 ; Indian Army, 10th January, 1905 ; Capt., 28th February, 1909.

Served in the Boer War, 1900-01, with 3rd Bn. (Queen's medal and 3 clasps).

Killed in action at Kissengeri, East Africa, 9th October, 1916.

BERTRAM LIONEL MADDISON

Born at Durham, 12th July, 1881, son of Thomas Maddison, of South Bailey, Durham.

Second Lieut., 4th December, 1901 ; Lieut., 27th August, 1904 ; Capt., 29th September, 1910 ; Major, 23rd January, 1916.

Served in the Boer War, 1902 (Queen's medal and 4 clasps). Joined the 2nd Bn. in France in February, 1915, and was wounded at Neuve Chapelle. On returning to France was posted to the 8th Bn. York and Lancaster Regt. as second in command. Was again wounded, 14th January, 1916, and after recovery appointed to the command on 12th May, 1916.

Killed in action at Thiepval, Somme, 1st July, 1916. Every officer in his battalion was either killed or wounded.

"No officer of the regiment who has given his life in this war is more worthy of our honour and respect. Few of us have had the welfare of the regiment more at heart more than he and to none was its honour more precious. To those who served under him, and to the friends who loved him, his cheerfulness and gentle unselfishness, handicapped as he was by ever-increasing deafness, remain an enduring example. He was a most delightful companion ; though he never led our amusements he entered into all of them and contributed to them a strong sense of humour and a delicate wit. He was satisfied to do his duty in that quiet, unselfish way that endeared him to all who served with him " (G.H.G.).

STUART LUMLEY WHATFORD, C.M.G., D.S.O.

Born at Eastbourne, 23rd July, 1879, son of J. Henry Whatford, of Eastbourne.

Second Lieut., 15th January, 1902 ; Lieut., 1st October, 1904 ; Capt., 9th October, 1910 ; Major, 23rd January, 1916 ; Bt.-Lieut.-Col., 1st January, 1919.

Served in the Boer War, 1900-02, with the 3rd Bn. Mounted Infantry. Operations in the Transvaal, 30th November, 1900, to end of war (Queen's medal and 5 clasps). On the outbreak of the Great War he was Adjutant to the 3rd Reserve Bn., and in April, 1916, was appointed 2nd in command of the 22nd Bn. Durham L.I., and was engaged with it in the battle of the Somme, till July 10th, when he was posted to the command of the 8th Bn. York and Lancaster, and took part in much of the fighting in which his battalion was engaged both in France and in

Italy. On being awarded the D.S.O., a letter from the Secretary of State for War records the King's high appreciation of his services. He was in command of his brigade from 2nd December, 1917, to 1st March, 1918, and was attached to the 22nd Machine Gun Bn. from 11th September, 1918, to 19th February, 1919, when he returned to the York and Lancaster, which he commanded till his death (six times mentioned in despatches, C.M.G., Distinguished Service Order and clasp, French Croix de Guerre avec Palme, Italian Croce di Guerra., Bt. of Lieut.-Col.). Killed in a motor-car accident between Cremona and Mantua, 30th August, 1919, when commanding the British troops in Fiumé.

His Brigadier, under whom he served for nearly three years, wrote as follows :—

"Everyone who came into contact with him respected and admired him. High courage, high moral, devotion to his men and to duty, combined with the qualities of a natural leader all went to make him an officer of exceptional value and capacity

In private life, his simple, straightforward, honourable and kindly character, endeared him to all of us. He was a man who stood out in the Division, and the officers and men of the 8th York and Lancaster's will be very genuinely grieved at his loss. In my experience I cannot recall another commanding officer of a battalion so much respected and looked up to by his men. He set them a very high example, the results of which were very apparent all these years, and perhaps never more so than during the difficult time at Fiumé, where the conduct and bearing of the battalion was most marked, and gained the admiration of the allied troops of occupation. Personally, I mourn his loss very much, for he was a real, loyal friend and comrade for whom I felt an affection one seldom experiences."

A brother officer writes:—"His alluring personality and inspiring influence will ever remain as a landmark in the annals of the Yorkshire Regiment, and every one of us were the better from coming into contact with him. I can only think the sudden curtailment of such a brilliant life, goes to refine each one of us for something better."

JOSEPH HAROLD STOPS WESTLEY, C.M.G., D.S.O.

Born at Northampton, 10th September, 1882, son of S. Westley, of Dunthorpe, Harrogate.

Second Lieut., 18th January, 1902 ; Lieut., 1st November, 1904 ; Capt., 20th January, 1911 ; Major, 18th January, 1917 : retired with rank of Lieut.-Col., 2nd April, 1920.

Served in the Boer War. Operations in the Transvaal, 1st April, to 31st May, 1902 (Queen's medal and 4 clasps). Served as Adjutant to the 2nd City of London Regiment (Royal Fusiliers) from September, 1911, to July, 1915, and proceeded to France with it on the 1st January, 1915. Took part in the 2nd battle of Ypres in May. Appointed Bde. Major to the 140th Infantry Bde., in July, 1915, and was present at the battle of Loos (mentioned in despatches, bronze star, and Distinguished Service Order). In February, 1916, was appointed D.A.A. and Q.M.G. to the 5th Division and was present at the battles of the Somme and Arras. In January, 1918, was D.A.A.G. to the 1st Division, and on 4th September was appointed A.A. and Q.M.G. to the 59th Division with which he took part in the final advance prior to the Armistice (mentioned in despatches and C.M.G.). Was A.A. and Q.M.G. at the British Base, Antwerp, January, 1919, to 23rd October, 1919.

CLARENCE EDWARD MOSS-BLUNDELL

Born at Norwich, 3rd June, 1882.

Second Lieut., 18th January, 1902 ; retired 11th November, 1903.

Served in the Boer War, 1902 (medal and 4 clasps).

FREDERICK CURTIS

Born at Woolwich, 3rd December, 1882, son of William Frederick de Hubbenet Curtis, Col., Royal Artillery.

Second Lieut., 18th January, 1902 ; Indian Army, 11th November, 1903 ; Lieut., 18th April, 1904 ; Capt., 18th January, 1911 ; Major, 18th January, 1917.

Served as Asst. Signalling Officer in the operations on the N.W. Frontier of India against the Mohmands in 1908 (medal and clasp). Served with the Egyptian Expeditionary Force in the Great War (mentioned in despatches).

GEORGE PRENDERGAST STEVENS

Born, 20th March, 1879, son of Major J. Stevens.

Second Lieut., 30th April, 1902 ; resigned, 3rd February, 1904.

ARCHIBALD FREDERICK BONE

Born, 31st May, 1882, son of F. S. Bone, of Dorking.

Second Lieut., 17th May, 1902 ; Indian Army, 1st December, 1903 ; Lieut., 17th August, 1904 ; Capt., 11th March, 1911 ; retired on half-pay, 18th March, 1915.

Served in the Boer War with the Imperial Yeomanry, and also with 4th and 1st Battalions (Queen's medal and 3 clasps, King's medal and 2 clasps).

GRANVILLE GEORGE ALGERNON EGERTON, C.B.

Born in London, 10th May, 1859, son of Colonel the Hon. Arthur Frederick Egerton, Grenadier Gds.

Second Lieut., 72nd Foot, 13th August, 1879 ; Lieut., 28th February, 1881 ; Adjt., 18th May, 1881—18th October, 1887 ; Capt., Seaforth Highlanders, 15th May, 1889 ; Major, 8th June, 1898 ; Bt.-Lieut.-Col., 16th November, 1898 ; Lieut.-Col., 19th Foot, 13th May, 1903 ; Bt.-Col., 12th February, 1904 ; Col., 28th March, 1907 ; Major-Gen., 10th December, 1912 ; retired, 17th June, 1919.

Served with the 72nd in the Afghan War from November, 1879, with the Kabul and Kandahar Field Forces, and was present in the operations around Kabul in December, 1879 (dangerously wounded). Accompanied Sir Frederick Roberts in the march to Kandahar, and was present at the battle there (medal and 2 clasps and bronze star). Served as Adjt. to 1st Bn. Seaforth Highlanders throughout the Egyptian War of 1882, and was present at the battle of Tel-el-Kebir (medal with clasp and Khedive's Star). Was present during the occupation of Crete in 1897. Served in the Soudan campaign of 1898, and took part in the battles of the Atbara and Khartoum (mentioned in despatches, Bt. of Lieut.-Col., medal and Khedive's medal with 2 clasps). Awarded the C.B. on the King's birthday, 1905. Was appointed to the command of the 52nd Lowland Territorial Division, 21st March, 1914, and with it embarked for Gallipoli in July, 1915 (mentioned in despatches and bronze star). Was later in December, 1915, appointed to the command of the troops in Sicily till 18th March, 1916. Inspector of Infantry, 18th April, 1916, to 3rd August, 1918 (mentioned in home despatches). He is in possession of a reward for distinguished and meritorious service.

JOHN WALKER, O.B.E., D.C.M.

Born at Guisborough, 30th April, 1870.
Pte., 18th January, 1888 ; Corpl., 1st January, 1890 ; Cr.-Sergt., 30th November, 1894 ; Sergt.-Major, 5th October, 1901 ; Qr.-Mr. and Hon. Lieut., 1st October, 1903 ; Hon. Capt., 1st October, 1913 ; Major and Qr.-Mr., 3rd June, 1917 ; Royal Guernsey Militia, 1st June, 1919.

Served in the Boer War, 1899-1902, and was present in the operations near Colesberg in January, 1900. Took part in the march along the Modder River including the Relief of Kimberley, the actions at Paardeberg, Kitchener's Kop, Poplar Grove and Driefontein, and occupation of Bloemfontein. Was in the advance on Dewetsdorp, and action at Leuukop. In the march from Bloemfontein to Pretoria, including actions at Brandfort, the Vet and Zand Rivers, Kroonstadt and Johannesburg. Also in the advance eastwards and actions at Diamond Hill and Belfast (mentioned in despatches, medal for distinguished conduct in the field, Queen's medal and 6 clasps King's medal and 2 clasps). During the war, 1914-18, was Qr.-Master to the 3rd Reserve Battalion (mentioned in home despatches, O.B.E.).

LAWRENCE PEEL

Born at Clitheroe, 18th September, 1884, 3rd son of William Peel, J.P., of Knowlmere Manor, Yorkshire.

Second Lieut., 10th October, 1903 ; Lieut., 18th February, 1905 ; Adjt., 1st December, 1906—1st March, 1910 ; Capt., 11th February, 1911.

Proceeded to France with 7th Division in 1914.
Killed whilst leading his cycle company in a night attack near Ypres, 23/24th October, 1914 (mentioned in despatches).

CHRISTOPHER CODRINGTON STEWART

Born in London, 4th October, 1884, only son of Major-Gen. Hopton Scott Stewart, Indian Army.

Second Lieut., 10th October, 1903 ; Indian Army, 6th February, 1905 ; Lieut., 10th January, 1906 ; Capt., 10th October, 1912.

Served in Mesopotamia and took part in the action at Kut-el-Amara, 28th September, 1915.
Killed at the battle of Ctesiphon, 22/24th November, 1915.
He was serving on Gen. Delamain's staff and was wounded in the arm, but refused to have it attended to. He was leading a small body of men in a counter attack when he was shot through the forehead (mentioned in despatches).

CECIL COURTNEY GODWIN

Born in London, 5th October, 1884, son of Lieut.-Col. Algernon Arbuthnot Godwin, J.P., late 103rd Foot, of Silverhow, Eastbourne.

Second Lieut., 21st November, 1903 ; Lieut., 18th February, 1905 ; Adjt., 16th January, 1911—29th January, 1913 ; Capt., 11th February, 1911 ; Bt.-Major, 3rd June, 1919.

During the war of 1914-18, was employed with the Egyptian Army, and took part in the operations in Darfur between 16th March, 1916, and 23rd November, 1916 (mentioned in despatches). Served in the Camel Corps in the operations in the Nymia Hills, Nuba mountains, Sudan (mentioned in despatches, 4th Class Order of the Nile).

ROBERT SHAW LEDGARD

Born at Scarcroft, Leeds, 17th January, 1884, son of Armitage Ledgard, of Scarcroft.

Second Lieut., 16th December, 1903 ; Lieut., 19th April, 1905 ; Capt., 28th March, 1911 ; Adjt., 29th January, 1913.

Went to the front with the Yorkshire Light Infantry in August, 1914, and was present in the fighting at Mons.

Taken prisoner at Le Cateau, 26th August, 1914 (bronze star and clasp).

HUGH CARLTON CUMBERBATCH, O.B.E., M.C., p.s.c.

Born at Winchfield, Hants, 19th May, 1884, only son of E. C. Cumberbatch, of Croxted House, Farnborough.

Second Lieut., 27th January, 1904 ; Lieut., 25th December, 1905 ; Capt., 19th July, 1911 ; Bt.-Major, 1st January, 1918.

In the Great War, served on the staff in France, and was present at the 2nd battle of Ypres and Loos in 1915, and 3rd battle of Ypres, 1917. Also took part in the Palestine campaign for nine months up to the Armistice (twice mentioned in despatches, Bt. of Major, Military Cross, Officer of the British Empire, and bronze star). Is in possession of a Staff College certificate.

WILLIAM KEITH ROLLO, M.C.

Born in Ceylon, 8th October, 1879, son of Keith Rollo, of Wana Rajah, Ceylon.

Second Lieut., 1st Foot, 12th August, 1899 ; Lieut., 22nd January, 1901 ; Indian Army, 14th March, 1903 ; 19th Foot, 13th February, 1904 ; Capt., 12th May, 1909 ; Major, 5th January, 1916 ; retired, 19th March, 1920.

Served in the Boer War, 1899-1901, including the battle of Stormberg and the operations around Wepener. Also in the eastern Transvaal, including the actions at Belfast and Lydenberg (medal and 4 clasps).

Served in the Great War, and was severely wounded at the battle of Neuve Chapelle, 11th March, 1915. Afterwards with the Signal Service in France from June, 1915, to January, 1916, and in Salonika from January, 1916, to August, 1918. Was O.C., 27th Division Signal Company from September 1918, to March, 1919, in Macedonia and South Russia. Took part in the operations against Bulgaria from September to December, 1918. O.C., Signals at Tiflis, December, 1918, to April, 1919 (four times mentioned in despatches, bronze star and Military Cross).

JOHN PONSONBY GILBERT

Born at Ajmere, 12th September, 1884, son of C. J. Gilbert.

Second Lieut., 2nd March, 1904 ; Indian Army, 25th January, 1906 ; Lieut., 2nd June, 1906 ; Capt., 2nd March, 1913.

Drowned in the wreck of the " Persia," 30th December, 1915.

WILLIAM JOHN BOVILL

Born at Motighari, India, 14th May, 1885, son of Col. Edward Bovill, M.D., F.R.C.S., India Medical Service (Bengal).

Second Lieut., 2nd March, 1904 ; Indian Army, 6th February, 1906 ; Lieut., 2nd June, 1906 ; Capt., 2nd March, 1913 ; Major, 2nd March, 1919.

Served in Mesopotamia, 1915 to 1918, including operations on the Tigris, 1917, recapture of Kut and fall of Baghdad (twice mentioned in despatches, bronze star and Chevalier of the Crown of Roumania).

FREDERIC LAWRENCE GORE, O.B.E.

Born at Brighton, 18th January, 1884, son of J. L. Gore, of the Hove, Brighton.

Second Lieut., 2nd March, 1904 ; Indian Army, 9th April, 1906 ; Lieut., 2nd June, 1906 ; Capt., 2nd March, 1913 ; Major, 2nd March, 1919.

Served in the Somaliland Expedition, 1908-10 (medal and clasp). Served in Mesopotamia during the war of 1914-18 (mentioned in despatches).

MARTIN LOUIS ALAN GOMPERTZ

Born at Cork, 23rd February, 1886, elder son of Major Alfred Clemons Gompertz, Hampshire Regt.

Second Lieut., 3rd December, 1904 ; Indian Army, 6th April, 1906 ; Lieut., 3rd March, 1907 ; Capt., 3rd December, 1913 ; Bt.-Major, 3rd June, 1919 ; Major, 3rd December, 1919.

Took part in the operations in East Africa in 1914, and was present at the fighting at Tanga (bronze star). Promoted Bt. Major for service in connection with the war in India. Served in the North West Frontier, 1919-20 (wounded when attached to the 100th Infantry).

LOUIS FRANK LANYON

Born at Mallow, Co. Cork, 26th May, 1885, 3rd son of Louis Mortimer Lanyon, District Inspector Royal Irish Constabulary, of Belmont Villa, Dundrum, Co. Dublin.

Second Lieut., 28th January, 1905 ; Lieut., 3rd October, 1906 ; Capt., 29th January, 1913 ; Bt.-Major, 1st January, 1919.

In the war of 1914-18, served in India with 1st Bn. till he joined the 2nd in France in January, 1917. Later was appointed to the staff at home (mentioned in home despatch, Bt. of Major).

HUGH LEVIN

Born at York, 16th January, 1886, son of Major L. H. M. Levin, 19th Foot.

Second Lieut., 28th January, 1905 ; Lieut., 3rd October, 1906 ; Capt., 23rd April, 1913 ; Bt.-Major, 3rd June, 1917.

In the war of 1914-18, went to Belgium with the 2nd Bn. Severely wounded at Gheluvelt, 29th October, 1914 (bronze star and clasp). For the remainder of the war was employed on the staff at home (mentioned in despatches, Bt. of Major).

JOHN MALLINSON

Born at Manchester, 9th October, 1884, son of John Mallinson, of Todmorden.

Second Lieut., 20th May, 1905 ; Lieut., 4th October, 1906 ; cashiered, 27th January, 1909.

LORN EDWARD HAMBLY HUMFREY

Born at Calcutta, 29th June, 1871, son of Lieut.-Col. J. C. T. Humfrey, 19th Foot and A.P.D.

Capt., Royal Garrison Regt., 27th September, 1902 ; 19th Foot, 19th July, 1905 ; resigned, 8th November, 1911.

Served in the Ashanti Expedition, 1895-96 (star). Served in West Africa in 1897-98 as Assist.-Inspector Lagos Constabulary, and was employed in the Hinterland (mentioned in despatches, medal and clasp). Served in South Nigeria, Aro Expedition, 1901-02, mentioned in despatches). In the war of 1914-18, served with the 1st Garrison Bn. King's Own Yorkshire L.I., from 24th February, 1916, and as Major, 1st Garrison Bn. South Staffordshire Regt., from 4th January, 1917.

CHARLES NORMAN JERVELUND

Born at Middlesbrough, 30th March, 1885, 2nd son of Albert N. Jervelund, of Coatham, Redcar.

Second Lieut., 16th August, 1905 ; Lieut., 27th April, 1907 ; Capt., 22nd January, 1914.

During the war of 1914-18, served in India till December, 1915. On the staff in France as a Brigade Major from April till October, 1918, and took part in the battle of the Somme, the 4th battle of Ypres, the battle of Courtrai, and operations in Belgium up to the Armistice.

BERNARD VIVIAN RAMSDEN

Born at Knowle, Warwickshire, 26th August, 1885, 3rd son of Richard Ramsden, F.R.G.S., of Siddinghurst, Chiddingfold, Surrey.

Second Lieut., 16th August, 1905 ; Lieut., 16th January, 1908 ; Capt., 13th October, 1914.

During the war of 1914-18, served with the West African Field Force up to April, 1915. Served in France from July, 1915, and took part in the operations on the Somme, including Montauban, Trônes Wood, and Guillemont. Was also in the fighting at Flers, 12th October, 1916. Served on the staff as Brigade Major from May, 1916, to February, 1917, and from December, 1917, to March, 1918, including the fighting south of Arras.

HAROLD EDMUND FRANKLYN, D.S.O., M.C., p.s.c.

Born at Cork, 28th November, 1885, elder son of Lieut.-Gen. Sir W. E. Franklyn, K.C.B., Colonel 19th Foot.

Second Lieut., 16th August, 1905 ; Lieut., 7th February, 1908 ; Capt., 30th October, 1914 ; Bt.-Major, 3rd June, 1916.

During the war of 1914-18, served in France on the staff. Was wounded at Neuve Chapelle in the attack of March, 1915 (six times mentioned in despatches, Bt. of Major, and of Lieut.-Col., when promoted substantive Major, Military Cross, Distinguished Service Order, bronze star, and Croix de Guerre).

STUART GRANT-DALTON, D.S.O.

Born at Bournemouth, 5th April, 1886, only son of Horace Grant-Dalton, of Shank's House, Wincanton.

Second Lieut., 24th January, 1906 ; Lieut., 14th February, 1908 ; Capt., 30th October, 1914 ; Wing-Commander Royal Air Force, 1st August, 1919.

Proceeded to France in April, 1915, as Adjt. 5th Bn., and was wounded at the 2nd battle of Ypres. Appointed to the Royal Flying Corps, 6th January, 1916, and served with it in Egypt till August, 1916. Was awarded the D.S.O., 27th July, 1916, " for conspicuous gallantry and resource. When on return from escort duty his observer, Sec.-Lieut.

Paris, discovered one of our machines which had been forced to land in enemy country owing to damage by hostile fire. Capt. Grant-Dalton, with great gallantry landed, destroyed the machine which was past repair and returned 90 miles to his aerodrome with his observer and the pilot of the other machine." Was wounded again in August, 1916 (foot amputated), and was awarded a clasp to his D.S.O. "He attacked two hostile aeroplanes although quite unsupported. Later, after being attacked by another enemy machine and wounded in three places, he brought his machine back and landed safely" (three times mentioned in despatches, 4th Class Order of the Nile, and Air Force Cross, bronze star).

Captain Grant-Dalton was on board the s.s. "Omrah" when it was torpedoed off Sardinia on the 11th May, 1918.

ORBELL OAKES

Born at Mhow, India, 7th November, 1880, 2nd son of Lieut.-Col. Orbell Henry Oakes, of Nowton Court, Bury St. Edmunds, late 29th Foot.

Second Lieut., Royal Garrison Regt., 28th January, 1903 ; Lieut., 19th Foot, 3rd October, 1906 ; Capt., 29th January, 1913.

Served in the Boer War, 1901-2, and took part in the operations in the Orange River Colony (Queen's medal and 4 clasps).

Killed in the attack on Neuve Chapelle, 12th March, 1915.

" In him the regiment has lost an excellent officer and a good comrade. Like many of our officers he was not the first of his family to join the regiment ; his uncle, George Oakes, served for over 31 years in the 2nd Battalion, which he commanded from 1888 to 1892 " (G.H.G.).

CUSACK GRANT FORSYTH, D.S.O.

Born at Leamington Spa, 4th May, 1887, 5th son of Lieut.-Col. Frederick Arthur Forsyth, 5th Fusiliers, of Leamington.

Second Lieut., 29th August, 1906 ; Lieut., 12th May, 1909 ; Adjt., 12th April, 1912 ; Capt., 30th October, 1914.

Went to Belgium in October, 1914, with 2nd Bn., and was wounded in the fighting at Ypres (twice mentioned in despatches, D.S.O., and Croix de Chevalier of the Legion of Honour). On return to duty, he took part in the battles of Festubert and Givenchy, and later was appointed Adjt. and 2nd in command of the 2nd Bn. Wiltshire Regt., with Lieut.-Col. Leatham as commanding officer, and was wounded at Hulloch (Loos) on the 25th September, 1915. Later, he went out to Egypt to command the 6th Service Bn. of the regiment. On returning to France with this battalion, he took part in the fighting on the Somme, and was killed near Thiepval on 14th September, 1916.

" This war has given many opportunities of distinction, and no one has made more of such opportunites than Cusack Forsyth. In particular, his work and its results as second in command to Colonel Leatham (when attached to a battalion of another regiment in order to bring it up to the standard of efficiency from which it had lapsed) show that he had all the qualities necessary to enable him to do well in the higher commands, which would undoubtedly have been his had he survived.

He had a keen interest and enjoyment in life and met everything in a cheerful, happy spirit. His memory will go down to future Green Howards as a type of devotion to duty " (G.H.G.).

THOMAS CHRISTIAN MINTOFT

Born at Lelham, Crieff, Perthshire, 6th November, 1886, son of T. Mintoft, Alne Low Hall, near York.

2nd Lieut., 29th August, 1906 ; Lieut., 22nd July, 1909 ;

Capt., 30th October, 1914.

During the war of 1914-18, served with 1st Bn. in India, and also in France with a Service Bn. Seconded to the West African Field Force, 15th May, 1918.

ALEXANDER CHARLES HOOTON

Born at Croydon, 1st March, 1887, son of E. C. Hooton, of Chepstow Rise, Croydon.

Second Lieut., 29th August, 1906 ; Lieut., 25th August, 1909 ; Capt., 31st October, 1914.

Was A.D.C. to Sir G. R. Le Hunte, G.C.M.G., Governor of Trinidad and Tobago, 9th November, 1910, and Private Secretary to Sir James Hayes-Sadier, C.B., K.C.M.G., Governor of the Windward Islands, 12th September, 1912.

During the war of 1914-18, served in India with 1st Bn. till December, 1915, when he was appointed Senior Supply Officer to the left bank column for the attempted relief of Kut. Assistant Provost Marshal to a division in January, 1916, and to a corps in November. A year later was appointed 2nd in command of 6th Bn. East Lancashire Regt., which he commanded at the first capture of Kirkut.

GEOFFREY BRADFORD WORSDELL, O.B.E.

Born at Chester, 16th February, 1883, only son of Wilson Worsdell, Greenesfield, Newcastle-on-Tyne.

Second Lieut., 26th September, 1906 ; Lieut., 25th September, 1909 ; Capt., 25th January, 1915 ; Bt.-Major, 1st January, 1918.

In the war of 1914-18, served in India with 1st Bn., and with the Signal Service in Mesopotamia (mentioned in despatches, Bt. of Major and O.B.E.).

GEORGE NOEL NEUMANN SMITH, M.C.

Born at Honiton, 23rd December, 1886, son of W. Fell Smith, of Deer Park, Honiton.

Second Lieut., 6th October, 1906 ; Lieut., 17th November, 1909 ; Capt., 18th February, 1915 ; Bt.-Major, 3rd June, 1919.

In the war of 1914-18, served in India on the staff. Joined the 2nd Bn. in France in October, 1916, and was wounded in December at Ransart, near Arras. Took part in the fighting on the Somme, October, 1916, and near Arras in April, 1917. Was later appointed a Staff Captain, and was wounded at Ypres in April, 1918 (mentioned in despatches, Military Cross and Croix de Guerre). He was awarded the M.C. "for leading a successful raid against the enemy's trenches with great courage and skill, and for setting a splendid example throughout." Served also in Macedonia, as D.A.Q.M.G. (mentioned in despatches, Bt. of Major).

HUMPHREY LANE WHEATLEY

Born at Tenby, Wales, 16th September, 1886, 2nd son of Lieut.-Col. Charles Robertson Elliott Wheatley, late Royal (Madras) Artillery.

Second Lieut., 6th October, 1906.

Killed at Cairo, 30th November, 1909, owing to a tramcar accident.

DOUGLAS HELIER MAGEE

Born at Nagpur, 2nd July, 1887, son of Col. Augustus Helier Magee, late 25th Foot and Army Pay Department.

Second Lieut., 7th November, 1906 ; Lieut., 29th September, 1910 ; Capt., 8th March, 1915.

Served during the war of 1914-18 with the Gold Coast Regt., and took part in the campaign in the Cameroons and in Togoland (wounded, loss of an eye).

HERBERT ARTHUR LILLEY, D.S.O.

Born at Rangoon, 13th November, 1887.

Second Lieut., 7th November, 1906 ; Lieut., 9th October, 1910 ; Capt., 8th March, 1915.

Took part in the operations against the Turkana Tribe, East Africa, between 2nd April, 1914, and 7th July, 1914, with the King's African Rifles (medal and clasp). Served in East Africa with King's African Rifles during the war of 1914-18 (twice mentioned in despatches, D.S.O.).

CECIL AUBREY BRADFORD

Born at Sutcombe, North Devon, 30th February, 1886, younger son of Lieut.-Col. Oliver John Bradford, late 39th Foot, of Welparke, Lustleigh, Co. Devon.

Second Lieut., 7th November, 1906 ; Lieut., 9th November, 1910 ; Capt., 8th March, 1915.

Attached to the Nigerian Regiment, he saw service in the Cameroons, 1914-15.

Drowned at sea on passage from Lagos to England, 24th April, 1917.

He was a good "all round" man, taking part in all athletic sports. He also did some big game shooting on the White and Blue Nile, procuring a quantity of good heads. A letter from Nigeria says : "I do want you to know how we all loved him. One couldn't help it, he was such a real 'white' man." A Government official writes : "To me he will always be one of the few men of whom the dedication of Kipling's 'Barrack Room Ballads' could be written, and a few lines of that short poem form in my mind the most suitable epitaph for a gallant gentleman, a loyal friend, and, I am sure, a splendid husband and father" (from "The Times.")

ALEXANDER EDWARD GUY PALMER, D.S.O., M.C.

Born in London, 26th March, 1886, son of Lieut.-Commander Cecil Brooke Palmer, R.N.

Second Lieut., 4th April, 1907 ; Lieut., 23rd November, 1910 ; Capt., 8th March, 1915.

During the war of 1914-18, served in France on the Staff (four times mentioned in despatches, Military Cross, bronze star, and Distinguished Service Order).

GUY LISTER NEVILE

Born at Skelbroke Park, Doncaster, 2nd October, 1886, 7th son of Percy Sandford Nevile, late 22nd Foot, of Skelbroke Park.

Second Lieut., 4th April, 1907 ; Lieut., 6th January, 1911 ; Adjt., 10th Service Bn., 22nd September, 1914—12th January, 1915 ; Capt., 8th March, 1915.

Killed at Givenchy, 15th June, 1915.

He was reporting missing for a long time, but as no news was received it is concluded he was killed. In the attack on Givenchy he led his men with a hunting horn.

BERNARD THORNELY BURBURY, M.C.

Born in London, 21st April, 1884, son of Samuel Hawksley Burbury, F.R.S., of 15, Melbury Road, Kensington, W.

Second Lieut., 6th Foot, 2nd March, 1904 ; Lieut., 19th Foot, 27th April, 1907 ; Capt., 29th September, 1913 ; Bt.-Major, 2nd June, 1917 ; Adjt., 5th Bn., 2nd March, 1920.

Served on the staff as Bde. Major, 71st Brigade, 8th December, 1915, to 27th June, 1917 (twice mentioned in despatches, Bt. of Major and Military Cross). Afterwards on the General Staff of the 40th Division and 5th Corps from 29th June, 1917, to 27th August, 1918. Present at the operations on the Somme in 1916, and at Cambrai in 1917. Was in command of the 2nd Battn. in September and October, 1918, including the fighting at Cambrai and on the Somme.

ROBERT BOULTON CORSER

Born at Olton, Warwickshire, 12th October, 1884, son of Benjamin Corser.

Second Lieut., 6th Foot, 27th April, 1904 ; Lieut., 19th Foot, 11th May, 1907 ; Capt., 12th February, 1914.

Proceeded to France with 2nd Bn. in October, 1914, and was wounded near Ypres, 1st November (bronze star and clasp). Was attached to 2nd Bn. Border Regt. in France, April and May, 1915, and to 7th Service Bn. from March to August, 1916. During the remainder of war, served on the staff at home.

HANS FREDERICK BLACKWOOD, M.C.

Born at Farnborough, 18th April, 1887, 3rd son of Lieut.-Col. Robert William Blackwood, 52nd Foot.

Second Lieut., 9th October, 1907 ; Lieut., 16th January, 1911 ; Adjt., 4th November, 1914—30th August, 1916 ; Capt., 8th March, 1915 ; Bt.-Major, 3rd June, 1919.

During the war of 1914-18, served with 1st Bn. in India. Went to France in 1916, and was seconded to the Machine Gun Corps in January, 1917 (awarded the Military Cross and Bt. of Major).

EVAN JOHN RICHARDSON

Born at Cheltenham, 9th January, 1888, son of J. Richardson, of Bath.

Second Lieut., 8th February, 1908 ; Lieut., 20th January, 1911 ; Capt., 14th March, 1915.

Joined 2nd Bn. in France on the 22nd March, 1915, and was killed in action at Hulloch (Loos) 25th September, 1915.

ROBERT EDWARD TALBOT HEWITT

Born, 11th June, 1887, youngest son of Thomas Hewitt, Southwood, Bexhill-on-Sea.

Second Lieut., 8th February, 1908 ; resigned, 17th March, 1909.

Became a planter in Ceylon, but came home and was appointed a tempy. Lieut. in the Royal Irish Regt., 26th July, 1916. Proceeding to France, he was wounded in March, 1917, and again in April, and was awarded a certificate for gallantry by the G.O.C. 16th Division on the 5th April, 1917.

Killed in action at Messines, 7th June, 1917.

His Colonel wrote : " He was popular with all and a gallant officer. I am very sorry, indeed, to lose him and his place will be hard to fill."

CHARLES BERNARD HACKETT

Born at Mean Meer, 18th April, 1886, son of Lieut.-Col. Charles Hackett, late 5th Foot.

Second Lieut., 27th May, 1908 ; resigned, 2nd August, 1911.

REGINALD GOULDHAWKE ATKINSON...

Born at Southsea, 22nd February, 1886, son of Capt. Alexander Henry Atkinson, 55th Foot, of St. Margaret's-on-Thames.

Second Lieut., 4th July, 1908 ; Lieut., 11th February, 1911 ; Capt., 15th March, 1915.

During the war of 1914-18, served in India with 1st Bn. till he joined the 8th Service Bn. in France in March, 1917, and was present in the fighting at Hill 60 (7th June, 1917). The battalion afterwards went to Italy, where he took part in the battle on the Asiago Plateau in June, 1918, and also the battle of the Piave in October, 1918 (mentioned in despatches, Croce di Guerra).

EWEN GEORGE SINCLAIR-MACLAGAN, C.B., C.M.G., D.S.O.

Born in Edinburgh, 24th December, 1868, son of R. E. Sinclair-Maclagan, of Glenquoick, Co. Forfar.

Second Lieut., Border Regt., 21st December, 1889 ; Lieut., 2nd March, 1892 ; Capt., 26th May, 1898 ; Adjt., 11th July, 1900—28th August, 1901, and 24th June, 1906—27th October, 1908 ; Major, 19th Foot, 28th October, 1908 ; Lieut.-Col., 28th March, 1915 ; Bt.-Col., 3rd June, 1915 ; Maj.-Gen., 1st January, 1919.

Served with the Waziristan Field Force in 1894-95 (medal and clasp). Served in the Boer War, 1899-1900, in the operations in Cape Colony and Natal in 1899, the Relief of Ladysmith, including the action of Colenso ; operations of 17th to 24th January, and action of Spionkop (severely wounded) ; Orange Free State, April and May, 1900 ; Cape Colony in May, 1900. Operations in the Transvaal, east of Pretoria, July, 1900 ; west of Pretoria, July to November, 1900 (mentioned in despatches, D.S.O., Queen's medal and 5 clasps). In the war of 1914-18, served in command of the 3rd Australian Brigade at Gallipoli (mentioned in despatches, bronze star). Afterwards, commanded the 4th Australian Division in France, being promoted a tempy. Major-General, 16th July, 1917 (four times mentioned in despatches, C.B., C.M.G., promoted substantive Major-General for service in the Field, Serbian Order of the White Eagle with swords, Croix de Guerre with palme, American Distinguished Service medal).

EDWARD PICKARD, D.C.M.

Born at Bradford, 4th February, 1873, son of George Pickard, of Bradford.

Pte., 16th October, 1891 ; Lce.-Corpl., 1st December, 1891 ; Corpl., 2nd June, 1892 ; Sergt., 12th August, 1895 ; Cr.-Sergt., 12th October, 1896 ; Sergt.-Major, 1st October, 1903 ; Hon. Lieut. and Qr.-Mr., 28th July, 1909 ; Hon. Capt., 4th June, 1917 ; Hon. Major, 3rd June, 1918 ; Major and Qr.-Mr., 8th August, 1918.

Served in the Boer War, 1899-1902, and was present in the operations near Colesberg in January, 1900. In the march along the Modder River, including the Relief of Kimberley, the actions at Paardeberg, Kitchener's Kop, Poplar Grove, and Driefontein, and occupation of Bloemfontein. In the advance on Dewetsdorp and action at Leuukop. In the march to Pretoria and actions at Brandfort, Vet and Zand Rivers, Kroonstadt and Johannesburg. In the advance eastwards and actions at Diamond Hill and Belfast (mentioned in despatches, medal for distinguished conduct in the field, Queen's medal and 6 clasps, King's medal and 2 clasps). Awarded the King's Coronation medal, 1911.

In the war of 1914-18, served as Qr.-Master to the 2nd Bn., and was present at all the operations in which it was engaged which included the 1st battle of Ypres, 1914, battles of Neuve Chapelle, Festubert, Givenchy and Loos in 1915, the Somme, July to September, 1916, Arras and 3rd battle of Ypres in 1917, St. Quentin, March and April, 1918, Ypres, April and May, Cambrai, 2nd battle of Le Cateau, Selle River and the Sambre, 1st to 11th November, 1918 (twice mentioned in despatches, bronze star and clasp, Belgian Croix de Guerre, promoted to Captain and Major, and granted higher rate of pay).

BRIAN CUFF

Born at Scarborough, 29th January, 1889, son of Robert Cuff, M.D., of Scarborough.

Second Lieut., 11th December, 1909; Lieut., 28th March, 1911; Capt., 22nd Foot, 10th June, 1915; Bt.-Major, 1st January, 1919.

Served in India with 1st Bn. during war of 1914-18, also with the Cheshire Regt. and on the staff (Bt. of Major).

RICHARD HERBERT PHAYRE

Born at Farnborough, Hants, 31st March, 1890, son of Lieut.-Col. Richard Phayre, O.B.E., late 19th Foot.

Second Lieut., 11th December, 1909; Lieut., 1st April, 1911.

Went to Belgium with 2nd Bn. in October, 1914.

Killed near Gheluvelt in the 1st battle of Ypres, 27th October, 1914.

" He was a young officer of great promise, keenly interested in his profession and his regiment. His younger brother, Lieut. C. F. Phayre, Royal Munster Fusiliers, was killed on the 27th August " (G.H.G.).

MANLIFFE UNSWORTH MANLY, M.C.

Born in Dublin, 22nd September, 1888, son of Joshua Carroll Manly, of Dublin.

Second Lieut., 25th December, 1909; Lieut., 25th May, 1911; Capt., Border Regt., 10th June, 1915.

In the war of 1914-18, served on the staff from 27th November, 1916, to end of the war (mentioned in despatches, Military Cross and clasp).

GEOFFREY LEE COMPTON-SMITH, D.S.O.

Born in London, 19th August, 1889, son of W. Compton-Smith, House Court, Kensington, W.

Second Lieut., 20th April, 1910; Lieut., 19th July, 1911; Capt., 23rd Foot, 10th June, 1915; Bt.-Major, 3rd June, 1917.

In the war of 1914-18, served with the Royal Welch Fusiliers as a tempy. Major and Lieut. Col., from October, 1915, to April, 1918 (three times mentioned in despatches, Bt. of Major and D.S.O.). Was wounded in July, 1916, and April, 1917. " He commanded his battalion with the greatest skill and determination. Immediately the objective was gained, he moved forward to supervise, consolidate, and cover the advance of another brigade. Although wounded he remained in the position and his personal example was of the utmost value to all." From April, 1918, to end of the war, he commanded a Service Bn. of the Liverpool Regiment.

CLEMENT REUBEN SMITH

Born at Sagaign, Burmah, 26th June, 1890.

Second Lieut., 20th April, 1910 ; Lieut., 12th April, 1912 ; Hampshire Regt., 16th November, 1912 ; Capt., 28th April, 1915 ; retired on half-pay, 13th December, 1916.

GEORGE BUSH

Born at Gosport, 28th August, 1889, son of Lieut. George Bush, Royal Marines.

Second Lieut., 18th February, 1911, from ranks of 13th Foot ; resigned, 5th April, 1913.

HARRY STEPHEN BAGNALL

Born in Dublin, 26th December, 1890, son of Lieut.-Col. Thomas Nock Bagnall, late 15th Foot and 3rd Bn. Jersey L.I.

Second Lieut., 4th March, 1911 ; Lieut., 23rd April, 1913 ; Capt., 27th September, 1915 ; Adjt., 30th August, 1916—18th February, 1920.

Served in India during war of 1914-18.

SAMUEL RICHARD WILFRED BENNEDIK

Born in Leeds, 17th January, 1891, son of Julian Bennedik, of Brooklands, Ilkley, Yorkshire.

Second Lieut., 4th March, 1911 ; Lieut., 29th September, 1913 ; Capt., 7th October, 1915.

Served in India during the war of 1914-18, and in the operations in North Russia in 1919 (mentioned in despatches).

WILLIAM CLAUD KENNEDY BIRCH, M.C.

Born at Landor, India, 24th August, 1891, son of Col. William James Alexander Birch, Indian Army, of Compton Lodge, Walton-on-Thames.

Second Lieut., 4th March, 1911 ; Lieut., 27th October, 1913 ; Capt., 15th April, 1916 ; Adjt., 17th June, 1917—20th November, 1917.

Lost his life in the fire at Hedge Street Tunnel near Ypres, 5th January, 1918.

At the beginning of the war he was attached to the Royal Flying Corps, and had gone out on a bombing expedition. His machine was hit many times and he was wounded in the arm. Finally, he was forced to land in a ploughed field. After many adventures he found his way to Flushing and disguised as a fireman under the name of " James Buckle," he worked his passage to England. He was reported missing, 15th January, 1915, and " not missing " ten days later. He rejoined the Flying Corps and was twice mentioned in despatches, and awarded the Military Cross. He rejoined the 2nd Bn. in March, 1917.

The Chaplain wrote the following account of his death, " We had an awful tragedy on last Friday night in the support trenches—a big

tunnel. It is believed that the electric light short circuited and a fire
broke out in two places (at 12.30 Saturday morning, January, 5th).
Major Birch and all the other officers at B.H.Q. were awakened but
alas, he, the acting Adjt. and all the officers in B. Company failed to get
out, and were burnt to death along with two other officers and a padre
and about 15 signallers and runners. A service was held shortly after.
The entrances were sealed up as soon as possible to stop the flames
and spread of the fire. At the enquiry, it was decided that no blame
attached to the regiment and that everything possible had been done.
These officers were really most of the flower of the regiment, three had
won Military Crosses. They were the bravest and best. One of the
men tells me that he (Major Birch) could have got out, and came to the
entrance steps, asked if all were out, was told " No," and so he went
back to get them and so gave his life." He was in command of the
battalion at the time with acting rank of Major.

His brigade commander, Br.-Gen. G. D. Goodman, wrote :—

" It was only the day before he died that, as I left him in the
forward area, I thought to myself how well he was doing in command
of his battalion, and how satisfied I was to have him there. I had already
recommended him for a permanent command, and in these days officers
of his stamp are not very many. He will be much missed, both in his
regiment and in the brigade, and was a very gallant soldier."

FRANK COOPER LEDGARD

Born at Scarcroft, Leeds, 15th October, 1891, son of
Armitage Ledgard, of Scarcroft.

Second Lieut., 25th March, 1911 ; Lieut., 27th October,
1913.

Proceeded to Belgium with 2nd Bn. in October, 1914.

Killed in action near Ypres, 23rd October, 1914. He was in charge
of the machine gun detachment of the battalion.

" Another very brave man was Lieutenant Ledgard, who has relatives in Leeds. On the day of a big German attack in October, he was
in command of the two machine guns. Operating against us were
eight machine guns and some artillery, and every few minutes he had
to change the position of the guns. Backwards and forwards along the
trenches, from one position to another, he was running with the heavy
machine gun on his shoulder, and perspiration streaming down his face.
Man after man in his section was hit as they mowed down the German
infantry, and eventually all were out of action except Lieutenant Ledgard
and Private Norfolk. Almost at nightfall the officer was hit by a shell,
and he died a great hero in the eyes of every Green Howard " (Yorkshire
Post).

HUBERT STANLEY KREYER, D.S.O.

Born at Kamptee, 4th July, 1890, younger son of Lieut.-
Col. Frederick Augustus Christian Kreyer, Indian Army.

Second Lieut., 25th March, 1911 ; Lieut., 22nd January,
1914 ; Capt., 15th April, 1916 ; Bt.-Major, 3rd June, 1919 ;
Adjt., 21st October, 1919.

Went to Belgium with the 2nd Bn. in October, 1914, and took part
in the fighting at Ypres. Was wounded in the attack on Neuve Chapelle,
11th March, 1915 (twice mentioned in despatches, bronze star and clasp
and Distinguished Service Order). Was awarded the D.S.O. " for
having shown conspicuous gallantry on several occasions in carrying
messages along the trenches under heavy fire. His commanding officer
considers that it was largely due to the service rendered by this officer
on one occasion that the battalion was extricated from a difficult position."
Rejoined 2nd Bn., 7th October, 1915, and remained with it till 20th March,

1916, when he was invalided home with a dislocated knee. Afterwards as Brigade Major of the 185th Infantry Brigade in the 2nd battle of the Marne and operations around Rheims (French Croix de Guerre). Took part in the final advance from 23rd August, to the Armistice (mentioned in despatches, Bt. of Major).

GERALD WILLIAM EDWARD MAUDE

Born at Rylstone, Co. York, 20th November, 1888, elder son of Lieut.-Col. William Wade Maude, 4th West Yorkshire Militia, of Skipton-in-Craven.

Second Lieut., 27th May, 1911 ; Lieut., 12th February, 1914 ; Capt., 2nd August, 1916.

Served in India with 1st Bn. during the Great War. Wounded in action at Dakka, Afghanistan, 17th May, 1919.

Died at Peshawar of pneumonia, 5th November, 1919.

" He was a soldier in the truest sense of the word. His devotion to his regiment, his *esprit de corps* was wonderful. He longed to see his battalion do something more than peace soldiering and he saw it. There was no better disciplinarian, no one more determined to uphold the traditions of the old regiment. He knew his work thoroughly and his courage and fearlessness on every occasion won for him the utmost confidence of his men " (G.H.G.).

LESLIE HANSON MARRIAGE, M.C.

Born at Chelmsford, 15th July, 1892, son of Jacob Marriage.

Second Lieut., 20th September, 1911 ; Lieut., 2nd September, 1914 ; Capt., 1st January, 1917.

Went to the front with the 2nd Bn., and was wounded near Ypres on 29th October, 1914 (bronze star and clasp). Served with the Motor Machine Gun Corps from 10th August, 1915, in France and was wounded (shell shock) in March, 1916. Commanded a Cadet battalion at home from November, 1916, till appointed to the Egyptian Expeditionary Force in November, 1917, and was at the crossing of the river Auja with the 52nd Division in December, and in the fighting on the Sinjil ridge, and at Burj Badavile with the 74th Division in March, 1918. Appointed 2nd in command of the 74th Battalion M.G.C., 74th Division, in April and moved with it to France the same month taking part in the battle of the Somme from Albert to the Hindenburg Line, in September, 1918, including the capture of Lille and Tournai in October and November. Promoted acting Lieut.-Col. of the battalion in December, 1918. Volunteered for service in North Russia, for which he sailed in May, 1919, and took part in the various actions on the Dvina river and railway sector with the 8th Bn. Machine Gun Corps up to the end of the campaign (Military Cross).

ERNEST GEOFFREY CARRINGTON LE SUEUR

Born at St. Helier's, Jersey, 21st January, 1891, younger son of Arthur Le Sueur, of St. Helier's.

Second Lieut., 20th September, 1911 ; Lieut., 22nd September, 1914 ; Capt., 1st January, 1917.

During the war of 1914-18, served in India with 1st Bn. Joined 2nd Bn. in France in June, 1917.

Killed in action, 26th July, 1917, when leading his company in a raid on the enemy's trenches.

WALTER ANFRID AUSCHAR CHAUNCY

Born at Northallerton, 28th August, 1892, son of Major William Auschar Chauncy, 19th Foot.

Second Lieut., 20th September, 1911 ; Lieut., 24th October, 1914 ; Adjt., 1st August, 1915—17th June, 1917 ; Capt., 1st January, 1917 ; Adjt., 3rd Bn., 13th March, 1920.

Proceeded to Belgium with 2nd Bn. in October, 1914, and was present in the fighting at Ypres, and at the battles of Neuve Chapelle, Festubert and Givenchy. Was wounded at Loos, September, 1915 (bronze star and clasp). Served with the Royal Air Force as Wing Adjt., and on the staff from February, 1917, to May, 1919.

PHILIP CHABERT KIDD

Born at Otley, Yorkshire, 18th July, 1892, son of Dr. Kidd, of Otley.

Second Lieut., 11th October, 1911 ; Lieut., 27th October, 1914.

Reported wounded and a prisoner near Ypres, 30th October, 1914. Supposed to have been killed as no further information about him has been received.

GEOFFREY BROUNCKER de MARIES MAIRIS, D.S.O.

Born at Walmer, Kent, 16th April, 1870, son of General Geoffrey Mairis, late Royal Marines.

Second Lieut., 3rd Foot, 9th September, 1893 ; Lieut., 25th June, 1896 ; Capt., 21st February, 1900 ; Adjt., 20th March, 1901—19th March, 1905 ; Major, 19th Foot, 4th November, 1911 ; Bt. Lieut.-Col., 3rd June, 1918 ; Lieut.-Col., 15th May, 1919.

Served in the Boer War, 1899-02, as Adjt., 2nd Bn. The Buffs, from 9th May, 1900, to end of the war. Operations in Natal, 1899, Relief of Ladysmith and action of Colenso ; operations of 17th to 24th January, 1900, and action of Spionkop ; operations of 5th to 7th February, 1900, and action at Vaalkranz ; operations on Tugela Heights, 14th to 27th February, 1900, and action at Pieter's Hill (mentioned in despatches, D.S.O., Queen's medal and 5 clasps, King's medal and 2 clasps).

In the war of 1914-18, served with 1st Bn. in India till appointed to the 6th Service Bn. Dorsetshire Regt., in December, 1916. Was transferred to 7th Service Bn. Yorkshire Regt. in February, 1917, and remained with it till its disbandment in March, 1918. Was present on the Somme from December, 1916, to March, 1917, at the battle of Arras and Arras front, April to September, 1917 ; at Ypres and Paschendaele front, October to December, 1917 ; Cambrai front, December, 1917, to March, 1918. Rejoined 6th Service Bn. Dorsetshire Regt. in March, 1918, as Lieut.-Col. commanding ; severely wounded at Le Sars, 25th March 1918 (twice mentioned in despatches, Bt. of Lieut.-Col. and Chevalier of the Legion of Honour).

AIDAN JAMES WHARTON BARMBY, O.B.E.

Born in London, 31st October, 1892, son of C. Barmby.

Second Lieut., 14th February, 1912 ; Lieut., 30th October, 1914 ; Adjt., 7th Service Bn., 7th September, 1914—4th July, 1916 ; Capt., 20th February, 1917.

In the war of 1914-18, served as Adjt. to 7th Service Bn. till 4th July, 1916 ; wounded, 9th July, 1916, at Mametz Wood. Afterwards on the staff of the Royal Flying Corps (mentioned in despatches, O.B.E.).

LESLIE CRAWLEY-BOEVEY

Born in London, 12th September, 1884, 2nd son of James Henry Crawley-Boevey, of the Mansions, Bramhall Gardens, S. Kensington.

Second Lieut., Hampshire Regt., 20th March, 1907 ; Lieut., 14th January, 1911 ; 19th Foot, 16th November, 1912 ; Capt., 10th June, 1915 ; Adjt., 9th Service Bn., 19th September, 1914 —March, 1915 ; 11th Service Bn., 25th November, 1915—26th January, 1916.

In the war of 1914-18, served in Egypt, March to May, 1916. In Macedonia, December, 1916, to January, 1918, and in Persia with General Dunsterville's Column, April to November, 1918.

WILLIAM ARTHINGTON WORSLEY

Born at Hovingham, 5th April, 1890, eldest son of Sir William Arthington Worsley, Bart., of Hovingham Hall, Yorkshire.

Second Lieut., 4th December, 1912 ; Lieut., 30th October, 1914 Capt., 17th June, 1917 ; Adjt., 18th February, 1920.

Went to Belgium with 2nd Bn. in 1914. Was wounded and taken prisoner at Gheluvelt, near Ypres, about 30th October, 1914 (bronze star and clasp).

HUGH GODFREY BROOKSBANK

Born at Healaugh, Old Hall, Tadcaster, 24th November, 1893, 3rd son of Sir Edward Clitheroe Brooksbank, Bart., of Healaugh, Old Hall.

Second Lieut., 5th February, 1913 ; Lieut., 31st October, 1914.

Went to Belgium with 2nd Bn. in October, 1914, and was severely wounded near Ypres on 1st November (twice mentioned in despatches). Died of his wounds at 26, Park Lane, London, 16th December, 1914.

A senior officer wrote of him : " A braver lad never stepped the earth ; he was left in command of ' B ' Company when all his seniors had been shot. He commanded it like a veteran and on two occasions he was largely responsible for the regiment being saved."

" His comrades will miss him sadly and an older generation will recall the loss we sustained in the death of his uncle, William Stafford Brooksbank, who died of smallpox at Bangalore, 18th June, 1891, while Adjutant of the same battalion " (G.H.G.).

WILLIAM THOMAS HOWES

Born in London, 1st July, 1870, son of Walter Frederick Howes, of Lowestoft.

Private, 13th February, 1889 ; Corpl., 23rd May, 1893 ; Sergt., 22nd February, 1897 ; Cr.-Sergt., 1st April, 1898 ; Sergt.-Major, 22nd April, 1905 ; Qr.-Mr. and hon. Lieut., 19th March, 1913 ; hon. Capt., 1st July, 1918 ; Capt., 8th August, 1918.

Served in the Tirah Campaign of 1897-98, and was present at the capture of the Sampagha and Arhanga Passes ; the reconnaissance of the Saran Sar, and action of 9th November, 1897. Operations at and around Dwatoi and action of 24th November, 1897. Operations against the Khani Khel Chamkanis, and in the Bazar Valley, 25th to 30th December, 1897.

Affair at Shinkamar, 29th January, 1898 (medal and 2 clasps). In possession of the medal for the Delhi Coronation Durbar, the Coronation medal of 1911, and the medal for long service and good conduct. During the war of 1914-18, served in India, and in the operations against the Afghans in 1919.

JOHN ROLAND FORBES ERRINGTON

Born at Bangalore, 15th July, 1894, eldest son of John Roland Errington, of Mysore.

Second Lieut., 17th September, 1913 ; Lieut., 4th November, 1914 ; Capt., 17th June, 1917.

In the war of 1914-18, served with the 1st Bn. in India, and with the Machine Gun Corps from 15th September, 1917.

ANDREW BEATSON-BELL

Born at Mussorie, India, 8th September, 1894, son of Lieut.-Col. John Beatson-Bell, Indian Army.

Second Lieut., 24th January, 1914 ; Lieut., 25th January, 1915.

During the war of 1914-18, served with the 1st Bn. in India. Appointed to Army Signal Service, 12th May, 1917, and served in the Waziristan Expedition, May-July, 1917, and in Mesopotamia in 1918.

ROBERT HENRY MIDDLEDITCH

Born at Bridge House, Cromford, Derbyshire, 24th January, 1895, son of H. H. Middleditch, of Wigswill Grange, Wirksworth, Derbyshire.

Second Lieut., 25th February, 1914 ; Lieut., 31st January, 1915.

Proceeded with 2nd Bn. to Belgium in October, 1914. Wounded and taken prisoner near Ypres, 30th October, 1914 (bronze star and clasp).

QUEEN ALEXANDRA

Appointed Colonel-in-Chief of the Regiment on the occasion of the King's birthday, 1914 (dated 22nd June, 1914).

The following telegram was sent by Queen Alexandra in reply to Lieut.-General Sir W. E. Franklyn, K.C.B., Colonel of the regiment :—

" Please accept my best thanks for your kind congratulations on my appointment as Colonel-in-Chief Alexandra Princess of Wales's Own Yorkshire Regiment. I hope you will inform all ranks of your distinguished regiment how proud I feel to accept this honour.

Alexandra."

JOHN DAMPIER HALLIFAX

Born, 3rd May, 1895, son of Captain Alfred Plassy Hallifax, late 19th Foot.

Second Lieut., 12th August, 1914 ; Lieut., 31st January, 1915.

Killed in action near Festubert, 17th May, 1915.

" He had an unusually charming personality and was exceedingly accomplished. His death was a great grief to his brother officers and to his men. The young heroes of this terrible war are many, and not one went to the front with more joyousness and enthusiasm than 'Jack' Hallifax. His father, the late Captain Plassy Hallifax, who lived for some time in Lakefield, Ontario, held a commission in the same regiment as that with which his son was for so short a time connected " (Toronto Newspaper).

ALFRED ERYK ROBINSON

Born at Scarborough, 19th September, 1894, son of Alfred Hind Robinson, late 11th Hussars.

Second Lieut., 12th August, 1914 ; Lieut., 31st January, 1915.

Wounded at Neuve Chapelle, 12th March, 1915, and again at Ypres, 12th December, 1917 (mentioned in despatches, bronze star).

RONALD CAMERON BENTLEY

Born at York, 3rd July, 1898.

Second Lieut., 14th August, 1914 ; Lieut., 18th February, 1915.

Joined 2nd Bn. in France, 6th January, 1915. Present at the battle of Neuve Chapelle, 11th March, 1915 (wounded). Again wounded at Hulloch, 25th September, 1915, and taken prisoner (bronze star). Carried the King's Colour in the Victory march through Paris, on 14th July, and through London on the 19th July, 1919.

GERALD FRANCIS HADOW

Born at Scarborough, 24th January, 1895, son of Colonel A. de S. Hadow, late 19th Foot.

Second Lieut., 15th August, 1914 ; Lieut., 8th March, 1915.

Took part in the battles of Neuve Chapelle and Festubert.

Killed in action at Givenchy, 15th June, 1915.

"He had reached the German barbed wire, and, finding he was practically alone, returned to his own trenches, which he reached untouched. Here he found his captain killed and all the other officers dead or wounded. His company went into action 180 strong and had 142 casualties. He returned to report to the C.O., and, on the way, was struck on the head by a piece of shell. A captain under whom he served wrote : 'I feel I have lost a young friend whom I had got to know and tested in perhaps the most severe time—war time—and he never failed. He was such a gallant little fellow and quite ready to die for the good cause.'"

BENJAMIN WILLIAMS, M.C., D.C.M.

Born at Hartlepool, 21st November, 1874.

Pte., January, 1893 ; Corpl., 16th February, 1894 ; Cr.-Sergt., 12th January, 1897 ; Sergt.-Major, 3rd Bn., 6th March, 1907 ; Qr.-Mr. and hon. Lieut., 25th August, 1914 ; hon. Capt., 25th August, 1917 ; Capt., 8th August, 1918.

Served in the Boer War, 1899-1902, and took part in the operations near Colesberg in January, 1900. In the march along the Modder River, including the Relief of Kimberley, the actions at Paardeberg, Kitchener's Kop, Poplar Grove, and Driefontein. In the advance on Dewetsdorp and action at Leuukop ; the advance on Pretoria and actions at Brandfort, Vet and Zand Rivers, Kroonstadt and Johannesburg ; the advance eastwards and actions at Diamond Hill and Belfast (mentioned in despatches, Distinguished Conduct medal, Queen's medal and 6 clasps, King's medal and 2 clasps). In the war of 1914-18, took part in the landing at Suvla Bay as Qr.-Mr., 6th Service Bn., and operations there till the evacuation of the Gallipoli Peninsula, 19th December, 1915 (bronze star) ; was with the 6th Bn. during operations in France and Belgium from July, 1916, to 1918. Afterwards served in the campaign in North Russia with 6th Bn.

FREDERIC CHARLES HATTON

Born at Parkhurst, 9th April, 1878, son of Qr.-Mr.-Sergt. Alfred C. Hatton, 19th Foot.

Dr., 3rd May, 1892 ; Corpl., 20th May, 1897 ; Sergt., 15th May, 1901 ; Col.-Sergt., 17th March, 1903 ; Qr.-Mr.-Sergt., 17th March, 1906 ; Sergt.-Major, 19th March, 1913. Second Lieut., 9th October, 1914.

Served in the Boer War, 1899-00. Present in the operations near Colesberg in January, 1900. In the march along the Modder River, including the Relief of Kimberley, the actions at Paardeberg, Kitchener's Kop, Poplar Grove and Driefontein (severely wounded, Queen's medal and 3 clasps).

Served with 2nd Bn. in Belgium and was killed in action near Ypres, 30th October, 1914.

" Born in the regiment, he joined it as a boy of 14, was a N.C.O. at 18, and a Colour-Sergt. at 24. He had been gymnastic instructor, drill instructor, orderly room clerk, clerk in a staff office, and Quarter-Master Sergt. He was a certified shorthand writer, and, like his father who was a sub-editor in Japan and his two brothers, who are well-known writers on military and medical subjects, had done journalistic work. In him we have lost a gallant and brave officer, whose interests were wrapped up in the regiment to which he devoted his life " (G.H.G.). Was in possession of the medal for long service and good conduct.

MARMADUKE THWAITES

Born, 17th July, 1881, son of Marmaduke Thwaites, of Richmond, Yorkshire.

Boy, 17th September, 1895 ; Dr., 1st November, 1895 ; Pte., 1st September, 1899 ; Corpl., 1st May, 1900 ; Sergt., 17th August, 1904 ; Cr.-Sergt., 11th March, 1906 ; Qr.-Mr.-Sergt., 15th May, 1913. Second Lieut., 9th October, 1914 ; Lieut., 8th March, 1915.

Served in the Boer War, 1901-2 ; operations in the Transvaal, 1901-2 (medal and 3 clasps). In possession of the medal for long service and good conduct. Went to Belgium with 2nd Bn. and was wounded at Ypres, 29th October, 1914.

Killed in the trenches at Hulloch, 29th September, 1915.

HARRY EBOURNE

Born at Birmingham, 15th February, 1887.

Boy, 25th Foot, 24th December, 1902 ; Dr., 1st September, 1903 ; Corpl., 23rd January, 1908 ; Sergt., 9th May, 1913. Second Lieut., 19th Foot, 7th November, 1914 ; Lieut., 14th March, 1915 ; cashiered, 15th April, 1918.

VICTOR JOHN BARBER

Born at Bristol, 4th December, 1891, son of Charles Taylor Barber, of Caistor-on-the-Sea, Great Yarmouth.

Second Lieut., 7th November, 1914, from ranks of 9th Foot ; Lieut., 15th March, 1915.

Served in India during the war, 1914-18, and in the operations in Afghanistan in 1919.

WALTER DERHAM

Born at Christchurch, 20th April, 1888, son of W. J. Derham.

Second Lieut., 7th November, 1914, from ranks of the North Staffordshire Regt. ; Lieut., 18th May, 1915 ; retired with a gratuity, 20th December, 1919, and granted the hon. rank of Captain.

Served with 1st Bn. in India during the Great War.

FRANCIS JOSEPH McGOVERN

Born at Halifax, Yorkshire, 27th April, 1892.

Second Lieut., 7th November, 1914, from ranks of the Duke of Wellington's Regt. ; Lieut., 10th June, 1915.

Served in Mesopotamia in 1916, and with the Army Signal Service from 12th May, 1917.

GEORGE ANTHONY TURTON

Born, 28th August, 1895, son of Lieut.-Colonel Ralph Douglas Turton, late 22nd Foot, of Larpool, Whitby.

Second Lieut., 11th November, 1914 ; Lieut., 10th June, 1915.

Served in Flanders, July to December, 1915, and was present at battle of Loos (bronze star). Royal Flying Corps, 30th June, 1915, to 31st March, 1918. Afterwards under Air Ministry.

HENRY DELROY McGRIGOR JAMES, M.C.

Born at Morant, Spanish Town, Jamaica, 12th April, 1875.

Second Lieut., 4th December, 1914, from Warrant Officer, Grenadier Guards ; Lieut., 10th June, 1915 ; placed on retired pay with rank of Major, 8th March, 1920.

Served in the Boer War, 1900-02 ; operations in Orange River Colony including action at Wittebergen. Operations in the Transvaal and Cape Colony (Queen's medal and 3 clasps, King's medal and 2 clasps). Served with the Machine Gun Corps in Mesopotamia during the War, 1914-18 (twice mentioned in despatches, Military Cross). Author of " Instruction in the Machine Gun," London, 1915.

ALBERT PARROT

Born, 19th June, 1888. Second Lieut., 9th January, 1915, from ranks of 8th Foot ; Lieut., 10th June, 1915.

Served in Mesopotamia during the Great War with the 2nd/6th Bn. Devonshire Regiment.

WILLIAM CREAD SHEAY, D.C.M.

Born in the parish of St. Luke, Middlesex, son of William Sheay.

Pte., 7th August, 1897 ; Sergt., 28th February, 1912 ; Co.-Sergt.-Major, 27th October, 1914. Second Lieut., 27th March, 1915.

Landed with the 2nd Bn. in Belgium in October, 1914. He commanded his company with great skill and resource from 30th October, to 15th November, 1914, after all the officers had been killed or wounded. Was afterwards on promotion for distinguished service, appointed Machine Gun officer (mentioned in despatches, bronze star and clasp, Russian medal of St. George, 1st Class). In possession of the medal for long service and good conduct.

Killed in action near Festubert, 16th May, 1915. Buried in Bethune town Cemetery.

"At the time of his death he was firing one of his machine guns in order to make sure it was trained on that part of the German parapet which our troops were not attacking ; a bullet ricochetted off the gun and hit him in the head. In him we lost without any exaggeration the best machine gun officer in the British army " (G.H.G.).

HUMPHREY WORTHINGTON WILSON, D.C.M.

Born at Carlow, 19th March, 1876, son of Sergt. James Wilson, late 89th Foot and Carlow Rifles.

Pte., 1st June, 1893 ; Corpl., 22nd September, 1894 ; Sergt., 10th January, 1898 ; Cr.-Sergt., 25th April, 1903 ; Sergt.-Major, 5th Bn., 1913. Second Lieut., 8th April, 1915 ; Lieut., 10th June, 1915.

Served with the 2nd Mounted Infantry in the Boer War, 1899-02, including the Relief of Kimberley, actions at Klip Drift, Paardeberg, Driefontein, and Sanna's Post ; operations near Thabanchu ; actions at Hout's Nek, Welkon Kopjes, Diamond Hill, and pursuit of De Wet, Relief of Eland's River ; operations in the Western Transvaal, October, 1900,—July, 1901, including action at Nooigedacht (mentioned in despatches, Queen's medal and 6 clasps, King's medal and 2 clasps, and Distinguished Conduct medal).

Killed in action in France, 4th October, 1915, when attached to 15th Foot as a temporary captain.

"He met his death while gallantly leading a charge against the German position—a most gallant and conscientious officer, whose loss to the regiment is greatly to be deplored " (G.H.G.).

ERIC WILLIAM LOYD

Born in London, 29th September, 1894, son of Lieut.-Col. Arthur Purvis Loyd, late 21st Hussars.

Second Lieut., 17th April, 1915 ; Lieut., 10th June, 1915.

Served in France from July, 1915, to 27th September, 1915, when he was wounded at St. Elie, near Hulloch. Served in Macedonia with Machine Gun Corps, and was present at the battle of Doiran, 9th May, 1917, and in the advance into Bulgaria in September, 1918. Subsequently served in Caucasia (mentioned in despatches, bronze star).

ARTHUR WILLIAM HAWKINS

Born at Putney, Surrey, 4th June, 1897, son of Henry Charlton Hawkins, Barrister-at-Law.

Second Lieut., 12th May, 1915 ; Lieut., 30th June, 1915.

Served in France from 1st October, 1915, to 20th December, 1915 (bronze star). Appointed to the Royal Flying Corps, 28th April, 1917, and with it served in Egypt and Mesopotamia, 1917-18, and in North Persia with the Bushire Field Force in 1919 (mentioned in despatches). Also again in Mesopotamia in 1919, and in the South Kurdistan campaign.

GEORGE ERNEST LISTER CRESSEY

Born in 1895, younger son of Dr. Cressey, of Tunbridge Wells.

Second Lieut., 12th May, 1915.

Killed at Hulloch, 26th September, 1915.

"He had joined the Kent Cyclists' Corps in August, 1914. Two months after being gazetted to the regiment he was sent to Belgium on special entrenching work. He was a young officer of much promise, whose loss is much to be deplored " (G.H.G.).

BASIL EVERY GILL

Born at Devonport, 24th November, 1893, youngest son of Thomas Husband Gill, Solicitor, of Penlee Cottage, Devonport.

Second Lieut., 12th May, 1915 ; Lieut., 26th July, 1915.

He joined the 2nd Bn. in France in September, 1915, and was shortly afterwards appointed acting adjutant. He was wounded at Mametz Wood on the 16th July, 1916, but remained at duty.

Killed, 18th October, 1916, on the Somme.

His Divisional Commander wrote :—

" I knew him well, and I always regarded him as one of the very finest boys in the Division. I know his regiment will miss him very sorely, and the Service is poorer without him. He had made a name for himself for his fine soldierly qualities and his unswerving devotion to duty."

GEORGE HALLIWELL CROSSE

Born, 23rd February, 1896, son of Canon Thomas George Crosse, The Vicarage, Faversham.

Second Lieut., 12th May, 1915 ; Lieut., 1st August, 1915.

Served in the war, 1914-18, with the Machine Gun Corps, and was wounded at Guillemont, 27th August, 1916; again at Bullecourt, 3rd May, 1917, and for the third time at Poelcappelle, 26th October, 1917.

HERBERT DACRES BEADON

Born at Newcastle-on-Tyne, 21st September, 1895, son of Dacres Carroll Beadon.

Second Lieut., 15th May, 1915, antedated from 4th February, 1916 ; Lieut., 27th September, 1915.

Took part in the 2nd battle of Ypres (wounded), being attached to the 2nd Bn. King's Shropshire L.I. from 15th March, 1915, to 19th November, 1915, in France. Served also with it in the Salonica Force from November, 1915, to 20th December, 1918, and on the Black Sea, South Russia, from December, 1918, to January, 1919 (bronze star).

WALTER HERBERT YOUNG, D.S.O.

Born at Southborough, Kent., 7th February, 1870, 4th son of Major-Gen. Charles Metcalfe Young, Royal Artillery (Bengal).

Second Lieut., 15th Foot, 23rd March, 1889 ; Lieut., 5th August, 1891 ; Capt., 27th November, 1897 ; Adjt., 20th June, 1901--19th June, 1904 ; Bt.-Major, 23rd August, 1902 ; Major, 29th April, 1908 ; Bt.-Lieut.-Col., 18th February, 1915 ; Lieut.-Col., 19th Foot, 15th May, 1915 ; retired, 15th May, 1919.

Served in the Boer War, 1900-02 ; operations in the Orange Free State, including action at Houtnek (Thoba Mountain) ; operations in the O.R. Colony, including actions at Biddulphsberg and Wittebergen, 1st—29th July, 1900 ; operations in the Transvaal, February to March, 1901. Operations in the O.R. Colony, 30th November, 1900,—February, 1901, March, 1901,—May, 1902 (twice mentioned in despatches, Bt. of Major, Queen's medal and 3 clasps, King's medal and 2 clasps). In the war of 1914-18, served with the 1st Bn. 15th Foot, and landed in France in September, 1914. Took part in all the fighting the battalion was engaged in, including the Aisne and 1st and 2nd battles of Ypres. On promotion to the command of the Green Howards, was present with them at the battle of Loos, and was wounded at Givenchy, 29th November, 1915. Present at the operations on the Somme, 1916. In April, 1917, was appointed to the command of a Training Reserve battalion (four times mentioned in despatches, Bt. of Lieut.-Col., bronze star and clasp and Distinguished Service order).

CYRIL ELCOMB BROCKHURST, M.C.

Born at Sidcup, 5th June, 1895, son of Charles Henry Brockhurst, of Beaumont, Jersey, C.I.

Second Lieut., 1st June, 1915, antedated from 31st March, 1917 ; Lieut. 27th September, 1915.

Commissioned to the 2nd/13th (Princess Louise's Kensington) Bn., the London Regiment in September, 1914, and proceeded to France with the 60th Division as a Company commander, 22nd June, 1916. Transferred to the Salonica front in November, 1916, and joined the Egyptian Expeditionary Force in August, 1917. Appointed Adjt. to the Bn., 11th September, 1917, and was wounded, 9th December, 1917. Awarded the Military Cross, 1st January, 1918, for service in Salonica. Appointed Staff Capt., 179th Infantry Bde., 5th November, 1918, and to the 234th Infantry Bde. in February, 1919, on disbandment of the 60th Division.

WILLIAM HENRY OSTLER HILL

Born in 1885. Second Lieut., 4th June, 1915, from Warrant Officer, Coldstream Guards.

Served in the war of 1914-18, with the Expeditionary Force in France from 3rd February, 1915. Distinguished himself at the battle of Neuve Chapelle, and was promoted to a commission for service in the Field.

Killed in action at Loos, 25th September, 1915.

WILLIAM DOUGLAS CLAYTON

Born at Wakefield, 24th February, 1895, son of Lieut.-Col. W. Kitson Clayton, C.M.G., R.A.M.C. (T.D.), of Broxbourne, Sandal, Wakefield.

Second Lieut., 16th June 1915 ; Lieut., 27th September, 1915.

Wounded at Givenchy-la-Bassee, 30th November, 1915 (shell shock). From July, 1916, served with 1st Bn. in India during the war, and during the operations in Afghanistan, 1919, as acting Adjutant.

THOMAS CHARLES GOODE, M.B.E.

Born, 27th January, 1880, son of Sergt. Valentine Goode, 19th Foot.

Pte., 27th August, 1897 ; Corpl., 24th November, 1900 ; Sergt., 8th June, 1903 ; Qr.-Mr.-Sergt. (O.R. Clerk), 6th February 1912. Second Lieut., 17th June, 1915 ; 13th Foot, 18th June, 1915 ; Lieut., 1st July, 1917 ; Adjt., 3rd August, 1917.

Served in the Boer War, 1899-02, including the operations round Colesberg in January, 1900. Took part in the march along the Modder River, Relief of Kimberley, actions at Paardeberg, Kitchener's Kop, Poplar Grove and Driefontein. Also in the march to the eastern Transvaal, including actions at Diamond Hill and Belfast (Queen's medal and

5 clasps, King's medal and 2 clasps). Appointed a member of the Order of the British Empire, 3rd June, 1919, for services in connection with the war in India.

THOMAS WALTER HAYES

Born at Cork, 27th June, 1875, son of John Hayes, of Derk House, Pallas Green, Co. Limerick.

Second Lieut., 17th June, 1915, from ranks of the East Surrey Regt. ; Lieut., 7th October, 1915.

Served in the Boer War, 1899-01. Operations in Natal and Transvaal. (Queen's medal and 3 clasps). Served in India during the Great War. In possession of the medal for long service and good conduct.

PHILIP CLOW

Born at Newcastle-on-Tyne, 8th March, 1878.

Second Lieut., 17th June, 1915, from ranks of Dorsetshire Regt. ; Lieut., 29th March, 1916.

During the war of 1914-18, served with Force " D " in Mesopotamia and was engaged at Shaiba. Served also in India. Took part in the operations against the Afghans in 1919.

FRANK CROWSLEY

Born at Kempston, Bedfordshire, 24th March, 1888, son of James Crowsley, of Kempston.

Second Lieut., 13th Foot, 17th June, 1915, from the ranks ; 19th Foot, 18th June, 1915 ; Lieut., 15th April, 1916.

During the Great War, served with the 1st Bn. in India, and in the operations against Afghanistan in 1919.

EDWARD COLLIS DOWNES

Born at Begbroke Rectory, Oxon, 18th July, 1893, son of the Revd. George Richmond Downes.

Second Lieut., 19th June, 1915 ; Lieut., 2nd August, 1916.

Proceeded to France with 8th Service Bn. Leicestershire Regt. in July, 1915, was wounded 4th February, 1916. In January, 1917, went to Mesopotamia and joined the 6th Service Bn. South Lancashire Regt., where he remained till December, 1918, proceeding thence to Salonika, being attached to a concentration camp there till May, 1919.

ARTHUR CYRIL LAWES PARRY, M.C.

Born at Poona, 11th January, 1893, son of the Revd. Arthur Audley Parry, Sandal Vicarage, Wakefield, Yorkshire.

Second Lieut., 22nd June, 1915 ; Lieut., 2nd August, 1916.

During the war of 1914-18, held a temporary commission from September, 1914, in the 9th Service Bn. Was present at the battle of Loos, in September, 1915. Was subsequently attached to the 2nd Bn. K.O. Royal Lancaster Regt. on the Macedonian front, and was present at the battle of Doiran. Was wounded, 23rd February, 1918, in the Struma Valley (mentioned in despatches, Military Cross and bronze star).

ARTHUR VIVIAN BURBURY, M.C.

Born in London, 20th May, 1896, son of Arthur Burbury, of 32, Campden Hill Gardens, Kensington.

Second Lieut., 14th July, 1915 ; Lieut., 2nd August, 1916.

Served with the Royal Flying Corps in the Great War, being graded as a Balloon officer, 1st October, 1915, and Flying officer, 16th March, 1917. Was awarded the Military Cross in September, 1916, for the following act :—" When observing from a balloon at a height of 3,000 feet, the cable was cut by a shell. He destroyed his papers, ripped the balloon, a most difficult operation in the air, and then got down in his parachute." Awarded the Croix de Guerre avec Palme in January, 1917. In April, 1917, he was shot down by anti-aircraft gun ; was wounded and taken prisoner. Repatriated in December, 1918. Served with the North Russia Expeditionary Force as S.O4 and Flying officer, Archangel front.

JOHN FERDINAND FAITHFULL

Born at Malmesbury, Wiltshire, 5th May, 1896, son of the Revd. Wyndham James Hamilton Faithfull, Oaksey Rectory, Malmesbury.

Second Lieut., 2nd September, 1915 ; Lieut., 2nd August, 1916.

Commissioned originally to the 6th Service Bn., and landed with it at Suvla Bay. Later took part in the Palestine Campaign, and was present at the 1st and 2nd battles of Gaza, and the taking of Beersheba and Jerusalem. With the 74th Division he was at the operations on the Somme in September, 1918, and at the capture of Lille in October (bronze star).

HENRY CLIFFORD LLOYD

Born at Bolton, 22nd May, 1888, son of Henry John Lloyd, Sherborne Manor Estate, Boscombe, Hants.

Second Lieut., 18th September, 1915 ; Lieut., 2nd August, 1916.

Served with the Mesopotamia Expeditionary Force.

JOHN GEORGE WYLDE

Born at Hendon, 28th January, 1891, elder son of John Arthur Wylde, Oakleigh Park, Lorring Road, London.

Second Lieut., 10th November, 1915, from Special Reserve ; Lieut., 2nd August, 1916.

Served in France from 16th August, 1915, and was wounded 1st July, 1916, in the attack on Montauban on the Somme (bronze star).

PERCY DARRAL DENMAN

Born, 4th November, 1875. Second Lieut., 29th September, 1915, from the ranks.

Served in France. Was wounded at Givenchy in June, 1915, and again at Hulloch, 26th September, 1915 (mentioned in despatches, bronze star).

Killed in action at Montauban, Somme, 1st July 1916.

He was promoted from Sergt.-Major 4th Bn. for distinguished conduct in the Field.

ERNEST PETTINGER DAVY

Born at Sheffield, 3rd July, 1897, son of Ernest Richards Davy, The Club, Sheffield.

Second Lieut., 24th November, 1915 ; Lieut., 28th August, 1916.

Joined 2nd Bn. in France in July, 1916, and was present at the operations on the Somme. Was transport officer to the battalion at the battle of Arras. A.D.C. to G.O.C. 30th Division, 1st August, 1917—30th January, 1918, when he was wounded at Chauny, near St. Quentin.

HAROLD NORMAN BRIGHT, M.C.

Born at Alverstone House, Forest Hill, 2nd March, 1894, son of John Milburn Bright, M.D., of Forest Hill.

Second Lieut., Manchester Regt., 4th January, 1916 ; 19th Foot, 18th July, 1917, antedated to 26th November, 1915 ; Lieut., 19th October, 1916.

Gazetted to a temporary commission in the 8th Service Bn. 26th February, 1915. With the 2nd Bn. in France from October, 1915, to April, 1917 (bronze star). Present at all the battles of the Somme, and was wounded at Arras, 2nd April, 1917 (awarded the Military Cross).

PERCY COLK

Born at Sheffield, 12th January, 1889, son of James Colk.

Second Lieut., 6th December, 1915, from the ranks ; Lieut., 19th October, 1916 ; retired with a gratuity, 13th March, 1920.

Served with 2nd Bn. at the battles of Ypres (wounded), Neuve Chapelle and Fromelles. Was wounded at Festubert, 18th May, 1915. Present at battle of Loos (bronze star with clasp and promoted to a commission for distinguished conduct in the Field). Took part in the operations on the Somme (wounded).

KENNETH ROBERT HENDERSON, M.C.

Born at Sutton Surrey, 29th May, 1895, son of R. C. Henderson, of Nithsdale, Sutton.

Second Lieut., 20th December, 1915, antedated from 30th March, 1916 ; Lieut., 1st July, 1917.

Served in France with Artists Rifles from 28th October 1914 (bronze star and clasp). Present with 2nd Bn. at Fromelles, 9th May, Festubert, 16th May (wounded), at Givenchy, 15th June, 1915 (wounded). Was again wounded 1st September, 1915, and for the fourth time on the Somme, 7th July, 1916. Served in the Russian Campaign with the 6th Bn. on the Archangel Front. The Military Cross was awarded in the London Gazette of the 21st January, with the following notice :—" He has carried out the duties of Company Commander of a mixed force at Bolshe-Ozerki, and has worked in a very efficient way. He has had continuous service on this front since November, 1918, and in the four engagements in which his company has taken part he has proved to be a fearless and good leader of men."

HUGH BERNARD MORKILL

Born at Ansthorpe Lodge, Whitkirk, Leeds, 1st October, 1896, son of H. S. Morkill, Newfield Hall, Bell Busk, Yorkshire.

Second Lieut., 22nd December, 1915 ; Lieut., 1st July, 1917.

Served with 2nd Bn. in France from July, 1916, to July, 1917. Afterwards with the Royal Flying Corps in Egypt, Palestine, and Mudros.

JOHN FOLLANSBEE BREDIN DELAP

Born at Paddington, 18th January, 1897, elder son of the Revd. Louis Bredin Delap, Benhall Vicarage, Saxmundham, Suffolk.

Second Lieut., 22nd December, 1915.

Killed at the village of La Barque, between Flers and Le Transloy, 18th October, 1916.

He was at the front for three months, and was killed in a night attack on the German trenches. An officer wrote of him, "Although one of the youngest, he was one of the most valuable officers we have had. I don't think he knew what fear was, or if he did he never showed it, which is still finer."

DOUGLAS DANA DREW KINNAIRD MOIR

Born at Halifax, N.S., 12th December, 1894, 2nd son of Major John Drew Moir, R.A.M.C., 55, Pembroke Villas, London.

Second Lieut., 22nd December, 1915.

Killed in action at Guillemont, Somme, 23rd July, 1916.

He received a temporary commission in the Norfolk Regiment, and passed into Sandhurst by nomination, 27th August, 1915.

NOEL FISHER McCARTHY

Born at Trincomalee, 11th November, 1895, son of Major J. McCarthy, 4, Leyland Road, Lee, London.

Second Lieut., 22nd December, 1915.

Killed in action at Le Sars, 18th October, 1916.

FRANK LAWRENCE JAMES SHIRLEY, M.C.

Born at Abingdon, 31st May, 1896.

Second Lieut., 22nd December, 1915 ; Lieut., 1st July, 1917 ; Flight Lieut., Royal Air Force, 1st August, 1919.

Served in France with the Royal Flying Corps, and was wounded over St. Quentin, 18th April, 1917. Present at the 1st battle of the Somme and enemy retirement in front of Peronne (mentioned in despatches, Military Cross). "He displayed great courage and skill on many occasions in photographing the enemy's position. On one occasion, although severely wounded, he completed his work and succeeded in landing his machine safely."

HENRY ROBERTSON WATT, M.C.

Born at Victoria, B.C., 26th September, 1896, son of Dr. A. T. Watt.

Second Lieut., 22nd December 1915 ; Lieut., 1st July, 1917.

Took part in the battle of the Somme, July to November, 1916, with 7th Service Bn. (mentioned in despatches). Awarded the Military Cross. "He displayed great courage and determination during a bombing attack on the enemy. Although wounded he continued to throw bombs until the trench was captured." With the 2nd Bn. he was at the 3rd battle of Ypres, near Sanctuary Wood, and at the battle of Amiens. Also at the battle of Arras with the Canadian Corps. Awarded a clasp to the Military Cross for "Having led his company to its objective with great dash and skill, he, with one sergeant, attacked a strong point, which he entered and shot the enemy inside. Later, although wounded, he rallied his company and organised bombing parties to meet the enemy's attack. He carried on in command for 48 hours after being severely wounded, setting a magnificent example of pluck and fine leadership." Was A.D.C. to Lieut.-Gen. Sir Arthur Currie, G.C.M.G., K.C.B., Commanding the Canadian Corps, 3rd December, 1917, to 8th September, 1918. Was wounded four times ; at Hebuterne, 22/8/16 ; at Le Transloy, 3/11/16 ; at Sanctuary Wood (Bodmin Copse), 31/7/17 ; and at Ecourt, St. Quentin (Canal du Nord, near Douai), 8/9/18.

HAROLD HOGARTH SCOBY

Born at York, 26th March, 1891, son of David Scoby.

Second Lieut., 27th December, 1915, antedated from 27th February, 1916 ; Lieut., 1st July, 1917.

Served with 2nd Bn. in France from 10th March, 1916, and was present at the fighting at Montauban and Trônes Wood, till wounded at Guillemont, 23rd July, 1916. Rejoined the battalion, 20th January, 1917, and remained with it till invalided, 31st March, 1917. Took part in the battle of the Somme in August and September, 1918, attached to 1st Bn. East Yorkshire Regt., and was wounded and taken prisoner at Gouzeaucourt, 10th September, 1918.

CHARLES BERJEW BROOK, D.S.O.

Born at Brantham, 7th March, 1895, son of C. B. Brooke, Colne House, Brantham, Essex.

Second Lieut., 4th January, 1916.

At the beginning of the war he was in the 3rd Suffolk Regt., and served with the Expeditionary Force in 1914 and 1915, being attached to the 1st Bn. Queen's (mentioned in despatches and awarded the Distinguished Service Order). Was severely wounded at Loos, 25th September, 1915.

Joined 2nd Bn., 18th April, 1916, and was killed in action at Montauban, Somme, 1st July, 1916, when acting as Captain.

JOHN BUCHAN FREELAND

Born at Toronto, 7th November, 1897, son of Edward B. Freeland, of Chestnut Park, Toronto.

Second Lieut., 18th January, 1916.

Was commissioned from the Royal Military College, Canada, and joined the 2nd Bn. on the 21st June, 1916. Took part in the fighting on the Somme, and was wounded at Trônes Wood, on the 8th July, 1916. Rejoined the battalion, 10th May, 1917.

Killed at Sanctuary Wood, Ypres, 26th July, 1917. His father received the following letter from Lieut.-Colonel C. V. Edwards, commanding the 2nd Bn. :—

"I write with great regret to inform you of the death in action of your son yesterday afternoon. He was taking part in an attack on the German lines, and was behaving with great gallantry at the time of his death. We are all extremely sorry to lose him. He had only been under my command for a few months, but in that time I was able to grasp what a good, sound fellow he was. He was the best working subaltern I had. In particular, his men came first in everything he did. His keynote was, I think, 'thoroughness.' The attack we carried out was successful, many Germans were killed and some few captured. Your son's platoon was in the thick of it, and was responsible for specially good work. I understand that he had moved forward to look for a machine gun which was commencing to fire from very close quarters when he fell. If he had come back, I would have recommended him for a Military Cross. We can ill afford to lose such men at a time like this. We know, however, that he had done his work well, and that his life he was not wasted.

I find it hard to write at all in cases like this ; a man ready and willing to give his life need, I think, have little said about him. We remember them all the same."

JOHN BROUGH GIRLING

Born, 27th July, 1896, son of E. J. Girling, Northcote, Woodside Park Road, London.

Second Lieut., 22nd January, 1916 ; Lieut., 22nd July, 1917.

Served with the 4th Bn. in France from 16th August, 1915, till wounded at Ligny Thilloy, on Somme, 18th October, 1916.

Transferred to Indian Army, 11th October, 1917.

RICHARD JOHN DARVALL

Born, 20th December, 1897, son of R. J. Darvall, Four Cedars, Tilehurst Road, Reading.

Second Lieut., 26th January, 1916 ; Lieut., 26th July, 1917 ; resigned his commission, 11th September, 1919.

WILLIAM EDGAR BUSH, M.C.

Born at Derby, 1st January, 1896, son of Arthur Bush, of Marston-on-Dove, Hilton, Derbyshire.

Second Lieut., 26th January, 1916 ; Lieut., 26th July, 1917.

Won a prize cadetship at Sandhurst in August, 1915. Was attached to 8th Service Bn. in France, and was engaged in the second battle of the Somme, Ypres Salient, October, 1916, Messines Ridge, June, 1917, and Menin Road, September, 1917 (wounded, awarded the Military Cross, 1st January, 1918, and clasp, 2nd April, 1919).

CHARLES RONALD STEELE, D.F.C.

Born at Sheffield, 9th November, 1897.

Second Lieut., 26th January, 1916 ; Lieut., 26th July, 1917.

Served in the war with the Royal Flying Corps, at the Somme, 1916, and on the St. Quentin front, and retreat in March, 1918 ; wounded at Berstangles, 24th August, 1918. Awarded the Distinguished Flying Cross. " A bold and skilful leader who inspires confidence in those who serve under him. On August 13th, while leading an offensive patrol of five machines, he observed six enemy scouts ; attacking these he shot down one out of control, his observer driving down a second. In this engagement he became separated from his patrol ; seeing this, eight scouts dived to attack him ; one of these his observer shot down out of control. Eventually, he rejoined his patrol and led them back to the aerodrome. In all, he had destroyed three enemy machines and driven down four others out of control " (London Gazette).

JOHN CHRISTIAN BARRACLOUGH

Born at Lowestoft, 24th July, 1897, son of H. C. Barraclough, M.D., of Lowestoft.

Second Lieut., 26th January, 1916 ; Lieut., 26th July, 1917 ; Flight Lieut., Royal Air Force, 1st August, 1919.

Served in the Royal Flying Corps as an observer to 25th Squadron R.F.C. in France, from February to August, 1916 (wounded).

HUGH RAYMOND BURN BAILEY

Born at Wembley, Middlesex, 2nd May, 1897, son of E. E. Bailey, of Trichinoply.

Second Lieut., 26th January, 1916 ; Lieut., 26th July, 1917.

Served with the 8th Service Bn. at the fighting at Ploegstreet Wood in 1916 (wounded), and with the 4th Bn. at Hill 60 and at Chemin des Dames in 1918.

Wounded and taken prisoner at Chemin des Dames, 27th May, 1918.

THOMAS THEODORE COLLETT

Born, 19th January, 1897, only son of the Revd. Thomas Collett, M.A., Vicar of Scotby, Carlisle.

Second Lieut., 26th January, 1916.

Wounded near Sailly-Saillisel on the 8th February, 1917, in the attack on the German trenches, when attached to the 7th Bn. Died of his wounds in a field hospital on the 15th February, 1917.

WALTER RAYES GAMBLE, M.C.

Born, 21st January, 1881. Second Lieut., 6th February, 1916, from ranks of 16th Lancers.

Promoted to a commission for distinguished conduct in the Field (mentioned in despatches, 15th June, 1916, and 25th August, 1916). Awarded the Military Cross "for conspicuous gallantry in action. He led the assault with the greatest dash and courage after his senior officer had been wounded."

Died of wounds in June, 1917.

ARTHUR EDWARD IRVING BELCHER, M.C.

Born in London, 22nd March, 1893, son of A. H. Belcher, of Lawn Road, Hampstead.

Second Lieut., 4th March, 1916 (antedated to 20th December, 1915) ; Lieut., 1st July, 1917.

Served in France with the Artists' Rifles, from October, 1914 (bronze star). Joined 2nd Bn. as temporary Second Lieut., 20th March, 1915, and was wounded at Givenchy. Present at battle of Festubert, also on the Somme during July and October, 1916. Took part in the fighting on the Western front from March to November, 1918. Was awarded the Military Cross "for conspicuous gallantry and devotion to duty while in command of the company in close support. Thanks to his coolness and good leadership his line was held intact, although the enemy had forced the front line. He also very gallantly led his company in a counter attack later in the day."

STANLEY GEORGE OUTWIN

Born at Shepherd's Bush, 17th February, 1893, son of William Outwin.

Second Lieut., 22nd March, 1916 (antedated from 15th February, 1918) ; Lieut., 22nd September, 1917.

Attached to the Machine Gun Corps, was present at the fighting at Beaumont Hamel on 1st July, 1916. Wounded near Ypres in September, 1916, and again at Grandecourt on the Somme in October, 1916. Took part in the fighting at Arras, April and May, 1917 ; at Ypres in September and October, 1917 ; and at Cambrai, November, 1917. Was also present at Bailleul in April, 1918, and at Ypres in September and October, 1918.

BRIAN DORVILLE STRATFORD TUKE

Born, 26th February, 1887. Temp. Lieut. Army, 19th September, 1914 ; Cyclists' Corps, 1st December, 1914 ; 19th Foot, 29th March, 1916 ; Royal Air Force, 1st August, 1919.

Served with the Army Cyclists' Corps in Gallipoli and afterwards at Salonika (mentioned in despatches, bronze star).

GEORGE CEDRIC HODGKINSON

Born at Rotheram, 7th January, 1896, youngest son of Reginald Edward Hodgkinson, Solicitor, of Rotheram.

Second Lieut., 4th April, 1916.

Was appointed to a regular commission from the 8th Bn. York and Lancaster Regt., to which he was gazetted as a temporary Second Lieut., 11th November, 1914. With this Battalion, he served in France, from 27th August, 1915, and remained with it till his death. He saw a lot of heavy trench fighting, south of Armentières, Bois Grenin, La Boutillerie, and Fleurbaix. He was wounded, 1st July, 1916, in the attack on Mouquet Farm.

Died at Heilly, near Amiens, 4th July, 1916.

No boy had greater zest for life than he had, but before he went to the front, he said, if he had to fall he hoped it would be at the head of his men in a big attack. A flattering notice as to his cricket and football abilities appeared in the " Field," of 29th July, 1916.

HERBERT HUDSON MORRELL

Born at Smethwick, 27th October, 1897, son of Thomas George Morrell, of Smethwick, Staffs.

Second Lieut., 7th April, 1916 ; Lieut., 7th October, 1917 ; placed on half-pay, 24th August, 1919.

Had been attached to a York and Lancaster Bn. for 14 months, when he was wounded at Salonika on 9th November, 1917.

HUBERT SAMUEL ALSTON TURNER

Born at St. John's Wood, 23rd June, 1897, only son of Herbert Turner, of 90, Clifton Hill, St. John's Wood.

Second Lieut., 7th April, 1916.

Killed at Sanctuary Wood, Ypres, 31st July, 1917.

His platoon commander wrote : " I was in a position to see how splendidly he was doing his duty. He died going forward at the head of his men, leading them with the greatest courage, setting a fine example to all ranks. I cannot say how deeply we all miss him."

WILLIAM SPENCER FITZROBERT SAUNBY

Born, 2nd April, 1898, son of Professor Robert Saunby, F.R.C.P., LL.D., of Edgbaston, Birmingham.

Second Lieut., 7th April, 1916.

Joined the Royal Flying Corps, 7th July, 1916. Reported missing, 17th November, 1916, and presumed to have been killed.

ROLAND MILTON HARRIS

Born at Little Haseley, 9th February, 1898, eldest son of Milton Harris, of Little Haseley, Wallingford, Oxford.

Second Lieut., 7th April, 1916.

Took part in the battle of the Somme, 8th September, 1916, to 28th October, 1916. Appointed to the Royal Flying Corps, 20th April, 1917.

Killed at Arras, 7th June, 1917.

GEOFFREY CHARLES KINDERSLEY

Born, 16th January, 1898, son of Captain Charles Porcher Wilson Kindersley, late Coldstream Guards, of Clyffe, Dorchester.

Second Lieut., 7th April, 1916 ; Lieut., 7th October, 1917 ; 11th Hussars, 11th June, 1918 ; resigned, 28th March, 1919.

Joined the 2nd Bn. on 28th February, 1917, and was present in the fighting at Arras in April. Was wounded, 31st July, 1917, at Ypres.

CHRISTOPHER GRAY ROBINS

Born at Hampstead, 24th June, 1898, son of Harold Gray Robins, of Brook House, Wendover, Bucks.

Second Lieut., 7th April, 1916 ; Lieut., 7th October, 1917 ; York and Lancaster Regt., 28th March, 1918.

Served with Salonika Force in 1917-18.

JAMES MORTON LEACH

Born at Leeds, 10th February, 1898, son of Frederick Leach, of Rockfield, Halton, Leeds.

Second Lieut., 7th April, 1916 ; Lieut., 7th October, 1917 ; resigned, 16th December, 1919.

Served in France with the Royal Flying Corps, attached to the 29th Squadron, from April to November, 1917. Was in the fighting near Arras and Ypres and his services were twice brought to the notice of Headquarters for gallant conduct. Wounded and taken prisoner at Comines, 15th November, 1917.

ROBERT PARLBY WALTON

Born, 2nd February, 1891, son of J. Herbert Walton, of Cape Town and formerly of Teddington.

Second Lieut., 7th April, 1916.

Served with the Union troops in the Johannesburg riots of 1912, and for ten months with the 1st Rhodesian Regiment in South Africa, including the occupation of Swakopmund, German South-West Africa, 14th January, 1915, and actions at Namib, 7th February, 1915, and Trekkopjes, 26th April, 1915 (wounded). Was attached to the 7th Service Bn., 14th June, 1916 (wounded in January, 1917).

Died of wounds in France, 7th December, 1917.

HENRY BELL

Born, 13th April, 1892, son of J. J. Bell, Tyne House, Brocklesby Road, South Norwood.

Second Lieut., 20th May, 1916, from the ranks.

Proceeded to Belgium with 2nd Bn., and served with it till commissioned for distinguished conduct in the Field. Was wounded at Horse Shoe Trench in July, 1916, and again on the Menin Road in September, 1917, when attached to the 8th Service Bn.

Died of wounds, 17th October, 1917.

GERALD BAYNES CRAWFORD

Born at Roundhay, Leeds, 2nd April, 1892, son of James Crawford.

Second Lieut., 25th May, 1916 ; Lieut., 25th November, 1917.

Was appointed to a commission in the Leeds Rifles, 2nd October, 1915. Served in France attached to 9th Service Bn. from November, 1917, to February, 1919.

ALFRED CHARLES STRUGNELL

Second Lieut., 14th June, 1916, from Sergeant 16th Lancers.

Was promoted to a commission for distinguished conduct in the Field.

Killed in action at the battle of the Somme, near Montauban, 1st July, 1916.

HENRY THORNE KNIGHTS

Born at Kirkleatham, 20th June, 1886, only son of Edward George Knights, Registrar of births and deaths, Redcar, Yorkshire.

Second Lieut., 14th June, 1916, from the ranks of 5th Lancers.

Was promoted to a commission for distinguished conduct in the Field. Attached to a Trench Mortar Battery, 15th September, 1916.

Killed in action, 19th October, 1916.

HAROLD ARTHUR BRYAN DONKIN

Second Lieut., 19th July, 1916. Removed from the Army, 8th October, 1916, the King having no further use for his services as an officer.

Died of pneumonia in France when serving with The Queen's (Royal West Surrey Regt.).

GEORGE CLARENCE KNOWLES

Born, 31st July, 1897, only son of Louis Knowles, of Kirkwood, Palmer's Green, London.

Second Lieut., 16th August, 1916.

Joined the 9th Service Bn. in France in October, 1916. Wounded at Hill 60 about 7th June, 1917.

Died of his wounds, 10th June, 1917 (mentioned in despatches).

A brother officer wrote : " We have lost our very dearest and best beloved boy in the Battalion. He was idolized by his men. In difficult times in the trenches and when in rest behind the lines he was always doing something for the care of his platoon, and his boldness and absolute disregard of danger when in action were superb. The greatest thing he could have done he did gloriously, and his faithfulness in little simple matters was part of his life."

LAWRANCE DARVALL, M.C.

Born at Uxbridge, 24th November, 1898.

Second Lieut., 16th August, 1916 ; Lieut., 16th February, 1918 ; seconded, Royal Air Force, 11th November, 1919.

Served with the Salonika Expedition, November, 1916, to March, 1918, attached to 14th Bn. King's Liverpool Regt., and with the Royal Air Force, April to August, 1918, in Egypt (Military Cross).

EDWARD FRANCIS JOSEPH BULFIN, M.C.

Born at Dover, 8th November, 1898, son of Lieut.-Gen. Sir E. S. Bulfin, K.C.B., C.V.O., Colonel, 19th Foot.

Second Lieut., 16th August, 1916 ; Lieut., 16th February, 1918.

Proceeded to France, 4th October, 1916, as A.D.C. to G.O.C. 60th (London) Division, and in the same capacity to Salonika, 19th December, 1916. Left for Egypt, 19th June, 1917, as A.D.C. to G.O.C. 21st Corps. Was attached to 2nd Bn. Leicestershire Regt., 1st May, 1918, and returned to 21st Corps, 19th December, 1918, again as A.D.C., and was present at battle of Gaza, capture of Jerusalem, operations in 1917, and in the operations in 1918 in Palestine and Syria (Military Cross).

FRANCIS CLIFFORD AINLEY

Born at Stainland, 23rd July, 1898, son of Dr. F. S. Ainley, of Crossfield House, Stainland, Halifax, Yorkshire.

Second Lieut., 16th August, 1916 ; Lieut., 16th February, 1918.

Served with 2nd Bn. in France from 10th April, 1918, till accidentally wounded, 22nd April. Rejoined the battalion, 17th June, 1918, and served with it on the Western Front till the Armistice.

HERBERT PHILLIPS

Born, 4th January, 1885, 3rd son of W. J. Phillips, of Walthamstow, E.

Second Lieut., 1st October, 1916.

Killed in action on the Somme (Switch Trench), 13th October, 1916. He enlisted in the regiment in 1901, and was transferred to the Army Reserve as a Corporal in 1914. On the outbreak of the war, he was appointed Qr.-Mr. Sergt. at the Depôt, and went to the front in July, 1916, receiving his commission shortly afterwards. " He was a smart, keen soldier, a strict disciplinarian, and an expert shot and signaller. He possessed all the qualities which characterised a gentleman, and was loved by all with whom he came in contact " (G.H.G.).

HARRY HARGREAVES

Born at Manchester, 24th October, 1881, son of James Hargreaves, of Manchester.

Second Lieut., 14th November, 1916, from Warrant Officer 20th Foot ; Lieut., 14th May, 1918.

Was commissioned from Co. Sergt.-Major for service in the Field. Present at the operations on the Somme in 1916, and at Arras, Messines, and Ypres in 1917 (wounded).

JOHN HENRY O'HALLORAN

Born at Manchester, 24th October, 1881, son of John Henry O'Halloran.

Second Lieut., 15th November, 1916, from Warrant Officer, 20th Foot ; Lieut., 15th May, 1918 ; retired with a gratuity, 12th December, 1919.

Served in Gallipoli from April to June, and again from August, 1915, to January, 1916. In Egypt to March, 1916. In Belgium and France from July, 1916, to April, 1917. Was promoted to a commission for service in the field. Was present in the fighting at Arras with the 2nd Bn., where he was wounded, 9th April, 1917 (bronze star).

FRANK HARTLEY

Born at Sheffield, 5th February, 1884, son of Thomas Hartley.

Pte., 13th July, 1903 ; Corpl., 31st August, 1905 ; Sergt., January, 1908 ; Cr.-Sergt., 11th March, 1914 ; Co. Sergt.-Major, February, 1915. Second Lieut., 21st December, 1916 ; Lieut., 21st June, 1918 ; retires on retired pay, 19th May, 1920.

During the Great War, served in India with 1st Bn., and in the operations against the Afghans in 1919, as Signalling Officer.

GEORGE BALL

Born at Hillsborough, Sheffield, 31st December, 1884.
Pte., 17th August, 1904 ; Corpl., 6th June, 1906 ; Sergt., 16th January, 1908 ; Col.-Sergt., 17th October, 1914 ; Co. Qr.-Mr.-Sergt., February, 1915. Second Lieut., 21st December, 1916 ; Lieut., 21st June, 1918.

During the Great War, served in India with 1st Bn., and in the operations against the Afghans in 1919.

ADOLPH ANDRÉ WALSER, M.C., D.F.C.

Born, 8th April, 1889. Capt., 10th City of London Regt., 27th October, 1913 ; Capt., 19th Foot, 27th December, 1916 ; Squadron Leader, Royal Flying Corps, 1st August, 1919.

Served with the Royal Flying Corps in France from 26th April, 1916, to 31st March, 1918 (twice mentioned in despatches, Croix de Guerre, Military Cross). Awarded the M.C. " as a brilliant and exceptionally able squadron commander, who, by his unsparing efforts and his fine personal example, has raised the morale of his squadron to a very high level. The comprehensive and detailed information obtained by Major Walser in the large number of low reconnaissances he has conducted has proved of the greatest value to his corps."

ERNEST VIVIAN FOX, M.C., D.C.M.

Born at Saltaire, 19th June, 1884, son of Smith Fox, of Saltaire, Shipley.

Second Lieut., 31st December, 1916, from Warrant Officer ; Lieut., 30th June, 1918.

Served with the 2nd Bn. in Belgium and France from October, 1914, to June, 1915, and was present at the battles of Ypres, Neuve Chapelle, Festubert and Givenchy. Was awarded the Distinguished Conduct medal for conspicuous gallantry during the winter of 1914-15, when he frequently made daring reconnaissances of the enemy's position at great personal risk. Served with the 6th Service Bn. from 18th September, 1915, to November, 1916, including the Dardenelles, Egypt and battle of the Somme. Awarded a clasp to the Distinguished Conduct medal for conspicuous gallantry in action. He assumed command of a company, and led his men with great courage and determination. He set a splendid example to his men throughout the operations. Promoted to a commission for distinguished service in the field. Served with the 7th Service Bn. from January, 1915, to May, 1917, including the battle of Arras, when he was wounded (15th May, 1917). Was awarded the Military Cross for " having, when in command of a bombing party, led his men with great gallantry and determination, driving the enemy back and improving our hold upon their trench. He was badly wounded, but remained in command until the objective was secured." Also in possession of the Russian medal of St. George, 2nd Class, and the bronze star with clasp. From 21st October, 1918, to 3rd November, 1919, served with the 1st Bn. Nigeria Regt.

GEORGE WALTER BIELBY, M.C.

Born, 28th February, 1885. Second Lieut., 31st December, 1916, from Warrant Officer. Dismissed the Service by sentence of a General Court Martial, 25th November, 1917.

Mentioned in depatches, 14th November, 1916, and promoted to a commission for service in the Field. Awarded the Military Cross " For conspicuous gallantry in action. He showed great skill and determination in carrying out a bombing attack, which finally gained the enemy trench. Later, he greatly assisted his company officer in the retaking of a lost trench."

RONALD MACDONALD, D.C.M.

Born, 20th February, 1881. Second Lieut., 3rd January, 1917, from Warrant Officer ; Lieut., 3rd July, 1918 ; seconded, King's African Rifles, 20th February, 1918.

Promoted to a commission for service in the Field. Served with 13th Service Bn. in the war. Was awarded the Distinguished Conduct medal " For conspicuous gallantry in action. He assumed command of his company and handled his men with great courage and determination. He set a splendid example throughout " (mentioned in despatches, 14th November, 1916). In possession of the medal for long service and good conduct.

Died at Blackpool, 29th February, 1920, on his way to join the 2nd Bn. at Tipperary.

DURHAM DONALD GEORGE HALL, M.C.

Born in London, 5th January, 1898, son of Sydney Donald Edward Hall.

Second Lieut., 5th January, 1917.

Served in France with the Royal Flying Corps from 16th March, 1916, to 3rd January, 1917. Awarded the Military Cross " For conspicuous gallantry in action. He has flown in the worst of weather and often at very low altitudes. On one occasion, he flew very low under a heavy fire from the ground, in order to range our artillery."

Died in France of wounds, 27th March, 1918.

JAMES WILSON

Second Lieut., 27th January, 1917, from ranks of Scots Guards ; Lieut., 27th July, 1918.

Promoted to a commission for distinguished conduct in the Field. Attached to Machine Gun Corps from 27th January, 1917.

JOSEPH AFFORD, M.C., D.C.M.

Born at Offord, Hunts, 18th April, 1888, son of Charles Afford, of Huntingdon.

Second Lieut., 3rd February, 1917, from Warrant Officer, 16th Foot ; Lieut., 3rd August, 1918.

Served in the battle of Ypres, 1914, with Bedfordshire Regt. (wounded). Present at Hill 60, April and May, 1915 ; at the battle of the Somme, 1916 (wounded at Longueval ; awarded the medal for distinguished conduct in the Field). Was again wounded at Falfermont Farm and also at Morval in September, 1916 (mentioned in despatches). Took part in the fighting at Messines in June and at Passchendaele Ridge. July to September, 1917, including the operations at White House in August, 1917. Awarded the Military Cross " for conspicuous gallantry and devotion to duty in successfully carrying out the task allotted to his company of capturing a house under heavy fire " (promoted to a commission for distinguished conduct in the Field, bronze star and clasp).

ROBERT POSTILL

Born, 29th August, 1893. Second Lieut., 5th February, 1917, from the ranks of 14th Foot ; Lieut., 5th August, 1918 ; retired on account of ill health caused by wounds, 1st May, 1919.

Proceeded to France with 1st Bn. 14th Foot, 7th September, 1914, and fought at the Aisne and the Marne (wounded at Parady, 20th October, bronze star and clasp). Was again wounded at Loos, 1st September,

1916. Was engaged on the Somme, November, 1916; at Messines, June, 1917, the advance east of Ypres, July, 1917, and in the fighting at Passchendaele Ridge (wounded, 27th August, 1917). Promoted to a commission from Sergeant for service in the Field.

PERCY SNELLING

Born at Horsford, Norfolk, 23rd December, 1889, son of Henry Snelling, of Hellesdon, Norwich.

Second Lieut., 16th February, 1917, from ranks of 12th Lancers ; Lieut., 16th August, 1918.

Proceeded to France with the 12th Lancers, and was at Mons, the Aisne, the Marne, and also in the fighting at Ypres in 1914 (bronze star and clasp). Wounded 28th October, at Ypres. Was present at the Somme in September, 1916. Promoted to a commission from Sergt. for distinguished conduct in the Field. Was with the 2nd Bn. in the fighting at Arras (wounded 9th April, 1917). Also at Ypres in August, 1917, and at Hill 70 in November, 1917.

ERNEST JOHN READINGS, M.C.

Born at Reading, 10th May, 1885.

Second Lieut., 19th February, 1917, from Warrant Officer, Duke of Wellington's Regt. ; Lieut., 19th August, 1918.

Served in France with 2nd and 8th Bns. Duke of Wellington's Regt. from 13th August, 1914 ,till promoted to a commission for distinguished conduct in the Field (bronze star and clasp). Was wounded at Hill 60 Ypres, 18th April, 1915, and again at Rancourt, 1st March, 1917. (Awarded Military Cross, 1st January, 1918.)

FREDERICK AUGUSTUS FOLEY, M.C.

Born at Fort Napier, Pietermaritzburg, 6th March, 1879, son of Sergeant-Major Foley, of the Buffs.

Second Lieut., 22nd February, 1917, from the ranks of the 3rd Foot ; Lieut., 22nd August, 1918 ; retired with a gratuity and rank of Captain, 22nd August, 1919.

Served in France with the Expeditionary Force from 13th August, 1914 (bronze star and clasp). Promoted to a commission from Sergt. for distinguished conduct in the Field. Was awarded the Military Cross, 16th September, 1918, when attached to 7th Bn. for the following act : " During a withdrawal he collected a party of stragglers, and on four successive occasions took up a position and checked the enemy, inflicting casualties. He afterwards amalgamated with Allied troops, and took a prominent part in further operations, shewing fine leadership and courage."

JAMES HOUGH PALIN

Born at Stoke-on-Trent, 1st January, 1884, son of George Palin, of Stoke-on-Trent.

Second Lieut., 5th March, 1917, from ranks of the Wiltshire Regt. ; Lieut., 5th September, 1918 ; retired on retired pay, 6th March, 1920.

Served with Royal Scots Fusiliers in France from 1st November, 1914, and was wounded at Kemmel, 16th December, 1914 (bronze star and clasp). Was again wounded at St. Eloi, 9th May, 1915. Took part in the second battle of Ypres and at Arras (wounded, 20th April, 1917). Was promoted to a commission for service in the Field.

ROBERT MULLANEY, M.C.

Born, 30th November, 1886. Second Lieut., 6th March, 1917, from Sergeant, 17th Lancers ; Lieut., 6th September, 1918.

Was promoted to a commission for service in the Field. Wounded in September, 1918, when attached to the East Yorkshire Regt. (Military Cross, 1st January, 1918).

FREDERICK WILLIAM HOLMES, V.C.

Born in Bermondsey, 27th September, 1889, son of Thomas George Holmes, of Birmingham.

Second Lieut., 14th March, 1917, from the ranks ; Lieut., 14th September, 1918.

Enlisted in the King's Own Yorkshire L.I. in 1908, and proceeded to France on the outbreak of the Great War. As a Lce.-Corpl. was awarded the Victoria Cross for having at Le Cateau, on the 26th August, 1914, carried a wounded man out of the trenches under heavy fire, and later assisted to drive a gun out of action by taking the place of a driver who had been wounded. He was also granted the Medaille Militaire for carrying a machine gun to a platoon of French soldiers, who were struggling against heavy odds. Was wounded 28th October, 1914 (twice mentioned in despatches, bronze star and clasp). Transferred, 6th October, 1915, to 1st Garrison Bn. of the Green Howards, and proceeded to India with it in December, 1915. Promoted Sergt. 10th October, 1915. On being commissioned was attached to the 9th Bn. Worcestershire Regt., and went to Mesopotamia in July, 1917. There, owing to an accident, he sustained a fracture of the skull in October, and was invalided home in January, 1918. Employed at Infantry Record Office, London, since October, 1918.

CUTHBERT CATTERSON

Born at Houghton-le-Spring, Co. Durham, 19th April, 1888, son of — Catterson, of Hemsworth, near Wakefield, Yorkshire.

Pte., 11th October, 1904 ; Corpl., 24th December, 1914 ; Sergt., September, 1916. Second Lieut., 7th April, 1917 ; Lieut., 7th October, 1918.

Served with 2nd Bn. in the first battle of Ypres and at Neuve Chapelle (wounded). Also with 6th Service Bn. at Gallipoli, Egypt and France, and was wounded at Stuff Redoubt (29th September, 1916) and at Hermies (1st May, 1917). Rejoined 2nd Bn. in April, 1918, and took part in all the fighting on the Western front till he was again wounded at Epinoy in September, 1918 (bronze star and clasp, promoted to a commission for service in the Field).

HENRY JOHN SMITH

Born, 21st January, 1889. Second Lieut., 9th April, 1917, from the ranks ; Lieut., 9th October, 1918 ; retired with a gratuity, 24th January, 1920.

Proceeded to Belgium with 2nd Bn. in October, 1914, and was wounded at Fleurbaix (bronze star and clasp). Served also in the Dardanelles, Egypt and France with 6th Service Bn. to April, 1917. Was wounded at Mesnil in December, 1916. Served again in France with 8th Service Bn., and was promoted to a commission for distinguished conduct in the Field. Wounded at Messines, 9th June, and again at Ypres, 20th September, 1917.

ALFRED MARGRETT

Born at East Dean, Gloucestershire, 19th November, 1888, son of Walter W. Margrett.

Second Lieut., 9th April, 1917, from the ranks of the 15th Foot; Lieut., 9th October, 1918; retired with a gratuity, 17th August, 1919.

Served in France with the Royal Dragoons in October, 1914, and was later transferred to the East Yorkshire Regiment (bronze star and clasp). Was wounded at Ypres, 13th May, 1915, and again at Loos, 15th November, 1916. Joined 2nd Bn., 15th April, 1917, having been promoted for service in the Field, and was present in the fighting at Arras and in the vicinity of Ypres up to 8th January, 1918.

EDWARD ALBERT GREENWOOD

Born in London, 6th January, 1885, son of Richard Greenwood.

Second Lieut., 15th April, 1917, from Warrant Officer; Lieut., 15th October, 1918; retired with a gratuity, 19th July, 1919, and hon. rank of Captain.

Embarked with 2nd Bn. for Belgium in 1914, and was wounded at Neuve Chapelle, 11th March, 1915 (bronze star and clasp). Joined the 7th Service Bn. in July, 1915, and served with it till promoted to a commission for distinguished conduct in the Field. Took part in the fighting at Arras in April, 1917, and was transport officer to the 2nd Bn. during the operations on the Western Front in 1918.

VERNUS FREDERICK BERNARD SANDERS, M.C.

Born at Coxbench, Derbyshire, 1st October, 1886, son of George Sanders.

Second Lieut., 16th April, 1917, from Warrant Officer, Sherwood Foresters; Lieut., 16th October, 1918.

Served in France from 29th September, 1914, and was present at the fighting at Ypres in October, and at Armentières in December, 1914 (wounded, bronze star and clasp). Went to the Dardanelles with 9th Bn. Sherwood Foresters and was at the landing at Suvla Bay and remained till the evacuation in December, 1915 (wounded, 9th August, 1915). Returned to France and was in the attack on Thiepval in September, 1916, and at Beaumont in November, 1916. Having been promoted to a commission for distinguished conduct in the Field, he took part with the 2nd Bn. in the fighting at Arras in April, 1917, and in the advance east of Ypres in July, 1917 (twice mentioned in despatches, and Military Cross). Carried the Regimental Colour in the Victory march through Paris on 14th July and through London on the 19th July, 1919.

JAMES BELL

Born, 9th June, 1886. Second Lieut., 18th April, 1917, from ranks of the Yorkshire Light Infantry. Placed on half-pay on account of ill health caused by wounds, 20th September, 1918.

Promoted to a commission from Acting Sergt.-Major, Yorkshire L.I. Took part in the fighting at Arras with the 2nd Bn. in April, 1917 (wounded).

HERBERT LOVEL HANNAM

Born at Monk Bretton, near Barnsley, 28th February, 1898, son of the Revd. William Robert Hannam, Felixkirk Vicarage, Thirsk, Yorkshire.

Second Lieut., 1st May, 1917 ; Lieut., 1st November, 1918 ; seconded, Indian Army, 3rd May, 1918.

Joined 2nd Bn. in France 11th June, 1917, and was wounded at Sanctuary Wood, Ypres, 31st July, 1917.

DOUGLAS BERTRAM RICHARDSON

Born at Ilkley, Yorkshire, 5th May, 1897, son of J. N. Richardson, M.D., of Hampton House, Ilkley.

Second Lieut., 1st May, 1917.

Served with the Royal Flying Corps (18th Squadron) in France, and was wounded 10th April, 1918.

GEORGE TWEEDALE MILNES

Born at West Town Vicarage, Dewsbury, 21st June, 1898, son of the Revd. Frederick George Milnes, Vicar of North Hykeham, Lincoln.

Second Lieut., 1st May, 1917 ; Lieut., 1st May, 1918.

Served with the Machine Gun Corps in France attached to the 20th Light Division from November 27th, 1917. With the 5th Army during its withdrawal in March, 1918, when he was wounded and reported missing at Voyennes on the Somme on the 23rd March, 1918.

FREDERICK CHARLES SHERWOOD

Born at Poole, 27th December, 1884, son of Charles Frederick Sherwood, of Talbot, Bournemouth.

Second Lieut., 19th May, 1917, from the ranks ; Lieut., 19th November, 1918.

Served in the Irish Rebellion of 1916, attached to the 4th Bn. Leicestershire Regt. as Regtl. Sergt.-Major. Served also in France with it and with the 7th Service Bn. from January to September, 1917. Was wounded at Fauvrecourt on the Somme (mentioned in despatches) 4th March, 1917, and again in the fighting at Arras on the 10th June, 1917. Promoted to a commission for distinguished service in the Field. Was employed with the East African Expeditionary Force from January to April, 1918, and in German and Portuguese E.A. from May, 1918, to May, 1919. Mentioned in the Portuguese Field Marshal's orders for work at Monopo, P.E.A., in July, 1919, and in Lieut.-Gen. Van Deventer's despatch of May, 1919. Is an interpreter in Swahili.

WALTER THOMAS ELLIS

Born at Hale, Surrey, 27th November, 1886, son of D. Ellis, of Horsham, Sussex.

Second Lieut., 22nd June, 1917, from Sergeant, 12th Lancers ; Lieut., 22nd December, 1918.

Served in France and Italy from 20th October, 1915 (bronze star). Promoted to a commission for distinguished conduct in the Field. Was wounded in November, 1918.

GEORGE FREDERICK PEARCE

Born at Haggerston, London, 28th September, 1881.

Second Lieut., 22nd June, 1917, from the ranks of the 9th Lancers ; Lieut., 22nd December, 1918 ; retired with a gratuity, 11th July, 1919.

Served with the 9th Lancers and 8th Service Bn. in France from January, 1915, to November, 1917, and in Italy from November, 1917, to end of the war. Was promoted to a commission for service in the Field (bronze star).

CHARLES THOMAS HEPWORTH, M.C.

Born at Shorncliffe, 27th July, 1886, son of Thomas Hepworth.

Second Lieut., 22nd June, 1917, from the ranks of the 12th Lancers ; Lieut., 22nd December, 1918 ; retired with a gratuity, 31st January, 1920.

Embarked with the Expeditionary Force in 1914, and was present at Mons, the battles of the Marne, the Aisne, first battle of Ypres and Neuve Chapelle, also second battle of Ypres, Loos (September-October, 1915), Passchendaele Ridge, Arras, and Somme, 1917. Served in Italy from 13th November, 1917, to 28th March, 1919, and took part in the great advance in September and October, 1918 (bronze star and clasp, and Military Cross). Was promoted to a commission from Sergt. in 12th Lancers for service in the Field. Was awarded the M.C. 19th November, 1917, under the following circumstances : "He showed great courage in patrol work after the occupation of the objective. Later, with a working party, he dug a long communication trench under continuous shell fire, and by his foresight and leadership got his party back without casualties."

PATRICK HARRY WHITWELL

Born, 16th March, 1893. Second Lieut., 3rd July, 1917, from the ranks for service in the Field.

Killed in action, 25th April, 1918.

WILLIAM HENRY ALLIS

Born, 3rd July, 1884. Second Lieut., 5th July, 1917, from Warrant Officer ; retired with a gratuity, 18th May, 1919.

Joined 10th Bn., 5th July, 1917, and was wounded 7th October, 1917, and again in April, 1918, when he was taken prisoner. Promoted to a commission for service in the Field.

CHARLES MORRIS

Born, 27th May, 1882. Second Lieut., 26th August, 1917, from ranks of the 17th Lancers ; Lieut., 26th February, 1919 ; retired with a gratuity, 14th February, 1920.

Served in the ranks of the 17th Lancers in France from 8th November, 1914, to August, 1916, and in the Machine Gun Corps from that date onwards. Promoted to a commission and seconded with the Machine Gun Corps, 26th August, 1917 (bronze star and clasp).

HENRY JOSEPH LUCAS, M.C., D.C.M., M.M.

Born at West Ham, 24th November, 1882, son of John Lucas, of West Ham.

Second Lieut., 29th August, 1917, from Warrant Officer ; Lieut., 28th February, 1919 ; retired with a gratuity, 14th July, 1919.

Embarked with 2nd Bn. in October, 1914, and was present at the fighting at Ypres (1914), Neuve Chapelle, Festubert, Givenchy, and Loos, 1915. At the Somme in 1916 and Arras 1917. Also during all the fighting on the Western Front from 3rd April, 1918, up to the Armistice. (Mentioned in despatches, promoted to a commission from Co.-Sergt.-

Major, bronze star and clasp, Military medal, medal for distinguished conduct in the Field and Military Cross.) He was awarded the D.C.M. "for gallantry on many occasions between 16th-25th October, 1914, in conveying messages under heavy fire along a firing line extending for 1,000 yards."

NORMAN MORANT

Born at Leeds, 5th October, 1893, son of Alfred Morant.

Second Lieut., 29th August, 1917, from ranks of the Scots Guards.

Served in France with Scots Guards and was present at the battles of Mons, the Aisne, Neuve Chapelle (March, 1915), Richebourg (May, 1915), Loos (September, 1915), and the Somme (September, 1916). Promoted to a commission and joined the 2nd Bn., 8th December, 1917. Was reported wounded and missing at Roupy, 22nd March, 1918, and died in a German Field Hospital at St. Quentin 27th March, 1918.

EDMUND CECIL BOYD SHANNON

Born, 11th September, 1898, son of Major William Boyd Shannon, D.S.O., 6th Service Bn.

Second Lieut., 12th September, 1917.

Joined the 2nd Bn. in France 18th October, 1917. Seconded to Indian Army 20th March, 1918.

JOHN STANLEY GRAHAM BRANSCOMBE

Born at Chester, 28th June, 1898, son of the Revd. Harry Stanley Branscombe, Marham Vicarage, Downham Market, Norfolk.

Second Lieut., 12th September, 1917 ; Lieut., 12th March, 1919.

Joined 2nd Bn. 25th November, 1917, and was wounded at Dickebusch 30th April, 1918.

HERMAN BYSSHE BAGSHAWE BICKNELL

Born at Northam, N. Devon, 16th January, 1889, son of Capt. Herman K. Bicknell, Oxford and Buckinghamshire L.I.

Second Lieut., 12th September, 1917.

Went to France 17th April, 1918, and was killed in action 28th May, 1918, when attached to East Yorkshire Regt. He was a nephew of Capt. E. G. C. Bagshawe, late 19th Foot, who was killed in France, 20th July, 1916.

ALBERT SHANN

Born at Adel, near Leeds, 23rd August, 1887, son of Joseph Shann.

Second Lieut., 26th September, 1917, from ranks of Royal Engineers.

He joined the Royal Engineers as a Pte. 4th October, 1910, and served with them in France from 14th August, 1914, being present at the battles of Mons, the Marne, the Aisne, first and second battles of Ypres, Neuve Chapelle (March, 1915), Loos (September, 1915), the Somme (July, 1916), and Messines (June, 1917). Was wounded at Hill 60, Ypres, 12th May, 1915. Joined 2nd Bn. 18th January, 1918, being promoted to a commission from Corpl. R.E.

Killed at Voormezeele, near Ypres, 8th May, 1918.

HARRY BRADBURY, M.C.

Born at Sheffield, 19th April, 1892, son of A. Bradbury, of Sheffield.

Second Lieut., 26th September, 1917, from ranks of the 5th Lancers ; Lieut., 26th March, 1919.

Served in France from 20th December, 1914, till 26th July, 1917. Promoted to a commission from Corpl. 5th Lancers and joined 2nd Bn. 19th January, 1918, and served with it till 30th March, 1918. Was awarded the Military Cross under the following circumstances : "During recent operations he was wounded in the first day of the attack, but remained at duty for eight days, showing great courage, till finally exhausted by his wound and lack of sleep and food. His pluck merits great praise" (bronze star).

ARNOLD LUPTON SHAW

Born at Harrogate, 19th January, 1896, son of F. W. Shaw, Registrar of births and deaths, Harrogate.

Second Lieut., 26th September, 1917, from ranks of the 5th Lancers ; Lieut., 26th March, 1919.

Proceeded with the 5th Lancers to France in August, 1914, and was present at the battles of the Aisne, Ypres, Somme (1916), and Arras (1917). Joined 2nd Bn. 18th January, 1918, having been promoted to a commission, and was wounded, 26th April, 1918, near Ypres (bronze star and clasp).

HERBERT EDWARD WEBB

Born at Richmond, Yorkshire, 5th April, 1882, son of James Webb, 19th Foot.

Boy, April, 1900 ; Corpl., April, 1901 ; Sergt., October, 1903 ; Clr.-Sergt., 30th July, 1907 ; Co.-Sergt.-Major, 30th October, 1914 ; Regtl.-Sergt.-Major 5th Bn. Northumberland Fusiliers, 2nd May, 1916 ; 2nd Lieut., 19th Foot, 14th October, 1917 ; Lieut., 14th April, 1919.

Present at the battle of the Somme (August to December, 1916), Arras (April, May, 1917), and at Ypres (October, 1917). Wounded at Armentières 11th April, 1918, when acting as Adjt. to 1st 4th Bn. (mentioned in despatches and promoted to a commission). Wounded and taken prisoner at Chemin des Dames, 27th May, 1918.

HARRY SPENCER VAREY, M.C., D.C.M.

Born at Burley Wood, Leeds, 24th May, 1886, son of George Varey.

Corpl., 16th January, 1908 ; Sergt., 25th January, 1911 ; Co.-Sergt.-Major, 19th June, 1915 ; 2nd Lieut., 28th November, 1917 ; Lieut., 28th May, 1919 ; retired with a gratuity and hon. rank of Capt., 12th August, 1919.

Landed with 7th Division in Belgium in October, 1914, and was present with 2nd Bn. at the battle of Ypres (bronze star and clasp). Took part in the battles of Neuve Chapelle (March, 1915), Festubert, Givenchy, and Loos, Guillemont (August, 1916), Le Sars, and the Somme (October, 1916), and in the advance east of Ypres in July, 1917. Awarded the Distinguished Conduct medal "for conspicuous gallantry and devotion to duty. Throughout the operations he set a splendid example to the men, and was of the greatest assistance in controlling the Company, which was short of officers. His coolness and courage under heavy fire was most marked." (Promoted to a commission for distinguished service.)

He also took part in the fighting on the Western Front, and was wounded in June, 1918, when attached to 1st Bn. East Yorkshire Regt. Was awarded the Military Cross "For conspicuous gallantry and devotion to duty on 18th September, 1918, at Villers Guislain. He led his Company to its objective, changing direction en route, and rushed the trenches, capturing many prisoners. As the troops on his right failed to get up, that flank was exposed, and, though the enemy made repeated attacks the whole of the 18th and 19th, enfilading the trench with machine gun fire, he held on in spite of heavy casualties."

HERBERT HUDSON

Born, 22nd May, 1882. Pte., January, 1900 ; Sergt., 1910 ; Co.-Sergt.-Major, 1916 ; 2nd Lieut., 28th November, 1917 ; Lieut., 28th May, 1919 ; retired with a gratuity, 29th November, 1919.

Served in the Boer War, 1900-02, with 1st Bn. (Queen's medal and 3 clasps, King's medal and 2 clasps). During the war of 1914-18 served in West Africa with the West India Regt., March, 1915, to April, 1916. In France from October, 1916, to June, 1917 (bronze star, promoted to a commission for service in the Field.

JOHN DUDLEY STANHOPE HOLROYD-SERGEANT, M.C.

Born at Sydenham, 15th November, 1898, son of Walter Holroyd-Sergeant, of Sydenham.

Second Lieut., 21st December, 1917 ; Lieut., 21st June, 1919 ; resigned his commission, 21st February, 1920.

Served in France with the 13th Service Bn. from April to July, 1918, and in North Russia on the Murmansk Front from October, 1918, to February, 1919, and on the Archangel Front from February to October, 1919. Awarded the Military Cross "on the early morning of 3rd April, 1919, he took up reinforcements to help the party in the block-house at the 4½ verst on Alexandrovo Road. Whilst his men were still in the sledges he met the party from the block-house retiring on Sved Mekrenga. At the same moment he was fired on from both flanks. Owing to his great coolness and the fine example set by him the whole party was extricated with only the loss of one sledge. Later, when in charge of a block-house, he was strongly attacked by the enemy, but repulsed them with heavy casualties, leaving over 100 prisoners in our hands, with four machine guns."

ALFRED MASON

Born at Malton, Yorkshire, 25th June, 1888, son of John Mason.

Second Lieut., 27th December, 1917, from Warrant Officer, 23rd Foot ; Lieut., 27th June, 1919.

In the war of 1914-18, served in the operations on the N.W. Frontier of India, 1914-15, in the Tochi Valley and Dejarat, and in Mesopotamia from August, 1916, to March, 1919, including the capture of Kut and Baghdad and the operations at Mile Plain, Adhaim and Sacacutan Pass (bronze star, promoted to a Commission for service in the Field).

JAMES ELLIS, M.C.

Born at Bradford, 25th November, 1888, son of D. Ellis, of Bradford.

Second Lieut., 9th January, 1918, from Warrant Officer ; Lieut., 9th July, 1919.

In the Great War took part in the first battle of Ypres (bronze star and clasp). Afterwards served with 6th Bn. from September, 1915, to June, 1916, in Gallipoli and Egypt. Was in France from July, 1916, to January, 1918, and was present at the battles of the Somme, Messines (1916), Poelcappelle, and Steenbeck (1917), Croisselles (1918). Wounded at Ypres 23rd November, 1914, and again at Croisselles 21st March, 1918. Promoted to a commission for service in the Field. Took part in the Russian Campaign on the Archangel Front under Major-Gen. Ironside with the 13th Bn., and was awarded the Military Cross and the Order of St. Anne of Russia under the following circumstances :—

" For marked gallantry and devotion to duty on June 8th-9th, 1919, near Alexandrovo. Although the Russian flanking party had withdrawn, he attempted to rush a hostile post with eight men. On June 15th, with a patrol of twelve other ranks, he kept up a running fight for three hours with an enemy patrol about 100 strong. A splendid leader, who can always get the best out of his men."

ALEXANDER WILLIAM McCARTHY

Born at St. Helier's, Jersey, 29th August, 1894, son of William McCarthy.

Second Lieut., 13th January, 1918, from the ranks ; Lieut., 13th July, 1919. Placed on half-pay on account of ill-health caused by wounds, 24th September, 1919.

Proceeded to Belgium with 2nd Bn. and was present at the first battle of Ypres (bronze star and clasp). Was afterwards posted to the 6th Bn., and took part in the landing at Suvla Bay. The Bn. was later transferred to Egypt and then France, when he was at the battle of the Somme (1916), and at Stuff Redoubt (29th September). Also in the fighting at Loos, Ypres, including Steenbecke, and Poelcappelle in 1917. Being posted to the 5th Bn., he was at Passchendaele Ridge, and at Hamel in March, 1918. During the fighting in 1918 was wounded at Ephy-on-Somme in April, 1918, when with the 10th Bn.

WILLIAM PETER BURKETT

Second Lieut., 26th January, 1918, from ranks of the 18th Foot.

Joined 2nd Bn. in France 26th January, 1918, on promotion for service in the Field. Shot dead by an Australian Pte. in France, 23rd April, 1918. Buried in Ebblinghem British Cemetery, west of Hazebrouck.

Second Lieut. Burkett noticed a man loafing near his billet at the 30th Divisional Wing Reinforcement Training Camp about 11 p.m. on the 23rd April, 1918. He asked him what he was doing, when the Australian said : " What's that to you !" and pulled out a revolver, fired at 2nd Lieut. Burkett, missed him, and ran away. He was then pursued by 2nd Lieut. Burkett and another officer, and when the Australian was being caught up, he turned and shot the former through the head.

ALBERT VICTOR WOOLLASTON

Born at Aston, 17th August, 1892, son of Charles Woollaston, of Aston, Birmingham.

Second Lieut., 24th February, 1918 ; retired with a gratuity, 15th June, 1919.

Served in the ranks of the 13th Hussars in France, 1914-15 (bronze star), and with Motor Machine Gun Corps in the Western Frontier Field Force, Egypt, 1916-17, and in Palestine and Egypt, November, 1917, to March, 1919. Promoted to a commission from Sergt. in the M.G.C. for service in the Field.

FREDERICK POOLE

Born at Chatham, 4th January, 1889, son of William Poole.

Second Lieut., 27th February, 1918, from ranks of the 3rd Hussars ; retired with a gratuity, 15th October, 1919.

Served with the 3rd Hussars in France from August, 1914, to November, 1917, and was present at the battles of Mons, the Marne, Ypres (1914), Neuve Chapelle (March, 1915), operations on the Somme (July, 1916), and before Arras in 1917; also operations before Lille, 1918 (bronze star and clasp and promotion to a commission).

CHARLES WALTER WYATT

Born at Taungo, Burmah, 27th January, 1892, son of Clr.-Sergt. Walter Wyatt, 19th Foot.

Second Lieut., 27th February, 1918, from the ranks ; retired with a gratuity, 15th June, 1919.

Served in France with 2nd Bn., and was wounded at the battle of Ypres, 31st October, 1914 (bronze star and clasp). Rejoined in April, 1915, and was present at the battle of Loos in September, 1915, and at the Somme in July, 1916. Served in Egypt with the Royal Air Force from 5th October, 1918, to 1st February, 1919.

FREDERICK MARCH, M.C., M.M.

Born, 24th December, 1892. Pte., 1st September, 1911 ; Corpl., June, 1915 ; Sergt., 3rd July, 1916 ; 2nd Lieut., 27th March, 1918 ; half-pay, 7th January, 1920, on account of ill-health caused by wounds.

Served with the 2nd Bn. in Belgium and France in 1914, and was present at the fighting round Ypres (bronze star and clasp). Was at the battles of Neuve Chapelle, Festubert, Givenchy, and Loos in 1915. On the Somme (Glatz Redoubt and Montauban), 1st July, 1916, Trônes Wood (7th July), and Guillemont (23rd August, 1916). In the Arras operations including Henin, Neuville Vitasse (April, 1917), and Inverness Copse, east of Ypres, 20th September, 1917. Took part with the 6th Bn. in the Russian operations on the Archangel Front under Major-Gen. Ironside (wounded). Awarded the Military Cross " on 23rd March, 1919, when his Company Commander was killed, he led the Company within 200 yards of the enemy in deep snow. He cooly walked up and down his lines under heavy fire, keeping his platoons in touch with each other. On being ordered to retire, he skilfully withdrew his command, bringing back all wounded. He shewed cool courage and ability to command."

FRANK TINHAM THEWLIS, M.C.

Born at Huddersfield, 7th August, 1893, son of Frederick Thewlis, of Richmond, Yorkshire.

Second Lieut., 27th March, 1918, from ranks of 3rd Dragoon Guards ; Lieut., 27th September, 1919.

In the war of 1914-18. Served in Egypt and France, including the first and second battles of Ypres, Loos (1915), Somme (1916), and Arras (1917). Was wounded at Hooge in June, 1915, and at Vermelles in January, 1916. Took part also in the fighting on the Western Front in 1918 (bronze star and clasp, promoted to a commission and Military

Cross). Is in possession of the Hon. Testimonial of the Royal Humane Society for having on the 3rd May, 1916, gone to the rescue of a child who was in imminent danger of drowning in the river at Beaurainville, France, and whose life he gallantly assisted in saving.

When attached to the 15th Bn. Yorkshire Light Infantry was awarded the Military Cross "for gallantry and devotion to duty. At Houplines on the night of October 8th-9th, 1918, when bringing rations up to the Bn., two horses alarmed by shell fire bolted towards the enemy lines. He rode forward and recovered them under heavy machine gun fire. At Houplines on the night of October 9th-10th, when bringing limbers up to the Bn., the transport came under shell fire, and his coolness and grip of the situation saved a stampede. He had his horse shot under him, and his courage and initiative alone ensured rations reaching the advanced troops."

FREDERICK GEORGE GLANVILLE WARE

Born, at Poplar, London, 20th February, 1892, son of H. J. Ware, of Farnham Royal, Buckinghamshire.

Second Lieut., 27th March, 1918, from ranks of 6th Dragoons ; Lieut., 27th September, 1919.

During the war of 1914-18, served with the Inniskilling Dragoons from November, 1914, to October, 1917, in France (bronze star). Promoted to a commission and joined 2nd Bn., 27th July, 1918, taking part in the fighting at Cambrai September to November, 1918.

CHARLES WILLIAM STIRK

Born at Leeds, 20th July, 1894.

Second Lieut., 11th May, 1918, from ranks of the Royal Horse Guards ; Lieut., 11th November, 1919.

Took part in the second battle of Ypres and Loos in 1915 (bronze star). Attached to Machine Gun Corps, was in the fighting on the Somme (1916), at Arras (1917), on the Somme in 1918, and Chemin des Dames. Promoted to a commission from Squad. Qr.-Mr.-Sergt. Machine Gun Corps for service in the Field.

Taken prisoner at Craon 27th May, 1918, when attached to 4th Bn.

ARTHUR THOMAS HUGHES

Born at Chelsea, 11th October, 1892.

Second Lieut., 27th June, 1918 ; Lieut., 27th December, 1919.

Served in the ranks for four years in the 5th Bn. Bedfordshire Regt., and 1st 8th Bn. Royal Warwickshire. Promoted to a temporary Commission, 27th June, 1917.

Took part in the operations on the Somme 1916-17, and before Ypres in 1917-18. Seconded Machine Gun Corps 27th June, 1918.

LEO MARRYAT O'CALLAGHAN

Born, 12th March, 1887. Boy, 12th January, 1903 ; Corpl., February, 1910 ; Sergt., May, 1913 ; Co.-Qr.-Mr.-Sergt., December, 1916 ; 2nd Lieut., 23rd July, 1918 ; Lieut., 23rd January, 1920.

Served in India during the Great War and in the operations in Afghanistan during 1919. Promoted to a commission for service in the Field.

BERTRAM SHIPLEY

Born at Pembroke Dock, 8th June, 1896.

Second Lieut., 9th October, 1918, from the ranks of the Machine Gun Guards ; Lieut., 9th April, 1920.

In the Great War served with the Coldstream Guards at the battle of the Marne and Aisne, first battle of Ypres, Festubert, Neuve Chapelle, Loos, third battle of Ypres, Somme, Passchendaele, and Cambrai (bronze star and clasp, and promoted to a commission).

WILLIAM CAREY FERGUSON-DAVIE

Born at Philadelphia, 25th March, 1900, son of Henry Herrick Ferguson-Davie.

Second Lieut., 16th July, 1919.

ROBERT GOULBORNE PARKER

Born at Edinburgh, 24th January, 1900, only son of Col. John William Robinson Parker, C.B., F.S.A., late 19th Foot, of Browsholme Hall, Yorkshire.

Second Lieut., 17th December, 1919.

Appendix.

Containing the Services of Officers of the 3rd Reserve and Territorial Battalions, and of Officers holding temporary commissions in the Regiment, who were attached to the 1st or 2nd Battalions during the Great War.

Officers of the 3rd Battalion.

———◆———

CHARLES RAMSAY WHITE, D.S.O.

Born at Leahurst, 11th May, 1881, 3rd son of William Knight Hamilton Ramsay White, of Leahurst, Tickhill, Rotherham.

Second Lieut., 18th February, 1900 ; Lieut., 12th June, 1901 ; Capt., 22nd October, 1904 ; Major, 2nd November, 1915 ; Lieut.-Col., 6th June, 1918.

Served in the Boer War, 1900-02. Operations in the Orange River Colony, September to 29th November, 1900. Operations in Cape Colony, south of the Orange River, June to August, 1900. Operations in the O.R.C., 30th November, 1900, to January 1902. Operations in Cape Colony, January to April, 1902 (Queen's medal and two clasps, King's medal and two clasps).

Was attached to 2nd Bn. from 25th November, 1914, and took part in the battle of Neuve Chapelle, 11th March, 1915 (wounded, mentioned in despatches). Served in the Gallipoli Expedition with the 6th Service Bn. Was also present in the fighting at Wonderwerk and Stuff Redoubt on the Somme in 1916 (mentioned in despatches), at Wytschaete (Messines), Poelcappelle, and Passchendaele in 1917 (mentioned in despatches. Distinguished Service Order, officer of the Ordre de la Couronne and Croix de Guerre (Belgic), bronze star).

WILLIAM HENRY GEORGE RALEY

Born, 3rd May, 1885, son of Lieut.-Col. William Emsley Raley, of Darley Hall, Barnsley, Yorks.

Second Lieut., 21st March, 1903 ; Lieut., 30th May, 1904 ; Capt., 3rd May, 1913.

Was attached to 2nd Bn. in France from 25th May, 1915 (mentioned in despatches).

Killed at Givenchy, 15th June, 1915.

In December, 1914, he went to France with the 5th Fusiliers, but was invalided home in January, suffering from blood-poisoning. He was killed leading his company out of the trenches to the attack. "A good officer and a keen sportsman, he will be much missed by his comrades." (G.H.G.)

WILLIAM FREDERICK IRVINE BELL

Born at Brighton, 11th September, 1884, son of W. A. Bell, of Blackrock, Brighton.

Second Lieut., 4th Bn., 19th June, 1905 ; Lieut., 3rd Bn., 1st February, 1909 ; Capt., 1st February, 1915.

Embarked for Zeebrugge with 2nd Bn. and was wounded in the fighting at Ypres, 22nd October, 1914, and again in January, 1915 (bronze star and clasp).

SAMUEL PALMER GLADSTONE

Born, 5th June, 1882, eldest surviving son of Arthur Gladstone, of Grosmount, Yorkshire.

Second Lieut., October, 1906 ; Lieut., 10th June, 1910 ; Capt., 10th February, 1915 ; resigned on account of ill-health, 5th May, 1915.

Joined 2nd Bn., 27th September, 1914, and took part in the first battle of Ypres (bronze star and clasp).

PHILIP HANBURY

Born at Teston, 5th June, 1879, son of Ernest Osgood Hanbury, of Teston, Kent.

Second Lieut., 31st December, 1907 ; Lieut., 16th June, 1909 ; Capt., 1st February, 1915 ; Adjt., 1st November, 1916, —16th July, 1917.

Joined 2nd Bn. in France, 10th April, 1915, and was present at the fighting at Fromelles, Festubert, Givenchy and Loos (mentioned in despatches, bronze star).

ARTHUR TEMPLE THORNE

Born, 20th March, 1889, son of L. T. Thorne, of Belmont, Surrey.

Second Lieut., 23rd July, 1910 ; Lieut., 1st May, 1912 ; Capt., 1st February, 1915.

Embarked with 2nd Bn. for Zeebrugge, and was wounded at Ypres, 30th October, 1914 (bronze star and clasp).

RICHARD WALMESLEY

Born in November, 1890, only son of John Walmesley, Hall of Ince, Lancashire.

Second Lieut., 13th August, 1910 ; Lieut., 1st March, 1912.

Accompanied 2nd Bn. to Zeebrugge and was killed in the fighting at Ypres, 23rd October, 1914.

WILLIAM HAROLD COLLEY, O.B.E.

Born at Grove House, Helperby, 31st July, 1888, 2nd son of William Colley, of Helperby, Yorkshire.

Second Lieut., 8th August, 1912 ; Capt., 1st February, 1915.

Proceeded to Belgium with 2nd Bn. and was wounded at Gheluvelt, 29th October, 1914. Rejoined in February, 1916, and was present at the fighting on the Somme, July to October, 1916. Also took part in the fighting on the western front in April, 1918 (twice mentioned in despatches, bronze star and clasp and Officer of the British Empire). Appointed to command of 16th Bn. Manchester Regt. in April, 1918.

MICHAEL DAY WADE MAUDE

Born at Rylstone, 29th September, 1890, younger son of Colonel W. Maude, The Fleets, Rylstone, Skipton-in-Craven.

Second Lieut., 7th June, 1913 ; Lieut., 17th May, 1914 ; Capt., 1st February, 1915.

Accompanied 2nd Bn. to Zeebrugge in October, 1914, and was present at the fighting round Ypres (bronze star and clasp). Took part in the operations on the Somme in October, 1916, and near Arras in April, 1917. Was severely wounded on 20th September, 1917, when attached to the 9th Service Bn. (twice mentioned in despatches).

Died of his wounds at the Military Hospital, Dover, 14th October, 1917.

"His remains were interred at Aldborough, near Boroughbridge, on 19th October, with military honours. The funeral procession was headed by the firing party and band of the 3rd Bn. and the regiment was represented by Lieut.-Col. Prior, Major Boyd Shannon, D.S.O., Major Gladstone, Capts. Hanbury, Montague, Walter and Wilkie, Lieuts. Scoby, Bright, and Somerset and 55 N.C.O.'s and men. Wreaths were sent by the officers of the depôt, the officers of the Reserve Bn., and by N.C. officers and men, as an expression of the deep sympathy of his old comrades with Capt. Maude's family in their sorrow." (G.H.G.)

STAMP BROOKSBANK

Born at Tadcaster, 16th January, 1887, eldest son of Sir Edward Clitherow Brooksbank, Bart., Healaugh Manor, Tadcaster.

Lieut., 17th September, 1914 ; Capt., 2nd December, 1915.

Attached to 2nd Bn. 10th January, 1915.

Killed at Hulloch, 25th September, 1915.

His brother, H.G. Brooksbank, 2nd Bn., died of wounds in London, 16th December, 1914.

JAMES RICHARD ANDERTON RIGBY

Born, 10th January, 1890, son of the Revd. James Rigby, M.A., B.C.L., Sheriff Hutton Vicarage, Yorks.

Second Lieut., 17th February, 1914 ; Lieut., 2nd February, 1915.

Attached to 2nd Bn. 10th April, 1915, and was killed at Breslau trench, Hulloch, 26th September, 1915.

NOEL TRACEY WRIGHT

Born in 1894, son of T. T. Wright, of Bombay, Deputy Auditor, B.B. and C.I. Railway.

Second Lieut., 15th August, 1914 ; Lieut., 2nd February, 1915 ; Capt., 15th June, 1915.

Attached to 2nd Bn. 15th December, 1914 (mentioned in despatches).

Died of wounds received at Hulloch, 1st October, 1915.

MALCOLM HEWLEY GRAHAM

Born at New Mill, near Huddersfield, 22nd November, 1894, son of Hewley S. Graham, of Oxley-Woodhouse, Huddersfield.

Second Lieut., 15th August, 1914 ; Lieut., 2nd February, 1915.

Attached to 2nd Bn. 5th March, 1915.

Killed at Givenchy 15th June, 1915, when leading his platoon in the attack

WEEVER KENNETH WALTER, M.B.E.

Born in London, 20th June, 1878, son of Weever James Walter, The Rise, Abbey Wood, Kent.

Second Lieut., 15th August, 1914 ; Lieut., 2nd February, 1915 ; Capt., 2nd December, 1915 ; Adjt., 16th July, 1917.

Attached to 2nd Bn. 6th January, 1915. Wounded at the battle of Neuve Chapelle, 13th March, 1915 (mentioned for home service, M.B.E. and bronze star).

FREDERICK CRESWELL PYMAN

Born, 2nd January, 1889, son of Frederick Haigh Pyman, of Dunsley, near Whitby, Yorkshire.

Second Lieut., 15th August, 1914 ; Lieut., 2nd February, 1915 ; Capt., 8th March, 1916.

Attached to 2nd Bn. 25th January, 1915. Wounded at the battle of Neuve Chapelle, 10th March, 1915 (mentioned in despatches, bronze star).

WILLIAM GRAY

Born at Seaton Carew, 18th August, 1894, son of Sir William Cresswell Gray, Bart., of Thorpe Perrow, Bedale, Yorkshire.

Second Lieut., 15th August, 1914 ; Lieut., 2nd February, 1915 ; Capt., 8th March, 1916.

Attached to 2nd Bn. 23rd March, 1915. Was wounded and taken prisoner at Vermelles, 25th September, 1915 (mentioned in despatches, bronze star). Interned in Holland in April, 1918.

ALAN PYMAN

Third son of Frederick Haigh Pyman, of Dunsley, near Whitby.

Second Lieut., 15th August, 1914 ; Lieut., 2nd February, 1915.

Attached to 2nd Bn. 10th April, 1915. Killed at Givenchy 15th June, 1915, when acting as machine-gun officer.

JOHN OSCAR PRITCHARD-BARRETT

Son of J. Pritchard-Barrett, and stepson of Lieut.-Col. Sir Neville Gunter, Bart., 3rd Bn.

Second Lieut., 15th August, 1914 ; Lieut., 2nd February, 1915.

Attached to 2nd Bn. 10th April, 1915, and was killed at Givenchy, 15th June, 1915.

JAMES AUSTEN PRESTON WILD

Born, 27th November, 1883. Second Lieut., 27th August, 1914 ; Lieut., 2nd February, 1915 ; Capt., 2nd December, 1915 ; resigned, 30th March, 1920.

Joined 2nd Bn. East Yorkshire Regiment in France 12th May, 1915, and took part in the 2nd battle of Ypres ,when he was wounded (25th May). Was attached to 2nd Bn. in France, 23rd May, 1916, to 9th June, 1916. Afterwards employed with a cadet battalion at home (bronze star).

GEORGE BINGLEY LANCASTER

Born at Barnsley, 30th May, 1879, son of Thomas Lancaster, The Cliffe, Monk Bretton, Barnsley.

Second Lieut., 29th September, 1914 ; Lieut., 2nd February, 1915 ; Capt., 8th March, 1916 ; half-pay, 4th February, 1917 ; retired on account of wounds, 18th September, 1917.

Attached to 2nd Bn. 25th May, 1915. Wounded at Vermelles, 17th September, 1915 (bronze star).

FRANCIS EDWARD FISH

Born at Heaton Chapel, Manchester, 24th March, 1876, son of Ralph Fish, of Manchester.

Capt., 1st October, 1914.

Joined 2nd Bn., 19th March, 1915. He obtained a commission in the 2nd Vol. Bn. (Scarborough) on 13th April, 1901, and was gazetted a Lieut. in the 3rd Bn. on 7th May, 1904, retiring 10th July, 1909. On the outbreak of the war he was gazetted back to the 3rd Bn. as a captain and embarked for France with a draft of 350 men for the 2nd Bn. in March, 1915. During the bombardment of Hartlepool in December, 1914, he had a narrow escape, being blown off his legs by the bursting of a shell.

Killed at Dead Cow Farm, Festubert, 17th May, 1915.

PERCIVAL ARMORER FORSTER, M.C.

Born at Ferryhill, Co. Durham, 27th December, 1887, son of Matthew Forster, Gosforth, Newcastle-on-Tyne.

Second Lieut., 10th October, 1914 ; Lieut., 2nd February, 1915 ; Capt., 2nd October, 1915.

Attached to 2nd Bn. 25th May, 1915. Took part in the attack on Loos, 25th September, 1915, and following days (mentioned in despatches, bronze star, and awarded the Military Cross).

HENRY ALBERT WILKINSON, M.C.

Born, 29th December, 1893, son of A. F. Wilkinson, Salisbury Road, High Barnet, London.

Second Lieut., 14th October, 1914 ; Lieut., 2nd February, 1915.

Present at Ypres in May, 1915, with 2nd Bn. East Yorkshire Regiment and was wounded at Wulvoerghem, 22nd July, 1915 (bronze star). Was attached to 2nd Bn. 28th November, 1915, and was again wounded at Carnoy, 10th February, 1916. Posted to the 7th Service Bn. in July, 1916, and took part in the operations on the Somme and before Arras, April and May, 1917 (wounded). Awarded the Military Cross for having, when in command of a newly-won position, led his men with great dash and gallantry against a strong enemy counter attack, which he successfully repulsed. At one moment, having outpaced his men, he faced the enemy with only one man. He was badly wounded, but insisted on being carried to battalion headquarters, under heavy shell fire, to report on the situation before proceeding to the comparative safety of a dressing station. Rejoining the 2nd Bn. in October, 1918, he was with it till the Armistice.

THOMAS TWEDDELL

Born at West Hartlepool, 31st March, 1895, son of A. Tweddell, Beckford House, W. Hartlepool.

Second Lieut., 23rd December, 1914 ; Lieut., 2nd December, 1915.

Attached to 2nd Bn. 18th June, 1915, to 7th September, 1915. Rejoined from hospital 13th February, 1916. Invalided 12th March, 1916. Severely wounded in June, 1918, when attached to East Yorkshire Regiment.

Death reported in "Times" of 20th July, 1918.

HORACE GORDON TOZER

Born at Stoke, Devonport, 9th September, 1895, son of J. C. Tozer, J.P., of Stoke House, Devonport.

Second Lieut., 17th February, 1915.

Attached to 2nd Bn., 21st June, 1915.

Killed at Gun Trench, Hulloch, 1st October, 1915.

WILLIAM EDWARD PERCIVAL WATERFIELD

Born, 5th February, 1889, son of Dr. W. H. Waterfield, East Stone House, Devon.

Second Lieut., 17th February, 1915 ; Lieut., 2nd December, 1915 ; relinquished his commission, 1st April, 1920.

Attached to 2nd Bn. 21st June, 1915. Gassed at Vermelles, 20th September, 1915 (bronze star).

ROBERT ALISTAIR FIELD, M.C.

Born at Wimbledon, 13th March, 1895, son of Joseph Louis Field, 18, Lansdowne Road, Wimbledon.

Second Lieut., 6th March, 1915 ; Lieut., 2nd December, 1915.

Attached to 2nd Bn. 1st October, 1915. Present at the battles on the Somme on the 1st, 8th and 23rd July, 1916, and 18th October, 1916 (twice mentioned in despatches). In the fighting at Henin, 30-31 March, 1917. Was awarded the Military Cross for displaying great courage and initiative during a bombing attack. Meeting an obstacle in the trench he went along the parapet under heavy fire, jumped into the trench again and killed one of the enemy.

Killed at Henin, near Arras, 2nd April, 1917.

His loss to the Regiment is expressed in the following lines, written by a brother officer who knew him well :—"Others in the battalion compelled our admiration, but he was our hero. Those of us who are not called upon to fight knew him as he was in billets and behind the line, and loved him as we knew him. Yet we picture him best as he was often described to us, 'passing along a hostile trench with a bomb in each hand, an unknown number of the enemy in front.' He was the best of companions, at all times eager that everyone should get the best out of our time in billets, cheery and optimistic in the most depressing trenches, absolutely fearless in battle. His judgment and decisions were those of an older man; yet they lacked nothing of the spirit and dash of his years, nor of the originality of himself. The battalion grieves for the loss of its bravest soldier : the officers and men the passing of one of the truest of friends."

Col. C. V. Edwards wrote :—"Your son was well known in this division and he had the reputation of being one of the bravest men in it. He had received the Military Cross for bravery on the Somme and we all thought he was likely to get further distinction. His loss is difficult to replace. We now have too few of his kind left. By nature he was all that an English gentleman should be, quiet, unassuming, but as brave as a lion. His men would have followed him anywhere " and again, " I write to tell you that I have forwarded your son's name for the Victoria Cross. He was as gallant a fellow as ever lived. He has performed many acts of bravery. Whether the Cross will be granted or not I cannot say. We trust it will be."

WILLIAM THORMAN FRY

Born in London, 18th June, 1890, son of T. H. Fry, The Elms, Belmont Hill, Blackheath.

Second Lieut., 13th March, 1915 ; Lieut., 2nd December, 1915 ; Machine Gun Corps, 4th December, 1916 ; retired on account of ill-health caused by active service, 17th April, 1918.

Served with the Honourable Artillery Company from September, 1914, to March, 1915, in France, including the battle of Ypres (bronze star). Was with the 2nd Bn. from 7th March to December, 1916, before Armentières. Took part in the battle of Messines with the M.G. Corps.

WILLIAM DICKENSON HUBBARD

Eldest son of Charles William Hubbard, of Sleaford, Lincoln.

Second Lieut., 20th April, 1915 ; Lieut., 8th March, 1916.

Was attached to 1/4th Bn. in France from 17th August, 1915, to 8th April, 1916, when he was posted to 2nd Bn.

Killed in action at Trônes Wood, Somme, 9th July, 1916, aged 23 years.

DONALD St. HERBERT LARNER

Second Lieut., 5th May, 1915 ; retired on account of wounds, 2nd March, 1918.

Was wounded in April, 1916, when serving with 8th Service Bn. Was attached to 2nd Bn. 19th January, 1917, and was again wounded at Agny, near Arras, 5th March, 1917.

ALFRED NEWBURY

Born at Southport, 5th October, 1882, son of Edmund Newbury.

Second Lieut., 7th May, 1915 ; Lieut., 10th October, 1916.

Was attached to 2nd. Bn. from 1st October, 1915, and took part in the battle of the Somme, July, 1916, and was present at Arras in April, 1917 (mentioned in despatches). Took part also in the fighting on the Western Front, from June to September, 1918 (wounded at Epinoy, 27th September).

ALFRED FRANCIS ROBINSON

Born, 8th April, 1887. Second Lieut., 8th May, 1915 ; Lieut., 10th October, 1916.

Posted to 9th Service Bn., November, 1915, till invalided with enteric, June, 1916. Was attached to 2nd Bn., in France from 21st March, 1917, and was wounded at Hénin, 1st April, 1917. Seconded to 6th King's African Rifles, 8th October, 1917, as Captain and Company Commander.

GEORGE FITZER KERSHAW

Born, 27th June, 1888, son of G. Kershaw, Moorland Mount, Cleckheaton.

Second Lieut., 8th May, 1915 ; Lieut., 1st July, 1917 ; relinquished his commission on account of ill-health, 8th August, 1918.

Was attached to 2nd Bn. from 1st January, 1916, and was wounded at Le Sars, 18th October, 1916.

ALYMER EADE

Born at Aycliffe, Durham, 28th January, 1892, son of the Revd. Charles John Alymer Eade, Aycliffe Vicarage, Darlington.

Second Lieut., 12th May, 1915.

Joined 2nd Bn., in France, 2nd October, 1915. Was appointed Adjt., 6th Service Bn., 30th October, 1916, to 14th July, 1917.

Wounded and missing at Poelcappelle, 9th October, 1917 ; presumed killed.

HENRY HUBERT FRASER

Born at Headingly, Leeds, 10th April, 1885, son of H. J. Fraser, of Ganthorpe House, York.

Second Lieut., 16th May, 1915 ; Lieut., 1st July, 1917.

Was attached to 2nd Bn., 26th November, 1915, to 17th October, 1916, and from 10th April ,1918, to 24th April, 1918, in France (wounded, 17th October, 1916, near Flers).

Reported missing, 27th May, 1918, when attached to 1/5th Bn. : Presumed killed.

HENRY JOSEPH WHITING

Born in Melbourne, 16th December, 1880, son of R. S. Whiting, Solicitor.

Second Lieut., 5th June, 1915 ; resigned his commission, 9th January, 1918.

Served in France with 2nd Bn., from 24th November, 1915, to 14th June, 1917. Present at the battle of the Somme, including actions at Montauban, Trônes Wood, and Guillemont, Flers, 12th and 23rd October ; also at Arras, including the fighting at Hénin, 26th March, 1917 ; Héninel, 9th April ; and Chérisey, 23rd April.

IAN KENNETH THOMSON

Born, 29th May, 1888, son of A. Thomson, Burgie House, Forres, N.B.

Second Lieut., 5th June, 1915 ; Lieut., 1st July, 1917 ; resigned his commission, 1st April, 1920.

Wounded, 2nd July, 1916, at Glatz Redoubt, near Montauban, Somme.

ROBERT MASTERS SOMERSET

Born, 6th March, 1894, son of N. Somerset, of Meirsbrook, Sheffield.

Second Lieut., 10th June, 1915 ; Lieut., 1st July, 1917 ; resigned his commission, 16th April, 1920.

Attached to 2nd Bn. from 7th February, 1916, and was wounded at Ligny-Thilloy, 8th October, 1916.

HUGH LOWENBERG CONSTABLE

Born, 15th September, 1880. Second Lieut., 11th June, 1915 ; Lieut., 1st July, 1917.

Joined 2nd Bn., 2nd October, 1915. Was seconded to Royal Engineers, 10th April, 1916, and engaged in mining operations, Carnoy, preparatory to Somme offensive. Also in operations prior to battle of Messines, 1917.

HUGH BLACKALL LAIRD

Born at Durris, Kincardineshire, 14th May, 1896, son of the Revd. David W. Laird, M.A., 26, Napier Road, Edinburgh.

Second Lieut., 26th June, 1915.

Joined 2nd Bn., 7th February, 1916.
Killed at Trônes Wood, Montauban, 8th July, 1916.

JOHN TRICKETT, M.C.

Born in 1893, son of John Trickett, Weaverham, Northwick, Cheshire.

Second Lieut., 26th June, 1915 ; Lieut., 1st July, 1917 ; relinquished his commission, 1st April, 1920.

Joined 2nd Bn. in June, 1916. Was wounded at Montauban, 1st July, 1916, and again at Trônes Wood, 8th July, 1916. Awarded the Military Cross. " Though hit and badly shaken he caught up his men again and led them through the enemy barrage. A week later he was severely wounded leading his platoon to the attack."

ARTHUR GALEN HILLABY

Born at Pontefract, 10th April, 1896.

Second Lieut., 26th June, 1915 ; Lieut., 1st July, 1917 ; retired on account of ill-health caused by wounds, 4th July, 1919.

Attached to 2nd Bn., 25th August, 1916, and was gassed at Ranzart, 11th November, 1916.

BERTRAM CUNLIFFE CAMM, M.C.

Born at Poppleton, near York, 2nd July, 1893, only son of N. C. Camm, of Brighouse, Poppleton, and Scarborough.

Second Lieut., 28th July, 1915 ; Lieut., 1st July, 1917.

Wounded at Fricourt on the Somme, 1st July, 1916, when attached to the 7th Service Bn. Joined 2nd Bn., 20th January, 1917, and was present in the fighting at Arras in April, 1917 (wounded at Hénin, 9th April). Was awarded the Military Cross under the following circumstances : " When the advance was held up by uncut wire he showed great coolness and ability under heavy fire of all kinds. He directed the digging, reorganised and opened up communications with both his flanks and throughout set a splendid example."

Lost his life in the fire at Hedge Street Tunnel, near Ypres, 5th January, 1918. See page 272 under W. C. K. Birch.

WILLIAM CHOCKLEY MILLS

Second Lieut., 4th August, 1915.

Attached to 2nd Bn., 26th November, 1915.
Killed at Guillemont, Somme, 23rd July, 1916.

ALAN MILLER

Born, 25th July, 1892, younger son of Lieut.-Col., David
Miller, Chief Inspector Postal Department, New Zealand.
Second Lieut., 4th August, 1915.
Attached to 2nd Bn., in August, 1916.
Killed at Le Sars, 14th October, 1916.
His commanding officer wrote: "He was most trustworthy and
zealous, a brave and good officer, and is a very great loss to the
battalion."

GEORGE ERNEST RICHARDS

Born, 8th October, 1897, son of F. E. Richards, of Nottingham.
Second Lieut., 11th August, 1915 ; Lieut., 1st July, 1917 ;
resigned his commission, 16th April, 1920.
Joined the 2nd Bn. in August, 1916, and was wounded at High-
wood, Somme, on 21st October, 1916. Posted to the 13th Bn. in
September, 1917, and was wounded at Bourlon Wood, 23rd November,
1917.

THOMAS HENRY THRISCUTT BALE

Born, 22nd December, 1885. Second Lieut., 20th August,
1915 ; Lieut., 1st July, 1917.
Took part in the fighting at Fricourt and Mametz in 1916, and at
Sailly-Saillisel on the Somme in February, 1917, when serving with the
7th Service Bn. Attached to 2nd Bn., 17th April, 1918.
Killed at Zillebeke, near Ypres, 25th April, 1918.

CEDRIC CHARLES BRAMWELL

Born, 4th June, 1897, son of C. J. Bramwell, Ravenhurst,
Westbury Road, New Malden.
Second Lieut., 20th August, 1915 ; Lieut., 1st July, 1917 ;
resigned his commission, 1st April, 1920.
Wounded (shell shock) at Guillemont (Trônes Wood), 23rd July,
1916.

BERNARD JOCELYN WILKINSON

Born, 13th May, 1893, 6th son of T. L. Wilkinson, of
Neasham Abbey, Darlington.
Second Lieut., 26th August, 1915.
Joined 2nd Bn., 5th May, 1916.
Killed at Montauban, 8th July, 1916.

MAURICE ANDRÉ CHRETIEN JUBERT

Born, 1st March, 1898, son of E. T. Jubert, of 4, Earldom
Road, Putney, London.
Second Lieut., 26th August, 1915 ; Lieut., 1st July, 1917 ;
resigned his commission, 16th April, 1920.
Wounded at Guillemont, 23rd July, 1916. He was studying at
Leipsic University in August, 1914, and on the outbreak of war was
detained as a civil prisoner until released by exchange.

JOHN PERRY

Born at West Hartlepool, 9th May, 1902, son of J. Perry,
of Carisbrook Road, W. Hartlepool.

Second Lieut., 26th August, 1915.

Joined 2nd Bn., 15th June, 1916, and during the fighting on the Somme was killed at Guillemont on the 23rd July, 1916.

LOUIS PARISOTTI

Born in London, 25th July, 1890, son of Luigi Parisotti, 5, Inverness Place, London, W.

Second Lieut., 1st September, 1915 ; Lieut., 1st July, 1917.

Joined 2nd Bn., 7th February, 1916, and was wounded at Glatz Redoubt, Somme, 1st July, 1916. Seconded to Indian Army, 30th October, 1917.

Killed in action on N.W. Frontier, India, when serving with the 4/39th Garhwal Rifles (2nd January, 1920).

HAROLD SPURGEON HOBBY, M.C.

Born, 2nd November, 1897, son of E. A. Hobby, Fairholme, Park Lane, Macclesfield.

Second Lieut., 5th September, 1915 ; Lieut., 1st July, 1917 ; Royal Air Force, 20th May, 1918.

Joined 2nd Bn. in May, 1916, and was wounded in August at Givenchy, again at Flers on 12th October, 1916, and for the third time at Battle Wood (Somme) on the 7th June, 1917. Awarded the Military Cross " for conspicuous gallantry and devotion to duty in taking charge of his company and completely reorganising it after the Commander had become a casualty. Although twice wounded, he refused to leave the line, and remained until the battalion was relieved, displaying great ability and cheerfulness in spite of his wounds, and setting a splendid example to his men."

JOHN SHEPHERD ALLISON BUNTING, M.C.

Born, 12th May, 1898, son of C. J. Bunting, of Shrewsbury House, West Hartlepool.

Second Lieut., 5th September, 1915 ; Lieut., 1st July, 1917 ; resigned his commission and granted rank of Captain, 2nd April, 1920.

Attached to 2nd Bn., 25th July, 1917. Took part in the retreat of the 5th Army in March, 1918, and was wounded at Ham, 27th March. Awarded the Military Cross. " When in command of a company he resisted for 24 hours repeated attacks of the enemy, inflicting great losses on them. In the rearguard action on subsequent days he rallied his men with skill and courage until finally wounded."

CHARLES WILLIAM JONES, M.C.

Born, 16th April, 1880. Second Lieut., 12th October, 1915 ; Lieut., 1st July, 1917.

Served in the Boer War, 1901-2, as a trooper in the Cape Mounted Rifles, and took part in the operations in Cape Colony and Orange River Colony (Queen's medal and clasps). Posted to the 8th Service Bn. in May, 1916, and was wounded at Contalmaison, 10th July, 1916, and again at Messines Ridge on 7th June, 1917 (mentioned in despatches). Awarded the Military Cross "For going on in broad daylight and carrying out a lengthy reconnaissance and furnishing a valuable report. He had on many previous occasions done fine work." Joined 2nd Bn., 17th August, 1917, and reposted to the 8th Service Bn. on the 28th.

HARRY GUISELIN ATKIN, M.C.

Born in Jamaica, 5th November, 1888.

Second Lieut., 4th Bn. South Staffordshire Regt., 30th November, 1915 ; Lieut., 1st July, 1917 ; transferred to 3rd Bn. Yorkshire Regt. in November, 1917 ; resigned his commission, 1st April, 1920.

Was attached to 7th Bn. in France from 3rd October, 1916, to 20th October, 1916, and to 6th Service Bn. from that date to May, 1918. Took part in the battle of Beaucourt (Somme), 17th January, 1917, and was at the battle of Messines, 7th June, 1917, also at Poelcapelle, 9th October, 1917. Joined the 2nd Bn., 21st June, 1918. Was in the fighting on the Western Front between then and November, 1918 (wounded).

THOMAS DALRYMPLE STRATHERN

Born, 26th November, 1887, son of W. Strathern, of White-haven, Cumberland.

Second Lieut., 9th December, 1915.

Joined the 2nd Bn., 21st June, 1916.

Killed at Montauban, 8th July, 1916.

PERCIVAL HENRY HART, M.C.

Born at Enfield, Middlesex, 5th August, 1891, son of James Hart, 41, Leighton Grove, Kentish Town.

Second Lieut., 1st March, 1917 ; Lieut., 1st September, 1918.

Joined 2nd Bn., 1st May, 1917, and from 20th September served with the 10th Service Bn. till its disbandment, 10th February, 1918. Rejoined 2nd Bn., and on 24th March was invalided home owing to an accident. Returned to France, 20th May, 1918, and was posted to 10th West Yorkshire Regt., and attached later to the 50th Trench Mortar Battery, 21st August to 31st October, 1918. Was awarded the Military Cross " for having led his two Stokes' guns in the attack on Neuvilly village on the night of October 10/11th, 1918, with great gallantry and determination. When all the officers had become casualties he took over command of the company, and displayed sound judgment, and after commanding for two days brought the company out, bringing also his two Stokes' guns. He showed fine leadership, and his services were invaluable to the battalion."

GILBERT PARKER SMITH

Born at Bury, Lancashire, 8th March. 1897, 3rd son of Henry Smith, of Clifton Avenue, W. Hartlepool.

Second Lieut., 1st March, 1917.

Joined 2nd Bn., 1st May, 1917.

Lost his life in the fire in Hedge Street Tunnel, near Ypres, 5th January, 1918. See page 272 under W. C. K. Birch.

JOHN WILLIAM BROWN

Born, 19th February, 1893. Second Lieut., 26th April, 1917.

Served in the ranks of the 15th Bn., West Yorkshire Regt., and proceeded with it to France in December, 1915. Was wounded on the Somme, 1st July, 1916. Posted to 2nd Bn., 11th June, 1917, and wounded again at Sanctuary Wood, Ypres, 31st July, 1917.

Died of his wounds, 1st August, 1917.

HAROLD CHILD, M.M.

Born, 25th July, 1891. Second Lieut., 26th April, 1917 ; Lieut., 26th October, 1918 ; resigned, 19th March, 1920, and granted rank of Captain.

Served in the ranks of the 15th Bn., West Yorkshire Regt., in France from December, 1915, to December, 1916 (Military medal for bravery); was wounded on the Somme, 31st July, 1917, when with 2nd Bn.; returned to France, 26th August, 1918.

LAWRENCE GOLIGHTLY

Born at Darlington, 29th April, 1895, son of G. Golightly, Thompson Street, Darlington.

Second Lieut., 30th May, 1917 ; demobilized, 30th March, 1919.

Served in the ranks of the 5th Bn., Durham Light Infantry, from April, 1915, to April, 1917, and took part in the 2nd battle of Ypres. Was also in the fighting on the Somme at Bazentin in September, 1916. Served with 2nd Bn. from 19th July, 1917, to 20th March, 1918 (bronze star).

ERNEST HOWARD

Born at Worksop, 23rd October, 1895.

Second Lieut., 30th May, 1917 ; Lieut., 30th November, 1918.

Took part in the fighting on the Somme in July, 1916. Attached to 2nd Bn., 6th August, 1917, and was in the retreat on the Western Front from March to May, 1918.

GEORGE FREDERICK LOCKWOOD

Born at Huddersfield, 25th November, 1887, son of Frederick Lockwood, of Huddersfield.

Second Lieut., 27th June, 1917.

Served in the ranks of the Yorkshire Dragoons in France from July, 1915, to January, 1917 (bronze star). Joined 2nd Bn. in August, 1917. Taken prisoner at Roupy on the St. Quentin-Ham Road, 22nd March, 1918.

FRANK BINGHAM

Born at Middlesbrough, 16th August, 1885, son of Frank Bingham, of Middlesbrough.

Second Lieut., 27th June, 1917 ; Lieut., 27th December, 1918.

Went to France with 12th Pioneer Bn., 1st June, 1916. Posted to 2nd Bn., 13th August, 1917, and was with it during the fighting on the Western Front from March to October, 1918.

WILLIAM WERGE VASEY

Born at Hartlepool, 12th January, 1894, son of William Vasey, of Hartlepool.

Second Lieut., 29th August, 1917 ; Lieut., 28th February, 1919.

Served in the ranks of the 20th Bn., Durham Light Infantry, from November, 1915, to May, 1917. Took part in the fighting on the Somme in September and October, 1916, and was present at Flers and Guedecourt (wounded 1st October, 1916). Posted to 2nd Bn., 18th October, 1917, and was taken prisoner at Roupy on the St. Quentin-Ham Road, 22nd March, 1918.

ABRAHAM WACHOLDER

Born at Hull, 27th November, 1893, son of Daniel Wacholder. Second Lieut., 29th August, 1917; Lieut., 28th February, 1919.

Attached to 2nd Bn., 18th October, 1917. Present at the fighting in March, 1918. Was wounded 29th March at Mazières.

FRANK LAYCOCK

Born at Sheffield, 27th December, 1897, son of Henry Laycock, of Sheffield.

Second Lieut., 31st October, 1917 ; Lieut., 30th April, 1919.

Served in the ranks of the 7th Bn., Suffolk Regt., from June, 1915, to April, 1917, and was present at the battle of Loos in September, 1915 (bronze star). Took part in the operations on the Somme in 1916, including Ovilliers, Pozières and Guedecourt, and in the fighting before Arras in April, 1917. Posted to 2nd Bn., 29th May, 1918, and served with it till October, 1918.

JOHN FAWCETT

Born, 2nd September, 1895, son of Robert Fawcett, of Great Broughton, Stokesley, Yorkshire.

Second Lieut., 30th January, 1918.

Served in the ranks of the 21st Bn., The King's Royal Rifles, from May, 1916, to July, 1917, in France, and was present at the operations on the Somme in September and October, 1916, and at Messines in June, 1917. Posted to 2nd Bn., 2nd May, 1918.

Killed near Ypres, 8th May, 1918.

WILFRED ALFRED STEWARD

Born, 26th April, 1897, son of Arthur Steward, of Sheffield.

Second Lieut., 30th January, 1918.

Posted to 2nd Bn., 2nd May, 1918. Present at the fighting on the Western Front between May and September, 1918 (wounded).

FRANCIS COODE

Born at Birmingham, 15th January, 1895.

Second Lieut., 30th January, 1918.

Served with the 2/6th Royal Warwickshire Regt., in France, and was present at the fighting at Laventie, 19th July, 1916. Posted to the 2nd Bn., 2nd May, 1918, and took part in the fighting on the Western Front from then onwards till wounded, 1st October, 1918.

JOHN WALKER

Born at Castleton, 18th July, 1889, son of Joseph Walker, of Castleton, Derbyshire.

Second Lieut., 26th June, 1918 ; demobilized, 9th April, 1919.

Posted to 2nd Bn., 16th October, 1918, and was present at the fighting south- east of Valenciennes, Artres, Preseau and Roisin. Was wounded at Meurain, 6th November, 1918.

Officers of the 4th Battalion.

WILLIAM WHITESMITH CONSTANTINE, M.C.

Born at Middlesbrough, 26th March, 1887, son of Joseph Constantine, Harlesly Hall, Northallerton.

Second Lieut., March, 1906 ; Lieut., 27th May, 1907 ; Capt., 5th October, 1913 ; Major, 13th June, 1916.

Served in France with 4th Bn. Gassed at Ypres, 24th May, 1915, and wounded at Martinpuich, Somme, 15th September, 1916. Posted to 2nd Bn., 2nd May, 1918, and to 9th Bn., King's Own Yorkshire Light Infantry in August (wounded). Awarded the Military Cross in 1916 " For conspicuous gallantry in action. Though wounded before the attack commenced he insisted in leading his company to the final objective, where, though again wounded, he continued with the greatest determination to control his company. He set a fine example " (bronze star).

HAROLD McLEAN HOLLINGWORTH, M.C.

Born in Sydney, 9th May, 1897, son of H. C. Hollingworth, of Marrockville, Sydney, N.S.W.

Second Lieut., 12th August, 1915 ; Lieut., 1st June, 1916 ; demobilized, 27th March, 1919.

Present at the operations on the Somme, 1916. Wounded at Butte de Warlincourt, 11th November, 1916. Also in the fighting at Arras, 1917, and the third battle of Ypres, where he was again wounded at Poelcappelle Station, 28th October, 1917. Took part in the final advance in 1918, and was posted to 2nd Bn., 18th October. Awarded the Military Cross.

JOSEPH ROBSON

Born at Todridge, Morpeth, Northumberland, son of Lancelot Robson, of Todridge.

Second Lieut., 16th November, 1915 ; Lieut., 1st June, 1916 ; demobilized, 27th March, 1919.

Enlisted in the Artists' Rifles, 15th June, 1915, and served in France, 15th June, 1916, to 24th September, 1916. Present at the battle of the Somme (wounded at Martinpuich, 17th September). Was at the fighting at Arras in 1917, and also at the third battle of Ypres. (Wounded at Wancourt, 23rd April, 1917). Took part in the Lys retreat and in the operations before Arras in 1918. Posted to 2nd Bn., 15th August, 1918, and remained with it till the Armistice.

VAUGHAN EDWARDES GARTH WILLIAMS

Born at Richmond, Yorkshire, 16th June, 1890, son of Dr. Howell Williams, of Frenchgate, Richmond.

Second Lieut., 12th January, 1916 ; Lieut., 12th July, 1917 ; demobilized, 1st February, 1919.

Served in France with 5th Bn. from October to November, 1916. With 6th Bn. from November, 1916, to May, 1918, including operations on the Somme, 1916-17, Messines Ridge and Ypres in 1917. Posted to 2nd Bn. in May, 1918, and was present with it in the fighting up to the Armistice.

Officers of the 5th Battalion.

JOHN STANLEY ROBSON

Born at Pocklington, 4th September, 1893, son of Thomas Robson, of Pembroke Lodge, Pocklington, East Yorkshire.

Second Lieut., 27th February, 1915 ; Capt., 27th May, 1918.

Served for six months in France with 19th Bn., Royal Fusiliers, and was wounded at Arras, 23rd April, 1917. Posted to 2nd Bn., 9th October, 1918, and served with it till the Armistice.

JOHN COPLAND STORY

Born at Largs, Ayrshire, 1st November, 1893, son of William Good Story.

Second Lieut., 7th May, 1916 ; Lieut., 18th December, 1917.

Served in the ranks from 17th April, 1915, to 6th May, 1916, in France, until promoted to a commission, including the operations at Ypres, April and May, 1915; The Bluff, Hill 60, in March, 1916. In the operations at Arras, April and May, 1917; advance East of Ypres in October, 1917. Was wounded at Broodseinde, Passchendaele, 4th October, 1917. Posted to 2nd Bn., 17th April, 1918, and shortly afterwards transferred to 1/4th Bn. Wounded and taken prisoner at Craonne, Chemin des Dames, 27th May, 1918.

THOMAS CLAUDE BAUMFIELD

Born at Nottingham, 20th July, 1899, son of Benjamin Baumfield, of Nottingham.

Second Lieut., 31st July, 1918 ; relinquished his commission on account of ill-health caused by wounds, 4th April, 1919.

Posted to the 2nd Bn., 16th October, 1918, and was wounded at Roisin on the 5th November.

Temporary Officers.

---+---

MARLBOROUGH EVELYN BEDFORD CROSSE

Born at Lucknow, 28th January, 1894, elder son of Marlborough Crosse, of Lahore, India.

Temp. Second Lieut., 14th November, 1914, from ranks of the Artists' Rifles.

Killed in action at Neuve Chapelle, 12th March, 1915, when in charge of Machine Gun Section, 2nd Bn.

GEOFFREY CUTTLE

Born at Wanstead, 20th April, 1893, son of George Cuttle, of the India Office.

Temp. Second Lieut., 14th November, 1914.

Served with the Artists' Rifles in France from October, 1914.
Killed in action at Neuve Chapelle, 11th March, 1915.

ALFRED JAMES PICKUP

Born in 1888, younger son of James Pickup, of Beechcroft, Beckenham.

Temp. Second Lieut., 14th November, 1914 ; Temp. Lieut., 15th June, 1915.

Proceeded to France with the Artists' Rifles in October, 1914, and was wounded at Armentières in December. With 2nd Bn., was present in the fighting at Neuve Chapelle (wounded) and Festubert.
Killed in action at Hulloch, 26th September, 1915.

HENRY LEWIS HOLLIS

Born, 11th August, 1889, son of H. T. Hollis, of Charlton, London.

Temp. Second Lieut., 14th December, 1914 ; Temp. Lieut., 10th June, 1915 ; relinquished his commission, 3rd January, 1920.

Was commissioned from the Artists' Rifles. Wounded at the battle of Neuve Chapelle, 11th March, 1915.

PERCY ROBINSON

Born at Middlesboro', 1st February, 1890, son of W. L. Robinson, of Middlesboro', Yorkshire.

Temp. Second Lieut., 8th Service Bn., 9th January, 1915.

Present at battles of Hulloch and Givenchy. Posted to 2nd Bn., 10th October, 1915, and was wounded, 21st January, 1916, at Carnoy, near Montauban. Rejoined the 8th Service Bn., and took part in the fighting on the Menin Road, and in Italy.

JOHN LLOYD-JONES

Born in London, 1st June, 1891, son of J. W. Jones, of Holloway.

Temp. Second Lieut., 10th March, 1915 ; Temp. Lieut., 18th June, 1915.

Went to France with the Artists' Rifles in October, 1914. With the 2nd Bn. was present at the battles of Neuve Chapelle, Fromelles, Festubert, and Givenchy (wounded). Was mentioned in despatches. He particularly distinguished himself on 17th May at Festubert while in charge of a bombing party. Three enemy snipers, concealed behind a fence, had caused several casualties amongst the men. Lieut. Jones crawled up, bomb in hand, and hurled the grenade with such excellent effect that two of the snipers were killed and the third had his hand blown off.

Died of pneumonia at Colwyn Bay, North Wales, 11th March, 1916, whilst on leave from the front.

EDWARD HUMBERT FISHER

Born at Leicester, 6th March, 1885, son of Edward Fisher, of Apsley Guise.

Temp. Second Lieut., 20th March, 1915.

Joined the Expeditionary Force in November, 1914, and was commissioned from the Artists' Rifles.

Killed in the trenches near Festubert by a sniper, 19th May, 1915.

WILLIAM BASIL CORNABY

Born, 6th April, 1892, at Hankow, China, son of the Revd. W. A. Cornaby, of Chorlton-cum-Hardy, Manchester.

Temp. Second Lieut., 30th June, 1915 ; Chinese Labour Corps, 9th March, 1918.

Took part in the battle of Loos with the 8th Service Bn. (wounded), and in the operations on the Somme (wounded at Fricourt, 2nd July). Attached to 2nd Bn. in October, 1916, till appointed to Labour Corps. Rejoined the Bn. in October, 1918, and served with it till the Armistice.

DAVID EDWARD BAWTREE

Temp. Second Lieut,. 8th Service Bn., 27th March, 1915 ; relinquished his commission, 3rd February, 1916.

Posted to 2nd Bn., 8th October, 1915, and left in December.

JOHN C—— McINTYRE

Son of A. McIntyre, of Ings Avenue, Skipton.

Temp. Second Lieut., 3rd April, 1915.

Enlisted at the beginning of the war in the Gordon Highlanders, and was later transferred to the Argyll and Sutherland Highlanders. Promoted to a commission in the 11th Service Bn. of the South Lancashire Regt., and finally posted to the Green Howards. Was severely wounded at Hulloch, 26th September, 1915, both legs being broken. Was captured and died of his wounds in the Field Hospital, Seclin, 5th October, 1915.

ARTHUR HORWOOD EAMES

Born at Hardham, Pulborough, 24th November, 1894, son of L. H. Eames, Upper Nash, Pulborough, Sussex.

Temp. Second Lieut., 5th April, 1915 ; Temp. Lieut., 10th June, 1915.

Joined the Artists' Rifles, 7th August, 1914, and served with them in France until date of commission. Took part in the fighting at Festubert and Givenchy (wounded) with 2nd Bn. Transferred to East Yorkshire Regt. in August, 1915, being granted a regular commission, 4th March, 1916.

Killed at Fricourt, 2nd July, 1916. He was leading his company against a superior force on the Somme, and the enemy's position was taken and the defenders captured.

FREDERICK WILLIAM SMITH

Born at Leyton, Essex, 7th March, 1896, son of Samuel Smith, of Traherne, Highgate Road, London.

Temp. Second Lieut., 28th April, 1915 ; 21st Bn. 60th Rifles, 8th April, 1916.

Gassed at Hulloch, 25th September, 1915.

JOHN WILFRED BANNER

Born at Sheffield, 22nd September, 1885, son of John Banner, of Oakledge, Breechfield Road, Sheffield.

Temp. Second Lieut., 3rd May, 1915 ; Temp. Lieut., 30th June, 1915.

Posted to the 1st Bn. in India, 14th December, 1915, and served with the Mesopotamia Field Force.

PERCY WAGNER FINCH

Born at Romford, 4th May, 1894, son of George Finch, of Heaton Grange, Romford.

Temp. Second Lieut., 5th May, 1915 ; Temp. Lieut., 30th June, 1915.

Enlisted in the 16th Bn. London Regt., 2nd September, 1914. Posted to 1st Bn., 14th December, 1915.

REAY CHOULER

Born at Doncaster, 14th April, 1891, son of George Thompson Chouler, Oakdale, Meanwood Road, Leeds.

Temp. Second Lieut., 13th May, 1915.

Was in the ranks of the 6th and 11th Service Bns. Posted to 1st Bn., 14th December, 1915. Seconded to the Indian Army (wounded, " Times," 4th October, 1918).

BERTRAM APPLEBY NUTTALL

Born at Longton, Staffs, 9th June, 1888, son of the Revd. E. A. Nuttall.

Temp. Second Lieut., 20th May, 1915 ; Temp Lieut., 27th September, 1916.

Served in the ranks of the 21st Bn. Royal Fusiliers, from 11th September, 1914, to 19th May, 1915. Was in France with 2nd Bn. from 28th November, 1915, to 12th January, 1916. Wounded near Givenchy by a mine explosion, 30th November, 1915. Served in India with 1st Bn. Duke of Wellington's Regt., 30th November, 1916, to 20th March, 1917, and in Mesopotamia with 1st Bn. Manchester Regt., from 1st April, 1917, to 30th May, 1917.

CYRIL FRANCIS WEBB

Temp. Second Lieut., 11th June, 1915, from ranks of Artists' Rifles.

Killed at Hulloch, 25th September, 1915.

JOHN THOMAS COLBERT

Born, 18th December, 1884. Temp Second Lieut., 1st June, 1915 ; Temp. Lieut., 17th July, 1916 ; relinquished his commission on account of ill-health caused by wounds, 25th March, 1919.

Served in the ranks of the 21st Bn. Manchester Regt., 6th November, 1914, to 1st June, 1915. Was wounded on 26th and 30th of September, 1916, at Stuff Redoubt, Somme, when with 6th Service Bn. Served with 2nd Bn. from 1st May, to 12th November, 1917.

ARTHUR RAYMOND VAUGHAN

Born at Middlesboro', 2nd September, 1892, son of William Vaughan, of Middlesboro'.

Temp. Second Lieut., 20th November, 1915 ; Temp. Lieut., 1st July, 1917 ; relinquished his commission on account of ill-health, contracted on active service, 20th March, 1919.

Was serving with the Yorkshire Hussars in Scarboro' when it was bombarded by the Germans in December, 1914. Attached to 2nd Bn. in France from January to April, 1917.

JACK PYMAN, M.C.

Born, 3rd November, 1894, son of J. W. Pyman, Raithwaite, Penarth, near Cardiff.

Temp. Lieut., Royal Defence Corps, 12th October, 1914 ; Army Service Corps, 4th December, 1916 ; Yorkshire Regt., 4th January, 1917.

Served with the A.S.C. in France from January to March, 1917. Wounded at Henin-sur-Cojeul, 2nd April, 1917, when attached to 2nd Bn. Was again wounded in October, 1918, when attached to West Yorkshire Regt.

Awarded the Military Cross " For conspicuous gallantry and devotion to duty. After leading his men forward with great gallantry and dash, he realized with excellent judgment that further progress was not possible without reinforcements, as his company had suffered heavy casualties. He immediately reorganised his men and consolidated the position he had won. He beat off a heavy counter-attack and retained his position, moving about from post to post under heavy fire and encouraging his men by his fine example and disregard of personal safety."

ERNEST ARTHUR BULL

Born in London, 13th March, 1885, son of S. W. Bull, 1, Windsor Road, Leyton, Essex.

Temp. 2nd Lieut., 5th December, 1915 ; Temp. Lieut., 1st July, 1917 ; Adjt., Suffolk Volunteer Rifles, 26th November, 1917.

Joined the Expeditionary Force in November, 1914, in ranks of the London Rifle Brigade, and was present at the 2nd battle of Ypres. Took part also in the operations on the Somme in September and October, 1916, and was wounded at Flers, 13th October, 1916.

JOHN FLESHER MYERS, D.C.M.

Born at Otley, Yorkshire, 27th March, 1877, son of T. Myers, of Otley.

Temp. Second Lieut., 30th April, 1916.

Joined the Regiment, 5th December, 1894, and retired on pension as a Sergt. in 1913. Appointed Co. Sergt.-Major, 4th Bn. in September, 1914, and Regtl. Sergt.-Major, 29th September, 1915. Was awarded the Distinguished Conduct medal, 1st January, 1916, for " Conspicuous gallantry and resource in holding, under heavy fire with a small party of men, until relieved, a trench which had been nearly obliterated by shell fire. He also displayed great bravery in leading forward men into a trench occupied by the enemy." Was also decorated with the Croix de Guerre for distinguished service by General Foch. Joined 2nd Bn., 17th May, 1916. Was wounded at Glatz Redoubt, Mariecourt, 1st July, 1916, when serving with 2nd Bn.

Killed on the Passchendaele Ridge, 9th October, 1917, when serving with 6th Bn.

JOHN THOMAS EVANS

Born at Sheffield, 24th May, 1890, son of George Evans.

Temp. Second Lieut., 7th May, 1916 ; Temp. Lieut., 7th November, 1917 ; relinquished his commission on account of ill-health caused by wounds, 22nd May, 1918.

Was commissioned from the ranks of the 8th Service Bn. Yorkshire L.I. With 2nd Bn. took part in the battles on the Somme on 1st, 8th, and 23rd July, and in October, 1916. Was wounded at Arras, 2nd April, 1917.

JOSEPH BRIAN CUTTS

Born at Tibshelf, near Alfreton, Derbyshire, 21st December, 1887.

Temp. Second Lieut., 29th January, 1916 ; Temp. Lieut., 25th August, 1916 ; relinquished his commission on account of ill-health caused by wounds, 24th May, 1919.

Took part in the fighting at Montauban, Trônes Wood, Guillemont, and Sailly-Saillisel. Wounded at Waterlow Farm, Guillemont, 23rd July, 1916, when serving with 2nd Bn.

LAMBERT HANSON-ABBOTT

Born in London, 26th September, 1893, son of P. Hanson-Abbott, of Streatham Hill, London.

Temp. Second Lieut., 27th September, 1915 ; Temp. Lieut., 28th August, 1916.

Was for eleven months a trooper in the 19th Hussars. Attached to 2nd Bn., 10th July, 1916, and was wounded at Trônes Wood, Guillemont, 23rd July, 1916. Was also wounded at Poelcappelle in October, 1917.

GEOFFREY ERNEST LAYTON-BENNETT

Born at Holmdene, Mill Lane, West Hampstead, 4th January, 1888, son of Ernest Layton-Bennett.

Temp. Second Lieut., 5th December, 1915.

Saw service in Flanders with the London Rifle Brigade, and was present at the 2nd battle of Ypres in May, 1915.

Killed at the storming of Montauban (Somme), 1st July, 1916, when serving with 2nd Bn.

WILLIAM JACKSON

Born, 2nd June, 1895, son of J. Jackson, of Bishop Auckland.

Temp. Second Lieut., 26th September, 1916 ; Temp. Lieut., 26th March, 1918.

Served in the ranks of the 19th Bn. Royal Fusiliers from November 15th, to March, 1916, in France, and with 2nd Bn. from November, 1916, to April, 1917, when he was invalided. Was wounded in May, 1918, when serving with the 1st/5th Bn.

GEORGE PERCY LUND, M.C., O.B.E.

Born at Bingley, 27th February, 1884, son of Tom Lund, San Remo, Morecambe.

Temp. Second Lieut., 26th September, 1916 ; Temp. Lieut., 26th March, 1918.

Served in the ranks of the 19th Bn. Royal Fusiliers from January, 1915, to May, 1916. Posted to 2nd Bn. in October, 1916. Present at the operations before Arras in April, 1917. Awarded the Military Cross: " He led his company most ably to their objective, and on reaching it, he assumed command of a mixed lot of men, established them in position and worked hard for the following three days in maintaining his position, setting a fine example to all ranks by his coolness and energy." With the 2nd Bn. he also took part in the fighting between March and May, 1918. In June, 1918, he took over command of the 6th Bn. and served with it in North Russia during the winter of 1918-19, and during the operations there (mentioned in despatches, officer of the British Empire).

HERBERT SMITH, M.C.

Born at Clifton, York, 8th December, 1888, son of Samuel Smith, of Clifton.

Temp. Second Lieut., 26th September, 1916 ; Temp. Lieut., 26th March, 1918 ; relinquished his commission on account of ill-health caused by wounds, 25th March, 1918.

Served in the ranks of the 19th Bn. Royal Fusiliers in France from November, 1915, to May, 1916. Attached to 2nd Bn. from November, 1916, and was wounded at Henin, near Arras, 2nd April, 1917. Awarded the Military Cross : " He displayed great courage and ability when his platoon became cut off, himself killing several of the enemy and extricating his men with great coolness. He has, at all times, led his men with great courage and determination."

THOMAS CONNELLY

Temp. Second Lieut., 26th September, 1916 ; Temp. Lieut., 26th March, 1918.

Served with 2nd Bn. from November, 1916, till wounded at Arras, 2nd April, 1917.

FRANK WHALEY

Born at Horton-in-Ribblesdale, 16th September, 1895, youngest son of the Revd. Frank Webster Whaley, Vicar of Horton-in-Ribblesdale.

Temp. Second Lieut., 26th September, 1916.

Served throughout the winter of 1915-16 with the 19th Bn. Royal Fusiliers in France. Posted to the 2nd Bn. in November, 1916.

Killed at Henin-sur-Cojeul, 31st March, 1917, in a night attack, after having personally captured a prisoner with a machine gun. His commanding officer writing of him said : " Your gallant son was killed leading his men, whilst setting them a fine example of courage under heavy fire. A shell fell near him, and he died at once. He had been in a tight corner during an attack on a village, and had extricated his men with skill. He was seen on a parapet encouraging his men and leading them with ability. We all feel his loss ; he was liked by everyone in the regiment."

THOMAS WILLIAM BARON, M.C.

Born at Duggleley, Malton, 11th April, 1880.

Temp. Second Lieut., 6th November, 1916 ; Temp. Lieut., 6th May, 1918 ; resigned his commission, 26th March, 1920.

Served for 16 months with 2nd Bn. Scots Guards in the South African War, and with the 8th Bn. Seaforth Highlanders in France from October, 1915, to September, 1916 (bronze star). Wounded at Hulloch, 12th February, 1916, and again at Martinpuich, 17th August, 1916. Took part in the fighting at Arras with 2nd Bn. in April, 1917. Awarded the Military Cross. " When, in command of the support company, he engaged three strong points held by snipers in strength, and in the face of heavy rifle fire and shell fire, finally succeeded in capturing the posts. He set a fine example throughout a most difficult operation." Was also in the fighting on the Western Front from October, 1918, to the Armistice. Posted to 1st East York Regt. as 2nd in command, 1st November, 1918 (mentioned in despatches).

H. B. WHITFIELD

Temp. Second Lieut., 14th November, 1916, from the ranks of the Royal Highlanders (T.F.) ; Temp. Lieut., 14th May, 1918 ; relinquished his commission on account of ill-health caused by wounds, 4th March, 1919.

Served with the 2nd Bn. from November, 1916, till wounded on the 8th March, 1917, near Arras.

HERBERT MELVILLE WRIGHT

Second son of Francis H. Wright, of Reading.

Temp. Second Lieut., 25th October, 1916.

On the outbreak of war, being too young to join, he served with a British ambulance attached to a division of the French army in the Vosges. On obtaining his commission, he joined the 2nd Bn. in January, 1917.

Killed at Henin-sur-Cojeul, 2nd April, 1917.

The Chaplain wrote : " He and his company commander were up against the strong post of the village, and in the thickest of the fight they fell. They won the day, and dug themselves in half a kilo. beyond the village."

LEONARD THOMAS WOOTTON

Temp. Second Lieut., 25th January, 1917 ; Temp. Lieut., 25th July, 1918 ; relinquished his commission on completion of service with rank of Captain, 26th March, 1920.

Joined 2nd Bn. in France, 16th April, 1917, and was wounded at Arras same month, and again on 4th September, 1917, near Westoutre, Ypres.

ERNEST JAMES RAPP

Born at Saltburn, 13th June, 1893, son of George James Rapp, of Saltburn.

Temp. Second Lieut., 9th Service Bn., 29th April, 1915, from ranks of 5th Bn. Durham L.I.

Present at the 2nd battle of Ypres and at St. Julien, and Hill 60. Wounded, 20th April, 1916, and again on 1st July, 1916, when employed with a trench mortar battery. Joined 2nd Bn., 29th August, 1916, and was wounded on the Somme, 13th October, 1916.

Killed at Agny, near Arras, 9th April, 1917.

HAROLD DEAN, M.C.

Son of William Dean, of Thornbury, Grove Hill, Middlesbrough.

Temp. Second Lieut., 25th October, 1916.

Served for some months in France in the ranks of the Royal Engineers. After being commissioned, joined the 2nd Bn. in December, 1916, and was present in the fighting at Arras in April, 1917. Wounded in August, 1917. Awarded the Military Cross for conspicuous gallantry.

Lost his life in the fire in Hedge Street Tunnel, near Ypres, 5th January, 1918, aged 30. See page 272 under W. C. K. Birch.

WILLIAM BRUCE TAYLOR

Son of Captain D. M. Taylor, of Halifax.

Temp. Second Lieut., 9th Service Bn., 7th July, 1916.

Was wounded in France in September, 1916. Joined the 2nd Bn., 20th January, 1917.

Killed at the battle of Arras, 9th April, 1917.

WILFRID HIGHMOOR MITCHELL

Temp. Second Lieut., 22nd November, 1916 ; Temp. Lieut., 22nd May, 1918.

Served with the 7th Service Bn. in France from 5th January, 1917, to 7th June, 1917, when he was wounded. Served with 1st Bn. in India from 8th April, 1918, and in Afghanistan in 1919.

RAYMOND ROBERT TAYLOR

Temp. Second Lieut., 25th January, 1917 ; relinquished his commission on account of ill-health caused by wounds, 9th December, 1917.

Joined 2nd Bn., 21st May, 1917, and took part in the fighting at Arras, where he was wounded on the 9th April, 1917.

EDWARD McLAUGHLIN

Temp. Second Lieut., 25th January, 1917 ; Royal Engineers (Cadet unit), 28th October, 1917.

Joined 2nd Bn., 16th April, 1917, and took part in the fighting at Arras.

RICHARD SAM BEAUMONT

Born, 24th December, 1893. Temp. Second Lieut., 1st March, 1917 ; Temp. Lieut., 1st September, 1918.

Served in the ranks of the 31st Bn. Royal Fusiliers from 4th December, 1915, to 1st November, 1916, in France. Joined 2nd Bn., 15th April, 1917, and served with it till 2nd August. Posted to 13th Bn., 28th April, 1918.

HERBERT JEFFRIES

Born at Louth, Lincolnshire, 2nd August, 1888, son of Henry Jeffries, of Louth.

Temp. Second Lieut., 1st March, 1917 ; Machine Gun Corps, 20th January, 1918.

Served in the ranks of the 30th Bn. Manchester Regt., from January, 1916, to February, 1917. Joined 2nd Bn., 1st May, 1917. Present at the fighting near Ypres, 31st July, 1917.

Died of wounds, 20th September, 1918. Buried in Doingt Communal Cemetery, S.E. of Peronne.

DAVID CUNNINGHAM

Born at Leeds, 1889, son of James Cunningham.

Temp. Second Lieut., 1st March, 1917.

Served in the ranks of the 1st City Bn. of the Manchester Regt. in France from November, 1915, to 1st July, 1916, when he was wounded at the battle of the Somme. Joined 2nd Bn., 1st May, 1917.

Died at Bailleul, 27th October, 1917.

DAVID GRAY

Born at Gateshead-on-Tyne, 12th June, 1891.

Temp. Second Lieut., 1st March, 1917 ; Temp. Lieut., 1st September, 1918 ; 2nd/6th Durham L.I., 7th April, 1919.

Served in the ranks of the 4th Bn. from 6th July, 1915, to November, 1916. Was in France with 2nd Bn. from 1st May, 1917, to 28th July, 1917, and from 18th January, 1918, to 25th May, 1918, when he was invalided. Present at the battle of St. Quentin, 21st to 30th March, and at Poelcappelle, Langemarck, and Ypres, 4th to 30th April, 1918.

WILLIE ROWELL

Born at Tudhoe Grange, Co. Durham, 7th September, 1888, son of Henry Rowell.

Temp. Second Lieut., 1st March, 1917 ; Temp. Lieut., 1st September, 1918.

Was commissioned from the ranks of the 2nd/4th Bn. Joined the 2nd Bn., 16th April, 1917, and was wounded at Roupy on the St. Quentin-Ham Road, 21st March, 1918. Rejoined 2nd Bn. in June, and took part in the fighting up to August, 1918.

ALEXANDER GRANT

Born, 1st October, 1892, son of William Grant, of Jesmond, Newcastle-on-Tyne.

Temp. Second Lieut., 1st March, 1917.

Was commissioned from ranks of the 30th Bn. Northumberland Fusiliers. Served with 2nd Bn. in France from 1st to 20th May, 1917. Rejoined in July, 1918, and was with it till 29th September.

EDGAR MOORE THOMAS

Born at Linthorpe, Middlesbrough, 2nd March, 1897, son of Ernest John Norman Thomas, of Marton-in-Cleveland, Yorkshire.

Temp. Second Lieut., 1st March, 1917 ; Temp Lieut., 1st September, 1918.

Was commissioned from the ranks of the 14th Reserve Bn. Joined 2nd Bn., 1st May, 1917, and was present at the battle on the Messines Ridge, 7th June, 1917.

JOHN SYMON

Born at Keith, 15th August, 1895, son of John Symon, of Keith, Banffshire.

Temp. Second Lieut., 30th May, 1917.

Served in the ranks of the 6th Bn. Gordon Highlanders in France from 9th November, 1914, to January, 1917. Was wounded at Loos, 29th September, 1915. Joined 2nd Bn., 8th August, 1917.

Lost his life in the fire at Hedge Street Tunnel, near Ypres, 5th January, 1918. See page 272 under W. C. K. Birch.

ROBERT ANDERSON CARTER

Born, 17th August, 1896. Temp. Second Lieut., 27th June, 1917.

Served in the ranks of the 5th Bn. Border Regt. in France from March, 1916, to February, 1917 (wounded at Flers, 15th September, 1916). Present at the fighting at the Butte de Warlincourt, 1st October, and 5th November, 1916. Joined 2nd Bn., 8th August, 1917, and transferred to Royal Flying Corps, 3rd January, 1918.

WALTER ORDISH HALL

Born, 30th July, 1893. Temp. Second Lieut., 27th June, 1917 ; Temp. Lieut., 27th December, 1918.

Served in the ranks of the 18th Hussars from 21st October, 1915, and was at the battle of the Somme, July to August, 1916. Posted to 2nd Bn., 13th August, 1917, and was present at the fighting on the Western Front from March to October, 1918, being wounded at Epinoy, 27th, September.

HAROLD VICTOR ROXBY

Born, 19th July, 1892. Temp. Second Lieut., 27th June, 1917 ; Temp. Lieut., 27th December, 1918 ; demobilized, 24th March, 1919.

Served in the ranks of the Yorkshire Hussars (Yeomanry) in France from 26th February, 1915. Joined 2nd Bn., 13th August, 1917, and was present at the fighting on the Western Front up to the Armistice.

JIM STEMBRIDGE

Born, 30th December, 1890. Temp. Second Lieut., 27th June, 1917.

Served with 6th Bn. Durham L.I. in France, including 2nd battle of Ypres, and on the Somme, 15th September, 1916, to 8th January, 1917. Joined 2nd Bn., 13th August, 1917.

Killed in action at Epinoy, 29th September, 1918.

WILLIAM JOHN COOPER

Born at Hull, 19th April, 1892, son of William John Cooper, of Barton-on-Humber, Lincolnshire.

Temp. Second Lieut., 27th June, 1917 ; Temp. Lieut., 27th December, 1918.

Served in the ranks of the Yorkshire and Durham Brigade Company A.S.C. (T.F.), and as Co. Sergt-Major from April, 1915, to March, 1917, with 50th Divisional Train in France. Present at the 2nd battle of Ypres in May, 1915, and at the fighting at Martinpuich and Flers in September, 1916 (mentioned in despatches). Joined 2nd Bn. in August, 1917, and was wounded at Ypres, 12th December, 1917 (bronze star).

LANCELOT FRANCIS SIMPSON, M.C.

Born, 23rd February, 1893, son of L. J. Simpson, of Pickering.

Temp. Second Lieut., 27th June, 1917 ; Temp. Lieut., 27th December, 1918.

Served for 21 months in the ranks of the 2nd Life Guards in France and was wounded at Hulloch, 24th January, 1916. Posted to 2nd Bn., 8th September, 1917, and took part in the fighting on the Western Front.

in 1918 up to the Armistice, the last six months as Adjutant. Awarded the Military Cross as follows : " During recent operations he showed great courage throughout and more than once saved a critical situation by rallying scattered men. His personal gallantry and coolness were of great service to the battalion."

ANDREW TAYLOR ROONEY, M.C.

Born, 8th July, 1892, son of J. B. Rooney, of Burnhope, Lancaster, Durham.

Temp. Second Lieut., 27th June, 1917 ; Temp. Lieut., 27th December, 1918 ; demobilized, 8th February, 1919.

Served in the ranks of the 9th Service Bn., from 25th August, 1915, to 10th January, 1917, in France. Was at the fighting at Scott's Redoubt near La Berselle, Somme, in July, 1916, at Contalmaison, 10th July, 1916, and Le Sars, 8th October, 1916. Posted to 2nd Bn., 8th September, 1917, and was present at the operations on the Western Front from March to April and from October to Armistice.

JAMES WILFRED WALKER, M.C.

Born, 2nd April, 1894, at Bridlington, son of James Walker, 3, Havelock Place, Bridlington.

Temp. Second Lieut., 27th June, 1917 ; Temp. Lieut., 27th December, 1918 ; relinquished his commission on account of ill-health caused by wounds, 26th February, 1920.

Served in the ranks of the 50th Divisional Train from 17th April, 1915, to 11th January, 1917, in France (bronze star). Posted to 2nd Bn., 7th September, 1917. Wounded and captured at Roupy on the St. Quentin-Ham Road, 22nd March, 1918 (Military Cross, 5th May, 1919).

GILBERT FARRAR

Born at Leeds, 16th April, 1893, son of Ramsden Farrar, of Leeds.

Temp. Second Lieut.,27th June, 1917 ; resigned his commission on account of ill-health contracted on active service, 6th November, 1918.

Served in the ranks of the Yorkshire Dragoons and took part in the Somme offensive of 1916. Joined 2nd Bn., 8th September, 1917, and was transferred to the 21st Trench Mortar Battery, 13th December, 1917. Wounded (shell shock) at Roupy on the St. Quentin-Ham Road, 22nd March, 1918.

ERNEST WILLIAM HARPER

Born at Leeds, 4th May, 1890. Temp. Second Lieut., 27th June, 1917.

Served in the ranks of the 13th Service Bn. in France from June, 1916, to 23rd January, 1917. Joined 2nd Bn., 7th September, 1917. Appointed Instructor 8th Corps School, 16th January, 1918.

JOSEPH FOREMAN

Born at Bear Park, 6th May, 1894, son of William Foreman, 8, Swan Street, Bear Park, Co. Durham.

Temp. Second Lieut., 27th June, 1917 ; Temp. Lieut., 27th December, 1918.

Served in the ranks of the 7th Service Bn. in France from 13th July, 1915, to 18th January, 1917. Attached to 2nd Bn., 8th September, 1917. Wounded at Roupy, 22nd March, 1918.

RICHARD NELSON PICKEN, M.B.E.

Born, 1st June, 1891. Temp. Second Lieut., 27th June, 1917 ; Temp. Lieut., 27th December, 1918.

Served in the ranks of the 18th Bn., Durham L.I., from 7th December, 1915, in Egypt, and from 2nd March, 1916, to 28th January, 1917, in France. Present at the battles of Serre Wood, 1st July, 1916, and Gommecourt, 13th November, 1916. Joined 2nd Bn., 8th September, 1917, and was wounded at Roupy, 23rd March, 1918. Rejoined, 16th October, 1918. Transferred to 9th Bn. Northumberland Fusiliers, 16th March, 1919 (mentioned in despatches).

JOHN JAMES COWNLEY, M.C.

Born, 23rd April, 1887, son of James Cownley, Swallow's Nest, Sheffield.

Temp. Second Lieut., 27th June, 1917 ; Lieut., 27th December, 1918.

Served in the ranks of the 8th Bn. North Staffordshire Regt., from 17th July, 1915, to 27th January, 1917, in France. Took part in the battle of Loos, and Bluff attack, Givenchy, 25th September, 1915 (bronze star). Present at the Somme, 1916, operations at La Boiselle, Contalmaison, High Wood, and Bazentin (wounded). Was slightly wounded at Grandecourt, 18th November, 1916. Joined 2nd Bn., 7th September, 1917, and was taken prisoner at Roupy, 21st March, 1918 (Military Cross, 5th May, 1919).

WILLARD BARBER

Born, 5th November, 1894. Temp. Second Lieut., 27th June, 1917.

Served in the ranks of the 10th Service Bn. from 9th September, 1915, to 29th January, 1917, in France. Present at battle of Loos, September, 1915 (bronze star), on the Somme, at Fricourt, Mametz Wood, and Flers. Also at Grandecourt. Received a distinction card from the G.O.C. 21st Division for good work in the Field. Joined the 2nd Bn., 7th September, 1917.

Lost his life in the fire at Hedge Street Tunnel, near Ypres, 5th January, 1918. See page 272 under W. C. K. Birch.

CHARLES ALFRED BARKER

Born, 29th July, 1893. Temp. Second Lieut., 27th June, 1917 ; Temp. Lieut., 27th December, 1918.

Served in the ranks of the 13th Service Bn. from 6th June, 1916, to 13th January, 1917, in France. Joined 2nd Bn., 7th September, 1917. Was wounded and captured at Roupy, 23rd March, 1918.

DONALD WILLIAM HARRIES LEAN

Born at Hathersage, Derbyshire, 28th July, 1893.

Temp. Second Lieut., 29th August, 1917.

Served in the ranks of the R.A.M.C. in France from 25th August, 1915, to 20th February, 1917 (bronze star). Joined 2nd Bn., 31st October, 1917. Wounded on 30th March, 1918, at Esmery-Hallon on the St. Quentin-Ham Road.

Dismissed the Service by sentence of a General Court Martial, 17th January, 1919.

JOHN FRANCIS CHALMERS PARK

Born, 7th October, 1893. Temp. Second Lieut., 29th August, 1917 ; Temp. Lieut., 1st March, 1919 ; 2/6th Durham L.I., 7th April, 1919.

Served in the ranks of the 15th Bn. West Yorkshire Regt. from 5th December, 1915, to July, 1916, in Egypt and France. Wounded at Serre on the Somme 1st July, 1916 Joined 2nd Bn. 31st October, 1917, and took part in the fighting on the Western Front between March and November, 1918.

NORMAN HOWARTH

Born at Toronto, 1st September, 1891, son of F. Howarth, of Roundhay, Leeds.

Temp. Second Lieut., 29th August, 1917 ; Temp. Lieut., 30th July, 1919.

Served in the ranks of the 15th Bn. West Yorkshire Regt. in Egypt and France from December, 1915, to July, 1916. Wounded at Serre on the Somme 1st July, 1916. Joined 2nd Bn. 31st October, 1917.

Missing at Roupy, 22nd March, 1918.

WILLIAM HILL PORTER

Born, 9th April, 1893, son of Thomas Porter, York House, Harrogate.

Temp. Second Lieut., 9th April, 1915 ; Temp. Lieut., 1st July, 1917.

Took part in actions at Bouchavesnes Wood, February, 1917, and at Bourlon Wood, November, 1917, when he was wounded on the 23rd. Joined 2nd Bn. 17th April, 1918, and transferred to 1/5th Bn. 26th April, 1918.

ARTHUR DOCKRAY, D.C.M.

Born, 28th March, 1894. Temp. Second Lieut., 26th April, 1917 ; Temp. Lieut., 26th October, 1918.

Served in the ranks of the 9th Service Bn. from August, 1916, to April, 1917, in France. Present at Contalmaison 10th July, 1916, and at Le Sars 7th October, 1916. Awarded the Distinguished Conduct medal "for conspicuous gallantry in action. With three men, he rushed an enemy machine gun, shooting the team and capturing the gun, thereby ensuring the success of the infantry attack." Joined 2nd Bn. 17th April, 1918, and transferred to 13th Bn. on 28th April. Was wounded in June, 1918.

CHARLES HENRY MARSDEN

Born, 20th December, 1892. Temp. Second Lieut., 29th August, 1917 ; Temp. Lieut., 1st March, 1919.

Served in France in the ranks of the 9th Service Bn. Suffolk Regt. from July to December, 1915, and from February to September, 1916. Present at the battle of Loos 25th September, 1915, gas attack at Ypres 19th December, 1915, battle of Beaumont Hamel 20th August, 1916. (Gassed at Ypres, 20th December, 1915, shell shock at Beaumont Hamel 29th August, 1916.) Joined 2nd Bn. 17th April, 1918. Transferred to 13th Service Bn. 28th October, 1918. (bronze star).

GEORGE AUGUSTUS BOWLER

Born, 29th August, 1896. Temp. Second Lieut., 30th May, 1917 ; Temp. Lieut., 30th November, 1918.

Served in the ranks of the 4th Bn. in France from 17th April, 1915, to 1st January, 1917. Present at the second battle of Ypres, Hooge May, 1915, Martinpuich, September, 1916, Eaucourt l'Abbaye, September, 1916, and Butte de Warlencourt November, 1916. Wounded at Polygon Wood 4th October, 1917, and again at Butte de Polygon 28th October, 1917. Joined 2nd Bn. 17th April and transferred to 13th Bn. 28th April, 1918 (bronze star).

BLANCKENBERG WAHL

Born, 25th January, 1886. Temp. Second Lieut., 1st March, 1917 ; Temp. Lieut., 1st September, 1918.

Served in the German West African Rebellion 1914-15. Posted to 9th Service Bn. 26th July, 1917, and was wounded at Inverness Copse 20th September, 1917. Joined 2nd Bn. 17th April, 1918, and transferred to 13th Bn. 28th April, 1918.

Taken prisoner by the Germans in June, 1918.

FRANCIS ERNEST STOKELD

Born, 11th August, 1896. Temp. Second Lieut., 26th September, 1917 ; Temp. Lieut., 26th March, 1919.

Served in the ranks of the 35th Field Ambulance in Gallipoli from July to September, 1915, and in France from March, 1916, to April, 1917. Joined 2nd Bn., 10th February, 1918, and took part in the fighting on the Western front till June, 1918 (bronze star).

CHRISTOPHER FRANK TURPIN

Temp. Second Lieut., 29th August, 1917 ; Temp. Lieut., 1st March, 1919 ; relinquished his commission, 26th March, 1920.

Was commissioned from a Cadet unit. Served with 1st Bn. in India during the war.

THOMAS PARKER LYNN

Temp. Second Lieut., 29th August, 1917 ; demobilised in March, 1919.

Was commissioned from a Cadet unit. Served with 1st Bn. in India during the war.

LESLIE BURNETT BARCHARD

Temp. Second Lieut., 29th August, 1917 ; 1/9th Bn. East Yorkshire Regt., May, 1918 ; relinquished his commission, 19th February, 1920.

Was commissioned from a Cadet unit. Served with 1st Bn. in India during the war.

ERNEST WILLIAM HECKLE

Temp. Second Lieut., 29th August, 1917 ; Temp. Lieut., 1st March, 1919.

Was commissioned from a Cadet unit. Served with 1st Bn. in India and in the operations in Afghanistan in 1919.

B. D. CROOKS

Temp. Second Lieut., 16th March, 1918 ; Temp. Lieut., 16th September, 1919.

Commissioned from Officers' Cadet unit. Served with 1st Bn. in India, and with the Royal Engineers in Persia.

H. O. URE

Temp. Second Lieut., 16th March, 1918.

Commissioned from Officers' Cadet unit. Served with 1st Bn. in India. Transferred to Army Signal Service.

JOHN EDWARD HIBBERT

Born at Gomersal, near Leeds, 2nd July, 1889, son of Edward Hibbert, of Gomersal.

Temp. Second Lieut., 30th May, 1917 ; Temp. Lieut., 30th November, 1918.

Served with the A.S.C. Motor Transport from 14th May, 1915, to 29th May, 1917, at home and in France. Joined 2nd Bn 10th February, 1918, from 10th S. Bn.

Taken prisoner 8th May, 1918, at Ypres.

JAMES DICKENSON SMITH, M.C., M.M.

Born at Swalwell, Co. Durham, 23rd July, 1891, son of J. D. Smith, of Stanley, Co. Durham.

Temp. Second Lieut., 29th August, 1917.

Enlisted in the 18th Bn. Durham L.I. 5th October, 1914, and served in Egypt and France from October, 1915, to July, 1916, and later with 3rd Bn. Durham L.I. Was present at the operations on the Somme in 1916 and at Arras in 1917 (wounded). Awarded the Military medal, the Military Cross, and the 4th class order of St. George of Russia. The following is the Gazette announcement of the M.C. :—" Hearing that an enemy post had been located, he decided to raid it with two N.C.O.'s and three men. After a personal reconnaissance, the post was surprised, fourteen of the enemy were killed and a prisoner captured. It was entirely due to his courage and initiative that the operation was successful."

Posted to 2nd Bn. 10th February, 1918. Wounded at Roupy 21st March, 1918.

ARTHUR OSWALD LISTER

Born at Shildon, Co. Durham, 14th September, 1891, son of Charles Lister, Sherburn Hill, Co. Durham.

Temp. Second Lieut., 12th July, 1915 ; Temp. Lieut., 19th July, 1916.

Posted to 2nd Bn. 29th August, 1916. Took part in the operations on the Somme (shell shock at Flers) 18th October, 1916. Rejoined 25th October. Invalided home 19th March, 1917.

THOMAS CHARLES WILLIAM SANDLAND

Born at Whittington Bks., Lichfield, 19th September, 1892, son of Major W. Sandland.

Temp. Second Lieut., 21st September, 1915 ; Temp. Lieut., 1st July, 1917 ; Royal Air Force, 7th November, 1918.

Served in the Staffordshire Yeomanry at Salonika and in France. Posted to the 2nd Bn. 10th February, 1918, from the 10th Service Bn. Wounded on the 26th April, 1918, near Ypres. Rejoined the battalion 17th May, and served with it till appointed to the Royal Air Force.

JOHN BEVAN

Born at Thorverton, Devonshire, 20th March, 1894, son of W. Bevan, R.E. Services, of Tower Hill, Haverfordwest.

Temp. Second Lieut., 30th May, 1917.

Served in the R.A.M.C. from July to October, 1915, in Gallipoli, and from March to December, 1916, in France. Present at Broodseinde Ridge 4th October, 1917, with 10th Bn. Posted to 2nd Bn. 10th February, 1918, and joined the Royal Air Force in April.

B——— READING

Temp. Second Lieut., 10th September, 1916.

Served previous to 1916 in the ranks of a service Bn. of the Royal Berkshire Regt. Posted to 2nd Bn. 10th February, 1918, and took part in the German offensive in March, 1918. Transferred to Royal Air Force in June.

HERBERT EDWARD READ, D.S.O., M.C.

Born at Kirby Moorside, 4th December, 1893, son of Herbert Read, of Roundhay, Leeds.

Temp. Second Lieut., 6th January, 1915 ; Temp. Lieut., 1st July, 1917.

Served with the 10th Service Bn. at Arras and Ypres April, 1917, to February, 1918. With 7th Bn. November, 1915 to March, 1916 (wounded at St. Eloi). Posted to 2nd Bn. 23rd February, 1918, and served with it as Adjt. during the fighting in March, April, and May (mentioned in despatches, Distinguished Service Order and Military Cross). Awarded the M.C. "for conspicuous gallantry and devotion to duty. Whilst leading a raid, a hostile covering party was encountered, which he attacked with the greatest promptitude and courage ; and although outnumbered, succeeded in killing one of the enemy and capturing an officer himself, in addition to inflicting severe casualties on the enemy. He withdrew his party under heavy fire with complete success, having contributed very largely to the success of the whole operation by a valuable reconnaissance, which he had made prior to the raid."

The D.S.O. was awarded under the following circumstances :—
"When his commanding officer was wounded he took command and successfully held his position for some time, surrounded by the enemy. He then organised the remnants of the battalion and fought a brilliant rearguard action. His behaviour at a most critical period of the battle was worthy of the highest praise."

COLIN DAVISON

Born at West Hartlepool, 24th August, 1893, son of R. C. Davison, of Linthorpe, Middlesbro'.

Temp. Second Lieut., 3rd January, 1916 ; Temp. Lieut., 3rd July, 1917.

Served in France with 10th Bn. and was wounded at Polygon Wood 4th October, 1917. Posted to 2nd Bn. 23rd February, 1918, and took part in the fighting during the German offensive till captured near Ypres on the 8th May.

CHARLES FREDERIC JAMESON, M.C.

Born at Ponteland, Newcastle-on-Tyne, 2nd October, 1898.

Temp. Second Lieut., 29th August, 1917 ; Temp. Lieut., 1st March, 1919.

Served before Ypres, October, 1917, and in the Cambrai sector, December, 1917, to January, 1918 (wounded at Ypres 7th November, 1917). Took part in the fighting with the 2nd Bn. during the German offensive of 1918, and was wounded near Armentières on 10th April. Afterwards served on the North Russian front with 13th Bn. Awarded the Military Cross under the following circumstances :—" During the enemy's attempted attack on Sred Mekrenga on March 17th, 1919, he showed a splendid example to the men. When the cavalry patrol fell back too rapidly, he rallied the British infantry patrol, and set them the necessary example with great coolness under heavy fire."

ALBERT LEE

Born at Goole, 19th May, 1878, son of W. T. Lee, of Goole. Temp. Second Lieut., 29th September, 1918.

Served in the ranks of 18th Bn. West Yorkshire Regt. in France from 7th October, 1916, to 25th March, 1917, including the offensive on the Ancre 13th November, 1916. Posted to 2nd Bn. 2nd April, 1918, and took part in the fighting on the Western front.

VICTOR WILLIAM WILLIAMS SAUNDERS PURCELL

Born, 26th January, 1896. Temp. Second Lieut., 13th November, 1914 ; Temp. Lieut., 13th May, 1917.

With 7th S. Bn. took part in the actions at the Bluff, St. Eloi, 14th February to 10th March, 1916, and at Sailley-Saillisel 8th February, 1917 (wounded). Posted to 2nd Bn. 17th April, and transferred to 1/4th Bn. 23rd April, 1918.

Taken prisoner in June, 1918.

ALBERT EDWARD MALINS

Born, 14th June, 1881, son of Arthur Malins, of Leamington Spa.

Temp. Second Lieut., 23rd November, 1915 ; Temp. Lieut., 1st July, 1917.

Posted to 2nd Bn. 17th April, 1918. Wounded (gas poisoning) 26th April, 1918, at Montreal Camp, Ouderdom Area, Ypres.

JOHN HALLIDAY

Born at Edenmouth, Parish of Ednam, 8th July, 1892, son of John Halliday, Eccles Mains, Kelso, N.B.

Temp. Second Lieut., 30th January, 1918.

Served in the ranks from 9th July, 1915, to 8th July, 1917, in France. Wounded at Loos 25th September, 1915, and again at Hulloch 9th December, 1915. Present at the fight at Oppy Wood 10th May, 1916, and in the operations on the Somme July to September, 1916, and Vimy Ridge, 9th April, 1917. Posted to 2nd Bn., 2nd May, 1918.

Wounded and missing at Dickebusche Lake, near Ypres, 8th May, 1918.

PETER AITCHISON

Born, 10th August, 1894, son of George Aitchison, Berry Hill, Bunkfoot, Perthshire.

Temp. Second Lieut., 30th January, 1918

Served in the ranks of the Royal Dragoons in France from 9th December, 1914, to 21st July, 1917. Present at the second battle of Ypres, Loos (wounded), and Somme 1916. Posted 2nd Bn. 2nd May, 1918.

Missing at Ypres, 8th May, 1918.

JOSEPH HENDERSON

Born, 19th July, 1894, son of A. Henderson, Kirkton, Kirk-manoe, Dumfries.

Temp. Second Lieut., 30th January, 1918.

Served in the ranks of the Gordon Highlanders in France from October, 1915, to July, 1917. Wounded at Hulloch in November, 1915, and at Arras 7th April, 1917 (bronze star). Posted to 2nd Bn. 2nd May, 1918. Wounded at Ridge Wood, Ypres, 8th May, 1918.

JOHN GREENBANK CAMPBELL

Born at Clapham, 3rd July, 1893, son of Thomas Campbell, Town Head, Austwick, near Lancaster.

Temp. Second Lieut., 30th January, 1918.

Served in the ranks of the 18th Bn. West Yorkshire Regt. and 8th Cyclist Corps in Egypt and France from 23rd December, 1915, to 13th July, 1917. Present at the operations on the Somme July to August, 1916. Gassed at Ypres in May, 1917. Posted to 2nd Bn. 2nd May, 1918. Killed at Ridge Wood, Ypres, 8th May, 1918.

HARRY CHILD

Born at Leeds, 12th January, 1892, son of John Child, of Bridlington.

Temp. Second Lieut., 30th January, 1918 ; demobilised 30th March, 1919.

Served in the ranks of the 21st Bn. 60th Rifles from 5th May, 1916, to 5th July, 1917, in France. Wounded at Ploegstreet 1st June, 1916. Present at the operations on the Somme 6th October, 1916, et seq. Posted to 2nd Bn. 2nd May, 1918, and took part in the fighting on the Western front up to the Armistice.

GEORGE McLAREN

Born, 2nd July, 1897, son of Duncan McLaren, of Dollar, Fifeshire.

Temp. Second Lieut., 30th January, 1918 ; demobilised, 6th February, 1919.

Served in the ranks of the Argyll and Sutherland Highlanders at Salonika from 6th November, 1916, to 18th July, 1917. Present at the action at Lake Doiran 8th-9th May, 1917. Posted to 2nd Bn. 2nd May, 1918, and took part in the fighting on the Western front up to the Armistice.

GEORGE ARCHIBALD TOMLIN, M.C.

Born in London, 19th June, 1881, 5th son of J. L. Tomlin, of Thiernswood, Richmond, Yorks.

Temp. Second Lieut., 5th December, 1914 ; Temp. Lieut., 11th November, 1916 ; demobilised, December, 1919.

Served with the 7th Service Bn. in the fighting at St. Eloi, on the Somme, and at Arras, Armentières, Cambrai, and Havrincourt Wood (mentioned in despatches and Military Cross). The latter gazetted as follows :—" When various dumps had blown up and ammunition was urgently required, he brought up limber loads by circuitous routes under heavy shell fire. It was through his ready resource, disregard of personal safety, and dogged determination that eleven limber loads of ammu nition were made available for the front line at a critical juncture." Was employed continuously as transport officer till disbandment of the 7th Bn. in February, 1918. Posted to the 2nd Bn. 11th May, 1918, on the Hulloch sector being attached to 32nd Bde. H.Q. as transport officer. Served under D.D. Remounts 1st Army August to November, 1918, when he rejoined 2nd Bn., and came home with the cadre in June, 1919. Served with the R.A.S.C. till demobilisation.

SIDNEY CRANSWICK, M.C.

Born at Hummanby, 20th October, 1882, son of John Cranswick, Field House, Hummanby, E. Yorkshire.

Temp. Second Lieut., 24th December, 1914 ; Temp. Lieut., 16th August, 1915 ; Temp. Capt., 23rd February, 1917.

Served in France from June, 1915, to May, 1918, with 6th and 7th Bns. Present at the fighting on the Somme July to October, 1916, Fricourt, Mametz, etc., Sailly-Saillisel February, 1917 (mentioned in despatches and Military Cross). Posted to 2nd Bn. 16th May, 1918, and served with it till 13th June on the Western front.

CLIVE LANE BAYLISS

Born at Wandsworth, 28th November, 1897, son of George Bayliss, of North Finchley, London.

Temp. Second Lieut., 22nd July, 1915 ; Temp. Lieut., 9th May, 1917.

Served in France with London Rifle Bde. 26th January to 6th March, 1915, and in Gallipoli with 6th Service Bn. from 24th October to 20th December, 1915, in Malta and Egypt from 20th December, 1915, to 26th June, 1916, and in France from 1st July to 18th August, 1916, and from 5th January, 1917, till wounded at Hill 70 (Loos) 28th November, 1917 (bronze star). Joined 2nd Bn. 16th May, 1918, and served with it in the fighting on the Western front till the end of June, when he proceeded to England to join the Indian Army.

ERNEST CHARLES GEORGE MOUNTFORD

Born, 19th June, 1879. Temp. Lieut. Gen. List, 31st July, 1915 ; Nigeria Regt., 25th August, 1915 ; Yorkshire Regt., 1st February, 1917.

Served in the Cameroons and Nigeria from September to December, 1915, with West African Frontier Force. Joined 2nd Bn. 16th May, 1918, and served with it till 5th November, 1918.

ARNOLD OUGHTRED VICK

Born, 29th March, 1890, 5th son of R. W. Vick, of Highnam, West Hartlepool.

Temp. Second Lieut., 11th November, 1914 ; Temp. Lieut., 1st July, 1917.

Posted to 6th Service Bn. in Egypt in March, 1916, and went with it to France in July, 1916. Was wounded at Wanderwerk, near Theipval, 14th September, 1916, and again at Stuff Redoubt 27th September, 1916. Joined 2nd Bn. 16th May, 1918.

Killed in action at Epinoy 27th September, 1918.

His company commander wrote :—" He did his work gallantly, and I am proud of him." A non-commissioned officer who was near him at the end, said :—" He knew no fear, and the men would follow him any-where. His total disregard of danger was most inspiring."

WILFRID DRESSER, M.C.

Born, 29th November, 1895, son of John Charles Dresser, of Darlington.

Temp. Second Lieut., 29th April, 1915 ; Temp. Lieut., 19th May, 1917.

Enlisted in the 4th Bn. and served with it in France from 17th September, 1914, till commissioned, including second battle of Ypres. Was posted to 5th Bn. West Yorkshire Regt. 17th August, 1915, and took part in the attack on Theipval (wounded), and was at Poelcappelle in October, 1917 (mentioned in despatches). Joined 2nd Bn. 16th May, 1918, and served with it in the fighting on the Western front till August, 1918, when appointed to the Staff.

ALICK WILLIAM TOVELL

Born at Chelsea, 13th June, 1891, son of E. A. Tovell, of Scarborough.

Temp. Second Lieut., 29th August, 1917 ; Temp. Lieut., 1st March, 1919 ; 9th Bn. Northumberland Fusiliers, 16th March, 1919.

Served in the ranks of the Norfolk Regt. in France from 10th October, 1915, to 12th March, 1916, and afterwards with 6th and 7th Bns. Wounded at St. Jean, Ypres, 5th March, 1916. Joined 2nd Bn. 16th May, 1918, and took part in the fighting on the Western front up to the Armistice.

LANCELOT HAROLD BARKER

Born at Coatham, Redcar, 24th October, 1896, son of L. H. Barker, of Redcar.

Temp. Second Lieut., 28th March, 1917.

Was commissioned from ranks of the Regt. Joined 2nd Bn. 16th May, 1918, and was wounded 31st August at the capture of Hamblain-les-Pres.

HAROLD CHARLES RATCLIFF

Born, 22nd March, 1889. Temp. Second Lieut., 29th August, 1917.

Served in the ranks of 5th Bn. Northumberland Fusiliers in France from 8th July, 1916, to 5th May, 1917. Took part in the operations on the Somme August, 1916, to January, 1917. Posted to 6th Service Bn. 18th October, 1917, and served with it till commissioned. Joined 2nd Bn. 16th May, 1918, and was shortly afterwards transferred to the Royal Air Force.

BENJAMIN SYDNEY APPLEYARD

Born at Thornton, Bradford, 3rd May, 1891, son of J. A. Appleyard, of Bowling, Bradford.

Temp. Second Lieut., 29th August, 1917.

Served in France in the ranks of the West Yorkshire Regt. from March, 1916, to August, 1916, and was present at St. Eloi 23rd March, Longueval Ridge 14th July, Delville Wood 23rd July, and Guillemont 17th August (wounded). Again wounded at Lens 27th November, 1917. Posted to 2nd Bn. 16th May, 1918.

Killed in action at Epinoy 29th September, 1918.

WILLIAM CHARLES NUNN

Born at St. John's Wood, 22nd March, 1895. Temp. Second Lieut., 29th August, 1917 ; relinquished his commission, 31st December, 1919.

Served in the ranks of the Duke of Cornwall's L.I. in France from 21st August, 1916, to 28th February, 1917, taking part in the battles of Delville Wood and Gueudecourt. Joined 2nd Bn. 16th May, 1918, and was attached to the 32nd T.M. Battery up to the Armistice. Transferred to 36th Bn. Northumberland Fusiliers 15th March, 1919.

ERNEST APPLEYARD, M.M.

Born, 26th March, 1886. Temp. Second Lieut., 26th April, 1917.

Served in the ranks two years and eight months. **Wounded at** Neuve Chapelle 13th September, 1916. Awarded the Military medal 10th November, 1916. Joined 2nd Bn. 16th May, 1918, and a month later was transferred to the Machine Gun Corps.

WILLIAM RALPH HALL

Born, 14th November, 1883. Temp. Second Lieut., 30th May, 1917 ; Temp. Lieut., 30th November, 1918.

Served in the ranks of the 17th Royal Fusiliers from 9th August to 24th December, 1916, in France. Present at the fighting at Beaumont Hamel 13th November, 1916. Posted to 2nd Bn. 16th May, 1918. Was wounded at Hulloch 24th June, whilst wiring. Rejoined 7th August and served till the Armistice.

CHARLES BIRD

Born at Middlesbro', 1st January, 1892, son of R. Bird, of Linthorpe, Middlesbro'.

Temp. Second Lieut., 30th May, 1917 ; Temp. Lieut., 30th November, 1918 ; 6th Bn. Durham L.I., 7th April, 1919.

Served in the ranks of the 4th Bn. from 11th November, 1911, to 29th May, 1917. Present at first battle of Ypres, at Loos, and the operations on the Somme. Wounded at Hooge 24th May, 1915. Joined 2nd Bn. 19th June, 1918, and was in the fighting up to September on the Western front (bronze star and clasp).

JOHN ORAM

Born at Longdon, Staffs., 10th August, 1892, son of Thomas Oram, of Lichfield.

Temp. Second Lieut., 29th August, 1917 ; Temp. Lieut , 1st March, 1919.

Served in the ranks of the 2/8th Bn. Worcester Regt. from 29th May, 1916, to February, 1917, in France. Posted to 2nd Bn. 25th June, 1918, and took part in the fighting up to the Armistice.

JOHN GAYLARD LAWRENCE

Born at Londonderry, 12th January, 1878, son of Lieut.-Col. William Wylly Lawrence, late 18th Foot.

Second Lieut., 18th Foot, 9th September, 1897 ; Lieut., 14th October, 1899 ; Capt., A.P.D., 29th October, 1903 ; Adjt., 6th Service Bn., 14th July, 1917.

Served in the Tirah Expedition (medal and clasp). Present at Messines, 1917 (wounded), and at third battle of Ypres. Joined 2nd Bn. as acting Lieut.-Col. 8th June, 1918, and served with it till appointed to command 7th Bn. Lincoln Regt. 20th October, 1918.

DAVID BRUCE ALMGILL

Born at Middlesbro', 27th December, 1895. Temp. Second Lieut., 6th January, 1916 ; Temp. Lieut., 6th July, 1917.

Served in the ranks of the York Hussars for sixteen months. Present at the operations on the Somme in 1916, at Ypres in 1917. Wounded at Hill 60, Messines Ridge, 7th June, 1917. Posted to 2nd Bn. in July, 1918, and served with it till October on the Western front.

GEORGE HENRY ROYCE

Born at Leicester, 4th September, 1890. Temp. Second Lieut., 26th September, 1917 ; Temp. Lieut., 26th March, 1919 ; 2/6th Durham L.I., 7th April, 1919.

In the ranks of the Leicester Regt. till commissioned. Joined the 7th Service Bn. 20th November, 1917, and 12th Bn. 12th February, 1918. Present at the operations in March, 1918, and in the Lys retreat in April, 1918. Joined 2nd Bn. in August, and took part in the advance up to the Armistice.

PERCY JOHN MAINWARING SYLVESTER

Born at Croydon, 1st February, 1891, son of Percy Sylvester, of Croydon, Surrey.

Temp. Second Lieut., 22nd September, 1914 ; Temp. Lieut., 29th September, 1915 ; Temp. Capt., 28th March, 1917.

Served in France from September, 1915. Present at Loos (1915), Somme July to September, 1916, Arras, Vimy, and Hindenburg Line, April, 1917, Passchendaele, Poelcappelle, October, 1917. Served with 2nd Bn. from 4th September to 12th October, 1918, when he was transferred to 9th Bn. West Yorkshire Regt. (bronze star).

FRED TENNEY

Temp. Second Lieut., Gen. List, 8th January, 1915 ; Temp. Lieut., Yorkshire Regt., 1st July, 1917 ; relinquished his commission on account of ill health caused by wounds, 17th April, 1919.

Posted to the 2nd Bn. 1st October, 1918, and was wounded and taken prisoner at Meurain 6th November, 1918.

WILLIAM ARTHUR HALL

Temp. Second Lieut., 28th August, 1918.

Posted to 2nd Bn. 16th October, 1918. Wounded at Roisin 5th November, 1918.

Died of his wounds (" Times," 3-12-18).

L. HOARE

Temp. Second Lieut., 16th March, 1918.

Commissioned from Cadet unit. Served with 1st Bn. in India. Transferred to Royal Air Force in June, 1918, and was employed as an observer in the Afghan Expedition, 1919. Was for ten days a prisoner in the hands of the Afridis in the Bazar Valley.

A. LYLE

Temp. Second Lieut., 19th August, 1918 ; Temp. Lieut., 19th February, 1920.

Commissioned from an Officers' Cadet unit. Served with 1st Bn. in India and in the operations in Afghanistan in 1919.

JOHN GEORGE ROBINSON

Born at Middlesbro', 10th May, 1895, son of Charles William Robinson, The White House, Coatham, Redcar.

Temp. Second Lieut., 26th June, 1918 ; demobilised 26th March, 1919.

Served in the retirement through Serbia, and in the advance in Macedonia through the Struma Main with the 6/7th Bn. R.M. Fusiliers. Posted to 2nd Bn. 20th October, 1918, and took part in the advance before the Armistice.

DENIS LEONARD, M.M.

Temp. Second Lieut., 26th June, 1918.

Joined 2nd Bn. 16th October, 1918.

Killed at Meurain, 6th November, 1918.

EDWARD WILLIAM TEASDALE

Born at Birmingham, 25th March, 1891, son of William Teasdale, of Bellingham, Northumberland.

Temp. Second Lieut., 26th June, 1918 ; demobilised, 3rd February, 1919.

Served in the ranks of the 6th Bn. Northumberland Fusiliers from 6th August, 1914, and was present at the second battle of Ypres, April, 1915 (wounded, bronze star), St. Eloi March, 1916, Ypres May, 1916, battle of the Somme September, 1916, Arras April, 1917, at the battle of Gussignies 6th November, 1918, with 2nd Bn., which he joined 16th October, 1918.

REGINALD SCOBY WILLIAMSON

Born at Yarm-on-Tees, 31st March, 1893, son of James Williamson, of Harrogate.

Temp. Second Lieut., 26th June, 1918.

Served in the ranks of the 8th Bn. Black Watch from 15th January, 1916, to November, 1917, and was present at the fighting before Arras 9th April, 1917, and at Ypres 12th October, 1917, also at Gussignies in November, 1918, with 2nd Bn., which he joined on 16th October. Transferred to 36th Bn. Northumberland Fusiliers 15th March, 1919.

FINIS.

INDEX.

www.ingramcontent.com/pod-product-compliance
Lightning Source LLC
Chambersburg PA
CBHW020806100426
42814CB00014B/353/J